KT-873-295

Psychology

The Essential Science

ALLYN AND BACON

Boston   London

Sydney   Toronto

Special project editor: Nancy Forsyth
Series editor: John-Paul Lenney
Production administrator: Peter Petraitis
Text design/art: Caliber Design Planning, Inc.
Photo research: Laurel Anderson/Photosynthesis
Cover coordinator: Linda Dickinson
Composition buyer: Linda Cox
Manufacturing buyer: Bill Alberti

Copyright © 1989 by Allyn and Bacon, A Division of Simon & Schuster, 160 Gould Street, Needham, Massachusetts 02194. All rights reserved. No part of the material protected by this copyright notice may be reproduced or utilized in any form or by any means, electronic or mechanical, including photocopying, recording, or by any information storage and retrieval system, without written permission from the copyright owner.

Library of Congress Cataloging-in-Publication Data

Baron, Robert A.
    Psychology : the essential science.

    Bibliography: p.
    Includes index.
    1. Psychology.   I. Title.
BF121.B32 1989   150   88-26262
ISBN 0-205-11432-6

Printed in the United States of America
10 9 8 7 6 5 4 3 2 1   93 92 91 90 89 88

Credits:
Photo credits:
Photos by John Curtis & David Dempster styled by Photosynthesis. **CHAPTER ONE** PAGE 6 (L-R) The Archives of American Psychology. Pg. 12L; J. Simon/The Picture Cube, C; M. Greenlar/The Picture Group, R; D. Budnick/Woodfin Camp & Associates. Pg. 15; Comstock. Pg. 17; L.L. Rue/Photo-Researchers Inc. Pg. 18; Courtesy Hunt Manufacturing Co. Pg. 24; John Curtis. Pg. 26; H. Morgan/Photo-Researchers Inc. **CHAPTER TWO** Pg. 33 L; R. Stuckey/Comstock, TR; J. Curtis, BR; L. Migdale/Photo-Researchers Inc. Pg. 34; M.C. Werner/Comstock. Pg. 35 L-R; Pierce & McCoy/Rainbow. Pg. 46T; Mazziota/Photo-Researchers Inc, B; P. Lynch/Photo-Researchers Inc. Pg. 48; Courtesy Dr. Neal Miller/Yale University. Pg. 53; J.B. O'Rourke/The Stock Market. Pg. 58; The Kobal Collection/Super Stock. Pg. 59; D. McCoy/Rainbow. Pg. 60L; T. Nebbia/Woodfin Camp & Associates, R; Reynolds Photography. **CHAPTER THREE** Pg. 74; B. Bachman/Photo-Researchers Inc. Pg. 76; D. Dempster/Off-Shoot. Pg. 77; The Kobal Collection/Superstock. Pg. 91 L; K. McCarthy/Off-Shoot, R; S. Uzell/The Stock Market. Pg. 92 L, R; D. Dempster/Off-Shoot. Pg. 97; Art Resource. Pg. 100; MOMA Film Stills Archive. **CHAPTER FOUR** Pg. 107; J. Curtis. Pg. 114; Biomedical Communications/Photo-Researchers Inc. Pg. 118; Bettmann Newsphotos. Pg. 122; G. Adler/Shooting Star. Pg. 123; J. Curtis. Pg. 128 T, B; J. Curtis. Pg. 130; North Wind Picture Archive (Inset; D. Dempster). **CHAPTER FIVE** Pg. 137 TL; B. Daemmrich, BL; Keller & Peet, R; J. Curtis. Pg. 140; J. Curtis. Pg. 142 L, R; K. McCarthy/Off-Shoot. Pg. 143; D. Dempster/Off-Shoot. Pg. 148; J. Curtis. Pg. 150 T; H. Morgan/Photo-Researchers Inc., B; S. Seitz/Woodfin Camp & Associates. Pg. 151;

(Photo credits continued on page 587)

To Bill and Sandra—
two people who recognize my strengths
and overlook my faults

Abbreviated Table of Contents

Contents

3

Sensation And Perception: Making Contact With The World Around Us   66

◥ 4 ▶

Consciousness: Awareness Of Ourselves And The World Around Us   104

◥ 5 ▶

Learning: How We're Changed By Experience   134

8

Human Development: Change Throughout Life 232

9

Motivation: The Activation (And Persistence) Of Behavior 272

10

Emotions: Their Nature, Expression, And Impact
302

11

Measuring Individual Differences: The Nature And Use Of Psychological Testing   336

12

Personality: The Uniqueness (And Consistency) Of Individual Behavior   368

Social Behavior and Social Thought: How We Think About And Interact With Others   466

Using the Essential Science: Making Psychology Part Of Your Life   502

Appendix/Thinking Like a Psychologist Revisited: The Use—and Abuse—of Statistics   524

Preface

On Doing and Teaching Psychology: Reflections of a Smiling Workaholic

We live in an age of word processors and desk-top publishing. Yet, despite these modern marvels, books are still written by people, not by machines. Since they are, books must necessarily reflect the skills, experience, and nature of their authors. *Psychology: The Essential Science* is certainly no exception to this rule. This book consciously reflects a theme that has been central to my entire career as a psychologist, one I can best summarize as follows: *There is absolutely, positively no substitute for hard work—but a touch of humor, too, can have its place*. In short, I have always believed that hard work is the most essential ingredient in a serious, scientific field such as psychology, and that an occasional smile can provide a much-needed boost to both affect and motivation. (I should add that a considerable body of research findings lend support to this view. Such research—including several studies I have conducted myself—indicates that humor can indeed exert a wide range of beneficial effects in many different contexts.)

Over the years I have applied this belief to teaching, writing, and even to research. Twenty years into my career as a teacher of psychology, I still work hard at preparing lectures, and still view my central task as that of stretching the minds of students. Yet I am also well known on campus for using (at unpredictable intervals) amusing illustrations that make important points about behavior.

While conducting research, I have always viewed myself as a serious scientist and have published scores of papers in leading journals. Most of this work has been programmatic in nature, and has dealt with serious topics such as procedures for reducing human aggression or (more recently) techniques for the effective resolution of organizational conflicts. On occasion, though, I've delved into questions of a somewhat lighter nature (e.g., Can humor play a beneficial role in negotiations? Should applicants wear perfume or cologne to job interviews?) In short, in my research, as in my teaching, I have always been committed to hard and careful work, but I have also found value in an occasional bit of whimsy.

The same basic theme—mounds of hard work with a dash of humor on the side—lies at the heart of the present text. On the one hand, I can honestly say that I have endeavored to make this book an accurate and comprehensive overview of psychology in the late 1980s. On the other hand, though, I have featured the lighter side of our field on occasion. To repeat, in a very real sense this text reflects not only my experience and nature, but also my personal approach to doing and teaching psychology.

Major Goals of This Text and How I Sought to Attain Them

Supported by a great deal of research on the value of goal-setting, I firmly endorse the view that it's easier to get somewhere is you know where you are going. Consistent with this view, I established several concrete goals—and strategies for attaining them—*before* beginning work on this text. The most important of these were as follows:

(1) Present a Broad, Accurate, and Up-to-Date Picture of Our Field.

This goal is one shared by most, if not all, authors of introductory texts. I do feel, though, that I have taken some special steps to attain it and that my personal background and experience have been very helpful in these efforts.

First, I should note that before preparing each chapter I obtained detailed input and suggestions from dozens of colleagues. These individuals kindly offered their views about the ideal content of each unit, suggested how it should be organized, and called my attention to important new lines of research. I paid close attention to these suggestions (as well to extensive reviews of each chapter after it was drafted) and feel that doing so has definitely helped me to attain the breadth, accuracy, and currency referred to above.

Second, my own broad set of professional experiences has proven invaluable to me in preparing a text that really does reflect the tremendous scope of modern psychology. I began my graduate career with basic training in experimental psychology. Later, I shifted into social psychology and worked in this area for a dozen years. During that period, though, I held two faculty positions in which I taught courses in developmental psychology, and I also conducted research on such topics as the impact of televised violence on young children. From 1979 to 1981 I served as a program director at the National Science Foundation. This provided me with a unique opportunity to gain wide exposure to virtually all areas of our field. Finally, in recent years, I have taught courses and conducted research in the area of industrial/organizational psychology. I feel that these experiences have helped me to prepare a text that does indeed provide an unusually broad introduction to the scope of modern psychology.

With respect to accuracy and currency, this is where the workaholic part of my personal nature played a positive role. I prepared each chapter with the relevant books and journals right on the desk beside me. The result: more than 30 percent of the references cited in this text are from 1985 or later, and many are from 1987 and even 1988.

(2) Present a Balanced Picture of Modern Psychology.

By ''balanced'' I mean three things: balance between what are sometimes known as the ''hard'' and ''soft'' areas of our field, balance between psychology as a science and psychology as a source of practical knowledge, and balance between new work on the cutting edge of our field and work that is now viewed as classic. Here, my experience in several areas of our field, and in both applied and basic research, has been helpful.

(3) Present Psychology in a Readable and Understandable Manner.

Prior to preparing this text, I have authored or co-authored some sixteen different books. One thing I've learned from this extensive writing experience is the following: a text students don't read and can't understand is of little value. Accordingly I've made concerted efforts to write this one with three major themes in mind:

(a) Never leave students wondering why anyone would be interested in this stuff. In other words, always try to explain the larger issues behind specific studies or lines of research, as well as the practical implications these may have.

(b) Never load a page or section with so many facts that the main points soon drop from view.

(c) Never add so may provisos and disclaimers that students conclude psychologists are incapable of giving straight answers and give up in despair. This last point, by the way, does not imply that I have glossed over complexities or inconsistencies in existing data. Rather, it means that wherever possible I've tried to offer at least *tentative* conclusions or suggestions.

(4) Represent Recent Major Trends in Our Field.

Psychology is everchanging, and I feel strongly that it is an author's duty to reflect trends whenever possible. Consistent with this approach, I've tried to take account of two major shifts in our field throughout the book: (1) Growing interest in cognition and cognitive processes, and (2) Growing interest in the application of psychological knowledge. Both trends were emphasized by colleagues who provided input on the text (both in the planning and draft stage), and both are represented in many chapters—wherever it seemed appropriate to introduce them.

Some Special Features of Psychology: The Essential Science

In recent years introductory psychology texts have become replete with a wide array of special features. Some of these seem quite useful; others appear to have been added without much concern for their ultimate value. *Psychology: The Essential Science,* too, has several unique features. All, however, are included for two reasons: first, they reflect my personal beliefs (based on my twenty years of teaching experience) that they do indeed add something ''extra''—they enhance the appeal or value of the text to students. Second, they were recommended or endorsed by many colleagues with extensive teaching experience who also felt they would be helpful. The most important of these features are summarized below.

(1) Representation of Recent Advances and New Lines of Research.

Psychology as a discipline has become so diverse, that representing all new findings and lines of research within the covers of a single text is all but impossible. I have tried, though, to include a sample of very recent work in each chapter. A small sample of these topics includes:

Physiological processes occurring during persuasion

Techniques for studying the living brain

Dominance and interpersonal attraction

Taste and odor perception in newborns

Cognitive mechanisms in the perception of pain

Sex differences in fantasies and daydreams

Thermoregulatory mechanisms and sleep

Counting by animals

Evidence suggesting that eyewitness testimony *is* often accurate

How alcohol affects memory

Heuristics in decision-making

Escalation of commitment in performance appraisal

Overconfidence in decision-making

Serial marriage

New evidence concerning the benefits of breast-feeding infants

Mood swings in adolescence

Effects of fragrance in work settings

The role of opioid peptides in eating disorders

Motivational factors in political leadership

Individual differences in affect intensity

Interviewers' mood and the evaluation of job applicants

Daily hassles as a source of stress

Effects of stress on decision-making

Self-monitoring and social behavior

Causes and effects of shyness

Self-focused attention and depression

New forms of family therapy

The dose-effect relationship in psychotherapy

Cultural differences in psychotherapy

Biases and errors in social cognition

Human factors in product design

Goal-setting and work motivation

Psychology and public health: Coping with AIDS

(2) Special Sections.

Three distinct types of special sections are included. The first two echo one aspect of the quest for balance described above: they represent efforts to highlight what is brand new in psychology and what is widely considered to be classic material. These sections are labeled, respectively, *Focus on Research: The Cutting Edge,* and *Focus on Research: Classic Contributions*.

The third type of section, *The Point of It All,* calls attention to potential or actual applications of psychological knowledge. As the title suggests, such inserts are designed to help answer one perennial question posed by students: What's the point of all this, anyway?

I should add that all special sections are clearly cited in the text so that their relevance to text materials is clear, and all appear at the end of sections, so they do not interrupt the reader's progress through each chapter.

(3) Special Treatment of All Illustrations.

A great deal of attention had been devoted to the illustrations. All graphs, tables, and charts were specially created for this text—none are simply redrawn or borrowed from journal articles. All contain the special labeling feature I originated more than ten years ago—the labels call a reader's attention to the key points being made and the key findings being illustrated in the chart. Photos and cartoons really *do* fit. They were chosen by me as the book was being written and each is tied closely to the points being made.

(4) Photos of Major Contributors to Our Field.

The inside front and back endpapers display portraits of many famous figures in psychology. Again, in the interests of balance, both historical and current contributors are included. Students often express interest in knowing what the famous psychologists look (or looked) like, so many will find this an interesting feature. The persons represented were chosen on the basis of a survey of more than five hundred psychologists. I conducted this survey with the aid of the publisher, Allyn and Bacon.

Some Concluding Words . . . And a Plea for Help

Those are the major goals I've sought and some of the steps I've taken to reach them. Looking back, I do feel that I've made at least measurable progress toward all of them. However, only you—my colleagues and readers—can determine whether, and to what extent, I've succeeded. I conclude, therefore, with a sincere request for help. Your comments, suggestions, and feedback will prove invaluable to me in many ways, and I would greatly appreciate receiving them. Please don't hesitate; share your reactions with me in any form you wish, and as often as you like. I really will take them carefully to heart—I really *will* listen!

Robert A. Baron
Department of Psychology
Rensselaer Polytechnic Institute
Troy, New York   12180–3590

Acknowledgments
Some Words of Thanks

Writing is a solitary task, and authors must spend much of their time isolated from the joys (and sorrows) of human contact. Converting the author's words into a book such as this one, though, requires the coordinated efforts of many individuals. In preparing this text I have been assisted by a large number of outstanding, talented people. While I can't possibly hope to thank all of them here, I'd like to express my appreciation to a few of those whose help has been most valuable.

First, my sincere thanks to the colleagues listed below. Those in the first group participated in focus groups during the initial planning stages of this book. Their insightful comments about teaching introductory psychology have guided me throughout the development of the text. I appreciate their candor and their willingness to share their teaching experiences and concerns. Those in the second group responded to questionnaires I mailed before writing a single word. Their suggestions about the content and features of the book were invaluable to me in planning and then preparing a text that reflects the current needs and preferences of many persons teaching introductory psychology. Colleagues listed in the third group read and commented upon various portions of the manuscript as I wrote them. Their suggestions were uniformly thoughtful, constructive, and informative, and this book has benefitted greatly from them in many ways.

Colleagues who participated in focus groups:

Michael Aamodt
Radford University

Yvonne Abatso
North Lake College

Glenn Albright
*City University of New York
Bernard Baruch College*

Irwin Aloff
MacCormac College

James Amirkhan
*California State University at Long
Beach*

J.C. Armstrong
Edinboro University of Pennsylvania

Joshua Bacon
Yeshiva University

Barbara Ann Bailey
Manhattan Community College

Roni Barrett
Loyola Marymount College

Kevin Barry
Iona College

Michael Berkowitz
Westchester Community College

H. Betancourt
Loma Linda University

William Blum
Ohlone College

Gordon F. Brown
Pasadena City College

Constance Campbell
Brookhaven College

Lester Campbell
Skyline College

Bernard Casella
Bergen Community College

Lawrence Chambers
Saint Xavier College

Scott Churchill
University of Dallas

Mel Ciena
Evergreen Valley College

Dennis Clare
College of San Antonio

Steven Cole
Texas Christian University

Daniel Conti
DePaul University

Catharine C. Cowan
Texas Wesleyan College

James V. Croxton
Santa Monica College

William Curtis
Camden County College

Diane Daniel
Montgomery College—Germantown

Nancy Dess
Occidental College

Lorraine Dieudonne
Foothill College

Steven Ducat
New College of California

Richard Eglsaer
Sam Houston State University

Karen Ensor
Patten College

Walter Falk
City Colleges of Chicago

Jana Flowers
Richland College

Alan D. Frankel
State University of New York at Purchase

Michael Fritche
University of Texas at Arlington

Daniel Gawronski
Calumet College

Kurt Geisiger
Fordham University

Charles P. Giles
North Lake College

Robert Glassman
Illinois State University

Donna Goetz
Elmhurst College

Lisa Gray-Schelberg
California State University at Dominguez Hills

Phyliss Grilinkhes-Maxwell
City College of San Francisco

Michael Haggerty
Mallinckrodt College

Howard Harris
Bronx Community College

Janice Hartgrave-Freile
North Harris County College

Linda Heath
Loyola University of Chicago

Alylene Hegar
Eastfield College

Walter Heimer
Long Island University—C.W. Post Center

Sid Hochman
Nassau County Community College

Jack Horowitz
West Los Angeles College

Joan Ingram
Northwestern University

R. Jackson
University of Texas at Arlington

Joann Jelly
Golden Gate University

Walter Jones
College of DuPage

George Kaluger
Shippensburg University

Harold Kassel
Daley College

Martin Keston
San Francisco State University

John Ketcher
Dallas Christian College

Elion Kinarthy
Rio Hondo Community College

Gary Kose
Long Island University—C.W. Post Center

Paul E. Kress
Simpson College

Velton Lacefield
Prairie State College

John D. Lawry
Marymount College

Steven Ledoux
State University of New York at Canton

Wayne Lesko
Marymount College

James Lewis
University of California at Los Angeles

Wayne Ludrigson
Texas Christian University

Steven Madigan
University of Southern California

Thomas Marhiez
Pepperdine University

Rick Marrs
Concordia College

Richard Maslow
San Joaquin Delta College

Edward McCrary III
El Camino College

Gerald Mikosz
Moraine Valley Community College

David Mitchell
Southern Methodist University

Pat Morris
Laney College

Ronald Murdoff
San Joaquin Delta College

Robert Osterman
Fairleigh Dickinson University

Michael Pallack
Georgetown University

Carlos Plazas
Saint Augustine Community College (Illinois)

Kathy Reinhardt
Saint Mary's College

Kathleen M. Rice
Saint John's University

Anthony L. Riley
American University

Robert Rios
New York Institute of Technology

Albert Roberts
Howard University

Seth Roberts
University of California at Berkeley

Kimberly Rodman
Katherine Gibbs School

Ann Romanczyk
Adelphi University

C. Cress Romano
Barat College

Frank Salamone
Elizabeth Seton College

Harold Schuckman
City College of New York—Queens College

Alan Schultz
Prince George's Community College

Jonathan Segal
Trinity College

Jerome R. Sehulster
University of Connecticut

Robert M. Seiden
Skyline College

Edward Serrano
East Los Angeles College

Laura Sidorwitz
Fashion Institute of Technology

Carol Ann Siefker
Mercy College

Robert Sigman
Columbia College

Charlotte Simon
Montgomery College—Rockville

Philip Stander
Kingsborough Community College of CUNY

Don Stanley
North Harris Community College

Stanley Starkman
Chicago State University

Charles Sternheim
University of Maryland

Gail Tanzer
MacCormac College

Philip Tecau
Golden Gate University

David Volckmann
Whittier College

Louis Tharp
Long Beach City College

Robert Wiater
Bergen Community College

William Threlfall
Chabot College

Alan Wolach
Illinois Institute of Technology

Russell Tracy
North Park College

Allen Young
Lincoln University

Gary Verett
Richland College

Virgil Young
University of the District of Columbia

Colleagues who provided input about the content and features of this text before it was written:

Hal S. Bertilson
Kearney State College

Stephen Link
Brookhaven College

Richard Bryan
Saint Leo College

Robert P. Markley
Fort Hays State University

Rosina C. Chia
East Carolina University

Don Meichenbaum
University of Waterloo

Raymond V. Coleman
Mount Wachusett Community College

Robert G. Meyer
University of Louisville

Jack Croxton
State University of New York at Fredonia

Bobby J. Poe
Belleville Area College

John M. Davis
Southwest Texas State University

Edward P. Riley
State University of New York at Albany

Joseph R. Ferrari
Mohawk Valley Community College

John S. Rosenkoetter
Southwest Missouri State University

Peter Flynn
Northern Essex Community College

James F. Sanford
George Mason University

Russell G. Geen
University of Missouri

David G. Schlundt
Vanderbilt University

Thomas T. Jackson
Fort Hays State University

Brent D. Slife
Baylor University

James J. Johnson
Illinois State University

Paul A. Susen
Mount Wachusett Community College

Nancy Kalish
California State University

James M. Thomas
University of Nebraska

J. Knight
Humboldt State University

William Wozniak
Kearney State College

Colleagues who reviewed various portions of the manuscript:

Daniel Ashmead
Vanderbilt University

John Best
Eastern Illinois University

William Barnard
University of Northern Colorado

Douglas Bloomquist
Framingham State College

Robert Bolles
University of Washington

Arnold Buss
University of Texas at Austin

Mark Cavanaugh
Nova University

Ernest L. Chavez
Colorado State University

Jonathan Cheek
Wellesley College

John S. Childers
East Carolina University

James R. Clopton
Texas Tech University

Robert H.I. Dale
Southeastern Louisiana University

G. William Farthing
University of Maine at Orono

Leslie Fisher
Cleveland State University

E. Scott Geller
Virginia Polytechnic Institute and State University

Robert Gifford
University of Victoria

Sherryl Goodman
Emory University

Tony Grasha
University of Cincinnati

Susan K. Green
University of Oregon

Charles Halcomb
Texas Tech University

Robert W. Hymes
University of Michigan at Dearborn

Elizabeth Lambert Johns
Northern Virginia Community College

Dennis Karpowitz
University of Kansas

Alan Kaufmann
University of Alabama

Harold O. Kiess
Framingham State College

T.C. Lewandowski
Delaware County Community College

Darwyn Linder
Arizona State University

Linda Musun-Miller
University of Arkansas at Little Rock

Denis Mitchell
University of Southern California

Richard Page
Wright State University

Paul Paulus
University of Texas at Arlington

Leslie Rescorla
Bryn Mawr College

Irwin Sandler
Arizona State University

James F. Sanford
George Mason University

Beth Shapiro
Emory University

Edward J. Shoben
University of Illinois

John Stern
Washington University

Newton Suter
San Francisco State University

James Tedeschi
SUNY Albany

Geoffrey Thorpe
University of Maine at Orono

Jean P. Volckmann
Pasadena City College

Benjamin Wallace
Cleveland State University

Russell H. Wiegel
Amherst College

David Louis Wood
University of Arkansas at Little Rock

Second, I wish to extend my gratitude to those scholars who provided me with photographs and responded to questionnaries on their work and who are featured on the endsheets as Masters of Psychology.

Third, I wish to express my appreciation to Nancy Forsyth, Alicia Reilly, and all the other members of the Special Projects Team at Allyn and Bacon—Sandi Kirshner, Diana Murphy, Susan Lewis, Carol Lou Kennedy, Ron Sohn, and Leslie Genser—for their help in countless ways. Their unflagging enthusiasm and virtual barrage of good suggestions have improved the final product in many ways, and I'm deeply indebted to them.

Fourth, my special thanks to Nancy Murphy for an outstanding and thoughtful job of copyediting on the entire manuscript. Her suggestions for changes in my prose, for additional illustrations, and for many other revisions were invaluable and added a fresh perspective to many portions of the text.

Fifth, I wish to thank Peter Petraitis, Paula Carroll, and the other members of the production team for guiding the book through a very complex production process so efficiently, for selecting an attractive internal design, and for devising such a striking cover. All in all, I feel this is the most attractive text with which I've ever been associated.

Sixth, I wish to express my deep appreciation to my good friend Bill Barke for all his support. It's really fair to say that without his confidence in me and in my understanding of psychology, the project would never have come to pass. And, of course, my sincere thanks to John-Paul Lenney, who served as my editor once the book was under way. It has been a pleasure working with him, and I look forward to doing so many more times in the future.

Finally, my warm thanks to Paul Paulus, Susan Green, Gene Smith, Chuck Hinderliter, and Ann Weber for their friendship and for their hard and excellent work in preparing the Study Guide, Instructor's Resource Manual, and Test Banks. These ancillary items are an extremely important part of the total project, and I am deeply indebted to those fine colleagues for their help.

To all these truly outstanding people, and to many others as well, my warmest personal regards and appreciation.

About The Author

Robert A. Baron is currently Professor and Chair of the Department of Psychology, Rensselaer Polytechnic Institute. A Fellow of the American Psychological Association since 1978, he received his Ph.D. from the University of Iowa (1968). Professor Baron has held faculty appointments at the University of South Carolina, Purdue University, the University of Minnesota, University of Texas, and Princeton University; he has won numerous awards for teaching excellence at these institutions. In addition, Professor Baron has been a Research Associate at the Fels Research Institute and a Visiting Fellow at the University of Oxford (England). From 1979 to 1981 he served as a Program Director at the National Science Foundation.

Professor Baron has published more than eighty articles in professional journals. He has served on the editorial boards of numerous journals (e.g., the *Journal of Personality and Social Psychology, Aggressive Behavior, Journal of Applied Social Psychology*), and is the author or co-author of some sixteen different texts in psychology. His book *Human Aggression* is considered to be a "classic," and his text *Social Psychology* (with Donn Byrne) has been the leading book in its field for many years. His texts on organizational psychology (*Behavior in Organizations*) and on human relations (*Understanding Human Relations*) have been widely adopted. Together, books by Professor Baron have been used by more than one million students.

At the present time Professor Baron's major research interests focus on applying the principles and findings of psychology to understanding behavior in work settings. His recent projects have dealt with such topics as techniques for reducing organizational conflict, and how the mood of interviewers affects their ratings of job applicants.

A long-time runner, Professor Baron's hobbies include woodworking, enjoying fine food, and music.

Psychology

C H A P T E R

Psychology: What It Is, and What It Isn't

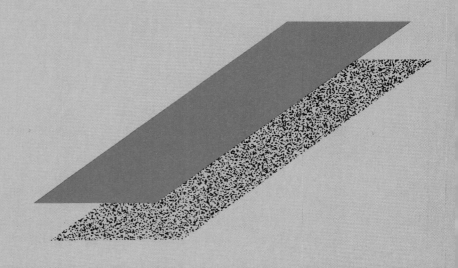

You're at a party, having a great time, when one of your friends walks up and asks you to introduce him to the attractive young woman with whom you've been talking. You begin to do so when, suddenly, your mind goes blank. Try as you may, you just can't think of her name. You feel your face growing red as you struggle to remember, but it's no good: you just can't do it. Why? How could you possibly forget a name you heard just a few minutes ago? Is there something wrong with your memory?

Your old car has broken down six times so far this year, virtually wrecking your budget with repair bills. Now, much to your disgust, you discover it has yet another serious problem. What should you do? You know the car is old and will probably develop other problems soon. But you've already spent so much on it that it seems a shame to junk it. Should you "throw good money after bad" and fix it again, or cut your losses and get rid of it now? And, whatever you decide, how can you avoid getting trapped in situations like this one in the future?

Tomorrow you face a very important job interview. In fact, it could hardly be *more* important, for this is the job you want—the one you've always hoped would come your way. How should you prepare? For example, what clothes should you wear? Should you use perfume or cologne? How should you act during the interview—is it best to be modest about your past accomplishments or to call them boldly to the interviewer's attention? These are only a few of the questions that pass through your mind as you get ready for this important event—one that may strongly affect the rest of your life or at least the next several years.

You're playing with your two-year-old cousin. She only comes up to your knee and can't dress herself, but she already speaks whole sentences. Moreover, she seems to understand practically everything you say—even complicated thoughts and ideas. You find this really surprising. How can such a little person know so much? No one seems to have actually taught her the meaning of hundreds of words, but she knows them all the same. Is it just part of human nature to master language so quickly? And what about animals—can they learn a language, too? You've heard about research with chimpanzees and dolphins; has it worked? Can they, too, master such skills?

One of your neighbors, Bill Thompson, has had a rough six months. First, he was passed over for a key promotion. Then his wife became seriously ill, leaving him to care, all alone, for their three young children. Now, as the icing on this bitter cake, a tree has fallen on his house during a storm, crushing half the roof. Yet, there's Bill, cheerful as ever, sunbathing on his front lawn as if he hasn't got a care in the world. How does he do it? How does he manage to handle stress that would wreck most people's health with such apparent ease?

Have you ever wondered about questions such as these? If you are like most persons, your answer is probably "Yes." In fact, the chances are good that it was your curiosity about such matters that led you to sign up for introductory psychology in the first place. If that's so, you won't be disappointed. Modern psychology is a tremendously diverse and fascinating field—one that delves into virtually every aspect of human behavior. Because it does, we're confident that you will find information on most, if not all, of your questions within the pages of this book (and in your classroom experiences). For example, a very small sample of the issues we'll consider are these:

Why do some people experience little or no difficulty in maintaining a stable weight, while others must continually fight (and often lose) the ''battle of the bulge''?

Can animals count, or is this ability possessed only by human beings?

Do our moods influence what we remember and the kind of decisions we make?

Why do some persons experience ''burn-out'' in their careers or jobs, while others do not?

What is intelligence? To what extent is it inherited?

Can a single individual actually have two or more personalities at the same time?

What are the causes of depression? Are people suffering from this problem actually more realistic about life than the rest of us?

What is hypnosis? Why are some persons much more susceptible to it than others?

Of course, we can't promise complete or final answers to these and many other fascinating questions. Psychology has made impressive progress during its short existence as an independent field, but as suggested by Figure 1-1, the topics it studies are highly complex. As a result, there are still many ''loose ends,'' and much remaining to be learned. Yet, we *do* know a great deal and will soon be sharing this knowledge with you. Before doing so, though, it is important to complete a few preliminary tasks. In essence, we wish to arm you with some basic facts about the nature and scope of psychology before turning to its actual findings. Our reason for adopting this strategy is simple: research on thinking and memory (which we'll cover in chapters 6 and 7) indicates that having a mental framework for new information makes it easier to absorb, store, and remember such material. So, think of the rest of this chapter as providing you with a kind of ''cognitive scaffold'' for understanding psychology—a framework to which you can attach new information as it is presented. Four types of information will prove helpful in this respect.

First, we'll offer a definition of psychology, and will consider several key questions relating to it (e.g., is it really scientific?). Second, we will tell you something about its scope—who psychologists are and what they do. Third, and perhaps most important, we'll describe the methods used by psychologists in their research—the techniques they employ to gain new information and insights about behavior. Finally, we'll describe the organization of this text, and some of its special features. After that, it will be back to our central task: sharing psychology's knowledge and insights with you.

Psychology: The Task It Faces Is Complex

FIGURE 1-1. Understanding (or predicting!) behavior is a complex task. (*Source:* The New Yorker.)

Psychology: A Definition, a Little History, and Some Questions about Its Nature

In science, it is often said, nothing exists in a vacuum. New methods, findings, and approaches do not stand in ''magnificent isolation.'' On the contrary, they usually spring from, and rest on, what went before. Psychology is certainly no exception to this general rule. When it emerged as an independent field of study in the late 1800s, it had important roots in several other fields, ranging from philosophy, on the one hand, through biology and physiology, on the other. Given these diverse origins, it is not at all surprising that disagreements over the nature of the new science soon developed. In other words, early psychologists did not always agree about what their field should study, or how its investigations should proceed. Since these controversies played an important role in the history of psychology and contributed to the modern definition offered below, we will touch on them briefly.

Psychology: Steps on the Road to a Modern Definition

Perhaps the best way of illustrating important shifts in how psychologists have defined their field is that of imagining a brief conversation between three major figures in the history of the field: Wilhelm Wundt, founder of the first psychological laboratory in 1879; William James, author of an early influential text, *Principles of Psychology* in 1890; and John B. Watson, founder of the behaviorist approach—one which dominated psychology for most of the twentieth century (refer to Figure 1-2). (Please note: to the best of our

Wundt, James, and Watson

FIGURE 1-2. Three important persons in the history of psychology: Wilhelm Wundt (left), founder of *structuralism;* William James (center), noted supporter of *functionalism;* and John B. Watson (right), founder of *behaviorism.*

knowledge, no such conversation ever took place, but if it did, the three persons involved might well have made comments such as these.)

WUNDT: In my opinion, psychology should be the study of conscious experience. Our task is that of analyzing the mind into its component parts, just as chemists analyze complex substances.

JAMES: I disagree. The mind isn't static, like a chemical compound. It is useful, and *used*. Our task is that of finding out how our psychological nature helps us adapt to a complex and changing world.

WATSON: You're both all wet. We can't see ''mind'' or ''conscious experience.'' We should restrict psychology to the study of overt behavior—actions we can see and measure scientifically.

As you can readily see, these three individuals held strongly contrasting beliefs about the nature of psychology. Wundt and other *structuralists* believed it should focus on conscious experience and on the task of analyzing such experience into its basic components. James and other *functionalists* felt that psychology should study the ways in which the ever-changing stream-of-conscious experience helps us adapt to, and survive in, a complex world. And Watson felt that psychology should focus solely on observable, overt activities—ones which can be measured in a scientific manner. Events and processes going on ''inside,'' such as thoughts, images, feelings, and intentions, have no place in the field. Which view prevailed? Clearly, the one suggested by Watson. For almost six decades, psychology was, by and large, defined as *the science of behavior*. In fact, if we had written this book in the late 1970s instead of the late 1980s, this is the definition we might have chosen.

In recent years, however, psychology has been greatly affected by what some term the ''cognitive revolution'' (e.g., Pribram, 1986). What this has involved, primarily, is vastly increased interest in many of those internal processes Watson and other *behaviorists* felt were beyond the realm of scientific study—processes such as thinking, expecting, remembering, and deciding, to name just a few. The reasons for this recent shift are complex, but among the most important is growing recognition by psychologists of two central facts: (1) thoughts and other mental processes strongly shape our overt actions, and (2) we don't simply *react* to the world around us; rather, we actively seek information about it and then process such input in complex ways. In the light of these facts, the suggestion that we should restrict psychology to the study of overt, observable actions makes little sense. If our mental processes affect behavior, and behavior, in turn, provides

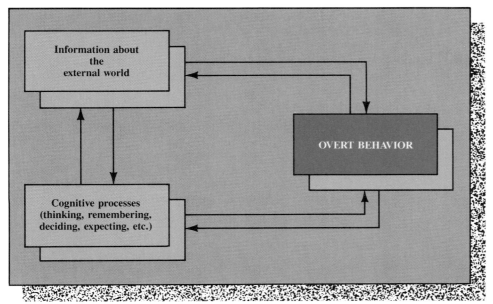

Cognitive Processes: A Central Topic in Modern Psychology

FIGURE 1-3. As indicated here, cognitive processes often affect our overt behavior. More-over, we actively seek information about the external world, and then actively process it once it is obtained. Because of these important relationships, psychology is now defined as the sci-ence of behavior and cognitive processes.

much of the input for such processes, the two are intimately related. Thus, a field of psychology that ignores mental or cognitive processes would be incomplete in very basic respects (refer to Figure 1-3).

At present, then, there is general agreement among psychologists that their field can be defined as *the science of behavior* only if the term "behavior" includes all of the cognitive processes mentioned above. Alternatively, and to make sure that such processes are given a role in the field, **psychology** can be defined as *the science of behavior and cognitive (mental) processes*. This is the definition we will adopt, for it suggests that modern psychology is concerned with everything we think, feel, or do; and that, in essence, is what our field *is* all about as we enter the 1990s.

Psychology: A Capsule History

Watson issued his call for a field of psychology focused on overt behavior as the decade of the "Roaring Twenties" got started. Yet much important work had already been com-pleted prior to that time. For example, tests designed to measure intelligence and other human characteristics had already been devised and had been put to widespread use (Terman, 1916). Similarly, Sigmund Freud had already published many aspects of his influential theories of human personality and psychological disorders (Freud, 1900, 1914). And much had already been learned about the functioning of our senses (Fechner, 1860) and the nature of human memory (Ebbinghaus, 1913). In the decades that followed, the pace of progress within psychology accelerated sharply. During the 1930s and 1940s C.L. Hull, B.F. Skinner, and other behaviorists uncovered a great deal of new informa-tion about *learning* and related topics (Hull, 1943; Skinner, 1953). Important work on conformity, leadership, and other aspects of *social behavior* was also performed at this time (e.g., Lewin, 1947; Sherif, 1935). During the 1950s the scope of psychology ex-panded greatly, and major advances were made with respect to knowledge about *human development* (Piaget, 1954), *motivation* (McClelland et al., 1953), functioning of the human brain (Lashley, Chow, & Semmes, 1951), and many other topics. The 1960s brought the emergence of many new interests and sub-fields (e.g., *environmental psy-chology*—the study of how our behavior is affected by the physical world around us), as well as continued rapid progress in all traditional areas of research.

During the 1970s and 1980s psychology has, in a sense, come into its own. Our field has gained increasing recognition as an active, diverse, and valuable branch of science. Moreover, its scope has expanded even further, to the point at which it now studies virtually every question about human beings and human behavior you can probably imagine. In addition, we have recently witnessed three important trends in psychology: (1) growing concern with *cognitive processes* (e.g., memory, thought, reasoning, deciding), (2) increasing attention to the *biological bases of behavior,* and (3) growing interest in the *application* of psychological knowledge. All three trends will be fully reflected in the chapters that follow.

Some Milestones in the Development of Psychology

FIGURE 1-4. As shown here, psychology's early years were marked by many important events, both within our field and outside it.

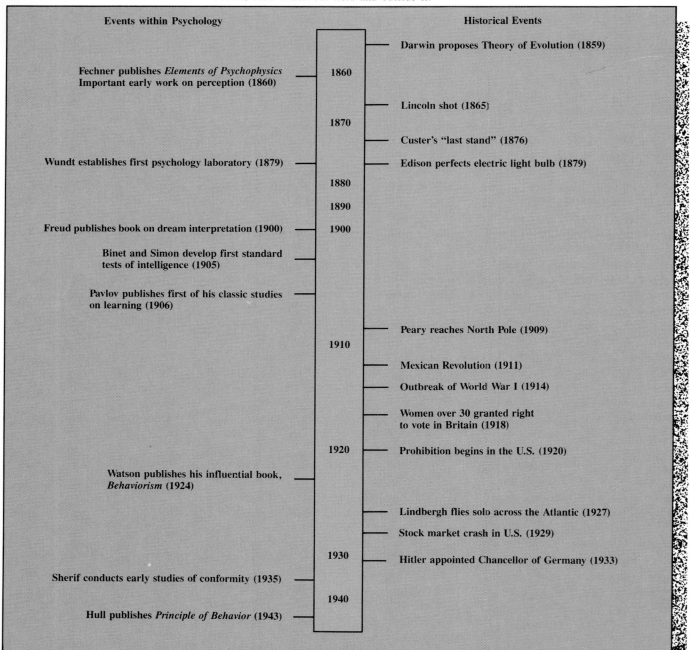

Events within Psychology		Historical Events
		Darwin proposes Theory of Evolution (1859)
Fechner publishes *Elements of Psychophysics* Important early work on perception (1860)	1860	
	1870	Lincoln shot (1865)
		Custer's "last stand" (1876)
Wundt establishes first psychology laboratory (1879)		Edison perfects electric light bulb (1879)
	1880	
	1890	
Freud publishes book on dream interpretation (1900)	1900	
Binet and Simon develop first standard tests of intelligence (1905)		
Pavlov publishes first of his classic studies on learning (1906)		
	1910	Peary reaches North Pole (1909)
		Mexican Revolution (1911)
		Outbreak of World War I (1914)
		Women over 30 granted right to vote in Britain (1918)
	1920	Prohibition begins in the U.S. (1920)
Watson publishes his influential book, *Behaviorism* (1924)		
		Lindbergh flies solo across the Atlantic (1927)
		Stock market crash in U.S. (1929)
	1930	Hitler appointed Chancellor of Germany (1933)
Sherif conducts early studies of conformity (1935)		
	1940	
Hull publishes *Principle of Behavior* (1943)		

Admittedly, this capsule overview of the history of our field has been extremely sketchy. This was by design; we did not want to begin by overwhelming you with endless strings of names and dates. The information you've just read should give you at least a rough idea of how our field has grown and developed during the present century. If you'd like to know more about the history of psychology, and its emergence as an independent field, please see the book by Schultz and Schultz (1987) listed in the ''For More Information'' section at the end of this chapter. And for a summary of some milestones in the development of our field, plus events occurring in the world at large, please refer to the time-line diagram in Figure 1-4.

Psychology: A Few Basic Questions

It's often said that ''There's no free lunch,'' and where definitions are concerned, this is certainly the case. Now that we've offered a definition of psychology, we must pause and ''pay our bill'' by commenting briefly on some of the questions this definition raises.

Is Psychology Really Scientific?   Twenty-five years of teaching experience suggests that some of you may wonder about our contention that psychology is scientific in nature. You may feel that, even today, it is really *not* a science in the same sense as chemistry, physics, or biology. While we certainly support your right to disagree, it's our firm belief that such reservations stem mainly from a basic misunderstanding about the word *science*.

Many persons seem to assume that this term refers to specific fields of study (e.g., physics, chemistry), and that only these can be described as truly scientific in nature. In fact, though, it refers mainly to a general approach to acquiring knowledge—one involving the use of certain *methods* plus adherence to several key *values* or *standards*. The methods consist primarily of *systematic observation* and *direct experimentation,* and we will describe them in detail in a later section. The standards involve commitment to such goals as *objectivity* (evaluating information on the basis of its merits rather than one's personal preferences), *accuracy* (gathering information as carefully and precisely as possible), and *skepticism* (accepting findings as true only after they have repeatedly been verified).

As you can readily see, these methods and values are largely independent of any specific field. In fact, they can be used to study a wide range of topics. In determining whether a given field is or is not scientific, then, the crucial question is this: does it make use of scientific methods and accept scientific values? To the extent it does, it may be viewed as scientific in nature. To the extent it does not, it should be seen as basically *non-scientific* in orientation. In short, it is the methods and values, *not* the topic being studied, that are essential (refer to Figure 1-5 on page 10). We should note, by the way, that it is possible for a specific field of study to adopt several of the values mentioned above without at the same time using scientific methods to acquire information. For example, *historians* certainly subscribe to the values of accuracy and objectivity. Since the topics they study cannot be observed directly, however, their field—valuable as it may be—is not essentially *scientific* in nature.

Given the criteria just described, is psychology really scientific? Our answer is straightforward: ''Definitely.'' In their efforts to understand behavior and mental processes, psychologists rely heavily on scientific methods, and adhere closely to the standards mentioned above.

This does not imply, however, that they are always perfect in such efforts. Sometimes psychologists (like other scientists) are tempted to accept their own informal observations of human behavior as true, even in the absence of confirming scientific data; and sometimes they find their personal preferences and non-scientific values intruding into their work (Howard, 1985). For example, a psychologist deeply committed to eliminating *sexism* (prejudice based on sex) from work settings may tend to notice more of this bias in the data he or she collects than would someone without such passionate views. Similarly, a psychologist with conservative political leanings may tend to interpret complex findings about the deterrent value of punishment as more supportive of stern treatment of criminals

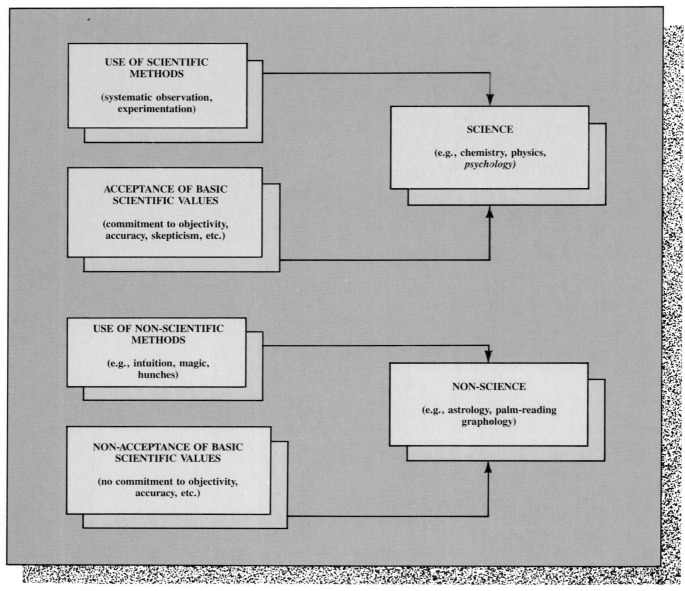

FIGURE 1-5. The term *science* refers to adherence to (1) a special set of methods, and (2) specific values. Fields that adopt these methods and values can be viewed as scientific in nature (upper panel). Fields that do not adopt them should be viewed as outside the realm of science (lower panel).

Psychology: Why It's Scientific

than colleagues holding different political views. Needless to add, such intrusions of non-scientific values into the scientific process must be vigorously resisted; only if they are can psychology retain its claim to scientific status (Baron, 1987). Fortunately, most psychologists are highly sensitive to such problems, and take active steps to prevent them. On our part, we'll do everything in our power to prevent our personal values or views from influencing our statements about psychology or the implications of its findings. Respect for *your* views make it impossible for us to do otherwise.

To conclude: psychology can be viewed as the *science* of behavior and mental processes because in their research psychologists are firmly committed to the scientific method and scientific values. The topics they seek to study certainly differ from those in older and more traditional fields of science, but the approach they follow is basically the same. And that, as we have already noted, is really the central issue.

Isn't Psychology Just Common Sense?   Have you ever listened to or watched one of those shows in which people describe their problems to a psychologist, who then

For Better or For Worse®   **by Lynn Johnston**

One Basic Problem with "Common Sense"

FIGURE 1-6. Unfortunately, *common sense* frequently offers contradictory suggestions about behavior. *(Source: Universal Press Syndicate, 1986.)*

offers suggestions or solutions? If so, you may already have asked yourself a second common question about psychology: "Isn't it just all common sense?" In other words, aren't the answers it supplies ones you could easily think of yourself, given enough time? Here are two replies we'd like you to consider.

First, if you stop and think about it for a moment, you'll quickly realize that common sense isn't really as useful a guide to human behavior as you may have assumed. Often it yields contradictory answers about important issues. For example, according to common sense, "Absence makes the heart grow fonder" (separation strengthens bonds of affection). But common sense also states, "Out of sight, out of mind" (bonds of affection are *weakened* by separation). Can both be true? Perhaps, but common sense doesn't explain why or how. As another example, consider these two statements: "Birds of a feather flock together" (similar persons are attracted to one another) and "Opposites attract" (*dis*similar persons are mutually attracted). Again, we are left with contradictory suggestions. (For another example, see Figure 1-6). Because of its scientific orientation, psychology can never be satisfied with such a state of affairs. Rather, it subjects suggestions about human behavior to careful study, in order to determine which, if any, are true. And, going further, it also tries to determine when such statements are accurate or inaccurate, and *why*, precisely, this is so. As you can see, this complex process of scientific inquiry yields a very different type of knowledge than that provided by common sense!

Second, before concluding that many of the findings reported by psychology are merely common sense, you should consider a phenomenon known as the *"I-knew-it-all-along effect."* This refers to a basic human tendency to react to new information by assuming that it really isn't so new, and that, in fact, we knew it all the time. Because of this tendency, people often perceive the results of psychological research as something they would have predicted anyhow. Of course, there is no way of knowing if this is actually the case. So, before you decide that the knowledge gathered by psychologists is often something you really knew all along (or something your grandmother could have told you), remember that in this case, as in many others, hindsight is a lot better than foresight. (For discussion of a third important question about psychology, please refer to "The Point of It All" section below.)

THE POINT OF IT ALL

Is Psychology Really Useful?

Over the years we've often heard students make the following type of remark: "Sure, psychology is interesting. But mainly, it seems like fun and games. Aside from helping people with mental problems, what use is it, anyway?" As you can guess from the title of this text, *Psychology: The **Essential** Science*, we have a ready answer. The major problems facing humanity

today (e.g., overpopulation, a rising tide of violence, adjusting to the computer age), are *not* ones that can be solved entirely through technological means (refer to Figure 1-7 on page 12). Rather, solutions to them will require major changes in human behavior and attitudes in addition to advances in engineering, technology, and the "hard" sciences. And what field is best suited to providing the information needed for producing such shifts? You guessed it: psychology. Perhaps we can best clarify this argument by applying it to each of the problems mentioned above.

First, consider overpopulation. How can this threat to continued human well-being and survival be avoided? Obviously, this can*not* be by technological means alone. Even if totally safe and effective contraceptives were developed, they would be of little use unless millions of persons recognize the dangers of unchecked population growth, decide to limit the size of their own families, and take active steps to do so.

Similarly, there is growing consensus around the world that neither super-weapons nor super-defenses will eliminate warfare or acts of violence. Only knowledge concerning the causes of such events, and the development of psychological principles and techniques that can be used in their control, will yield the lasting peace and personal safety we all desire.

Finally, consider the problems posed by the computer revolution. What happens to people who have lost their jobs to automation or robots? How can entire workforces be trained to make effective use of the marvelous technology now at their disposal? And, turning the issue around, how can such technology be adapted so that it is most useful to the persons who will employ it? These are only a few of the questions for which no straightforward technological solutions are possible. Rather, information about human beings—their needs, attitudes, and cognitive capacities—is essential if we are to meet the challenge of this historic transition.

In sum, there appear to be powerful reasons for seeking scientific knowledge about human behavior and cognitive processes: such information is essential to the well-being and continued survival of humanity. But this is only part of the total picture. The knowledge currently being gathered by psychologists is useful in many other, less dramatic contexts as well; indeed, it is of practical value in virtually every sphere of human activity.

At this point, we should note that we are not alone in such beliefs. Many psychologists have become increasingly concerned with *application* in recent years—with putting the findings and principles of their field to use in a wide variety of settings. A few examples are: (1) basic knowledge about perceptual processes (how we perceive the world around us) has been used to design more effective traffic signs, (2) scientific knowledge about memory has been used to clarify legal matters (e.g., the accuracy of eye-witness testimony), and (3) information about how children develop has been used to design more effective child-care centers. We could list many other examples, but by now the main point should be clear: in a very real sense, psychology *is* the essential science. With it, the future, troubled and turbulent as it may be, offers hope and challenge. Without it, the years ahead may prove bleak indeed.

Psychology: Essential for Human Welfare

FIGURE 1-7. None of the problems illustrated here can be solved entirely through technological means. Knowledge of human behavior and cognitive processes is also essential.

Psychology: "Who" and "What"

Now that we've defined psychology and presented some information about its basic nature, we're ready for some related issues. In this section, we'll indicate (1) just who psychologists are and (2) what they do.

Who: The Background and Training of Psychologists

The terms "psychiatrist" and "psychologist" seem quite similar, and many persons think that they mean the same thing. In reality, though, they refer to two different groups of professionals. Psychiatrists are physicians who, after completing medical studies and receiving the M.D. degree, go on to specialize in the treatment of mental disorders.

In contrast, psychologists receive their training in graduate programs of psychology, where they earn both a master's degree and, in most cases, a Ph.D. (Doctor of Philosophy) degree. The latter degree usually requires a minimum of four years of study. In addition, if they choose to specialize in certain topics (e.g., the treatment of psychological disorders), one or more years of practical experience in a hospital, clinic, school, or business may also be required. Throughout their graduate education, psychologists focus mainly on the principles and findings of their field. However, most also receive extensive training in statistics, research methods, and related subjects (e.g., physiology, sociology, management sciences).

Clearly, then, psychologists and psychiatrists receive different kinds of training. Why are the two fields often confused? The main reason is that many psychologists specialize in the diagnosis, study, and treatment of disturbed behavior. As a result, they tend to focus on many of the same problems, and perform many of the same activities, as psychiatrists. Indeed, members of the two fields often work closely together in the same mental health institutions. Since only *some* psychologists focus on abnormal behavior, though, the two fields overlap only partially, and they remain largely independent and separate professions.

Now that we've clarified the difference between psychologists and psychiatrists, here are a few facts about psychology itself:

   1.   At last official count (Stapp, Tucker, & VandenBos, 1985), there were more than 103,000 psychologists in the U.S. alone.

   2.   Of these, 61.8 percent were male, and 37.8 percent were female. This represents a marked increase in the proportion of females from psychology's earliest days, when only 10 percent were women (Furumoto & Scarborough, 1986).

   3.   Unfortunately, despite many efforts to increase the representation of minority groups in psychology, such persons still account for only a little more than 5 percent of the total in the U.S.

   4.   Among today's psychologists, more than 48 percent received their Ph.D. degree between 1970 and 1979; thus, as you can see, psychology experienced its own population explosion during that turbulent decade. By comparison, only 24 percent received their degrees during the 1960s, the next most prolific decade.

What: Specialties Within Psychology

Before reading any further, stop and answer the following question: What, precisely, do psychologists do? If you are like most people, your answer probably included phrases such as "helping people," "doing therapy," or perhaps even "psychoanalysis." In one sense, this is not entirely inaccurate, for the largest single specialty within psychology— clinical psychology—is indeed concerned with such matters. However, even this group accounts for only 38 percent of the total, so it is clear that psychologists have many other interests. In fact, psychology is divided into a number of different branches or specialties, each focusing on somewhat different topics. A number of these (but by no means all) are listed in Table 1-1 on page 14, along with some comments about their major interests or concerns. Please see the accompanying chart (Figure 1-8 on page 14) for the percent of psychologists who identify themselves as belonging to each of these specialties. After examining this material, we're sure you'll reach two conclusions: (1) psychologists are a highly diverse lot, with many different interests; and (2) they do indeed focus on virtually every aspect of behavior and mental processes you can imagine.

One final point: although psychology does have a number of different specialties, the lines between them are anything but firm. On the contrary, the interests of the various groups overlap, and each area often draws upon the others in its efforts to understand behavior and cognitive processes. Thus, for example, social psychologists have recently made extensive use of the findings of cognitive psychology (a branch of experimental psychology) in their efforts to understand social thought—how we think about other persons. Similarly, clinical psychologists have frequently based new forms of therapy on basic principles of learning developed by their colleagues in experimental psychology.

TABLE 1-1

Some of the Major Specialties Within Psychology

Branch or Specialty	Major Focus/Interests
Clinical psychology	Studies the causes and treatment of behavior disorders
Counseling psychology	Assists individuals in dealing with a wide range of personal problems (e.g., career plans, interpersonal relations)
Developmental psychology	Studies changes in behavior and cognitive processes throughout the entire span of life
Educational psychology	Studies all aspects of the educational process (e.g., techniques of instruction, learning disabilities, changes in curricula)
Experimental psychology	Focuses on basic psychological processes such as perception, learning, motivation
Cognitive psychology	A branch of experimental psychology that studies all mental processes (e.g., memory, reasoning, problem-solving)
Industrial/Organizational psychology	Studies behavior in work settings (e.g., selection of employees, evaluating performance, work motivation, leadership)
Personality psychology	Focuses on stable individual differences—characteristics or traits persons show across a wide range of situations
Physiological psychology	Investigates the biological bases of behavior, especially the structure and function of the central nervous system
School psychology	Performs such tasks as counseling students and administering tests; also assists in the training of teachers
Social psychology	Focuses on all aspects of interpersonal behavior (e.g., attraction, social influence, aggression) and social thought

FIGURE 1-8. The percentage of psychologists currently working in different branches of the field. As you can see, a large majority are in fields that have traditionally been viewed as applied in orientation (e.g., clinical, counseling, school psychology). *(Source: Based on data from Stapp, Tucker, & VandenBos, 1985.)*

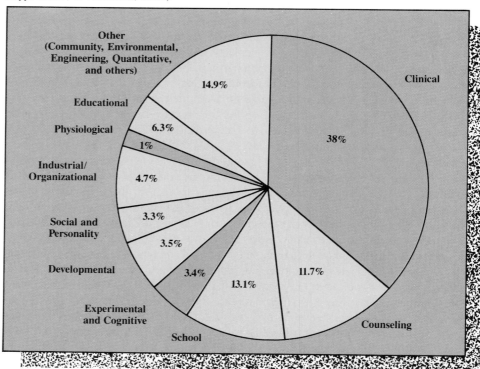

The main point to remember is this: Despite the existence of many specialized interests, psychology remains a unified field with shared values and goals, and one in which knowledge flows freely among its various branches.

Adding to What We Know: The Nature of Psychological Research

Now that we know who psychologists are and what they do, we can turn to what is perhaps the most important question in this chapter: how does psychology accomplish the task of adding to our knowledge of behavior and cognitive processes? As we noted earlier, common sense is not the answer; while it can sometimes serve as a useful starting point, it is too inconsistent and vague to serve as a firm foundation for scientific knowledge. Recognizing this fact, psychologists long ago turned to more systematic techniques for conducting their research. In this section, we will describe these procedures and will consider the ethical issues they sometimes raise.

Naturalistic Observation: The Scientist as Explorer

Almost everyone finds the giant panda of China fascinating; here, at least in outward appearance, is a teddy bear come to life! For this reason, zoos throughout the world have sought eagerly to add these beautiful animals to their collections (refer to Figure 1-9). Unfortunately, these efforts have usually produced disappointing results. The pandas, when finally obtained, seemed to pine away in captivity. Even worse, they have adamantly refused to mate, despite the best efforts of experts and their keepers. Given the small and declining numbers of pandas still present in the wild, these events seemed to spell disaster for a species humanity would dearly love to preserve. Could anything be done to change the situation? There seemed only one way to find out: **naturalistic observation** of pandas in their natural habitat. In other words, scientists would go to locations where the pandas live (mountainous regions of western China) and observe their natural patterns of behavior in the wild. Fortunately, efforts along these lines (Schaller, 1986) have added greatly to our knowledge of these impressive animals. And this information, in turn, promises to be of major use in efforts to help the pandas survive.

As this example suggests, naturalistic observation is often used to study animal behavior. However, it is sometimes applied to human beings as well. For example, Heslin and Boss (1980) quietly observed the behavior of people greeting or saying good-bye to friends, lovers, and relatives at airports. The observations they gathered yielded intriguing insights into what actually goes on in this emotion-packed situation. Of course, the data obtained through naturalistic observation is often informal in nature, and this can reduce its scientific value. Still, it can be a useful way to begin the study of certain topics, and may be the *only* way to proceed with respect to others, as was true with the giant panda.

Case Studies: Generalizing from the Unique

As we'll note in more detail in later portions of this book (see chapters 11 and 12), human beings are unique: each possesses a distinctive combination of traits, abilities, and characteristics. Given this fact, is it possible to learn anything about human behavior *generally* from the detailed study of one or perhaps a few individuals? Several famous figures in the history of our field have believed this is so, and have adopted the **case method** of research in their own work. For example, Freud based his entire theory of personality on detailed study of a few interesting cases. In a similar manner, Jean Piaget, an influential *developmental psychologist,* observed his own children closely in order to learn how youngsters change as they grow older.

Is the case method really useful? In the hands of talented investigators such as Freud and Piaget, it does seem to yield valuable insights into key aspects of human behavior. We should note, however, that it is subject to several practical problems that tend to lessen its appeal. First, working very closely with specific persons may make it

Studying Pandas in Their Natural Habitat

FIGURE 1-9. Naturalistic observation has proven helpful in understanding the behavior of the giant panda, and may help in saving this beautiful animal from extinction.

difficult for a researcher to maintain scientific objectivity; despite his or her best efforts, the investigator may become emotionally involved with the persons being studied. Second, the particular cases encountered by a given researcher may be "special" in some respect, with the result that principles based upon them are not truly general in scope. For example, some of Freud's findings appear to be limited by the fact that he worked only with persons from a specific culture (late-nineteenth-century Vienna).

Because of such problems, the case method should be employed with considerable caution. Indeed, it is currently viewed by most psychologists as a source of interesting ideas and hypotheses rather than as a basis for rigorous scientific knowledge.

Surveys: The Science of Self-Report

You are probably already familiar with another research method often used by psychologists—the **survey approach.** This involves asking large numbers of individuals to complete questionnaires designed to provide information on some aspect of their behavior, attitudes, or both. Such surveys (or *polls*) are often conducted to measure public reactions to specific events (e.g., some action by the President) or voting preferences prior to elections. The results are then often presented on network news and in newspapers. Surveys are often repeated over long periods of time in order to track shifts in public opinion or attitudes. For example, some surveys of *job satisfaction*—individuals' attitudes toward their jobs—have continued for several decades (Quinn & Staines, 1979). In a similar manner, changing patterns of sexual behavior and sexual attitudes have been tracked by the Kinsey Institute for more than forty years.

Advantages of the survey method are obvious: large amounts of information can be gathered with relative ease, and shifts over time can be readily noted. Moreover, as shown in Figure 1-10, findings obtained in this manner can be quite revealing—or even downright surprising. But the disadvantages, too, are apparent. First, people may fail to respond accurately or truthfully. They may provide answers that place them in a favorable light rather than ones reflecting their true views (e.g., they may report that they dislike

FIGURE 1-10. Recent surveys indicate that after rising for several decades, premarital sexual activity among young persons decreased during the early 1980s. *(Source: Based on data from Gerrard, 1986.)*

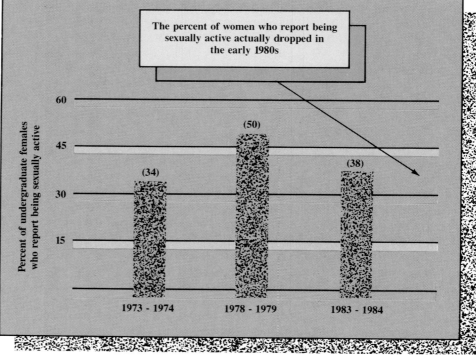

fast food when in fact they really love it; they may report being happier and better adjusted than they actually are). Second, results of surveys are useful only if the persons questioned are representative of larger groups to whom the findings are to be generalized. Unfortunately, such representative samples are often difficult to obtain. In sum, the survey method can be a highly useful method of conducting research, but only when safeguards designed to lessen such problems are employed.

Informal (and Ineffective) Use of the Correlational Method

FIGURE 1-11. Every year, there are efforts to predict the duration of the present winter by determining whether groundhogs can or cannot see their shadows. As you can guess, there is probably no relationship between these variables, so such predictions are doomed to failure.

The Correlational Method: Knowledge Through Systematic Observation

Late each winter, many television news programs present the following scene: a newscaster is shown standing in a field with a farmer. Both watch as a small, furry animal (a groundhog) emerges from its burrow, looks around, and then darts back inside (refer to Figure 1-11). These events are followed by speculations about whether the groundhog was able to see its own shadow. If it could, the newscaster and farmer conclude that winter will soon be over. If it could not, they suggest that it will last for six more weeks. After these remarks, the camera returns to the studio.

What do these events have to do with psychological research? Actually, quite a bit. *Prediction*—the ability to forecast future events from present ones—is an important goal of science, and psychologists, too, often seek it. But how can this goal be attained? One answer involves the establishment of *correlations*. To the extent that changes in one factor (or *variable* as the term is used in psychology) are associated with changes in another, they are said to be *correlated*. And the stronger such correlations, the more successfully one variable can be predicted from the other. (See the appendix on pages 524–538 for more about correlations.)

The amusing TV scene described above is based on this principle. The presence or absence of a small animal's shadow on a certain date is, according to folklore, correlated with the length of the winter season. Hence, the latter can (supposedly) be predicted from the former. Needless to say, this particular correlation is tenuous at best. As you already know from your own experience, however, some events are indeed closely related to others, and so can be used as effective predictors of them. For example, it has been found that the higher the scores attained by applicants on certain kinds of tests (e.g., college entrance examinations, medical boards), the higher their grades tend to be after admission. Similarly, it has been observed that the greater the number of hours of violent television shows watched by children, the higher is their likelihood of behaving aggressively when they become teenagers (Eron, 1987). It has even been found that taller candidates for political office are more likely to win election (Feldman, 1971).

Of course, in many instances, accurate predictions can be obtained only when several factors (and the correlations between them) are taken into account at once. For example, if you wished to predict the likelihood that particular dating couples would later marry, it would probably be necessary to consider many factors, such as (1) the current intensity of their feelings for one another, (2) the similarity of their backgrounds, and (3) the compatibility of their future career plans and life goals. Perhaps a specific example will help to illustrate the way psychologists use the **correlational method** to uncover important new facts about behavior.

Imagine that a researcher wished to test the following **hypothesis** (an as yet untested prediction about behavior): the higher the concentration of *negative ions* in an office or factory, the better the performance of the people working there. (Ions are charged particles found in the atmosphere at all times; however, their concentration can vary greatly from one location to another as well as over time.) At first glance, this might seem to be an unusual topic for research. In fact, though, there are several reasons why it might be worth investigating. First, advertisements for devices such as the one shown in Figure

FIGURE 1-12. Devices like the one shown here, which generate negative ions, have been advertised as producing beneficial effects on people's moods, cognitive processes, and behavior. Tens of thousands have been sold, many for use in factories and offices where, the purchasers hope, they will increase productivity.

1-12 are common, and these ads often claim that exposure to negative ions yields important benefits, such as improved mental efficiency and enhanced moods. Second, many persons seem to believe such claims: tens of thousands of these devices (negative ion generators) are sold each year. In short, in the absence of sound scientific evidence, consumers have found it necessary to rely on common sense, advertising claims, and other non-scientific sources of information in deciding whether to purchase and use such devices. Clearly, this is one case where the potential value of systematic psychological research is obvious!

But how, precisely, can such research be conducted? How can we determine whether exposure to negative ions really does affect human behavior? One approach to this task involves use of the *correlational method*. The researcher could visit a number of different work settings (offices, factories) and in each would measure the concentration of negative ions in the air. (This could be accomplished by means of a special meter.) In addition, she would also gather information on performance or productivity in each setting. Daily output, number of errors, and similar measures might be useful in this respect. The researcher would then subject these two sets of data to **statistical analysis** to determine if there is any *correlation* between them. (Please refer to the Appendix on pages 524–538 for more information about statistics and their use in psychology.) Correlations can range from −1.00 to +1.00, and the larger the departure from 0.00 (no correlation), the stronger the relationship between the variables under study is assumed to be. For example, if the psychologist obtained a correlation of +.80 between concentration of negative ions and some measure of performance, she would at least tentatively conclude that performance can indeed be predicted from ion concentration: the higher the level of negative ions, the higher performance tends to be. And if she found a correlation of −.80, she would also conclude that performance can be predicted from ion concentration. In this case, though, the higher the concentration of ions, the *lower* work performance would tend to be.

The correlational method of research offers important advantages. It can be used to study behavior in many real-life settings. It is highly efficient and can yield large amounts of interesting data in a relatively short period of time. And, as we have already noted, the ability to make accurate predictions is one of the key goals of science. Unfortunately, though, this research method suffers from one drawback that lessens its appeal, at least to a degree: the findings it produces are not conclusive about cause-and-effect relationships. In other words, the fact that two variables are correlated (that changes in one are accompanied by changes in another) does not in any sense guarantee that there is a causal link between them—that changes in the first *cause* changes in the second. (For an amusing illustration of this point, please see Figure 1-13).

To see why this is so, let's return to our example. Imagine that the psychologist actually finds a moderately strong correlation between negative ions and work performance. Does this mean that a high concentration of ions *causes* people to work harder or more efficiently? Perhaps. But it may also be the case that both the concentration of negative ions and good performance are related to a third factor, and it may be *this* variable that produces changes in performance. For example, the concentration of negative ions might increase with the effectiveness of the air conditioning in the offices and factories studied. (The more effective the air conditioning, the more comfortable the employees, and so the better their performance.) If our psychologist conducted her study during the summer, it might be this factor—not negative ions—which accounts for higher performance. Similarly, it could be that the concentration of negative ions is lowered by harmful substances in the air (e.g., chemical fumes in the factories, or too many people and not enough oxygen in the offices). Here, again, the correlation between negative ions and work performance would stem from the effects of a third factor, which is actually the one affecting employees' output.

In instances such as this one, the fact that correlation does not necessarily imply causation is relatively easy to spot. In other cases, though, it is more difficult, and we can easily slip into this error. For example, it has sometimes been reported that in major cities, crime rates increase with degree of crowding. Does this mean that crowding causes crime? Not necessarily. Both of these factors may be related to a third: level of income. The lower people's income, the more crowded the conditions in which they live. And the lower their income, the more likely they are to be exposed to many other factors that might increase the rate of crime, such as broken homes and exposure to many other persons behaving in an antisocial manner (please see Figure 1-14).

By now, we trust that the main point is clear. The existence of even a strong correlation between two factors should *not* be interpreted as a definite indication that they are causally linked. Such conclusions should be accepted only if they are supported by additional confirming evidence.

Correlation Does Not Equal Causation

FIGURE 1-13. The fact that changes in one variable are accompanied by changes in another does *not* guarantee that there is a causal link between them. Contrary to what Ziggy thinks, there's no basis for concluding that weather is responsible for problems with his car. *(Source: Universal Press Syndicate, 1985.)*

FIGURE 1-14. The fact that two variables are closely correlated does *not* necessarily mean that changes in one cause changes in the other. For example, as shown here, a correlation between degree of crowding in cities and rates of crime does *not* prove that crowding somehow causes crime. Instead, both factors may be affected by a third variable: income.

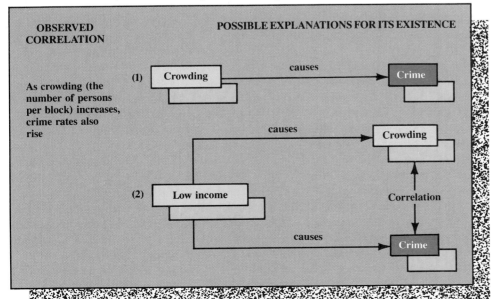

Why Correlation Doesn't Equal Causation

Experimentation: Knowledge Through Intervention

Now, at last we come to a method of research preferred by many psychologists: **experimentation.** There are several reasons for this preference, but perhaps the most important is this: in contrast to the other methods we have considered, experimentation yields relatively definitive evidence on causality. This, in turn, is extremely valuable from the point of view of another major goal of science: *explanation*. Briefly, scientists do not wish merely to describe the world around them and the relationships between different variables or factors in it. They want also to be able to explain *why* such relationships exist— why, for example, people possessing certain personality traits are more likely to suffer heart attacks than persons not possessing such traits, why some kinds of information are easier to remember than others, why some people have difficulty in maintaining a stable weight while others do not. Because it often yields information useful in answering such questions, experimentation is frequently the method of choice in psychology. But please take note: there are no hard-and-fast rules in this regard. Rather, most psychologists select the research technique that seems most suited to the topic they wish to study and the resources available to them.

Unfortunately, most persons seem to view experimentation as both mysterious and complex. Actually, this is far from the case. In its basic logic, experimentation is surprisingly simple. To help you understand its use in psychological research, we will first describe its basic nature—how experimentation actually proceeds. Then, we will comment briefly on two conditions essential for its success. Finally, we will consider some of the complex ethical issues raised by the use of experimentation in psychological research.

Experimentation: Its Basic Nature.   Reduced to its bare essentials, the experimental method involves two basic steps: (1) the presence or strength of some factor believed to affect behavior is *systematically varied;* and (2) the effects, if any, of such variations are measured. The logic behind these steps can also be simply stated: if the factor varied does indeed influence behavior or cognitive processes, individuals exposed to different levels or amounts of it should show contrasting patterns of behavior. Thus, exposure to a small amount of the factor should result in one level of behavior, exposure to a larger amount should result in a different level, and so on.

Generally, the factor systematically varied by the researcher is termed the **independent variable,** while the aspect of behavior or cognitive processes studied is termed the **dependent variable.** In a simple experiment, then, subjects in different groups are exposed to contrasting levels of the independent variable (e.g., low, moderate, high). Their behavior is then carefully measured and compared to determine whether it does in fact vary with different levels or amount of the independent variable. If it does—and if two other conditions we will mention below are met—it can be tentatively concluded that the independent variable does indeed affect the form of behavior or mental process being studied.

Perhaps a concrete example will help clarify this process. Let's return to the topic considered earlier—the influence of negative air ions on work performance. How could this be investigated by means of experimentation? Again, the answer is straightforward. The independent variable in this research—the one believed to affect behavior—is the concentration of negative ions. Thus, a researcher studying this issue would arrange for different groups of subjects to be exposed to contrasting levels of this factor (e.g., low, moderate, and high concentrations of negative ions). Such conditions could be produced in her laboratory by means of appropriate ion-generating equipment (such as that noted above). The dependent variable would be some measure of subjects' performance. For example, participants could be asked to work on a fairly simple task such as proofreading— finding errors in a typed manuscript. Our *hypothesis* might be that the higher the concentration of negative ions to which they are exposed, the greater their speed in performing this task (i.e., the more lines of type they will read). Alternatively, we could employ a different dependent measure: some index of subjects' accuracy (e.g., the percent of errors they correctly identify). Whatever our dependent measure, if ion concentration does affect performance, we would expect differences between subjects exposed to low, moderate,

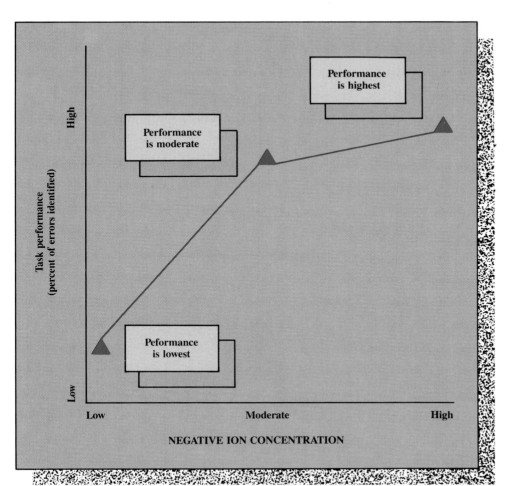

FIGURE 1-15. In the experiment shown here, the *independent variable* was negative ion concentration. The *dependent variable* was a measure of task performance (e.g., the percent of errors correctly noticed by subjects while proofreading). Results indicated that as ion concentration rose, performance improved. Thus, it can tentatively be concluded that negative ion concentration affects performance on this task.

and high ion levels. If (as shown in Figure 1-15) such differences were actually found, we could conclude, tentatively, that negative ion concentration does indeed affect performance, at least on the type of simple task studied.

Experimentation: Two Requirements for Its Success.   As we noted earlier, before we can conclude that an independent variable has caused some change in behavior, two conditions must be met. We will now describe these for you.

The first involves **random assignment of subjects to groups.** According to this principle, all participants in an experiment must have an equal chance of being exposed to each level of the independent variable. The reason for this rule is simple: if participants are *not* randomly assigned to each group, it may later be impossible to determine whether differences in their behavior stemmed from differences they brought with them to the study, or to the effects of the independent variable. In our ion example, imagine that all participants exposed to a high concentration of negative ions are experienced proofreaders, while those exposed to a moderate or low concentration of ions are people who have never performed this task before. If we now found that the first group of subjects outperformed the remaining two, what can we conclude? Actually, very little: we can't tell whether this difference stems from exposure to the higher level of negative ions or to their expertise in proofreading. In order to avoid such problems it is necessary to assure that initially, all participants in an experiment have an equal chance of being exposed to any level of the independent variable—they must be *randomly assigned* to each experimental group.

The second condition essential for conducting a successful experiment is this: insofar as possible, all factors that might also affect subjects' behavior, aside from the independent variable, must be held constant. To see why this is so, consider the following situation. In our ion experiment, the equipment used to generate different concentrations of ions also affects temperature. Thus, when subjects are exposed to a high concentration of ions, they are also exposed to higher temperatures (e.g., 77–78° Fahrenheit) than when they are exposed to a moderate concentration (74–75° F) or a low concentration (71–72° F). As before, the results of our study indicate that the higher the level of ions,

FIGURE 1-16. When factors other than the independent variable are not held constant, it may be impossible to interpret the results of an experiment. In the example shown here, the independent variable of interest was ion concentration. However, temperature, too, was permitted to vary. As a result, it is impossible to determine whether any results obtained stem from the influence of ions, temperature, or both. In short, *confounding of variables* exists.

Confounding of Variables in an Experiment

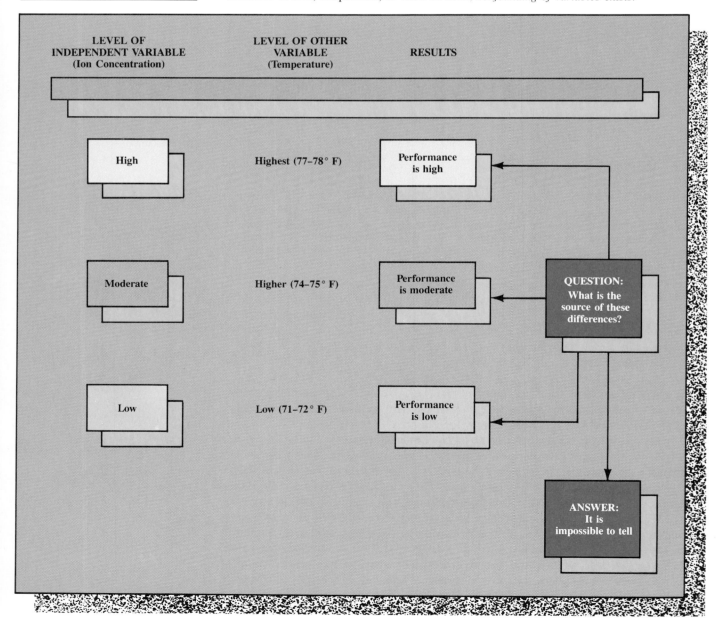

the better the subjects' performance. What can we conclude *now*? Again, very little. There is no way of knowing whether our results stem from the impact of negative ions, the impact of temperature, or both. In short, the independent variable is **confounded** with another variable the experimenter never wished to study (please refer to Figure 1-16).

In the case we have just described, confounding of variables is relatively easy to spot. Often, though, it can enter in more subtle and hidden ways. For this reason, experimenters must always guard against its impact. Only when confounding is prevented can the results of an experiment be interpreted with confidence as indicating a causal link between the independent and dependent variables.

Before concluding, we should note that research concerned with the impact of negative ions on several aspects of behavior has actually been performed (e.g., Baron, 1987a,b). Such research indicates that exposure to negative ions does *not* produce the uniformly beneficial effects suggested by advertisements. Instead, high concentrations of such particles seem to intensify whatever reactions are already occurring in a given situation. For example, if individuals are in a pleasant mood, negative ions enhance such feelings; if they are in a bad one, negative ions intensify *these* reactions (Baron, Russell, & Arms, 1985). Similarly, negative ions may increase performance on simple tasks people already know how to perform, but may interfere with performance on more complex ones they are just learning (Baron, 1987b). In view of such results, it seems important to view negative ion generators—and claims about their beneficial effects—with a healthy degree of caution.

Theory: An Essential Guide to Research

Over the years, we have often heard the following question from students in our classes: ''How do psychologists come up with the ideas for all those studies?'' Given the broad range of topics covered in introductory psychology, this question is hardly surprising. Our answer involves several different points.

First, as we have already seen, the need for systematic research on a given topic can be suggested by practical considerations. Should people buy and use ion generators? Only careful research can yield a satisfactory answer. Second, research projects often derive from informal observation of the world around us. Psychologists notice some interesting or puzzling aspect of behavior, and then plan investigations to shed new light upon it. Third, and most important, the idea for psychological research may derive from specific **theories.**

In simple terms, theories represent efforts by scientists in any field to answer the question, ''Why?'' In short, they involve attempts to understand *why* certain events or processes occur as they do. In this sense, theories go beyond mere observation or description of various aspects of behavior; they seek to *explain* them. The development of accurate theories is a major goal of all science (Howard, 1985), and psychology is no exception to this rule. Thus, a great deal of research in our field is concerned with efforts to construct, refine, and test such frameworks. But what *are* theories? In essence, they consist of two major parts: (1) several basic concepts and (2) statements concerning relationships between these concepts. Perhaps a concrete example will clarify matters.

Imagine that we observe the following: after individuals have made a decision, they tend to stick to it even in the face of growing evidence suggesting it was wrong. For example, they continue to hold a corporate stock that has dropped in value, and so increase their financial losses, or they remain in a romantic relationship which now yields more pain than joy (see Figure 1-17 on page 24). (We will consider this tendency, which is known as *entrapment* or *escalation of commitment* in Chapter 7.) Certainly, knowing about this tendency is useful in itself. It allows us to predict what may happen in many situations where people make errors of judgment. And it also suggests the possibility of intervening in some manner to prevent such outcomes. For example, we might caution people against the dangers of ''sticking to their guns'' once they learn that a decision is a poor one. These two accomplishments—*prediction* and *intervention* (or *control*)—are major goals of science. Knowing about the occurrence of entrapment, however, does not indicate *why* it takes place. It is at this point that *theory* enters the scientific process.

Theories in Psychology: Seeking Answers to the Question "Why?"

FIGURE 1-17. In psychology, as in other fields of science, theories seek to explain various aspects of human behavior, not simply to observe or describe them. For example, why do people sometimes remain in intimate relationships which have become sources of pain rather than love and satisfaction? Psychological theories offer intriguing answers.

In older fields, such as physics or chemistry, theories often take the form of mathematical equations. While this is also true to some extent in psychology, many of the theories we will consider in this book involve verbal assertions. For example, a theory designed to account for escalation of commitment might state: "When individuals make decisions that result in losses, they are reluctant to admit they made a mistake, for this will cause them to 'lose face' and look foolish in the eyes of others. As a result, they feel they have no choice but to stick to their original commitment." Note that this theory, like all others, consists of the two parts mentioned above: several basic concepts (e.g., losses, pressures to justify past actions) and assertions about the relationships between these concepts (e.g., as losses increase, pressures to justify previous decisions intensify).

Once a theory has been formulated, a crucial process begins. First, **hypotheses** (predictions) are derived from the theory in accordance with basic principles of logic. Then, such hypotheses are tested in actual research. If they are confirmed, confidence in the theory's accuracy is increased. If, instead, such predictions are disconfirmed, confidence in the theory's accuracy is reduced. The theory may then be altered so as to generate new hypotheses which, in turn, are subjected to test. If these, too, are disconfirmed, additional changes may be made in the theory, or it may be rejected as a scientific dead end. Until such conclusions are reached, the process involves a cycling and recycling between the theory, predictions derived from it, and the findings of ongoing research. (See Figure 1-18 for a summary of this process.)

One additional point: theories are useful, from a scientific point of view, only to the extent that they lead to *testable predictions*. If they do not generate hypotheses that can

Theories: The Source of Much Research in Psychology

FIGURE 1-18. Predictions derived from a theory are tested in actual research. If these are confirmed, confidence in the theory is increased. If they are disconfirmed, the theory may be modified, and new predictions tested. If these, too, are disconfirmed, confidence in the theory's accuracy is reduced and, ultimately, it may be rejected.

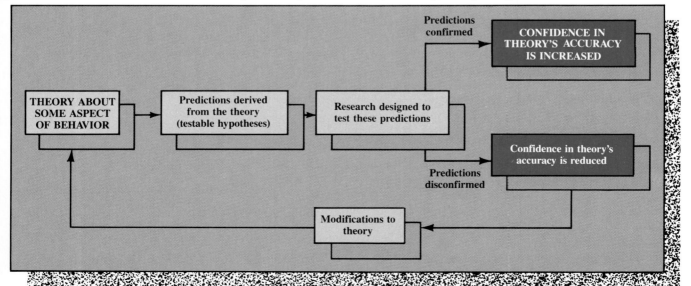

A Theory That Can't Be Tested
Is No Theory at All

FIGURE 1-19. Contrary to what the character in this cartoon believes, theories that can't be tested are useless from the point of view of science. *(Source: Field Enterprises, Inc.)*

be examined in actual research, they are *not* scientific in nature. For example, consider the following ''theory'': the reason you are so unlucky in love is that you were a scoundrel in one of your previous lives, and you are now paying for your misdeeds. Obviously, there is no way to verify or refute the view that you have had previous existences (that you have experienced *reincarnation*), or that there is some mechanism in the universe that acts to ''even the scales'' across these many lives! Thus, such a ''theory'' is not a theory at all; it does not generate predictions testable by scientific means. In sum, the character in Figure 1-19 is definitely wrong: theories are *not* useful when they can't be tested. In fact, just the opposite is true: theories belong within the realm of science only when they can be confirmed or refuted through actual research.

The Ethics of Psychological Research: Must the Quest for Knowledge and the Rights of Individuals Clash?

Strange as it may seem, the phrase ''psychological research'' has a sinister ring for some people. When they hear it, they visualize frightening scenes in which diabolical scientists twist the psyches of unwilling subjects around their fingers, wringing facts and admissions from them they'd prefer not to reveal. That such concerns are not restricted to some outlandish ''fringe'' is suggested by the fact that at least one U.S. senator (William Proxmire) has gone on record as stating that certain types of psychological research (studies dealing with romantic love) are inappropriate and should be stopped. Moreover, to back up his objections, he has awarded the infamous ''Golden Fleece Award'' to several psychologists whose research he found particularly objectionable and wasteful of public funds. Are such anxieties well-founded? Is psychological research really harmful to the people and animals who participate in it, and therefore unethical? While we don't wish to gloss over a complex and serious issue, our answer is a confident ''No.'' The vast bulk of psychological research conducted today is performed in accordance with the ethical principles acceptable both to society and to science. Perhaps the best way of illustrating this fact is to consider some of the major objections to psychological research and explain how each is defused by current research practice.

The first objection is that in their research, psychologists violate their subjects' right to privacy. In other words, they obtain information participants do not wish to reveal. While this may sound reasonable (especially if one is given to fantasies of all-powerful psychologists who literally hypnotize their subjects into submission), this concern overlooks a very basic fact: in virtually all psychological studies research participants are not identified as individuals. Rather, the data from many subjects are combined, and no record of names or other identifying information is retained. The reason for this is that as a science, psychology is primarily concerned with establishing general principles—ones that apply to human beings generally. Thus, there is little if any reason to focus on specific persons. The fact that data from many individuals are combined goes a long way toward protecting research participants from the invasions of privacy feared by some critics.

A second objection sometimes raised about psychological research is that it exposes both human and animal subjects to potential physical and psychological harm. Given that psychologists do sometimes expose research participants to stressful or unpleasant conditions, this objection seems, at first glance, to have some merit. However, it ignores the fact that at present, all plans for research in psychology must be reviewed and approved by standing committees (Institutional Review Boards) in the setting where such research is conducted (universities, research institutes, government agencies). Such IRBs, as they are usually termed, subject each planned project to careful scrutiny and approve only those which take adequate safeguards to protect the safety and well-being of subjects. Indeed, recent evidence suggests that such bodies are quite conservative in this respect, and grant approval only when risk is held to a minimum and all procedures are consistent with accepted scientific standards (Ceci, Peters, & Plotkin, 1985). As evidence that such research is carefully screened, consider the following question: when was the last time you read or heard about harm to a participant in a psychological investigation? Given the huge number (many thousands) of studies performed by psychologists each year, this record of protecting the welfare of participants is impressive.

A third objection to psychological research raises even more complex issues than those we have already considered. This criticism centers around the fact that sometimes psychologists find it necessary to conceal the purposes of a research project, or certain of its aspects, from participants—a procedure known as **deception.** The reason for doing so is this: knowledge of these aspects of the research would alter subjects' behavior, so little could then be learned about the topic under investigation. For example, imagine that before participating in a study concerned with the causes of prejudice, participants were told about this purpose. They might then lean over backwards to avoid demonstrating any prejudice, and so render the study useless. Similarly, suppose that in a study concerned with factors that interfere with problem-solving, subjects were given a description of each of these factors. This might result in a situation where participants take great pains to overcome the effects of such factors.

In cases such as these, most psychologists feel it is appropriate to withhold such information from participants temporarily, provided that (1) before agreeing to take part in a study, subjects are given as much information as possible about the study and their role in it (informed consent); and (2) they are provided with thorough **debriefing** after it is completed—full information about all of its aspects once they have fulfilled their role as participant. We should note, though, that not all psychologists share this conviction. Some (e.g., Baumrind, 1985) believe that deception, even if temporary and for excellent scientific reasons, is not justified. They feel that the use of such procedures reduces subjects' faith in science generally, and in psychology in particular, and so jeopardizes continued public support for psychological research. While such arguments should not be ignored, existing evidence seems to point to more optimistic conclusions. Persons who have taken part in studies employing deception actually report more positive feelings about psychology and its research than do persons who have not been exposed to such procedures (Smith & Richardson, 1983). And it appears that a thorough debriefing at the conclusion of studies employing deception does eliminate negative feelings or effects subjects may have experienced during the investigation itself (Smith & Richardson, 1985).

These and related findings suggest that psychological research *can* in fact proceed—that it *can* be used to increase our understanding of behavior and cognitive processes. However, potential dangers exist. Thus, we must be constantly on guard to prevent their occurrence and to protect the rights and well-being of all individuals who, through their time, effort, and cooperation, help us to advance the essential science.

A Note on Research with Animals

If you were given a tour through the research facilities of any large psychology department, you would soon encounter rooms filled with rats, pigeons, or monkeys, as well as equipment for studying their behavior (refer to Figure 1-20). Obviously, then, psychologists conduct a great deal of research with animals. Why? Aren't they primarily interested in human beings? The answer to this question is, "Yes, but there are important reasons for studying animal behavior, too."

First, knowledge about the behavior of species other than our own can be of immense practical value. Understanding the needs and preferences of animals on which we depend for food and other products can help us establish conditions under which they

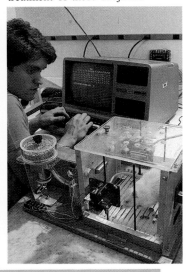

FIGURE 1-20. Psychologists often conduct research with animals. When they do, they follow detailed guidelines for the humane treatment of these subjects.

The Study of Animal Behavior: An Important Part of Modern Psychology will thrive. Similarly, understanding the behavior of various pests can help us to combat them more effectively, perhaps without the use of dangerous chemicals that may poison us as well as them.

Second, because they often have much shorter lifespans than human beings, some animal species provide a useful means for studying *development*—changes during a life-span. Studies that might require decades with human beings can be performed in much shorter periods with mice or rats. Similarly, the behavioral effects of various environmental conditions may become apparent only across several generations. Here, again, animals with a relatively short span of life may provide a practical alternative to long-term research with humans.

A third reason for conducting research with animals is implicit in our comments thus far: it may simply be impossible (for health or safety reasons) to conduct certain types of research with human participants. In such cases, researchers must perform their studies with animals or not study the problem at all. For example, imagine that a psychologist had reason to believe that a particular portion of the brain plays a key role in certain types of learning disability. Obviously, he or she could not investigate this hypothesis by inflicting neural damage on human subjects—even volunteers!

Guidelines for the humane treatment of animals in *all* research—medical, psychological, or biological—have been established by appropriate government agencies and by the American Psychological Association. While no human endeavor is perfect, psychologists adhere closely to such rules, and do their best to conduct their studies in the safest and most humane manner possible.

Using This Book: A Displaced Preface

Before concluding, we'd like to explain several features of this text. Such information is often included in a preface, but since many readers seem to skip such messages, presenting it here may prove useful.

First, we've taken several steps to make this text easier to read and more convenient to use. One of these concerns *organization*. Past experience tells us that one reason students find some textbooks undecipherable is a lack of careful attention to this issue; they don't see how the author got from point A to point B. To lessen this problem, we've tried to arrange the materials within each chapter in as orderly and logical a manner as possible. Further, to help you grasp this organization, an outline is presented at the start of each chapter. Please examine the outline before reading each chapter, for, as we noted before, having a mental framework to hold new information really *does* help. In addition, we've made use of very distinct headings. Major sections begin with prominent headings like the one above (''Using This Book: A Displaced Preface''). Within each major section, sub-sections start with smaller headings, such as the one on page 25 (''The Ethics of Psychological Research: Must the Quest for Knowledge and the Rights of Individuals Clash?'').

Second, we've included a number of other features designed to help in your studying. All chapters conclude with a summary. Within the text, key terms or concepts are printed in **dark type like this,** and they are defined in a glossary (''Key Terms'') at the end of the chapter. All figures and tables have been specially prepared for this text and are as clear as possible. In addition, many contain special labels which call your attention to the key findings being illustrated.

Finally, two types of special sections are included. The first, ''Focus on Research,'' appears in two forms: ''Classic Contributions'' and ''The Cutting Edge.'' As you can guess, the former describes research that started new lines of research or changed the thinking of psychologists about some topic. The latter describes recent studies carried out at the frontiers of our field. The second type of insert, labeled ''The Point of It All,'' is designed to indicate how the findings and principles of psychology are currently being put to practical use, or how they may be used in the future. Such sections also consider the implications of psychological knowledge for society.

It is our hope that these and other features of this text will help you to understand psychology, and also help you to share our excitement with it. In any case, may your first formal contact with the "essential science" be as stimulating, enjoyable, and beneficial as ours was almost thirty years ago.

Summary and Review

Psychology: A Definition and Some History

Psychology is the science of behavior and cognitive processes. It studies virtually every aspect of what we do, feel, and think. Because it adopts scientific methods and values, it can be viewed as essentially scientific in nature, and its findings go far beyond mere common sense. Important facts about human behavior were uncovered in the late nineteenth and early twentieth centuries. However, psychology did not attain anything approaching its modern form until the 1920s, when John B. Watson suggested that it should be concerned only with observable activities—ones that can be subjected to scientific observation and measurement.

Psychology: Who and What

At present there are over 100,000 psychologists in the U.S. alone. Many different branches of psychology exist, each focused on specific aspects of behavior. However, these specialties are unified by shared goals and values and by the ready flow of information among them.

The Nature of Psychological Research

In order to obtain new information about behavior and cognitive processes psychologists make use of several different research methods. These include *naturalistic observation*—the study of behavior in natural settings, the *case method*—detailed study of a small number of interesting cases, and *surveys*—procedures in which many persons are asked to describe their attitudes or behavior. Two additional approaches of somewhat greater importance in modern psychology are the *correlational method* and *experimentation*. In the first, two or more variables are carefully observed to determine whether changes in one are associated with changes in the other. To the extent such correlations exist, one variable can be predicted from the other.

In *experimentation,* one or more independent variables are systematically varied by a researcher in order to determine if changes in this factor produce changes in one or more aspects of behavior or cognitive processes.

Many research projects conducted by psychologists are designed to test *hypotheses* derived from specific *theories*. Theories consist of several basic concepts and assertions concerning relationships between these concepts. If hypotheses (predictions) derived from a theory are confirmed by research findings, confidence in its accuracy is increased. If such predictions are disconfirmed, the theory may be revised and then tested once again. Thus, there is a continuous interplay between theories, hypotheses derived from them, and the results of ongoing research.

Some critics contend that psychological research is unethical because it invades the privacy of participants or exposes them to potential harm. However, many safeguards protect the rights and well-being of subjects. Occasionally, it is necessary to withhold information about the purposes of a study or some of its procedures from participants—a practice known as *deception*. Most psychologists believe this is permissible if the persons involved are informed about all the procedures to which they will be exposed prior to participation *(informed consent)* and then given a full explanation of the study after its completion *(debriefing)*.

Psychologists often conduct research with animals. This is so for several reasons: (1) information about the behavior of various species may be of practical as well as scientific value, (2) their relatively short lifespans make animals highly useful in the study of development, and (3) they must sometimes be employed in place of humans in studies involving risks to health or safety. Animal subjects must always be treated in the most humane manner feasible.

 Key Terms

Behaviorism The view that psychology should study only observable (overt) behavior.

Case Method A method of research in which detailed information about specific individuals (cases) is used to formulate general principles about some aspect of behavior.

Confounding of Variables A situation that arises when factors other than the independent variable in an experiment are not held constant.

Correlational Method A method of research in which two or more variables are observed, to determine whether changes in one are accompanied by changes in the other. To the degree that this is so, one variable can be accurately predicted from the other.

Debriefing Providing participants in psychological research with complete and accurate information about all purposes and procedures of a study following its completion.

Dependent Variable The aspect of behavior that is measured in psychological research.

Experimentation A method of research in which one or more variables are systematically varied in order to determine whether such changes affect some aspect of behavior or cognitive processes.

Functionalism An early approach suggesting that psychology should focus on the contribution of our mental processes to our survival in a complex and ever-changing world.

Hypothesis The prediction about behavior or cognitive processes under investigation in psychological research.

Independent Variable The factor that is systematically varied in an experiment.

Informed Consent Providing potential subjects with as much information as feasible prior to obtaining their consent to take part in psychological research.

Naturalistic Observation A method of research involving careful observations of behavior in natural settings.

Psychology The science of behavior and cognitive processes.

Random Assignment of Subjects to Groups Assuring that all participants in psychological research have an equal opportunity of being assigned to any of the experimental conditions.

Statistical Analysis Mathematical procedures used to evaluate the results obtained in psychological research.

Structuralism An early view suggesting that psychology should focus on the task of analyzing conscious experience into its component parts.

Survey Approach A method of research in which large numbers of persons answer questions about some aspect of their attitudes or behavior.

Theories Frameworks in science for explaining various phenomena. Theories consist of two major parts: basic concepts and assertions concerning relationships between these concepts.

For More Information

American Psychological Association. (1978). *A career in psychology*. Washington: American Psychological Association.

    This booklet provides information on the various branches of psychology and on the type of training required to become a psychologist. You can obtain a free copy by writing to the American Psychological Association, 1200 Seventeenth St. NW, Washington, DC 20036.

Drew, C.J., & Hardman, M.L. (1985). *Designing and conducting behavioral research*. Elmsford, NY: Pergamon Press.

    A clear and relatively brief description of how psychologists and other behavioral scientists plan and conduct research projects. If you'd like to learn more about this topic, this is a good place to start.

Schultz, D.P., & Shultz, S.E. (1987). *History of modern psychology*, 4th ed. San Diego: Harcourt Brace Jovanovich.

    A concise overview of major developments in the history of psychology. Contemporary trends (e.g., growing interest in cognitive processes) are given special attention.

CHAPTER

2

Biological Bases of Behavior: A Look Beneath the Surface

"Did you hear about Jenni and David?" Carla asks her friend Pam.

"Yeah, I sure did," she replies. "A real bad accident out on the Interstate. Hit a big truck. But they're both O.K., aren't they? Fred told me they're out of the hospital."

"Well, you're half right, anyway." Carla answers. "They're back home, but whether they're all right is something else again."

"What do you mean?" Pam asks, a puzzled look on her face.

"Hm . . . it's kind of hard to describe. They both have different problems. . . ."

"Well come on, *tell* me!" Pam says, a note of irritation in her voice. Carla often delivers information one tiny piece at a time, and today she has no patience for this tactic.

"O.K., O.K. It seems to have something to do with the fact that they both had pretty bad head injuries. Jenni was thrown out of the car and landed on her left side; she really got bumped on the head. And now she does some real strange things, like, sometimes, when you talk to her, she doesn't seem to understand a word you're saying. If you repeat it a few times, she catches on. But it's weird, real weird."

"No kidding!" Pam comments. "What else?"

"Well, sometimes I get the feeling she really doesn't know where her own arms and legs are. Yesterday I had lunch with her, and when she got up, she seemed to forget she had her right leg up on a chair—practically fell over."

"Mm, that's *strange* all right," Pam says, shaking her head. "But what about David? Does he have the same problems?"

"No, he understands everything you say, and isn't any clumsier than usual." At this comment, both friends laugh, for David is famous for tripping over his own feet, dropping things, and generally acting like a big, overeager puppy. "But there *is* something different about him. . . . I guess it's that he seems so bland—just kind of stares in front of him all the time. Remember how he used to get so excited?" Pam nods in agreement. "Well, he's not like that any more. Really, it's kind of spooky. He still *looks* the same, but when I'm with him, I'd swear it's a different person."

"Did he get hurt on the side of the head, too?" Pam asks.

"No. That's the funny part. He stayed in the car, but was thrown against the roof; he got hit on the top of his head, near the front. Hm . . . I wonder if that's why he has different problems than Jennifer."

"Well, I don't know," Pam remarks, shaking her head, "I'm no doctor. But I can tell you one thing: from now on I'm going to wear my seat belt!"

What happens when you experience rage, joy, or sexual desire? How can you remember events that took place months or even years in the past? How do you know you are hungry, thirsty, or tired? What happens when you think, reason, or daydream? If you are like most people, you have wondered about questions such as these, at least occasionally. And like most people, you have probably assumed that the answers involve *something* going on inside your body—probably within your brain (please see Figure 2-1).

If you have reasoned in this manner, you are in good company. In fact, your basic conclusion is central to a major branch of our field—**physiological psychology** (sometimes known as *psychobiology* or behavioral neuroscience). Physiological psychologists, too, believe that conscious experience—in fact, everything we think, feel, or do—is a result of (or is at least influenced by) biological processes within our bodies. Thus, they focus their attention on the task of studying the inner processes responsible for our feelings, actions, and thoughts. If we can understand these, they suggest, our knowledge of behavior and cognitive processes will be enhanced. We agree. In fact, we feel that trying

All Aspects of Behavior Have a
Biological Basis

FIGURE 2-1. *Physiological psychologists* believe that conscious experience—everything we feel, think, or remember—is a result of biological processes occurring within our bodies.

to understand human behavior without a basic grasp of its biological roots is like trying to solve a puzzle from which several crucial pieces have been removed. In this chapter, therefore, we will present a brief introduction to the biological structures and physiological processes that play a crucial role in behavior. In order to accomplish this, we will touch on several related topics.

First, we will describe the structure and function of **neurons,** the building blocks of which our nervous system—and therefore, ultimately, our consciousness—is composed. Next, we will turn to the **nervous system** itself, devoting special attention to the brain—that magnificent organ that is responsible for much that makes us uniquely human *and* much that we share with other forms of life. After that, we'll examine the **endocrine system,** internal glands regulated by the nervous system that play an important role in several aspects of behavior. Finally, we'll consider the role of *genetic factors* in human behavior, and the relatively new (and still controversial) field of **sociobiology.**

One last point before we start: throughout this chapter, we will be using terms and describing processes that may, at first glance, seem more at home in a text on biology than in a text on psychology. *Please don't be confused!* Our interest is not in these structures and processes themselves but their relationship to behavior. So, as we hope you'll soon see, we aren't departing from the course charted in Chapter 1; we're simply starting with an important "port of call" you may not have realized was on our route.

"Is That All There Is?" A Note on Levels of Analysis.   A popular song of the 1970s posed the question in this heading over and over again. While the song itself pondered the meaning of life, these words can also be applied to the view that, in the final analysis, everything we think, feel, or do can be understood in terms of biological processes. Is that really all there is? Can all of our feelings, hopes, plans, and desires—the human spirit—be explained in these terms? Most psychologists would answer "Yes." In other words, they accept what philosophers describe as a *reductionist* view. Does this mean that you should drop introductory psychology and switch to biology or chemistry? Hardly. Two major points argue strongly against such a reaction, and *for* a field of psychology that investigates human behavior from several different perspectives.

First, while psychologists do assume that human behavior stems, ultimately, from underlying biological processes, they realize that we are very far from being able to put

Interpreting Complex Stimuli Requires Higher Levels of Neural Organization

FIGURE 2-2. Single neurons can detect movement and orientation in space. However, interpreting such movement (e.g., recognizing that it involves coordinated actions by the members of a marching band) involves complex interactions between large numbers of neurons.

this principle into practice. We simply do not know enough about the brain, the nervous system, and other biological systems to explain complex forms of behavior purely in such terms. Until such knowledge is available, it seems reasonable to continue studying behavior at other levels of analysis than the biological.

Second, and perhaps even more important, growing evidence indicates that the nervous system itself (and hence behavior, too) is *hierarchically organized* (Van Essen & Maunsell, 1983). While relatively simple functions or aspects of behavior can be related to the functioning of single neurons or small groups of neurons, more complex behaviors are quite another story: they involve coordinated activity in millions of cells in various portions of the nervous system. Moreover, new capacities, not readily predictable from the properties of single neurons or specific structures, emerge at higher levels of organization. For example, single neurons can detect the fact that various objects are moving across our visual field. However, the ability to grasp the *meaning* of such motion (e.g., the fact that it is produced by the members of a marching band) emerges only from subtle and complex interactions between countless neurons in many regions of the brain (see Figure 2-2).

So, to return to our initial question, Is that all there is? We can answer "Yes, indeed"; all of our feelings, thoughts, and actions involve biological events and processes. But this by no means implies that there is no value in the many topics we will consider in later chapters—everything from our ability to solve problems and use language to the capacity to feel love or experience deep depression. On the contrary, understanding how these reactions and abilities emerge from underlying biological bases is part of the challenge of modern psychology. Having clarified these points, let's begin at the beginning with a consideration of *neurons*—the building blocks for all aspects of our behavior.

Neurons: From Small Beginnings . . .

Suppose you were walking along the street when you happened to see a crisp, new $20 bill. What would happen next? Almost certainly, you would stop in your tracks, bend down, and pick it up. Then, perhaps smiling, you would continue on your way, thinking about your good fortune and what you might have done recently to deserve it! At first glance, this sequence of events seems simple. But how does it actually unfold? How did

FIGURE 2-3. Neurons occur in many different forms, but all show the basic structures presented here: a cell body, an axon (with its terminal buttons), and one or more dendrites.

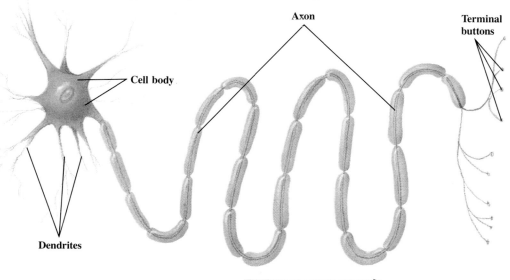

The Basic Structure of Neurons

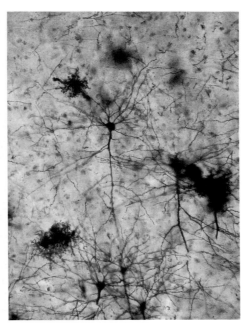

FIGURE 2-4. Actual human neurons, as you can see, vary greatly in shape.

the information received by your eyes travel to your brain? And then how did appropriate messages of some sort move from your brain to various parts of your body, so that you could react in an appropriate manner? The answer involves **neurons**—cells within our bodies that are specialized for the tasks of receiving, moving, and processing information.

Neurons: Their Basic Structure

Although neurons take many forms in different parts of the body, most show three basic parts: (1) a **cell body,** (2) an **axon,** and (3) one or more **dendrites.** Dendrites carry information toward the cell body, while axons carry information away from it. Thus, in a sense, neurons are "one-way" channels of communication. Information usually moves from dendrites or the cell body toward the axon, and then outward along this structure. A simplified diagram of a neuron is shown in Figure 2-3, and some actual neurons are shown, magnified, in Figure 2-4.

In many neurons, the axon is covered by a sheath of fatty material known as *myelin*. The myelin sheath is interrupted at several points by small gaps. As we will soon note, both the sheath and the gaps in it play an important role in the neuron's ability to transmit information.

Near its end, the axon divides into several small branches. These, in turn, end in round structures known as **terminal buttons** which closely approach, but do not actually touch, other cells of the body (other neurons, muscles, or glands). This region is called the *synapse,* and the manner in which information manages to cross this small space will be described below.

Neurons: Their Basic Function

In considering how neurons function, two questions arise: (1) how does information travel within a single neuron and (2) how is information transmitted from one neuron to another, or from neurons to other cells of the body?

Communication Within Neurons: The Action Potential.   The answer to the first question is complex, but it can be summarized as follows. When a neuron is at rest (i.e., not transmitting information), there are more positively charged particles (especially

The Action Potential: How Neurons ''Fire''

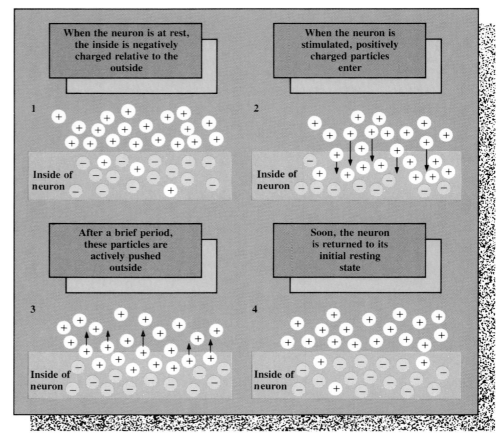

When the neuron is at rest, the inside is negatively charged relative to the outside

1

Inside of neuron

When the neuron is stimulated, positively charged particles enter

2

Inside of neuron

After a brief period, these particles are actively pushed outside

3

Inside of neuron

Soon, the neuron is returned to its initial resting state

4

Inside of neuron

FIGURE 2-5. (1) When a neuron is at rest, there are more positively charged particles (sodium ions) outside it than inside. As a result, a tiny negative electric charge exists across the cell membrane. This is known as the *resting potential*. (2) When the cell is stimulated, positively charged particles enter, thus eliminating the resting potential. (3) A few milliseconds later, positively charged particles are actively pumped outside. (4) The resting potential is then restored, and the neuron is ready to ''fire'' once again.

sodium ions) outside it than inside it. Conversely, there are more negatively charged particles within it than outside (refer to Figure 2-5). As a result, the interior of the cell acquires a tiny negative charge (about 70 thousandths of a volt, or 70 millivolts) relative to the outside. This is known as the *resting potential,* and it is not an accidental or chance occurrence. It results from the fact that the cell does active work to hold positively charged particles (mainly sodium ions) outside. When the neuron is then stimulated, this situation changes radically. The cell membrane alters so that the positively charged sodium ions can readily enter. As they do, the resting potential is reduced and then eliminated. In fact, the inside of the cell may actually become positive relative to the outside, a reversal of the original state of affairs.

After a very brief period (1 or 2 milliseconds), the membrane regains its resistance to positively charged particles (i.e., sodium ions). Further, those inside the cell are actively pumped back outside. As a result, the resting potential is gradually restored, and the cell becomes ready to ''fire'' once more. Together, these swings in electric charge—from negative to positive and back again—are termed the **action potential.** And it is the passage of this electrical disturbance along the cell membrane that constitutes the basic ''signal'' of our nervous system.

Note, by the way, that the action potential (or *nerve impulse,* as it is often termed) is an *all-or-none* affair. Either it occurs at full strength or it does not occur at all; there is nothing in between. Also, in neurons possessing a myelin sheath, the action potential does not travel along the entire axon; rather, it jumps from one small gap in the sheath to another. This greatly increases its speed, which can reach 200 meters per second (about 224 miles per hour).

Communication Between Neurons: Synaptic Transmission.   Earlier we noted that neurons closely approach, but do not actually touch, other neurons (or other cells of the body). How, then, does the action potential cross this tiny gap? Existing evidence suggests the following answer.

When a neuron is stimulated, the action potential produced travels along its membrane from the dendrites or cell body to the axon, and then to the terminal buttons. At this point, the information it carries must somehow cross the **synapse**—a region of close approach between the terminal buttons of one neuron and the membrane of another cell. How is this accomplished? The answer is largely through chemical means.

Located within the terminal buttons are many round or oval structures known as **synaptic vesicles.** Arrival of the action potential causes these vesicles to approach the cell membrane, where they empty their contents into the synapse (refer to Figure 2-6). The chemicals thus released—usually known as *transmitter substances*—travel across the synapse until they reach special *receptors* in the membrane of the other cell. These receptors are complex protein molecules whose structure is such that transmitter substances fit like chemical ''keys'' into the ''locks'' they provide. When they contact receptors, transmitter substances produce one of two effects. If they are *excitatory* in nature, they stimulate production of an action potential in the second neuron. This then travels away from the point of origin—from the dendrite or cell body toward the axon—and excites another neuron. In contrast, if transmitter substances are *inhibitory* in nature, they make it more difficult for this second neuron to conduct an action potential. In other words, they may reduce the likelihood that it will fire.

The fact that transmitter substances produce either excitatory or inhibitory effects seems to suggest that there are only two types. In fact, though, many different transmitter substances exist. Moreover, these seem capable of exerting contrasting effects, depending on where in the nervous system they occur. For example, **acetylcholine,** one important transmitter substance, seems to produce mainly excitation in the brain. Indeed, the death of neurons sensitive to acetylcholine seems to play a role in the occurrence of *Alzheimer's disease*—a fatal illness that involves progressive loss of memory and other cognitive functions. However, in other parts of the nervous system, away from the brain, it may exert an inhibitory effect. Similarly, **norepinephrine,** another important transmitter substance, produces inhibitory effects within the brain, but excitatory ones in other locations.

FIGURE 2-6. (1) Terminal buttons found on the ends of axons contain many *synaptic vesicles.* (2) When an action potential reaches the terminal buttons, these vesicles approach the cell membrane. (3) Then they release their contents (*transmitter substance*) into the synapse.

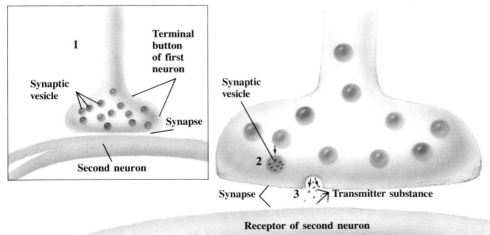

Basic Steps in Synaptic Transmission

TABLE 2-1

Many Different Transmitter Substances Play a Role in the Transmission of Information by the Nervous System

Transmitter Substance	Where Found	Effects
Acetylcholine	Brain, spinal cord, autonomic nervous system, target organs of the parasympathetic system	Excitation in brain and autonomic nervous system; excitation or inhibition of target organs
Norepinephrine	Brain, spinal cord, target organs of sympathetic system	Inhibition in brain; excitation or inhibition of target organs
Dopamine	Brain	Inhibition
Serotonin	Brain, spinal cord	Inhibition
GABA	Brain, spinal cord	Inhibition
Glutamic acid	Brain, spinal sensory nerves	Excitation
Aspartic acid	Spinal cord, brain	Excitation

A summary of the effects of several important transmitter substances is presented in Table 2-1. As it suggests, communication between neurons is far from a simple matter.

Incidentally, direct evidence for release of transmitter substances from synaptic vesicles exists. For example, in one ingenious study, Heuser and his colleagues (1979) stimulated neurons from a frog's leg (by mild electric current) and then dropped them against a super-cooled block of pure copper. The intense cold literally froze the biochemical reactions we have been discussing so that they could be studied with an electron microscope. As you can see from Figure 2-7, the events described earlier were clearly visible. Many synaptic vesicles could be seen approaching the cell membrane, while others had already opened, thus releasing the transmitter substance through the cell membrane.

At this point, you may be wondering about an obvious question we haven't yet considered: what happens to transmitter substances after they cross the synapse? The answer is relatively clear. Either they are taken back into the terminal buttons of the

FIGURE 2-7. When stimulated and then frozen instantaneously, neurons from a frog's leg clearly show the key events involved in synaptic transmission. Synaptic vesicles can be seen approaching the cell membrane and releasing molecules of transmitter substance into the synapse. *(Source: Heuser, 1977. Courtesy Dr. J.E. Heuser.)*

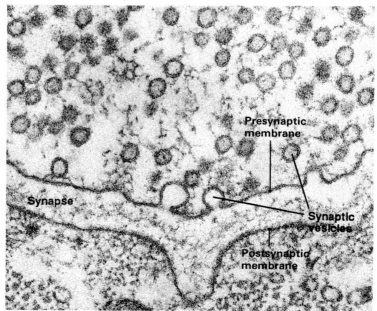

neuron which released them (a process known as *re-uptake*) or they are deactivated by substances present at the synapse (various enzymes). Thus, they are quickly put out of commission in one way or another.

One final point: our comments so far have greatly simplified reality. In contrast to the "one-on-one" situation we have been describing, most neurons actually form synapses with many other neurons, not just one. Thus, at any given moment a neuron may receive a complex pattern of excitatory and inhibitory influences from many neighbors. Whether it conducts an action potential or not, then, depends upon the total pattern of this input—at any given instant and across time. And as we shall soon see, it is the total pattern of activity in our brain and other parts of our nervous system that seems to be responsible for everything we think, feel, know, or do.

(Is there any practical use for understanding the process through which neurons communicate with each other and with other cells of the body? Definitely. For information on this issue, please see "The Point of It All" section below.)

THE POINT OF IT ALL

Drugs and Synaptic Transmission

In the late twentieth century, drugs are big business—*very* big business. And the medical portion of this huge industry is by no means the largest part. Each day, hundreds of millions of human beings take drugs, not to combat illness or improve their health, but for another reason: to change the way they feel. To mention just a few specific uses, people consume drugs to encourage sleep or to fight fatigue, to calm jittery nerves or to increase their energy, to chase away the blues, or simply to "turn on" (refer to Figure 2-8). We will return to the problems that stem from the use (and abuse) of such substances in later chapters. Here, we simply wish to call your attention to an important link between the topics we have been discussing (the structure and function of neurons) and the effects of many drugs. Stated simply, the link is this: in many cases, it seems, drugs affect our feelings or behavior by altering the process of synaptic transmission. In short, they produce their effects by changing the complex biochemical events that take place when one neuron communicates with another. This can occur in several ways.

Some drugs seem to either stimulate or inhibit the release of transmitter substances at synapses. For example, *atropine*, which is often used to dilate the pupils prior to eye examinations, produces such effects by interfering with the action of *acetylcholine*, a key transmitter substance in many parts of the nervous system. More dramatically, *botulinim toxin*, a substance sometimes found in canned foods that have decayed, totally blocks the release of this key transmitter substance. The result: essential bodily functions are interrupted, and death may result. So powerful is this toxin that less than one one-millionth of a gram can prove fatal.

Other drugs mimic the effects of transmitter substances, either stimulating or inhibiting activity in various portions of the nervous system. For example, *nicotine*, a drug found in

THE DECAFÉ

FIGURE 2-8. When individuals take certain drugs to change the way they feel, they often become dependent on them for such effects. As you probably know, the drug involved here—*caffeine*—increases feelings of alertness. (*Source:* The New Yorker.)

Drugs: One Common Form of Dependence

tobacco, stimulates neural receptors normally affected by acetylcholine, and so, in small doses, acts as a mild stimulant. Still other drugs serve as *false transmitters*, occupying receptors normally stimulated by natural transmitter substances, but failing to trigger action potentials in the neurons involved. (In a sense, they act like keys that fit into a lock, but won't turn.) The poison *curare* operates in this manner. It replaces acetylcholine at many synapses between neurons and muscle cells. As a result, total paralysis occurs, and persons who receive this drug may suffocate because they are unable to breathe.

Some drugs inhibit the re-entry of transmitter substances into terminal buttons. *Cocaine* and *amphetamines* seem to function in this manner. They prevent the re-uptake of such transmitter substances as *dopamine* and *norepinephrine*. As a result, these substances remain in the synapse, where they continue to stimulate activity in the neurons they contact. This helps explain why persons taking such drugs often experience feelings of tremendous excitement and energy.

A very different mechanism seems to be involved in the impact of various *opiates* (morphine, heroin). Recent findings indicate there are special *opiate receptors* within the brain—neurons that are associated with feelings of well-being and other pleasurable sensations, plus *analgesia*—a lessening of pain. Why do such receptors exist? Apparently, because the body produces its own opiate-like substances during times of stress. These *opioid peptides* or *endorphins* lessen pain, and so help us cope with a wide range of stressful activities (e.g., fighting, mating, other actions requiring intense exertion). Recent evidence, which we'll consider in more detail in Chapter 9, suggests that they also play an important role in regulating the intake of many kinds of foods and may also be related to alcoholism and other "ingestion disorders" (Bertino et al., 1988; Hubbell, Czirr, & Reid, 1987.)

Other substances, such as alcohol, tranquilizers, and barbiturates seem to produce their effects by inhibiting activity in many neurons, although the precise mechanisms through which this occurs are not yet known. And still others, such as some drugs used to treat depression, may affect the sensitivity of certain types of neural receptors to several transmitter substances (McNeal & Cimbolic, 1986).

As we're sure you can readily see, understanding how drugs produce their effects can yield important practical benefits. First, such knowledge can aid in the development of effective antidotes for various poisons. Second, and perhaps of even greater importance, drugs are often abused (e.g., alcohol, heroin, cocaine), and understanding how they affect neurons and the nervous system may suggest ways of treating their harmful effects, perhaps even how to counter addiction to them. Finally, knowledge of how various drugs produce their effects is currently providing valuable clues about the causes of serious psychological disorders. For example, recent studies designed to discover just how *antidepressants* (drugs that combat depression) work promise to shed new light on changes in individual nervous systems that may produce this serious problem (McNeal & Cimbolic, 1986). In these and other ways, basic knowledge about how neurons function—how they transmit information—is already making substantial contributions to human health and welfare.

The Nervous System: What It Is and How It's Studied

Earlier, we noted that neurons are the building blocks of the *nervous system*—the structure that regulates all of our internal bodily functions and provides us with our abilities to think, feel, do, and act. But just what is the nervous system? And how do physiological psychologists and other *neuroscientists* go about studying its functions? It is on these questions that we will focus next.

The Nervous System: Its Major Divisions

While the nervous system functions as an integrated whole, it is often divided into two major portions—the peripheral and central systems (please refer to Figure 2-9 for summary of these and other major divisions of the nervous system). The **central nervous system** consists of the *brain* and the *spinal cord*. Since we will soon describe the brain in great detail, we won't examine it here. The spinal cord runs through the middle of a column of hollow bones known as *vertebrae*, which you can feel by moving your hand up and down the middle of your back.

The spinal cord has two major functions. First, it carries sensory information from receptors throughout the body to the brain and conducts information from the brain to effectors (muscles and glands). Second, it plays a key role in various **reflexes.** As you probably already know, these are seemingly automatic actions evoked rapidly by particular stimuli. Common examples include withdrawing your hand from a hot object, an eye-blink in response to a rapidly approaching object, and the knee-jerk reaction tested by

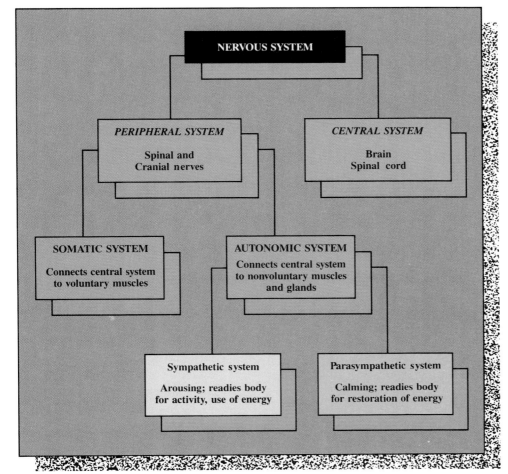

FIGURE 2-9. The nervous system is divided into several major components.

physicians during routine check-ups. In their simplest form, reflexes involve neural circuits in which information from various receptors is carried to the spinal cord where it stimulates other neurons (*interneurons*). These then transmit information to muscle cells, thus producing reflex actions. Please note: reflexes are usually much more complex than this. Hundreds or even thousands of neurons may play a role in their occurrence, and input from certain areas of the brain may also be involved. However they arise, spinal reflexes offer an obvious advantage: they permit us to react to potential causes of harm much more rapidly than would be true if we had to actively consider how to respond in such situations.

The **peripheral nervous system** consists of *nerves* (bundles of axons from many neurons) that connect the central nervous system with sense organs and with muscles and glands throughout the body. Some of these nerves (*spinal nerves*) are attached to the spinal cord, and serve all of the body below the neck. Others (*cranial nerves*) are directly attached to the brain. They serve sensory receptors and muscles in the neck and head (e.g., eyes, ears, mouth).

The peripheral nervous system is further divided into two parts: the somatic and autonomic systems. The **somatic nervous system** connects the central nervous system to voluntary muscles throughout the body. Thus, when you engage in almost any voluntary action (e.g., phoning for a pizza, reading the rest of this chapter), portions of your somatic central nervous system are involved. In contrast, the **autonomic nervous system** connects the central nervous system to internal organs, glands, and muscles over which we do not seem to have direct control (e.g., those in our digestive system).

Unfortunately, we can't stop dividing things here. The autonomic nervous system, too, consists of two parts, and these operate in distinct ways. The first, known as the

The Autonomic Nervous System: An Overview

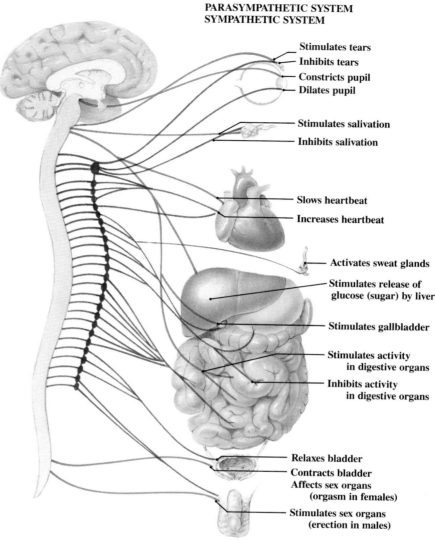

PARASYMPATHETIC SYSTEM
SYMPATHETIC SYSTEM

Stimulates tears
Inhibits tears
Constricts pupil
Dilates pupil

Stimulates salivation
Inhibits salivation

Slows heartbeat
Increases heartbeat

Activates sweat glands
Stimulates release of glucose (sugar) by liver
Stimulates gallbladder
Stimulates activity in digestive organs
Inhibits activity in digestive organs

Relaxes bladder
Contracts bladder
Affects sex organs (orgasm in females)
Stimulates sex organs (erection in males)

FIGURE 2-10. The autonomic nervous system consists of two major parts: the *sympathetic* and *parasympathetic* systems. Some of the functions of both are shown here.

sympathetic division, prepares the body for using energy, as in vigorous physical activity. Thus, stimulation of this division increases heartbeat, raises blood pressure, releases sugar (for energy) into the blood, and increases the flow of blood to muscles used in physical actions. The second portion of the autonomic system, known as the *parasympathetic division,* operates in the opposite manner, stimulating processes that serve to restore or conserve the body's energy. Activation of this system lowers blood pressure, slows heartbeat, and diverts blood away from skeletal muscles (e.g., those in your arms and legs) to the digestive system. (See Figure 2-10 for a summary of the structure and function of the autonomic nervous system.)

At first glance, it may appear that these two parts of the autonomic nervous system compete with one another in a head-on clash. In fact, this is far from the case. The sympathetic and parasympathetic systems actually function cooperatively. For example, after an individual eats a large meal on a warm day, the parasympathetic division may stimulate digestion while, at the same time, the sympathetic system stimulates sweating in order to eliminate excess heat. Similarly, both systems are involved during sexual relations. (Among males, the parasympathetic system stimulates erection, while the sympathetic system stimulates ejaculation.)

Before concluding, we should emphasize one further point. While the autonomic nervous system plays an important role in the regulation of internal bodily processes, it does so mainly by transmitting information to and from the central nervous system. Thus, it is the central nervous system, ultimately, that "runs the show."

The Nervous System: How We Know What We Know about It

Suppose you were a neuroscientist, interested in unraveling some of the mysteries of the human mind. Imagine that you suspect a certain portion of the brain plays a vital role in memory. How would you go about testing this possibility? In short, how might you attempt to acquire new information about the function of this structure? Unfortunately, there are no simple answers to this question. As we noted in Chapter 1, all research methods offer advantages, and all suffer from certain drawbacks. However, several useful strategies for obtaining such information do exist, and, when combined, they often yield the knowledge we seek.

Tracing Neural Pathways.   A basic question often raised about the nervous system is this: what structures or portions are connected, so that information can flow between them? One useful tactic for gaining information on this issue involves *degeneration studies*. Here, the axons of certain neurons are cut. When this is done, the portion beyond the cut soon dies. Since certain chemicals stain only dying tissue, the actual route taken by such axons can be traced. In this way, the incredibly complex maze of intertwined axons present in much of the nervous system can be at least partially disentangled.

Observing the Effects of Damage.   If a particular part of the nervous system plays a role in a specific form of behavior, then damage to this area should affect the behavior in question. This reasoning underlies a major technique used by neuroscientists in their research: brain *lesions*. Here, some portion of the brain (or other part of the nervous system) is surgically damaged, and the changes in behavior (if any) are observed. For example, suppose a specific structure deep within the brain is believed to play a key role in the regulation of eating. If damage to this structure does in fact produce feeding disturbances, evidence that it actually affects such behavior would be obtained.

As you can guess, the subjects in such research are always laboratory animals who, of course, are treated as humanely as possible. However, it is sometimes possible to study the behavior of persons who have accidentally suffered damage to a specific part of the nervous system. In such cases, important clues concerning the role of specific areas or structures can be obtained.

Electrical Recording of Brain Activity.   If a particular part of the brain or nervous system plays a role in some form of behavior, this part should be active during the behavior. Consistent with this reasoning, neuroscientists attempt to study the nervous system by recording electrical activity within the brain. Sometimes this involves measuring the electrical activity of the entire brain by means of *electroencephalograms*. In other cases, it involves implanting tiny electrodes in specific locations within the brain. The activity of groups of neurons, or even of specific neurons, can then be measured. In order to implant these electrodes precisely, equipment such as that shown in Figure 2-11 is often used. Such *stereotaxic apparatus* allows researchers both to locate specific structures in the brain and to place electrodes in them.

A related technique involves delivering tiny electric currents to specific brain areas. This may be used to map connections between various areas or structures. If delivery of an electric current at one point produces increased activity at another, the two must be connected. In addition, stimulation of specific portions of the brain can sometimes result in certain behaviors (e.g., eating, drinking, aggression). Obviously, this suggests that such structures play a role in these behaviors. (For more information on the effects of electrical stimulation of the brain, please see the "Classic Contributions" insert on page 44.)

FIGURE 2-11. In order to place electrodes in precise locations in the brains of anaesthetized laboratory animals, physiological psychologists often use *stereotaxic apparatus* such as that shown here.

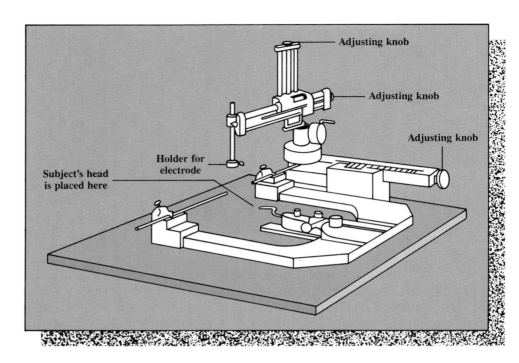

Adjusting knob

Adjusting knob

Adjusting knob

Holder for electrode

Subject's head is placed here

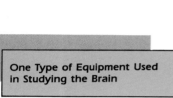

One Type of Equipment Used in Studying the Brain

FOCUS ON RESEARCH: Classic Contributions

Electrical Stimulation of the Brain: Of Pleasure . . . and Pain

In the early 1950s James Olds, assisted by a graduate student, Peter Milner, was attempting to determine whether electrical stimulation of the *reticular formation*, a specific structure in the brain, would increase arousal and so facilitate learning. This was an interesting topic, but their attention was soon diverted to something entirely different. By a lucky accident, the electrodes they placed in the brain of one of their subjects (laboratory rats) missed its mark and ended up in another structure, the *hypothalamus*. We say "lucky," because the effects produced by stimulation of this region were both profound and enlightening. When given tiny shocks of electricity to the brain each time it entered one corner of its cage, the rat quickly returned there time and time again. In fact, it soon appeared to be "coming back for more" over and over again. When Olds and Milner then arranged conditions so that subjects received such brain stimulation each time they pressed a lever, even more dramatic results were uncovered. Rats would stand in front of the lever and press it over and over again (see Figure 2-12). Indeed, hun-

dreds or even thousands of presses per hour were soon reported (e.g., Olds, 1973; Olds & Milner, 1954). In contrast, when electrodes were placed in other brain locations, opposite effects were obtained: animals would press the lever once, and then avoid it altogether. In short, it appeared that Olds and Milner had discovered discrete "pleasure" and "pain" centers within the brain.

Subsequent research has generally confirmed Olds and Milners' findings. Moreover, intriguing light has also been shed on how and why such effects occur. At first glance, it is tempting to assume that electrical brain stimulation produces sensations similar to those produced by the satisfaction of various needs (e.g., eating when we are hungry, making love when we feel passionate). Contrary to such suggestions, reinforcing brain stimulation often elicits precisely those behaviors that should be *reduced* if this were the case. Animals receiving such stimulation often engage in eating, drinking, or mating—something they would be unlikely to do if brain stimulation duplicated the satisfaction of such needs or drives. It appears, therefore, that brain stimulation may produce its reinforcing effects because it resembles the feedback organ-

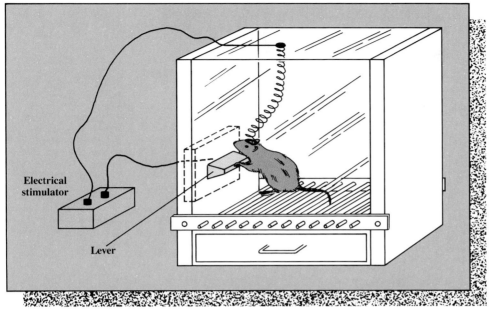

Electrical
stimulator

Lever

Electrical Stimulation of the
Brain: Its Reinforcing Effects

FIGURE 2-12. When pressing a lever delivers tiny pulses of electricity to portions of their brain, animals often engage in such behavior at a very high rate.

isms receive from engaging in such *appetitive behaviors* (i.e., from eating, drinking, mating). In other words, brain stimulation is more like the feelings generated by chewing and swallowing than those of a full stomach at the end of a meal (Carlson, 1986). Several types of evidence offer support for this conclusion. For example, it has been found that animals who respond at a high rate to receive brain stimulation in one session sometimes fail to do so at later sessions. If they are given a few pulses "free of charge" (without pressing a lever or performing some other activity), however, they begin working for brain stimulation once again. This seems similar to the *priming effect* most of us experience upon eating one potato chip—once we are reminded of how good this feels

(how much we enjoy crunching potato chips), we find it hard to stop.

Interestingly, when human beings receive direct brain stimulation during medical procedures (e.g., brain surgery), they do not report intense feelings of pleasure or being "turned on." More subtle effects, such as feeling mildly amused, are common (Deutsch, 1972).

To conclude: many complexities remain, and we are far from a full understanding of just how electrical stimulation of the brain produces its effects. One conclusion does seem clear, however: feelings of pleasure and pain are manifestations of activities and processes occurring deep within the brain. Thus, they are as firmly rooted in our biological nature as other aspects of our behavior and conscious experience.

Studying the Living Brain: CATs, PETs, and MRIs.   In recent years, several new and extremely promising techniques for studying the nervous system (especially the brain) have been developed. All were designed for medical diagnosis and are safe for use with fully conscious human beings.

The first of these techniques is known as *computerized axial tomography*, or *CAT*, scans for short. In this procedure, an individual places his or her head in a doughnut-shaped ring containing an X-ray tube. X-rays are sent through the person's brain as the ring is moved up or down with the aid of a computer. The result is a three-dimensional picture of the brain—one showing much greater detail than was previously available.

A second procedure is *positron emission tomography*, or *PET*. Here, individuals receive an injection of a slightly radioactive form of glucose. This is absorbed by brain cells in such a manner that the most active cells retain the greatest amount of glucose. As

PET Scans: Reflections of Human Consciousness?

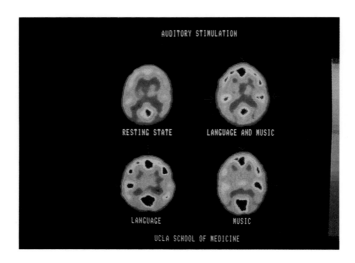

FIGURE 2-13. Positron emission tomography (PET) reveals patterns of activity in the human brain as an individual performs different tasks. The photos shown here were prepared as an individual engaged in various activities.

a result, it is possible to determine how much activity is going on in various portions of an individual's brain while he or she reads, listens to music, tries to solve a problem, or engages in just about any other activity the researcher wants to test. PET scans are often produced in vivid colors (see Figure 2-13), so the result is a glowing picture of the human brain in action.

The most recent development with respect to studying the human brain is *magnetic resonance imaging (MRI)*. The equipment used for this procedure resembles that used for CAT scans. However, it uses a strong magnetic field rather than x-rays to form images of the living brain. The level of resolution obtained with such equipment is truly impressive— much greater than that previously available. For this reason, it is extremely useful in diagnosing many brain disorders. And, since more detailed information about such disorders (e.g., the precise location of injuries or tumors) can help clarify the relationship between the brain and behavior, MRI scans promise to contribute much to basic scientific knowledge.

 ## The Brain: Where Consciousness Dwells

If there can be said to be a ''governing organ'' of the body, it is the brain. And what an amazing structure it is! Into slightly more than three pounds it crams an array of functions and capacities that even today, might well bring wistful tears to the eyes of computer scientists. After all, what computer, no matter how huge or advanced, is currently capable of (1) storing seemingly *unlimited* amounts of information for years or decades, (2) rewriting its own ''programs'' in response to new experiences, and (3) controlling a vast number of internal processes and external activities simultaneously, many of which are, themselves, highly complex? Moreover, even if such a computer existed, it would not, as far as we can tell, reproduce the emotional experiences, imagery, and creativity generated by the human brain. So, in an important sense, this section is the most central in our discussion; it is here, in the brain, that the essence of our humanity seems to dwell. (Please refer to Figure 2-14.)

The brain is a complex structure, and can be described in many different ways. Often, though, it is divided for discussion into three major components: portions concerned with basic bodily functions and survival; portions concerned with motivation and emotion; and portions concerned with language, planning, foresight, and many other activities we view as uniquely human.

FIGURE 2-14. A photo of an actual human brain. Note that the brain shown here has been split from top to bottom to reveal its inner structure.

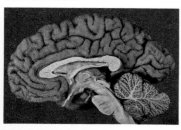

Survival Basics: The Brain Stem

Let's begin with the basics—those portions of the brain that regulate basic bodily processes and that we share with many other forms of life on earth. These are located in the

The Human Brain

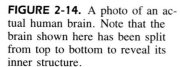

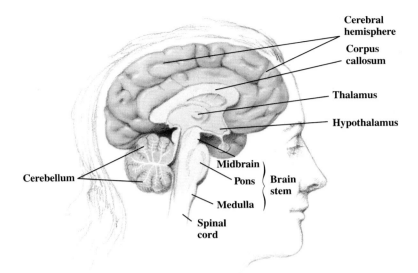

Basic Structure of the Human Brain

FIGURE 2-15. Note that in this simplified drawing, the brain has been split down the middle, as in Figure 2-14, in order to reveal its inner structure.

brain stem, the portion that begins just above the spinal cord and which continues into the heart of this complex organ (refer to Figure 2-15).

Two of these structures, the **medulla** and the **pons,** are located just above the point where the spinal cord enters the brain. Major sensory and motor pathways pass through both of these structures on their way to higher brain centers or down to effectors in different parts of the body. In addition, both the medulla and pons contain a central core consisting of a dense network of interconnected neurons. This is known as the **reticular activating system,** and it plays a crucial role in arousal and sleep. The medulla also contains several *nuclei*—collections of neuron cell bodies—that control vital functions such as breathing, heart rate, and blood pressure, as well as coughing and sneezing. It receives input directly from receptors throughout the body, and exerts its effects through nerve fibers within the spinal and cranial nerves.

Behind the medulla and pons is the **cerebellum** (refer again to Figure 2-15). It is primarily concerned with the regulation of motor activities, serving to ''smooth'' muscular movements so that they occur in an integrated fashion. Damage to the cerebellum results in jerky, poorly coordinated movements. Indeed, if such damage is severe, it may be impossible for an individual even to stand, let alone walk or run.

Above the medulla and pons, near the end of the brain stem, is a structure known as the **midbrain.** It contains an extension of the reticular activating system, as well as primitive centers concerned with vision and hearing. Eye movements and certain visual reflexes (e.g., our ability to follow moving objects) seem to be regulated here.

Emotion and Motivation: The Thalamus, Hypothalamus, and Limbic System

Ancient philosophers identified the heart as the center of our emotions. While this is a poetic belief still reflected on many valentine cards, modern science indicates that it is wrong. If there is indeed a center for appetites, emotions, and motives, it actually is deep within the brain in several interrelated structures.

Perhaps the most fascinating of these is the **hypothalamus.** Less than one cubic centimeter in size, this tiny structure exerts profound effects upon our behavior. First, it regulates the autonomic nervous system, thus influencing such reactions as sweating, salivating, shedding tears, secreting digestive juices, and changes in blood pressure. Second, it plays a key role in the process of *homeostasis*—keeping the body's internal environment at optimal levels. Consistent with this general function, portions of the hypothalamus seem to play a role in the regulation of eating and drinking. Thus, damage to one part of the hypothalamus turns normal laboratory animals into gluttons who, upon awaking from their operation, stagger over to the food tray and begin shoveling in enormous quantities of food. Such excessive eating often continues until their bulk reaches

The Hypothalamus: Its Role in Eating

FIGURE 2-16. Damage to part of the hypothalamus often turns animals into gluttons who overeat and gain large amounts of weight. This rat shows such effects.

gigantic proportions (see Figure 2-16). In contrast, damage to another part of the hypothalamus seems to turn normal subjects into animal gourmets who will consume only the best and tastiest diet. Indeed, animals who have suffered such damage often refuse to eat or drink at all, and will starve if not forced to consume nourishment.

Such effects occur because the hypothalamus contains special sensors that continually monitor various aspects of the blood (e.g., the amount of nutrients it contains, its temperature). Destruction of such sensors interferes with the careful balance needed to maintain weight and other bodily characteristics at stable levels. (Please note: the regulation of eating and drinking is actually much more complex than this, and involves other parts of the body, including the liver and pancreas. We'll return to this topic in Chapter 9, where many factors—social as well as biological ones—that play a role in human eating and body weight will be considered.)

The hypothalamus also influences such activities as mating and aggression and controls important glands within the body. We will return to these functions in a later section of this chapter.

Above the hypothalamus, quite close to the center of the brain, is another important structure, the **thalamus.** This has sometimes been called the "great relay station" of the brain, and with good reason, for it receives input from all of our senses except olfaction (smell) and transmits this information, both specifically and diffusely, to other portions of the brain.

Finally, we should mention a set of structures which, together, are known as the **limbic system.** The functions of this system are not yet entirely clear. However, it seems to play an important role in emotions. For example, early research (Kluver & Bucy, 1939) indicated that damage to part of the limbic system (the *amygdala*) can sharply reduce an organism's level of aggression. Indeed, animals with such damage are often totally placid even in the face of strong provocation or other stimuli that would normally elicit aggression. In contrast, electrical stimulation of the amygdala can sometimes elicit rage and violent attacks from previously tame or placid animals. On the basis of such findings, some physicians have considered performing operations on violent human beings to remove portions of the limbic system, and so reduce their aggression. Little evidence for the effectiveness of such procedures exists, and as you can guess, they are in the "gray" area of medical ethics (Valenstein, 1980). Finally, we should note that recent research suggests that the limbic system may be involved both in our subjective feelings of emotion and our overt behaviors related to these feelings (Carlson, 1986).

The Cerebral Cortex: A Uniquely Human Structure

Now, at last, we come to "center stage"—the portion of the brain in which, as far as we can determine, our most uniquely human activities take place. Fittingly, this structure— the **cerebral cortex**—is one we do *not* share with most other species. While other organisms possess a cortex, it is much smaller in surface area, shallower, and less complex than our own. Thus, it seems to be the cerebral cortex that accounts for our ability to reason, plan, remember, and imagine—in short, for our impressive information-processing capacity.

Much of the human brain consists of the two *cerebral hemispheres,* structures that entirely cover the remainder of this organ. Indeed, together, they make up more than 80 percent of the brain's total weight. Please note that the two hemispheres are mirror images of each other. Thus, many of the structures we will describe are double, appearing in both the left and right hemispheres.

The *cerebral cortex* is a layer of grey matter lying on top of these hemispheres, and from the point of view of sheer space, it is remarkably efficient: all of its varied information-processing capabilities are contained in a layer less than one-fourth of an inch thick. Within this thin covering, though, lie billions of neurons, all intricately interconnected with each other and with other portions of the brain.

The cerebral hemispheres are folded into a number of ridges and grooves, which greatly increase its surface area. Each hemisphere is usually divided, on the basis of the largest of these *fissures,* into four distinct regions or *lobes.* The *frontal lobe,* which occupies the area of the brain nearest the face, is bounded by the deep *central* fissure. Lying along this fissure, just within the frontal lobe, is the primary *motor cortex,* an area concerned with the control of body movement (please refer to Figure 2-17). Damage to this area does not produce total paralysis. Instead, it often results in a loss of control over fine movements, especially of the fingers. This illustrates an important fact about the human brain: while a specific area may normally perform a particular function, other regions can often "take up the slack" if it is damaged and may gradually come to perform these functions. Such *plasticity,* as this is often termed, is greater if damage occurs at a young age than after maturity is reached, but it seems to operate to a degree throughout life.

The Cerebral Cortex

FIGURE 2-17. The cerebral cortex is divided into four major *lobes* (left drawing). Specific areas are concerned with sensory and motor functions (right drawing).

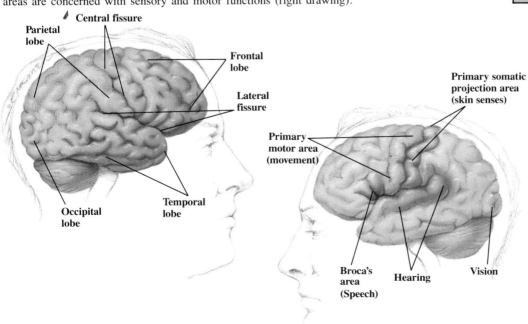

Across the central fissure from the frontal lobe is the *parietal lobe*. This contains the *somatosensory cortex,* in which information from the skin senses (touch, temperature, pressure, and so on) is represented (please see Figure 2-17 on page 49). Discrete damage to this area produces a variety of effects, depending, in part, on whether injury occurs in the left or right cerebral hemisphere. If it involves the left hemisphere, individuals may lose the ability to read or write, or they may have difficulty knowing where parts of their own body are located. (You may recall that one of the characters in this chapter's opening story suffered from such effects.) In contrast, if damage occurs in the right hemisphere, individuals may seem unaware of the left side of their body; for example, males may "forget" to shave this side of their face. The fact that injuries to the parietal lobe in the left and right hemisphere yield contrasting effects upon behavior calls attention to a basic fact: where the brain is concerned, there is an important degree of **lateralization of function.** That is, the two hemispheres are somewhat specialized for the performance of different tasks or functions; they do not duplicate one another entirely. We will return to this topic below (page 51).

The *occipital lobe* is near the back of the head. It's primary functions are visual, and it contains a sensory area which receives input from the eyes. Damage to this area often produces a "hole" in the field of vision: objects in a particular location can't be seen, but the rest of the visual sense is intact. As with other brain structures, injury to the occipital lobe may produce contrasting effects, depending on which cerebral hemisphere is affected. Injuries to the right hemisphere may result in a strange situation in which a person can point to objects and avoid bumping into them, but can't name them or describe their purpose. Persons with certain injuries to the left hemisphere can name familiar objects but can't identify basic elements in a visual scene (e.g., they can't point to matching angles or curves).

Finally, the *temporal lobe* is located along the side of each hemisphere (again, please refer to Figure 2-17 on p. 49). The location makes sense, for this lobe is concerned primarily with hearing and contains a sensory area that receives input from the ears. Damage to the temporal lobe, too, can result in intriguing symptoms. When such injuries occur in the left hemisphere, individuals may lose the ability to understand spoken words. When damage is restricted to the right hemisphere, in contrast, they may be able to recognize speech but may lose the ability to recognize other sounds (melodies, tones, rhythms).

Speech and the Cerebral Cortex.   At several points in this discussion, we've mentioned disorders in verbal abilities resulting from damage to the cerebral cortex. At this point, we'd like to pull such information together to provide you with a basic understanding of the physiological bases of this essential human capacity. Much of the evidence has been obtained through the study of individuals who have suffered brain damage through head injuries, brain tumors, or strokes.

The mechanisms underlying speech and related abilities are complex, but two major areas of the brain seem most important in this respect. The first, *Wernicke's area,* is located in the left temporal lobe—the one intimately related to our sense of hearing. The second, *Broca's area,* is located in the left frontal lobe, just in front of the primary motor cortex. (Please note that among right-handed persons these areas are found only in the left hemisphere; among some—but not all—"lefties" they are found in the right hemisphere.) Damage to Wernicke's area produces two major symptoms: poor comprehension of spoken words and the production of meaningless speech. Such persons cannot readily understand what is said to them, and when they speak, they say things no one else can comprehend. For example, when asked to name some common objects (e.g., toothbrush, pen, quarter), one patient responded with "stoktery," "minkt," and "spentee" (Kertesz, 1979). Careful research suggests that Wernicke's area stores memories of the sequences of sounds contained in words. Such memories allow us to recognize words when we hear them, and then play a role in our ability to utter them ourselves.

In contrast, persons with damage to Broca's area can comprehend speech fairly well, but they cannot produce it. Some evidence suggests that this area contains memories for the sequences of muscular movements needed to speak words. Thus, when damage occurs, the persons involved can understand speech but cannot speak clearly themselves.

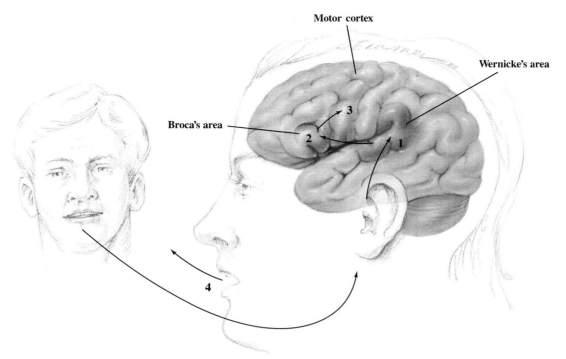

FIGURE 2-18. Spoken words induce activity in *Wernicke's area* (1), which seems to contain memories for the sequence of sounds in various words. Such information is then transmitted to *Broca's area* (2), where the sequence of muscle movements needed to produce speech is stored. When motor areas in the frontal lobe are then activated (3), actual speech occurs (4).

Human Speech: One Possible Model

In addition, such persons have difficulty using proper grammar; for instance, when asked to describe a picture showing a boy hit with a baseball, they may state, "Boy is hurting to it." And, as you might guess, they also experience difficulties with articulation, often altering the sequence of sounds in words (e.g., lipstick becomes "likstip").

Putting these and other findings together, it appears that the brain mechanisms responsible for our ability to speak function in the following manner. When we hear spoken words, activity in Wernicke's area permits us to recognize them and to understand their meaning. Then such information is transmitted to Broca's area, where memories of the sequence of muscular movements necessary to produce words are stored. When such information is sent to motor areas in the frontal lobe that control movements of the mouth, lips, and tongue, recognizable speech is produced (refer to Figure 2-18).

We should hasten to add that even this is a greatly simplified description of the neural mechanisms underlying speech. Many other parts of the brain are involved and must be considered in any complete picture of these complex processes.

One final point: if you examine Figures 2-17 and 2-18, you will notice that the areas labeled as primarily sensory or motor in nature make up only a small part of the total area of the cortex. The remainder—perhaps three-fourths—consists of *association areas*. When these areas lie close to a primary sensory area, they receive input primarily from this area. However, when they are farther away, they receive input from many sources. It is in these association areas that foresight, imagination, memory, and other cognitive activities seem to take place.

Lateralization of the Cerebral Cortex: Two Minds in One Body?

The brain, we have already noted, is a double organ. Like the lungs or kidneys, it consists of two parts that are essentially mirror images of each other. Yet, as we have also noted, these two hemispheres do not seem to function in identical ways. What are the differences

FIGURE 2-19. Although the two hemispheres of the brain seem to be specialized for the performance of somewhat different tasks, they don't compete as the character in this cartoon seems to believe. Rather, they complement each other under normal conditions. *(Source: NEA, Inc.)*

between them? A growing body of evidence points to the following conclusion: in many persons (but by no means all), the left hemisphere specializes in verbal activities (speech, reading, writing) and in the analysis of information. In contrast, the right hemisphere specializes in synthesis (putting isolated elements together, perceiving things as a whole) and in the comprehension and communication of emotion (see Figure 2-19). Two lines of research, one conducted with normal, uninjured persons, and the other performed with persons whose cerebral hemispheres have been isolated from each other through surgery (for important medical reasons) lend support to these suggestions.

Research with Normal (Non-injured) Persons: Brain Activity and the Communication of Emotion

Since the development of PET scans and related procedures, it has been possible to study the activity occurring in people's brains as they perform various tasks. Such studies lend support to the view that the right and left hemispheres are specialized for different tasks. For example, when individuals speak or work with numbers, activity in the left hemisphere increases. In contrast, when they work on perceptual tasks (e.g., ones in which they compare shapes), activity rises in the right hemisphere (e.g., Springer & Deutsch, 1985). Similarly, individuals recognize words or strings of letters more quickly or accurately when these are presented to the left hemisphere than to the right hemisphere. Conversely, they can more readily detect differences in the tilt of a line when it is presented to the right than to the left hemisphere (Bryden & Ley, 1983).

Other evidence indicates that the right and left hemispheres differ in their ability to recognize and communicate emotion. For example, in one interesting study Ley and Bryden (1979) presented drawings of faces showing various emotions to subjects. These were presented one at a time, in such a manner that information about them reached either the right or left hemisphere. (When you look straight ahead, visual stimuli to the left of center reach only the *right* hemisphere, while stimuli to the right of center reach only the *left* hemisphere. There appears to be no strong reason for this arrangement; it's just the way the nervous system is hooked up.) After each face was presented, Ley and Bryden showed subjects either the same face or a different one in the center of the visual field, so that information about this face reached both hemispheres. At this point, subjects were asked whether the second face showed the same emotion as the first. (Please note: the faces were presented for very brief periods of time to prevent information from moving from one cerebral hemisphere to the other.) Results were as follows: when the emotions shown on the faces were clear, subjects made fewer errors when the first face had stimulated the right hemisphere than when it had stimulated the left hemisphere. When the emotions were neutral or mild, however, no differences of this type occurred (please see Figure 2-20). So it appeared that, at least with respect to strong or clear emotions, judgments made by the right hemisphere were more accurate than those made by the left hemisphere. Other studies report corresponding findings for hearing; again, judgments made by the right hemisphere alone are more accurate than those made with the left hemisphere alone (Bryden, Ley, & Sugarman, 1982).

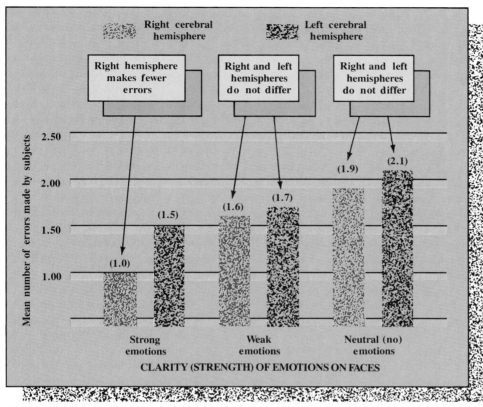

FIGURE 2-20. When the emotions shown on drawings of faces were clear (i.e., strong), subjects made fewer errors in making judgments about them with the *right* cerebral hemisphere than with the *left* hemisphere. However, when the emotions shown on the faces were neutral or weak, there were no differences between the two hemispheres in terms of accuracy. *(Source: Based on data from Ley & Bryden, 1979.)*

At this point, we should add that not only do the two cerebral hemispheres seem to differ with respect to interpreting emotions in others; they may also play different roles in contrasting emotional experiences themselves (Springer & Deutsch, 1985). Growing evidence suggests that the left hemisphere is more active during positive emotions, while the right hemisphere is more active during negative ones (refer to Figure 2-21). Thus, individuals suffering from depression (intense negative moods) often show higher activity in the frontal lobes of their right hemispheres than do persons not suffering from this problem. Similarly, when individuals are exposed to events that place them in a positive mood (e.g., they receive good news or are told to think about positive events), they demonstrate

FIGURE 2-21. Growing evidence suggests that the two cerebral hemispheres may play different roles in emotional experiences. The left may be more active during positive emotions, while the right may be more active during negative ones.

greater activity in the left than in the right cerebral hemisphere. When exposed to events that place them in a negative mood, however, the opposite pattern occurs: activity is higher in the right hemisphere (Miller, 1987).

Such findings have led some researchers to suggest that the two hemispheres operate in a *reciprocal* manner where emotions are concerned (Sackeim et al., 1982). Strong activity in one hemisphere (resulting from some emotion-provoking experience), induces activity in the other hemisphere. The result: extreme swings in mood are usually prevented. Only when some disturbance (e.g., injury, biochemical imbalances) occurs does this system of "checks-and-balances" fail, so that severe shifts in emotional experience follow.

At this point, we should insert an essential note of caution: at present, these possibilities, though fascinating, are largely speculative in nature. Much additional research is needed before firm conclusions concerning any emotional specialization of the two hemispheres can be reached. Still, the potential value of such knowledge for the treatment of depression and other emotional disorders indicates that careful attention to these possibilities is certainly worthwhile. (Do the two cerebral hemispheres also function differently in complex cognitive tasks? For evidence that they do, please see "The Cutting Edge" section below.)

FOCUS ON RESEARCH: The Cutting Edge

Brain Activity and Attitudes: The Physiology of Persuasion

What happens when individuals make up their minds about some issue or idea—when they form clear attitudes? One possibility is as follows: initially, their views are unformed, so they think carefully about the issues involved. Then, as their attitudes develop, they cease such analysis, and have a more "gut level" or emotional reaction (e.g., they become convinced that they are right!). If this is indeed the case, such events might be reflected in shifting patterns of activity in the two cerebral hemispheres. At first, activity might be high in the left hemisphere—the one which seems to be specialized for analytical thinking and related activities. After individuals have made up their minds, however, activity in the left hemisphere would decrease, while activity in the right hemisphere would rise. Does this actually happen? Evidence gathered by Cacioppo, Petty, and Quintanar (1982) suggests that it does.

These researchers exposed subjects to eight statements—four with which they agreed and four with which they disagreed (e.g., "Driving 55 miles per hour to conserve energy," "Reducing foreign imports to curb inflation"). After reading each statement, subjects were asked to close their eyes and think about it. Half were asked to think for 20 seconds and half were asked to think for 90 seconds.

During this period, electrical activity in both hemispheres was carefully observed. It was expected that those given more time for thought would show greater activity in the right cerebral hemisphere—after all, they would have had time to reach a conclusion concerning each statement. Results offered clear support for this prediction (see Figure 2-22). Further, the longer subjects thought about each statement, the greater the activity in the right hemisphere.

In other studies the same researchers noted that after listening to taped persuasive messages designed to change their views on various issues, individuals with relatively high activity in the right cerebral hemisphere reported more polarized (i.e., more extreme or definite) views about these messages than individuals with relatively low activity in this hemisphere. It was as though persons with high activity in the left hemisphere had not yet made up their minds, while those with high activity in the right hemisphere had already done so.

While these results are far from conclusive, they do suggest that the two cerebral hemispheres function somewhat differently during complex cognitive tasks such as persuasion. If further research confirms this possibility, additional insights into both the nature of persuasion and the functioning of the cerebral hemispheres may be attained.

LIVERPOOL JOHN MOORES UNIVERSITY
Aldham Robarts L.R.C.
TEL. 051 231 3701/3634

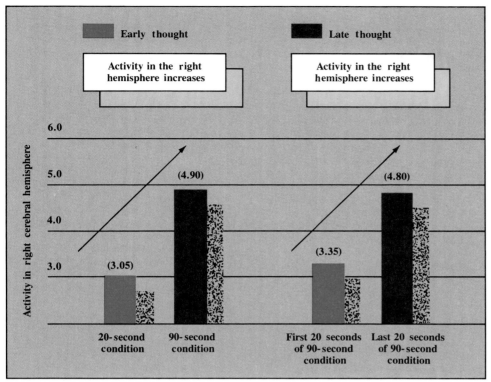

Activity in the Two Cerebral Hemispheres During Exposure to Attitude Statements

FIGURE 2-22. Subjects given 90 seconds to think about attitude statements showed more activity in the right cerebral hemisphere than subjects given 20 seconds to think about such statements (left graph). Also, activity in the right cerebral hemisphere was greater near the end of the 90-second period than at the beginning (right graph). These findings suggest that activity in the right hemisphere may increase as individuals become more certain of their views. (Numbers have been transformed to show higher values for rising activity.) *(Source: Based on data from Cacioppo, Petty, & Quintanar, 1982.)*

Research with Split-Brain Subjects: Isolating the Two Hemispheres

Under normal conditions the two hemispheres of the brain communicate with each other through the **corpus callosum**—a wide band of nerve fibers between them. Sometimes it is necessary to sever this link for medical reasons, for example, to prevent the spread of epileptic seizures from one hemisphere to the other. Careful study of individuals who have undergone such operations provides intriguing evidence on specialization of function in the two halves of our brain (Gazzaniga, 1984, 1985; Sperry, 1968).

For example, consider the following simple demonstration. A woman whose corpus callosum has been cut is blindfolded and handed a common object, such as a pencil. She is then asked to identify it. If it is placed in her right hand (from which sensory information reaches the left hemisphere), the task is easy, and she can promptly say "pencil." If, instead, it is placed in her left hand (from which sensory information travels to the right hemisphere), she is stumped. Additional research has uncovered other interesting effects. If a photo of a spoon is flashed to a split-brain patient's left cerebral hemisphere, the person can readily name it. If it is flashed to the right cerebral hemisphere, however, he cannot. But while he can't name the object, he can select it with his left hand from an assortment of common objects (refer to Figure 2-23 on page 56).

Finally, consider these results (Gazzaniga, 1985). Words such as "Dad," "dope," and "home" are flashed to the right hemisphere of split-brain patients (the words are presented to the left visual field). Subjects are asked to rate each word's likability by pointing to one of seven cards. They perform this task with ease, and large

Some Intriguing Effects of
"Splitting the Brain"

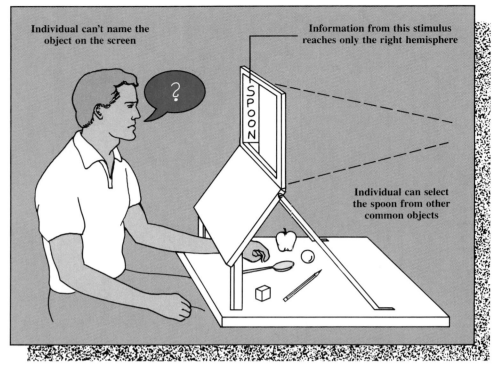

FIGURE 2-23. When the name of a common object, in this case, a spoon, is flashed on a screen so that information about it reaches only the right cerebral hemisphere, a split-brain patient cannot name it. However, he can select the object from among several other objects with his left hand.

differences in the ratings assigned to various words are noted. The same patients are then asked to indicate their ratings by saying a number (from one to seven). Subjects find this task more difficult. (After all, their left hemisphere, which plays a key role in such verbal responses, has never seen the words!) When urged to guess, however, they assign ratings virtually identical to those assigned by pointing. Apparently, their left hemisphere is somehow aware of the reaction to the words experienced by the right hemisphere, and responds accordingly. Yet subjects cannot verbally report the words they have seen, or indicate why they are assigning them the numbers they have chosen.

All these puzzling findings make sense if we assume that the right and left hemispheres are indeed specialized for different functions, and that one major difference between them is that the left is more skilled in certain types of verbal tasks. In fact, this is the interpretation usually offered for such results (Sperry, 1968). A word of caution, is needed, though: when the corpus callosum is severed, other effects—some of which are quite unknown—may also result. As a result, the unusual reactions of split-brain patients may stem from other conditions, as well as from the fact that their two cerebral hemispheres are no longer in direct communication.

Despite such complications, research with individuals who have undergone such operations does seem to support the view that the two hemispheres perform somewhat different functions. And when such evidence is combined with the findings obtained with normal persons (described above), the total picture becomes compelling: there does indeed seem to be at least a partial division of labor between the two cerebral hemispheres. In one sense, then, the suggestion that we possess two minds (or at least two brains) in a single body is not as far fetched as it might at first seem.

The Endocrine System: Chemical Regulators of Bodily Processes

In an earlier section we noted that the hypothalamus plays an important role in regulating the activities of certain glands. These are the **endocrine glands**—ones that secrete special

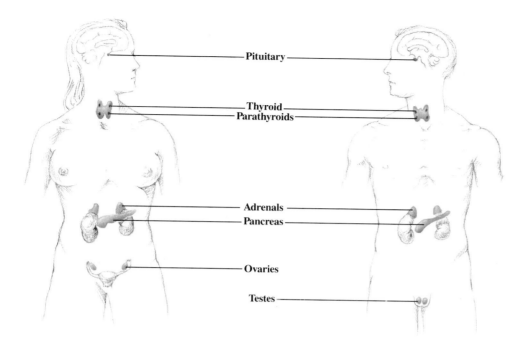

FIGURE 2-24. *Endocrine glands* are located throughout the body. The hormones they produce exert profound effects upon many bodily functions.

Location of the Endocrine
Glands

chemicals known as *hormones* directly into the bloodstream (see Figure 2-24). Such hormones, in turn, exert profound effects upon a wide range of processes related to the basic functioning of our bodies.

The relationship between the hypothalamus and the endocrine glands is complex. Basically, though, the hypothalamus exerts such influence through its impact on the *pituitary gland*. This gland is located just below the hypothalamus and is closely connected to it. The pituitary is sometimes described as the master gland of the body, for the hormones it releases control and regulate the actions of other endocrine glands. For example, the pituitary secretes *ACTH,* a substance that stimulates the outer layer of the adrenal gland (the *adrenal cortex*) to secrete cortisone. This hormone, in turn, affects cells in many parts of the body. The pituitary also secretes hormones that affect sexual development and basic bodily functions relating to metabolism and excretion.

A dramatic illustration of effects resulting from hormones secreted by the endocrine glands is provided by a disorder known as the **adrenogenital syndrome.** Because their adrenal glands produce too much *androgen,* genetic females are born with what appear to be male sexual organs (Money & Erhardt, 1972). Even when given corrective surgery and raised as girls, they seem to retain some masculine characteristics (e.g., they describe themselves as ''tomboys'' and prefer to play with toy trucks and guns rather than dolls). As we'll note in Chapter 9, sexual identity is affected by a host of social and environmental variables as well as biological ones, so these findings are far from conclusive. Still, they point to the possibility that early exposure to androgens shapes brain development in subtle but important ways—ways that are reflected in later behavior. It is hard to imagine more compelling evidence for the importance of the endocrine glands and the hormones they secrete. (Please refer to Table 2-2 on page 58 for a summary of the major endocrine glands and their effects. For more information on the adrenogenital syndrome and related disorders, please refer to Chapter 9.)

Genes and Behavior

Do you resemble your parents physically? The chances are good that you do, at least in some respects (see Figure 2-25). The reason for such similarity is obvious: you have inherited certain characteristics from them. Nearly all cells of your body contain twenty-three pairs of **chromosomes,** and within each pair one was contributed by your father and

The Endocrine System: A Summary of Its Major Effects

TABLE 2-2
Some Effects of Hormones Produced by Endocrine Glands

Gland	Effects or Functions It Regulates
Adrenal Glands	
ADRENAL MEDULLA	Produces *epinephrine* and *norepinephrine*. Both play an important role in reactions to stress (e.g., increased heartbeat, raised blood pressure)
ADRENAL CORTEX	Produces hormones that promote release of sugar stored in the liver. Also regulates the excretion of sodium and potassium
Gonads	
OVARIES	Produce hormones responsible for secondary sex characteristics of females (e.g., breast development); also regulate several aspects of pregnancy
TESTES	Produce hormones responsible for secondary sex characteristics of males (e.g., beard growth); also affect sperm production and male sex drive
Pancreas	Produces hormones (e.g., insulin, glucagon) that regulate metabolism
Parathyroid	Produces hormones that regulate levels of *calcium* and *phosphate* within the body (these substances play an important role in functioning of the nervous system)
Pituitary Gland	
ANTERIOR	Controls activity of gonads; regulates timing and amount of body growth; milk production in females
POSTERIOR	Releases hormones that control contractions of uterus during birth and the release of milk from mammary glands; also regulates excretion of water
Thyroid	Produces *thyroxin,* which regulates rate of metabolism and controls growth

FIGURE 2-25. Because of heredity, children often resemble their parents in many ways. (Shown here are Marlene Dietrich and her daughter Maria.)

Heredity and Physical Appearance

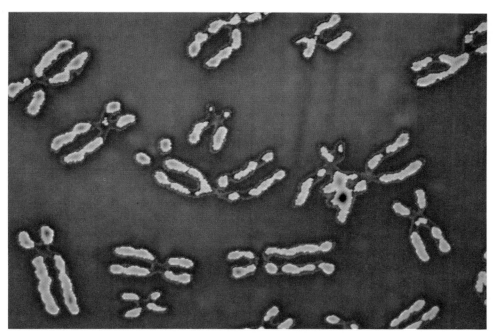

FIGURE 2-26. Almost all the cells within your body contain twenty-three pairs of chromosomes (your *gametes*—eggs or sperm—are an important exception). Within each pair, one chromosome came from your mother and one from your father.

one by your mother (refer to Figure 2-26). These chromosomes, in turn, contain hundreds of **genes,** and these, as you probably already know, exert profound effects upon the structure and functioning of your body. In a sense, they constitute nature's blueprint—chemical instructions for producing a fully functioning human being out of the tiny spark of life produced by the union of your father's sperm and your mother's egg.

Now consider a second question: do you resemble your parents with respect to behavior? Do you share their traits, preferences, and views of the world, as well as their height or eye-color? Again, the chances are good that you do, at least to a degree. Does this mean that behavior, too, is inherited? Not necessarily. You may think, act, and feel like your parents because they have raised you, shaped your world, and served as your models for many years. On the other hand, such similarities may also exist because your nervous system and body resemble theirs in many respects. Both you and your parents may, for example, possess taste buds and related sensory systems that lead to a preference for vanilla ice cream over chocolate. Similarly, both you and they may possess bone or muscle structure that makes dancing, playing tennis, or swimming feel especially good—or bad. The result: your feelings about these activities may be similar to those of your parents.

So, to what extent is our behavior shaped by genetic factors, and to what extent is it shaped by experience or current conditions? As you can see, this is an exceedingly complex question, with no simple answers. Some aspects of behavior may well involve a strong genetic component, while others may be shaped primarily by experience and environmental factors. The key question, then, is determining the extent to which a given form of behavior is shaped by each of these factors. This task can be accomplished through certain types of research we will now describe.

Disentangling Genetic and Environmental Effects: Some Research Strategies

In one sense, human beings have been conducting applied research on genetic effects for thousands of years. They have bred dogs, horses, sheep, and cattle so that these animals show characteristics people find desirable (e.g., obedience in dogs, speed or strength in

FIGURE 2-27. Both of the animals shown here were produced through selective breeding. Their appearance suggests that many physical characteristics are certainly inherited.

Selective Breeding: Some Bizarre Results

horses, docility in cattle). Such efforts have involved *selective breeding*—procedures in which animals demonstrating desirable characteristics are bred with each other. If such characteristics are indeed inherited, then over many generations the desirable traits should become stronger and stronger. This has indeed turned out to be true in many instances (refer to Figure 2-27). The conclusion: many behavioral characteristics are strongly affected by heredity.

Similar principles have also been applied to the scientific study of the *nature-nurture* question. Careful breeding has produced strains of laboratory animals whose genetic makeup is virtually identical. When different strains are then exposed to the same environmental conditions, differences in their reactions can be explained largely in terms of genetic factors. In this way, the relative contributions of genetic and environmental factors can be at least partially distinguished.

With human beings, of course, selective breeding is out of the question. Here, efforts to assess the relative roles of genetic and environmental effects have often involved comparisons of identical twins, especially identical twins separated early in life and raised in contrasting environments. Since such twins have identical genes, any differences between them must be due to contrasting experiences and environments. Similarly, to the extent they demonstrate similarity in various behaviors, despite being raised in different environments, the greater the importance of genetic factors. Recent research of this type (e.g., Bouchard, 1987) has yielded some surprising findings: even identical twins reared in very different environments show remarkable similarities. Indeed, their personalities, and even many of their preferences and attitudes, are amazingly alike. We will review such research in detail in Chapter 11. At the moment, we merely wish to call your attention to the fact that it points to the following conclusion: many aspects of our behavior are influenced by genetic factors.

Sociobiology: Genetics and Social Behavior

Why do we find certain characteristics in others attractive? What accounts for the fact that individuals will sometimes sacrifice their own safety—or even their lives—to help others? Why do men typically spend less time in child-rearing activities than women? Most psychologists would answer these questions in terms of learning and experience (e.g., we find certain characteristics attractive because we have been taught, by our culture, that they are desirable). Another, and very different set of answers, is provided by the field of **sociobiology** (Daly & Wilson, 1983; Wilson, 1975).

Briefly, sociobiologists suggest that social behavior, too, is at least partly determined by genetic factors. Thus, human beings—like the members of other species—behave in certain ways because they possess inherited tendencies to do so. Presumably, over the course of many generations, patterns of social behavior that help individuals survive and reproduce become increasingly common. The reason for this is simple: individuals showing such patterns have a better chance of transmitting their genes to the next generation than individuals not showing these patterns. In sum, according to sociobiologists, many aspects of social behavior, as well as physical structure, are shaped by the laws of *natural selection* first proposed by Charles Darwin (1871).

Perhaps, at this point, the nature of sociobiology can best be clarified by returning to one of the questions mentioned above. How does sociobiology account for the fact that we find certain characteristics attractive? It argues that these traits (e.g., smooth skin, good physique) are associated with health and reproductive capacity. For this reason, individuals who demonstrated a preference for such characteristics in potential mates in the dim-and-distant past had more offspring than other persons. The result: many of us now possess strong preferences for these traits.

Do such explanations of complex human behavior make sense? At present, sociobiology is quite controversial. Indeed, many psychologists object strongly to its assertion that many forms of social behavior can be understood in terms of genetic factors. Some evidence, though, offers support for several of its predictions. For example, according to sociobiology women, but not men, should find *dominance* in prospective mates sexually attractive. The reasoning behind this assertion is as follows: females invest much more of their physical resources in each offspring than males. As a result, they should be more discriminating than males in choosing sexual partners, and should prefer ones possessing characteristics that will enhance their children's chances of survival. Dominance is one of these. Males, in contrast, have less physical investment in creating each offspring; for them, the dominance of potential mates should be largely irrelevant. In sum, sociobiology predicts that females should strongly prefer dominant males to non-dominant ones, but that males should show no preference for dominant females. Interestingly, both these predictions have been confirmed in at least one recent study (Sadalla, Kenrick, & Vershure, 1987).

These researchers conducted a series of investigations in which male and female subjects either watched videotapes in which a member of the opposite sex showed a high level or low level of dominance, or they read descriptions of a stranger indicating that this person was either dominant or non-dominant. For example, the description of a dominant male playing tennis stated, ''All of his movements tend to communicate dominance and authority. He tends to psychologically dominate his opponents, forcing them off their games and into mental mistakes.'' The description of a non-dominant male stated: ''Strong opponents are able to psychologically dominate him, sometimes forcing him off his game.'' After watching the videotapes or reading the descriptions, subjects rated the sexual attractiveness and dating desirability of the persons involved. Results were identi-

Dominance and Sexual Attraction: Findings Predicted by Sociobiology

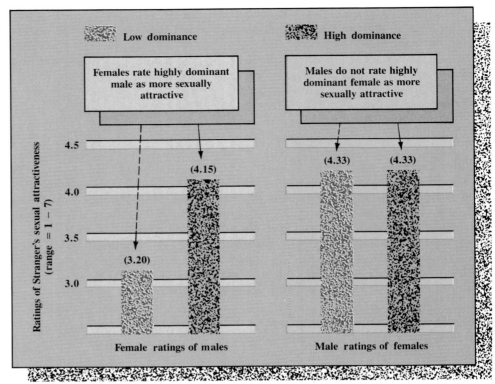

FIGURE 2-28. Female subjects rated males who showed a high level of dominance as more sexually attractive and more desirable as a dating partner than males who showed a low level of dominance. In contrast, males did not find dominant females more desirable in these respects. Such findings offer support for predictions derived from sociobiology. *(Source: Based on data from Sadalla, Kenrick, & Vershure, 1987.)*

cal in both types of study: female subjects assigned significantly higher ratings to dominant than to non-dominant males. Similar differences did *not* emerge in males' ratings of females (refer to Figure 2-28).

These findings do not necessarily support the view that females' preference for dominant males is genetically determined. Learning and experience, too, are likely to play important roles in this respect, and no specific attempt to assess the impact of such factors was made by Sadalla and his colleagues. Still, these and related findings (Kenrick, 1987; Rushton, 1985) suggest that sociobiology offers a new perspective on the potential impact of genetic factors on many forms of human behavior. Although it remains controversial, therefore, it should certainly not be ignored.

Summary and Review

Neurons: Their Structure and Function

Neurons are the building blocks of the *nervous system*. They communicate with one another through the release of *transmitter substances* at the *synapse*. Many drugs exert their effects by affecting this process. For example, they may block the release of various transmitter substances, or they occupy and thus block receptor sites that would normally be stimulated by these substances.

The Nervous System

The nervous system consists of two major parts: the *central nervous system* and the *peripheral nervous system*. The former is composed of the *brain* and the *spinal cord*. The latter consists of nerves connecting the brain and spinal cord to muscles and glands throughout the body. Two major components of the peripheral nervous system are the *somatic* and *autonomic* systems.

Several techniques for studying the nervous system exist. These include (1) recording electrical activity in various structures, (2) electrically stimulating such structures to determine how this affects behavior, (3) observing the effects of damage to various portions of the nervous system, and (4) obtaining detailed images of the brain or records of metabolic activity in it during the performance of various tasks.

The Human Brain

The brain can be divided into three major parts which are concerned, respectively, with (1) basic bodily functions; (2) emotions and motivation; and (3) thought, planning, language, and many other aspects of conscious experience. The brain has two *cerebral hemispheres* that are mirror images of each other in terms of structure. However, growing evidence suggests that the two hemispheres are somewhat specialized for different tasks. The left hemisphere appears to play a dominant role in verbal activities (e.g., speech, reading) and in the analysis of information. The right hemisphere seems to play a key role in synthesis (combining information or experiences into a whole) and in the communication of emotion.

The Endocrine System

Many bodily functions are regulated by the *endocrine system,* internal glands that release various hormones directly into the bloodstream. The *hypothalamus* regulates many of these glands through its impact on the *pituitary*—sometimes known as the ''master gland'' of the body. The hormones produced by endocrine glands exert profound effects on development, metabolism, and many other basic bodily processes.

Genes and Behavior

Human behavior is affected by *genetic* factors as well as by experience and current environmental conditions. A key task of psychological research is determining the relative importance of each of these factors in specific aspects of behavior. With animals this can be accomplished by comparing subjects from different genetic strains. Among humans such efforts often focus on comparisons of identical twins reared in different environments.

Sociobiology contends that many aspects of human social behavior are shaped by genetic factors. While this suggestion remains controversial, some research findings offer support for predictions derived from a sociobiological perspective.

Key Terms

Acetylcholine An important transmitter substance found in the brain and other parts of the nervous system. The death of cells normally sensitive to this substance seems to play a role in *Alzheimer's disease*.

Action Potential A rapid shift in the electrical charge across the cell membrane of neurons. It is through the rapid movement of this disturbance along the membrane that information is communicated within neurons.

Adrenogenital Syndrome A disorder in which the adrenal glands of a female fetus produce too much androgen. As a result, such infants are born with sexual organs resembling those of males, and even after corrective surgery these individuals may continue to show masculine characteristics in their behavior.

Autonomic Nervous System That part of the peripheral nervous system that connects internal organs, glands, and muscles not under voluntary control to the central nervous system.

Axon The part of the neuron that carries information (action potentials) away from the cell body.

Cell Body The part of a neuron (or other cell) containing the nucleus.

Central Nervous System A crucial part of the nervous system, consisting of the brain and spinal cord.

Cerebellum A part of the brain concerned with the regulation of motor activities.

Cerebral Cortex The outer covering of the cerebral hemispheres.

Chromosomes Threadlike structures containing genetic material (i.e., genes) found in nearly every cell of the body.

Corpus Callosum A band of nerve fibers connecting the right and left cerebral hemispheres.

Dendrites The part of the neuron that carries information (action potentials) toward the cell body.

Endocrine Glands Glands that secrete hormones directly into the bloodstream.

Genes Biological ''blueprints'' that shape development and basic bodily processes.

Hypothalamus A small structure deep within the brain that plays a key role in regulating the autonomic nervous system, in emotion, and in regulating several important forms of behavior (eating, drinking).

Lateralization of the cerebral hemispheres Refers to the fact that the two hemispheres of the brain appear to be specialized for somewhat different functions.

Limbic System Several structures deep within the brain that play an important role in emotional reactions.

Medulla A structure in the brain concerned with the regulation of vital bodily functions (e.g., breathing, heartbeat).

Midbrain A part of the brain containing primitive centers concerned with vision and hearing. It also plays a role in the regulation of visual reflexes.

Nervous System The complex structure which regulates bodily processes and overt behavior and which is responsible for all aspects of conscious experience.

Neurons Cells specialized for communicating information that are the basic building blocks of the nervous system.

Norepinephrine An important transmitter substance producing inhibitory effects within the brain but excitatory effects in other parts of the nervous system.

Peripheral Nervous System That portion of the nervous system that connects internal organs, glands, and muscles to the central nervous system.

Pons A portion of the brain through which sensory and motor information passes and which contains structures related to sleep and arousal.

Reflexes Rapid, seemingly automatic actions evoked by a particular stimulus (e.g., withdrawal of the hand from a hot object).

Reticular Activating System A structure within the brain concerned with sleep and arousal.

Sociobiology A branch of biology that studies the evolution of social behavior. Sociobiologists contend that patterns of behavior that help members of a given species survive and reproduce become part of that species' genetic inheritance.

Somatic Nervous System That portion of the nervous system that connects voluntary muscles to the central nervous system.

Synapse A region where the axon of one neuron closely approaches the dendrites or cell body of another neuron, or the cell membrane of other types of cells within the body (e.g., muscle cells).

Synaptic Vesicles Structures found in the terminal buttons of axons, containing various transmitter substances.

Terminal Buttons Structures on the end of axons that play an important role in the transmission of information across synapses.

Thalamus A structure deep within the brain that receives a great deal of sensory input from other portions of the nervous system and then transmits such information to the cerebral hemispheres and other parts of the brain.

For More Information

Carlson, N.R. (1986). *Physiology of behavior,* 3rd ed. Boston: Allyn and Bacon.
   A comprehensive, accurate, well-written, and lavishly illustrated introduction to the field of physiological psychology. All the topics introduced in this chapter (e.g., methods for studying the brain, neural regulation of eating, drinking, and other basic activities, lateralization of the cerebral cortex) are considered in detail. In addition, many other issues (e.g., sleep and waking, the physiology of learning) are also examined. If you'd like to know more about the biological bases of behavior, this is an excellent source to consult.

Fincher, J. (1981). *The brain: Mystery of matter and mind.* Washington: US News Books.
   This book provides a brief and clearly written introduction to the structure and function of

the human brain. Included are chapters on the role of the brain in speech, intelligence, and memory. With many beautiful color illustrations, the book is designed for readers who have no prior exposure to physiology or physiological psychology.

Gazzaniga, M.S. (1985). *The social brain*. New York: Basic Books.

An intriguing review of split-brain research. The author marshals an impressive array of evidence to support his contention that the mind has a *modular organization*—one in which many different mental systems coexist and operate simultaneously. An intriguing place to start if you'd like to know more about the biological foundations of behavior.

Logue, A.W. (1986). *The psychology of eating and drinking*. New York: W.H. Freeman.

Why do some people gain weight while others do not? What are the causes of eating disorders such as anorexia, bulimia, and alcohol abuse? To what extent are eating and drinking behaviors influenced by environmental factors and heredity? These are only some of the questions addressed in this relatively brief text. If you'd like to know more about how physiological, social, and genetic factors combine to determine what and how much we eat, this is a good place to begin.

C H A P T E R

Sensation and Perception: Making Contact with the World Around Us

"You guys are really going to love this!" Duan Potibut says with a smile as she places a steaming bowl before her two friends, Pam Glick and Todd Sherman. "My grandmother used to make it all the time in Bangkok."

"Umhh! smells terrific," Pam comments, peering into the dish. "And all those beautiful colors. Red, green, yellow, white . . . if it tastes as great as it smells, we're really in for a treat."

"I'll say." Todd agrees enthusiastically. "Heck, it looks so good, I could polish it all off myself."

Smiling, Duan serves large portions onto each person's plate. There is silence for a few moments as all three friends eat with gusto.

"Duan, this is *delicious,*" Pam comments. "It's got so many good things in it, I don't know which I like best."

"Right," Todd agrees. "You'll have to give us the recipe so we can make it ourselves."

"Sure, but you'll have to go to some special stores to get all the ingredients."

"I was just wondering about that," says Pam, between bites. "I recognize a lot of it, but what's this brown stuff?"

"Oh, that's what we call 'wood ears.' It's a kind of fungus that grows on dead trees."

At this remark, Todd's fork pauses in mid-air, and he looks slightly uncomfortable. But after a few seconds he goes back to eating—more slowly than before, however.

"And what's this, Duan?" Pam asks, pointing to a plump white morsel on her plate. "It's not shrimp, is it?"

"No, that's octopus. It's very important in this dish," Duan answers. Now Todd stops eating altogether. "Octopus?" he asks weakly. "No kidding? Gee, I didn't realize. . . ."

"What's wrong with *you*?" Pam says, grinning. "You were practically inhaling it a minute ago. What difference does it make, as long as you like it?"

"I know, I know," Todd replies. "But *octopus*—ugh!"

"Oh, shut up!" Pam warns. "Just eat." Then, turning to her hostess, she asks, "One more question, Duan. What's in this sauce? It's great, but I don't think I've ever had it before."

"Mostly *nam pla*—you know, fermented fish paste. It's used in lots of Thai dishes."

Now Todd turns visibly green. Pushing back his chair, he rises to his feet. "I'm sorry," he stammers weakly. "I really have to go . . . I'm feeling kind of sick. . . ." Then he rushes to the door.

"What's the matter?" Duan asks, turning to her friend Pam. "Did I say something wrong?"

"Not a thing," Pam replies with a laugh. "Todd's just like that. Real picky about what he eats. I guess the idea of octopus, wood ears, and fermented fish really got to him. But not me. I love it. In fact, how about some more?" And with these words she holds out her dish for a second helping.

One old saying that really *does* seem to be true is, "Everyone sees the world through different eyes." Exposed to the same events or stimuli, different persons often react in sharply contrasting ways; they *do* seem to see the world through different eyes. Further, and perhaps even more surprising, the same individual can react differently to identical events or stimuli on different occasions. (Recall Todd's sudden shift from enjoyment to nausea!) How can this be so? Don't we know the world around us in a direct and simple manner? The answer provided by several decades of psychological research is clear: we definitely do *not*. Contrary to what common sense might suggest, we do not know or understand the external world in a simple, automatic way. Rather, we actively construct a picture of it through several complex processes.

When discussing our efforts to make sense out of the world around us, psychologists often distinguish between two key topics: **sensation** and **perception.** Sensation refers to the information brought to us by our various senses (our eyes, ears, and so on). In contrast, perception refers to the process (or processes) through which we then interpret and organize such information.

As evidence for the occurrence of such interpretation, consider Todd's reactions in the preceding story. Until he learned what was in the dish, he thoroughly enjoyed eating it. Once he found out it contained fungus, octopus, and (for him) other exotic ingredients, his reactions changed dramatically; in fact, he couldn't take another bite. At first glance, this is puzzling. The information supplied by his senses remained constant—the food smelled, looked, and tasted the same before and after Duan's comments. Yet, Todd's *interpretation* of this sensory input shifted radically. This is an example of the active process of perception. (For another example, please see Figure 3-1.) If you need still further convincing, consider the following. (1) Have you ever sailed blithely through a red light or a stop sign which, you realized later, you saw but somehow ignored? (2) Have you ever listened to a speech or lecture which you could hear quite clearly but still could not understand? (3) Have you ever read a 3-D comic, looked through a ViewMaster, or attended a 3-D movie? In all of these cases, you may well have been aware of a noticeable gap between the information supplied by your senses and your interpretation of this input.

Since our understanding of the world around us can strongly shape our actions, *sensation* and *perception* are very important aspects of human behavior. Indeed, they play a role in virtually every topic we will consider in later chapters. For this reason, we will devote careful attention to both of them here. In addition, we'll consider two questions relating primarily to perception: (1) to what extent is such processing of input from our senses learned or innate? and (2) can we form perceptions about events or objects in the external world in the total absence of sensory input about them? (In other words, is there really such a thing as *extrasensory perception*?)

FIGURE 3-1. As shown here, our interpretation of information brought to us by our senses can shift in important ways over time. (*Source:* The New Yorker, *1976.*)

"When I fell in love with you, suddenly your eyes didn't seem close together. Now they seem close together again."

Perception: The Active Interpretation of Sensory Input

Sensation: The Raw Material of Understanding

The sight of a gorgeous sunset, the fragrance of sensuous perfume, the sound of beautiful music, the pleasant glow produced by a warm bath—what do these experiences have in common? If you recall our comments in Chapter 2, you already know the answer: ultimately, all are based upon complex biological processes occurring within the nervous system. This highlights an intriguing paradox: although you live within a surging sea of physical energies (e.g., light, heat, sound), your brain cannot react directly to these forces. Rather, it can only respond to intricate patterns of action potentials conducted by your neurons. The first task we face in terms of knowing the external world, then, is *transduction*—converting the many forms of energy in the external world into signals the nervous system can use and understand. As you already know, we possess highly developed equipment for accomplishing this task—**sensory receptors** in our eyes, ears, nose, tongue, and elsewhere. Before turning to the nature and function of these receptors, however, we will first describe two concepts that have proven useful in the study of sensation generally: *thresholds* and *sensory adaptation*.

Thresholds: How Much Stimulation Is Enough?

Perhaps the simplest question we can ask about each of our senses is this: what level of stimulation can it detect? In other words, how much physical stimulation (energy) is necessary for us to experience a sensation? Psychologists refer to this value as the **absolute threshold,** and it turns out to be impressively low for most aspects of sensation. Thus, as shown in Table 3-1, we can hear a watch ticking from twenty feet away in a quiet room; we can smell a single drop of perfume in an empty three-room apartment; and on a dark night, through clear, unpolluted air, we can see a dim candle thirty miles away (Galanter, 1962). In fact, our ability to detect weak stimuli is so great that if it were even slightly better in certain respects, we would encounter some unsettling problems. For example, just a minor improvement in our ability to detect sounds would allow us to hear individual air molecules bumping into our eardrums. So, from the perspective of sheer capacity to detect, we seem to be well equipped indeed.

Absolute Thresholds: Some Complications.   Our comments so far seem to suggest a definite relationship between physical stimulation and sensation: if enough energy is present, we will detect the presence of a stimulus. In fact, the situation is far more complex than this. For one thing, our sensitivity to stimuli varies from moment to moment. Thus, a stimulus we can detect at one time will not necessarily be detected at another. For this reason, psychologists usually define the absolute threshold as that magnitude of physical energy we can detect 50 percent of the time. While this definition takes account of fluctuations in our sensitivity to various stimuli, it does not address the intriguing question of why such fluctuations occur. The answer seems to involve several different factors.

TABLE 3-1

As Shown Here, Our Senses Can Detect Very Low Levels of Stimulation

Sense	Absolute Threshold Equivalent (Weakest Stimulus that Can Be Detected)
Vision	Candle thirty miles away on a clear, dark night
Hearing	Tick of a watch twenty feet away in a quiet room
Taste	Teaspoon of sugar dissolved in two gallons of water
Smell	One drop of perfume in a three-room apartment; a single molecule of an odorous substance
Touch	A bee's wing falling on the cheek from a height of one centimeter
Warmth or Cold	A one- to two-degree (Celsius) change in skin temperature

Absolute Thresholds for Each of Our Senses

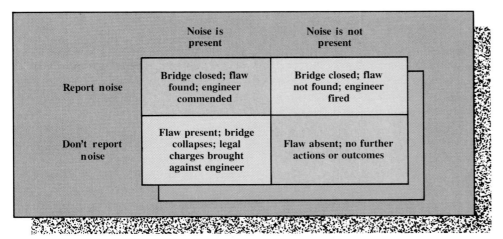

FIGURE 3-2. Should an engineer conclude that he or she heard a faint sound that may mean that a bridge is unsafe? His or her decision would be influenced by the possible outcomes outlined above.

First, as living organisms, countless changes are occurring within our bodies all the time. It is hardly surprising that as a result of these, our sensitivity to external stimuli varies, too.

Second, more complex factors such as our motivation to detect various stimuli and the relative rewards and costs associated with detecting or failing to detect them also play a role. Such factors are taken into careful account by **signal detection theory,** an approach to sensation suggesting that complex *decision mechanisms* come into play whenever we try to determine whether we have, or have not, detected a specific stimulus. Perhaps a concrete example will help clarify the nature of these mechanisms.

Imagine that you are a safety engineer whose job it is to inspect bridges. While examining a span which carries heavy traffic during rush hour, you think you hear a faint sound indicating a serious flaw in the bridge. What should you do? If you decide that you heard the noise, you will close the bridge and inconvenience thousands of commuters. If the flaw is then discovered (you really *did* hear that noise), you will be commended for doing a good job. If the flaw is not found, though, you'll be blamed for taking needless action. In contrast, if you decide you did not hear the noise, you won't close the bridge. Then, if the flaw is really there (you did hear the sound), there's a risk that many motorists will plunge to their death when the bridge fails. Alternatively, if the sound wasn't there and you don't close the bridge, you have made the right choice. What should you do? As you can see, deciding whether you heard the sound or not is likely to be influenced by the rewards and costs associated with each alternative. In this case, there's real danger to passing motorists, so you'd probably choose to avoid taking chances: you'd close the bridge even if the noise was extremely faint and you weren't at all sure you heard it. But what if you were new on the job and had just gone deeply into debt buying a house for your growing family? Here, the fear of making a foolish decision, which could cost you your job, might weigh more heavily in the balance; you would avoid reporting the noise unless you were quite certain you had heard it. (See Figure 3-2 for an overview of all the options in this situation.)

In sum, deciding whether we have detected a given stimulus is far more complex than you might at first assume. Often it involves much more than a simple relationship between the amount of physical energy present in a stimulus and the resulting psychological sensations.

Difference Thresholds: Are Two Stimuli the Same or Different?   Have you ever tasted a dish you were cooking, added salt to it and then tasted it again to see if you could detect any change? If so, you are familiar with another basic question relating to our sensory capacities: how much change in a stimulus is required before a shift can be noticed? Psychologists refer to this as the **difference threshold,** and it, too, provides valuable information about our ability to detect aspects of the physical world. Obviously, the smaller the change we can detect, the greater is our sensitivity. As you might guess, we are more sensitive to changes in some types of stimuli than others. For example, we sometimes can notice very tiny shifts in temperature (less than 1 degree Fahrenheit) and in the pitch of sounds (a useful fact when trying to tune an instrument), but we are somewhat less sensitive to changes in loudness or to smells.

Stimuli Below Threshold: Can They Have an Effect?   Now for a question we're sure you will find intriguing: what about stimuli below threshold? Can they affect us even if we are unaware of their presence? Surprisingly, the answer seems to be "Yes," at least in certain respects. For example, consider the results of an intriguing study conducted by Wilson (1979).

In this investigation subjects wore earphones and received different "programs" in each ear. On one side they heard a voice reading literary passages. On the other, they heard brief "melodies" (sequences of tones). Subjects were told to listen to the voice, repeat what it said out loud and, at the same time, check for errors in a written copy of the passage being read. After the passage ended, subjects were presented with six tone melodies, three of which they had previously heard and three they had not heard before. They were then asked to indicate whether each of these melodies was "old" or "new." Not surprisingly, they performed at chance level: subjects had been kept so busy while the melodies were presented that they couldn't tell which ones they had heard before. In one sense, then, the melodies were below threshold; subjects were unable to recognize them. When asked to indicate how much they liked or disliked each melody, however, very different results emerged: subjects rated the "old" melodies (ones they had previously heard) more favorably than the "new" ones (unfamiliar melodies they had not heard before; see Figure 3-3). This suggests that these stimuli must have "registered" at some level; after all, ratings of the two types of melodies differed significantly.

Please note: the tones used by Wilson (1979) were *not* below threshold in the traditional meaning of this term. They were loud enough to be detected by all subjects. However, because of the instructions to listen to the voice, subjects could not pay attention to the melodies and were not (apparently) aware of them. Thus, these stimuli were "below threshold" in terms of conscious awareness, if not in terms of subjects' potential ability to detect them. This fact renders interpretation of Wilson's findings complex. Still, since detection of all stimuli seems to depend, in part, on decision mechanisms and related cognitive factors, this study seems relevant to the question posed on page 69: can stimuli below threshold affect us in any manner?

Related findings have been obtained for visual stimuli (random shapes) presented so briefly that subjects could not report having seen them (Kunst-Wilson & Zajonc, 1980). Thus, it appears that even stimuli that are below absolute threshold (or at least below our threshold for conscious awareness of them) are capable of affecting our behavior. How can this be so? One possibility is that our threshold for conscious experience—for being able to report "Yes, I noticed that"—may be higher than our threshold for simple positive or negative reactions. Thus, weak stimuli can affect our feelings while we remain unaware of their presence (Zajonc, 1984).

This reasoning, in turn, suggests one potential use for sub-threshold stimuli: perhaps they can be included in advertising to influence potential customers. This idea was put into practice in the 1950s by a commercial firm which flashed such messages as "Eat popcorn" and "Drink Coca-Cola" on the screen in front of movie audiences. Although these stimuli were presented so briefly ($\frac{1}{3000}$ of a second) that audience members were not aware of their presence, popular press reports claimed that sales of both products in theater lobbies rose substantially right after the messages. Unfortunately, it is impossible to assess such claims: no full report of the study was ever published— it was merely summarized in popular magazines such as *Life* (Brean, 1958). We do know, however, that systematic research on such effects in subsequent years has generally yielded negative results (George & Jennings, 1975; McBurney & Collings, 1984). In other words, such procedures simply don't work: it doesn't seem possible to induce people to buy various products by exposing them to subliminal messages. This is hardly surprising; as we'll see in Chapter 15, changing people's behavior is usually

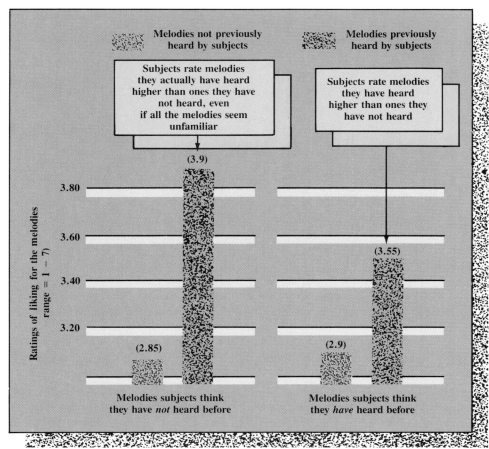

Evidence for the Impact of Subliminal Stimuli

FIGURE 3-3. Subjects were unable to tell melodies they had previously heard from ones they had not heard. However, they still assigned higher ratings to the familiar ones. These findings suggest that even stimuli that are below our threshold for conscious awareness can affect us in at least some ways. *(Source: Based on data from Wilson, 1979.)*

a complex and difficult task. The mildly positive or negative reactions which might potentially be induced by subliminal stimuli are far too weak to produce such effects. So rest easy: there's little danger that advertisers or anyone else will soon be able to send you marching to the nearest store in robot-like fashion to purchase products they wish to promote!

Sensory Adaptation: "It Feels Great Once You Get Used to It"

You step into a hot bath and feel practically scalded for a moment or two; then you settle down with a sigh. You jump into a lake and for a moment feel chilled; soon, though, the water seems comfortable (see Figure 3-4 on page 74). Your car's turn signal fails to go off, and you drive for miles with it on. If you've ever had experiences such as these, you are already familiar with the process of **sensory adaptation.** It refers to the fact that our sensitivity to an unchanging stimulus tends to decrease over time. Actually, this is quite useful, for if such adaptation did not occur, you'd constantly be distracted by such sensations as those produced by your clothing, the feel of your tongue in your mouth, and bodily processes such as eye blinks and swallowing. Sometimes, though, adaptation can be less helpful. For example, after about a minute our sensitivity to most odors drops by some 70 percent; clearly, this can pose a danger in situations where smoke or a harmful chemical is present. In general, though, the process of adaptation permits us to concentrate on *changes* in the world around us, and that is what is usually most important for survival.

Now that we've considered some basic aspects of sensation, we'll turn to our major senses. We'll describe how each sense operates and some of its special features.

Sensory Adaptation: Reduced
Sensitivity to Constant Stimuli

FIGURE 3-4. If you've ever entered water that at first felt very cold, but found that soon it seemed much warmer, you are already familiar with a basic fact about sensation: our sensitivity to unchanging stimuli tends to decrease over time.

Vision

Light, in the form of energy from the sun, is the fuel that drives the engine of life on earth. Thus, it is hardly surprising that we possess exquisitely adapted organs for detecting this stimulus: our *eyes*. A simplified diagram of the human eye is shown in Figure 3-5; please refer to it often as we proceed.

The Eye: Its Basic Structure.   Light enters the eye through the *pupil,* a round opening whose size varies with lighting conditions: the less light present, the wider the pupil opening. These adjustments are executed by the *iris,* the colored part of the eye,

FIGURE 3-5. A simplified diagram of the human eye. Light enters through the *pupil* and is focused by the *lens* on the *retina,* a structure containing light-sensitive receptors (the *rods* and *cones*).

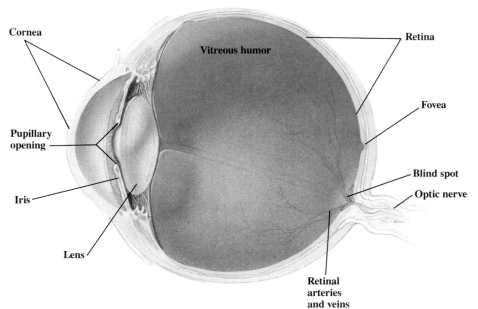

The Human Eye

which is actually a circular muscle which contracts or expands to let in varying amounts of light. Light rays then pass through the *lens*—a clear structure which permits us to focus on objects at varying distances from our eyes through adjustments in its shape. The actual sensory receptors of the eye are found in the *retina* at the back of the eyeball. This postage-stamp-size structure contains two types of light-sensitive receptor cells: about 6.5 million **cones** and about 100 million **rods.** Cones, which seem to function best in bright light, play a key role in color vision and in our ability to notice fine detail. In contrast, rods play an important role in vision under lower levels of illumination. Interestingly, the rods and cones are actually located at the back of the retina—the part farthest away from incoming light. Light must pass through two other types of cells—*ganglion cells* and *bipolar cells*—before reaching these receptors. Also, while several rods synapse with a single bipolar cell, many (but not all) cones have their own bipolar cell. This is one reason why cones are superior in detecting fine detail. Neural information from the rods and cones is carried from the eye to the brain by the *optic nerve*. Since no receptors are present where this nerve exits the eye, a *blind spot* in our visual field exists at this point.

Light: The Physical Stimulus for Vision.   At this point we should call your attention to some important facts about *light,* which is the physical stimulus for vision. First, light visible to us is only a small portion of the whole *electromagnetic spectrum*. As shown in Figure 3-6, this spectrum ranges from radio waves at the slow or long-wave end to cosmic rays at the fast or short-wave end. Visible light occupies only a narrow band in the entire spectrum.

Second, certain physical properties of light are related to our psychological experiences of vision. *Wavelength*—the distance between successive peaks and valleys of light energy—is related to *hue* or color. As shown in Figure 3-6, as wavelength increases from about 400 nanometers (a nanometer is one-billionth of a meter), our sensations shift from violet through blue, green, yellow, orange, and finally red. The *intensity* of light (the amount of energy it contains) is related to its brightness. The extent to which light contains only one wavelength, rather than many, is related to *saturation;* the fewer the number of wavelengths mixed together, the more saturated or ''pure'' a color appears. For example, the deep red of an apple is highly saturated, while the pale pink of a delicate flower is low in saturation (see Figure 3-7 on page 76).

Basic Functions of the Visual System: Acuity, Dark Adaptation, and Eye Movements.   How sensitive are our eyes? We have already mentioned our ability to detect tiny amounts of light (refer to page 70). Another important aspect of vision is **acuity,** the ability to see fine details. Acuity can be measured in several different ways.

FIGURE 3-6. Notice that visible light—the only stimuli we can see—constitutes a small part of the total electromagnetic spectrum.

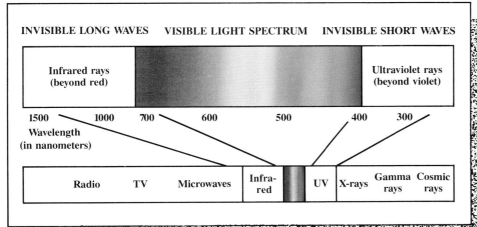

The Electromagnetic Spectrum

Light: Its Physical and Psychological Properties

FIGURE 3-7. Sensations of *hue* (color) are related to the wavelengths of light reaching us from any source (in this case, a beautiful bouquet of flowers). Sensations of *brightness* are related to the amount of energy in the light. Finally, *saturation* (purity of color) involves the number of different wavelengths that stimulate our visual receptors. For example, the pastel flowers are low in saturation, while the deep red ones are highly saturated.

For example, eye doctors often use the familiar *Snellen chart* to determine if patients can recognize familiar letters from given distances. Acuity can also be measured in terms of *resolution* (how small a separation between lines an individual can notice) and *detection* (how small a stimulus a person can detect). Since cones, which are sensitive to fine detail, are concentrated near the center of the retina in an area known as the *fovea*, acuity is higher near the center of our field of vision, and it is lower toward the edges (at the periphery).

Another aspect of visual sensitivity involves the process of **dark adaptation**—the increase in sensitivity that occurs when we move from bright to dim environments. This increase is impressive: the dark-adapted eye is about 100,000 more sensitive to light than the light-adapted eye. Actually, dark adaptation occurs in two steps. First, within a period of five minutes or less, the cones reach their peak sensitivity. After about ten minutes, the rods begin to adapt. This process is complete in about twenty minutes. At one time it was thought that dark adaptation was entirely a function of chemical changes within the rods and cones. However, more recent findings suggest that additional mechanisms at higher levels within the nervous system (e.g., visual centers in the brain) probably also play a role.

When you get to the end of this sentence, stop reading and stare at the last word for several seconds. Did your eyes remain motionless while you did this? If you think carefully about your sensations, you will probably realize they did not. Instead, your eyes tended to move about. Such movements are involuntary: they occur whether we wish them to or not. And they seem to play an important role in the operation of our visual system. Specifically, they assure that the stimuli reaching our visual receptors (the rods and cones) are constantly changing. This is beneficial, for if such change failed to occur, these receptors might undergo sensory adaptation, with the result that vision would be impaired.

Such movements are not the only ones made by our eyes. In addition, we show what are termed **saccadic movements.** These are jumps by our eyes from one fixation point to the next. They are fast, frequent, and seem to have pre-determined locations. That is, our eyes don't jump about randomly; they move from one spot we wish to examine to the next. Such movements are apparent in reading. Moreover, it has been found that the saccadic movement patterns made by effective and ineffective readers differ sharply (refer to Figure 3-8). The saccadic movements of good readers move smoothly across the materials being read; those of poor readers are smaller in size and move backward as well as forward. We will have more to say about the importance of eye movements in our later discussion of *illusions*. Incidentally, reading also involves another type of eye movement, *pursuit movements,* which are smoother in form than saccadic movements.

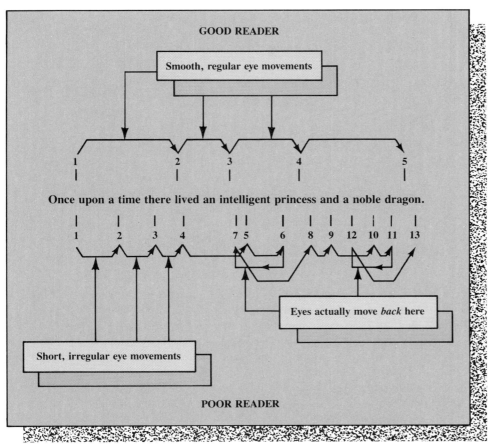

FIGURE 3-8. The eye movements of effective readers are smooth and usually cover several words. In contrast, the eye movements of poor readers are shorter, somewhat jerky, and go back over materials already completed.

Color Vision. Can you imagine a world without color? If you ever watch black-and-white movies or television, you can. And if you do, you probably realize that a world without color would be sadly restricted, for color—vivid reds, glowing yellows, restful greens—is a key aspect of our visual experience. It is for this reason, of course, that computerized systems for adding color to classic black-and-white films have recently been developed (see Figure 3-9). For many persons, though, the absence of color is a

FIGURE 3-9. Because color is such an important part of our visual world, its absence from black-and-white films has long been viewed as a drawback by some persons. Recently, computer-assisted techniques for adding color to classic films has been developed. Reactions to such efforts have been mixed. (Still below is from ''It's A Wonderful Life,'' a film that has been colorized.)

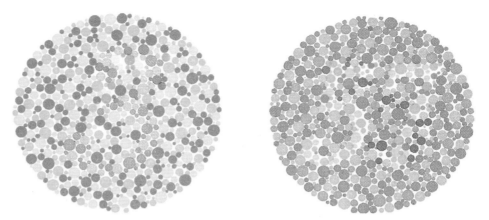

FIGURE 3-10. What do you see in each of these circles? (Answers for normal and color-blind individuals differ. Normal responses are 3 and 57.)

reality. About 8 percent of males and 0.4 percent of females suffer from some degree of *color weakness;* they are less sensitive than the rest of us either to red and green or to yellow and blue. And a few individuals are totally *color blind*—for them, the world exists only in varying shades of white, black, and gray. Intriguing evidence on how the world actually appears to people suffering from color weakness has been gathered from rare cases in which individuals have normal color vision in one eye, and impaired color vision in the other (e.g., Graham & Hsia, 1958). For example, one such woman indicated that to her color-impaired eye all colors between red and green appeared yellow, while all colors between green and violet seemed blue. (If you'd like to check your own color vision, please see Figure 3-10.)

How does the visual system normally function to provide our rich sense of color? Two theories provide a useful answer. The first, known as **trichromatic theory,** suggests that we have three different types of cones, each of which is most sensitive to red, green, or blue. Presumably, different patterns of activity in these receptors under different light conditions provide us with the neural signals responsible for color. In fact, careful studies of the human retina suggest that we do possess three groups of receptors. While these cannot be neatly divided into types that are primarily sensitive to red, green, or blue, because they actually overlap quite a bit, this suggests that at the level of the retina different types of receptors do contribute to our sense of color (Rushton, 1975).

Unfortunately, though, trichromatic theory leaves some key questions unanswered. For example, how do we perceive yellow, which seems (subjectively) as basic a color as red, green, and blue? And how can three types of receptors account for our ability to discriminate between hundreds or thousands of different colors? In addition, trichromatic theory cannot explain the occurrence of **negative afterimages.** These are sensations of *complementary colors* that occur after staring at a stimulus of a given color. (Complementary colors are ones which, when combined, produce white or gray.) For example, after staring at a red object, if you shift your gaze to a neutral background, sensations of green may follow. Similarly, after staring at a yellow stimulus, sensations of blue may occur. (You can demonstrate negative afterimages for yourself by following the instructions in Figure 3-11.)

All these issues are handled more effectively by a second theory of color vision, **opponent process theory.** According to this framework, above the level of the retina we possess six kinds of cells that play a role in sensations of color. Two of these handle red and green: one is stimulated by red light and inhibited by green light, while the other is stimulated by green light and inhibited by red. (This is where the phrase *opponent process* originates.) Two additional types of cells handle yellow and blue (again, one is stimulated by yellow and inhibited by blue, the other shows the opposite pattern). The remaining two types handle black and white—again, in an opponent process manner. Each of these six types of cells is stimulated in different patterns by the three types of cones. It is the overall pattern of such stimulation that yields our complex and eloquent sensations of color.

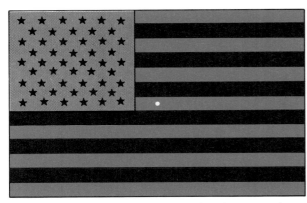

FIGURE 3-11. Stare at this stimulus for about one minute. Then shift your gaze to a blank sheet of white paper. Do you see a negative afterimage?

**Negative Afterimages:
A Demonstration**

In sum, our impressive ability to respond to color appears to stem from two mechanisms, one present at the level of the retina and the other present in the ganglion cells and beyond. For additional information on how the visual system handles sensory input from our eyes, see the "Classic Contributions" section below.

FOCUS ON RESEARCH: Classic Contributions

Information Processing in the Visual System: Feature Detectors in the Visual Cortex

Imagine the following scene: we are in a darkened laboratory. A cat sits facing a screen, on which various visual stimuli can be projected. The cat is awake and alert, but a tiny electrode has been implanted into its brain in the area most directly involved with input from the visual system, the occipital lobe. In fact, the electrode is placed so it can record the activity of a single neuron. Now a stimulus, consisting of a light horizontal bar against a darker background, is presented. Nothing happens. Next, a bar tilted at a 45 degree angle is flashed; again there is little or no response from the neuron. Now the bar is shown in a vertical orientation. Suddenly the neuron bursts into activity. We have found a specific cell in the visual cortex that responds only to a specific type of visual stimulus. The electrode is moved to another cell in the cortex, and the process is repeated. Many different stimuli, varying in size, shape, color, and movement are projected, and the neural activity produced by each is observed.

The procedures just described were actually used by Hubel and Wiesel (1979) in a series of studies which earned them a Nobel Prize. Taken as a whole, the results of their careful research indicate that there are neurons at various levels within the visual system that respond only (or at least primarily) to stimuli possessing certain features. Three types of such cells have been identified.

One group—known as **simple cells**—responds to bars or lines presented in certain orientations (horizontal, vertical, and so on). A second group—**complex cells**—responds to moving stimuli. For example, such cells may react maximally to a vertical bar moving from left to right, or to a tilted bar moving from right to left, but remain relatively inactive when other visual stimuli are presented. Finally, there are **hypercomplex cells**—neurons that respond to even more complex features of the visual world, such as length, width, and even certain aspects of shape, such as corners and angles. Thus, such cells may fail to respond to a thin bar moving from right to left, but may respond strongly to a thick bar moving from lower to higher regions of the visual field. Or they may respond to a shape containing a right angle but fail to respond to one containing a smaller angle. (Refer to Figure 3-12 on page 80 for examples of visual stimuli detected by simple, complex, and hypercomplex cells.)

The findings uncovered by Hubel and Wiesel plus many other researchers (e.g.,

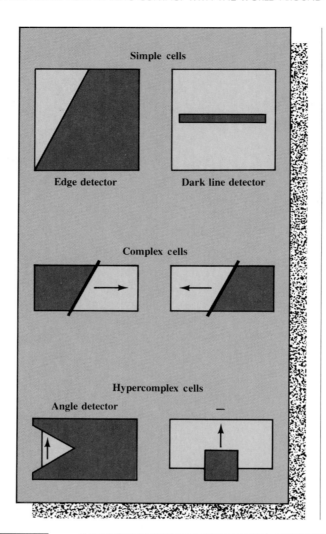

Devalois, Yund, & Hepler, 1982; Heggelund, 1981) have important implications. First, they suggest that the visual system is quite *selective*. Certain types of input have a greater chance than others of reaching the brain and undergoing further processing. Second, since nature is rarely wasteful, the existence of cells specially equipped to detect certain features of the external world suggests that these features may be the building blocks for many complex visual abilities (e.g., reading, identifying complex visual patterns such as faces, and the like). Further research on these and related topics may add substantially to our understanding of how, visually, we come to know the world around us.

FIGURE 3-12. Visual stimuli that produce activity in simple, complex, and hypercomplex cells of the visual cortex.

Feature Detectors in the Visual Cortex

Hearing

The murmur of laughing voices, the roar of a jet plane, the rustling of leaves, and that quintessential sound of the late twentieth century—the "beep, beep" of a personal computer—clearly, we live in a world full of sound. And, as with vision, we are well equipped to receive it. A simplified diagram of the human ear is shown in Figure 3-13; please refer to it as you proceed through the discussion below.

The Ear: Its Basic Structure. In common speech we use the term *ear* to refer to the visible portion—the part to which we attach *ear*rings. However, this is only part of the entire ear. Inside, out of sight, is the *eardrum*—a thin piece of tissue which moves ever so slightly in response to sound waves striking it. When it moves, the eardrum causes three tiny bones within the *inner ear* to vibrate. The third of these is attached to a second membrane, the *oval window,* covering a spiral-shaped structure known as the **cochlea.** The cochlea is filled with fluid, and movements in this fluid produced by vibration of the oval window cause tiny *hair cells* to bend and rub against another membrane within the cochlea. These are the true sensory receptors for sound; the neural messages they transmit move to the brain through the *auditory nerve.*

Sound: The Physical Stimulus for Hearing. When we discussed light, we noted that relationships exist between certain of its physical properties (e.g., wavelength,

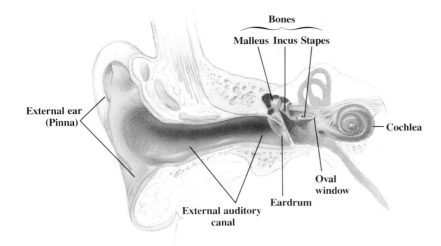

Bones

Malleus Incus Stapes

External ear
(Pinna)

Cochlea

Oval
window

Eardrum

External auditory
canal

The Human Ear

FIGURE 3-13. A simplified diagram of the human ear. Sound waves (alternating compressions and expansions in the air) enter through the external auditory canal and produce slight movements in the eardrum. This, in turn, produces movements in fluid within the *cochlea*. As this fluid moves, tiny *hair cells* shift their position, thus generating the nerve impulses we perceive as sound.

intensity) and psychological aspects of vision (hue, brightness). Similar relationships exist for sound, at least with respect to two of its psychological qualities: *pitch* and *loudness*.

Sound waves consist of alternating compressions and expansions of the air (or, more precisely, of the molecules which compose it). The faster these sound waves occur (the greater their *frequency*), the higher the perceived *pitch*. Frequency is measured in terms of cycles per second or *hertz* (Hz); we can hear sounds ranging from about 20 Hz to about 20,000 Hz. The greater the *amplitude* (magnitude) of these waves, the greater their *loudness* to us. A third psychological aspect of sound—its *timbre*—is somewhat harder to describe. Timbre refers to a sound's quality. For example, a piece of chalk squeaking across a blackboard may have the same pitch and amplitude as a note played on a violin, but it will certainly have a different quality! In general, the timbre of a sound is related to its *complexity*—how many different frequencies it contains. However, other physical aspects of the source of the sound may be involved, too, so the relationship is not a simple one.

Basic Aspects of the Auditory System: Pitch Perception and Sound Localization. If you've ever tuned a guitar or tried to sing in harmony with other persons, you know that our ability to detect differences in pitch is impressive. Most persons can easily tell when two sounds have the same pitch and when they do not. How do we manage to make such fine distinctions? Two explanations, based on two different mechanisms, seem to provide the answer.

Place theory suggests that sounds of different frequencies cause different portions of the *basilar membrane* (the floor of the cochlea) to vibrate. These vibrations, in turn, stimulate the hair cells—the sensory receptors for sound. Specifically, high-frequency sounds cause parts of the basilar membrane close to the oval window to vibrate, while low-frequency sounds cause parts near its end to vibrate. This theory has been verified through actual observation: sounds of different pitch *do* produce activity in different parts of the basilar membrane (Von Békésy, 1960). Unfortunately, though, no portion of the basilar membrane seems sensitive to sounds of very low frequency (e.g., ones of only a few hundred cycles per second). This suggests the need for an additional explanatory mechanism.

Such a mechanism is provided by **frequency theory,** which suggests that sounds of different pitch cause different rates of neural firing. Thus, high-pitched sounds produce high rates of activity in the auditory nerve, while low-pitched sounds produce lower rates. This theory seems to be accurate up to sounds of about 1,000 Hz—the maximum rate of firing for individual neurons. Above that level, the theory must be modified to include the *volley principle*—the assumption that sound receptors for other neurons begin to fire in volleys. For example, a sound with a frequency of 5,000 Hz might generate a pattern of activity in which each of five groups of neurons fire 1,000 times in rapid succession (i.e., in volleys). Since our daily activities regularly expose us to sounds of many frequencies, both theories are needed to explain our ability to respond to this wide range of stimuli.

You are walking down a busy street, filled with many sights and sounds. Suddenly, your name is called by a familiar voice. You instantly turn in the direction of this sound and spot one of your friends. Simple, right? You do it all the time. But *how,* precisely, do you accomplish this feat? How do you know where to turn in order to spot your friend? Research on *localization*—this ability of the auditory system to locate the source of a given sound—suggests that two factors play a role.

The first stems from the fact that you have two ears, placed on opposite sides of your head. As a result, there is a slight difference in the time it takes for a sound to reach each ear, except when it comes from directly in front or directly in back of you. This difference is truly tiny—often less than one millisecond (one thousandth of a second). Yet, small as it is, it provides an important clue as to sound localization (see Figure 3-14). Second, there is also a difference in the intensity of a sound upon reaching the two ears. For example, a sound behind you and to your left will not only reach your left ear sooner than your right ear, it will also be slightly *louder* in your left ear. Again, such differences are tiny, but our auditory system seems to be constructed so as to take full advantage of them. When you consider how rapidly you process such information, then respond to it by turning in the proper direction, it seems nothing short of marvelous in its efficiency.

FIGURE 3-14. Because your ears are located on opposite sides of your head, sounds coming from anywhere other than directly behind or in front of you reach one ear a fraction of a second before reaching the other. This, plus the fact that a sound is slightly louder at the nearer ear than at the other, helps you locate the source of sounds very accurately.

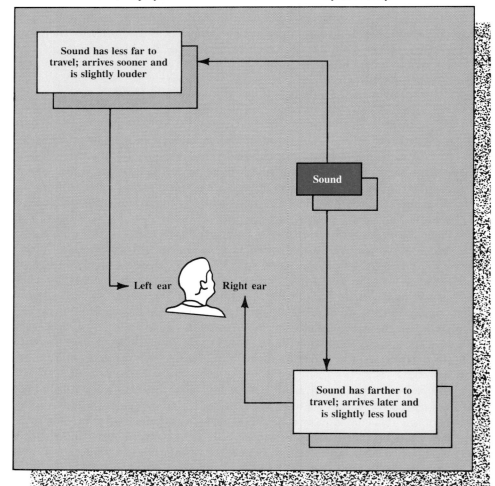

Sound has less far to travel; arrives sooner and is slightly louder

Sound

Left ear   Right ear

Sound has farther to travel; arrives later and is slightly less loud

Localization of Sounds: How We Do It

Touch and Other Skin Senses

What is the largest sensory organ you possess? If you said anything except "my skin," think again. In fact, not only is the skin the largest sensory organ, it also produces the most varied experiences—everything from the pleasure of a soothing massage or a warm bath to the pain of serious injury and the sting of biting cold. Actually, there are several skin senses rather than one: touch (or pressure), warmth, cold, and pain.

Since there are specific sensory receptors for vision and hearing, it seems reasonable to expect this also to be true for the various skin senses—one type of receptor for touch, another for warmth, and so on. Indeed, microscopic examination of the skin reveals several different types of receptors. This fact led early researchers to suggest that each type must be responsible for a specific sensory experience (warmth, cold, touch, and so on). However, this prediction was not confirmed. In some unsettling studies, several brave researchers first located patches of their own skin that seemed especially sensitive to various kinds of stimulation. Then they actually snipped these patches out and examined them under a microscope. The results were disappointing; specific types of receptors were *not* found at spots highly sensitive to touch, warmth, or cold. It seems, therefore, that such sensations stem from the total pattern of nerve impulses reaching the brain rather than from the activity of any one type of receptor.

The physical stimulus for sensations of touch is a stretching of or pressure against the skin. Psychologists often distinguish between **passive touch,** in which an object is placed against the skin, and **active touch,** in which we bring our hand or other body part in contact with an object. As you might guess, we are considerably more accurate at identifying objects through active than passive touch. One more interesting fact: women are significantly more sensitive to touch than men (see Figure 3-15 on page 84). Whether this reflects differences in the sensory systems of the two sexes or merely the fact that women learn to pay more attention to such sensations is not yet clear.

Surprisingly, it appears that sensations of warmth and cold are not opposites or "mirror images" of each other: such sensations are detected at different locations. Whatever the sensory receptors for temperature, though, we are extremely sensitive to it. Indeed, we can sometimes detect changes of less than one degree Celsius (Kenshalo, 1978).

Pain: Its Nature and Control.   Throbbing joints, aching muscles, cuts, scrapes, and bruises. For most of us, pain is an all-too-common experience. Despite its discomfort, though, it plays an important adaptive role: without pain, you would be unaware that something is amiss inside your body or that you have suffered some type of injury.

Sensations of pain seem to originate in *free nerve endings* located throughout the body (in the skin, around muscles, in internal organs, and so on). Apparently, damage to body tissues releases substances that stimulate such neurons. The neural messages they then transmit are responsible for our sensations of pain.

Actually, two types of pain seem to exist. One can best be described as quick and sharp—the kind of pain you experience when you receive a cut. The other is dull and throbbing—the pain you experience from a sore muscle or an injured back. The first type of pain seems to be transmitted through large sensory nerve fibers, which also carry information from the other skin senses. The second type is carried by smaller fibers which conduct neural impulses more slowly. The discovery of these two distinct pain systems led to the formulation of an influential view of pain known as the **gate-control theory** (Melzack, 1976).

Briefly, gate-control theory suggests that there are neural mechanisms in the spinal cord that sometimes close, thus preventing pain messages from reaching the brain. Apparently, pain messages carried by large sensory fibers can activate this "gate" (cause it to close), while messages carried by small fibers (the ones related to dull, throbbing pain) cannot. This may be one reason why sharp pain is relatively brief, while an ache persists for longer periods. In a sense, the former type is self-terminating: its initiation tends to close the spinal "gate," and so brings the sensation to an end. The gate-control theory

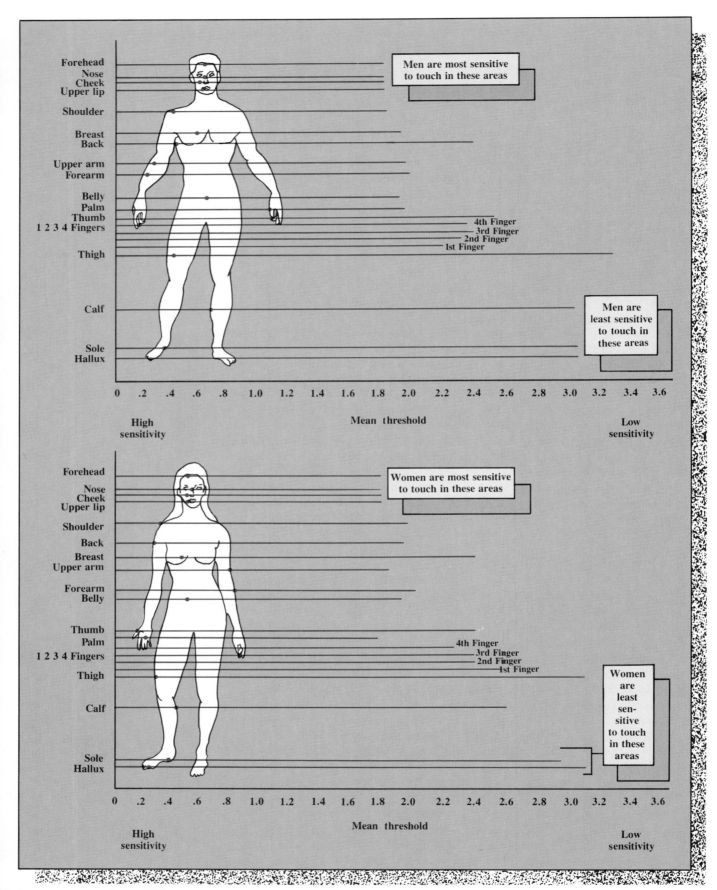

FIGURE 3-15. As you can see from these two diagrams, we are much more sensitive to touch at some points on our bodies than others. Also, by comparing the two drawings, you can see that women are considerably more sensitive to touch than men. (Please note: Higher numbers on the vertical axis indicate *lower* sensitivity.) *(Source: Adapted from Weinstein, 1968.)*

Differences in Sensitivity to Touch

FIGURE 3-16. *Acupuncture*—in which thin needles are inserted into parts of the body as a means of reducing pain—may succeed because it somehow closes the spinal "gate," thereby preventing pain messages from reaching the brain. Please note, though, that the effectiveness of acupuncture is still somewhat in doubt.

Acupuncture and the Gate-Control Theory of Pain

also helps explain why such techniques as rubbing the skin near an injury, applying ice-packs or hot water bottles, and even *acupuncture* may sometimes work (see Figure 3-16). Presumably, all these tactics stimulate activity in large nerve fibers, closing the spinal "gate." The result: sensations of pain are reduced.

At this point, we should note that sensations of pain are also affected by mechanisms within the brain. First, as we saw in Chapter 2, the brain produces substances (endorphins) which seem to lessen sensations of pain (e.g., Akil et al., 1984). Second, in response to painful stimuli, the brain may transmit messages that either close the spinal "gate" or tend to keep it open. This may be one reason why your emotional state often affects the intensity of pain you experience. For example, when you are anxious (as many persons are when sitting in a dentist's chair), pain is intensified. In contrast, when you are calm and relaxed, such sensations may be reduced. A dramatic illustration of the role of higher-level mechanisms in sensations of pain is provided by a study conducted by Craig and Prkachin (1978).

These investigators exposed female volunteers to a series of electric shocks. After receiving each shock, subjects rated its discomfort. Half performed these activities in the presence of another person (actually an accomplice of the experimenters) who supposedly received the same shocks they did, and who always announced a rating 25 percent lower than the rating stated by the subject. In other words, the accomplice reported finding the shocks much less painful. The other half of the participants (the control group) rated the shocks in the presence of an accomplice who did *not* announce her own ratings out loud.

Results were quite revealing. First, subjects exposed to information indicating that the accomplice found the shocks low in painfulness reported significantly less discomfort than subjects who did not receive such information. Even more intriguing, these subjects actually showed *lower physiological arousal* in response to the shocks than those in the control group (refer to Figure 3-17 on page 86). These and related findings (e.g., Craig, 1979) suggest that although it is a basic sensory experience, pain can be strongly affected by social or cognitive factors. It is hard to imagine a more compelling illustration of the two-way flow of information between sensory receptors and higher centers of the brain.

Smell and Taste: The Chemical Senses

Last, but certainly not least, we come to the *chemical senses:* smell and taste. Although these are separate senses, it is reasonable to consider them together for two reasons. First, both respond to substances in solution (substances that have been dissolved in a liquid). Second, the two are intimately related in everyday life.

Taste and Smell: How They Operate.   The stimulus for sensations of smell is molecules of various substances in the air. Such molecules enter the nasal passages during breathing or during active sniffing, where they dissolve in moist nasal tissues. This brings

The Role of Higher Mental Processes in Sensations of Pain

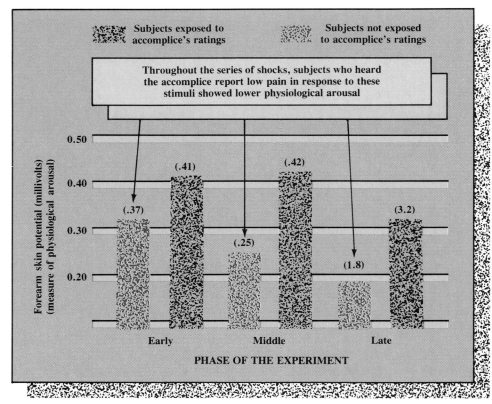

FIGURE 3-17. Subjects who heard another person (an accomplice) announce that she found a series of electric shocks to be relatively non-painful showed lower physiological arousal in response to actual shocks than subjects who did not receive such information. These findings suggest that reactions to painful stimuli can be strongly affected by social or cognitive factors. *(Source: Based on data from Craig & Prkachin, 1978.)*

them in contact with *receptor cells* contained in the *olfactory epithelium* (refer to Figure 3-18). Human beings possess about five million receptors sensitive to odors; dogs, in contrast, possess more than one hundred million.

Efforts to develop a useful technique for classifying odors have generally failed. Some evidence suggests that such sensations may be related to the shapes of the odor molecules (Amoore, 1970). However, little evidence for this view exists, and at present no satisfactory method exists for dividing odors into groups or categories. (Perfumers often divide the fragrances they manufacture into the following categories: fresh, floral, spicy, and musky.)

The sensory receptors for taste are located inside small bumps on the tongue known as *papillae*. Within each papilla is a cluster of **taste buds,** arranged on either side (refer to Figure 3-19). Each taste bud, in turn, contains several receptor cells that are responsible for sensations of taste. Human beings possess about ten thousand taste buds. In contrast, chickens have only twenty-four; catfish would be the winner in any "taste-bud counting contest"—they possess more than 175,000, scattered over the surface of their body. Thus, in a sense, catfish can "taste" with their entire skin (Pfaffmann, 1978).

When we chew foods, we often have the strong impression that we can distinguish a large number of flavors. In fact, there appear to be only four basic tastes: sweet, salt, sour, and bitter. Why, then, do we believe we are sensitive to many more? The answer lies in the fact that when we eat, we are aware not only of the taste of the food in our mouth, but also of its smell, its texture, its temperature, the pressure it exerts on our tongue and mouth, and many other sensations. When these are removed from the picture, only the four basic tastes mentioned above remain.

Have you ever noticed that some foods seem to taste stronger when in contact with one part of your tongue than another? If so, you will not be surprised to learn that sensations of taste do seem to vary in this regard. We seem to be most sensitive to sour

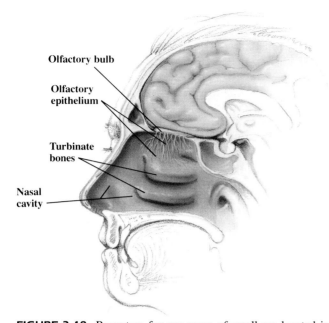

FIGURE 3-18. Receptors for our sense of smell are located in the *olfactory epithelium,* found at the top of the nasal cavity. Molecules of odorous substances are dissolved in moisture present in the nasal passages. This brings them into contact with *receptor cells* whose neural activity gives rise to sensations of smell.

tastes on the sides of the tongue, to sweet and salt tastes on the front, and to bitter at the back. The middle of the tongue seems to be a kind of ''blind spot'' for taste; we have little sensitivity to taste there.

Smell and Taste: Some Interesting Findings. Perhaps because they are difficult to study, smell and taste have received far less attention from researchers than vision and hearing. However, this does not imply that these senses are not important. Indeed, individuals who have lost their sense of smell (a state known as **anosmia**) often become deeply depressed. Many even turn to suicide rather than face a world in which they cannot smell a rose and in which all foods taste very much alike (Douek, 1988).

FIGURE 3-19. (A) *Taste buds* are located inside small bumps on the surface of the tongue known as *papillae*. (B) Within each taste bud are a number of individual *receptor cells*.

A taste bud (A)

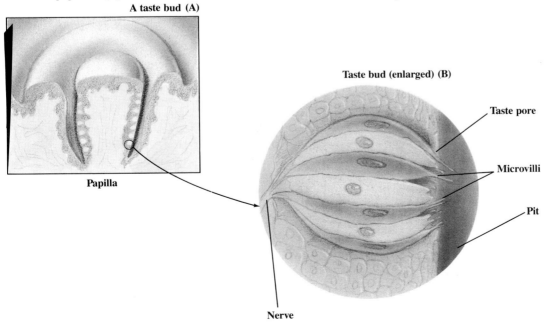

Papilla

Taste bud (enlarged) (B)

Taste pore

Microvilli

Pit

Nerve

Despite this relative lack of attention, many interesting facts have been uncovered about smell and taste. With respect to smell, it appears that we are not very good at identifying different odors (Engen, 1986). For example, when asked to identify thirteen common fragrances (e.g., grape, smoke, mint, pine, soap), individuals were successful only 32 percent of the time. Even when brand-name products were used, accuracy rose only to 44 percent. Interestingly, women were more accurate in both respects than men. However, there is one way in which our sense of smell *is* very impressive: once exposed to a specific odor, we can recognize it months or even years later (Engen & Ross, 1973; Engen, 1986).

With respect to taste, two phenomena, known as *cross adaptation* and *cross enhancement,* are of interest. The first refers to the fact that after becoming adapted to the taste of one substance, we are less sensitive to the same taste in other foods. For example, after drinking a glass of lemonade, you may fail to notice a hint of sourness in a salad dressing. Cross enhancement is just the opposite. Here, tasting one food may intensify certain components of another. You may have experienced this yourself if you've ever tasted dessert before a meal. After a bit of a sweet cake or pie, even an excellent wine served along with your meal may taste sour or bitter. The moral of cross adaptation and cross enhancement is clear: consider carefully the order in which you eat various foods. If you don't, the enjoyment you ruin may be your own! (Does knowledge about the chemical senses—smell and taste—have any practical use? For some evidence that it does, please see ''The Point of It All'' section below.)

THE POINT OF IT ALL

Fragrance: Its Potential Effects in Work Settings

Fragrance is big business—*very* big business. Billions of dollars are spent each year on perfumes, colognes, and related grooming aids. In addition, artificial scent is added to many household products—everything from cleaning aids to paper napkins. At first glance, you might assume that fragrance is used primarily in social settings or at home. However, a recent survey indicates that more than 90 percent of women and almost 80 percent of men wear perfume or cologne to work at least part of the time (*Newsweek,* 1984). Why? The answer is simple: most people believe that wearing the right fragrance enhances their appeal to others. Are such beliefs justified? And does the use of fragrance have any impact on human behavior in work settings? Recent investigations have begun to provide some answers.

First, several studies (e.g., Baron, 1983, 1986) indicate that wearing perfume or cologne to *job interviews* can have strong effects upon the ratings individuals receive. Moreover—and

this may surprise you—such effects are not always favorable. For example, it appears that while *female* interviewers assign slightly higher ratings to job applicants who wear perfume or cologne than to ones who do not, *male* interviewers react somewhat differently. They assign significantly *lower* ratings to applicants who wear perfume or cologne than to applicants who refrain from using fragrance. One reason why this may be so is that males may realize that they are easily influenced by applicants' personal appearance (at least, more easily influenced than females). Thus, they may interpret the use of such grooming aids as an attempt to bias their judgments. Little wonder, then, that they tend to down-rate applicants who use artificial fragrance. In any case, the moral of such research is clear: if you choose to wear perfume or cologne to an interview, do so in moderation and with caution (see Figure 3-20).

On the other hand, some evidence (Baron, 1988) indicates that introducing a pleasant fragrance into the air of work set-

FIGURE 3-20. While most people seem to believe that wearing fragrance enhances their personal appeal, research findings are consistent with the conclusion suggested by this cartoon: a little can go a long way, so moderation is best! *(Source: Universal Press Syndicate.)*

cathy   **by Cathy Guisewite**

Scent in Work Settings: Use with Care

tings may produce several beneficial effects. In this research, popular brands of air freshener were either sprayed or not sprayed into rooms where subjects worked on various tasks. Results indicated that the presence of a pleasant aroma produced several positive outcomes. For example, it increased subjects' confidence in their own ability to perform various tasks, and it raised the goals they set for themselves on these tasks. In addition, the presence of pleasant scents enhanced subjects' mood, and so increased their willingness to compromise with an opponent during negotiations. Of course, these results are only preliminary and must be replicated under other conditions before being accepted with confidence. Nevertheless, they suggest that introducing pleasant aromas into work settings may be one inexpensive and noncontroversial tactic for improving employees' performance and satisfaction. Stay tuned for further developments!

Perception: Putting It All Together

Stop for a moment and look around you. Do you see a meaningless swirl of colors, brightnesses, and shapes? Of course not. Now flip on the radio and tune it in to any speaking voice. Do you hear an incomprehensible babble of sounds? Certainly not (unless, of course, you've tuned to a foreign language!). In both cases you "see" and "hear" more than the units of information brought to your brain by your senses: you see meaningful objects and hear recognizable words. So, in an important sense, the information transmitted by your eyes, ears, and other senses is only part of the picture. Once it arrives, you somehow *organize* and *interpret* sensory input into a meaningful grasp of your immediate surroundings. The process through which you accomplish this marvelous feat is known as **perception,** and it is to this important topic we turn next.

Perception: Some Organizing Principles

Look at Figure 3-21; what do you see? A black cross against a white background? A white cross against a black background? Either interpretation of this drawing is possible, but one or the other will almost certainly occur. This simple fact points to an important principle of perceptual organization: the **figure-ground relationship.** What this means, simply, is that when you examine the world around you, you tend to divide it into two parts: *figure,* which has a definite shape and a location in space; and *ground,* which has no shape, seems to continue behind the figure, and has no definite location. This principle, and the others described below, were first studied systematically by *Gestalt psychologists*—a group of German psychologists who worked in the early decades of this century. They were intrigued with what they felt were innate tendencies of the human mind to impose order and structure on the physical world, and to perceive sensory patterns as well-organized wholes, rather than as separate isolated parts (*Gestalt* means "whole" in German). These scientists sought to identify basic principles and believed they had succeeded. While many psychologists currently question their conclusion that the tendencies they studied (e.g., figure-ground) are entirely innate, there is little doubt that they exist and do affect our perceptions. In this regard, Gestalt psychologists made a lasting contribution to the field. One could say that they changed our perceptions about the nature of perception!

But the figure-ground relationship was not the only *organizing principle* of perception noted by the Gestaltists. In addition, they called attention to a number of principles known as **laws of grouping.** These describe basic ways in which we group items together perceptually. Several of these "laws" are illustrated in Figure 3-22 on page 90. As you can see from examining this figure, they *do* seem to offer a good description of our perceptual tendencies. For example, try as you may, you probably can't perceive diagram A, which illustrates the *law of similarity,* as consisting of vertical columns of crosses and zeros. Rather, you probably see it as horizontal rows of these two figures. This principle suggests that we tend to group similar objects together, and apart from dissimilar ones. As another example, we doubt that you can help perceiving diagram C as a circle, despite the gap it contains. This illustrates the *law of closure:* when a space is enclosed by a line, it tends to be perceived as a simple, enclosed figure. See Figure 3-22 for a description of other laws of grouping.

FIGURE 3-21. What do you see when you look at this drawing? In all probability, you see either a black cross against a white background, or a white cross against a black background. Since this is an *ambiguous figure,* your perceptions may switch back and forth between these two possibilities. It is much less likely that you will simply see a circle with alternating light and dark slices. This illustrates our strong tendency to divide the perceptual world into two parts: *figure* (a cross) and *ground* (the background).

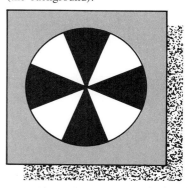

Figure Versus Ground: A Simple Demonstration

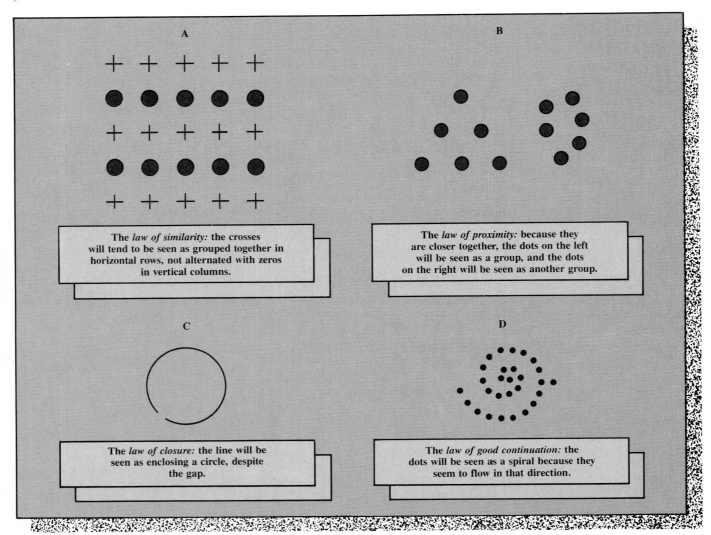

FIGURE 3-22. We seem to possess strong tendencies to group stimuli together in certain ways. Several of these *laws of grouping* are illustrated here.

Laws of Perceptual Grouping

Please don't misunderstand: the principles outlined by Gestalt psychologists are *not* hard-and-fast rules that exist without exception. Rather, they are merely *descriptions* (fairly good ones) of ways in which we usually tend to perceive the world around is. Whether they are indeed innate, as the Gestaltists believed, or are learned, as some newer evidence suggests, is still open to debate. In any case, these principles are readily visible in the natural world, and they do seem to "work." For two illustrations of this point, please examine Figure 3-23. Can you see the value to lobsters of blending into their environment, and to combat soldiers in wearing the kind of uniform shown here? A Gestalt psychologist might suggest that both types of camouflage work because they make it harder for an observer to perceive the wearers as *figures* against a back*ground*.

Constancies and Illusions: When Perception Succeeds —and Fails

Perception, we have repeatedly noted, is more than the sum of all the sensory input supplied by our eyes, ears, and other receptors. It is the *active* organization and interpretation of such input. It yields final products that depart from "raw," unprocessed sensations in important ways. Up to now, we have emphasized the potential benefits of such active interpretation. We now wish to make the following point: perception, like any other powerful process, can function as a two-edged sword. On the one hand, it can, and often does, help us adapt to a complex and ever-changing environment. On the other hand,

FIGURE 3-23. Many types of natural camouflage operate by making it harder to perceive an animal as a *figure* against the background of its natural habitat (left). The same principle is used in designing special uniforms for combat soldiers (right photo).

The Figure-Ground Relationship and Camouflage

though, it sometimes leads us into serious error in our efforts to understand the world around us. As examples of the actual benefits and potential costs of perception, we will now consider two important phenomena: **constancies** and **illusions.**

Perceptual Constancies: Stability in the Face of Change.   Try this simple demonstration. Hold your right hand in front of you at arm's length. Now, move it toward and away from your face several times. Does it seem to change in size? Probably not. Now, also hold your left hand in front of your face at a distance of about 20 cm (about 8 inches); again move your right hand in and out. Does it seem to change in size now? Again, probably it does not. You have just had some first-hand experience with **size constancy.** This refers to the fact that the perceived size of an object remains the same when the distance is varied, even though the size of the image it casts on the retina changes greatly. Under normal circumstances, such constancy is impressive. Indeed, it may even hold true when you look down from great distances, as from a plane. The trees, houses, cars and trucks you see cast tiny images on the retina. Yet you may perceive them as being of normal size. What accounts for this powerful tendency? Two explanations seem most useful.

First, this effect may rest on a principle known as **size-distance invariance.** This suggests that when you estimate the size of any object, you somehow take account of the size of the image it casts on your retina and the apparent distance of the object. From these data you almost instantly calculate the object's size. Only when the cues that normally reveal an object's distance are missing do we run into difficulties in estimating the object's size. (We will return to such cases below, in our discussion of illusions.)

Second, we make use of *relative size*. That is, we notice the size of an object compared to other objects whose size we know. This mechanism seems especially useful in estimating the size of unfamiliar things. For example, look at the two photos in Figure 3-24 on page 92. You'd probably be unable to estimate the size of the bamboo trees shown on the left. But from the picture on the right you can readily accomplish this task, since you know the usual size of human beings.

Size is not the only perceptual feature of the physical world that does not change directly, in a simple one-to-one relationship with the information transmitted by our sensory receptors. In addition, we experience *shape* and *brightness* constancy. **Shape constancy** refers to the fact that the shape of an object does not alter as the image it casts on the retina changes. For example, you perceive a pencil as having the same shape whether you look at it head-on (directly at the point or eraser) or from the side, despite the fact that the retinal images in the two instances are vastly different.

Brightness constancy involves the fact that we perceive the brightness of an object as constant even when viewed under different lighting conditions. Thus, a dark-green sweater looks dark indoors or outdoors in bright sunlight. Apparently, this is due to

FIGURE 3-24. Can you guess the height of the bamboo trees from the photo on the left? You probably cannot. When cues concerning *relative size* are added, however, as on the right-hand photo, you can easily perform this task.

the fact that we automatically compare objects with other, nearby objects; and a dark-green sweater reflects less light than many other objects, whether indoors or out.

Whatever their basis, perceptual constancies are highly useful. Without them, we would spend a great deal of time and effort calculating the size of objects and re-identifying them each time we view them from a different perspective. Thus, the gap between our sensations and our perceptions provided by the constancies is clearly beneficial.

Illusions: When Perception Fails.   Now we come to the other edge of the sword—cases in which perception provides false interpretations of sensory information. Such cases are known as **illusions,** a term used by psychologists to refer to perceptions that are incorrect. (By the way, don't confuse illusions with *mirages,* which occur when physical conditions distort a stimulus, so that we are led to perceive things that aren't really there. The water you can often see on the dry road ahead of you on a hot day is one example of a mirage.)

FIGURE 3-25. Three powerful visual illusions. In drawing A, known as the *Müller-Lyer illusion,* the bottom line looks longer than the top line. Actually, they are equal in length. In drawing B, the *Ponzo illusion,* the top horizontal line looks longer; again, both lines are equal. Finally, in drawing C, known as the *horizontal-vertical illusion,* the vertical line looks longer; check with a ruler to see that it's not!

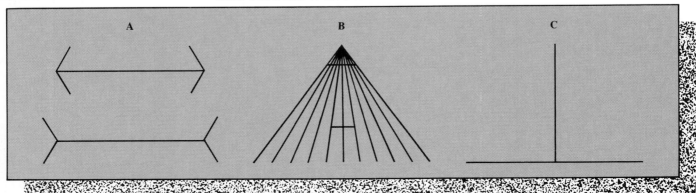

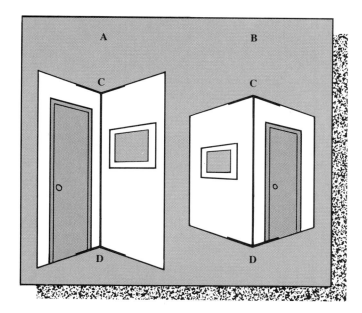

FIGURE 3-26. Our experience with corners, plus the size-distance invariance may account, in part, for the Müller-Lyer illusion. We know that line CD in drawing A is usually farther away than line CD in the configuration shown in drawing B. Since the size of the image cast on your retina by vertical line CD in both drawings is the same (the line is the same length in both), we perceive the vertical distance as greater in drawing A than in B.

Countless illusions exist, for there are many cases in which our efforts to impose order and meaning on sensory input lead us into error. However, most fall under two major headings: illusions of size and illusions of shape or area. Three well-known illusions of the first type are presented in Figure 3-25. As you can see, the effects are powerful. Moreover, they persist even if you *know* they are illusions. This raises an intriguing question: why do they occur? What causes our interpretation of such stimuli to be directly at odds with physical reality? One answer is provided by the *theory of misapplied constancy*. It suggests that when looking at illusions such as those in Figure 3-25, we interpret certain cues as suggesting that some parts are farther away than others. Our powerful tendency toward size constancy then comes into play, with the result that we perceptually distort the length of various lines. This interpretation is illustrated in Figure 3-26. As you can see, past experience suggests that the corner shown by lines arranged like those in drawing A is usually farther away than that drawn by lines like those in drawing B. Since the size of the retinal image cast by line CD in both drawings is identical, we interpret this vertical line as longer in A than in B. (For discussion of a second explanation for such illusions, based primarily on eye movements, please see ''The Cutting Edge'' section below.)

FOCUS ON RESEARCH: The Cutting Edge

Eye Movements and Illusions of Size

Earlier, we noted that our eyes are constantly in motion. Even when we attempt to hold them steady and stare at a specific point or object, the eyes make small movements around this target. And when we examine complex visual stimuli such as the drawings in Figures 3-25 and 3-26, they jump from point to point as we scan the entire item. Do such movements play a role in the occurrence of visual illusions? Research conducted by Coren (1986) suggests that they do.

Coren reasoned that our judgments concerning the length of lines may depend, in part, on the size of the *saccadic movements* our eyes make as we examine such stimuli. The bigger these jumps, the longer we perceive the lines as being. In order to test this prediction, Coren asked subjects to examine the simple patterns shown in Figure 3-27, and then to adjust two other dots so that they seemed as far apart as the dots shown in A and B. He reasoned that because subjects would try to see both the dot (the target) and the X (an extraneous stimulus) at once, their *fovea* (the region of greatest acuity) would

FIGURE 3-27. Because our eyes must make larger saccadic movements in examining drawing A than in examining drawing B, we tend to perceive the distance between the dots as greater in A than in B. In fact, this distance is the same in both cases. *(Based on materials developed by Coren, 1986.)*

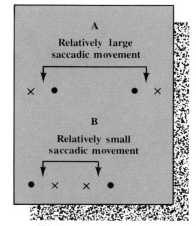

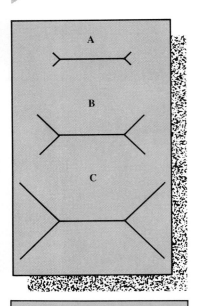

Eye Movements and the Size of the Müller-Lyer Illusion

fall between these two stimuli. Thus, the saccadic movements of their eyes would be larger when viewing A than B. This, in turn, would lead them to perceive the distance between the dots as greater in A than in B. Results supported this prediction. Although the distances are actually identical, subjects overestimated the distance between the dots in A and underestimated the distance in B.

In additional studies, Coren reasoned that if the distance between the target stimulus and the extraneous stimulus became too large, subjects would give up the strategy of trying to see both at once. Then the type of illusion shown in Figure 3-27 would decrease as the distance between these two stimuli continued to rise. As you can see from Figure 3-28, this prediction, too, was confirmed. When the wings on the standard Müller-Lyer illusion were increased in size, the illusion at first grew stronger. Beyond a specific point, though, it actually became *weaker*.

The findings uncovered by Coren suggest that eye movements do indeed play a role in certain illusions. Apparently, the more visual effort we expend in scanning a stimulus, the larger it appears to be. As in many other spheres of life, then, effort seems to color our judgment and perceptions.

FIGURE 3-28. The length of the horizontal line seems to increase from drawing A to drawing B, but then to decrease from B to C. Actually, all three lines are identical in length, only the "wings" are different. This shift in the magnitude of the illusion seems to reflect different patterns of eye movements we make when examining these stimuli. *(Based on materials used by Coren, 1986.)*

Some illusions of shape or area are shown in Figure 3-29. As you can readily see, these are also compelling. For example, try as you may, you probably can't see the letters in drawing C as vertical—but they are! Another common illusion of area you have probably noticed yourself is the *moon illusion*. This refers to the fact that the moon often appears larger when near the horizon than when directly overhead. Why is this the case? In part because when the moon is near the horizon, we can see that it is farther away than trees, houses, and other objects. When it is overhead, such cues are lacking. Thus, the moon appears larger when near the horizon because we can see that it is very far away. Once again, our tendency toward size constancy leads us astray. Other illusions of shape, such as the one shown in drawing B of Figure 3-29, may arise from the fact that when one point on the retina is stimulated, other nearby points are inhibited. This may cause us to perceive the line as bent.

Some Key Perceptual Processes: Pattern and Distance

Perception, it can be argued, is an eminently *practical* process: it provides living organisms with the information they need for survival in their normal habitat. Of course, the specific nature of such information varies greatly with different species. For example, frogs must be able to detect small moving objects because they feed on insects, while porpoises need sensory input that will enable them to navigate safely through turbulent and often murky ocean waters. However, it is probably safe to say that virtually all living creatures need information about the following issues: (1) what's out there? and (2) how far away is it? Human beings are no exception to this general rule, and we possess impressive perceptual skills in both areas.

Pattern Recognition: What's Out There?   As you read the words on this page, you are somehow recognizing small black marks as specific letters and collections of such marks as familiar words. How do you accomplish this task? One possibility, suggested by *prototype-matching theory*, goes something like this. As you read, you automatically compare each letter (and perhaps the words, as well) to abstract representations of these stimuli in your memory known as **prototypes.** For example, you have a prototype in memory for each letter of the alphabet, based on all examples of the letter you have previously encountered. If the stimulus you now see matches any of these proto-

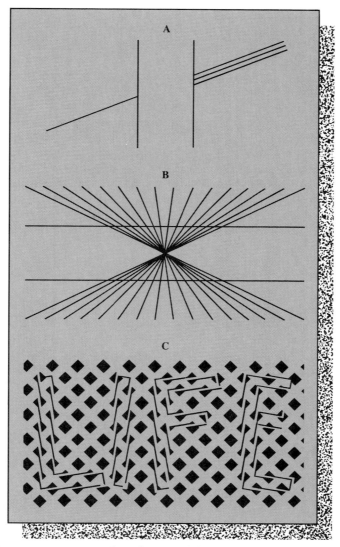

FIGURE 3-29. Illusions of shape or area, too, can be quite powerful. In drawing A, known as the *Poggendorf illusion,* which of the three lines on the right continues the line on the left? Check your answer with a ruler. In drawing B, are the horizontal lines straight or bent in the middle? Again, check for yourself. Finally, in the third, are the letters tilted or vertical? When you check, you'll see why sometimes you can't believe what you think you see!

types, you recognize it quickly. If it does not, you are puzzled and will not be sure what you have just seen.

While some evidence supports this view (e.g., Franks & Bransford, 1971), two other approaches are currently the subject of greater interest among psychologists. These are termed *bottom-up* and *top-down theories* of pattern recognition, and, as their names suggest, they adopt somewhat opposite perspectives on the basic question of how we recognize patterns of visual stimuli.

The *bottom-up* approach is based on an idea we considered in Chapter 2: *hierarchial organization* of the nervous system. It suggests that our ability to recognize specific patterns (e.g., letters of the alphabet) is built up from simpler capacities at lower levels of organization. For example, our ability to recognize a specific letter, such as *A*, and to distinguish it from other letters, such as *P* or *E*, rests on activation of specific groups of *feature detectors,* which, when stimulated, activate other neurons that may be described as *letter detectors*. (As you may recall, we considered feature detectors in the ''Focus'' insert on page 79.) In short, bottom-up theories suggest that pattern recognition is constructed from simpler perceptual abilities through a discrete series of steps (Marr, 1982).

In contrast, *top-down* theories take note of the fact that our perceptions are often shaped by our expectations. Our past experience tells us what to expect in certain situations, so we proceed in accordance with these; we don't bother to analyze every feature of most stimuli we encounter. This can save lots of time and accounts for the speed with which pattern recognition often occurs (e.g., the speed with which you can read the words on this page). However, top-down processing can lead us astray. Nearly everyone has had the experience of rushing over to another person who appears to be an old friend, only to realize he or she is actually a stranger. In such cases, our tendency to process information quickly from the "top down" can indeed result in errors.

Which of these approaches is correct? Current evidence indicates that both play a role in pattern recognition. When we have strong expectations or we are in a familiar context, we often opt for speed and adopt a top-down approach. However, when dealing with unfamiliar situations or stimuli, bottom-up processing often dominates. And in many situations both may occur at once. In sum, as we have stated before, our efforts to make sense out of the world around us tend to take whatever form is most efficient or cost-effective in a given context.

Distance Perception: How Far Away Is It?   "Reach out and touch someone," says a commercial most of us have heard hundreds of times. While we may not all be excellent at communication (the process to which this ad refers), we *can* indeed accomplish this task from a purely physical point of view—we are excellent at judging depth and distance. One reason for our success in this respect lies in the fact that we make use of many different cues in forming such judgments. These can be divided into two major categories, *monocular* and *binocular*, depending on whether they can be seen with only one eye or require the use of both eyes.

Under the first category (**monocular cues** to depth or distance), are the following:

1. *Size cues:* the larger the image of an object on the retina, the larger it is judged to be; in addition, if an object is larger than other objects, it is often perceived as closer.
2. *Linear perspective:* parallel lines appear to converge in the distance; the greater this effect, the farther away an object appears to be.
3. *Texture gradient:* the texture of a surface appears to become smoother as distance increases.
4. *Atmospheric perspective:* the farther away objects are, the less distinctly they are seen—smog, dust, haze get in the way.
5. *Overlap* (or *interposition*): if one object overlaps another, it is seen as being closer than the one it covers.
6. *Height cues (aerial perspective): below* the horizon, objects lower down in our field of vision are perceived as closer; *above* the horizon, objects higher up are seen as closer.
7. *Shading:* patterns of light and shadow often provide important cues to depth; for example, if part of an object sticks out, it will cast a shadow on adjacent areas.

In understanding monocular cues to distance, a picture does indeed seem to be worth a thousand words. So please examine Figure 3-30 and see how many monocular cues you can spot.

Turning to **binocular cues,** two seem most important:

1. *Convergence:* in order to look at close objects, your eyes turn inward, toward one another; the greater this movement, the closer such objects appear to be.
2. *Retinal disparity (binocular parallax):* your two eyes observe objects from slightly different positions in space; the difference between these two images is interpreted by your brains to provide another cue to depth.

By using the wealth of information provided by both monocular and binocular cues, we can usually perceive depth and distance in a highly accurate manner (Gibson, 1979).

FIGURE 3-30. How many monocular cues to depth or distance can you find in this famous painting by Pieter Brueghel, ''The Return of the Hunters''?

Monocular Cues to Depth in a Masterpiece

The Plasticity of Perception: To What Extent Is It Innate or Learned?

Imagine that you have been blind from birth. Now, through a miraculous operation, your sight is suddenly restored. What will you see? An orderly world filled with the things you have previously imagined? Or a chaotic swirl of colors, brightnesses, and meaningless shapes? We're sure you'll agree this is an intriguing question. In fact, it is one variation on an issue we considered in Chapter 2 and will meet again and again in this book: to what extent are various aspects of human behavior learned, and to what extent are they innate? Several kinds of evidence are relevant to this **nature-nurture controversy** as it pertains to perception.

Perception: Evidence That It's Innate

Let's begin with evidence suggesting that at least some aspects of perception are innate. Two lines of research are informative here. One of these involves people born blind (or blinded soon after birth) whose sight is later restored by medical procedures. If the ability to interpret sensory information is innate, then such persons should be able to see clearly immediately after recovery from the operation. Only a small number of such cases have been studied, and results vary greatly from one person to another. Still, there is some indication that many of these individuals can make at least partial sense out of the visual world soon after their sight is restored. For example, they can detect objects, fixate on them, and follow them with their gaze as they move (Von Senden, 1960). This suggests that some aspects of visual perception may indeed be innate. One final word of caution: complications exist even with respect to this limited interpretation. To mention one, it is difficult to know just when recovery from the medical procedure is sufficient to allow normal vision. This leaves open the question of when the patient should be tested for perceptual abilities.

A second form of evidence suggesting that certain aspects of perception may be innate is provided by research with very young organisms, those just a few hours or days old. Such studies indicate that some perceptual abilities are present at birth, or shortly afterward. For example, in one recent investigation (Adams, 1987) infants slightly more than three days old were exposed to squares of colored light (blue, green, yellow, red) and to gray light of equal brightness. Results indicated that the infants spent more time looking at all of the colored stimuli than at the colorless gray.

In perhaps an even more surprising study Balogh and Porter (1986) exposed newborns just a few hours old to one of two aromas (ginger or cherry) for about twenty-four hours. (One odor was present on a gauze pad in each infant's bassinet.) After the initial exposure, two pads, each containing a different smell, were placed in the bassinet, and the amount of time the infant spent orienting toward each one during brief test periods was observed. As you can see from Figure 3-31 on page 98, female infants showed a marked

Odor Recognition in Human Infants

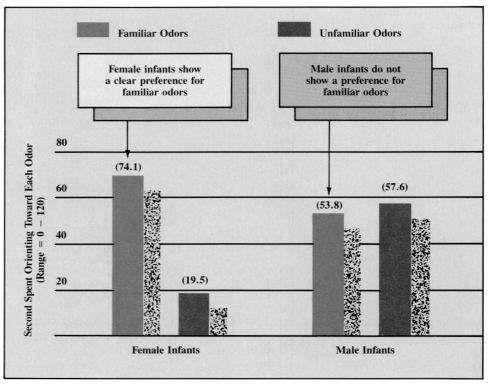

FIGURE 3-31. Female infants only a little more than a day old spent more time orienting toward a familiar odor than toward an unfamiliar one. Male infants of the same age did not demonstrate such a preference. The findings for females suggest that they are capable of differentiating between odors at birth or very shortly thereafter. *(Source: Based on data from Balogh & Porter, 1986.)*

preference for the familiar odor—the one to which they had previously been exposed. Male infants showed no preference. While it is not certain why this sex difference occurred, other research suggests that females are superior to males in identifying specific odors at all ages, from early childhood to old age (Doty et al., 1984). Thus, it appears that this difference may be present at or soon after birth. In any case, studies such as this one suggest that some aspects of perception are innate or, at least, appear very early in life.

Perception: Evidence That It's Learned

On the other hand, there is considerable evidence for the view that key aspects of perception are learned. In a famous series of studies Blakemore and Cooper (1970) raised kittens in darkness except for brief periods during which they were exposed to either horizontal or vertical stripes. When the kittens were later released from their restricted environment, they showed what seemed to be permanent effects of their earlier experience. Those who had been exposed only to vertical lines would respond to a long black rod when it was held in an upright position; when it was held horizontally, however, they ignored it. In contrast, kittens exposed only to horizontal lines would only respond to a rod when it was held in a horizontal position, and ignored it when presented vertically. Additional evidence indicated that there was no damage to the kittens' visual systems—these were intact, at least at lower levels of organization. However, their restricted visual experience seemed to result in permanent deficits in their perceptions.

Additional evidence for the role of learning in perception is provided by studies in which volunteers have worn special goggles that invert their view of the world and reverse right and left. At first, such persons are confused, and experience great difficulty carrying out normal activities. After a few days or weeks, however, they adapt and can do everything from reading a book to flying a plane (e.g., Kohler, 1962). Such findings suggest that we do indeed learn to interpret the information supplied by our sensory receptors, and we are quite flexible in this regard.

A Resolution and Some Final Words

Where does all this leave us? The findings we've reviewed so far offer no simple resolution. Moreover, additional evidence, provided by studies in which animals' early sensory experience has been restricted, fails to clarify matters greatly. For example, in one ingenious project, Wiesel (1982) placed goggles that admitted only diffuse light over the eyes of very young kittens. When the goggles were later removed, the kittens could distinguish colors and brightness, but not shapes (e.g., distinguish a circle from a square). These results are strikingly similar to those obtained in studies of people who have suddenly acquired sight through medical procedures. Some aspects of visual experience seem to be present without previous sensory experience, while others develop only through experience with the external world.

Confronted with this mixed evidence, most psychologists accept the following conclusion: perception is influenced both by innate factors *and* by experience. It *is* plastic in the sense that it can be, and often is, modified by our encounters with physical reality. Moreover, such plasticity becomes increasingly evident as we move from simpler to more and more complex perceptual tasks (e.g., from recognizing colors to identifying the traits and motives of other persons; see Chapter 15). However, perception also seems to rest, quite firmly, on certain aspects of our biological nature, and it may be strongly affected by innate tendencies and principles. We realize that this is not the most satisfying kind of answer; most persons prefer definite replies to hedged ones. As far as we can tell, though, conclusions along these lines are the most accurate. And in the ''essential science,'' after all, it is truth—not simplicity—that is the ultimate goal.

Extrasensory Perception: Perception Without Sensation?

MAN CHANGES PLANS, ESCAPES DEATH.   Charles Thompson had a narrow brush with death yesterday. He was a scheduled passenger on Transcontinental Flight 361 to Denver, but within minutes of departure he canceled his plans. ''I woke up with a bad feeling about this trip this morning,'' Thompson noted. ''It felt like something was trying to tell me not to travel. The feeling got stronger all day, so finally I just decided to stay home.'' It's fortunate for Thompson that he did, for Flight 361 crashed shortly after take-off, killing all 186 people on board. ''I never believed in telling the future or stuff like that before,'' Thompson added, ''but after this, I guess I'll pay attention to all my hunches.'' . . .

Have you ever seen a story like this one in the newspaper? If so, you've probably wondered about the following question: Do we really possess a ''sixth sense''? In other words, can we sometimes gain information about the external world without use of our five basic senses? As you probably know, many persons believe we can. They accept the existence of **extrasensory perception** (or *ESP*)—literally, perception without a basis in sensation (Frazier, 1984–85). What, precisely, is ESP? Does it really exist? These are the questions on which we'll now focus.

ESP: The Claims

Parapsychologists—individuals who study ESP and other *paranormal events* (events outside our normal experience or knowledge), suggest that ESP actually takes several distinct forms. First, there is *precognition,* the ability to foretell future events. This is the kind of ESP illustrated in the fictional newspaper account above. Somehow Mr. Thompson ''knew'' his flight would be disastrous, and he avoided tragedy by staying home. Fortune-tellers and even stock market analysts often earn handsome livings from the supposed ability to make such predictions. A second form of ESP is *clairvoyance,* the ability to perceive objects or events that do not directly stimulate your sensory organs. While playing cards, if you somehow know which one will be dealt next, you are experiencing clairvoyance. A third type of ESP is known as *telepathy,* the direct transmission of

Telepathy: Entertaining, But Unproven

FIGURE 3-32. Can one individual read another's thoughts? Many people believe *telepathy* is possible.

thoughts from one person to another. This is the skill supposedly possessed by ''mind-readers'' such as the one shown in Figure 3-32. While playing cards, if you can tell which ones the other players have picked up, you are experiencing telepathy. Finally, there is *psychokinesis,* the ability to affect the physical world purely by thought. This is not actually a form of ESP, but it is often linked with it, so it should be mentioned here.

ESP: Does It Really Exist?

The idea of a mysterious ''sixth sense'' is intriguing; indeed, it has been used to amuse, entertain, and astound people for thousands of years. But does it really exist? Many persons are passionately convinced it does (Bowles & Hynds, 1978). They point to hundreds of studies, conducted mainly by parapsychologists, which seem to indicate that some people *can* demonstrate such abilities as clairvoyance and telepathy. For example, it has been reported in such studies that if a special deck of cards containing various symbols is carefully shuffled, subjects can predict the order of the symbols' occurrence at better than chance levels. Moreover, they can do this whether the experimenter knows which card will be presented next or not—in short, they can demonstrate both clairvoyance and telepathy (Rhine & Pratt, 1962).

Despite such reports, psychologists remain skeptical about the existence of ESP. Several factors contribute to such doubts. First, after decades of research and hundreds of investigations, ESP remains elusive. It cannot be reliably reproduced (replicated) across various studies; certain procedures may yield evidence for ESP at one time but not at others. Since the ability to replicate results is an important requirement of science, this pattern casts serious doubt on the existence of ESP.

Second, it is not clear what physical mechanism could account for ESP. As we noted in Chapter 2, ultimately all aspects of our behavior stem from biological processes, and these, in turn, must have a basis in chemical or physical events. How does ESP fit into this picture? The answer is simple: it doesn't. At the present time, we know of no physical process that could generate precognition, clairvoyance, telepathy, or psychokinesis. In fact, such phenomena, if they exist, would require a major restructuring of our view of the physical world. This is not to imply, of course, that our conception of physical reality is perfect or complete—far from it. Major changes in our knowledge are still occurring, and there is no basis for ruling out the possibility that, someday, a mechanism that accounts for ESP could be discovered. Still, the absence of such a process at present weighs heavily against any current acceptance of ESP as a proven fact.

Third, much of the support for ESP has been obtained by persons already deeply convinced of its existence. As we noted in Chapter 1, scientists are far from immune to being influenced, in their observations, by their own views or beliefs. And such effects don't imply fraud or overt ''faking'' of data; on the contrary, they can be quite subtle. For example, consider a researcher who conducts several careful studies of telepathy. The first six experiments fail, while the last one yields positive results. What does he or she conclude? If he or she already accepts the existence of ESP, the researcher may reason as follows: ''My first six studies were poorly conducted, so telepathy could not appear. The seventh corrected these problems, so its results are the important ones.'' In contrast, a researcher who does not believe in ESP might stop after the first three or four failures and conclude that telepathy does not exist. Because of such factors, studies suggesting that ESP exists may represent a small sample of all research conducted on this topic: only those few experiments that yield positive results find their way into print. Many ''failures'' are simply not reported.

In view of these and other considerations, most psychologists remain quite skeptical about the existence of ESP. They don't deny the possibility that someday, convincing evidence for such effects may be obtained; rather, they simply note that currently, it is not available. Unless and until it is, our view remains, ''Interesting, very interesting—but not yet conclusive.''

Summary and Review

Sensation: Detecting the External World

Information about the external world is supplied by our *sensory receptors,* which transform physical energy (e.g., light, sound) into neural impulses our brains can interpret. Our ability to detect the presence of various stimuli is determined both by the physical energy the stimulus contains and several other factors (e.g., the relative costs and benefits associated with detecting or failing to detect the stimulus). All these factors are taken into account in *signal detection theory.*

Sensory receptors for vision are rods and cones, found in the *retina,* located at the back of each eye. Two different mechanisms appear to play a role in color vision. One operates at the level of the retina, while the other operates at higher levels of organization in the visual system.

Sound waves are transformed into neural impulses in the ear by tiny *hair cells* located in the *cochlea.* Our ability to discriminate sounds of different pitch (i.e., sound frequency) stems from two facts: (1) sounds of different frequencies stimulate different parts of the *basilar membrane,* and (2) the rate of neural impulses transmitted by sensory receptors for sound rises with increasing frequency.

The skin is the largest single sensory organ in the body. Through it we can detect touch, pressure, pain, warmth, and cold. The *gate-control theory* of pain suggests that a neural mechanism in the spinal cord can block transmission of some pain signals to the brain. The *chemical senses,* smell and taste, interact closely in our daily life. We can recognize a large number of different odors, but there appear to be only four distinct sensations of taste: sweet, salt, sour, bitter.

Perception: Interpreting the External World

Perception is the process through which we actively organize and interpret information supplied by our sensory receptors. *Gestalt psychologists* established that we divide the world into figure and ground, and that we tend to group objects together according to simple principles (e.g., similarity, closure). Because perception is an active process, there is often a gap between sensory experience and resulting perception. In the case of the *constancies* this difference is useful, and it helps us perceive stability in the face of changing sensory input. However, in the case of *illusions* it can lead us to false conclusions about the external world. Our impressive ability to make accurate judgments of depth or distance stems from our use of many different cues. Our ability to recognize various patterns may involve comparing current sensations with existing *prototypes.* It may also involve *bottom-up processing,* in which higher and higher levels of organization within the nervous system come into play in recognition, or *top-down processing,* in which our expectations play a greater role in shaping perception. A number of cues play a role in our ability to judge distance. These include both *monocular cues* (involving only one eye) or *binocular cues* (involving both eyes).

Perception: Innate or Learned?

Some evidence suggests that certain aspects of perception are innate or present shortly after birth. These include the perception of color and the ability to distinguish between different aromas. Other evidence (e.g., the effects of early sensory restriction) indicates that perception is learned. At present, most psychologists assume this process is influenced by both types of factors.

ESP: Myth or Reality?

Belief in the existence of *extrasensory perception*—abilities to foretell future events, read others' minds (*telepathy*), or perceive objects that do not stimulate our senses (*clairvoyance*)—is common among the general public. However, most psychologists remain skeptical about ESP. Such effects cannot be reliably reproduced in careful research, and there is no known physical mechanism which could account for ESP. For these and other reasons, psychologists view ESP as an interesting but unproven phenomenon.

 # Key Terms

Absolute Threshold The smallest amount of a stimulus that we can detect 50% of the time.

Active Touch Our ability to detect and recognize objects we touch with our hands or other body parts.

Acuity The visual ability to see fine details.

Anosmia A condition in which some portion of the sense of smell is lost.

Binocular Cues Cues to depth or distance resulting from the fact that we have two eyes.

Brightness Constancy The tendency to perceive objects as having a constant brightness when they are viewed under different conditions of illumination.

Cochlea A portion of the inner ear containing the sensory receptors for sound.

Complex Cells Neurons in the visual cortex that respond to stimuli which move in a particular direction and which have a particular orientation in space.

Cones Sensory receptors in the eye that play a crucial role in sensations of color.

Constancies Our tendency to perceive physical objects as unchanging despite shifts in the pattern of sensations these objects induce.

Dark Adaptation The process through which our visual system increases its sensitivity to light under low levels of illumination.

Difference Threshold The amount by which two stimuli must differ in order to be just noticeably different.

Extrasensory Perception Perceptions that are not based on input from our sensory receptors. Included under the heading of ESP are such supposed abilities as *telepathy* (reading others' minds) and *clairvoyance* (perceiving distant objects).

Figure-Ground Relationship Our tendency to divide the perceptual world into two distinct parts—discrete figures and the background against which they stand out.

Frequency Theory A theory of pitch perception suggesting that sounds of different frequencies (heard as differences in pitch) induce different rates of neural activity in the hair cells of the inner ear.

Gate-Control Theory A theory of pain suggesting that the spinal cord contains a mechanism that can block transmission of pain to the brain.

Illusions Instances in which perception yields false interpretations of physical reality.

Hypercomplex Cells Neurons in the visual cortex that respond to complex aspects of visual stimuli, such as width, length, and shape.

Laws of Grouping Simple principles describing how we tend to group discrete stimuli together in the perceptual world.

Monocular Cues Cues to depth or distance provided by one eye.

Nature-Nurture Controversy An ongoing debate concerning the extent to which various aspects of behavior are determined by genetic factors or experience.

Negative Afterimage A sensation of complementary color that occurs after staring at a stimulus of a given hue.

Opponent Process Theory A theory that describes the processing of sensory information related to color at levels above the retina. The theory suggests that we possess six different types of neurons, each of which is either stimulated or inhibited by red, green, blue, yellow, black, and white.

Passive Touch Our sensitivity to being touched at various points on the body.

Perception The process through which we

organize and interpret input from our sensory receptors.

Place Theory A theory suggesting that sounds of different frequency stimulate different areas of the basilar membrane, the portion of the cochlea containing sensory receptors for sound.

Prototypes Representations in memory of various objects or stimuli in the physical world.

Rods One of the two types of sensory receptors for vision found in the eye.

Saccadic Movement Movement of the eyes from one point of fixation to another.

Sensation Input about the physical world provided by our sensory receptors.

Sensory Adaptation Reduced sensitivity to unchanging stimuli over time.

Sensory Receptors Cells of the body specialized for the task of transduction—converting physical energy (light, sound) into neural impulses.

Shape Constancy The tendency to perceive a physical object as having a constant shape even when the image it casts on the retina changes.

Signal Detection Theory A theory suggesting that there are no absolute thresholds for sensations. Rather, detection of stimuli depends on their physical energy and on internal factors such as the relative costs and benefits associated with detecting their presence.

Simple Cells Cells within the visual system that respond to specific shapes presented in certain orientations (e.g., horizontal, vertical, etc.).

Size Constancy The tendency to perceive a physical object as having a constant size even when the image it casts on the retina changes.

Size-Distance Invariance Refers to the fact that when we estimate the size of any object, we take simultaneous account of the size of its image on the retina and its apparent distance from us.

Taste Buds Structures containing sensory receptors for taste.

Trichromatic Theory A theory of color perception suggesting that we have three types of cones, each primarily receptive to different wavelengths of light.

For More Information

Coren, S., & Girgus, J.S. (1978). *Seeing is deceiving: The psychology of visual illusions*. Hillsdale, NJ: Erlbaum.
> A fascinating discussion of visual illusions and why they occur. If you'd like to know more about this intriguing topic, this is a good place to start.

Matlin, M.E. (1988). *Sensation and Perception*. Boston: Allyn and Bacon, 1988.
> A clear and well-written summary of current knowledge about sensation and perception. The chapters on the development of perception and the impact of learning and motivation on perception are especially interesting.

C H A P T E R

Consciousness: Awareness of Ourselves and the World Around Us

"Hey Mark—what are you doing?" Joe Stamm shouts suddenly to his friend. "You're on the road to the bridge!"

"Oh no!" Mark exclaims, a glazed look in his eyes. "How did I do *that*?"

"I don't know," Joe groans, "but we're in for it now. There's no turning back until we get across. There goes half an hour, at least. And we'll have to pay the toll both ways. No chance of being on time for that meeting, either. What a drag!"

"I just wasn't paying attention," Mark comments, shaking his head. "I guess I'm so used to making that turn on the way home every night that I didn't think about what I was doing."

"No kidding! Daydreaming about Sally again, I suppose," Joe answers scathingly.

"No, really, I wasn't!" Mark answers quickly. But slightly embarrassed, he continues. "I wasn't thinking about Sally, but I *was* imagining Steve's reaction when he finds out I closed the Patterson deal. I could just see his face, burning with envy. Hey, it was great!"

"I'm sure it was," Joe replies, "but he'll get a big laugh when we show up half an hour late. You *know* how Bill Dickinson hates to be kept waiting."

"Don't rub it in. I feel bad enough already. I've got to stop daydreaming so much—it's been getting me into too much trouble lately. But," Mark says, glancing at his friend, "it sure is fun!"

Have you ever had an experience like this? Probably you have. Most of us tend to perform many different activities on what seems to be "automatic pilot." We can drive for miles while our thoughts are focused on distant times and places. We can shower, dress, and even eat an entire meal without paying much attention to what we are doing. Indeed, many actions we perform are so automatic and removed from consciousness that we are only dimly aware we performed them (refer to Figure 4-1). In short, we spend much of our time being less aware of the external world and our own behavior than we could be.

This shift between being "on automatic" and being more fully conscious of both internal and external stimuli is not the only indication that **consciousness**—your current awareness of yourself, your behavior, and the world around you—can, and often does, change sharply over the course of a single day. Consider what happens when you fall asleep, when you dream, or when you are affected by a drug (e.g., alcohol, tranquilizers). In these cases, too, your consciousness is different than under normal, awake conditions (Wallace & Fisher, 1987).

Since such shifts in *states of consciousness* have profound effects upon behavior, feelings, and thoughts, they are clearly important to psychology's major goal: understanding all aspects of human behavior. You may be surprised to learn, therefore, that from about the 1920s until as late as the 1960s, consciousness was largely ignored by our field. It was even viewed by many psychologists as a slightly "shady" topic—one to be avoided by serious scientists. Many factors contributed to this state of affairs, including the lack of scientific methods for studying consciousness phenomena, but perhaps most important was the dominance of *behaviorism*. As you may recall from Chapter 1, Watson and other behaviorists held that psychology should focus firmly on overt, observable actions. Since consciousness cannot be directly observed, they literally read this topic out of the field.

Needless to say, this is no longer the case. Most psychologists now define their field as being intimately concerned with cognitive processes as well as overt behavior, so consciousness has re-emerged as an important topic of study. (We say "re-emerged" because early in its history, before the arrival of behaviorism, psychology *did* attempt to study consciousness; indeed, many early psychologists identified this as the major task of

FIGURE 4-1. As shown here, we perform many actions without directing full conscious attention to them. *(Source: Universal Press Syndicate, 1984.)*

Automatic Processing Strikes Again!

their new field. It's hard to imagine a more dramatic illustration of the fact that even in science, the pendulum of opinion swings widely over time.)

Given that psychologists have only studied states of consciousness in a systematic manner for about two decades, we don't yet have a complete picture of this complex and fascinating subject. However, knowledge has accumulated rapidly, so we *do* know quite a bit about several of its major aspects. In the remainder of this chapter we'll summarize psychology's current knowledge about the following topics: controlled and automatic processing (the distinction between operating ''on automatic'' and operating in a more conscious manner), daydreams and fantasies, sleep and dreams, hypnosis, and the impact of various drugs upon consciousness.

Controlled and Automatic Processing: The Limits of Attention

Have you ever tried to carry on separate conversations with two different persons at once? If so, you already know a basic fact about human consciousness: our attentional capacities are limited. We simply don't have the ability to focus on several different stimuli or events at once. Rather, we find it necessary to shift back and forth between events which we wish to make the center of our current perceptions. If this is the case, how do we manage to perform two or more activities at once—for example, driving while daydreaming or drying dishes while planning the next day's activities (see Figure 4-2)? The answer seems to lie in the fact that there are two contrasting ways of controlling ongoing activities—two levels of attention to, or conscious control over, our own behavior (Logan, 1980, 1985).

The first of these is the kind of ''auto pilot'' described in the opening story. In such **automatic processing** you initiate an activity, then perform it with relatively little conscious awareness. Processing of this type seems to make little demand upon your attentional capacity. Thus, several activities, each under automatic control, can occur at the same time (Shiffrin & Schneider, 1977; Shiffrin & Dumais, 1981). In contrast, **controlled processing** involves more effortful and conscious control of behavior. In this case you direct your full attention to the task at hand and concentrate on it. Obviously, processing of this type *does* consume attentional capacity; as a result, only one such task can usually be performed at a time.

Research on the nature of these two mechanisms suggests some interesting differences between them. First, it appears that within limits, neither the accuracy nor the speed of automatic processing is strongly affected by *attentional load*—the number of different objects or items with which we must deal. This fact was first demonstrated by Schneider and Shiffrin (1977) in a series of well-known experiments. For example, in one of these studies subjects were asked to search for numbers contained in a list of letters. On some

FIGURE 4-2. How can we perform two different activities at once? The answer seems to involve the fact that we can operate at two different levels of attention to our own behavior: *automatic processing* and *controlled processing*.

Doing Two Things at Once: Automatic versus Controlled Processing trials they searched for a single target (e.g., the number *7*). On others, they searched for as many as four different targets simultaneously (e.g., the numbers *1, 4, 7, 8*). After many practice trials, participants were able to search for the four targets almost as quickly as they could search for one. They had shifted to *automatic processing* in performing this task.

In other sessions, however, the same subjects were asked to perform a slightly different task. This time they searched for letters located within a list of other letters. In addition—and this was the crucial change—the targets of their search did *not* remain constant: a letter that was a target on some trials could be a nontarget (a distractor) on others. As before, subjects sometimes searched for a single letter (target), and sometimes for several letters. Results were quite different than in the earlier case: even after more than two thousand practice trials, subjects still needed more time to search for four targets than for one. One interpretation of these findings is as follows: when the targets of

Conditions under which Automatic Processing Can or Cannot Develop

FIGURE 4-3. When the targets for which they searched remained constant, automatic processing developed, and after practice subjects could search for multiple targets as quickly as for a single target. When the targets varied, however, automatic processing did not develop. Even after practice, subjects searched for multiple targets more slowly than for single targets. *(Source: Based on data from Schneider & Shiffrin, 1977.)*

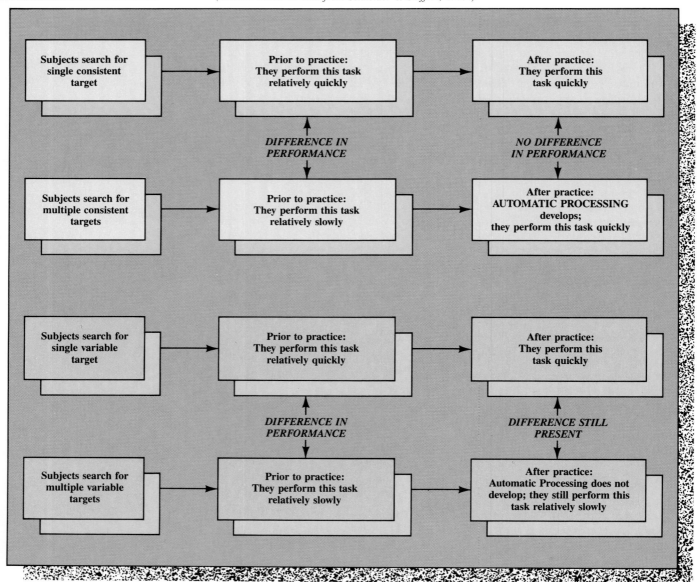

subjects' search varied, they could not shift to automatic processing. Therefore, looking for several targets required more time than looking for one. (Please refer to Figure 4-3 for a summary of Schneider and Shiffrin's procedures and results.)

A second difference between controlled and automatic processing involves the extent to which each can be modified or controlled. In general, it appears that automatic processing is much more difficult to modify than controlled processing. For example, in another study Shiffrin and Schneider (1977) told subjects to ignore targets appearing in certain locations in the stimulus arrays they examined. Subjects using controlled processing in their search activities (those for whom the targets varied from trial to trial) were able to do this quite easily, and their performance did not decrease. Those using automatic processing (subjects for whom the targets remained consistent) experienced greater difficulty; it was as if they could not turn off their "automatic pilots" and continued to respond to these stimuli even though they were told to ignore them. Additional findings (e.g., Logan, 1980, 1985) indicate that automatic processing is not totally outside voluntary control. For example, skilled typists can stop their typing, which is largely automatic, in response to a signal to do so or an error. In general, though, automatic processing is less easily modified than conscious, controlled processing. So, in sum, both types offer advantages and involve disadvantages. Automatic processing is rapid and efficient but relatively inflexible. Controlled processing is slower but is more flexible and open to change. Clearly, both have their place in our efforts to deal with information from the external world.

Two final points need to be made. First, automatic and controlled processing are *not* hard-and-fast categories. Rather, they represent ends of a continuum; on any given task, individuals may be operating in a *relatively* controlled or a *relatively* automatic manner. Second, recent findings indicate that the occurrence of automatic processing is not restricted to simple search tasks involving visual stimuli. On the contrary, it appears that this mechanism can develop even with respect to complex social judgments about other persons (Bargh, 1984). For example, Smith and Lerner (1986) found that automatic processing can develop, and develop quickly, when individuals are asked to indicate whether persons having certain traits are suited to particular occupations, whether specific persons are likable or not likable, and whether political statements are pro- or anti-liberal in nature. With respect to occupational judgments, subjects responded more quickly and showed other signs of automatic processing when the target occupation remained constant throughout the session than when several target occupations were employed. These findings suggest that we may shift to automatic processing even in situations where such a strategy seems inappropriate. After all, in making important judgments about others, conscious, controlled processing would seem preferable.

In sum, there seems little doubt that we have a strong tendency to adopt automatic processing whenever feasible. Given our limited capacities for attending to various stimuli and processing information about them, this offers major benefits. At the same time, though, our tendency to turn our "automatic pilot" on can exact important costs. Whatever the balance between these pluses and minuses, the important point to remember is this: even during waking activities, when most of us contend that we are in a "normal" state of consciousness, we can and often do shift back and forth between contrasting levels of awareness.

Daydreams and Fantasies: Self-Induced Shifts in Consciousness

Freud once stated: "A happy person never fantasies, only an unsatisfied one" (1908, p. 146). If that statement is true, most of us must be unhappy indeed, for a great majority of seemingly normal, well adjusted persons regularly engage in **daydreams** and **fantasies** (Singer, 1975). Further, it is clear that for many persons (like Mark in our opening story) such experiences can be quite intense, blotting out external stimuli and reality, at least temporarily. What do people daydream or fantasize about? And do these internally generated shifts in consciousness have any function? It is on these and related questions that we now focus.

FIGURE 4-4. Many daydreams are concerned with such basic themes as success, anger, guilt, or sex. However, as shown here, the specific content of these altered states of consciousness is unique for each individual. *(Source:* The New Yorker, *1986.)*

The Content of Daydreams and Fantasies: Some Major Themes

Think back for a moment: what was the content of your last daydream? If you are like most people, it can probably be placed under one of these headings: failure or success (e.g., you imagined receiving straight As, or you landed a desirable job), aggression or hostility (e.g., you fantasized about ''evening the score'' with someone you dislike), sexual or romantic fantasies, guilt (e.g., you tortured yourself once again over something you should or shouldn't have done), or problem-solving (e.g., you fantasized about working on some task; Singer, 1975). Of course, many other themes exist; these are simply the most common ones reported (please refer to Figure 4-4).

While most people report daydreams, and many of them have the type of content just mentioned, large individual differences exist with respect to such activities. First, people differ greatly in the frequency with which they daydream or fantasize (Lynn & Rhue, 1986). While some report spending up to half their free time in such activities, others indicate that they rarely have fantasies or daydreams. Similarly, the intensity of such experiences also varies greatly. Some individuals report that their fantasies and daydreams are so vivid and lifelike that they are almost hallucinations; for others, these experiences are pale and less involving. Interestingly, among persons who report a high frequency of daydreaming, three distinct patterns or styles seem to exist. For one group, daydreams focus on achievement and accomplishment; these individuals report fantasies centering around self-examination or self-evaluation. A second group has daydreams that focus primarily on failure and self-doubts. Finally, a third group reports elaborate daydreams which vary greatly in content but are mainly positive (e.g., fantasies about enjoyable experiences or pleasant interactions with other persons).

Daydreams and fantasies begin in early childhood—children, of course, have an extremely rich fantasy life—and they persist throughout life. However, some shift in their content seems to occur. Daydreams with negative content (e.g., ones focused on anxiety) and ones focused on future events decrease with age. In contrast, daydreams with mainly positive content, especially ones involving the successful solution of problems, increase. Finally, confirming what you always suspected about middle-age, daydreams with sexual content also decline somewhat with age (Giambra, 1974). For more information on the actual content of daydreams or fantasies, please see ''The Cutting Edge'' section.

FOCUS ON RESEARCH: The Cutting Edge

The Sexual Fantasies of Women and Men

At some time or other, nearly everyone has sexual fantasies. But what, precisely, are these? What do people think about when they have erotic daydreams? Until recently, little evidence was available on this issue (e.g., Griffitt & Hatfield, 1985). Now, however, detailed information on this intriguing topic has begun to accumulate. Especially revealing findings in this respect have recently been reported by Arndt, Foehl, and Good (1985).

These researchers asked several hundred undergraduates to indicate the frequency with which they had had each of a large number of different sexual fantasies during the past year. In addition, subjects completed questionnaires designed to assess various aspects of personality, and they reported on their sexual behavior during the past year. Results indicated

that while both males and females reported a high frequency of sexual fantasies, the two sexes differed in terms of the specific content of these fantasies. Among females, fantasies with a romantic theme or ones emphasizing either watching or being watched during sexual activities were most common. In contrast, among males fantasies involving being excited by a woman's legs or breasts and being sexually stimulating to females were the most frequent (refer to Table 4-1).

In addition, males and females differed in terms of the relationship of their sexual fantasies to various aspects of their personality. Among women, specific fantasy themes were correlated with certain personality traits. For example, women who reported a high frequency of romantic fantasies (e.g., "I'm a very glamorous woman and an extremely handsome man is having sex with me") were found to be impulsive. Similarly, women who re-

TABLE 4-1

As shown here, sexual fantasies are common among both sexes, but their specific content differs for women and men.

Fantasy of Female Students	Percent of Respondents	Fantasy of Male Students	Percent of Respondents
A man is kissing my breasts	92	I'm excited by a woman's shapely legs	96
I'm in a secluded place. A man gently removes my clothes and has sex with me	90	I'm kissing a woman's large breasts	91
I'm a very glamorous woman, and an extremely handsome man is having sex with me	71	I get a woman so excited that she screams with pleasure	87
A man and I are having sex in a place where there is danger of being caught	65	A woman tells me that she wants my body	86
I'm at a party where famous men admire my charms	65	Two women are exciting me sexually	84
I'm wearing skin-tight clothes. Men are staring at me	51	Several women are admiring my nude body	65
An older man is seducing me	46	I'm at a party where everyone is having sex with everyone else	62

Some Common Sexual Fantasies

(SOURCE: Based on data from Arndt, Foehl, & Good, 1985.)

ported a high frequency of fantasies in which suffering played a role (e.g., "I'm made to suffer before a man will satisfy me sexually") were low in submissiveness and moodiness. Among males, in contrast, few if any relationships between sexual fantasy and personality were noted.

Finally, the two sexes also differed with respect to the relationship between sexual fantasies and both sexual behavior and sexual satisfaction. Female subjects reporting a high frequency of sexual fantasy also reported higher levels of sexual behavior, greater frequency of orgasms, and a greater degree of sexual satisfaction than subjects who reported a low frequency of such fantasies. Again, corresponding relationships were weaker in the case of males. Overall frequency of

sexual fantasies was not significantly related to level of sexual behavior, and only one theme (being sexually stimulating to women) was related to frequency of orgasms: men who reported a high frequency of such fantasies also reported more orgasms with sexual partners.

In sum, it appears that sexual fantasies are common for both sexes. However, the findings reported by Arndt, Foehl, and Good (1985) suggest that these daydreams may play a more important role in actual sexual behavior and sexual satisfaction among females. Why this may be so is still an open question, but at first glance, at least, these results seem consistent with the informal observation that females are often more closely in touch with their feelings and internal experiences than males.

Daydreams and Fantasies: What Do They Accomplish?

If people spend a considerable amount of time engaging in daydreams and fantasies—manipulating the content of their own consciousness—it seems reasonable to suggest that these activities must serve some useful functions. But what, precisely, do these activities accomplish? No clear-cut answer to this question has as yet emerged, but existing evidence points to several interesting possibilities.

First, and most obvious, daydreams and fantasies may serve as a kind of safety valve, permitting individuals to escape, briefly, from the stress and boredom of everyday life. In other words, these states of consciousness may provide individuals with "psychological breathing space," and this, in turn, may make them better able to cope with reality when they return to it.

Second, as suggested by the cartoon in Figure 4-5, daydreams and fantasies often provide us with a ready means of altering our own moods in a positive direction. If you've ever felt happier after a daydream filled with desirable activities and events, you are already familiar with such benefits.

Third, it is possible that daydreams and fantasies help individuals find solutions to actual problems in their lives. Fantasizing about various behaviors and the outcomes they will produce may assist many persons in evaluating real alternatives. Further, as they imagine themselves saying or doing different things, and then imagine others reacting in various ways, they may become better prepared for dealing with a wide range of situations. The overall result: daydreams and fantasies may assist individuals in formulating useful plans of action. Moreover, since this can be accomplished without the risks of actual trial and error, it is doubly useful.

Fourth, fantasies may play an important role in the self-regulation of behavior. By imagining negative outcomes, individuals may strengthen their inhibitions against dangerous or prohibited behaviors (Bandura, 1986). Similarly, by daydreaming about potential rewards, many persons may increase their motivation and their actual performance on various tasks. Finally, individuals may use specific fantasies to affect their emotional state. For example, they may increase their righteous indignation by daydreaming about real or imagined wrongs at the hands of others. And growing evidence suggests that many persons can increase both their sexual arousal and pleasure through self-generated erotic fantasies (Stock & Geer, 1982). Indeed, in recent surveys more than two-thirds of men and women report that they seek to increase their enjoyment of lovemaking through sexual fantasies (Byrne & Kelley, 1986; Singer, 1975).

In sum, fantasies and daydreams may be much more than a pleasant diversion—

FIGURE 4-5. As shown here, daydreams and fantasies often help individuals improve their own moods or emotions. *(Source:* The New Yorker.*)*

sempé

Fantasies and Daydreams: One Means of Enhancing Current Moods

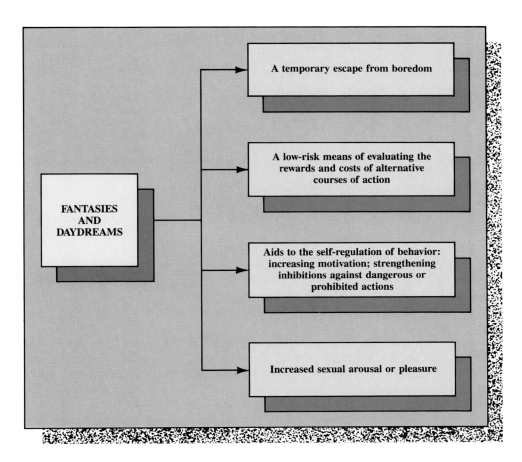

Fantasies and Daydreams: Their Potential Benefits

FIGURE 4-6. As shown here, fantasies and daydreams may serve several functions.

they may actually yield substantial benefits to those who choose to induce them. (Please see Figure 4-6 for a summary of the potential effects and benefits of these altered states of consciousness.)

 ## Sleep: The Pause That Refreshes?

What single activity occupies more of your time than any other? While you may be tempted to respond with such words as "studying" or "working," think again. If you are like most people, the correct answer is probably **sleep.** A majority of human beings spend fully one-third of their entire lives asleep, and for some the proportion is even higher (Dement, 1974; Webb, 1975). Obviously, any activity that occupies so much of our time *must* be important in several respects, so efforts to understand the nature of sleep have been under way in psychology for several decades. What has this research revealed? Just what happens when we sleep, and when we dream, and what are the functions of these processes? We will focus now on these topics.

Sleep: How It's Studied

How would you describe sleep? Clearly, this is a difficult task. Most of us realize that we are in a different state while asleep than when awake, but we're not quite sure about the nature of this difference. For this reason, asking individuals about their own experience with sleep is not a useful technique for studying it. Fortunately, another much more rigorous approach exists. As a person shifts from a waking state to being asleep, complex changes in the electrical activity of the brain take place. These changes can be measured with great precision, and the resulting **electroencephalogram (EEG)** reveals much about the nature of sleep. Thus, in a typical research project on this process, volunteer subjects are fitted with electrodes so that researchers can study their EEGs, as well as other changes in bodily functions such as respiration, muscle tone, heart rate, and blood pressure. The changes which occur as individuals fall asleep and remain in this state are then

An Important Technique for
Studying Sleep

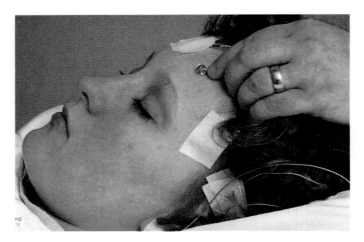

FIGURE 4-7. In many studies of sleep, electrodes are attached to volunteer subjects so that electrical activity of their brains can be recorded throughout the night. Investigations of this type have added greatly to our understanding of the nature of sleep.

recorded. In this way, revealing information about the normal course of sleep, as well as factors affecting it, can be obtained. (Please see Figure 4-7.)

Sleep: Its Basic Nature

What has such research revealed? Perhaps the best way of answering is by describing the changes in brain activity and other bodily processes which occur during a single night's sleep. As you will soon see, this involves regular movement, or cycling, through several different stages of sleep.

When you are fully awake and alert, your EEGs contain many *beta waves*— relatively high frequency (14 to 30 Hz), low voltage activity. As you enter a quiet, resting state (for example, just after getting into bed), beta waves are replaced by *alpha waves*— EEG activity that is somewhat lower frequency (8 to 13 Hz) but slightly higher in voltage. The presence of alpha waves reflects the fact that individual neurons (or groups of neurons) are firing individually, in a *synchronous* manner. As you begin to fall asleep, the alpha waves are gradually replaced by even slower, higher-voltage *delta waves*. The appearance of delta waves seems to reflect increasingly large numbers of neurons firing in unison. In a sense, it is as if the brain has moved from a state in which a number of different messages are being processed to a state in which only a single message is being quietly murmured by many different cells.

Although such phrases as ''drifting off to sleep'' suggest that the onset of sleep is gradual, it is actually quite sudden. One instant you are awake and aware of your surroundings; the next you are asleep, no longer experiencing such awareness. Sleep is not solely an either–or phenomenon, however. EEG records obtained from thousands of volunteers indicate that it can actually be divided into four different stages. The transition from wakefulness to sleep occurs with the onset of *Stage 1* sleep. During this stage, a mixed but relatively slow (and low-voltage) EEG pattern emerges. Breathing slows, muscle tone decreases. and in general the body relaxes. At this point, individuals can still be readily awakened by external stimuli. If not awakened, they progress through stages 2, 3, and 4. As shown in Figure 4-8, these stages are marked by an increasing frequency of delta waves, further slowing of all major bodily functions, and by the fact that it becomes increasingly difficult to awaken an individual at each of these successive stages. Almost everyone shows the same pattern of shifts in falling asleep; indeed, departures from pattern are often a sign of physical or psychological disorders (e.g., Empson, 1984).

So far, the pattern we have described probably sounds consistent with your own experience of sleep: you change from being awake to being more and more deeply asleep. About ninety minutes after the process begins, however, several dramatic changes occur. You enter what seems to be a distinct type of sleep known as **REM** (for *rapid eye-movement*) **sleep.** REM sleep differs from the other stages in several respects.

First, during REM sleep the electrical activity of the brain resembles that shown when you are awake but resting. Delta waves disappear, and fast, low-voltage activity

FIGURE 4-8. As an individual falls asleep, the electrical activity of the brain changes in an orderly manner. High-frequency, low-voltage *alpha waves* present during waking restfulness are gradually replaced by low-frequency, higher-voltage *delta waves*. The scale on the bottom will give you some idea of the actual speed and magnitude of these variations in brain activity.

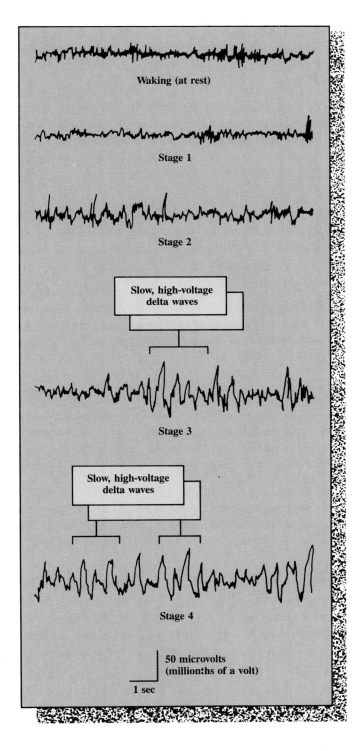

Stages of Sleep

Waking (at rest)

Stage 1

Stage 2

Slow, high-voltage delta waves

Stage 3

Slow, high-voltage delta waves

Stage 4

50 microvolts (millionths of a volt)

1 sec

returns. Second, your eyes begin to move about rapidly beneath your closed lids, as if you were watching moving objects or other activity. It is these rapid eye-movements that give REM sleep its name. Third, there is an almost total suppression of the muscle responses of the body. Indeed, muscle relaxation is so great that a state bordering on paralysis seems to exist. Yet, males may experience erections and females corresponding changes in their sexual organs. This combination of signs of activation along with signs of profound relaxation has led some researchers to describe REM sleep as *paradoxical* in nature, and in several ways this description seems fitting.

These observable shifts in brain activity and bodily processes are accompanied, in many cases, by one of the most fascinating phenomena of sleep: *dreams*. An individual awakened during REM sleep often reports dreaming. In some cases eye movements during such sleep seem related to the content of the dreams (Dement, 1974). Thus, it is as if an individual is ''following the action'' in a dream with his or her eyes! Periods of REM sleep continue to alternate with the other stages of sleep throughout the night. The duration is variable, but the REM periods increase in length toward morning. Thus, while the first REM period may last from five to ten minutes, the final one—from which many people awake—may last thirty minutes or more (Hartmann, 1973).

Two additional facts about REM sleep are of interest. The proportion of total sleep time occupied by REM sleep decreases with age, so that children spend more time in this state than do adults. Second, REM sleep occurs only among mammals. It is absent among fishes, reptiles, and amphibians, and it occurs only very briefly among a few birds of prey. Thus, it seems related to the development of brain structures found in mammals.

Sleep Disorders: Why, Sometimes, There's No Rest for the Weary

Do you ever have trouble falling asleep or staying asleep? If so, you are in good company: almost 40 percent of adults report they sometimes have this problem—generally known as **insomnia** (Bixler et al., 1979). Further, such problems seem to increase with age, and they are somewhat more common among women than men. While many persons report insomnia, however, it is not clear that the problem actually exists in all cases. When the sleep habits of self-proclaimed insomniacs are carefully studied, it turns out that many of them sleep as long as persons who do not complain of such problems (Empson, 1984). Thus, either many self-labeled insomniacs sleep more than they realize, or the duration of sleep is not closely related to its quality—a possibility that agrees with informal experience. (Many individuals find it possible to feel refreshed after only a few hours of ''good'' sleep, but may still feel fatigued after many hours of restless, fitful sleep.) No sure-fire cure for insomnia exists, but many persons find the following tactics to be helpful: (1) reading just before going to sleep, (2) arranging their schedule so they go to sleep at the same time each night, and (3) a warm bath or other relaxing treatments. Unfortunately, sleeping pills, which are used regularly by millions of persons, do not seem effective. They may induce sleep at first, but tolerance to them quickly develops, so that larger and larger doses are needed. Further, some drugs used for this purpose seem to interfere with REM sleep, and this can lead to other sleep disturbances. (For another technique that some persons might find helpful in overcoming insomnia, please see Figure 4-9.)

Unfortunately, insomnia is far from the only problem associated with sleep. Several other *disorders of initiating and maintaining sleep* (*DIMS,* for short) also exist. First, there are disorders of *arousal*. The most dramatic of these is **somnambulism**—walking in one's sleep. Actually, this is less rare than you might guess; almost 25 percent of children experience at least one sleepwalking episode (Empson, 1984). A second sleep disorder of this type is *night terrors*. In this disorder, which is more common among children than

FIGURE 4-9. Most people have difficulty falling asleep on some occasions, and when they do, they use many techniques to overcome this problem (e.g., warm baths, sleeping pills). Another approach to such difficulties—one you may well have experienced yourself—is shown here. (*Source: King Features Syndicate, 1977*).

An Unusual Technique for Overcoming Insomnia

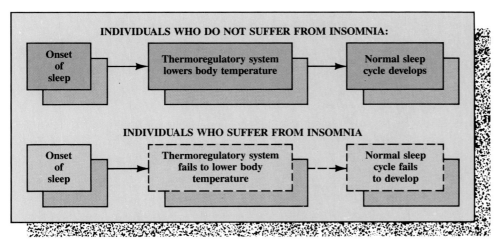

INDIVIDUALS WHO DO NOT SUFFER FROM INSOMNIA:

Onset of sleep → Thermoregulatory system lowers body temperature → Normal sleep cycle develops

INDIVIDUALS WHO SUFFER FROM INSOMNIA

Onset of sleep → Thermoregulatory system fails to lower body temperature ⇢ Normal sleep cycle fails to develop

Body Temperature and Insomnia

FIGURE 4-10. Growing evidence indicates that many cases of insomnia may stem in part from disturbances in the brain mechanisms that regulate internal body temperature (the *thermoregulatory system*). Among insomniacs, these mechanisms fail to lower body temperature after the onset of sleep, activation remains high, and normal sleep cycles cannot develop. *(Source: Based on suggestions by Sewitch, 1987.)*

adults, individuals awaken from deep sleep with signs of intense arousal (e.g., a racing pulse, rapid respiration) and feelings of intense fear. Yet, they have no memory of any dream relating to these feelings. Night terrors seem to occur primarily during Stage 4 sleep. (In contrast, *nightmares,* which most persons experience at some point in their lives, occur during REM sleep and involve recall of vivid dreams.) Both somnambulism and night terrors appear to be related to disturbances in the functioning of the autonomic nervous system, which plays a key role in regulating brain activity during sleep.

Another, and especially disturbing, type of sleep disorder is *apnea*. Persons suffering from apnea actually stop breathing when they fall asleep. Needless to say, this causes them to wake up or at least to move from a deep stage of sleep (e.g., Stage 4) to a stage closer to waking. Since this process can be repeated literally hundreds of times during the night, apnea can seriously affect the health of persons suffering from it by depriving them of needed rest.

Finally, there are several disorders known as **hypersomnias** in which affected individuals appear to sleep too much. The most serious of these is *narcolepsy,* a condition in which individuals fall deeply asleep suddenly, in the midst of waking activities (Empson, 1984). Such attacks, which are accompanied by almost total paralysis, are often triggered by a strong emotion. Thus, when a person with this sleep disorder becomes excited or upset, he or she may suddenly fall down in a deep sleep, practically in mid-sentence. Obviously, such reactions can pose a serious threat to the health, safety, and even careers of narcoleptics.

Given their adverse effects upon both physical and psychological well-being, sleep disorders have been the subject of a great deal of study. One interesting finding which has emerged from such work is the existence of a close relationship between brain mechanisms that regulate internal body temperature (the *thermoregulatory system*) and mechanisms that regulate sleep (Sewitch, 1987). Several lines of evidence point to such a link. As individuals fall asleep, body and brain temperature decreases. Further, internal temperature rises again as the time for awakening approaches. Third, individuals who describe themselves as "poor sleepers" have a higher body temperature during the night than ones who report being "good sleepers" (Rechtschaffen, 1968). Finally, individuals deprived of sleep show a downward trend in body temperature, almost as if their bodies were attempting to attain the conditions normally present during sleep (Horne, 1978). Together, these findings suggest that in some cases insomnia may stem from disturbances in internal thermoregulatory mechanisms—disturbances that prevent body temperature from decreasing in normal fashion as individuals fall asleep (refer to Figure 4-10). As researchers in this area have put it (Sewitch, 1987), the result may be that persons suffer-

Prolonged Sleeplessness: Does It Have any Effects?

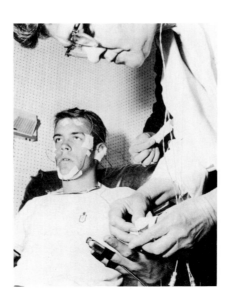

FIGURE 4-11. Even after going without sleep for eleven days, Randy Gardner was alert and seemingly normal. Findings such as this raise the intriguing question: Why do we sleep?

ing from insomnia face a situation in which their brains are asleep, while their bodies remain active and awake. Little wonder, then, that such people experience difficulty in obtaining a good night's rest!

Sleep: What Functions Does It Serve?

It seems reasonable to assume that any activity that fills as much of our lives as sleep must serve crucial functions. But what, precisely, are these? What benefits do we gain from the hours we spend asleep? Several possibilities exist.

The most obvious of these is suggested by the fact that when, for some reason, you don't attain the amount of sleep that is normal for you (large individual differences exist in this respect), you often feel tired and irritable the next day. This seems to indicate that sleep serves a basic restorative function: it provides the rest you need to recover from the previous day's activities. Contrary to this seemingly reasonable view, however, even prolonged deprivation of sleep does not seem to produce large or clear-cut effects upon behavior. For example, in one famous demonstration, seventeen-year-old Randy Gardner stayed awake for 264 hours—11 entire days! His motivation was simple: he wanted to earn a place in the *Guinness Book of Records,* and he did! Although he had some difficulty staying awake this long and in performing certain tasks, he remained alert and active throughout the entire period (see Figure 4-11). On the first night after his ordeal, he slept fifteen hours. The next night he returned to his usual eight-hour cycle. Further, he seemed to suffer no lasting physical or psychological harm from his long sleepless period. On the basis of this and related evidence, one well-known sleep researcher (Webb, 1975) remarked that the major effect of sleep deprivation is to make us go to sleep, and that sleep evolved merely to keep us quiet at night—a dangerous time for human beings. While this may be true, at least to a degree, other findings indicate that we should not too quickly downplay the value of sleep or the harmful effects that may result from sleep deprivation (Wallace & Fisher, 1987). In particular, it appears that prolonged lack of sleep may interfere with the performance of tasks requiring sustained attention and complex forms of information processing. Perhaps, then, sleep *is* necessary for efficient cognitive functioning. Its effects are not obvious, though, so we must look carefully if we wish to find them.

A second possible function of sleep involves its role in learning and memory. Some evidence indicates that REM sleep may be especially important in the integration of newly acquired information with existing memories and information (McGrath & Cohen, 1978). When individuals are deprived of REM sleep (by waking them up whenever they enter this state), they seem to show reduced ability to retain newly learned information or responses. Such effects do not seem to occur when individuals are deprived of other sleep stages, so these effects seem to be linked primarily with REM sleep.

A third function of sleep is suggested by the results of research concerned with the relationship between sleep and current mood (e.g., Berry & Webb, 1983). For example, in one investigation Berry and Webb (1985) asked forty women whose average age was 59.5 years to rate their own mood on several nights just before going to sleep. During the night, several measures of their sleep were obtained (e.g., the length of time before they fell asleep, number of awakenings during the night, sleep efficiency—the percent of the time spent in bed actually asleep–and length of time until their first period of REM sleep). When these measures were correlated with subjects' reported moods, several interesting findings emerged. First, the more cheerful subjects reported feeling, the shorter the period until their first REM sleep both on the following night and the preceding night. Second, the more anxious subjects were, the longer the period until their first REM sleep period, again on both the following and the preceding nights. Finally, the more anxious they reported being, the lower their sleep efficiency. In sum, the more positive subjects' moods on a given night, the better their sleep. And the better the sleep subjects attained, the more positive their moods on the following day. These results, in turn, point to the following, tentative conclusion: one possible function of sleep is that of countering the effects of negative life experiences, thus restoring our mood to a positive state (refer to Figure 4-12). That this may be the case is also suggested by two other findings: (1) patients suffering from depression enter REM sleep more quickly than persons not suffering from depression (Kupfer, 1977), and (2) insomniacs suffer from more psychological problems than other persons (Kales et al., 1974). Incidentally, and related to our comments about the link between body temperature and sleep, it has been found that depressed persons do not show as great a fall in body temperature during sleep as nondepressed persons (Sewitch, 1987).

We should hasten to add that the evidence outlined above is far from conclusive. Still, it seems possible that one function of sleep is that of helping us recover, emotionally, from the unavoidable stresses and pains of life. Perhaps Shakespeare was close to the mark when he described sleep as the mysterious process that ''knits up the ravell'd sleave of care.''

Dreams: Stimulation in the Midst of Sleep

Without a doubt, the most dramatic aspect of sleep is that of **dreams**—those jumbled, vivid, and often disturbing images that fill our sleeping minds. What are these experiences? And why do they occur? Psychologists are still seeking final answers to these

FIGURE 4-12. The more cheerful and less anxious individuals felt on a given night, the better they slept. Furthermore, the better they slept, the more cheerful and less anxious they felt the next day. These findings suggest that one function of sleep is to counter the effects of unpleasant or stressful experiences. *(Source: Based on data from Berry & Webb, 1985.)*

Mood and Sleep: Two-Way Effects

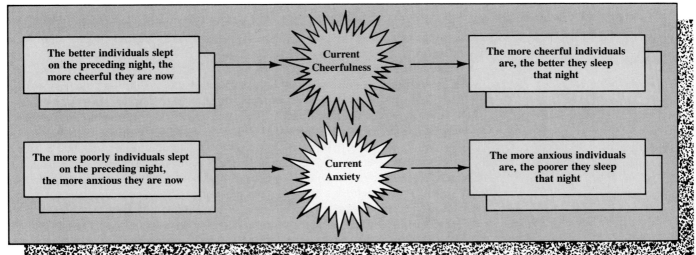

puzzling questions. In ancient times, dreams were viewed as messages from the gods—communications which foretold future events, contained instructions, or provided dire warnings. After Freud's important work in the late nineteenth century, they were seen as deriving from a different source: hidden (and often repressed) desires or motives. As we will soon see, psychologists now account for the occurrence of dreams in very different terms—ones relating primarily to the basic nature of our nervous system and several cognitive processes (Foulkes, 1985). Whatever their precise origins, dreams are certainly intriguing events, well worth our careful attention.

While individuals differ greatly in frequency of dreaming (or, at least, in the number of dreams they remember), everyone seems to have such experiences on at least some occasions (Cohen, 1973). Moreover, while most dreams occur during REM sleep, some seem to unfold at other times. Dreams during non-REM sleep, though, tend to be less vivid and less detailed than those during REM sleep. Also, while some dreams are indeed powerful in their emotional effects, most seem to be quite ordinary in content. For example, they may focus on recent events, on planned activities, or on unsolved problems actually facing the dreamer. Contrary to what you might expect, only a small proportion of dreams are sexual in content (Hall, 1984).

What is the function of such experiences? Are dreams merely an accident of evolution—a byproduct of the normal operation of your sleeping nervous system? Or do they serve important psychological functions? As we noted above, one answer to such questions was proposed by Freud, who viewed dreams as a kind of ''safety valve'' through which individuals find release for unacceptable wishes or impulses. Indeed, Freud believed that much could be learned about a person's hidden anxieties or desires through careful study of his or her dreams.

While such suggestions are fascinating, they have not been supported by systematic research. As we have just noted, the content of most dreams is highly consistent with individuals' waking behavior (Cohen, 1973). Thus, there is little evidence for the view that they primarily serve as a release for the expression of unacceptable impulses. Additional evidence, though, suggests that dreams may provide other psychological benefits. First, they may play a role in information processing or problem solving. Although dreaming about one's problems rarely yields workable solutions to them, some progress in this direction does occasionally take place (Dement, 1975). Moreover, REM sleep tends to increase after periods of intense learning. Since most dreams occur during such sleep, this finding suggests that dreams may play some role in the processing or retention of new information. On the other side of the coin, some researchers suggest that dreams may be related to forgetting—they may somehow help us ''erase'' unneeded or unwanted information from long-term memory (Crick & Mitchison, 1983). At present there is little evidence for this possibility, but it is certainly an intriguing one worthy of further study.

Second, dreams may provide the sleeping brain with periodic stimulation—input it needs to continue normal functioning throughout the night. The fact that a much higher proportion of infants' than adults' sleep is REM sleep provides indirect support for this possibility. It seems reasonable to expect that the need for stimulation provided by REM sleep would be greater before the nervous system is fully developed than after such development has ceased.

While evidence we have just described suggests that dreams do indeed serve *some* useful function, we should note, in all fairness, that not all psychologists share this view. In fact, some believe that dreams are merely neural ''accidents.'' Specifically, some researchers (e.g., McCarley & Hobson, 1981) suggest that dreams simply reflect efforts by the cerebral cortex to make sense out of what is, essentially, random activity in the sleeping brain. According to this view, dreams have no significance in and of themselves.

A closely related but in some ways even more intriguing theory of the nature of dreams has recently been proposed by Foulkes (1985). Foulkes, too, assumes that dreams are triggered by spontaneous and diffuse activity in the nervous system. However, he relates such activity to basic cognitive processes. While the activation within our brains may be largely random, Foulkes reasons, our cognitive systems (e.g., memory, cognitive frameworks we use in interpreting new experiences) are definitely *not* random. Thus, these systems seek to interpret this brain activity in meaningful ways. This is why dreams usually have a plot and generally unfold in ways that make at least some sense: once

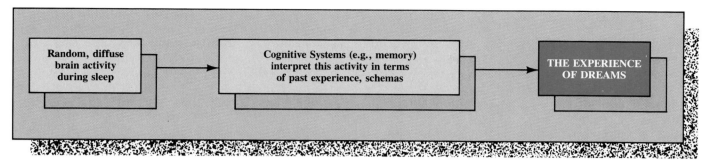

FIGURE 4-13. According to a theory proposed by Foulkes (1985), dreams represent efforts by our cognitive systems (e.g., memory) to make sense out of essentially random and diffuse activity within the sleeping brain. *(Source: Based on suggestions by Foulkes, 1985.)*

Dreams: A Modern View

activated, your cognitive system imposes structure on the diffuse activation from which dreams are constructed (refer to Figure 4-13).

According to Foulkes, dreams do *not* contain messages from the unconscious, as Freud proposed, nor do they foretell the future or demonstrate any other aspects of ESP (refer to Chapter 3). Yet they may still tell us something about the person who experiences them. Dreams, after all, reflect the memories and knowledge of the dreamer. Further, since they are shaped by basic cognitive systems, they may reveal much about how these work—about the basic nature of the human mind itself, if you will.

In the context of this theory, do dreams have a function? Foulkes suggests that they may actually have several. First, dreams may assist you in integrating specific knowledge or experiences with more general knowledge acquired in the past. Second, they may help you to combine knowledge acquired through your various senses (e.g., the sight, smell, taste, and feel of a newly experienced food). Third, since they often contain events that could have happened to you but didn't, they may help to prepare or to "program" your mind for dealing with new, unexpected events. Finally, since dreams usually refer to the dreamer, they may help you relate newly acquired knowledge to your own self-consciousness.

At the present time little evidence for these intriguing possibilities exists. Since dreams are certainly cognitive events, however, it makes good sense to attempt to understand them in terms of memory and other cognitive processes. By relating dreams to basic aspects of human cognition, Foulkes has broadened our perspective on this intriguing topic. In this respect, at least, his theory offers an important contribution to modern efforts to solve one of the oldest remaining mysteries of human behavior. (As we have just seen, modern research casts strong doubt on widely held views concerning the nature of dreams. For an additional example of how systematic research by psychologists can help correct persistent, but often false, beliefs about human behavior, please see "The Cutting Edge" section below.)

FOCUS ON RESEARCH: The Cutting Edge

Lunar Madness: The "Transylvania Effect" Revisited

Does the moon exert an effect upon human behavior? Many people believe it does. In fact, in a recent survey (Rotton & Kelly, 1985) almost half of the undergraduates polled reported their belief that at least some people act strangely when the moon is full! Given the plots of many Hollywood epics, this is hardly surprising.

After all, most persons have seen actors or actresses turn into frightening monsters under the influence of lunar rays (refer to Figure 4-14). Is there any basis to such beliefs? Do people actually enter an altered state of consciousness when the moon is full? A major study conducted by Rotton and Kelly (1985) casts serious doubt on this possibility.

These researchers subjected the results of all the research conducted on this

Hollywood's View of the "Transylvania Effect"

FIGURE 4-14. Does the moon affect human behavior? Many movies suggest that this is the case!

topic—some thirty-seven separate studies dealing with "moon madness"—to highly sophisticated statistical analysis. The analyses performed were complex, but the purpose was straightforward: to determine whether any evidence was provided for the occurrence of lunar effects. In their investigation Rotton and Kelly examined the potential impact of phases of the moon on a wide range of behaviors—admissions to mental hospitals, calls to crisis centers, suicides and other types of self-harm, homicides, and other criminal offenses. Although they did not specifically examine altered states of consciousness, it seems reasonable to suggest that many of the behaviors included in their study would be preceded by such shifts. For example, many persons who commit homicide report, later, that they were "not themselves" when they carried out this violent crime.

The results of the project were both clear and conclusive: little, if any, evidence was found for an impact of the moon on human behavior. While there were slightly more criminal actions when the moon was full than when it was in other phases, this trend was *not* statistically significant. Further, the incidence of "lunar madness" was *not* higher when the moon was close to the earth than when it was farthest away, and the incidence of such behaviors was *not* higher near the equator than farther away from it. (The distance between the moon and the earth is slightly less at the equator than elsewhere.) Moreover, in examining the findings of all thirty-seven previous studies, Rotton and Kelly (1985) found that some reported a higher incidence of behaviors linked to "lunar madness" when the moon was full, while others reported a *lower* incidence of these behaviors at such times.

On the basis of these negative results, Rotton and Kelly conclude there are no scientific grounds for the contention that the moon influences human behavior or human consciousness. In fact, at the end of their article they break with the strong tradition in psychology of calling for additional research. Instead, they express the hope that their paper will put an *end* to further studies of "lunar madness," for in their view, at least, such research has been "much ado about nothing!"

Hypnosis: Externally Induced Alterations in Consciousness

"You are becoming drowsy. Your eyes feel heavy; you can't keep them open. You feel yourself drifting peacefully in space. Now you are asleep, but you can still hear the sound of my voice. . . ." Have you ever heard a hypnotist say such things to a volunteer who, right before your eyes, then seemed to enter a deep trance? (Refer to Figure 4-15.) If so, you have probably wondered about this process. Is hypnosis real? Or is it just an act, a clever trick perpetrated by the hypnotist and a subject? If it is real, what is it, and how does it work? These are some of the questions we'll now consider.

Hypnosis: Its Basic Nature

Perhaps we should begin by noting that there is not complete agreement among psychologists at present about the essential nature of **hypnosis.** On one hand, many researchers accept what is often described as a *trance view of hypnosis:* they define it as involving an altered state of consciousness during which an individual demonstrates heightened susceptibility to suggestions or commands of the hypnotist (Barber, Spanos, & Chaves, 1974; Wallace & Fisher, 1987). In contrast, others accept a *non-trance* or *social definition:* hypnosis involves a social interaction in which one person (the subject) responds to suggestions by another person (the hypnotist), which involve behavior, perceptions, or memories (Kihlstrom, 1985). As you can see, this latter view makes no mention of a trance or an altered state of consciousness; it contends that all of the effects observed while an individual is in a hypnotic trance can also occur in its absence if such a person has positive views about hypnosis and is predisposed to accept suggestions of the hypnotist (Barber, 1969; Kilhstrom, 1985). Since research evidence for both views exists, we won't attempt to choose between them. Instead, we'll focus on the major effects of

FIGURE 4-15. Hypnotism has long had a place in the world of entertainment, but is it real? Psychologists have tried to answer this question through systematic research.

Hypnotism: Show-Business Trick or Genuine Shift in Consciousness?

hypnosis—changes in hypnotized individuals reported by supporters of both the trance and the social definitions.

First, it is generally agreed that persons who are successfully hypnotized enter a state of increased *suggestibility*. They will carry out various actions suggested by the hypnotist and will experience feelings and perceptions suggested by this person, even if these are not consistent with actual external conditions. For example, a deeply hypnotized person may fail to smell a bottle of ammonia held under his or her nose if the hypnotist indicates that it contains water. Similarly, such persons will feel their arms getting heavier and heavier if the hypnotist tells them this is the case. Such heightened suggestibility is so central to the concept of hypnosis that several scales have been developed to assess it (e.g., the Stanford Hypnotic Susceptibility Scales). Individuals completing such tests are given a variety of suggestions, ranging from simple (e.g., ''Your eyelids are becoming very heavy, so heavy you can't keep them open any longer'') to ones that are quite demanding and difficult (e.g., ''After the session is over, you will hear a tapping noise. When you do, you will feel like changing chairs.'') The more of these suggestions a subject follows, the greater this person's assumed susceptibility to hypnosis.

Second, hypnosis often involves *dissociation*—a division of consciousness. For example, if hypnotized individuals are asked to put their arms into icy water, they will do so and report no pain. However, if asked to describe their feelings in writing, they may indicate they did experience pain (Hilgard, 1979). Such effects suggest that during hypnosis consciousness is divided into different levels; experiences at one level may be *dissociated* from experiences at other levels.

Third, hypnotized individuals frequently demonstrate distortions in the way they process information. For example, they may accept inconsistencies or incongruities that unhypnotized individuals notice and question. Moreover, hypnotized subjects often experience shifts in perception; for example, they may experience reduced visual acuity, make unusual errors in estimating depth or distance, and experience time as passing more slowly than normal.

Finally, persons undergoing hypnosis often demonstrate lessened awareness of the world around them, a sense of unreality, and loss of volition—an inability to initiate actions by themselves. They can carry out suggestions or commands from the hypnotist, but if left to their own devices, they will sit quietly with little or no activity. Does this mean that hypnotized persons are totally under the control of the hypnotist—they will do or say anything this person suggests? Evidence on this question is not conclusive, but in general it appears that even deeply hypnotized individuals will avoid doing anything that may harm themselves or others. Since people aren't always aware of their own motives or desires, however, this is a difficult issue to resolve in any final sense. Consider the following example: Joe is ordered by a hypnotist to jump into a vat of Jello and go for a swim. He obeys, but then reports being angry and embarrassed by being ''forced'' to perform these actions. Does this mean the hypnotist has been successful in forcing Joe to behave in ways contrary to his own will? Perhaps. But it is also possible that Joe is actually angry at himself for some real or imagined misdeed, and wanted punishment in this manner. As you can see, determining whether hypnosis can actually coerce individuals into actions they would not otherwise perform is complex, to say the least.

Before concluding, we should mention one other possible effect of hypnosis: its impact on memory. Some research findings (but by no means all; Orne et al., 1984) suggest that certain aspects of memory can be enhanced by hypnosis. For example, in one recent study on this issue (McConkey & Kinoshita, 1988), subjects previously identified as being high or low in susceptibility to hypnosis were exposed to sixty different visual patterns (simple black-and-white drawings). Later—one day or one week afterwards—they were asked to write the names of as many of these stimuli as they could remember. Prior to these memory tests they were exposed or not exposed to procedures designed to induce hypnosis. Results indicated that on both occasions subjects exposed to hypnosis remembered more of the patterns than subjects not exposed to hypnosis. Further, such effects were strongest among persons previously found to be highly susceptible to hypnosis.

Why does hypnosis improve memory in at least some instances? One possibility is that hypnotized subjects are more willing than non-hypnotized subjects to offer guesses. Since some of these are correct, total recall increases. Another is that hypnotized individuals may simply try harder—they are more motivated to perform well and please the experimenter. Regardless of the mechanisms involved, the possibility that memory can sometimes be enhanced through hypnotism has important implications. For example, to the extent such effects occur, hypnosis might be employed to increase the accuracy of eyewitnesses to various crimes (Orne et al., 1984). We'll return to this possibility in Chapter 6, where we consider many aspects of human memory.

Hypnosis: Is It Real?

Now let's consider another important question: is hypnosis real? Are the effects we have just described genuine, or are they merely simulated by persons pretending to be hypnotized? For several reasons this, too, is a difficult question to answer. First, when asked to pretend that they are hypnotized, subjects often act in ways very similar to those demonstrated by persons exposed to hypnosis (Orne & Evans, 1965). Second, many of the effects supposedly induced by hypnosis are internal ones; hypnotized and unhypnotized individuals may act in much the same manner, but those who are hypnotized report that they *feel* differently. For example, unhypnotized subjects indicate that in responding to suggestions from a hypnotist, they simply decide to do what this person wants. In contrast, hypnotized persons report that the behaviors they perform seem to happen without their conscious will or effort. Because of such complexities, the existence of hypnotism is still somewhat controversial. However, several intriguing findings seem to suggest it is a real phenomenon.

First, while hypnotized individuals and persons merely simulating hypnosis do often behave in the same manner, important differences between them exist. For example, in one intriguing study Orne and his colleagues (Orne, Sheehan, & Evans, 1968) told hypnotized subjects and other persons pretending to be hypnotized that during the next forty-eight hours, their right hand would rise to touch their foreheads whenever the word "experiment" was heard. After receiving this suggestion, subjects left the laboratory, where they encountered a secretary who mentioned the word "experiment" three times. As you can see from Figure 4-16, simulating subjects followed the hypnotist's suggestions much less frequently than those who were actually hypnotized. Moreover, when only those subjects most susceptible to hypnosis were considered, this effect was even more pronounced.

Several other studies support the finding that persons simulating hypnosis behave differently from ones who are actually hypnotized (e.g., Gray, Bowers, & Fenz, 1970). For example, persons who have been hypnotized and told that they cannot see a chair still walk around it, just as sleepwalkers might. In contrast, those told to pretend that they are in a trance often purposely bump into the obstacle (Bowers, 1976). Similarly, individuals placed in a trance and left alone in a room gradually emerge from this altered state of consciousness; simulators remain in their false "trance" until the experimenter returns

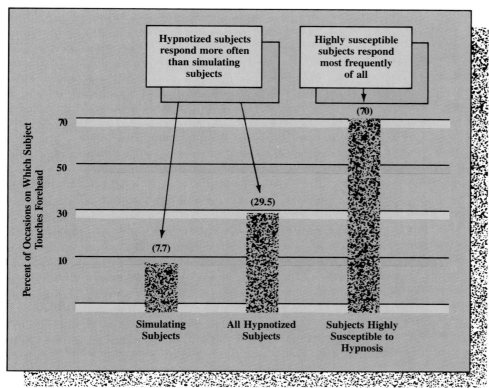

FIGURE 4-16. Hypnotized and nonhypnotized subjects were told that they would touch their forehead with their right hand whenever they heard the word "experiment." Those actually undergoing hypnosis responded much more frequently than subjects who merely pretended to be hypnotized. This tendency was even greater among individuals highly susceptible to hypnosis. *(Source: Based on data from Orne, Sheehan, & Evans, 1968.)*

(Evans & Orne, 1971). Together, such experiments indicate that hypnotism constitutes a genuine shift in consciousness.

In addition, susceptibility to hypnosis seems to change with age. It peaks between nine and twelve years of age, and then decreases slowly until the mid-thirties (Morgan & Hilgard, 1973). After that, it seems to level off, or perhaps to rebound slightly. Since there is no obvious reason why hypnotic susceptibility should change with age if it is purely a "faked" phenomenon, these changes also suggest that it is at least partially real.

In sum, taking all available evidence into account, it appears that hypnosis may be a genuine phenomenon. This is not to say that all effects attributed to it are real; there is much room for deception and for the impact of *demand characteristics*—doing what an experimenter wants or expects just because he or she expects it. Still, there do seem to be grounds for assuming that for some people, on some occasions, hypnotic inductions work—they induce a genuine shift in state of consciousness.

Hypnosis: Who Is Susceptible and Who Is Not?

Can anyone be hypnotized, or are some persons more susceptible to this process than others? The answer seems clear: large individual differences in hypnotizability exist. About 15 percent of adults are highly susceptible, while 10 percent are highly resistant, and the rest are somewhere in between. In addition, it appears that several traits or characteristics are related to hypnotic susceptibility (e.g., Council, Kirsch, & Hafner, 1986; Lynn & Rhue, 1986).

First, persons who tend to have vivid and frequent fantasies (*fantasy-prone individuals*) are more readily hypnotized than persons who do not have such fantasies or who have them less frequently. For example, in one recent study on this topic, Lynn and Rhue (1986) exposed individuals previously found to be high, medium, or low in fantasy-

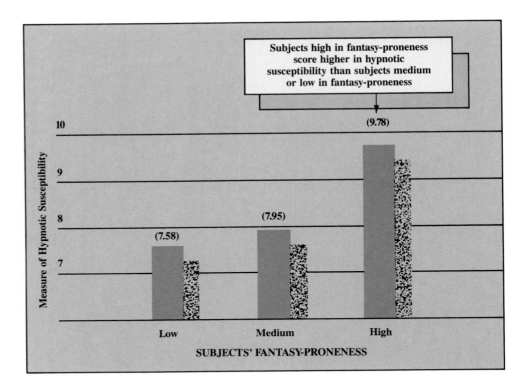

Fantasy-Proneness and Hypnotic Susceptibility

FIGURE 4-17. In one recent study, individuals high in fantasy-proneness (persons with a rich and vivid fantasy life) were found to be higher in hypnotic susceptibility than individuals who rated medium or low on this characteristic. *(Source: Based on data from Lynn & Rhue, 1986.)*

proneness to hypnosis, and then measured their hypnotic susceptibility. Results indicated that those high on this dimension were more strongly influenced by suggestions from the hypnotist than those medium or low in fantasy-proneness (refer to Figure 4-17). Interestingly, persons high in fantasy-proneness also scored highest on scales designed to measure vividness of mental imagery and creativity.

Second, there is some indication that persons high in the trait of *absorption*—the tendency to become deeply involved in sensory and imaginative experiences—are higher in hypnotic susceptibility than those who are low in this characteristic (e.g., Farthing, Venturino, & Brown, 1983). However, we should note that one recent study (Council, Kirsch, & Hafner, 1986) suggests that this may be true only when absorption is measured when individuals expect to be exposed to hypnosis. If absorption is measured in a context unrelated to hypnosis, it may not be closely linked to hypnotizability.

Third, *expectancies* concerning the impact of hypnotism, too, seem important. To the extent individuals expect to be influenced by hypnotic suggestions, they are. To the extent they do not anticipate such effects, these do not occur (Council, Kirsh, & Hafner, 1986). Thus, to some extent, at least, hypnotizability may be a function of faith: individuals are susceptible to such procedures only to the extent that they believe they will work.

Pulling these diverse findings together, it seems reasonable to suggest that individuals who are most susceptible to hypnosis are ones who (1) have a rich, vivid, and active fantasy life; (2) become deeply absorbed in activities they perform; and (3) expect to be influenced by hypnotic inductions. Do you fit this description? To the extent you do, you may be a suitable subject for hypnosis. (Does hypnosis have any practical benefits? For information suggesting that it does, please see "The Point of It All" section below.)

THE POINT OF IT ALL

Hypnosis: A Useful Therapeutic Tool?

Hypnosis has a long history in the world of entertainment; millions of people have watched with interest as noted hypnotists put others into a deep trance, and then have seemingly bent their will to their own. But does it have any practi-

cal value apart from such uses? Some evidence indicates that it does. In recent years psychologists have attempted to use hypnosis to help individuals solve personal problems.

First, it has been applied to the treatment of many ailments that seem to have a behavioral or psychological basis, such as asthma, migraine headaches, and skin disorders (Kihlstrom, 1985). Results in this respect have been promising. For example, Bowers (1983) describes the case of a forty-year-old woman who suffered from dozens of painful sores all over her body. Medical treatment over a twenty-year period had failed to help. Bowers hypnotized this person, and told her to imagine herself swimming in a shimmering liquid that would purify and cleanse her skin. The result: she became virtually free of sores. Similar successes have been reported in the treatment of warts, asthma, and other illnesses. Of course, such results are open to question: is it hypnosis or some other factor (e.g., patients' belief that they will improve) that is responsible for the beneficial outcomes? At present, it is difficult to tell. Still, some of the effects produced seem too dramatic to ignore.

While doubts remain about the effectiveness of hypnosis in treating some ailments, there is currently greater agreement about its usefulness in another respect: as a technique for reducing persistent pain (Hilgard & Hilgard, 1983). Hypnotism has been found to be effective in reducing sensations of pain and the emotional upset which often accompanies pain (Gillett and Coe, 1984). For example, in one recent study (Price & Barber, 1987), subjects rated their reactions to uncomfort-

ably hot water both before and after undergoing hypnosis. When they received repeated post-hypnotic suggestions that they would not be bothered by the heat and would be able to dissociate themselves from such sensations, they reported almost a 50 percent drop in experienced pain. Other findings suggest that the pain-reducing (*analgesic*) effect of hypnosis is somewhat greater among persons who are highly susceptible to hypnotism than among those who are less susceptible. However, this difference is not large, so hypnosis may be an effective analgesic for many persons. In one dramatic application, hypnosis was found to be successful in reducing pain experienced by children undergoing chemotherapy for the treatment of cancer (Hilgard & LeBaron, 1984). We should note, by the way, that the use of hypnosis as an analgesic is not a new idea. Prior to the development of chemical anesthetics, hypnosis was often used for this purpose in connection with surgery (Fromm & Shorr, 1979).

Of course, until more is known about hypnosis—its basic nature and how it works—caution should be the byword in putting it to clinical use. At present, though, it seems to offer a promising and intriguing new weapon in the arsenal for enhancing human welfare.

Drugs and Consciousness

As we noted in Chapter 2, drugs are big business in the late twentieth century. In fact, we seem to live at a time when the use of such substances is at an all-time high. Each day, millions of human beings use drugs to change the way they feel—to alter their mood or state of consciousness (refer to Figure 4-18). In this final section we will review the mind-altering effects of a number of these drugs, and we will consider some factors that play a role in drug use.

Consciousness—Altering Drugs: An Overview

While many different drugs affect consciousness, many seem to fit under one of three major headings: **depressants, stimulants** and **hallucinogens.** Please note that these categories are based on the *psychological* effects of various drugs and do not refer to the chemical nature of these substances. Thus, drugs that act as depressants or as stimulants may, and often do, differ greatly in their chemical formulas.

Depressants.   Drugs in the first category reduce activity in the central nervous system. Perhaps the most important of these is *alcohol*, undoubtedly the most widely consumed drug in existence. While small amounts of alcohol seem, subjectively, to be stimulating, larger doses act as a depressant. They interfere with coordination and normal functioning of our senses (often with tragic results when driving) and may disrupt information-processing in several respects. Perhaps the most impressive effect of alcohol is that of lowering social inhibitions. Thus, after consuming large quantities of this drug, individuals often become more aggressive (Jeavons & Taylor, 1985) and seem to appreciate blunter types of humor (Weaver et al., 1985). Overall, it appears that alcohol interferes with an individual's ability to foresee negative consequences and to recall accepted standards of behavior. Thus, actions tend to become more extreme in the presence of this drug (Steele & Southwick, 1985). (Refer to Figure 4-19.)

How alcohol exerts these effects has not yet been fully determined. Some evidence suggests that it acts directly on the cell membrane of neurons, reducing their ability to

Drugs: All-Too-Common Means of Altering Consciousness

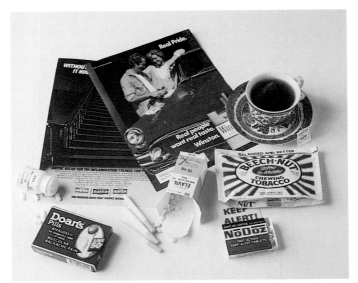

FIGURE 4-18. Each day, hundreds of millions of people take drugs to change the way they feel—to alter their state of consciousness.

conduct nerve impulses. Such effects seem to be most pronounced among neurons in the reticular activating system. Reduced activity in these neurons disrupts activity in the cerebral cortex, and this, in turn, yields the changes in behavior and consciousness noted above.

Barbiturates, contained in sleeping pills and relaxants, constitute a second important type of depressant. These drugs, too, depress activity in the nervous system, and so reduce overall activation and mental alertness. Initially, such drugs produce feelings of relaxation and euphoria—a kind of drunkenness without alcohol. They often go on to generate feelings of confusion, memory lapses, and reduced ability to concentrate. Wide swings of emotion and loss of motor coordination may occur after prolonged use or large doses. Barbiturates seem to produce their effects by reducing the release of excitatory transmitter substances at synapses in several parts of the nervous system.

Perhaps the most dangerous depressants of all are the *opiates*. These drugs (morphine, heroin, and related substances) greatly reduce activity in the nervous system. They produce lethargy and a pronounced slowing of almost all bodily functions. They also alter consciousness, producing intensely pleasurable sensations and a dream-like state among many users. The essence of such reactions is captured by the fact that many heroin-users describe the initial effects of this drug as something akin to a ''whole-body orgasm'' (Wallace & Fisher, 1987). The costs associated with such pleasurable sensations are high,

FIGURE 4-19. Alcohol, especially consumed in large quantities, reduces inhibitions and thereby leads to extreme forms of social behavior.

Alcohol: An Inhibition-Reducing Depressant

however. Heroin and other opiates are highly addicting, and withdrawal from them often produces agony. As we noted in Chapter 2, the brain produces substances closely resembling opiates in chemical structure (*opioid peptides* or *endorphins*), and it contains special receptor sites for them. This suggests one possible explanation for the discomfort experienced by opiate users during withdrawal. Opiates taken regularly soon overload endorphin receptor sites within the brain. As a result, the brain stops producing these substances. When the drugs are no longer taken, neither opiates nor endorphins are available (Snyder, 1977). The result: an important internal mechanism for regulating pain and discomfort is severely disrupted. If you needed one more reason for avoiding such drugs, this should provide it. Their use is virtually certain to damage (perhaps permanently) the intricate and precisely balanced processes within your brain that make bearable the unavoidable stress and discomfort of life.

Stimulants. Drugs which increase arousal and induce feelings of energy and self-confidence—effects opposite to the ones we have been discussing—are known as *stimulants*. As we saw in Chapter 2, *amphetamines* and *cocaine* produce such effects by inhibiting the re-uptake of transmitter substances (especially norepinephrine) at synapses in the nervous system. As a result, neurons that would otherwise stop firing continue to respond. Such drugs raise blood pressure, heart rate, and respiration—all the signs of activation or arousal produced by the sympathetic nervous system. In addition, they yield short periods of pleasurable sensations—twenty to forty minutes during which users feel incredibly powerful and energetic. They pay dearly for such feelings, however, for as the drug wears off they often experience an emotional "crash" marked by strong anxiety, depression, and fatigue.

It is interesting to note that at one time cocaine was widely hailed as valuable for medical purposes. Indeed, Freud (1885) believed that it was valuable as a local anesthetic and could be used in the treatment of such varied ailments as asthma, indigestion, and even addiction to alcohol or morphine. During the nineteenth century cocaine was added to many patent medicines, the kind sold out of the back of a wagon in town squares or by mail (see Figure 4-20). Since continued use of cocaine can produce harmful results, such as loss of appetite, paranoia, and *formication* (the sensation of countless insects crawling over one's skin), the dangers of such old remedies are apparent.

Other stimulants in common use include *caffeine,* found in coffee, tea, and many soft drinks; and *nicotine,* found in tobacco. It is interesting to note that the use of various stimulants seems to be interrelated. Thus, individuals who smoke also tend to consume more caffeine than other persons (Istvan & Matarazzo, 1984).

Hallucinogens. Perhaps the drugs with the most profound effects upon consciousness are the *hallucinogens*. All such drugs produce marked shifts in consciousness, but the most dramatic effects are yielded by LSD. After taking this substance, many persons report profound changes in perception of the external world. Objects and people seem to change color or shape; walls may sway and move; and many sensations seem more intense than normal. Perhaps most dramatic of all, there may be a strange blending of sensory experiences known as *synesthesia*. Music yields visual sensations, while colors produce feelings of warmth or cold. Such effects may sound exciting or even pleasant, but many others produced by LSD are quite negative. Objects, people, and even one's own body may seem distorted or threatening. Users may experience deep sorrow or develop intense fear even of close friends and relatives. Perhaps worst of all, the effects of this drug are quite unpredictable; there is no way of determining in advance whether LSD will yield mostly pleasant or mostly unpleasant sensations. In fact, the same person may experience radically different effects at different times. Unless you are willing to gamble with your own physical and mental health, therefore, LSD is certainly a drug to avoid.

In contrast, marijuana usually produces much milder effects. These include mild arousal (increased blood pressure and pulse rate), a perceived increase in the intensity of various stimuli (sounds, colors, tastes, smells), and distortions in the sense of time (e.g., users often estimate that more time has elapsed during a given period than is actually the case). Unfortunately, marijuana also interferes with the ability to judge distances, which

Patent Medicines: More Potent Than You Might Suspect

Liver Troubles Corrected by Guy's Tonic.

When the Bowels are confined, the Tongue coated with a yellowish-brown fur, when you have a splitting frontal Headache, and the Appetite is either depraved or altogether lost, when you are irritable and peevish, and sleep badly at night, then your Liver is out of order.

Now when you feel like this, and that it is with you not an uncommon occurrence, do not delay, but tone up the Liver and Digestive Organs by a few doses of Guy's Tonic, and you will find prompt and permanent relief.

Mr. J. CLARKSON makes the following interesting Statement—

"I am anxious you should publish my case on account of the obstinacy and severity of the Symptoms. For years I had been suffering fearfully from an inactive sluggish Liver, accompanied by Indigestion and Low Spirits.

"I consulted some of the best Physicians in England, and although all pronounced it the same, 'a torpid, inactive Liver, aggravated by Indigestion,' their treatment and remedies were alike unavailing. I positively spent £185 in Doctors' bills. You, Sirs, may not know the misery of taking bottle after bottle of Doctors' physic, without the slightest relief from pain or amelioration of one single Symptom. I am thankful to state, however, that I was completely cured by taking your wonderful Guy's Tonic.

"I saw an advertisement of yours stating 'Improvement follows the first dose.' This I can say was truthfully so in my case; I had not taken the first dose of Guy's Tonic ten minutes before I felt its beneficial influence on the Liver and Digestive Organs. The distressing Despondency and Nervousness disappeared as if by magic; the dull, aching pain between the Shoulders, constant Headache, tenderness about the Liver, flushing of the Face after meals, Drowsiness, Giddiness, Flatulency, and the other Symptoms have not returned, and it is now eighteen months since my Restoration took place."

Thousands of Voluntary Testimonials are on File. The Originals may be inspected by anyone interested at 12, Buckingham Palace Road, London, the Head Office of Guy's Tonic Company.

Stomach Troubles Cured by Guy's Tonic.

"Point Cot
"I have used Guy's Tonic in my family for Stomach troub
"and its effects have been such that I never fail to recomme
"Tonic is far away the best Tonic I have ever tried. (Rev.) '

Doctors Recommend Guy's Tonic.

"Mowbray House, Norfolk Str
"I often use Guy's Tonic myself with advantage, and o
"prescribes it as one of the best Tonics he can give.
"EDWIN H. STOUT, Manager

Guy's Tonic is a British Preparation of sin
It is now employed in Hospital Practice, a
mended by Medical Men.
A new size (Six Ounce) Bottle of Guy's T
now on sale at all Chemists' and Stores.

FIGURE 4-20. Patent medicines of the nineteenth century often contained cocaine as a "secret ingredient." Needless to say, the unregulated consumption of such remedies could be extremely harmful to an unsuspecting public.

can have tragic effects when users attempt to drive cars or operate other equipment. Other effects reported by some, but not all, persons include reduced inhibitions, increased sexual pleasure (which may simply reflect increased sensitivity to all sensations), and feelings of relaxation.

At the present time marijuana is one of the most widely used drugs throughout the world. Despite its popularity, though, it involves potential dangers. First, as we have already noted, the perceptual distortions it produces can yield tragedy when users attempt to drive or work power machinery. Second, because it is still illegal in many nations, it is often blended with other substances; thus, users never know exactly what they are getting. Third, there is some indication that long-term use of marijuana may result in passivity—a general lack of energy or motivation (Baumrind, 1984). Finally, marijuana may also impair several kinds of learning or information processing. The pleasure some people find in this drug, therefore, must be weighed against potential dangers in its use. For a summary of the effects of a wide range of different drugs, please refer to Table 4-2.

Consciousness-Altering Drugs: Some Factors Affecting Their Use

While use of drugs to alter states of consciousness is widespread, not everyone chooses to follow this route. Why? What factors predispose an individual toward or away from the use of such substances? This is a complex issue, still under active study. Before concluding, though, we will mention some factors which seem to play a role in this process.

First, it appears that individuals who use one type of drug often use others, as well. One possible explanation for this finding might be termed the *escalation hypothesis*—the suggestion that the use of fairly mild drugs leads in many cases to the use of stronger and

TABLE 4-2

As shown here, drugs can produce a wide range of effects and can alter consciousness in many ways.

Drug	Effects
Depressants	
ALCOHOL	Reduced inhibitions and anxiety; interferes with information processing; leads to extreme forms of social behavior
BARBITURATES	Reduced anxiety, tension; feelings of euphoria
OPIATES	Lethargy, slowing of many bodily functions; dream-like state, "rush" of pleasure
Stimulants	
AMPHETAMINES	Increased alertness, activation; feeling of heightened energy
COCAINE	Tremendous surge of energy; restless activity; feelings of unlimited power or energy
CAFFEINE	Increased alertness, clarity of thought; wakefulness
TOBACCO	Increased alertness; reduced nervousness (calming effect)
Hallucinogens	
MARIJUANA	Feelings of relaxation; heightened sensory experiences; euphoria; mild hallucinations
MESCALINE	Distortion of sensory processes; hallucinations
LSD	Feeling of exhilaration; distortion of sensory processes

more dangerous ones as individuals require greater and greater stimulation to get their "kicks." A second, and perhaps more reasonable, possibility is that several variables (e.g., personal unconventionality, friends who demonstrate deviant or illegal behavior, low parental control) may predispose individuals toward the use of a wide range of drugs. Recent evidence offers stronger support for this second possibility (Hays et al., 1987). It appears that when individuals are exposed to certain kinds of life experiences, the likelihood increases that they will use a wide variety of drugs.

Second, there seems to be a link between specific personality traits and the use of several drugs. In particular, the higher individuals' need for change and stimulation (the higher their *sensation-seeking*), the more likely they are to use various drugs. Moreover, contrary to what you might expect, this is not restricted to the use of stimulants; persons high in sensation-seeking are also more likely than others to use depressants such as alcohol. These findings suggest that persons with a high need for stimulation or change simply enjoy *any* change in their feelings or consciousness. Thus, they may be more likely than others to "experiment" with many different drugs.

To conclude: whether, and to what extent, specific persons use drugs to alter their own state of consciousness seems to depend on many different factors. Thus, predicting whether a given individual will use—or abuse—such substances is definitely a complex task.

Summary and Review

Controlled and Automatic Processing

Consciousness refers to our awareness of ourselves and the world around us. Even during normal activities we often enter what may be viewed as an altered state of consciousness when we make use of *automatic processing*. Activities controlled in this manner proceed without conscious attention and can be performed in an efficient manner. However, they are not readily open to modification. In contrast, *controlled processing* requires careful attention to the task at hand, and such activities proceed more slowly. This state is more flexible than automatic processing, however.

Daydreams and Fantasies

Everyone has *daydreams* or *fantasies,* but individuals differ greatly in the frequency or vividness of such self-induced shifts in consciousness. While the content of daydreams and fantasies varies greatly, several themes are common (e.g., success or failure, guilt, problem-solving). Both men and women report having frequent sexual fantasies, but the sexes seem to differ with respect to the specific content of such fantasies.

Sleep and Dreams

Sleep occupies almost one-third of our lives. It is not a unitary process. Rather, we seem to cycle through several stages of sleep each night. *REM sleep,* named for the rapid eye-movements that accompany it, is different from other stages of sleep. Sleep affects your mood, and your current mood, in turn, affects the quality of sleep. Sleep disorders include *insomnia, night terrors,* and *apnea.* Recent findings suggest that insomnia may stem from disorders in thermoregulatory mechanisms within the brain. Most *dreams* occur during REM sleep. Several explanations for the occurrence of dreams exist, but at present most psychologists believe they reflect efforts by our cognitive systems (e.g., memory) to make sense out of random, diffuse activity in the sleeping brain.

Hypnotism

Hypnotism involves interaction between two persons in which the hypnotist makes suggestions that change the behavior, perceptions, or consciousness of the subject. There is currently disagreement among psychologists as to whether the effects produced by hypnotism require entry into a trance state. However, there is general agreement that hypnotized individuals show increased susceptibility to suggestions or commands from others, distortions in perception and information processing, and *dissociation*—a division of consciousness. Not all persons can be hypnotized. Those who have a rich and vivid fantasy life and who can readily become deeply absorbed in various activities seem to be most susceptible to this process. In recent years, hypnotism has been used to treat a wide range of behavioral disorders, with promising success.

Drugs and Consciousness

Some individuals use drugs to alter their state of consciousness. *Depressants* such as alcohol and barbiturates reduce activity in the central nervous system. They induce pleasurable feelings of relaxation, but they also interfere with both motor and cognitive processes. *Stimulants,* such as caffeine, nicotine, or cocaine, increase neural activity. These drugs yield feelings of energy, exhilaration, and self-confidence, but they may be followed by deep depression, fatigue, and anxiety when the drug wears off. *Hallucinogens* such as marijuana or LSD affect perceptions and other aspects of consciousness. The effects of LSD are unpredictable and may be pleasant or intensely frightening to the same person at different times. Marijuana, a widely used drug, produces weaker effects (e.g., intensification of many sensations, mild distortions in the sense of time). However, because it interferes with ability to judge distances, it should never be used by persons who plan to drive. Drug use seems related to many factors, such as lack of parental control when young and the presence of others who behave in an unconventional manner. It may also be linked to individuals' need for change and stimulation (*sensation seeking*).

Key Terms

Automatic Processing Processing of information without conscious awareness.

Consciousness Awareness of external and internal stimuli (yourself, your behavior, and the world around you).

Controlled Processing Processing of information with conscious awareness.

Daydreams (Fantasies) Imaginary scenes and events that occur while you are awake.

Depressants Drugs that reduce activity in the nervous system and therefore slow many bodily and cognitive processes (e.g., alcohol, barbiturates).

Dreams Cognitive events, often vivid and detailed, that occur during sleep. Most dreams take place during REM sleep.

Electroencephalogram A record of electrical activity occurring within the brain. EEGs play an important role in the scientific study of sleep.

Hallucinogens Drugs that exert profound effects upon states of consciousness (e.g., marijuana, LSD).

Hypersomnia Sleep disorder involving excessive amounts of sleep or an overwhelming urge to fall asleep (e.g., narcolepsy).

Hypnosis An interaction between two persons in which one (the hypnotist) induces changes in the behavior, feelings, or cognitions of the other (the subject) through suggestions. These may be delivered while the subject is in an altered state of consciousness (a trance).

REM Sleep A stage of sleep in which brain activity resembling waking restfulness is accompanied by profound muscle relaxation and rapid eye-movements. Most dreams occur during periods of REM sleep.

Sleep A process in which important physiological changes (e.g., shifts in brain activity, slowing of basic bodily functions) are accompanied by profound alterations in consciousness.

Somnambulism A sleep disorder in which individuals actually get up and move about while still asleep.

Stimulants Drugs that increase activity in the nervous system (e.g., amphetamines, caffeine, nicotine).

For More Information

Bowers, K.S. (1983). *Hypnosis for the seriously curious,* 2nd ed. Monterey, CA: Brooks/Cole.
A brief and well-written introduction to this fascinating topic. Scientific evidence concerning the existence of hypnosis is reviewed, and factors that seem to make individuals susceptible or resistant to hypnosis are considered. An excellent place to start if you'd like to know more about hypnosis.

Coleman, R.M. (1986). *Wide awake at 3:00 a.m.: By choice or by chance?* New York: W.H. Freeman.
An up-to-date discussion of a subject not discussed in this chapter: biological rhythms. The information on "day people" and "night people," as well as on several related topics, makes fascinating reading.

Dement, W.C. (1975). *Some must sleep while some must watch.* San Francisco: W.H. Freeman.
An excellent summary of existing knowledge about sleep. While the book is more than a decade old, much of the information it presents is still accurate, and its clear writing style makes it highly recommended.

Wallace, B., & Fisher, L.E. (1987). *Consciousness and behavior,* 2nd ed. Boston: Allyn and Bacon.
A very readable summary of current information about many aspects of consciousness. The chapters on hypnosis, sleep and dreams, and consciousness-altering drugs all expand in useful ways the coverage in this chapter.

CHAPTER

5

Learning:
How We're
Changed by
Experience

"Ready?" Gary Scolan calls out to his friend Earl Ketterer.

"Uh, no, not quite . . ." Earl replies slowly. And, in fact, he really *isn't* ready. Blind dates terrify him. How can he go through with it? His palms are sweating, he can't swallow, and his stomach feels as though it's tied in knots.

Just then, Gary sticks his head into the bathroom. "C'mon, already! You look good enough. You know Jan hates me to be late."

"I d-don't know," Earl stammers, "I'm not feeling well . . . maybe you should go without me."

"Oh come on, don't start that stuff again! It's only a blind date." Gary has a note of irritation in his voice.

"That's right, kid around—these things don't bother you. But it's different for me. I get so nervous. . . . No, go ahead without me."

Gary looks at his friend with sympathy. He knows about Earl's fear of meeting new people, and he realizes that it causes him a lot of pain. But he can't for the life of him figure it out.

"What's it all about, Earl?" he asks. "Why do you get so up tight about these things? You're an O.K. guy."

"I don't know," Earl replies, shaking his head. "I really try, but nothing helps. I get so nervous I can hardly stand it."

"But *why*?" Gary asks. "What can happen? If you don't hit it off, it's no big deal."

"Yeah, but suppose I do something really dumb, and make a fool of myself. I couldn't stand it! No leave me here. I'll only ruin everything anyway."

Sitting down, Gary becomes more serious. "O.K., you don't have to go if you don't want to. But tell me what's *really* bothering you. How did you get like this in the first place?"

"I don't know, I just don't know," Earl answers, a look of misery on his face. After a brief pause, he continues. "Well, maybe I *do*. I think it all started when I was in the fourth grade. I was in a class play, and I got sick right on stage. Threw up all over myself and three other kids. Yech! It was awful!" Earl shudders visibly. "Since then, I get real nervous whenever I think people are watching me. And it seems to be getting worse, not better."

"Whew!" Gary mutters with a whistle. "Heavy stuff! But you've got to get over it somehow. I mean, you can't let something that happened so long ago ruin your life. It makes no sense."

"I know, I've got to get it out of my system some way."

"Well, look, try not to think about it. Let's just go out and have some fun. I promise I'll cover for you if any touchy situation develops, O.K.?" And with this, Gary takes Earl by the arm and, ignoring his protests, steers him toward the door and their evening's adventure.

Do you remember the first time you drove a car, tried to play a musical instrument, or operated a computer? If so, you probably recall that your performance on any of these tasks was far from perfect. In fact, you probably had great difficulty keeping the car in lane, hitting the right notes, or getting any correct responses out of the gleaming screen in front of you. If you persevered, though, the situation soon changed. Each of the tasks seemed easier, and you made fewer and fewer errors. This illustrates an important principle about behavior: all organisms—especially human beings—have the capacity to profit from experience. Under normal conditions, they can acquire the behaviors, skills, and knowledge needed to function in a complex world.

Psychologists refer to such changes as **learning.** Specifically, they define this process as follows: *learning is any relatively permanent change in behavior (or behavior potential) produced by experience.* This definition seems straightforward, but several

FIGURE 5-1. Learning plays an important role in all the activities shown here and in virtually any others you can imagine.

points about it are worth noting. First, the term *learning* does not apply to temporary changes in behavior such as those stemming from fatigue, drugs, or illness. Second, it does not refer to changes resulting from maturation—the fact that you change in many ways as you grow and develop. Third, learning can result from *vicarious* as well as from direct experiences. In other words, you can be affected by observing events in the world around you as well as by participating in them (Bandura, 1986).

Finally, the changes produced by learning are not always positive in nature. As you well know, people are as likely to acquire bad habits as good ones, and in some cases the results of learning can be devastating for the person involved. (Recall poor Earl, who acquired an intense fear of certain social situations.)

So, to repeat, learning involves lasting changes in behavior resulting from experience—from our direct or vicarious interactions with the world around us. Defined in these terms, there can be no doubt that learning is a key process in human behavior. Indeed, it seems to play a role in virtually every activity we perform—from mastering complex skills to falling in love (refer to Figure 5-1). While its effects are diverse, however, many psychologists believe it occurs in only three major forms: **classical conditioning, operant conditioning,** and **observational learning.** We will focus on all three in this chapter.

Classical Conditioning: Learning That Some Stimuli Signal Others

Imagine the following situation. You're visiting friends. It's 7:00 a.m., and you are drifting somewhere between sleep and waking. In the next room you hear a soft click. Then, almost immediately, you are practically knocked out of bed by a loud noise. You are about to rush out of your room to find out what's happened, when you figure it out: your friends have switched on the bathroom fan, and, being old, it is extremely noisy. You try to go back to sleep, but your heart is pounding so hard that you decide to get up, too.

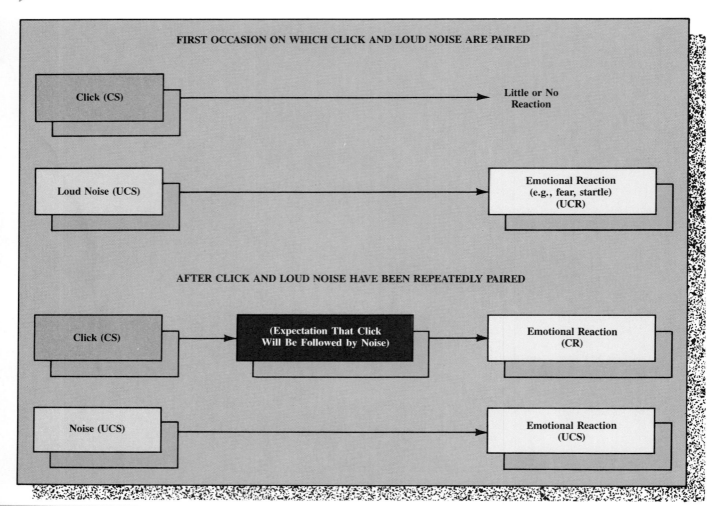

FIRST OCCASION ON WHICH CLICK AND LOUD NOISE ARE PAIRED

Click (CS) ──────────────────────────→ Little or No Reaction

Loud Noise (UCS) ──────────────────────────→ Emotional Reaction (e.g., fear, startle) (UCR)

AFTER CLICK AND LOUD NOISE HAVE BEEN REPEATEDLY PAIRED

Click (CS) → (Expectation That Click Will Be Followed by Noise) → Emotional Reaction (CR)

Noise (UCS) ──────────────────────────→ Emotional Reaction (UCS)

FIGURE 5-2. At first, a soft click would have little effect on your behavior (top diagram). After the click has been paired with a loud noise on several occasions, you might react emotionally to the click alone (lower diagram). This reaction would be the result of classical conditioning.

Classical Conditioning: A Simple Example

Since you are staying with your friends for two weeks, the same events are repeated each morning. Would there be any change in your behavior during this period? The chances are good there would be. Gradually, you might begin to respond not just to the sound of the fan, but to the soft click as well. The reason is simple: since it is always followed by the noisy fan, the click comes to serve as a signal for the onset of this loud, irritating sound. In other words, hearing the click, you expect the fan noise to follow, and you react accordingly—you are startled and you experience increased arousal (refer to Figure 5-2).

This simple incident provides an everyday example of *classical conditioning,* the first type of learning we will consider. In classical conditioning a stimulus which is initially unable to elicit a response gradually acquires the ability to do so as a result of repeated pairing with a stimulus that *can* elicit such a reaction. Learning of this type is quite common, and it seems to play a role in such varied reactions as strong fears, some aspects of sexual behavior, and perhaps even racial or ethnic prejudice (Baron & Byrne, 1987). Despite this fact, though, it was not the subject of careful study until the early twentieth century, when Ivan Pavlov, a Nobel Prize-winning physiologist, identified it as an important behavioral process.

The Nature of Classical Conditioning: Pavlov's Early Work

In one of those strange twists of fate which seem so common in the history of science, Pavlov did not set out to investigate classical conditioning. Rather, his research was

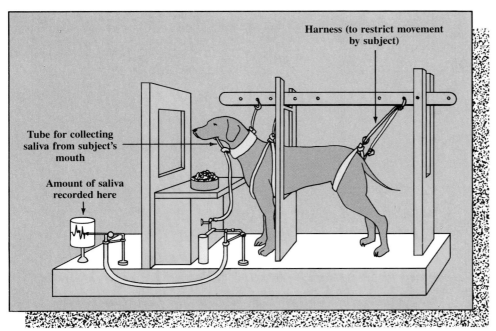

FIGURE 5-3. Pavlov used equipment similar to this in his early experiments on classical conditioning. A tube inserted in the dog's mouth carried drops of saliva to an instrument which kept a precise record of this reaction.

concerned with the process of digestion. During his investigations he noticed a curious fact: the dogs which were subjects in his studies often began to salivate when they saw or smelled food, before they actually tasted it. Indeed, some even salivated at the sight of the pan where their food was kept or at the sight of the person who usually brought it. This suggested to Pavlov that these stimuli had somehow become *signals* for the food itself: the dogs had learned that when the signals were present, food would soon follow. Pavlov quickly recognized the potential importance of this process and shifted his attention to it.

The procedures he used to study such learning were relatively simple. Dogs were placed in the apparatus shown in Figure 5-3. On *conditioning trials,* some neutral stimulus (a bell) which had previously been shown to have no effect upon salivation was presented. This was followed, almost at once, by a second stimulus known to produce a strong effect on salivation (dried meat powder squirted directly into the dog's mouth). The bell was termed a **conditioned stimulus (CS)** because it did not at first produce salivation. The meat powder was termed the **unconditioned stimulus (UCS)** because it produced salivation even the first time it was presented. Similarly, salivation in response to the bell was termed a **conditioned response (CR),** while salivation to the meat powder was termed an **unconditioned response (UCR).** For an example of a stimulus which will almost certainly elicit a conditioned response from *you,* please see Figure 5-4 (page 140).

The basic question, of course, was this: would the bell sound gradually acquire the ability to elicit salivation as a result of its repeated pairing with the meat powder? In other words, would it evoke a conditioned response from subjects when it was presented alone? The answer was clear: it did. After the bell had been paired with the meat powder on a number of occasions, the dogs would salivate upon hearing it, even when the bell was not followed by a squirt of meat powder.

Classical Conditioning and Human Behavior. "O.K.," we can almost hear you saying, "so dogs learn to salivate to a bell or other stimulus that is presented right before they receive food. So what? What does this tell us about people?" The answer is: quite a bit. As Figure 5-5 (page 140) suggests, classical conditioning is actually a common form of learning among human beings as well as other organisms. In fact, as we noted earlier, it plays a role in such important reactions as fear, prejudice, and even certain forms of sexual behavior. As an example of such effects, let's consider the role of classical conditioning in learned fear.

**A Familiar (and Powerful!)
Conditioned Stimulus**

FIGURE 5-4. Does this photo cause you to salivate? If it does, this is the result of classical conditioning. Your reaction is produced by the sight of this stimulus, even though you can't taste it.

Imagine the following scene. An eleven-month-old child named Albert is shown a white laboratory rat. His initial reactions are positive: he smiles and attempts to pet it. Just as he reaches out for the rat, though, an iron bar is struck to make a loud noise right behind his ear. Albert's reaction to this sound is immediate: he jumps, cries, and shows every sign of being terrified. These procedures are repeated again and again. Each time the rat is presented, the terrifying noise follows. The result: Albert soon begins to cry and to show other signs of fear whenever the rat is presented, even when it is *not* followed by the noise.

This sequence of events was actually performed by Watson and Raynor (1920) nearly seventy years ago in a study that is now a classic in psychology. The study itself certainly fails to meet the rigorous standards followed in modern psychological research. Precise control was not maintained over several factors which might have affected the results; for example, the intensity of the loud noise was not precisely measured, and data were collected from only one subject. Moreover, serious questions can be raised about the ethics of this investigation. Is it appropriate to badly frighten a young child, even if doing so will yield new information about a basic form of learning? Reasonable people can disagree—and disagree quite strongly—over this point. Still, with all its drawbacks Watson and Raynor's study suggests that human beings can sometimes acquire strong fears through classical conditioning, and this is an important finding.

The story does not end there, however. In recent years many other investigations have uncovered similar effects. In one example of such research (Hygge & Ohman, 1978), adult subjects viewed a series of slides, including pictures of snakes. For one group (those undergoing conditioning), each time a snake photo appeared, it was followed by a mild but unpleasant electric shock to the fingers. For another group, an equal number of shocks were presented, but these were *not* paired with the snakes in a consistent manner. The results of such procedures were clear: subjects who received a shock each time they saw a picture of a snake soon reacted emotionally to such photos, showing signs of

FIGURE 5-5. As shown in this cartoon, classical conditioning is common among human beings as well as other species. Do you also react to the sound of opening cans or bottles? *(Source: King Features Syndicate, Inc.)*

**Classical Conditioning and
Human Behavior**

increased arousal even when these stimuli were not followed by shocks. In contrast, those who received random shocks did not demonstrate such reactions. The persons participating in such studies did not report strong fear of snakes initially. Thus, they seemed to acquire such reactions during the experiment as a result of classical conditioning. (Please note: these reactions are quite weak and quickly fade once the experiment is over.)

To mention just one more example of the impact of classical conditioning on human behavior, some evidence suggests that articles of clothing or other stimuli that are repeatedly paired with sexual arousal or pleasure may become conditioned stimuli for such reactions (Griffitt & Hatfield, 1985). To the extent they do, persons who have undergone such learning may seek such stimuli to intensify their reactions, and may even find it difficult to enjoy sexual relations without them. Certainly, such effects are far removed from Pavlov's experiments with ringing bells and salivating dogs. But they, too, may rest, at least in part, on the same process of classical conditioning.

Classical Conditioning: Some Basic Principles

So far, we've merely described the basic nature of classical conditioning—what this process is all about. At this point, we'll take a closer look at some of the principles that govern its occurrence.

Acquisition: The Course of Classical Conditioning.   We've already noted that classical conditioning is usually a gradual process: a conditioned stimulus gradually acquires the capacity to evoke a conditioned response as a result of repeated pairing with an unconditioned stimulus. In fact, such conditioning often occurs as shown in Figure 5-6. At first, it proceeds quite rapidly. After a number of pairings of the CS and UCS, it slows down. Finally, it levels off as conditioning nears completion. As we will soon see, though, there are some important exceptions to this general rule; in some instances conditioning can occur very quickly—even after a single pairing between a CS and a UCS

FIGURE 5-6. As the number of pairings between a CS (conditioned stimulus) and UCS (unconditioned stimulus) increase, the strength of the CR (conditioned response) rises gradually.

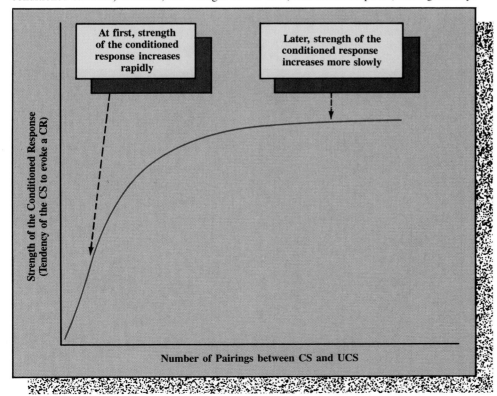

Acquisition of a Conditioned Response

(Rescorla, 1988). One additional point: in order for classical conditioning to occur, the CS must precede the UCS; if the CS occurs after the UCS is presented, little or no conditioning will occur.

Extinction: Getting Rid of "Excess Baggage."   Imagine that you are back visiting your friends with the noisy fan. After a few days of listening to this racket each morning, you can't bear it any longer and ask them to get the fan repaired. Being good hosts, they do, so now the sound of the switch is no longer followed by a loud racket. Will you continue to react strongly to this click? In all likelihood, you won't. Gradually, the click will cease to evoke conditioned responses from you. This process, through which the effects of prior conditioning are reduced and finally disappear, is known as **extinction.** It plays an important role, for if extinction did not occur, we would soon become walking collections of useless—but persistent—conditioned responses.

Interestingly, the course of extinction is not entirely smooth. If a CS that has ceased to produce conditioned reactions is presented again at a later time, it may evoke such responses once more, although in weakened form. This is known as *spontaneous recovery*. If extinction is then continued (the CS is presented repeatedly but no UCS follows), such reactions decrease and finally disappear entirely.

Generalization and Discrimination: Responding to Similarities and Differences. Suppose that because of several painful experiences, a child has acquired a strong conditioned fear of wasps: whenever he sees one, or hears one buzzing, he shows strong emotional reactions and heads for the hills! Will he also react in the same manner to similar insects, such as bees? He almost certainly will. The reason lies in a process called **stimulus generalization,** the tendency of stimuli similar to a conditioned stimulus to evoke similar conditioned responses (e.g., Honig & Urcuioli, 1981; Pearce, 1986). As you can readily see, stimulus generalization often serves a useful function. In this example, it may save the boy from several additional stings. To mention just one additional example, sirens on police cars, fire trucks, and ambulances do not sound exactly alike. Yet, because of stimulus generalization, we react strongly to all of them.

FIGURE 5-7. Many organisms turn *stimulus generalization* to their benefit. They mimic the appearance of poisonous species and thereby increase their own chances of survival. Because of *stimulus generalization,* predators perceive the harmless organism as poisonous, too, and seek other prey. For example, as illustrated below, the sea slug (left) mimics the appearance of the poisonous sea anemone (right) to ward off predators.

Stimulus Generalization: A Tool for Survival

Stimulus Generalization: One Questionable Use

FIGURE 5-8. Mail-order businesses sometimes try to profit from *stimulus generalization*. They design their ads to resemble letters from the IRS or other government agencies.

Many animals turn the existence of stimulus generalization to their advantage. For example, some insects which are totally harmless mimic the coloring of more dangerous species and so ward off would-be predators. Similarly, some frogs that would make a tasty mouthful for birds show markings highly similar to those of poisonous species, so increasing their chances of survival (refer to Figure 5-7).

Stimulus discrimination is, in a sense, the other side of the coin. It refers to the fact that when stimuli similar to a CS in some manner are *not* followed by a UCS, reactions to them are weakened and soon disappear. You have probably encountered many examples of such stimulus discrimination. For example, some mail-order companies attempt to capture consumers' attention by putting their ads in envelopes resembling ones used by the U.S. Internal Revenue Service (see Figure 5-8). Since many people have received refund checks or notices of tax audits in such envelopes, they often have strong emotional reactions to them. Thus, they are unlikely to throw these ads away at first. After receiving a number of such bogus letters, though, most persons learn to notice the difference between them and the ones actually sent by the IRS. Once they do, their treatment of the promotional letters is quite different than it was initially!

Classical Conditioning: A Cognitive Perspective

During his early experiments Pavlov (1927) observed the following curious events. A dog was conditioned to the ticking of a metronome. (This sound had been repeatedly paired with the presentation of food.) When the metronome was turned off, the dog didn't take this event lying down. Instead, it sat in front of the machine and proceeded to whine and beg. Why? If conditioning involves only the development of an *association* between the CS and UCS, then the dog should respond only to the CS. The fact that it appeared to beg for the ticking sound suggests that classical conditioning involves more than just this. In fact, this and several related findings point to the following conclusion: regular pairing of a CS with a UCS provides subjects with valuable information—it indicates that whenever a CS is presented, a UCS will shortly follow. Thus, as conditioning proceeds, subjects acquire the *expectation* that a CS will be followed by a UCS.

In this context, the dog's behavior is easy to understand. During conditioning, the dog learned that the ticking of the metronome signaled the delivery of food. Then, without any warning, this fickle machine stopped working. Obviously, *something* had to be done to get it started, so the dog acted on its expectancies: it whined and begged for it to tick again. The suggestion that *cognitive processes* such as these play a role in classical conditioning is supported by several types of evidence. First, as we noted in our discussion of acquired fears (see page 140), conditioning fails to occur when a UCS is paired with a CS in a random manner. Under such conditions, of course, subjects cannot acquire any firm expectation that a UCS will indeed follow presentation of a CS. The UCS–CS pairing must be consistent for conditioning to occur.

Second, it is supported by a phenomenon known as *blocking*. This refers to the fact that, sometimes, conditioning to one stimulus may be prevented by previous conditioning to another stimulus. For example, suppose that subjects are first conditioned to a tone: each time it occurs, food is presented. Then, a second stimulus (e.g., a light) is added to the situation. It, too, occurs just before the presentation of food. If classical conditioning occurs in an automatic manner, simply as a result of repeated pairings of a CS and UCS, then the light, too, should become a conditioned stimulus: it should elicit salivation when presented alone. In fact, this is not the case. Why? Again, an explanation in terms of expectancies is helpful. Since the food is already predicted by the tone, the light provides no new information. It is therefore of little value to subjects and fails to become a conditioned stimulus.

Findings such as these suggest that classical conditioning involves much more than the formation of simple associations between specific stimuli. Indeed, modern views of such conditioning conceive of it as a complex process in which organisms form rich representations of the *relationships* existing between a wide variety of events—including many aspects of the physical setting or context in which the CS and UCS are presented (Balsam & Tomie, 1985; Rescorla, 1988).

We should add that this cognitive perspective on classical conditioning has also been extended to several of its basic aspects. For example, one recent theory of stimulus generalization suggests that memory and other cognitive events play a role in this process (Pearce, 1986). Specifically, during conditioning organisms form a representation, in memory, of the stimuli that preceded the UCS. When they then encounter different stimuli at later times, they compare these with the information stored in memory. The greater the similarity between current stimuli and such memory representations, the stronger the response now evoked. In short, both memory and active comparison processes play a role in what might, at first, seem to be an automatic function.

Probably, you do not find the suggestion that cognitive processes play a role in human classical conditioning surprising. You know that *you* have expectancies about what events go together or are likely to follow one another. But does it make sense to talk about expectancies and other cognitive events for animals? Ten or fifteen years ago, many psychologists would have answered ''no.'' Now, most hold the opposite view (Pearce, 1987). So, don't be surprised to find further references to the role of cognitive processes throughout this chapter; in many cases, they are essential for full understanding of basic forms of learning. (Can *any* neutral stimulus become a CS for virtually *any* UCS? Or is it easier to condition some stimuli than others? For some surprising conclusions about these questions, please see the ''Classic Contributions'' section below.)

FOCUS ON RESEARCH: Classic Contributions

How General Are Conditioning Principles? Biological Constraints on Learning

At the turn of the century when psychologists began the systematic study of learning, they noticed that some species could master certain tasks more quickly than others. Such findings sparked little interest, though, because early researchers saw their task as that of establishing *general principles of learning*—principles which would apply equally well to all organisms and to all stimuli. For several decades it was widely assumed that such principles existed. Beginning in the 1960s, though, some puzzling findings began to accumulate. These results suggested that all organisms do *not* learn all responses or all associations between stimuli with equal ease. Perhaps the most dramatic evidence pointing to such conclusions—and certainly the research that got many psychologists thinking about this issue in a new way—was reported by Garcia and his colleagues (e.g., Garcia, Hankins, & Rusiniak, 1974; Braverman & Bronstein, 1985).

In perhaps the most famous of these studies, Garcia and Koelling (1966) allowed two groups of rats to sip water containing saccharine, an artificial sweetener. Next, the rats in one of these groups received an injection that made them sick to their stomachs. Those in the other group received a strong electric shock to the foot. Both groups were then tested for a learned aversion to the sweet taste. Traditional principles of conditioning suggest that both should acquire a negative reaction to the sweet liquid; after all, in both cases the stimulus was followed by a strong UCS (nausea in one case, electric shock in the other). But this was *not* what Garcia and Koelling found. Instead, rats who received the nausea-inducing injec-

tions showed much more conditioning (as measured by a tendency to avoid the sweet-tasting water) than those who received the electric shock (refer to Figure 5-9).

Another interesting finding was that, although the rats who received the injections did not become ill immediately, they still acquired an aversion to the sweet taste. This seemed to contradict the widely held belief that classical conditioning could occur only if the UCS followed the CS within a very short interval. (It is interesting to note that these results were so surprising that Garcia and Koelling experienced great difficulty in getting them published. Reviewers were reluctant to recommend that their paper be accepted by leading journals.)

In another part of their study, Garcia and Koelling exposed two new groups of rats to a combination of light and noise when they drank water. All rats in one group then received nausea-producing injections, while those in the other re-

FIGURE 5-9. Rats quickly acquired an aversion to a sweet-tasting liquid when it was followed by an injection that made them ill. In contrast, they did *not* readily acquire an aversion to the sweet taste when it was followed by an electric shock. In contrast, rats learned to avoid a light-noise combination when it was paired with shock, but *not* when it was followed by a nausea-inducing injection. These findings indicate that classical conditioning cannot be established with equal ease for all stimuli and for all organisms. *(Source: Based on data from Garcia & Koelling, 1966.)*

Evidence for the Existence of Biological Constraints on Learning

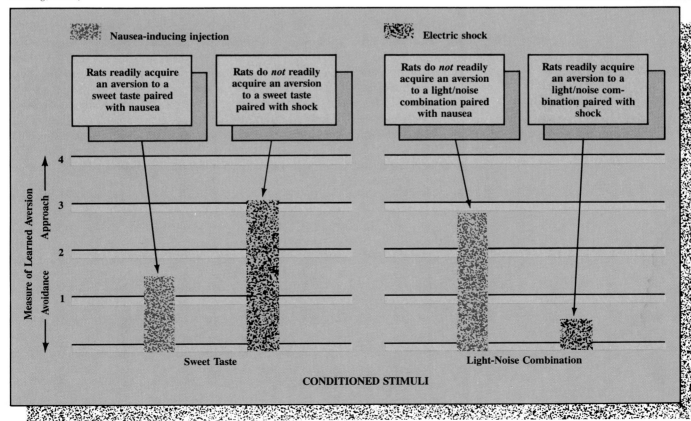

ceived electric shock. Again, traditional principles of conditioning suggest that both groups should learn to avoid the light-noise combination, yet results indicated that subjects exposed to the shocks acquired a much stronger aversion than those who received injections. In short, it seemed as though the rats found it easier to associate the light and noise with shock than with later physical illness.

Similar findings were soon reported in many different studies (Braverman & Bronstein, 1985). Together, such evidence points to three important facts. First, conditioning can sometimes occur even when there is a long delay between a CS and a UCS (this can be as long as several hours; Andrews & Braverman, 1975). Second, some types of conditioning occur very rapidly—perhaps after a single pairing between a CS and a UCS. Third, and perhaps most important of all, classical conditioning cannot be established with equal ease for all stimuli and all organisms. Important differences exist among species, so that types of conditioning readily accomplished by some are only slowly acquired by others. And often, the types of conditioning most readily accom-

plished by one species are the very ones it needs to survive in its normal habitat. For example, rats eat a varied diet and are most active at night. Thus, it is especially useful for them to be able to associate specific tastes with later illness, since in many cases they can't see the foods they eat. In contrast, birds depend heavily upon vision for finding food. For a bird it is more useful to be able to form associations between visual cues and later illness. This, too, has been shown to be the case (Wilcoxon, Dragoin, & Kral, 1971).

In sum, contrary to earlier beliefs, all types of conditioning are not equally easy to establish for all organisms. Rather, there are *biological constraints* on this and other forms of learning such that each species seems to come equipped with a nervous system which facilitates those types of learning it finds most useful. This is not to say that classical conditioning is a different process for different species. On the contrary, the basic principles described earlier seem to apply in most instances. However, important differences among species do exist and should not be overlooked. In many cases, they can, and do, matter greatly. ◀

Classical Conditioning: A Note on Its Applications

Before concluding this discussion of classical conditioning, we should call attention to the fact that knowledge about it has been put to many practical uses. We have already mentioned that this form of learning plays a key role in many acquired fears. This, in turn, has led to the development of several effective procedures for reducing such reactions. For example, in one procedure, known as **flooding** (or *implosive therapy*), a person suffering from a specific fear (e.g., fear of dogs, fear of open spaces) is told to imagine contact with the objects or events he or she dreads. Because such thoughts or images are frightening, the individual undergoing flooding often tries to change the subject or think about other matters. It is the therapist's task to keep the fear-inducing images uppermost in the subject's mind—in fact, to make sure the patient is deluged with them (hence the term *flooding*). Because no actual harm then follows (no UCS is paired with the CS), these images and thoughts gradually lose their capacity to evoke emotional reactions. In short, extinction occurs, and the participant's conditioned fear gradually disappears (Agras et al., 1974; Stampfl & Levis, 1967). (Refer to Figure 5-10.)

A second intriguing application of knowledge about classical conditioning is in connection with eating disturbances, such as *anorexia nervosa*. Persons suffering from this disorder literally starve themselves to a point at which their health is adversely affected. Recent investigations (Bernstein & Borson, 1986) suggest that many individuals suffering from this problem experience gastrointestinal discomfort after eating. The result: they acquire a strong aversion to food they have just consumed (recall our discussion of Garcia's research). Unfortunately, such persons also seem to be fairly finicky to begin with—they eat a restricted range of food even before they develop anorexia. For this reason, aversion to even a few of these may reduce their caloric intake to dangerously low levels. We'll return to anorexia and other eating disturbances in Chapters 9 and 13. For now, the main point is this: knowledge about classical conditioning has turned out to be far more useful to human welfare than Pavlov or other early researchers probably ever guessed.

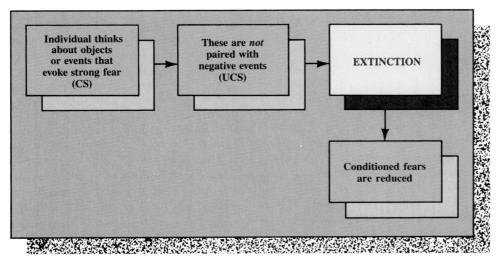

FIGURE 5-10. During *flooding* (or implosive therapy), individuals with intense fears of specific stimuli are made to think about the objects or events they dread. Since these stimuli (which are CS's) are not followed by actual harm (no UCS is present), extinction occurs, and the persons gradually lose their fears.

 ## Operant Conditioning: Learning Based on Consequences

When Kara Eaton started her campaign for state office, her speeches contained many remarks about the need for higher spending. She would note, with considerable passion, that the state's schools were in serious trouble, its roads and bridges were falling apart, and that the salaries paid to its employees were far below the national average. The crowds she addressed, however, weren't favorably impressed by these views. Whenever Kara mentioned raising taxes, many persons present would shake their heads, boo, or get up to leave. Now, several months later, Kara's speeches have a different flavor. She rarely if ever mentions the need for higher spending. Instead, she emphasizes *efficiency*— getting full value from every tax dollar spent. And when she makes such remarks, people smile, applaud, and cheer.

What happened here? Why did Kara change the nature of her speeches? The answer should be obvious: she changed her remarks in response to the *consequences* they produced. Statements that yielded hisses and boos from voters decreased in frequency, while those that yielded applause and cheers increased. In short, Kara learned to perform behaviors that produced positive outcomes and to avoid behaviors that yielded negative ones. This process is known as **operant conditioning** (or *instrumental conditioning*), and it is the second major form of learning we will consider.

The Nature of Operant Conditioning: Principles of Reinforcement

How, precisely, do we learn from the consequences of our own actions? Psychologists generally agree that operant conditioning occurs in response to two major types of events.

First, it involves the impact of **positive reinforcers.** These are stimuli or events which strengthen responses that precede them. In other words, if you perform some action and a positive reinforcer follows, your tendency to perform it again increases (see Figure 5-11 on page 148). Some positive reinforcers seem to exert such effects because they are related to a basic biological need. Such *primary reinforcers* include food (when we are hungry), water (when we are thirsty), and sexual pleasure. In contrast, other events acquire their capacity to act as positive reinforcers through association with primary reinforcers. Among such *conditioned reinforcers* are money, status, and praise from others.

Obviously, subjective reactions to such events are positive, but please note: an event that serves as a positive reinforcer at one time or in one context may have quite a

Positive Reinforcement in Action

FIGURE 5-11. Actions that yield pleasant outcomes (positive reinforcers) tend to be repeated. The person shown here will probably order this dish again when she sees it on the menu of another restaurant.

different effect at another time. For example, food may be a positive reinforcer when you are hungry, but a very unpleasant occurrence when you are in an airplane during a thunderstorm! Also, at least where people are concerned, large individual differences sometimes exist: an event which serves as a positive reinforcer for one person may fail to operate in a similar manner for another (refer to Figure 5-12).

Second, operant conditioning stems from the impact of **negative reinforcers.** These are unpleasant stimuli or events which strengthen responses permitting us to escape from or avoid them. Thus, if you perform some action which permits you to escape from the presence of a negative reinforcer, your tendency to perform this action will increase. Again, some negative reinforcers exert their effects the first time they are encountered (e.g., intense heat, biting cold, electric shock). Others seem to acquire their impact as a result of association with unpleasant events (e.g., public embarrassment, harsh criticism from others). One simple example of operant conditioning based on negative reinforcement can be seen every April 15 in the United States, when millions of citizens rush to mail their tax forms to avoid the even more unpleasant consequences that will follow if they miss this deadline.

At this point, we should clarify a matter about which there is often much confusion. Contrary to what common sense seems to suggest, **punishment** is not the same as negative reinforcement. Punishment occurs in situations where some response is followed by unpleasant stimuli or events, or by the omission of positive events. In such cases, we must *learn not to perform* these actions, or negative consequences will follow. In situations involving negative reinforcement, in contrast, we must *learn to perform* certain responses in order to avoid unpleasant outcomes or escape from them. Perhaps the following example will help clarify matters.

Imagine that your boss warns you against making personal calls from the office. In order to avoid her anger and perhaps the loss of your job, you must refrain from this activity, at least when she is present. This is an example of the impact of punishment: to

FIGURE 5-12. A stimulus that acts as a positive reinforcer for one person does not necessarily have the same effect on others. *(Source: King Features Syndicate, Inc.)*

Individual Differences with Respect to Positive Reinforcers

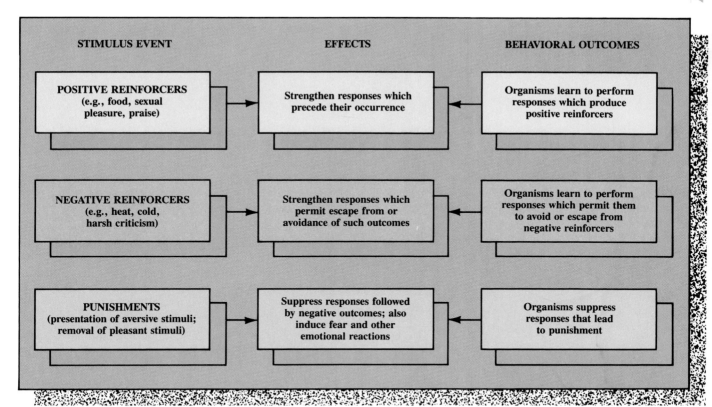

STIMULUS EVENT	EFFECTS	BEHAVIORAL OUTCOMES
POSITIVE REINFORCERS (e.g., food, sexual pleasure, praise)	Strengthen responses which precede their occurrence	Organisms learn to perform responses which produce positive reinforcers
NEGATIVE REINFORCERS (e.g., heat, cold, harsh criticism)	Strengthen responses which permit escape from or avoidance of such outcomes	Organisms learn to perform responses which permit them to avoid or escape from negative reinforcers
PUNISHMENTS (presentation of aversive stimuli; removal of pleasant stimuli)	Suppress responses followed by negative outcomes; also induce fear and other emotional reactions	Organisms suppress responses that lead to punishment

FIGURE 5-13. *Positive reinforcers* strengthen responses that precede them. *Negative reinforcers* strengthen responses that permit us to escape from or avoid them. *Punishment* involves situations in which specific responses are followed by negative outcomes.

Positive Reinforcement, Negative Reinforcement, and Punishment: An Overview

avoid unpleasant outcomes, you suppress a form of behavior you might otherwise demonstrate. Now, despite your boss's warnings, imagine you *do* make personal calls from your desk. One day, you are talking to a friend when your boss suddenly enters the room. To head off her anger, you quickly change what you are saying to create the impression that you are speaking to an important customer. In short, you adopt a form of behavior which enables you to avoid unpleasant outcomes. This is an example of the impact of negative reinforcement. (Please see Figure 5-13 for a summary of the nature and effects of positive reinforcement, negative reinforcement, and punishment.)

Operant Conditioning: Some Basic Aspects

In classical conditioning, the responses performed are generally involuntary; they occur in response to a UCS, and later to a CS, in an automatic manner (e.g., salivation to the taste of food, blinking the eyes in response to a puff of air). In operant conditioning, in contrast, the responses are more voluntary; they are emitted *spontaneously* by organisms in a given environment. In order to understand the nature of operant conditioning, then, we must address two basic questions: (1) why are certain behaviors emitted in the first place? and (2) once they occur, what factors determine the frequency with which they are repeated?

Shaping, and a Few More Words on Biological Constraints.   In order to study operant conditioning under laboratory conditions, psychologists often use two basic types of apparatus. The first is known as a *maze* or *runway* (see Figure 5-14 on page 150). Here, subjects (usually rats) must learn which ways to turn in order to get to some reward (usually food) located at the end of the maze. Since making correct responses yields positive reinforcement, the frequency of such responses usually rises over trials (successive opportunities to run through the maze). The second type of equipment is known as a

Runways: Tools for Studying Operant Conditioning

FIGURE 5-14. Psychologists often use equipment like this runway to study various aspects of operant conditioning.

Skinner box, after its originator, B.F. Skinner. Skinner is a major figure in the history of psychology, for both his research and his outspoken support of the behaviorist perspective. We'll consider his contributions to psychology at several points in this chapter. Subjects (usually pigeons or rats) in a Skinner box must press a lever or peck a bar in order to obtain small pellets of food (see Figure 5-15). Since this is the only response that yields reinforcement, it quickly increases in frequency, and subjects may spend long periods working for their reward.

The responses measured in mazes and Skinner boxes are both simple and natural for the organisms involved: rats often run through tunnels and pecking is common among pigeons. What about behaviors that organisms *don't* spontaneously emit? How can they be established? The answer involves a procedure known as **shaping,** which was first systematically studied by Skinner. In essence, it is based upon the principle that a little—gradually—can go a long way. In shaping, reinforcement is delivered to subjects for each small step toward the final goal—the *target behavior* we'd like them to perform. So, at first, anything even remotely resembling the target behavior is followed by positive reinforcement. Gradually, closer and closer approaches to the final behavior are required before reinforcement is administered. This sounds simple, but does it actually work?

FIGURE 5-15. Another type of equipment often used to study operant conditioning is a Skinner box. A subject can obtain reinforcement, such as pellets of food, by performing simple responses such as pushing a lever or pecking at a disk or bar.

A Skinner Box

Absolutely. If you've ever seen elephants climb on one another into a giant pyramid or tigers jump through burning hoops, you've seen the impressive results that can be achieved through shaping techniques (refer to Figure 5-16). In modified form, shaping can even be applied to human behavior. For example, when working with a beginning student, a skilled dance teacher or ski instructor may praise even simple accomplishments (e.g., performing a basic step, standing on the skis without falling down). As training progresses, however, the teacher requires better and better performance before administering such verbal reinforcement.

As we've already noted, shaping techniques can produce dramatic effects. But consider this question: can they be used to establish virtually *any* form of behavior in *any* organism? If you recall our earlier discussion of biological constraints on classical conditioning, you can probably guess the answer: no. Just as there are biological constraints on classical conditioning, there are constraints on shaping and learning based on consequences. Perhaps this is most clearly illustrated by the experience of two psychologists, Keller and Marian Breland (1961), who attempted to put their expertise in techniques of operant conditioning to commercial use. To do so, they trained various animals to perform unusual tricks, and then exhibited them at state fairs. At first, things went well. Using standard shaping techniques, the Brelands trained chickens to roll plastic capsules holding prizes down a ramp and then peck them into the hands of waiting customers, and pigs to behave in a thrifty manner, depositing silver dollars into a ''piggy'' bank. As time went by, though, their star performers gradually developed some unexpected responses. The chickens began to seize the capsules and pound them against the floor, and the pigs began to throw coins onto the ground and root them about instead of making ''deposits'' in their bank. In short, despite careful training the animals showed what the Brelands termed *instinctive drift*—a tendency to return to the type of behavior they would show under natural conditions. Such findings indicate that operant conditioning, too, is subject to biological constraints. While the power of positive and negative reinforcers is great, natural tendencies are important, too, and can influence the course and results of operant conditioning in many cases.

Shaping: An Effective Technique

FIGURE 5-16. Through *shaping,* animals can be trained to perform many unusual tricks.

Schedules of Reinforcement: Different Rules for Delivery of ''Payoffs.''   As you probably already realize, reinforcement is often an uncertain event under natural conditions. Sometimes a given response yields reinforcement, but sometimes it does not. For example, smiling at an attractive stranger sometimes produces a return smile and additional positive outcomes. On other occasions, however, it may be followed by a suspicious frown or other rejection. Similarly, putting a coin in a pay phone usually permits you to dial and place your call. Sometimes, though, you merely lose the money.

In such cases, the occurrence or nonoccurrence of reinforcement seems to be random or unpredictable. In many other cases, though, its presence is governed by rules. For example, paychecks are delivered on certain days of the month, while free pizzas or car washes are provided only to customers who have purchased a specific amount of products or services. Do such rules—known as **schedules of reinforcement**—affect behavior? Several decades of research by Skinner and other psychologists suggest that they do. Many different types of schedules of reinforcement exist (e.g., Ferster & Skinner, 1957; Honig & Staddon, 1977). We will concentrate on four of the most important ones here.

In the first of these, known as a **fixed-interval schedule,** the occurrence of reinforcement is controlled by the passage of time: the first response made after a specific period has elapsed brings the reward. When placed on schedules of this type, subjects generally show a pattern in which they respond at low rates immediately after delivery of a reinforcement, but then gradually respond faster and faster as the time when the next reward can be obtained approaches (refer to Figure 5-17 on page 152). A good example of behavior on a fixed-interval schedule is provided by students studying. After a big exam, little studying takes place. As the time for the next test approaches, the rate of such behavior increases until, the night before the exam, few other activities may be occurring. (Incidentally, in research concerned with the effect of schedules of reinforcement, interest

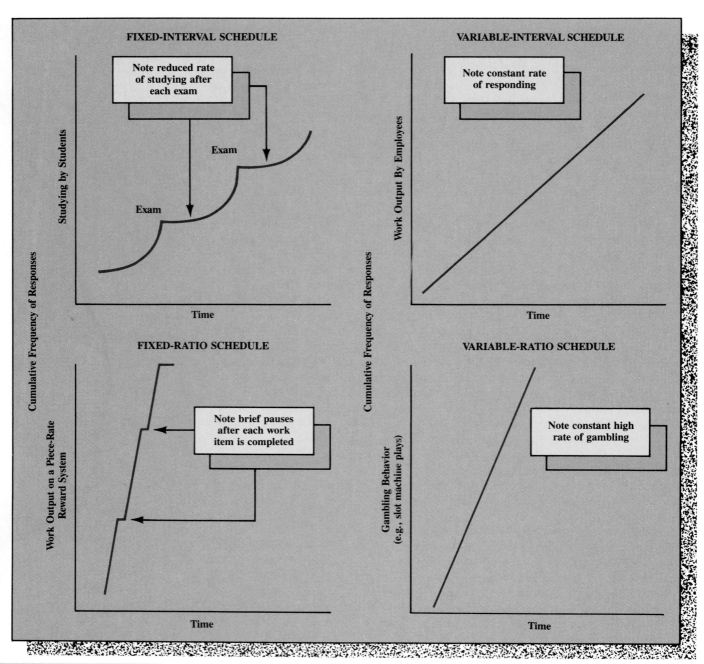

FIXED-INTERVAL SCHEDULE

Note reduced rate of studying after each exam

Exam

Exam

Studying by Students

Cumulative Frequency of Responses

Time

VARIABLE-INTERVAL SCHEDULE

Note constant rate of responding

Work Output By Employees

Time

FIXED-RATIO SCHEDULE

Note brief pauses after each work item is completed

Work Output on a Piece-Rate Reward System

Time

VARIABLE-RATIO SCHEDULE

Note constant high rate of gambling

Cumulative Frequency of Responses

Gambling Behavior (e.g., slot machine plays)

Time

FIGURE 5-17. Rates of responding vary under different schedules of reinforcement. Note that the steeper the line in each diagram, the higher the rate at which responses are performed.

Schedules of Reinforcement: A Summary of Their Effects

has been focused on the *rate* at which organisms perform specific responses. This is what is shown in Figure 5-17. The steeper the line in each diagram, the faster the rate of responding.)

Reinforcement is also controlled mainly by the passage of time in a **variable-interval schedule.** Here, though, the period which must elapse before a response will again yield reinforcement varies around some average value. In some cases reinforcement can be obtained after a very short time has passed, while in other cases the interval is longer. An example of behavior on a variable-interval schedule is provided by employees whose supervisor checks their work at irregular intervals. Since the employees never know when such checks will occur, they must perform in a consistent manner in order to obtain positive outcomes (e.g., praise) or avoid negative ones (e.g., criticism). This is precisely what happens on variable-interval schedules: organisms respond at a steady rate without the kind of pauses observed on fixed-interval schedules (refer again to Figure 5-17).

Reinforcement is determined in a very different manner on a **fixed-ratio schedule.** Here, it occurs only after a fixed number of responses have been performed. Individuals who are paid on a piecework basis (a fixed amount is paid for each item produced) are operating on a fixed-ratio schedule. Generally, such schedules yield a high rate of responding, with a tendency toward brief pauses immediately after each reinforcement (see Figure 5-17). The pauses occur because individuals take a slight ''breather'' after earning each unit of reinforcement.

Finally, reinforcement occurs after completion of a variable number of responses on a **variable-ratio schedule.** Since organisms confronted with a variable-ratio schedule cannot predict how many responses are required before reinforcement will occur, they usually respond at high and steady rates. The effect of such schedules upon human behavior is readily apparent in gambling casinos, where high rates of responding occur in front of slot machines and other games of chance. Variable-ratio schedules also result in behaviors that are highly resistant to extinction—ones that persist even when reinforcement is no longer available. In fact, resistance to extinction is much higher after exposure to a variable-ratio schedule of reinforcement than it is after conditions in which every response is followed by reinforcement. This phenomenon is known as the *partial reinforcement effect* and seems to occur for the following reason. During exposure to a variable-ratio schedule, many responses are *not* followed by reinforcement. Thus, during extinction it is harder for organisms to recognize that reinforcements are no longer available, and to realize that no amount of responding will do any good (Capaldi, 1980).

Stimulus Control of Behavior: Signals About the Usefulness (or Uselessness) of Responses. Imagine that you own an old and temperamental car. During the winter there are days when it will start and days when it will not start no matter what you do. After a while, you learn that on days when it *will* start, turning the key in the ignition results in a strange grinding sound. On days when the grinding sound is absent, the car never starts. Will these conditions have any effect on your behavior? Probably they will. When you hear the grinding sound, you will persevere in your efforts to start the car, trying again and again. On days when the sound is absent, you may quickly get out of the car and seek another way of getting to work or school.

This is an example of what psychologists sometimes term the *stimulus control* of behavior. Briefly, stimuli associated with the occurrence of reinforcement come to serve as useful *signals,* indicating whether operant behavior should be performed or omitted. If you'd like a first-hand illustration of such stimulus control, just pick up the nearest telephone. The dial tone tells you that certain responses (pushing the buttons, dialing) are likely to yield reinforcement; if it is absent, no amount of dialing will allow you to complete your call.

Punishment: When Behavior Yields Aversive Outcomes

Punishment is a frequent occurrence in everyday life. Parents punish their children for behaviors they find objectionable. Businesses demote or fire employees who perform at poor levels. And most societies establish legal codes that specify punishments for particular crimes. It is widely assumed, therefore, that punishment *works*—that it can change human behavior in important ways.

Surprisingly, psychologists have long expressed serious doubts about the usefulness of punishment. Early studies (e.g., Estes, 1944; Skinner, 1938) suggested that when a response is followed by punishment, it is not eliminated; rather, it is merely suppressed and may return when punishment is discontinued. Further, punishment appears to have several harmful side effects that limit its usefulness. First, it can create strong fear which may interfere with effective performance. If you ever had a frightening, punishment-prone teacher, you know about such effects from first-hand experience. Second, punishment can arouse anger or hostility in those who receive it, especially if they feel it is unfair (Baron, 1983). Third, punishment indicates what responses should be avoided, but it provides little information about what reactions would be more effective in a given situation.

For these and other reasons (e.g., the belief that positive reinforcement exerts stronger effects), punishment has long been out of favor among psychologists as a technique for changing human behavior. Recent evidence, however, suggests that it may be time to reconsider such conclusions. It appears that punishment *can* exert lasting effects upon a wide range of behavior in at least some instances (Walters & Herring, 1978). In order to be effective, though, several conditions must be met. First, punishment must be relatively strong; weak punishment seems to exert only weak and temporary effects. Second, it must quickly follow the undesirable behavior. Delay weakens the impact of punishment. Third, it must be consistent; punishing a behavior on some occasions but not on others may fail to eliminate its occurrence. Finally, the probability of punishment, too, must be high. Punishments that have a low probability of occurring tend to have little effect on behavior.

In addition, growing evidence supports the view that, if used with care, punishment can produce beneficial effects in many practical settings (e.g., Arvey & Ivancevich, 1980). In one recent study Schanke (1986) examined the impact of *vicarious* (witnessed) punishment on the behavior of employees. Subjects were hired to do a specific job (look up and record stock market information) and were paid on an hourly basis. After completing two hours of work, those in one group saw another person (actually an accomplice) receive a cut in pay from $5.00 to $3.50 per hour, supposedly because of poor performance. Those in a second group did not witness such punishment. Results were clear: subjects who observed the accomplice receive punishment showed a sharp increase in work output (refer to Figure 5-18). Moreover, these differences were still present one week later, when performance was measured again. Finally—and this is an important point—subjects' reported satisfaction with their job did *not* decrease as a result of witnessing the accomplice's punishment.

These and related findings suggest that punishment can be useful in some contexts. But please don't misunderstand: we're not recommending its careless or widespread use. Rather, we merely wish to correct a possible previous imbalance by noting that punish-

FIGURE 5-18. When individuals saw another employee receive a cut in pay because of poor performance, their own productivity increased. These findings suggest that *vicarious* punishment can sometimes exert beneficial effects in work settings. *(Source: Based on data from Schanke, 1986.)*

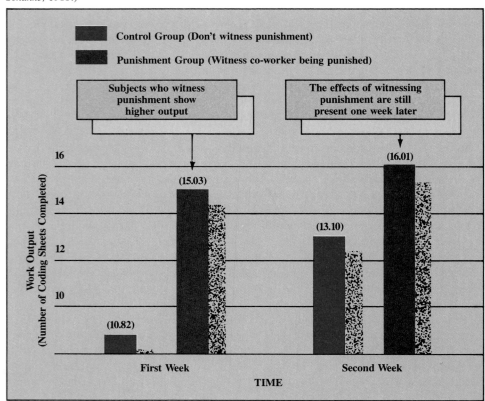

Punishment: Some Beneficial Effects

ment, like many other principles of behavior, is something of a two-edged sword. It can be, and has been, used to inflict needless suffering on innocent victims. But it can also be used to change behavior in ways that benefit individuals and society. The crucial point, of course, is precisely how, by whom, and when it is used.

Operant Conditioning: A Cognitive Perspective

Now, to come full cycle, we'll briefly address the following question: do cognitive processes play a role in operant conditioning as they do in classical conditioning? This is a point on which some psychologists disagree. Skinner and other behaviorists contend, even today, that there is no need to introduce cognition into the picture; if we understand the nature of the reinforcers available in a situation, and the schedules on which they are delivered, we can accurately predict behavior. In contrast, many psychologists (a large majority, it appears) believe that no account of operant conditioning can be complete without attention to cognitive factors. Several types of evidence support this conclusion.

First, and perhaps most dramatic, is the existence of a phenomenon known as **learned helplessness.** This refers to the lasting effects produced by exposure to situations in which nothing an organism does ''works''—no response it performs yields reinforcement or provides escape from negative events. After such an experience, both people and animals seem, literally, to give up. And here is the unsettling part: if the situation changes so that some responses they can perform *will* work, they never discover this fact. Rather, they remain in a seemingly passive state and simply don't try. Such effects have been observed among animals (Seligman, 1975) and humans (Tennen & Eller, 1977), and they have important implications. For example, as we will see in Chapter 13, they may play a key role in *depression,* a serious psychological disorder. While it is not yet clear why learned helplessness occurs (McReynolds, 1980), it does not seem possible to explain it entirely in terms of reinforcement. Rather, cognitive factors, such as reduced expectancies, seem to be involved. This suggests the importance of such factors in operant conditioning.

Second, several studies indicate that in some cases beliefs about schedules of reinforcement may exert stronger effects upon behavior than do the schedules themselves. For example, in one study (Kaufman, Baron, & Kopp, 1966) three groups of subjects performed a manual response on a variable-interval schedule (the period between reinforcements varied, but averaged one minute). One of the groups was told this schedule would be in effect. Two other groups were given false information: one was told that they would be rewarded every minute (a fixed-interval schedule), and the other was told that they would be rewarded after an average of 150 responses (a variable-ratio schedule). Although all groups actually worked on the same schedule, large differences in their behavior emerged. Those who thought they were working on a variable-ratio schedule showed a high rate of responses (259 per minute). Those told they would be rewarded on a fixed-interval schedule showed a very low rate (6 responses per minute); and those who were correctly informed that they would work on a variable-interval schedule showed an intermediate rate (65 per minute). As noted recently (Bandura, 1986, p. 129), these results suggest that people's behavior may sometimes be more accurately predicted from their beliefs than from the actual consequences (i.e., reinforcements) they experience. (For even more dramatic evidence on the role of cognitive factors in operant conditioning, please see ''The Cutting Edge'' section below.)

FOCUS ON RESEARCH: The Cutting Edge

Can Animals Count? Keeping Track of Reinforcements During Conditioning

Suppose you performed the following

experiment. Rats are permitted to run through a simple maze (runway) for a food reward. But you don't give them a reward on every trial. Rather, you train them on two different sequences: RRN (food, food, no food), and NRRN (no food, food, food, no food). Will they run more slowly on the final trial—the one that is not reinforced? Capaldi and Miller (1988) asked this question in the first of several studies concerned with the following issue: can animals count? They reasoned that if the rats could count, they would run more slowly on the final N trials in both series. This would be so because they would keep track of the fact that after two R trials, no reward would be available. Results were clear: the rats *did* run more slowly on the final N trials than on any others. Moreover, this was true even after several other aspects of the situation were changed (e.g., the amount of time they were permitted to eat on R trials was altered).

The researchers did not stop there, however. They also asked the following question: can rats also count one type of food reward while ignoring another? (This is equivalent to your counting the oranges in a bowl while ignoring the apples or pears.) In order to examine this possibility, rats were trained to run a simple maze for two kinds of rewards: Corn Pops or Honey Smacks (two different breakfast cereals). Rats in one group received these rewards in two sequences: RRN and NRRN. Those in a second group (Group Identical) were trained on RRN and RRRN: a food event identical to the others in the series was substituted for the first N in the NRRN series. For example, if on the other R trials Corn Pops were presented, the same was true now; if, instead, Honey Smacks had been presented, *this* was the reward used. Finally, in a third group (Group Different) rats were trained on the following sequences: RRN and R'RRN. Here, a *different* food event was substituted for the first N in the NRRN series. Thus, if Corn Pops were given on the other R trials, a Honey Smacks reward was given now, in the R' trial.

Capaldi and Miller reasoned that if rats can count one type of food reward while ignoring others, then subjects in Group Different should run more slowly on the final N trial of *both* the RRN and R'RRN sequences, because they would count the R' event separately from the two R events. Thus, in either case, they would know that after two Rs the next trial

FIGURE 5-19. Rats who received an initial food reward which was different from the others they received (Group Different) ran more slowly on the final nonreinforced trial of both three- and four-trial sequences (RRN, R'RRN). In contrast, rats who received an initial food reward which was the same as the others they later received (Group Identical) ran more slowly on the final, nonreinforced trial of the four-trial sequence. These findings indicate that rats can count one type of reinforcement while ignoring another. *(Source: Based on data from Capaldi & Miller, 1988.)*

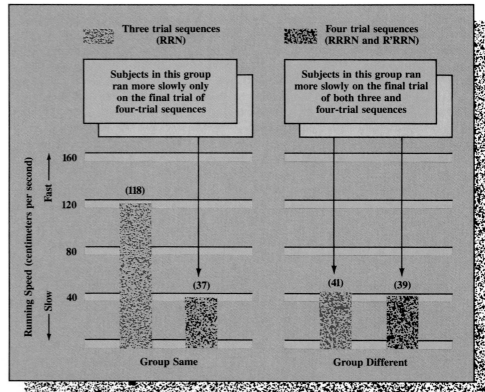

would not result in a food reward. In contrast, subjects in the Group Identical should run more slowly only on the N trial of the RRRN series. They would not run slowly on the N trial of the RRN sequence because they would not be able to tell whether another R or an N trial would follow two Rs. As shown in Figure 5-19, results supported all these predictions. The rats were indeed able to count one type of food reward while ignoring another!

The studies conducted by Capaldi

and Miller (1988) suggest that animals *can* keep count of their reinforcements. Given this fact, it is difficult to view operant conditioning solely in terms of the occurrence of positive and negative reinforcers. Rather, organisms (even rats!) appear to be engaging in active information processing throughout such learning. Clearly, such activities must be taken into account if we are to fully understand this important way in which we are affected by our experience.

Applying Operant Conditioning

Because positive and negative reinforcement exert powerful effects upon behavior, procedures based on operant conditioning have been applied to many practical problems. Indeed, they have been used in so many different settings it would be impossible to describe them all here. Instead, we'll simply present a brief overview of some of these uses.

First, principles of operant conditioning have been applied to the field of education. Here, the most impressive use to date involves *computer-assisted instruction*. In this technique, students interact with sophisticated computer programs which provides immediate reinforcement of correct responses. The programs are paced according to each pupil's progress, and permit individuals to enter branch programs designed to provide special help in areas of weakness. Given the color graphics, synthesized speech, and other effects available on current equipment (see Figure 5-20), computer-assisted instruction helps convert the dull task of studying into an exciting adventure in learning. While it is still too soon to assess fully the impact of such procedures, early results are promising, so in some form such instruction seems here to stay.

Second, operant conditioning has been adapted to the treatment of many psychological problems. Since we'll examine several forms of therapy based on operant conditioning in Chapter 14, we will consider only one concrete example here. Let's return to a serious disorder we've already mentioned while discussing applications of classical conditioning—*anorexia nervosa*. How can operant techniques be used to deal with this problem? Consider an individual who has been hospitalized because her unwillingness to eat is seriously affecting her health. In order to help this person, we might first identify some behavior that she likes to perform, such as watching a favorite T.V. program. Then, we would make this activity available only when she eats a minimum amount of food. At first, the patient would only have to eat a small amount of food in order to gain access to a television. In accordance with principles of shaping, however, the amount she must eat would gradually be increased. Such procedures have actually been used with considerable

FIGURE 5-20. One important use of operant conditioning principles has been in *computer-assisted instruction*.

Operant Conditioning Applied to Education

Biofeedback: One Intriguing Application of Operant Conditioning Principles

FIGURE 5-21. During *biofeedback*, small changes in blood pressure, heart rate, or other bodily processes are detected and converted into audible or visible signals (e.g., tones, flashing lights). Under these conditions, individuals can learn to alter processes that are not usually under voluntary control.

success (Stunkard, 1976), so this is one important way in which knowledge of operant conditioning has already contributed to human welfare.

Third, operant conditioning provides the basis for **biofeedback**—a procedure which is sometimes successful in treating high blood pressure and other effects of stress (Miller, 1980). In biofeedback, small changes in basic bodily processes, such as blood pressure and heart rate, are detected by electronic equipment, then converted into a signal that can be readily detected by the subject, such as a flashing light or an audible tone (refer to Figure 5-21). An individual undergoing biofeedback is told to try to make the signal stay on as much as possible. Conditions then are arranged so that only desirable changes in bodily functions (e.g., reduction in blood pressure) produce this effect. Amazing as it may seem, many persons are indeed able to produce such changes, although most are unclear about how they attained this goal. In short, they are able to bring basic bodily processes under what amounts to voluntary control.

The results of early studies on the effectiveness of biofeedback were highly encouraging. Indeed, they suggested that this technique might soon prove valuable in treating a wide range of serious illnesses such as high blood pressure (Miller, 1978). Unfortunately, this promise has not been fulfilled, and it now appears that enthusiastic claims for the potential of biofeedback were probably somewhat exaggerated (Miller, 1985). At present, then, it is probably best viewed as an intriguing and potentially valuable application of operant conditioning principles, but one still in its early stages of development.

Finally, techniques of operant conditioning have been applied to many issues and problems in work settings. For example, they have been used to improve the performance

FIGURE 5-22. Unfortunately, good performance is not always followed by positive reinforcement in work settings. In fact, the outcomes shown here are sometimes more common! (*Source:* The New Yorker.)

"By God, I'm so pleased with the way you handled that lousy, thankless job I gave you, Frawley, that I'm going to give you another one."

Operant Conditioning: How *Not* To Use It!

of sales personnel (Luthans, Paul & Baker, 1981) and to increase employees' use of safety practices in their work (Reber & Wallin, 1984). Perhaps the most intriguing use of operant procedures in work settings, however, has involved efforts to answer an age-old question: why are some persons more effective in the role of leader or manager than others? In order to answer this question, the actual on-the-job behavior of managers has been carefully observed and then analyzed within the framework of operant conditioning (Komaki, 1986). The results of such research indicate that effective managers are ones who pay close attention to their subordinates' performance, and then provide contingent rewards and punishments. That is, successful managers take extra effort to determine just how well employees are performing and reward them accordingly. This may sound like common sense, but, as Figure 5-22 suggests, this is *not* the case in many work settings. Instead of yielding rewards, good performance is often "recognized" by even tougher work assignments and other negative outcomes! Clearly, both businesses and employees can profit greatly from closer attention to basic principles of operant conditioning.

Observational Learning: Learning from the Behavior and Outcomes of Others

You are at a formal dinner party. Next to your plate are five different forks, including two you've never seen before. Which ones do you use for what dishes? You have no idea. In order to avoid making a complete fool of yourself, you watch the other guests as the first course arrives. When several reach unhesitatingly for one of the unfamiliar forks, you do the same. Now, thank goodness, you can concentrate on the food!

Have you ever had an experience like this? Even if you have not, you have probably encountered situations in which you acquired new forms of behavior, information, or even abstract rules and concepts from watching other persons. Such **observational learning** is a third major way we learn, and it is a common part of everyday life (Bandura, 1977, 1986). Indeed, a large body of research findings suggest it can play a role in almost every aspect of behavior (refer to Figure 5-23 on page 160). Perhaps a few more examples will help:

(1) A new employee watches while an experienced one performs a task; under the guidance of this person, she then tries to repeat the action.

(2) A couple watches a torrid X-rated videotape containing several lovemaking techniques they have never before seen. Later, they try the same techniques themselves.

(3) A child watches her mother wash dishes, do the laundry, and cook meals. From such experience, she forms the impression that these are the right kinds of activities for females to perform.

In these and countless other instances, we appear to learn *vicariously,* merely by watching the actions of other persons and the consequences they experience. More formal evidence for the existence of observational learning has been provided by hundreds of studies, many of them performed with children. Perhaps the most famous of these are the well-known "Bobo doll" experiments conducted by Bandura and his colleagues (e.g., Bandura, Ross, & Ross, 1963). In these studies one group of nursery-school children saw an adult engage in unusual aggressive actions against a large inflated "Bobo doll." The model knocked the doll down, sat on it, and repeatedly punched it in the nose. Another group of children were exposed to a model who behaved in a quiet, nonaggressive manner. Later, both groups of youngsters were placed in a room with several toys, including a Bobo doll. Careful observation of their behavior revealed that those who had seen the aggressive adult (model) often imitated this person's behavior: they, too, punched the toy, sat on it, and even emitted verbal comments similar to those uttered by the model. In contrast, children in the control group rarely if ever demonstrated such actions. While you may not find these results surprising, they point to an important possibility: perhaps children acquire new ways of aggressing through exposure to media violence (violent television programs and movies). We'll return to this issue below. For the present, let's consider the nature of observational learning itself.

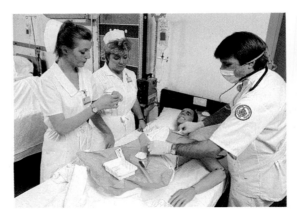

FIGURE 5-23. In many cases we acquire new forms of behavior, information, and even concepts from watching other persons.

Given that this process exists, what factors affect its occurrence? What conditions determine whether, and to what extent, we acquire behaviors, information, or even concepts from others? According to Bandura (1986), who is still the leading expert on this process, four factors are most important.

First, in order to learn through observation you must direct your *attention* to appropriate *models* (other persons performing some activity). Obviously, if you ignore them completely, such learning cannot occur. And, as you might expect, you don't choose such models at random, but focus most attention on people who are attractive to you, who possess signs of knowing what they're doing (ones high in status or past success), and whose behavior seems relevant to your own needs and goals (Baron, 1970).

Second, you must be able to *remember* what the persons have said or done. Only if you can retain some representation of their actions in memory can you perform similar actions at later times, or acquire useful information from them.

Third, you must be able to convert these memory representations into appropriate actions. Bandura terms this aspect of observational learning *production processes*. This involves two issues: (1) your own physical abilities—you must be able to perform the behavior in question, for, if you can't, having a clear representation of it in memory is of little use; and (2) your capacity to monitor your own performance and adjust it until it matches that of the model.

Finally, *motivation* plays a role. People often acquire information through observational learning but do not put it to immediate use in their own behavior. They may have no need for such actions (e.g., you watch someone tie a bow tie but have no plans to wear one yourself), or the observed behaviors may involve a high risk of punishment (e.g., you observe an ingenious way of cheating during an exam but are reluctant to cheat). Only if the information or behaviors acquired are useful will observers put them to actual use. Please refer to Figure 5-24 for a summary of the factors affecting observational learning.

As you can see, observational learning is a complex process—far more complex than simple *imitation*. Understanding its nature, though, seems to be well worth while, for it plays an important role in many aspects of behavior. As we noted above, perhaps this point is most forcefully illustrated by a controversy that has persisted in psychology, and in society as a whole, for almost three decades: whether children (and perhaps adults) are made more aggressive by long-term exposure to violence on television shows or in movies.

A large body of evidence suggests that this may actually be the case (Bandura, 1986; Friedrich-Cofer & Huston, 1986). Apparently, when they are exposed to new ways of aggressing against others—techniques they have not previously seen—children and adults can add these new behaviors to their repertoire. Later, when angry, irritated, or frustrated, they may put such behaviors to actual use in assaults against others.

Of course, exposure to media violence—whether on the evening news, in movies, or on television programs—has other effects as well. It may convey the message that violence is an acceptable means of handling interpersonal difficulties; after all, if heroes and heroines can do it, why not viewers? It may elicit additional aggressive ideas and thoughts, for example, convince viewers that violence is even more common than it is (Berkowitz, 1984). And it may also lessen emotional reactions to aggression and the harm it produces, so that such outcomes seem less upsetting or objectionable (Thomas, 1982). When these are coupled with new behaviors and skills acquired through observational learning, the overall effect can be disturbing: an increased tendency among many persons to engage in acts of aggression (Eron, 1987).

FIGURE 5-24. Observational learning is affected by several factors or subprocesses. The most important of these are summarized here.

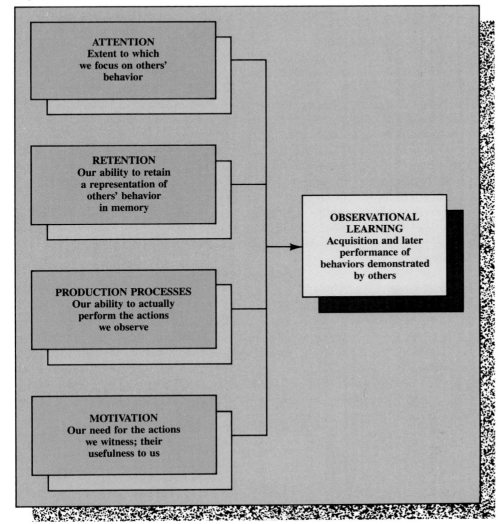

Key Factors in Observational Learning

We should hasten to add that not all findings support such conclusions (Freedman, 1986), and that the effects of exposure to media violence, when they occur, seem to be modest in scope. Given the fact that many children spend more time watching television and videotapes than they do in any other single activity, however, the potential influence of such experience on aggression and other forms of behavior seems worthy of careful attention (Liebert, Sprafkin, & Davidson, 1982).

Summary and Review

Classical Conditioning

Learning is any relatively permanent change in behavior produced by experience. One basic form of learning, *classical conditioning,* occurs when, through repeated pairing one stimulus (a CS) becomes a signal for the occurrence of another stimulus (a UCS). This process plays an important role in many forms of human behavior, such as the acquisition of strong fears. After conditioning has occurred, stimuli similar to the CS may also evoke conditioned responses; this is known as *stimulus generalization.* Conversely, if one stimulus is followed by a UCS while a similar stimulus is not, *stimulus discrimination* may develop: one stimulus will evoke a conditioned response while the other stimulus will not. Classical conditioning is not equally easy to establish with all stimuli for all organisms. Rather, there are important *biological constraints* on such learning, so that members of a given species acquire some types of conditioning more readily than other types of conditioning. Cognitive factors, such as *expectancies* about the occurrence of various stimuli, play an important role in classical conditioning.

Operant Conditioning

Operant conditioning occurs when behavior is affected by its consequences. Actions which yield positive results *(positive reinforcement)* or which permit escape from or avoidance of unpleasant outcomes *(negative reinforcement)* increase in strength or frequency. In contrast, responses which are followed by negative outcomes, or which result in the omission of positive ones, are suppressed. This is known as *punishment.* Rules determining the delivery of reinforcement *(schedules of reinforcement)* exert strong effects upon behavior. Cognitive processes also play an important role in operant conditioning. For example, an individual's beliefs concerning schedules of reinforcement may exert stronger effects upon behavior than the schedule actually in effect. Similarly, certain animals seem capable of counting and can even keep track of two different reinforcers at the same time. Operant conditioning has been put to practical use in *computer-assisted instruction,* in several types of *therapy,* in *biofeedback,* and in efforts to enhance work productivity.

Observational Learning

Observational learning occurs when we acquire behaviors, information, or concepts by watching others. In order for such learning to occur, we must direct attention to other persons *(models),* retain a representation of their behavior, and be able to convert these representations into overt actions. In addition, we must be motivated to perform the behavior we have witnessed. Observational learning plays a role in many forms of behavior. For example, individuals may acquire new ways of aggressing against others through exposure to media violence.

 Key Terms

Biofeedback   A procedure in which small changes in bodily processes are detected and magnified by electronic equipment into an audible or visible signal.

Classical Conditioning   A basic form of learning in which one stimulus comes to serve as a signal for the occurrence of a second stimulus. During classical conditioning, organisms acquire information about the *relations* between various stimuli, not simple associations between them.

Conditioned Response (CR) In classical conditioning, the response to the conditioned stimulus.

Conditioned Stimulus (CS) In classical conditioning, the stimulus which is repeatedly paired with an unconditioned stimulus.

Constraints on Learning Refers to the fact that all forms of conditioning are not equally easy to establish with all organisms.

Extinction The process through which a conditioned stimulus gradually loses the ability to evoke conditioned responses when it is no longer followed by the unconditioned stimulus.

Fixed-Interval Schedule A schedule of reinforcement in which a specific interval of time must elapse before a response will yield reinforcement.

Fixed Ratio Schedule A schedule of reinforcement in which reinforcement occurs only after a fixed number of responses have been emitted.

Flooding Procedures for eliminating conditioned fears based on principles of classical conditioning. During flooding an individual is asked to think about fear-inducing objects or events. Since no unconditioned stimulus then follows, extinction of these fears eventually takes place.

Learned Helplessness The reduced ability of organisms to learn that certain responses will yield reinforcement following exposure to a situation in which no response produces such outcomes.

Learning Any relatively permanent change in behavior (or behavior tendencies) resulting from experience.

Negative Reinforcers Stimuli which strengthen responses which permit organisms to avoid or escape from their presence.

Observational Learning The acquisition of new forms of behavior, information, or concepts through exposure to others and the consequences they experience.

Operant Conditioning A process through which organisms learn to repeat behaviors which yield positive outcomes or which permit them to avoid or escape from negative outcomes (also termed instrumental conditioning).

Positive Reinforcers Stimuli which strengthen responses which precede them.

Punishment Refers to situations in which negative outcomes follow specific responses.

Schedules of Reinforcement Rules determining when and how reinforcements will be delivered.

Shaping A technique in which closer and closer approximations to desired behavior are required for the delivery of positive reinforcement.

Stimulus Generalization The tendency of stimuli similar to a conditioned stimulus to evoke conditioned responses.

Unconditioned Response (UCR) In classical conditioning, the response evoked by an unconditioned stimulus.

Unconditioned Stimulus (UCS) In classical conditioning, a stimulus which can evoke an unconditioned response the first time it is presented.

Variable-Interval Schedule A schedule of reinforcement in which a variable amount of time must elapse before a response will yield reinforcement.

Variable-Ratio Schedule A schedule of reinforcement in which reinforcement is delivered after a variable number of responses have been performed.

For More Information

Bandura, A. (1986). *Social foundations of thought and action: A social cognitive view*. Englewood Cliffs, N.J.: Prentice-Hall.
> This highly sophisticated book is written mainly for people with advanced training in psychology. However, the chapters on enactive learning (learning through direct experience) and observational learning are outstanding. If you are prepared to exert some effort, this is a very useful source of additional information about learning.

Hall, J.F. (1989). *Learning and memory*. Boston: Allyn and Bacon.
> This is a brief and clearly written overview of current knowledge concerning several aspects of learning and memory. The chapters on classical and instrumental conditioning expand on materials presented in this chapter.

CHAPTER

6

Human Memory: Of Things Remembered . . . and Forgotten

"Well, I did it again," Fran Jackson says to her friend Ed. "There I was, at my sister's wedding, meeting all her new in-laws. She introduced me to her husband's brother, and a minute later, Valerie Clanton walked up and wanted to meet him, too, and *I couldn't remember his name!* It was so embarrassing. I just stood there, like a dummy, turning red. Ooh!"

"Sounds pretty bad," Ed agrees, shaking his head. "I wouldn't have wanted to be you."

"You sure wouldn't. But that kind of thing *never* happens to you. I remember that party at Joe's house—you must have met twenty different people in the first half hour. But did you forget a single name? No way! You reeled 'em off as though you had written them down. I'm just the opposite. Introduce me to someone, and a minute later I can't remember their name. It's funny; if I can get through the first couple of minutes, I'm O.K. Why doesn't that happen to you? What is it, some kind of gift or something?"

"Naturally! You now how gifted I am!" Ed replies, laughing. "But seriously, it's really pretty simple. I just *try* to remember, that's all."

"What do you mean, *try* to remember?" Fran asks, a puzzled look in her eyes.

"Well, first, do you even *listen* when someone tells you their name? I've watched you lots of times, and I don't think you do. Your mind seems to be on something else, like what other people are saying, who's hitting it off with whom, stuff like that. If you want to remember someone's name, you've got to listen to it. Otherwise, it can't get inside your head in the first place."

Smoothing her hair, Fran comments, "You know, you may have something there. I really *don't* pay much attention to names—it's *people* that interest me. But it's got to be more than that. Even if I do listen, how can I remember a whole string of names the way you do?"

"See, you're not listening even now! I just said I *try* to remember. That means I don't just stand there, hoping for the best. When I hear a new name, I say it to myself over and over. I usually try to visualize it, too—you know, imagine it written down. And sometimes I try to think of something about the person that reminds me of their name. Take Pete Mendoza, for instance. When I met him, I noticed that he's got what I'd call a pretty hefty nose. So, remembering his name is easy: I just visualize that big schnozzola!"

At this remark, Fran chuckles. "What a character you are! Who else would come up with stuff like that? But I guess it works, at least for you. Anyway, from now on, I'm going to concentrate on names when I hear them, the way you do. And I think I'll try repeating them to myself, too. I'm not sure it'll help, but anything's worth a try!"

FIGURE 6-1. We often experience difficulties in remembering some things, while forgetting others. *(Source: United Press Syndicate.)*

Memory: Far from Perfect

Memory, we're sure you'll agree, is a funny thing. Sometimes, you may seem unable to retain important facts or information for even a few seconds. Yet, on other occasions you are able to remember events or actions from years ago vividly and in great detail. Indeed, this is often true even when you might prefer to forget them! (Refer to Figure 6-1.) Does this mean you have more than one type of memory—different mechanisms for retaining information over time? And if so, how do these systems operate? Further, what happens when you forget? Is the information lost forever, or is it still "in there" but somehow beyond your cognitive reach? And, to pose the ultimate question, how do you manage to store all the varied facts, skills, and experiences of a lifetime within the confines of your three-pound brain?

The answers to such questions are essential to a full understanding of human behavior, for memory plays a central role in all of our cognitive processes. Without some mechanism for retaining information over time we would be unable to speak or to reason, to solve problems, to recognize persons or objects, to drive, to play a musical instrument, or to carry out virtually any other form of complex human activity. Understanding the nature of memory, therefore, is and always has been a central topic in psychology. In fact, it was the focus of some of the earliest systematic research in our field—research conducted more than one hundred years ago by Hermann Ebbinghaus (1885). Using himself as subject, Ebbinghaus attempted to study the nature of memory by learning and then recalling hundreds of lists of *nonsense syllables* (meaningless letter combinations, such as *ner* or *pxt*). Some of his findings have withstood the test of time and are valid even today, so Ebbinghaus's feats of patience were definitely *not* wasted. (One of these findings: at first, we forget materials we have learned quite rapidly. Later, forgetting occurs more slowly.)

While the studies Ebbinghaus conducted were ingenious in many respects, modern research on memory has gone far beyond these simple beginnings. In fact, it is probably safe to say that, at present, we have a fuller grasp of memory than of any other basic cognitive process. For this reason, be prepared for some surprises: in many respects, facts psychologists have discovered about memory are as unexpected as they are fascinating. In order to provide you with a broad introduction to this intriguing body of knowledge, we'll proceed in the following manner. First, we'll describe a basic model of human memory—one that is widely accepted as providing a useful overview of this complex process. As we'll soon see, this model suggests that we possess three different memory systems. After describing the model, we'll examine each of these systems in turn. Once that task is complete, we'll consider the operation of memory in *natural settings* (e.g., its role in eye-witness testimony). Then we'll turn to a topic we're sure will be of interest: techniques for improving memory. Finally, we'll examine current evidence concerning memory disorders and what these tell us about the biological nature of memory.

Human Memory: An Information-Processing Approach

In science, the way a topic is approached often shapes the questions asked about it and the ways it is studied. Memory is no exception to this rule. In recent years, most efforts to understand this essential process have proceeded within a framework known as the **information-processing approach** (Klatzky, 1984). This perspective derives partly from computer science and related fields, and it suggests that memory can best be understood by tracing the manner in which information is stored and then is retrieved for later use. Consistent with the operation of modern computers, then, memory is generally studied in terms of three basic operations: encoding, storage, and retrieval.

Encoding refers to the way in which information is entered into memory. It is analogous to the fact that when you wish to put information into a computer, you must first convert it into a form the computer can recognize. **Storage** refers to the manner in which such information is then retained in memory. In computers this involves changes in tiny electrical circuits; for human beings it involves changes in the structure of the brain, although the nature of these alterations is not yet clear. Finally, **retrieval** refers to various procedures or mechanisms which allow us to locate and then use information previously stored in memory. Refer to Figure 6-2 for a summary of these stages.

Please don't misunderstand: the information-processing approach does *not* imply that human memory operates the same way modern computers do. It merely suggests that examining memory in terms of the three operations mentioned above (encoding, storage, retrieval) is a useful way to proceed. So think of the information-processing approach as a convenient way of discussing memory—*not* as a model of what it is or how it works.

Having said this, we should add that at present, the most widely accepted model of human memory is one that rests firmly on the information-processing perspective (Atkinson & Shiffrin, 1968). According to this framework, we actually possess three distinct memory systems: sensory memory, short-term memory, and long-term memory. These differ in many ways, but the model suggests that the key task for each is to understand how information is encoded, stored, and then retrieved.

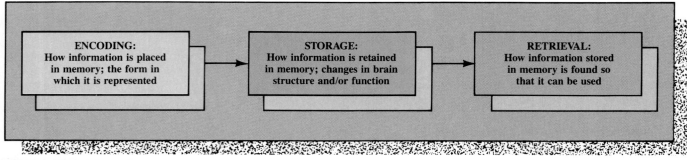

ENCODING: How information is placed in memory; the form in which it is represented	STORAGE: How information is retained in memory; changes in brain structure and/or function	RETRIEVAL: How information stored in memory is found so that it can be used

The Information-Processing Approach: An Overview

FIGURE 6-2. The *information-processing* approach suggests that memory can best be understood in terms of three stages: *encoding, storage,* and *retrieval.*

The first of these three types of memory, **sensory memory,** provides temporary storage of information brought by our senses. Since we have several different senses, we actually have several types of sensory memory. Sensory memory can hold quite a lot of information—in fact, all the data currently reaching the brain from our eyes, ears, and other sense organs. However, it retains such information only briefly—less than a second in the case of vision, and no more than a few seconds in the case of hearing (e.g., Cowan, 1984). If you've ever listened to a brief melody and then been able to hum it immediately afterwards because you still seemed to "hear" it, you are familiar with sensory memory and its role in everyday life.

The second system described by Atkinson and Shiffrin (1968) is **short-term memory (STM).** This is the type of memory you use when you look up a phone number and dial it immediately. In contrast to sensory memory, short-term memory has limited capacity; in fact, it can hold only a few items at any time, perhaps no more than about nine (MacGregor, 1987). It also stores information for short periods of time—twenty seconds or less. Short-term memory is sometimes known as *working memory,* and this term makes good sense: it seems to hold information or facts we are currently using.

Finally, we also possess **long-term memory.** This is what we usually have in mind when we use the term "memory," for this system allows us to retain vast amounts of information for long periods of time. It provides a means of storing information in a relatively permanent way (refer to Figure 6-3).

How does information move from one memory system to another? We'll return to this complex question in more detail below, but here, we can note that the Atkinson and Shiffrin model (plus recent refinements of it) suggests the following answer: through the operation of active *control processes.* For example, information is transferred from sensory memory to short-term memory when we make it the focus of our attention—we decide it is important to us in some way. Similarly, information moves from short-term to long-term memory when we *rehearse* it in certain ways—we think about its meaning or its relationship to other information already in long-term memory. So, as Ed in our opening story suggested, we retain information when we actively try to do so! (Please see Figure 6-4 for a summary of the Atkinson-Shiffrin model and our three types of memory.) We should add that the framework we have just described is not the only model of memory in existence—far from it (e.g., Craik & Lockhart, 1972; Matlin, 1983a). We'll refer to some of these other models in later sections. Since the Atkinson-Shiffrin model is the one which currently enjoys widest acceptance, though, it provides a good context for our discussion of memory.

FIGURE 6-3. Long-term memory allows us to store large amounts of information for very long periods of time. Without such a memory system, performers such as these could not possibly remember the lines for many different plays.

Long-Term Memory in Action

Sensory Memory: Gateway to Consciousness

You are waiting in a busy airport. Many different activities are occurring around you: people are rushing to and fro; passengers are moving through security; people are talking, laughing, crying, hugging. At one point, your gaze passes over a large television screen containing flight information. You look away, but then, almost at once, your eyes snap

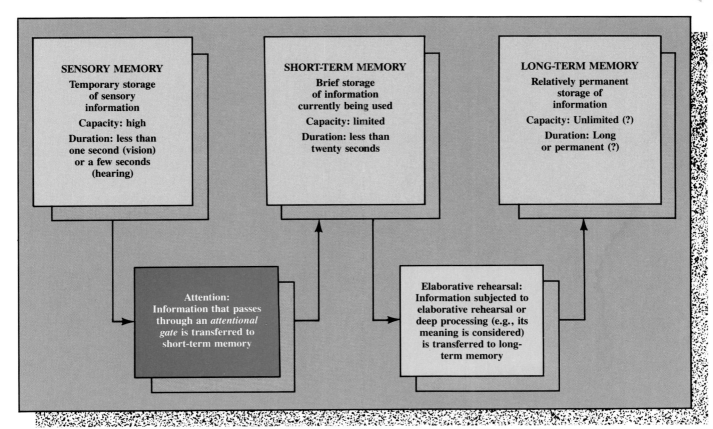

FIGURE 6-4. Many psychologists believe that we actually possess three distinct memory systems: *sensory memory, short-term memory,* and *long-term memory.* Information is transferred from one of these storage systems to another through several *control processes* (e.g., attention, rehearsal, elaborative rehearsal). *(Based on a model proposed by Atkinson & Shiffrin, 1968.)*

One Widely Accepted Model of Human Memory

back to it. Something seemed different. . . . Now what was it, you wonder? Groaning, you quickly note that your flight has been delayed *again*. Dejectedly, you settle back in your chair for an even longer wait.

At first blush, this incident may seem more closely related to the trials of modern air travel than to memory, but think again: what made you glance back at the screen? The answer involves our simplest memory system: sensory memory. As we hope you'll recall, this system holds information from our senses very briefly—just long enough, it appears, for us to determine that some aspect of this input is worthy of further attention. Without such memory, you would have had no reason to return your gaze to the television screen, for as soon as your eyes moved away from it, all traces of the screen and its contents would vanish. In this and countless other situations, sensory memory is useful indeed; without it, we'd be able to react only to stimuli reaching us at a given instant, and the "double-takes" we perform each day would be impossible.

But how much can sensory memory hold? And how long does such information last? Existing evidence suggests that the capacity of sensory memory is quite large—indeed, it may hold a representation of virtually everything we see, hear, taste, or smell (Reeves & Sperling, 1986). Such information, however, is held only for brief periods of time. For example, visual sensory memory seems last no more than a single second, while for hearing, sensory memory lasts somewhat longer—perhaps up to ten seconds (Cowan, 1984). Impressive evidence pointing to these conclusions was first gathered almost three decades ago by Sperling (1960) in several experiments.

In one of these studies, subjects were shown nine letters arranged in rows of three on a card. These stimuli were presented very briefly—for only 50 milliseconds (.05 seconds). Subjects were then asked to report all the letters. Under these procedures, their

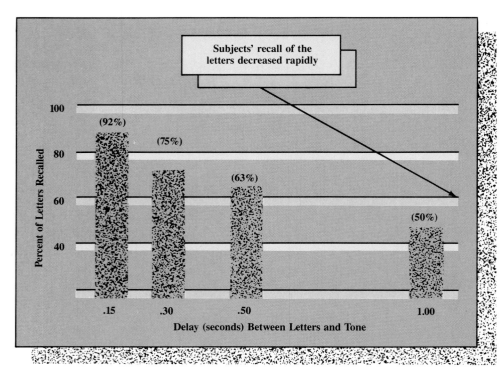

FIGURE 6-5. When subjects heard a tone, they tried to report letters in one of three rows on a card they had seen for 50 milliseconds. If the tone indicating which row to report was sounded immediately after presentation of the card, their performance was nearly perfect. If delayed even briefly, however, their ability to report the letters decreased sharply. These findings indicate that visual sensory memory is very brief indeed. *(Source: Based on data from Sperling, 1960.)*

memory was not impressive: they could recall only about four or five of the nine letters. However, subjects reported the impression that right after seeing the card they could in fact remember all of the letters; however, their visual image of them faded quickly, so by the time they had named four or five, it was gone. To see if this was actually true, Sperling used an ingenious technique. Immediately after presentation of the letters, he sounded a tone that was high, medium, or low in pitch. The high tone meant that subjects should report the first row, the medium tone indicated that they should report the second, and so on. Results were clear: under these conditions, subjects demonstrated near-perfect scores. Their subjective impressions were correct: right after seeing the card, they *did* retain an ''image'' of it for a brief period of time. This was sensory memory in action!

How quickly does such information fade? To check on this issue, Sperling repeated the above procedures, but delayed presentation of the tone for various periods of time. The results indicated that sensory memory is indeed brief. When the tone was delayed only .10 second, subjects' performance dropped appreciably; when it was delayed for an entire second, their ability to remember the letters all but disappeared (refer to Figure 6-5).

These findings, confirmed in many later studies, point to two conclusions: sensory memory exists, and it can store an impressive amount of information. However, it is *very* short-lived in duration. Where sensory memory is concerned, then, it appears to be very much a matter of ''now you see it, now you don't.''

Short-Term Memory: The Workbench of Consciousness

Imagine you are in a restaurant sampling food you've never had before. One of the dishes is truly delicious, so you ask the waiter for its name in his native tongue. He tells you, and you repeat it several times until you get it right. Five minutes later, you decide to write it down; you get out your pen and paper only to discover that you can't remember the name at all! Have you ever had an experience like this? If not, remember the last time you looked up a phone number and forgot it while dialing, or the last time you were introduced to someone and, a moment later, couldn't remember her name. Such experiences point to the existence of a second memory system—one that holds a limited amount of information for a short period of time (usually twenty seconds or less). Short-term memory, like sensory memory, is very important. Indeed, some experts view it as a kind of workbench for consciousness or the mind—a ''place'' where information you are using right now can be stored temporarily, and then discarded when no longer required. What kind of information does short-term memory hold? How long does it last? It is on such questions that we now focus.

How Does Information Enter Short-Term Memory?

Actually, there are two routes into the short-term memory system. One involves the transfer of information from *long-term memory*. In other words, information stored in long-term memory is retrieved for use in short-term memory. We'll discuss long-term memory in detail in the next section, so we won't focus on this route here. Second, information can also enter short-term memory from sensory memory. Since sensory memory seems to hold representations of much of what we see or hear, it is obvious that not all information is transferred. Which portion gets through? The answer seems to involve *attention*—active selection of the information in sensory memory that is most important or noticeable. To return to our airport example, you probably wouldn't notice changes in flight times other than your own, for they are of little interest or importance to you (see Figure 6-6). Changes in *your* flight, though, are quickly noticed and selected for further processing: they enter short-term memory, where you think actively about them. Intriguing information on how this transfer actually takes place has recently been reported by Reeves and Sperling (1986).

These scientists asked subjects to watch streams of letters presented on the left side of the visual field. Then, whenever they spotted a target (the letters *C, U,* or a square), subjects were to shift their attention to the right side of the visual field, where a stream of numerals was being presented. Their task was then to report the first four numbers they

FIGURE 6-6. So much activity takes place in a busy airport that you can't possibly be aware of all of it at once. Yet, you will readily notice changes in the departure or arrival time of your own flight. This is due to *attention*—the active selection of certain information present in sensory memory.

Attention: Gateway to Short-Term Memory

Transfer of Information from Sensory to Short-Term Memory

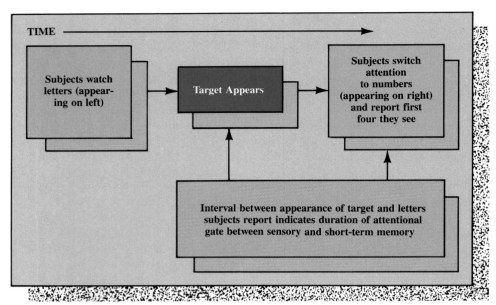

FIGURE 6-7. In research on short-term memory (Reeves & Sperling, 1986), subjects watched a stream of letters. When they noticed a target (e.g., the letter *C*), they were to shift their attention to a stream of numbers, and report the first four they saw. By measuring the time between appearance of the target and the first letter subjects reported, a measure could be obtained of how long an *attentional gate* between sensory memory and short-term memory remained open. Results indicated that this gate stayed open for about 400 milliseconds. *(Source: Based on data from Reeves & Sperling, 1986.)*

saw. Reeves and Sperling reasoned that the time between occurrence of the signal and the first number subjects reported would reveal the speed with which they could shift their attention from the letters to the numbers. In addition, they also suggested that this interval would provide information on how long the *attentional gate* between sensory memory and short-term memory remained open after subjects noticed a target. Reeves and Sperling actually found that the "gate" remained open for about .40 second. Further, they also found that subjects could not report the numbers they saw in correct order, even though they thought they could. This suggests that there is some loss of information during the transfer from sensory to short-term memory (refer to Figure 6-7).

In sum, the research conducted by Reeves and Sperling (1986) suggests that only a small portion of the information present in sensory memory is ever transferred to short-term memory. Given the large amount of input supplied by our various senses, and the limited capacity of short-term memory, this makes eminent sense. In this respect, as in many others, our cognitive system seems to function in ways which maximize our ability to make sense out of the world around us.

Short-Term Memory: Some Basics

Now that we know something about how information enters short-term memory, let's consider some of its basic features—what, precisely, it holds, how much it can retain, and how long it can retain information. In sensory memory, information is represented in a form similar to that reported by our senses; thus, people "hear" sounds and "see" visual stimuli which have previously been presented for brief periods of time. Information is represented somewhat differently in short-term memory. Most verbal input (what we read, the words others speak) seems to be stored *acoustically,* by how it sounds (Salame & Baddeley, 1982). This is indicated by the fact that shortly after learning lists of words or letters, individuals tend to confuse ones that sound alike (e.g., *P* and *T*), rather than ones that look alike (e.g., *O* and *D*).

There is some indication, however, that information is also represented *semantically* in short-term memory—in terms of its meaning. When asked to recall words they have just memorized, people often confuse ones with similar meanings as well as ones that sound alike. In sum, we seem to store information in different ways in our working memory.

Now for another issue: just how much can short-term memory hold? As you know from your own experience, the answer is not much. In fact, careful research on this question indicates that, in general, short-term memory can hold no more than five to seven separate items (Miller, 1956). Note the word ''separate,'' though. Although short-term memory can hold only a small number of items, each of these, in turn, can represent several facts or pieces of information. For example, most persons can retain no more than seven words in short-term memory at once. However, if each of these words consists of the first letters of several other words (e.g., S.A.P.P. for Society of Amalgamated Pickle Packers), quite a bit of information can be contained in this small number. The process of combining separate pieces of information into larger ones is known as *chunking*, and recent evidence suggests that, depending on how we search through information in short-term memory, it may be useful and may begin to occur when as few as four separate items are present (MacGregor, 1987).

Another basic issue relating to short-term memory concerns duration: how long does information in this system last? Again, your own experience suggests a reasonable answer: not very long. Unless it is actively rehearsed (repeated again and again), information entered into short-term memory fades quickly. Indeed, it may be almost totally gone within twenty seconds. Convincing evidence for this conclusion was first gathered by Peterson and Peterson (1959) in a famous investigation. Please see the ''Classic Contributions'' section below for a description of this important research.

FOCUS ON RESEARCH: Classic Contributions

How Long Is Short-Term Memory? Rehearsal Is the Key

Suppose you are about to check into a motel. You know that you'll need to enter your auto's license plate number in the register. Assuming it's not a number you have specially ordered (e.g., your name, birthdate), how do you remember it? The answer is simple: you repeat it to yourself over and over as you enter the building and fill out the form. Research findings suggest, in fact, that this is a highly effective strategy; as long as it is constantly rehearsed, information can remain in short-term memory almost indefinitely. But suppose that on the way into the motel something distracts you, preventing you from repeating the license number to yourself. What will happen? The chances are good that you'll quickly forget the number. Situations like this one suggest that where short-term memory is concerned, the key to persistence involves rehearsal. But how long does short-term memory last in the absence of this activity? The answer was provided three decades ago by Peterson and Peterson (1959).

In order to measure the duration of short-term memory, and the impact of rehearsal on it, these researchers used the following procedures. Subjects first listened to a *trigram*—a combination of three consonants such as *TMS* or *DKV*. Then they heard a three-digit number (e.g., *265*). Subjects were told that when they heard the number, they should immediately begin counting backwards by threes, and continue in this manner until they heard a special signal. At the signal, they should try to recall the trigram. Peterson and Peterson reasoned that counting backwards would prevent participants from rehearsing the trigrams. Thus, by presenting the special signal after varying amounts of time, it would be possible to determine how quickly information is lost from short-term memory in the absence of rehearsal. (Remember: when rehearsal is permitted, there is little loss, even over extended periods of time.) As you can see from Figure 6-8, results left little doubt about the appropriateness of the term *short* in short-term memory. When rehearsal was prevented, a considerable amount of information was lost after only three seconds, and by eighteen seconds, subjects' ability to accurately recall the trigram had virtually disappeared.

Additional findings suggest that the

LIVERPOOL JOHN MOORES UNIVERSITY
Aldham Robarts L.R.C.
TEL. 051 231 3701/3634

Duration of Short-Term Memory

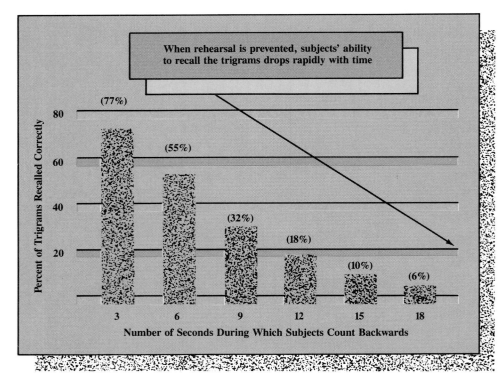

When rehearsal is prevented, subjects' ability to recall the trigrams drops rapidly with time

FIGURE 6-8. After listening to *trigrams*, subjects counted backwards by threes until they heard a signal indicating that they should stop, and try to recall the trigrams. Results indicated that under these conditions, which prevented rehearsal of the trigrams, subjects' ability to recall the trigrams decreased quickly. In fact, it was virtually gone after eighteen seconds. These findings suggest that in the absence of rehearsal, short-term memory is indeed short! *(Source: Based on data from Peterson & Peterson, 1959.)*

greater the extent to which rehearsal is prevented (e.g., by even more distracting tasks), the more rapid is the loss of information from short-term memory (Reitman, 1974). Further, most individuals seem aware of this important fact; when left to their own devices, a large majority actively rehearse information they wish to retain in short-term memory (Reitman, 1974). The moral of such findings is clear: if you want to remember a phone number, license plate, stranger's name, or any other new piece of information even for a brief period of time, there's only one solution: rehearse, rehearse, and then rehearse some more!

Forgetting from Short-Term Memory: Why Does It Occur?

As we've just seen, when rehearsal is prevented, information is quickly lost from short-term memory. But why is this the case? This leads us to a basic question about memory generally: what is the cause of **forgetting**—the loss of information from a memory system? We will consider this question more closely with respect to long-term memory, but it is worth introducing here. Many potential explanations for forgetting have been suggested, but two have received the most attention: decay and interference.

Decay refers to the possibility that forgetting occurs because *engrams*—the electrical or structural changes in our brain produced by learning—fade away over time (see Figure 6-9 for an illustration of this suggestion). In contrast, **interference** refers to the possibility that as new items or pieces of information enter memory they somehow interfere with or displace some which are already present. Such interference can actually occur in two different ways. Items learned first can interfere with items learned later; this is known as *proactive interference*. An example of proactive interference is when you study

One Popular View of Forgetting

FIGURE 6-9. Whether they know it or not, the characters in this cartoon accept the view that forgetting occurs because information stored in memory gradually fades away over time. *(Source: King Features Syndicate, 1978.)*

definitions for a psychology course and, later, these interfere with your efforts to memorize definitions of similar vocabulary for another course. Second, items being learned now can interfere with memory for items learned previously; this is known as *retroactive interference*. An example: you memorize one person's phone number at a party. When you try to memorize another number, you forget the first one. (Incidentally, both of these examples refer primarily to long-term memory; the difference between proactive and retroactive interference is easier to illustrate in this context.)

Which of these explanations—decay or interference—is correct? Since we'll return to this issue in a later section, we won't consider it in detail here. However, the answer currently accepted by most psychologists goes something like this: interference is crucial in forgetting from short-term memory (and other memory systems), but there is some indication that simple decay, too, can play a role (Matlin, 1983a; see pages 183–184 for further discussion).

Long-Term Memory: The Storehouse of Consciousness

Can you remember your first day at school? Your first trip to the dentist? Your first love? Even though these events occurred years ago, the chances are good that you have vivid memories of them. The fact that you do points to the existence of a third memory system—one which permits us to store vast quantities of information in a relatively permanent manner. This is known as **long-term memory,** and evidence concerning its accuracy is nothing short of startling. For example, in one study, Standing, Canezio, and Haber (1970) found that subjects who had viewed each of 2,560 pictures for a few seconds were able to recognize them accurately a year later: they could indicate whether they had seen each picture about 63 percent of the time. Similarly, when persons who had graduated from high school thirty, forty, or even fifty years earlier were asked to match the names with the photos of their classmates—people they hadn't seen for decades—they were able to do so with impressive accuracy (Bahrick, Bahrick, & Wittlinger, 1975). (Refer to Figure 6-10.) In some respects, therefore, long-term memory is quite impressive.

At the same time, though, we have all experienced situations in which, no matter how hard we tried, we could not remember some item or piece of information, despite having previously learned it very well. To make matters worse, at such times we often feel that the fact, name, or item we want is somewhere ''there'' but is just beyond our reach. This is known as the **tip-of-the-tongue phenomenon,** and research findings indicate that it is quite real. When individuals are given the definitions of uncommon English words (e.g., sampan, geode, charisma) and report that they can ''almost'' think of the word, they are quite successful in supplying its first letter and indicating how many syllables it has (Brown & McNeil, 1966). Such findings suggest that the information being sought *is* present in memory but can't be located. As we'll soon see, *retrieval* is indeed a crucial issue where long-term memory is concerned; after all, information that can't be found is as useless to us, in a practical sense, as information that is actually gone.

**Evidence for the Long-Term
Accuracy of Long-Term Memory**

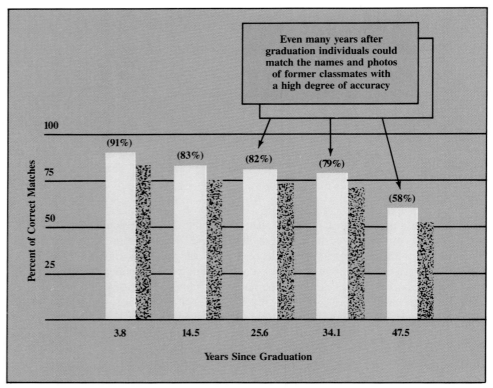

Even many years after
graduation individuals could
match the names and photos
of former classmates with
a high degree of accuracy

FIGURE 6-10. Individuals could match the correct names with photos of former high school classmates even if they hadn't seen these people for nearly fifty years. Such findings suggest that information stored in long-term memory can remain accurate over long periods of time. *(Source: Based on data from Bahrick, Bahrick, & Wittlinger, 1975.)*

So, we are left with a mixed picture of long-term memory. On the one hand, it is impressive in its capacity to store huge quantities of information for long periods of time. On the other hand, it often lets us down just when we seem to need it most (for example, during exams or while delivering a speech to a large group). How does this memory system operate? How is information entered in long-term memory and later retrieved? These are only a few of the questions we'll now consider.

Long-Term Memory: Some Basic Facts

Perhaps the first question is this: how does information enter long-term memory from short-term memory? The answer seems to involve a process we discussed previously: rehearsal. In this case, though, the rehearsal does not consist simply of repeating what we wish to remember. Rather, for information to enter long-term memory, **elaborative rehearsal** seems to be required. This is rehearsal in which we think about the meaning of the new information and attempt to relate it to information already in memory. For example, if you wish to commit the facts and findings presented in a section of this chapter to long-term memory, you should not simply state them to yourself over and over again (maintenance rehearsal). Instead, you should think about what they mean and how they relate to things you already know. In contrast to maintenance rehearsal, elaborative rehearsal requires considerable mental effort. Little wonder, then, that serious studying is such hard work!

If elaborative rehearsal is required for information to enter long-term memory, then anything that interferes with such rehearsal should also interfere with such memory. Many factors might produce such effects, but one with which many persons have had direct experience is *alcohol*. Informal observation suggests that when consumed in sufficient quantities, this drug interferes with long-term memory. For example, individuals often claim that they can't remember events that occurred while under its influence (the "morning after" effect). Research findings lend support to this claim: alcohol *does* seem to impair human memory (Birnbaum & Parker, 1977). But why is this the case? One possibility, suggested by an investigation carried out by Birnbaum and her colleagues (Birnbaum et al., 1987), is as follows: perhaps alcohol interferes with long-term memory by preventing elaborative rehearsal, or at least elaborative processing of incoming information (Birnbaum et al., 1987). Let's examine the evidence pointing to this conclusion.

In one of their studies Birnbaum and her colleagues had male subjects in two groups consume drinks either containing or not containing alcohol. (Subjects did not know which they received, and the aroma of alcohol was concealed by peppermint flavoring.) They then read lists of common words aloud. Some of the words were read only once, while others were read three or five times. After completing this task, subjects were asked to indicate how often they had read each word aloud. Results indicated that the actual frequency with which the words were read had a smaller effect on the judgments of the subjects who received alcohol than on the judgments of those who did not. Thus, in one sense, individuals who had consumed alcohol were less accurate in remembering than those who had not consumed this drug (refer to the left-hand graph of Figure 6-11).

In an additional study, two groups of subjects again either consumed or did not consume alcohol. In this instance, however, the alcohol was presented only *after* subjects had read the lists. Birnbaum and her colleagues reasoned that if this drug affects input into memory, then the effects previously uncovered should not appear. Since information concerning the frequency of the words had already been entered into memory before subjects drank alcohol, long-term memory for frequency of the words should not be

FIGURE 6-11. Individuals who drank alcohol before reading lists of words aloud were less able to report accurately the frequency of the words they had read than were subjects who did not drink alcohol (left graph). Such differences were not found when subjects drank alcohol *after* reading the words (right graph). These findings suggest that alcohol may interfere with processes through which information is entered into long-term memory (e.g., elaborative rehearsal). *(Source: Based on data from Birnbaum et al., 1987.)*

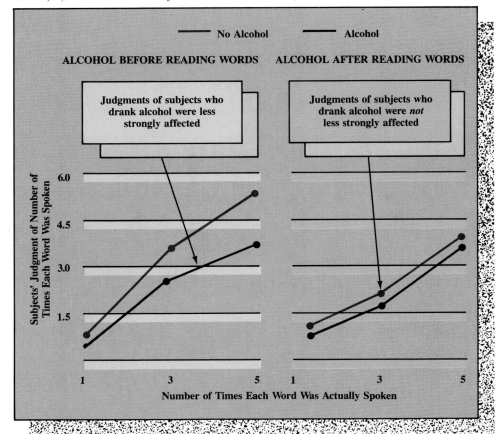

Alcohol and Human Memory

affected. This is precisely what happened: under these conditions (when alcohol was consumed *after* reading the words), subjects who drank alcohol did not differ from those in the control (no-alcohol) group (refer to the right-hand graph of Figure 6-11).

In sum, the findings reported by Birnbaum and her colleagues suggest that alcohol can indeed affect human memory. Moreover, it appears that such effects may derive, at least in part, from interference with the processes through which information is entered into long-term storage.

Now that we've mentioned elaborative rehearsal, this is a good place to introduce a related concept—**levels of processing.** This term refers to an intriguing approach to memory, different in certain respects from the one we've adopted so far. This approach (Craik & Lockhart, 1972) suggests that information can actually be processed in several ways, and these can be arranged along a dimension ranging from *shallow processing* through *deep processing.* Shallow processing involves such things as simple sensory judgments—for example, do two words or two letters look alike? A deeper level of processing might involve the way words sound—for example, do they rhyme? A deep level of processing would involve attention to meaning, and how the word or letter relates to ideas and concepts already in memory. Considerable evidence suggests that the deeper the level of processing which takes place when we first encounter new materials, the more likely we are to remember them—the more likely they are to enter long-term memory (refer to Figure 6-12). For example, in one well-known study (Craik & Tulving, 1975) subjects were asked to read a list of words and then to answer questions about the words. Some of the questions referred to the words' appearance (e.g., are they printed in capital or small letters?). For others, the questions involved their sound (e.g., do they rhyme with other words?). For still other words, the questions concerned meaning (e.g., do these words fit into specific sentences? Are they nouns or verbs?). Later, subjects' ability to remember which words had been on the list was assessed. Results offered support for the levels of processing view: subjects were most accurate in recognizing words about which they had been asked questions relating to meaning (deep processing), and they were least accurate in recognizing words about which they had been asked questions pertaining merely to appearance (shallow processing).

As you can readily see, the activities required by a deep level of processing are the ones required by elaborative rehearsal. Thus, there seems to be general agreement among

FIGURE 6-12. According to the *levels of processing* approach, the more effort we expend in processing new information, the more likely it is to be placed in long-term memory. Thus, thinking about the meaning of printed words produces better recall of them at later times than merely noticing whether they are written in capitals or small letters.

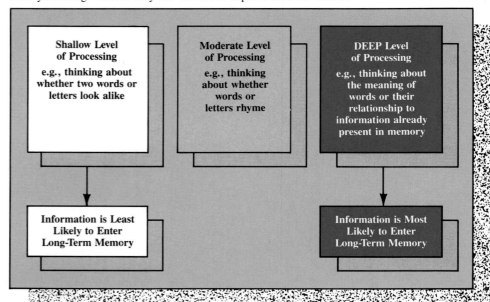

Levels of Processing and Long-Term Memory

memory researchers on this point: if you wish to enter some fact or item into long-term memory, there is only one way to do so: hard, mental effort.

Retrieval: Finding What's There

As we've already noted, the major limitations of short-term memory are all too obvious: this memory system has a limited capacity, and information is quickly lost unless it is rehearsed in a continuous manner. Long-term memory, of course, does not suffer from these problems. It has a seemingly limitless capacity—you can go on learning and storing new information throughout your entire life. And it can retain information for very long periods of time, perhaps indefinitely. Is it, then, a perfect memory system? Definitely not. All too often you find it impossible to remember information you need, when you need it. Only later—maddeningly!—does it sometimes pop effortlessly into your mind (Payne, 1987). Why is this the case? If long-term memory has such a huge capacity, why does it let you down in such cases? The answer involves the process of *retrieval*. As we've noted before, the information you seek is there, all right; you just can't find it. So, to understand the nature and operation of long-term memory we must consider retrieval.

Actually, where long-term memory is concerned, it is difficult to separate retrieval from the issue of *storage*—the form in which information is first entered into memory. The reason for this is as follows: the way information is initially placed in long-term memory plays an important role in determining how readily it can later be retrieved. In general, the better *organized* materials are, the easier it is to retrieve them at later times. For example, consider a study by Bower and his colleagues (Bower et al., 1969) in which subjects were asked to memorize words falling into four distinct categories (e.g., minerals, animals). For some subjects the words were presented in an organized manner (refer to Figure 6-13). Thus, *birds* and *mammals* were presented under the general heading "animals," and appropriate entries were placed under each subtitle. For other subjects the words were arranged randomly; they were also presented in tree-like structures like the one in Figure 6-13, but the words occurred in any position, at random. When subjects were asked to recall the words, those who had viewed them in an organized manner did much better. In fact, they recalled an average of seventy-three words on the first trial, while subjects in the control group (organization lacking) recalled only twenty-one. Simi-

FIGURE 6-13. Subjects were much more successful in remembering words which had been presented in the organized manner shown here than when the same words had been presented in the absence of such organization. *(Source: Based on materials used by Bower et al., 1969.)*

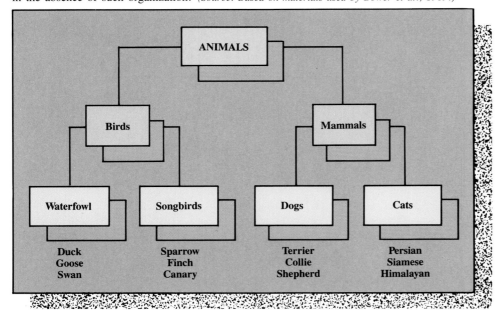

The Role of Organization in Long-Term Memory

lar results have been obtained in many other studies (Matlin, 1983a). Thus, it appears that one key to the effective retrieval of information stored in long-term memory is organization. This may require extra work initially, but benefits in later retrieval can be great.

Retrieval Cues: Stimuli Which Help Us Remember. After an interval of several years, you return to a place you once knew well—a school you attended, a neighborhood where you once lived, or a favorite restaurant you haven't visited for a long time. Once there, memories of days gone by come flooding back, with no apparent effort on your part to bring them to mind. Have you ever had this kind of experience? If so, you are already familiar with the operation of what psychologists term *retrieval cues* (see Figure 6-14). These are stimuli which are associated with information stored in memory, and so can help us retrieve it. As our example indicates, such cues can be aspects of the external environment—a place, sights or sounds, smells (Engen, 1986), or even another person. One ingenious study illustrating this point was conducted by Smith, Glenberg, and Bjork (1978). They had people memorize some words in one environment (a windowless room with a large blackboard, in the presence of an experimenter dressed in a coat and tie), or in a different environment (a tiny room with two windows, and an experimenter dressed in a flannel shirt and jeans). Later, subjects' memory for the lists of words was tested in each location. Results indicated that subjects remembered more words when returned to the place where they originally learned them. Thus, words initially memorized in the first room were remembered better there than in the second room, and vice versa.

In addition, certain aspects of the materials to be remembered can serve as retrieval cues. In this respect, *category names* are often helpful. Once individuals have such categories, locating the information in them (items fitting under the categories) becomes easier. An experiment by Tulving and Pearlstone (1966) demonstrated such effects

FIGURE 6-14. If you have ever returned to a place you once knew well but haven't visited for years, you may have experienced an unexpected flood of memories. This is due to the presence of many *retrieval cues*.

Retrieval Cues: An Important Aid to Memory

clearly. These researchers asked subjects to memorize forty-eight different words. The words were grouped together into named categories. Subjects were told that they didn't have to remember the categories, only the words. Later they were asked to recall the forty-eight words. Some subjects were given the category names at this time, while others were not. As you might expect, those given the category names performed much better—they remembered more of the original words. Apparently, when subjects learned the words, they organized them according to the categories supplied by the experimenters. When asked to recall them, the categories served as retrieval cues which helped subjects remember the correct information. Interestingly, when individuals are not supplied with category names or other means of organizing materials they wish to memorize, they often develop their own organization. For example, when Rubin and Olson (1980) asked graduating college students to list all the faculty they could remember, they showed a strong tendency to group such persons by department. Thus, subjects listed all the psychology faculty together, all the chemistry faculty together, and so on, even though they were not asked to do this. Such findings indicate that although most persons have not heard the term *retrieval cues,* they often use them to enhance their recall of important information.

Finally, even an individual's own internal state can serve as a retrieval cue in some cases. Suppose that while studying for an exam you drink lots of coffee. Thus, the effects of caffeine are present while you memorize facts, names, findings, or formulas. On the day of the test, should you also drink lots of coffee? If you do, the effects of caffeine will again be present. And if these act as a retrieval cue, your memory will be enhanced (refer to Figure 6-15). Several studies indicate that this may be the case. That is, when your internal state at the time you attempt to remember specific information is the same as it was when you first learned it, your memory will be enhanced. Such effects are known as *state-dependent retrieval* (Eich, 1980, 1985). However, this only seems to be true under conditions of free recall—when you try to remember the information in the absence of category names or other external cues. Such findings offer another explanation for why

FIGURE 6-15. If you drink lots of coffee while studying for an exam, your internal state may become associated with the information you memorize. If you also drink coffee on the day of the exam, this internal state will be reproduced and may serve as a useful *retrieval cue* (upper panel). In contrast, if you don't drink coffee while studying, you should probably not drink it on the day of the exam. If you do, your internal state will be different than when you studied and will not serve as a retrieval cue for the information you need to remember (lower panel).

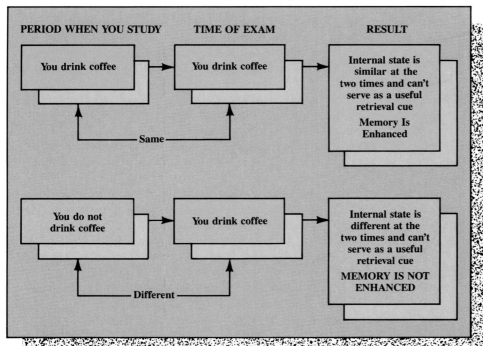

Internal States as Retrieval Cues

people who consume large amounts of alcohol or other drugs sometimes report that they cannot remember what they said or did while under the influence of these drugs. Since a person's internal state on the ''morning after'' is quite different than it was while under the influence of the drug, important retrieval cues are absent and memory may be impaired. Of course, drug-induced forgetting can also stem from the physiological impact of the drug. But changes in internal states and the absence of appropriate retrieval cues, too, may play a role.

In sum, many different stimuli can serve as retrieval cues. Which do we actually use, and which are most helpful? According to the **encoding specificity principle** (Tulving & Thomson, 1973), this depends on what information we enter into memory in the first place. If, when learning some information, certain aspects of your physical surroundings are part of the ''package'' you encode, these will later serve as useful retrieval cues. If your internal state is part of what is encoded, then *this* will later serve as an effective retrieval cue. The key point seems to be a close match between the conditions under which you first learned some information and the conditions under which you attempt to recall it. The specific nature of individual retrieval cues seems to be of less importance.

Retrieval from Semantic Memory: Recall of General Knowledge.   Studying for a test, memorizing phone numbers, trying to recall the items on a shopping list; these are common situations in everyday life in which we try to remember specific items or information acquired in specific contexts. Because such information is linked to specific times, places, or contexts, it is often described as **episodic memory.**

In contrast, we also use memory to recall more general knowledge. Such information often seems so familiar that we can no longer remember just when and how we acquired it, yet it can be of great importance. Psychologists refer to this as **semantic memory,** and it is truly impressive, both in the wealth of information it contains, and in the speed with which it seems to operate. For example, suppose you are asked to indicate which of the following statements is true or false. You can do so with amazing speed:

A dog is an animal.
Trees are plants.
Alligators have feathers.
The sun rises in the west.
Politicians have halos.

How can you respond so quickly? How can you search through semantic memory and find just the information required in less than a second (the average time most people need)? One explanation, known as *spreading activation theory,* suggests that the answer lies in the fact that individual bits of information do not float around freely or at random in memory (Collins & Loftus, 1975). Rather, they exist in networks of *associations*. The more similar in meaning facts or concepts are, the stronger the connections between them. Thus, when one fact or concept is activated (e.g., by a question about it), such activation spreads to related concepts or ideas. In short, our general knowledge of the world exists in a richly interrelated framework, and it is the existence of this conceptual framework that allows us to demonstrate such great efficiency in dealing with specific aspects of semantic memory.

Evidence for the kind of spreading activation just described is provided by studies in which subjects are asked to indicate whether each item on a list is or is not a word (e.g., olvan, randel, hammer, orange, blom). When the words on the list are unrelated, as in the example, subjects can respond quite quickly. However, when some of the words are related (e.g., hammer, nail), subjects respond even more rapidly (refer to Figure 6-16). One explanation for such results is that activation from the first word spreads to related words or concepts. Such activation then facilitates recognition of these words or concepts (Neely, 1977).

Interestingly, as in many other areas of life, there can sometimes be ''too much of a good thing'' with respect to semantic memory. When words or concepts activate large numbers of related concepts, memory for the original words—the ones which got the

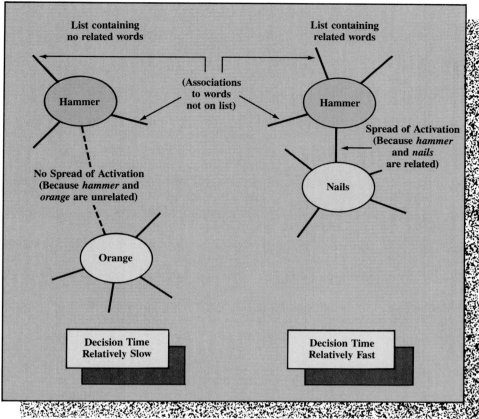

FIGURE 6-16. When subjects were asked to determine whether each item on a list is a word or not a word, they made such decisions more quickly when some of the words were closely related to each other (e.g., hammer, nail). Such findings can be explained in terms of the *spread of activation* from the first related word to the second.

entire process started—may actually be impaired. In such cases, it is as if our minds became clogged with too much related but irrelevant information (Nelson, Bajo, & Canas, 1987). This appears to be the exception rather than the rule, however. In general, the existence of a richly interconnected semantic framework for our general knowledge about the world seems to facilitate, not hinder, memory and other cognitive processes.

Forgetting from Long-Term Memory: Why Does It Occur?

If long-term memory can retain information for months or years, why do we sometimes seem to lose items from it? In short, assuming that information is ever lost from long-term memory (an assumption many psychologists question), what accounts for this occurrence? As was true with short-term memory, two possibilities have received most attention: (1) information simply fades or *decays* with the passage of time; (2) some items entered into memory interfere with others, thus preventing their recall. Which view is correct? Although no final answer to this question yet exists, most psychologists believe that forgetting from long-term memory is largely a matter of interference. A great deal of evidence points to this conclusion, but here we'll simply mention two findings that argue strongly against the view that forgetting is due to decay of memory traces.

First, consider the occurrence of *reminiscence* and *hypermnesia*. **Reminiscence** refers to an experience we've all had: we try to remember some information but fail; later, though, we remember it with ease. **Hypermnesia** refers to the fact that our memory for certain types of information (especially pictorial items) actually seems to improve with the passage of time (Payne, 1987). Obviously, the existence of both reminiscence and hypermnesia argue against the notion that information in memory simply decays with the passage of time. On the contrary, they suggest that information we can't remember is still there; it simply can't be located.

Second, consider an old but still informative study by Jenkins and Dallenbach (1924). These researchers asked two subjects to learn a list of ten nonsense syllables. In one condition, both individuals then went to sleep. In another, they continued with their normal activities. Their recall of the nonsense syllables was tested after one, two, four, and eight hours. Results were clear: forgetting was more rapid when subjects stayed awake than when they went to sleep. This finding, too, argues against the view that forgetting from long-term memory is produced by the gradual decay of information over time.

On the other side of the coin, a large number of studies indicates that interference between items accounts for such forgetting (Matlin, 1983a). Both proactive and retroactive interference seem important in this respect. (Do you remember the difference between these? Proactive interference occurs when old information interferes with recalling new information; retroactive interference occurs when new information interferes with the recall of old information.) One way of thinking about the role of interference in long-term memory is as follows: imagine that a book you are looking for in a library has been pushed behind the shelf. Now, you can't find it because other books block your view. This certainly oversimplifies things, but it may help you grasp the role of interference in forgetting. In sum, forgetting from long-term memory seems to be primarily a matter of interference. Unlike old soldiers, old memories do not seem to fade away; rather they are obscured or hidden by other information also present in memory.

Memory in Natural Contexts

So far, our discussion of memory has focused on somewhat artificial tasks: recall of nonsense syllables, lists of words or numbers. Of course, we *do* have to remember such items in some real-life contexts; for example, many students would describe chemistry formulas as close to nonsense syllables, at least at first, and lists of names, dates, and terms must be memorized in many other courses. Still, the research we've described does not seem closely related to many tasks of daily life. For example, when you read a book, magazine, or newspaper, you often retain some of the information you've encountered,

FIGURE 6-17. When you see a play, read a book, or have a conversation with others, you usually remember only part of what you saw, read, or heard. How does memory operate in such natural contexts? This question has been the subject of an increasing amount of research.

but not in a word-for-word form. Similarly, when you attend a meeting or have a conversation with another person, you remember some of the information presented but, again, not all of it. How does memory operate in such contexts? (Refer to Figure 6-17.) Does it involve principles not apparent in the traditional kinds of research we've already described? Recent research has focused on such questions, with intriguing results.

Distortion and Construction in Memory for Natural Events

When individuals are asked to memorize lists of nonsense syllables or meaningless numbers, they rarely show perfect performance. Usually they are unable to reproduce all the items they tried to learn. Since the items are unfamiliar, this is far from surprising. When individuals are asked to remember more familiar stimuli, such as sentences, stories, or the events in films, however, different results are often obtained. Forgetting of specific facts may also occur, but it is more frequent for errors to take two other forms: *distortion* and *construction*.

Distortion and the Influence of Schemas.   Distortion refers to changes introduced into the information we remember. For example, after a conversation one of the participants may remember that he said ''no'' to a request from the other person, while she remembers that he said ''yes.'' Similarly, when individuals are asked to remember, and perhaps to evaluate, the performance of others, what they recall may depart from reality in important ways. For example, if they like the person they are evaluating, they may remember his or her performance as being better than it actually was; if they dislike this person, they may recall it as being worse (Williams & Keating, 1987).

What accounts for such effects? One answer involves the operation of **schemas** (Wyer & Srull, 1986). These are cognitive frameworks, developed through experience, which act like mental scaffolds: they provide structures for processing and storing new information. Many different types of schemas seem to exist. For example, you may have separate schemas for specific groups of persons (e.g., men, women, blacks, whites) and for various situations (e.g., you know what usually happens in college classrooms or on a visit to a dentist).

Once they are formed, schemas exert strong effects on the way information is encoded, stored, and then retrieved. This, in turn, can introduce important errors into memory systems. Perhaps such effects are most apparent with respect to encoding. Some evidence suggests that information which is consistent with our schemas is encoded more readily than information which is inconsistent with such frameworks (Fiske & Taylor, 1984). Since only information that is noticed and encoded can later be remembered, this can be an important source of memory distortion. For example, consider an individual whose schema for members of a minority group includes the belief that they are immoral. When reading the newspaper, she will notice and encode information consistent with her schema (e.g., reports of violent crimes carried out by such persons). In contrast, she will be less likely to notice and encode information which contradicts this view (e.g., reports of heroism or achievement by members of this group; Fiske & Taylor, 1984). As you can readily see, such effects can have serious practical results (refer to Figure 6-18). And, as we have already noted, they seem to occur in a wide range of contexts.

Construction and Inference.   Unfortunately, distortion is not the only type of error that can affect our memory for everyday events or experiences. In addition, such memory is also often affected by *construction*. This refers to the fact that we often fill in the details when recalling natural events; we add to what actually had been experienced. Why do we do this? The answer seems to involve our strong desire to have a clear understanding of the world around us. In order to make sense out of our experiences, we tend to fill in details in ways that make the overall pattern most complete and sensible.

In most cases, such additions to memory are relatively simple and undramatic. For example, we ''remember'' the eye-color of a character in a story when in fact this detail was absent. Sometimes, however, the tendency to complete our picture of the world can lead us to ''remember'' statements or even actions by others they never performed. As we

Schemas and Memory Distortions

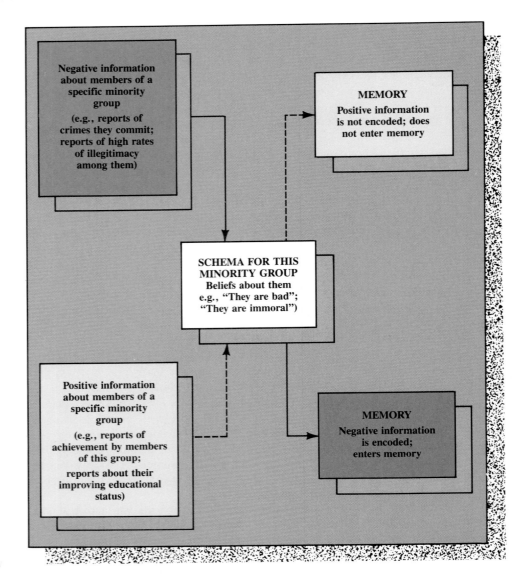

FIGURE 6-18. *Schemas,* cognitive frameworks developed through past experience, often determine what information is noticed and stored in memory. One example would be an individual whose schema for members of a specific minority group contains the belief that such persons are immoral. As a result, she notices information consistent with this view quite readily, but she tends to ignore information inconsistent with it. The result: she remembers only negative information about these persons.

will see in the next section, where we discuss *eyewitness testimony,* memory errors of this type can be serious indeed (Wells & Loftus, 1984).

But adding details or even entire incidents is only part of the total picture. In addition, our memory for natural events is often affected by the process of *inference.* Given certain types of information, we infer other ''facts'' or events because we think that logically, they must have occurred (Conway & Ross, 1984). For example, imagine that someone you know suddenly leaves her husband. Will this affect your memory about this person? Perhaps you add details to your recollection of previous incidents—ones which are consistent with your inference that she has been unhappy for a long time and probably showed this in her behavior. In this and many other situations, the inferences we draw can introduce errors into our memory systems.

Eyewitness Testimony: Distortion and Construction in Action

If you've ever watched the exploits of ''Perry Mason'' or other television attorneys, you already know that eyewitness testimony plays an important role in many legal proceedings. At first glance, this makes a great deal of sense: after all, what better source of information about events could there be than persons who were actually present? (Refer to Figure 6-19.) After reading the last section, though, you may now realize that there may be more to this situation than meets the eye! Given the possibilities for error in human

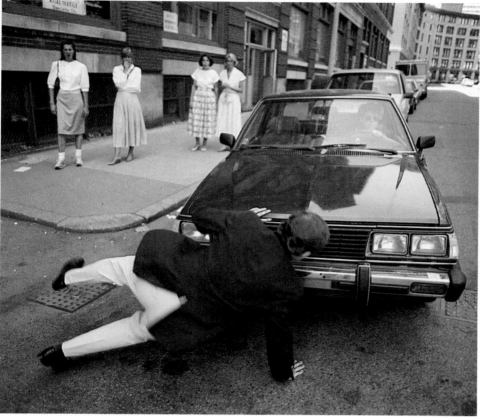

FIGURE 6-19. Can eyewitnesses to an accident provide accurate information about it? Research on this question suggests that the answer is probably, "sometimes."

memory already described, it is reasonable to ask the following question: are eye-witnesses really accurate? Unfortunately, a growing body of evidence suggests that the answer to this question is "no," or, at best, "sometimes" (Wells & Loftus, 1984).

Perhaps the most unsettling findings on this issue are ones reported by Loftus and her colleagues in a series of related studies. For example, in one of these investigations—designed to see if witnesses could be influenced by leading questions—subjects saw a series of slides about an imaginary traffic accident (Loftus, Miller, & Burns, 1978). One of the slides showed a red sports car (a Datsun) halted at a stop sign. Later, subjects were asked the following question: "Did another car pass the red Datsun while it was stopped at the yield sign?" Finally, subjects were shown two slides: the one they had previously seen and one showing the Datsun at a yield sign. They were asked to choose the one which had previously been presented. The results? Most subjects chose the picture with the yield sign. Apparently, their memories had been influenced by the experimenter's leading question.

In another study, Loftus (1979), staged a theft at a busy train station. A female accomplice left a bag unattended, and while she was gone a male accomplice reached inside and removed an article. When the woman returned, she stated, "My tape recorder is missing!" Then, she asked eye-witnesses to give her their phone numbers; most agreed to do so. One week later, an individual who identified himself as an insurance agent phoned these witnesses and asked them for details of the crime. Although there actually was no tape recorder, more than 50 percent remembered seeing it. Moreover, many persons gave details concerning its shape and color!

These and related findings suggest that eyewitness testimony is not as accurate as the legal system often assumes. Rather, it appears to be subject to several types of error. Considering the powerful impact on jurors which eyewitness testimony often exerts (Leippe, 1985), the dangers of accepting such evidence at face value become apparent. Is

Improving the Accuracy of
Eyewitness Testimony

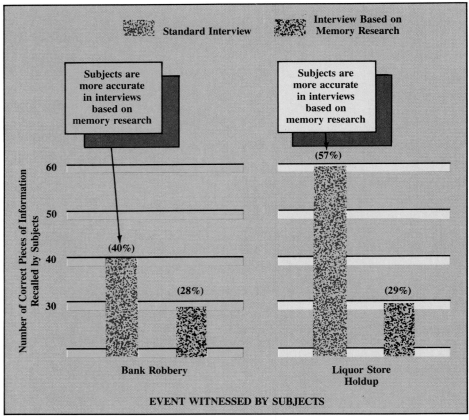

FIGURE 6-20. When procedures based on scientific findings about human memory were employed, the accuracy of eyewitnesses was substantially improved over that obtained through standard techniques for questioning such persons. These findings indicate that under appropriate conditions the accuracy of eyewitnesses *can* be improved. *(Source: Based on data from Geiselman et al., 1985.)*

there any way of improving this situation? Fortunately, recent findings indicate that there are. For example, Geiselman and his colleagues (Geiselman et al., 1985) had professionals in law enforcement (e.g., detectives, CIA investigators) interview subjects who had watched four films depicting crimes (e.g., a bank robbery, a liquor store holdup). In one condition, the interview was conducted in a standard manner, the way police officers would normally proceed: subjects were asked to describe the film in their own words, and then were asked specific questions about the events in it. In another condition, procedures based on the findings of basic research on memory were used to improve the witnesses' accuracy. Thus, steps were taken to increase the overlap between the context at the time of encoding and during retrieval. Subjects were told to report everything, even partial information, and they were also asked to describe the events they had seen in a variety of different orders. Results were quite encouraging: subjects were more accurate in describing the films when questioned in this manner than in the standard interview (refer to Figure 6-20). It appears, then, that the accuracy of eyewitness testimony *can* be improved through procedures based on current knowledge about the nature of human memory. (For even more encouraging evidence with respect to eyewitness testimony, please see ''The Cutting Edge'' section on page 189.)

Before concluding, we should mention one additional technique for improving the accuracy of eyewitness testimony: hypnosis. (Recall that we mentioned this possibility in Chapter 4, in our discussion of hypnosis.) Because some research findings suggest that certain types of memory can be enhanced through hypnosis (McConkey & Kinoshita, 1988), it has been proposed that hypnotizing eyewitnesses to a crime may help such persons remember crucial evidence. Is this actually the case? Some findings seem to offer support for this hypothesis (Reiser & Nielson, 1980), but existing evidence, taken as a whole, is unconvincing (Kihlstrom, 1985). Thus, it seems unwise to jump to the conclusion that hypnosis can serve as an important aid to justice, ''refreshing'' the memories of witnesses, victims, or defendants about crucial, crime-related events. Hypnosis may indeed enhance some types of memory under some conditions (McConkey & Kinoshita, 1988), but, at present, claims about its usefulness in courtroom proceedings remain unproven.

FOCUS ON RESEARCH: The Cutting Edge

How Accurate Is Eyewitness Testimony? Evidence from an Actual Crime

During the past two decades psychologists have gathered impressive evidence pointing to the conclusion noted above: eyewitness testimony is not very accurate. Given what we know about human memory and errors in recalling natural events, this conclusion makes good scientific sense. Yet there is one problem in interpreting research on this issue. In general, findings have been obtained in *simulations*—studies in which students and other subjects read or watched artificially created events. In such research participants usually know they are witnessing a contrived event, and they realize that the consequences of their reports are minimal. Would findings be any different if actual eyewitnesses to a real crime were considered? The results of a recent study by Yuille and Cutshall (1986) indicate that they would.

In order to examine the accuracy of real eyewitnesses, Yuille and Cutshall obtained the cooperation of the police in a large Canadian city. Immediately after a violent crime occurred (a shooting incident in which a thief was shot and killed by a gun store owner), police officers conducted standard interviews with the twenty-one eyewitnesses. During these interviews they first asked witnesses to describe what they had seen, and then posed specific questions about these events. Four to five months later, the researchers contacted the witnesses and asked them to participate in additional interviews; thirteen persons agreed. These interviews were similar to the ones conducted by the police, with one important exception: two misleading questions were added. These involved the headlight on the thief's car ("Did you see the broken headlight?") and the color of the car ("Did you see the yellow quarterpanel?"). In fact, there was no broken headlight, and the color was not yellow.

Results were dramatic, to say the least. First, contrary to many laboratory studies, eyewitnesses were highly accurate. As shown in Figure 6-21, this was true with respect to their descriptions of actions, people, and objects related to the crime. Moreover, this high level of accuracy did not decline over time; witnesses were almost as accurate after five months, during the interviews conducted by the researchers. In addition, and perhaps even more encouraging, the misleading questions used in the follow-up interviews failed to affect these actual eyewitnesses. Ten of the thirteen replied negatively to both, or indicated that they hadn't noticed, and the remaining three persons expressed uncertainty.

Why are these findings so different from those in simulation studies? Yuille and Cutshall (1986) believe that the high levels of accuracy they observed are due, in part, to the emotional impact and uniqueness of this event. Seeing an actual shooting may be so arousing that vivid memories were produced among witnesses. This is similar to what are often termed **flashbulb memories**—vivid images of what we were doing at the time of some dramatic event such as the assassination of President Kennedy (Brown & Kulik, 1977) or the tragic explosion of the space shuttle *Challenger*. In addition, Yuille and Cutshall note that the actual witnesses realized that their reports had extremely important consequences; this, too, may have enhanced their accuracy.

If these suggestions are correct, lower levels of accuracy may occur among eyewitnesses to less unique or less arousing crimes, a possibility worthy of careful study in further research. Such possibilities aside, the findings reported by Yuille

Eyewitness Testimony: It *Can* Be Accurate

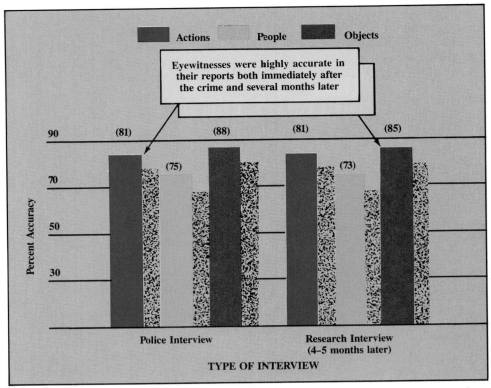

FIGURE 6-21. Contrary to the results of many laboratory studies, eyewitnesses to an actual crime were highly accurate in remembering information about events in the crime and the people involved. Moreover, they did not show any decrease in accuracy after several months. These findings suggest that eyewitness testimony can be quite accurate, at least in cases where the crimes observed are unique and emotionally arousing. *(Source: Based on data from Yuille & Cutshall, 1986.)*

and Cutshall suggest that it may be time for another look at eyewitness testimony. Perhaps, when the chips are down, eye-witnesses *can* be quite accurate. If so, this is certainly good news for the fairness of our legal system.

Improving Memory: Some Useful Techniques

While few of us share the problems shown by the person in Figure 6-22, we are aware that memory is far from perfect. Yet, some people seem immune to such difficulties and are able to perform great feats of memory. For example, actors and actresses can recite the lines of many different plays; great conductors know every note played by every instrument in dozens of symphonies. And some waiters and waitresses remember complex orders from many different customers at once. How do they do it? Are some persons born with a special gift, or can almost anyone learn to improve his or her memory? Existing evidence points to the latter conclusion: with a little hard work, almost anyone can remember more information, more accurately, than he or she ever thought possible. Some useful techniques in this regard are summarized below.

Elaborative Rehearsal: Think About What You Want to Remember. Earlier, we noted that if you wish to remember something, it is important to think about it in certain ways. In particular, it is useful to ask questions about it, to consider its meaning,

"Refresh my memory, Miss Lockland. Who am I?"

FIGURE 6-22. While memory usually isn't this bad, there is little doubt that it's far from perfect. *(Source: The New Yorker, 1986.)*

and to examine its relationship to information you already know. Following these steps takes effort, we admit, but the results in improved recall can be impressive. Try to use this method as you study this text and others; it's almost certain to help.

Imagery: Often, a Mental Picture Is Worth Many Words. Suppose you were learning to speak a foreign language. Would it be easier to remember words relating to specific objects (table, apple, house) or ones standing for abstract concepts (justice, honor, truth)? In all likelihood, memorizing words in the first group would prove easier. The reason for this involves the role of *imagery* in memory. We generally find it easier to remember information associated with a vivid mental image (Pavio, 1969). If you wish to improve your memory, therefore, it is often useful to employ this basic principle. In fact, imagery plays an important role in several **mnemonics**—strategies for improving memory. One of these, known as the *method of loci,* involves the following steps. Suppose you want to remember a series of points you hope to make in a speech. First, imagine walking through some familiar place, say, your home. Then form a series of images in which each item you wish to remember is placed in a specific location. Perhaps the first point is, ''Tax rates are too high.'' You might imagine several persons impoverished by excessive taxes begging for assistance near your front door. The second point is, ''Government spending is excessive.'' Here, you could visualize a huge pile of money being shoveled out a window in your living room. You could continue in this way until each point you wished to make is associated with a specific location. Then, by taking an imaginary walk through your house, you would ''see'' each of these images, and so have a means of remembering the points in your speech (refer to Figure 6-23).

Organization: Information That Is Structured Is Easier to Remember Than Information That Is Not. As we hope you'll recall, information that is well organized at the time it is encoded is usually easier to remember than information that is not well organized. So, if you wish to remember a large array of facts, dates, or terms, it is often helpful to organize them in some manner. This can involve placing them in outline form or in a logic tree, in which large categories are at the top, with smaller and smaller

Mnemonics in the Supermarket

FIGURE 6-23. This person didn't make a grocery list and is trying to recall the items he needs. If he had used the *method of loci* and mentally ''placed'' each item in a different room of his home, he would now be able to remember them by taking an imaginary stroll through each room.

categories underneath, like branches. Again, some effort is required to come up with an appropriate organization, but it is time well spent; for your ability to remember the information will be greatly increased.

Mediation: Develop Your Own Internal Codes.   When you were in elementary school, you may have learned the nine planets by means of the *first-letter technique:*

TABLE 6-1

In addition to the techniques described in the text, the procedures listed here can also sometimes be useful in improving memory.

Technique	Description
Rhymes	Information to be remembered is included in a short statement that rhymes (e.g., ''*I* before *E* except after *C*.'')
Peg Method	Objects which rhyme with numbers are chosen (e.g., ''one is a gun,'' ''two is a shoe,'' etc.), and the items to be remembered are converted to images involving these peg words.
Keyword Method	Words that sound like the ones to be memorized (e.g., foreign vocabulary) are identified. Then individuals form images of the to-be-memorized keywords interacting with the English words (e.g., to learn *golova*, the Russian word for ''head,'' choose *Gulliver* and imagine Gulliver with his head tied down by the tiny Lilliputians).

Additional Techniques for Improving Memory

Mary's Violet Eyes Make John Stay Up Nights Pondering (Mercury, Venus, Earth, Mars, Jupiter, Saturn, Uranus, Neptune, Pluto). This seems to be a very useful technique; more than half of first-year medical students report using it when preparing for anatomy exams (Gruneberg, 1978). The first-letter technique is only one way in which *mediation* can be used to enhance memory. Others involve adding extra words or images to material in order to make it more memorable. Another is known as the use of *narrative*. Here, a story which links the items to be remembered together is constructed. Since the story will have a plot that ties the parts together, this can be helpful.

Many other techniques for improving memory exist, but most are related to the ones we have described so far. For a description of several of these procedures, please see Table 6-1. Good luck!

The Physiology of Memory: In Search of the Engram

Let's begin with a simple assumption: when you acquire new information and commit it to memory, *something* must happen in your brain. But what, precisely, is this? This question has tantalized psychologists, physiologists, and other scientists for decades. Indeed, after thirty years of work on this issue a famous physiological psychologist, Karl Lashley (1950), admitted with a tinge of despair that he could not identify any specific area of the brain as critical to memory. Only within the last decade has an answer to this puzzle begun to emerge. Since important clues have come from the study of persons suffering from memory disorders, we'll turn to this type of evidence first.

Amnesia and Other Memory Disorders: What They Tell Us About the Nature of Memory

Amnesia, as you probably already know, is the loss of memory. In humans, it is often the result of an accident resulting in brain injury, although it can also stem from drug abuse or from serious forms of mental illness. Two major types exist. In *retrograde amnesia* memory for events prior to the accident is impaired. In *anterograde amnesia,* in contrast, memory loss occurs only for events following the accident. Both types of amnesia seem to be related to damage to the temporal lobes and hippocampus, and recent evidence suggests that the amygdala and portions of the thalamus, too, may be involved (Carlson, 1986). Given the complex interconnections between parts of the brain, the fact that several structures may play a role in memory disorders is hardly surprising.

But what does amnesia tell us about the nature of memory? Actually, quite a lot. Some of the most dramatic information in this respect is based on the careful long-term study of a patient known as H.M. who, because of severe epileptic seizures, underwent surgery to remove large portions of his temporal lobes (Scoville & Milner, 1957; Corkin, et al., 1981). After his operation H.M. experienced severe anterograde amnesia. He could remember events that had occurred before his operation but little that happened after it. For example, when his family moved to a new home, he could not find his way back to it, even after several months of practice. He could not name people he had met repeatedly since his operation. And he could read the same magazine over and over again with continued enjoyment, because as soon as he put it down, he forgot what it contained. As H.M. himself put it: ''Every day is alone in itself. . . . It's like waking from a dream; I just don't remember'' (Milner, 1970, p. 37).

While demonstrating such impairments, though, H.M. can carry on normal conversations, can repeat seven numbers, and can perform simple arithmetic without paper and pencil. These findings suggest that his short-term verbal memory is intact, as is his long-term memory for events prior to his operation. Thus, his major problem seems to be an inability to transfer new information from short-term memory to long-term memory.

The story does not end there. Although H.M. showed severe anterograde amnesia, his ability to learn has not been totally eliminated. For example, when asked to trace the outline of geometric figures seen in a mirror, his performance quickly improved (refer to

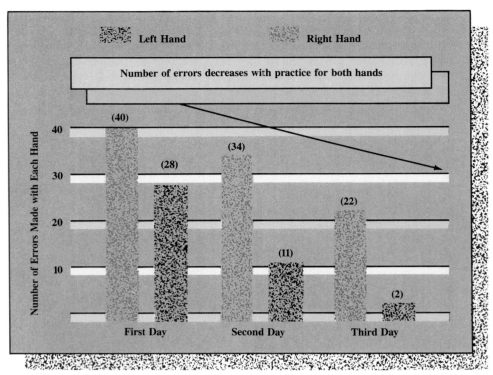

FIGURE 6-24. H.M., an individual suffering from anterograde amnesia, could learn to trace the outlines of geometric figures seen in a mirror. Moreover, his performance improved with practice and did not decrease even after several days. These findings suggest that such persons can enter new information into long-term memory, even though they remain unaware of its presence. *(Source: Based on data from Milner, 1965.)*

Figure 6-24). Moreover, these improvements were maintained for several days. Similarly, he showed evidence of learning on several other tasks, such as recognizing incomplete drawings or solving various puzzles (Cohen & Corkin, 1981). Interestingly, though, after performing such tasks on one occasion, H.M. typically denied any prior experience with them when asked to perform them again at later times (Cohen & Corkin, 1981). It appears, then, that persons such as H.M. suffering from anterograde amnesia may actually remember more than they realize or can report (Graf, Squire, & Mandler, 1984). One possible interpretation of these results is that information acquired by amnesics is indeed entered into long-term memory. Once there, however, it cannot readily be recalled to consciousness. In short, such persons can learn but are unable to report what they learned or even report that they learned it.

Memory and the Brain

Additional clues to the biochemical nature of memory are provided by studies directly concerned with changes in the brain and nervous system produced by learning. Presumably, such changes in structure or function are related to the way in which neurons store information. The picture provided by such research is still unclear, but the outlines of an overall pattern are beginning to emerge. For example, it appears that, at least in some species, learning triggers the release of specific neurotransmitters at certain synapses, and as a result these synapses become more efficient in transmitting neural impulses (Davis & Squire, 1984). Similarly, the number of neuron receptor sites—places where transmitter substances can stimulate nerve impulses—may increase as a result of learning (Lynch & Baudry, 1984).

Additional evidence indicates that persons suffering from *Alzheimer's disease,* whose symptoms often include amnesia, show a decrease in acetylcholine (an important transmitter substance) in their brain (Coyle, Price, & Delong, 1983). This suggests that acetylcholine may be involved in memory, although here, too, findings are complex (Squire & Davis, 1981).

So, at present, growing evidence suggests that when information is acquired and stored in memory, complex neurochemical events occur within the brain and other portions of the nervous system. It also appears that the reason earlier attempts to identify such changes have failed is that the techniques for measuring them were simply not available. Such procedures do exist today or will soon be developed. Thus, the chances now seem better than ever that in the not-too-distant future we will finally crack the biochemical code of memory. When we do, the potential benefits for persons suffering from amnesia and other memory disorders will probably be immense.

Summary and Review

Human Memory and Information Processing

Memory is our ability to retain information over time. At present, it is frequently studied from an *information processing* perspective, in terms of *encoding* (the manner in which information is entered into memory), *storage* (the manner in which it is retained), and *retrieval* (how it is located for later use).

Different Memory Systems

One widely accepted model of memory suggests that we possess three memory systems: *sensory memory, short-term memory,* and *long-term memory.* Sensory memory stores representations of information brought to us by our senses for very brief periods of time. Short-term memory holds limited amounts of information for relatively brief intervals (up to about twenty seconds). Information that is not actively *rehearsed* is rapidly lost from short-term memory.

In a sense, long-term memory is our ultimate memory system, for it seems to have unlimited capacity and can retain information for an entire lifetime. Information stored in long-term memory can often be located by means of appropriate *retrieval cues.* These can involve aspects of the physical environment, category names, and even an individual's internal state *(state-dependent retrieval).* Information related to specific events or contexts is stored in *episodic memory.* More general information is stored in *semantic memory.* Loss of information from long-term memory appears to be primarily due to *interference* rather than to simple *decay* of memory traces.

Memory in Natural Contexts

Memory for natural events is often affected by two processes: distortion and construction. *Distortion* refers to changes in information stored in memory, usually to make it more consistent with other information or with existing *schemas. Construction* refers to our tendency to add information in order to complete gaps in memory. Both processes seem to operate in *eyewitness testimony.* Many studies indicate that such testimony is not as accurate as was once assumed. However, some evidence suggests that memory for an actual crime may be quite accurate, even over long periods of time.

Improving Memory

Many techniques for improving memory exist. One of the most effective of these is *elaborative rehearsal,* procedures in which the meaning of information to be retained and its relationship to information already present in memory is carefully considered. Several other *mnemonics* (techniques for improving memory) involve the use of *imagery.* For example, in the *method of loci* items to be remembered are associated with familiar physical locations (e.g., the rooms in one's home). Then, an imaginary walk through these locations brings the items to mind. *Mediation,* in which internal codes are developed for items to be remembered, is also useful.

The Physiology of Memory

Insights into the biochemical processes that play a role in memory are provided by studies of individuals suffering from *amnesia* and other memory disorders. Such persons experience difficulty in transferring information from short-term memory to long-term memory. Even if they succeed in performing this task, they may be unable to retrieve such information for current use. Alterations in the brains of persons suffering from *Alzheimer's disease* and other illnesses suggest that deficits in the production of various neurotransmitters, such as acetylcholine, or reduced sensitivity to them may contribute to amnesia and other forms of memory loss.

Key Terms

Amnesia A disorder involving loss of memory.

Decay The suggestion that forgetting occurs because memory traces fade with the passage of time.

Elaborative Rehearsal Rehearsal involving efforts to understand the meaning of words or other materials and their relationship to information already in memory.

Encoding The process through which information is placed in a form that can be entered into memory.

Encoding Specificity Hypothesis The suggestion that cues present at the time information is encoded can facilitate recall if they are also present at a later time.

Episodic Memory Memory for personally experienced events associated with specific places or contexts.

Flashbulb Memory Vivid memory for what an individual was doing at the time some emotionally arousing event took place.

Forgetting The loss of information from memory. (In the case of long-term memory, this involves inability to retrieve information in memory.)

Hypermnesia Improvements in memory over time or repeated efforts to recall previously learned materials.

Information-Processing Approach The view that human memory can best be understood in terms of the operations of encoding, storage, and retrieval.

Interference The suggestion that forgetting occurs because various items or pieces of information stored in memory actively interfere with one another.

Levels of Processing A view suggesting that the more cognitive effort we expend with respect to new information, the more strongly it will be entered into memory and the more readily it will be recalled at later times.

Long-Term Memory The memory system that permits us to store large (perhaps unlimited) amounts of information over long periods of time.

Memory The retention of information over time.

Mnemonics Specific procedures for improving memory.

Reminiscence A phenomenon in which information that can't be remembered at one time *is* remembered later.

Retrieval The process through which information stored in memory is located.

Retrieval Cues Stimuli associated with information stored in memory which often play a key role in its retrieval (in bringing such information into conscious experience).

Schemas Cognitive frameworks developed through experience that affect the way in which incoming information is encoded, stored, and retrieved.

Semantic Memory Memory for general knowledge not associated with specific times or contexts.

Sensory Memory A memory system that retains representations of sensory input for brief periods of time.

Short-Term Memory The memory system that holds information we are currently using.

Storage The process through which information is retained in memory.

Tip-of-the-Tongue Phenomenon The feeling that you can ''almost'' remember some item or information.

For More Information

Matlin, M. (1983). *Cognition*. New York: Holt, Rinehart & Winston.
> A brief and well-written introduction to cognitive processes. The chapter on memory is easy to understand and expands considerably on many of the points we have discussed.

Solso, R.L. (1988). *Cognitive psychology,* 2nd ed. Boston: Allyn and Bacon.
> An excellent, clearly written introduction to all aspects of cognitive psychology, including memory. The chapters on models of memory, organization of memory, and mental imagery are especially interesting.

Wells, G.L., & Loftus, E.F. (1984). *Eyewitness testimony: Psychological perspectives*. Cambridge: Cambridge University Press.
> This book contains chapters written by several researchers who have focused their attention on eyewitness testimony. While it is aimed primarily at a professional audience, you should be able to understand many of the points made. This is an excellent source to consult if you'd like to know more about this intriguing aspect of memory.

C H A P T E R

Language and Thought: Thinking, Deciding, Communicating

"Look, I don't care *what* you say! Corvettes are the best, period." And with this pronouncement, Larry Redmond folds his hands across his chest to indicate that, as far as he's concerned, the matter is closed.

"Larry, you are one confused person," his cousin Mark replies. "I don't know where you get these ideas. If you bothered to look at the facts, you'd know the only thing they have going for them is power. They've got the biggest engines around, but that's it. In every other way Corvettes are junk, pure junk."

"Ha!" Larry comments. "What makes you an expert, anyway? Have you ever owned one?"

"What does owning one have to do with it? I can read, can't I? And statistics say they guzzle gas and spend more time in the shop than on the road. Just the other day I was reading an article in *Consumer Reports,* and it said. . . ."

"Aw, come off it. If that stuff is right, then why do all the people I know who have a 'Vette love 'em so much? Talk to Bob Augustino—*he'll* tell you. Says it's the greatest car he's ever owned, and he's had a few in his day. And Pete Grady says the same."

"O.K., so you know two people who own Corvettes and both of them are happy. Big deal! What does that prove? With those big payments every month, what else could they say? I mean, how stupid they'd look if they admitted they blew that much money on a lemon."

"Now that's the dumbest thing you've said so far. Why would they keep spending for something they didn't like? Anyway, what it all comes down to is this: would you rather believe the things people you know tell you or some stuff printed in a magazine? I know what comes through to *me,* loud and clear."

"That's right—make up your mind by listening to two people and ignore statistics based on thousands. Good move, Larry, good move." Then, after a brief pause, Mark continues, "You know what? As far as I'm concerned, there's something wrong with your thinking. You wouldn't know the truth if it came up and hit you in the face. I can't take any more of this. So long!" And with these parting words, Mark storms off, fuming visibly over his cousin's refusal to listen to reason.

FIGURE 7-1. As suggested by this cartoon, people do not think in a totally rational manner, even with respect to very important matters. *(Source:* The New Yorker.*)*

"Let me see now! Shall I give you the minimum or the maximum?"

Human Cognition: Far from Perfect

Who is right—Mark or Larry? Sitting there calm and collected at your desk, the answer probably seems obvious: Mark, of course. He based his opinions on facts, or at least on his memory of them. In contrast, Larry derived his views from the opinions of two people he knew—persons who own Corvettes and so have powerful reasons for believing they are worth their price. But take a mental step back from this situation, and think again: in which of these ways do *you* usually operate? In reasoning about various events, in making decisions, and in solving the problems posed by daily life, do you proceed in a rational manner, gathering all relevant facts and evaluating them systematically? Or, like Larry, do you sometimes jump to conclusions, pay too much attention to some kinds of input and not enough to others? Unless you are the exception that proves the rule, the answer to this question, too, should be clear: you probably do not act logically all the time. (Please refer to Figure 7-1.)

Human cognition—the process through which we combine, organize, and use information from memory and current experiences—is far from perfect. In fact, it is subject to a wide range of errors and to several forms of bias. Thus, when we think, reason, make decisions, solve problems, or use language, we do not always do so in ways that appear completely rational to an outside observer. In short, where information processing is concerned, we are definitely *not* like computers which have been programmed for maximum accuracy and efficiency.

Having said this, we should hasten to restore the balance. While our ability to perform complex cognitive tasks is indeed far from perfect, it is impressive. Most of our decisions are correct ones; we manage to cope with even fairly complex problems; and our ability to use language as a tool of communication remains light-years beyond that of even the most sophisticated computers. In short, while our ability to think, reason, and decide is not perfect, it is generally good enough for us to steer a course through the complexities of life in the late twentieth century. Still, the ways in which we depart from ''total rationality'' are of interest for two reasons. First, they call our attention to the types of pitfalls that can lead us seriously astray. Second, they often tell us a great deal about the nature of human cognition—how we actually think, reason, make decisions, and use language. For both of these reasons, such errors will serve as a basic theme throughout this chapter and will be examined in our discussion of each of the topics we will consider: **thinking, decision-making, problem-solving,** and **language.**

Thinking: Forming Concepts and Reasoning to Conclusions

What are you thinking about at this moment? Probably, the words on this page and the ideas they evoke. But perhaps you are also thinking that you are too warm or too cold, about your date next weekend, about that problem with your car. . . . The list could be endless, for at any given moment consciousness usually consists of a swirling, shifting pattern of thoughts and impressions. How can we hope to understand this complex process? In order to do so, psychologists have often adopted two strategies. First, they have focused on the basic ways in which thought is organized—the *concepts* we use to group or classify objects, events, or ideas. Second, they have examined the nature of *formal reasoning*—how we attempt to draw conclusions from known facts or assumptions.

Concepts: Categories in the Mind

What do the following objects have in common: a country home, a skyscraper, an ancient pyramid? Although they all look different, you probably have no difficulty in replying: all are *buildings* (refer to Figure 7-2). Now consider these items: a plate of sushi (slices of

> **Concepts: Mental Categories for Diverse but Related Objects**

FIGURE 7-2. What do the objects in each row of photos have in common? You probably have no difficulty labeling those in the top row ''buildings'' and those in the bottom row ''foods.'' This is because you already have well-developed *concepts* for such items.

raw fish over rice); a tray of pastries; a ripe apple. What do *these* have in common? Again, you probably have no difficulty in answering: all are *foods*. One reason you can reply so quickly is that you already possess well-developed **concepts** for both groups of stimuli. In short, you possess a mental framework for categorizing these diverse items as somehow belonging together.

Because concepts are such a familiar part of our mental life, we usually take them for granted. Actually, though, they form an important cornerstone of thought. Without them, each stimulus we encounter would seem unique. Thus, it would be impossible to think generally about groups of related objects or events—to realize that all automobiles need servicing, that doctors generally keep patients waiting, or that most parties are fun. In sum, concepts help us to impose order and meaning on what might otherwise be a chaotic external world.

How Concepts Are Formed: The Traditional View.   That we possess many concepts is obvious. It seems only natural to categorize our experience in various ways and to treat stimuli which are not identical as somehow equivalent (Medin & Wattenmaker, 1986). But how are such concepts formed? How do we acquire mental categories for trees, politicians, pizzas, and pickles? One possibility involves the process of *hypothesis testing*. On the basis of experience with various objects, we formulate an initial assumption about the attributes an object must possess in order to be included in a given concept. We then put this hypothesis to the test by determining whether items that possess these attributes do or do not seem to fall within the category. Perhaps a concrete example will help illustrate this process.

Imagine that you go to work in a pretzel factory where large, soft pretzels are twisted by hand. At the end of the first day, your supervisor tells you that your work is improving, but your pretzels still lack "pizzazz." You are upset by this negative feedback, so you compare your pretzels with those of an experienced employee. At first, you can't see any difference between yours and hers except that the ones she makes have a tighter twist in the center. This leads you to hypothesize that only pretzels with a tight center have "pizzazz." You test this possibility by making yours the same way. At the end of the next day, though, your supervisor reports that your pretzels still lack "pizzazz." Redoubling your efforts, you now notice another difference between your pretzels and those of the experienced worker: the ends on her pretzels stick out beyond the edge. You test this alternate hypothesis by making yours the same way. The result: success! Your supervisor now praises your pretzels as having "pizzazz." You've gained a new concept—one that may be labeled "pretzels with pizzazz." (Please see Figure 7-3 for a summary of such hypothesis testing.)

How Concepts Are Formed: A Modern Approach.   Is this really how we form concepts—through trial and error? For many years, psychologists believed this was so. During the past decade, however, another and markedly different view has emerged from research findings (Medin & Smith, 1984; Rosch & Mervis, 1975). This newer approach suggests that, while hypothesis testing may indeed play a role in the development of *logical concepts*—those consciously created for a specific purpose—it is probably not directly relevant to **natural concepts**—ones we use in everyday life (Medin & Smith, 1984; Rosch, 1975). What are the differences between logical and natural concepts? And if the latter are not formed through hypothesis testing, how *do* they emerge?

Logical and Natural Concepts: How They Differ.   As we just noted, logical concepts are created for a specific purpose, such as the concept for "pretzels with pizzazz." Perhaps their most important use is in *classification schemes* employed by many branches of science. For example, is a tomato a vegetable or a fruit? Botanists developed a system which precisely specifies the attributes for fruits and for vegetables. (According to this system, by the way, a tomato is a fruit.) Similarly, as we will see in Chapter 13, psychologists and other professionals who treat psychological disorders have a standardized system for classifying such problems—one with clearly defined criteria for many different conditions.

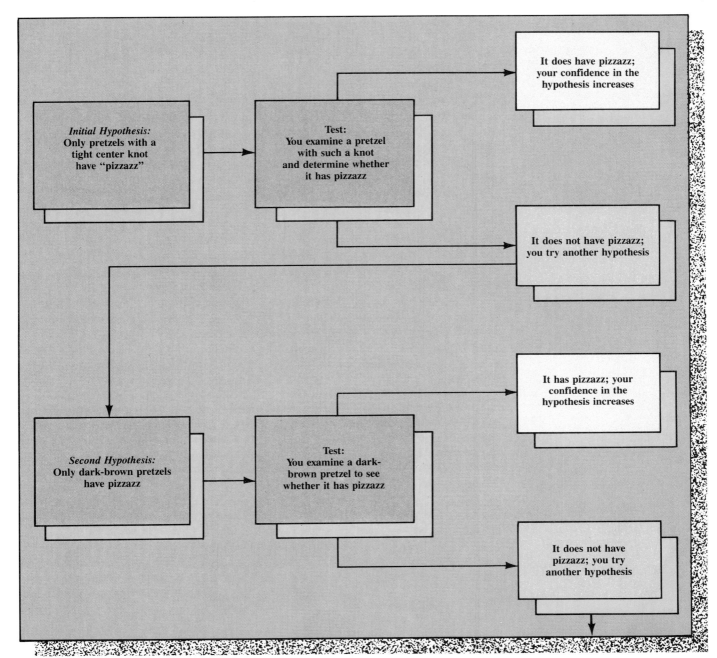

FIGURE 7-3. What, exactly, is a pretzel with ''pizzazz''? In order to find out, you begin with the hypothesis that only ones with a tight knot in the middle qualify. If this is shown to be false (a pretzel with a tight knot is described as *not* having pizzazz), you shift to a second hypothesis: pretzels which are dark brown in color have pizzazz. If this is also shown to be false (a light brown one has pizzazz), you try still a third idea: only pretzels with lots of salt qualify. By testing various hypotheses, you will eventually form a clear concept of the ideal pretzel, or at least one with pizzazz.

Hypothesis Testing in Concept Formation

In contrast, other concepts are quite different, including many we use in everyday life. These natural concepts do not seem to be based on specific, concrete sets of attributes. Rather, they are ''fuzzy'' or ill-defined in nature. Consider the following questions:

Is an elevator a vehicle?
Is chess a sport?
Is a psychologist a scientist?

As you can see, these all relate to common concepts: ''sport,'' ''vehicle,'' and ''scientist.'' What specific attributes are necessary for inclusion in each? If you find yourself puzzled, don't be surprised: the boundaries of these concepts are somewhat fuzzy, so the questions are difficult to answer.

Natural Concepts: How They Are Formed.   How, then, are natural concepts formed? The answer seems to involve the development of **prototypes**—the best or clearest examples of such categories (Rosch, 1975). Prototypes emerge out of your experience with the external world, and once they do, new items you encounter are compared with them. The more attributes such items share with existing prototypes, the more likely they are to be included within the concept.

That you possess prototypes for many natural concepts is readily apparent. For example, consider the following words, each naming a familiar concept: furniture, clothing, weapons. What objects come to mind as you read them? If you are like most people, you probably think of tables and chairs, shirts or dresses, and guns or knives, respectively. These are familiar, best examples of these concepts—*prototypes* for them. You are much less likely to think of a hide-a-bed, high-heel boots, or brass knuckles. These items are definitely *not* prototypes for the concepts involved (refer to Figure 7-4).

In short, in determining whether specific stimuli fit within a natural concept, we seem to adopt a *probabilistic* strategy. The more similar an object or event is to those already in the category, especially to prototypes for the category, the more likely we are to include a new item within the concept. In everyday situations, then, concept membership is not an all-or-none decision; rather, it is graded, and various objects are recognized as fitting within a category to a greater or lesser degree (Medin & Wattenmaker, 1986).

Natural Concepts, Family Resemblance, and Knowledge of the World.   Before concluding, we should note that recent evidence points to the necessity for expanding our concept of ''concepts'' still further. Prototypes developed through experience may

Prototypes: Clear Examples of Specific Concepts

FIGURE 7-4. The objects in the top row are all *prototypes* for the concepts named on the left. They are ''best examples'' of these concepts. In contrast, the objects in the bottom row are *not* prototypes for the same mental categories, although they do fit into the categories.

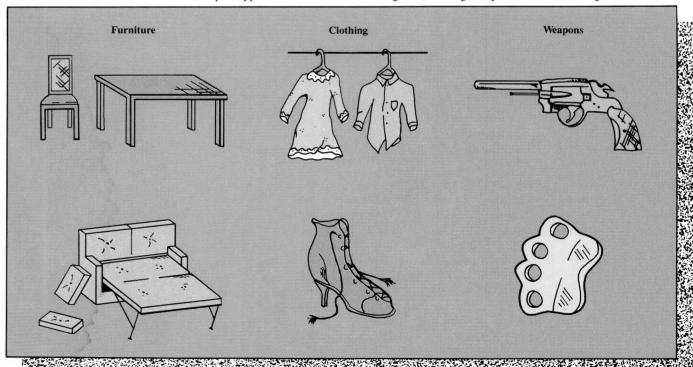

Furniture   Clothing   Weapons

well be important in determining whether specific events or objects are included within a given category, but this is far from the entire story. In addition, your more general knowledge of the world, and especially your knowledge about *relationships* between various attributes, is important, too (Medin, Wattenmaker, & Hampson, 1987). You know through experience that certain things seem to go together, and you use such knowledge in constructing natural categories. For example, you know (or at least you believe) that, where people are concerned, certain traits tend to occur together. Impulsive people may also be exuberant or energetic, but they are rarely inhibited or timid. Similarly, reserved people may be discreet or withdrawn; they are rarely boisterous or dominating.

On the basis of such knowledge, you develop categories for two types of people: ones who are *introverted* and ones who are *extroverted*. In assigning people to one or the other, you don't expect each person to show all of the traits. On the contrary, you proceed in terms of what has been termed *family resemblances* (Mervis & Rosch, 1981). People, objects, or events included in a category are similar in some respects, but there is no single set of characteristics they all share. This is analogous to human families, where all members share some characteristics, but it is difficult to point to a single set of attributes all have in common, hence the term *family resemblance* to describe one type of natural concept.

In sum, in developing natural concepts we pay attention not only to specific characteristics or attributes, but also to the relationships between them. As Medin and his colleagues have aptly put it (Medin, Wattenmaker, & Hampson, 1987, p. 277), our natural categories consist not merely of bricks (specific attributes of the objects or events involved), but of mortar, too (our understanding of the relationships between them).

Reasoning: From A to C by Way of D?

An important task you often face is drawing conclusions from facts you believe to be true. In other words, you engage in formal **reasoning.** While the ultimate goal of such thought is always the same—drawing accurate conclusions—it occurs in several different forms. The following examples illustrate this basic fact:

Bob is a better lover than Tom.
Tom is a better lover than Fred.
Is Bob a better lover than Fred?

Anyone who dislikes this psychology text is lacking in good taste.
Valerie dislikes this text.
Therefore, Valerie is lacking in good taste.

All stockbrokers love chocolate.
All persons who love chocolate are generous to a fault.
Therefore, all stockbrokers are generous to a fault.

The first set of statements illustrates **linear reasoning**—reasoning in which we must compare items and determine their relative order. The second illustrates **propositional reasoning,** in which we consider the truth of "if . . . then" statements. Finally, the third set of statements illustrates **syllogistic reasoning,** in which we determine whether a conclusion follows logically from two statements we assume to be true. (The answers, by the way are: (1) yes, Bob is a better lover than Fred; (2) yes, Valerie lacks good taste, and (3) yes, all stockbrokers are generous to a fault. These conclusions follow logically if we assume that the statements which preceded them are accurate—which in the case of (3) is false; of course, they are not; see Figure 7-5.)

Obviously, reasoning is a crucial form of thought, and one in which we engage on a daily basis. But can we reason in an accurate manner? Discouragingly, the answer appears to be "sometimes." In relatively simple cases such as the ones above, we *can* often do a good job of reaching useful conclusions. Sometimes, though, we face a more difficult task; in many situations our reasoning may be subject to several forms of bias. Two of the most important of these are described next.

FIGURE 7-5. In *syllogistic reasoning* a conclusion follows logically from two statements we assume to be true. If we assume that (1) all stockbrokers love chocolate, and (2) all persons who love chocolate are generous, then we might logically (although falsely!) conclude that all stock brokers must be generous.

Syllogistic Reasoning: Not Infallible

The Confirmation Bias: In Search of Positive Evidence. Suppose you were asked to perform the following task. You are told that the series of numbers *2, 4, 6* conforms to a simple rule. Your task is to guess the rule by making up other "triples" and asking whether they, too, are correct. What would be your first guess? If you are like the subjects in a study conducted by Wason (1968), you might suggest *8, 10, 12.* Suppose the experimenter then tells you that this series, too, fits the rule. What would you conclude? If you are like Wason's subjects (and most people), you might reason that the rule is "consecutive even numbers." Then, you would go on to guess *14, 16, 18; 20, 22, 24;* and so on. This is precisely what happened in Wason's study; subjects proposed such numbers frequently—much more often than numbers that did not comply with this rule.

This result probably strikes you as quite reasonable; after all, if a rule works, why not stick with it? In fact, though, the rule Wason used was much simpler: *any* series of increasing numbers was correct. Thus, if subjects guessed *3, 4, 5* or even *1, 2, 3,* they would have been informed they were correct. Yet they rarely made such suggestions. Once subjects developed a hypothesis, they stuck with it and never learned that, in fact, another rule applied.

These results, and those of many other studies, illustrate an important type of error in our reasoning, one known as the **confirmation bias,** more recently called the **positive test strategy** (Klayman & Ha, 1987). Briefly, this refers to our strong tendency to test conclusions or hypotheses by examining only instances in which some property or event is expected to occur, rather than instances in which the event or property is *not* expected to occur. In other words, once individuals have formed a hypothesis or reached a conclusion, they tend to concentrate on gathering evidence which will confirm rather than refute it. Perhaps a concrete example will help clarify matters.

Imagine that a politician wants to increase his standing in the polls. His campaign manager suggests that the best way of doing so is by kissing babies. The politician tests this hypothesis by kissing every baby in sight. Sure enough, his ratings go up. On the basis of this evidence, he concludes that kissing babies is indeed a highly effective strategy for gaining votes and continues to use it in all his campaigns. He never stops kissing babies to see if his ratings drop; and he never tries alternate strategies to see if they, too, might raise his standing. In short, he is "locked in" by the confirmation bias to planting his lips firmly on every soft infant cheek he encounters (refer to Figure 7-6).

Please don't misunderstand: the positive test strategy does not necessarily result in errors; indeed, in many cases it is an eminently reasonable way to proceed. However, in some situations, it can prevent us from discovering that some of our conclusions or working hypotheses are false, and this can prove costly indeed.

Belief Perseverance: Don't Bother Me with the Facts; My Mind's Already Made Up. If you found the tendency to search for confirmation of hypotheses or conclusions unsettling, prepare for more of the same. Growing evidence suggests that we are subject to another, perhaps even stronger form of bias: **belief perseverance** (Anderson, Lepper, & Ross, 1980). This is our tendency to cling to beliefs or conclusions we have reached even when these are strongly refuted by additional evidence. Such effects have been observed in several different contexts. For example, in one convincing study on this topic (Lord, Ross, and Lepper, 1979), subjects who either supported or opposed capital punishment read descriptions of two studies on this topic. One study supported the benefits of capital punishment, while the other discredited such benefits. In other words, one study confirmed subjects' initial views (whatever these were), while the other refuted them. Subjects were then asked to rate the quality of the two studies. As you can probably predict, both groups (those favoring and those against capital punishment) rated the study that confirmed their beliefs as higher in quality and more convincing than the one that contradicted them. Thus, they not only ignored evidence contrary to their beliefs—they tended to dismiss it!

Can the tendency toward belief perseverance be reduced? Fortunately, recent evidence suggests that it can. In two related studies, Lord, Lepper, and Preston (1984) again had subjects who either supported or opposed capital punishment read descriptions of studies whose results confirmed or refuted their beliefs. One group of subjects was in-

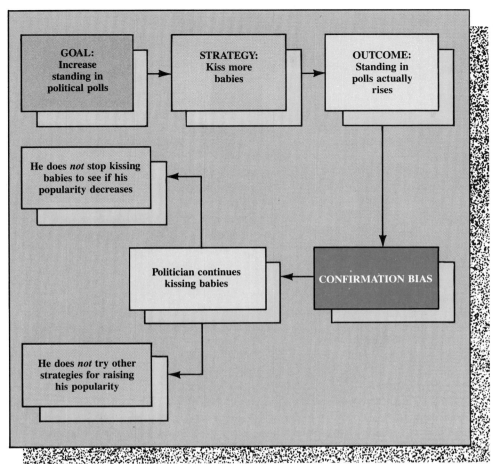

The Confirmation Bias: An Example

FIGURE 7-6. In order to increase his standing in the polls, a politician tries kissing more babies. His popularity increases. Because of the confirmation bias, he concludes that his hypothesis has been confirmed, and he goes on kissing babies. He does *not* try withholding his kisses to see if his popularity plummets, nor does he try other strategies to see if they work equally well.

structed to be as objective and unbiased as possible in evaluating this evidence. This did *not* do the trick. Subjects still rated evidence contrary to their own beliefs as less convincing than evidence confirming their beliefs. In contrast, another group of subjects was asked to consider the opposite point of view in making their evaluations. Specifically, they were told to ask themselves "whether you would have made the same high or low evaluations had the same study produced results on the *other* side of the issue." This procedure *did* reduce the tendency toward belief perseverance. These subjects did not rate the study that confirmed their beliefs as more convincing than the contradicting one (refer to Figure 7-7 on page 208).

These results permit us to conclude on an optimistic note. While the tendency to cling to our beliefs is strong, it *can* be overcome. When reason and beliefs "square off," the outcome is not always a foregone conclusion; but with a little help, reason and the weight of existing evidence can indeed carry the day.

Decision-Making: Choosing the Best Alternatives

Reasoning is hard work; in fact, it's an activity many people go out of their way to avoid. In some respects, though, it is far less difficult than another cognitive task you perform many times each day: making decisions (refer to Figure 7-8 on page 208). Think for a moment about how often you must choose among alternatives. From the moment you

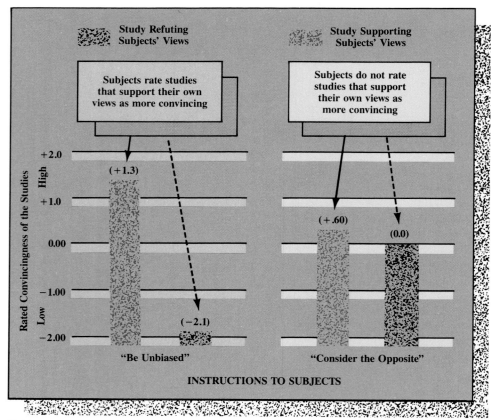

FIGURE 7-7. When subjects were asked to be as unbiased as possible, they still rated studies that supported their views as more convincing than ones that refuted these views. However, when asked to imagine what their reactions would have been had the studies reported exactly opposite results, this tendency toward *belief perseverance* was eliminated. *(Source: Based on data from Lord, Lepper, & Preston, 1984.)*

wake up until you turn out the light and go to sleep, life presents a series of choices: what clothes to put on, what to eat for lunch, whether to attend a class or meeting, to phone or not to phone that attractive person you met at the party last week—the list is practically endless.

If you were a perfectly rational decision-maker, you would make each of these choices in a cool, almost mathematical way. Specifically, you would consider the *utility* or value of each alternative (your subjective evaluation of the outcomes it may yield), and the probability that such results will actually occur. Then, taking these two factors into account, you would make your decision. As you know from your own experience, this is rarely, if ever, the case. Usually, you don't pause to reason about such matters in a systematic manner. Instead, decisions are generally based on hunches, intuition, and a

FIGURE 7-8. Making decisions is rarely easy, even in situations where the issues at stake are less than earth-shaking in importance. *(Source: King Features Syndicate.)*

host of other factors, many of which seem only weakly linked to the situation at hand. The impact of several such factors will now be considered.

Heuristics: Useful—But Fallible—Rules of Thumb

In many situations, we have to make decisions quickly, on the basis of incomplete information—far less than we would prefer. How do we proceed in such cases? The answer seems involve the use of several rules of thumb known as **heuristics** (Kahneman & Tversky, 1982). In a sense, these are shortcuts extracted from past experience—simple guidelines which help us to make reasonably good choices in a quick and efficient way. Several heuristics exist, but perhaps the ones we use most often are availability and representativeness.

Availability: What Comes to Mind First?   Because it's somewhat easier to grasp, let's start with the **availability heuristic.** Simply stated, this refers to the tendency to make judgments about the frequency of various events or objects in terms of how readily you can bring examples of them to mind. The more easily you can remember such instances, the more frequent or likely you judge the events or objects to be. And since judgments of probability play an important role in your decisions, the availability heuristic is quite important in this respect.

A good example of the availability heuristic in operation is provided by a study conducted by Tversky and Kahneman (1974). They presented lists of names like the one in Table 7-1 and then asked subjects whether the lists contained more men's or women's names. Although the numbers of male and female names were roughly equal, nearly 80 percent of the subjects reported that women's names were more frequent. Why? Because the women named in the lists were more famous, so their names were more readily remembered.

Interestingly, the availability heuristic also plays a role in the tendency of many persons to overestimate the chances of being a victim of violent crime, an airplane crash, or natural disasters (earthquakes, floods). Because such events are given extensive coverage in the mass media, individuals can bring vivid examples of them to mind quite readily. The result: they conclude that such incidents are more frequent than they actually are (Tyler & Cook, 1984). (Refer to Figure 7-9 on page 210.)

Representativeness: What's Typical Is Likely.   Suppose you tossed a coin into the air six times. Which of the following patterns of heads and tails would be most likely: *T H H T H T, H H H T T T,* or *H H H H H H?* If you are like most people, you probably believe that the first pattern is the most probable and that the third one (all heads) is the least likely. In fact, the probability of each of these specific sequences is the same. What led you astray is another rule of thumb we use for estimating the likelihood of various events—the **representativeness heuristic** (Kahneman & Tversky, 1972).

TABLE 7-1

Does this list contain more men's or women's names? The answer may surprise you: the number of male and female names is about equal. Because of the *availability heuristic*, though, most persons tend to guess that female names are more common.

Louisa May Alcott	Henry Vaughn	Allan Nevins
John Dickson Carr	Kate Millet	Jane Austen
Emily Dickinson	Eudora Welty	Henry Crabb Robinson
Thomas Hughes	Richard Watson Gilder	Joseph Lincoln
Laura Ingalls Wilder	Harriet Beecher Stowe	Emily Brontë
Jack Lindsay	Pearl Buck	Arthur Hutchinson
Edward George Lytton	Amy Lowell	James Hunt
Margaret Mitchell	Robert Lovett	Erica Jong
Michael Drayton	Edna St. Vincent Millay	Brian Hooker
Edith Wharton	George Nathan	

(SOURCE: Based on materials used by Tversky & Kahneman, 1974.)

The Availability Heuristic: A Compelling Example

Mass Media and the Availability Heuristic

FIGURE 7-9. Dramatic events such as earthquakes and airplane crashes often receive extensive coverage in the news. As a result, we can bring vivid examples of them to mind quite easily, and this causes us to tend to overestimate the frequency of such occurrences.

According to this principle, we judge the likelihood of events or objects in terms of how representative they seem of *prototypes,* our best or most typical examples of some concept. So why do you judge *T H H T H T* to be more likely than *H H H H H H?* Because you assume that the outcome of tossing a coin will be random, and the first of these patterns looks more like a random outcome.

Perhaps the powerful impact of representativeness on our judgments and decisions is most evident in the fact that it causes us to overlook other important information. In particular, the representativeness heuristic can lead us to ignore information about **base rates**—the relative frequency of different objects or types of events in the world around us. For example, imagine that you read the following description of a young woman:

> Pam is bold, energetic, and carefree. However, she is also quite disciplined, and she will work very hard to reach goals that are important to her. She spends most of her spare time skiing, visiting night clubs, and going to parties.

Is Pam more likely to be a professional dancer or a schoolteacher? You probably guessed that she is a dancer; after all, she sounds more typical of dancers (or at least of your stereotype of them) than of teachers. Now, suppose you received information about base rates: you learned that there are one hundred times as many teachers as dancers. Would this change your judgment? If you were a totally rational decision-maker, it would: after all, the odds are much greater that *any* young woman is a teacher. Because of the representativeness heuristic, though, it's unlikely that you would change your guess. The fact that Pam sounds more typical of dancers than teachers would overwhelm information about base rates and would perhaps lead you into error.

Other Influences on Decision-Making: Entrapment and Overconfidence

While heuristics play an important role in decision-making, they are not the only factors that affect this process. Several others, too, are worthy of our attention. Among the most intriguing of these are **entrapment** (or *escalation of commitment*) and **overconfidence.**

Entrapment: Throwing Good Money (or Love, or Effort) after Bad. Consider the following situation: Ralph Hagerty is a senior executive at Apex Industries. A year ago he hired Connie Langford as his chief assistant. Unfortunately, things haven't worked out well. Despite Ralph's best efforts to train her, Connie has been a disappointment in every respect. What should he do? Fire her and cut his future losses, or keep her as his assistant and hope things will eventually improve?

From a totally rational perspective, this decision sounds easy: Ralph should fire his assistant and seek another one. But think again: if he chooses this course of action, he'll experience serious losses. First, he'll have to admit that he made a mistake hiring Connie, something most persons are reluctant to do. Second, he'll have to view all his efforts in training her as a waste of time.

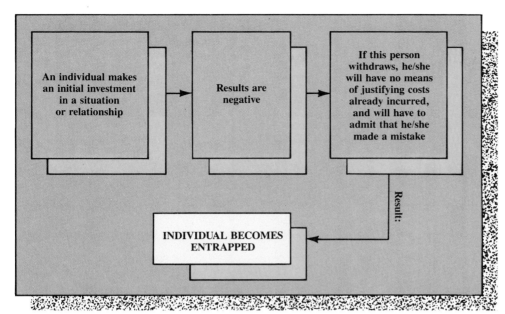

FIGURE 7-10. When individuals make costly investments in some situation or relationship, they may become *entrapped* in it. They come to feel that they have no choice but to continue, for if they withdraw, they will be unable to justify the costs they have already experienced.

Unfortunately, situations like this one are all too common. Indeed, they are readily visible in labor disputes, unhappy marriages, long and costly wars, and many other contexts (refer to Figure 7-10). In all such situations, decision-makers feel *entrapped* (Brockner & Rubin, 1985). They come to believe that they have no choice but to continue in the situation or stick to their original decision; if they don't, they will have no way of justifying the losses they have incurred as a result of their earlier judgments or decisions (refer to Figure 7-11).

Research findings suggest that entrapment (or *escalation of commitment,* as this phenomenon is sometimes termed), occurs in a wide range of settings, from tragic international events (e.g., the United States' involvement in the Vietnam war) through important business decisions. As one example of such effects, consider a recent study by Schoorman (1988). He reasoned that the tendency to stick to prior decisions and to attempt to justify them would occur in the context of evaluating employees' performance—a key task in most organizations. Specifically, Schoorman predicted that managers would evaluate persons whom they had previously hired (or had recommended be hired) more favorably than persons in whose hiring they had not been directly involved. This would be the case because by evaluating such persons positively the managers could justify their earlier decisions. Similarly, Schoorman also predicted that managers would evaluate per-

FIGURE 7-11. Labor disputes and other types of conflict often continue long past the point at which either side can hope to achieve any gains.

Escalation of Commitment in Performance Appraisal

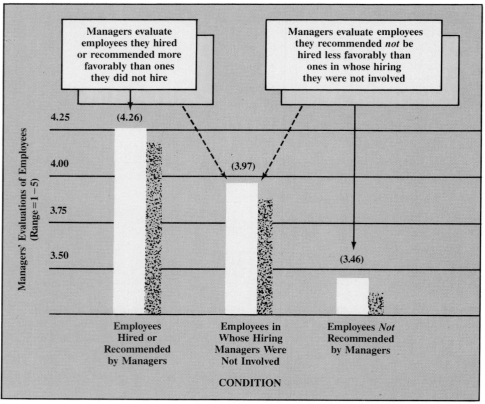

FIGURE 7-12. Managers rated employees they had hired or recommended be hired more favorably than ones in whose hiring they had not been directly involved. Similarly, they rated employees they recommended *not* be hired less favorably than employees in whose hiring they had not been involved. These findings illustrate the impact of tendencies toward entrapment or escalation of commitment. *(Source: Based on data from Schoorman, 1988.)*

sons they had previously recommended *not* be hired less favorably than ones in whose hiring the managers had not been involved.

To test these predictions, Schoorman asked managers in a large organization to evaluate the performance of clerical workers. Information on whether the manager had been involved in the hiring of a person, and whether the manager had agreed or disagreed with the decision to hire the person, was also obtained. As you can see from Figure 7-12, results supported both hypotheses. Managers evaluated employees they had hired or recommended more favorably than ones in whose hiring they had not been involved. And they evaluated employees they had recommended *not* be hired less favorably than ones in whose hiring they had not been involved. In short, their previous decisions seemed to bias their later evaluations of employees. Since ratings by supervisors play an important role in the assignment of raises and promotions in most companies, it is clear that the tendency to become entrapped by or committed to past decisions can have important practical effects (Bazerman et al., 1984; McCain, 1986).

Can such tendencies be overcome? Schoorman suggests that they can. For example, newly appointed managers might be asked to review the records of all their subordinates. Those they find acceptable would remain in their present jobs, while those they find unacceptable would be transferred. This procedure might lessen the tendency for the managers to evaluate the persons they subsequently hire in more favorable terms. Regardless of whether such tactics succeed, Schoorman's (1988) research and many other studies on entrapment or escalation of commitment underscore the following point: where decision-making is concerned, we are often far from totally rational.

Overconfidence: Misplaced Optimism in Decisions. How good are you at making decisions? Are your choices usually correct or incorrect? Do you think you are better in this respect than a computer programmed with all the relevant information would be? Since we have been discussing errors and bias in decision-making, you are well-prepared for such questions: "no," you may answer, "I guess I'm not as good at making decisions as I once thought." But people who haven't read a discussion like this tend to take a different stand: they usually greatly *overestimate* their success in decision-making. They believe their judgments and decisions are much more accurate and efficient than they actually are (Lichenstein & Fischoff, 1980). Why is this the case? One possibility is as follows: it is generally easier to remember successful decisions or judgments than unsuccessful ones; thus, in keeping with the availability heuristic, we tend to overestimate our success at such tasks (Dawes, 1976).

Regardless of its origins, overconfidence in your ability to make correct judgments or decisions can be costly (Arkes, Dawes, & Christensen, 1986). For example, existing evidence suggests that in deciding which individuals to hire for specific jobs, the best way to proceed is probably by statistical formulas that take account of as many different qualifications on the part of applicants (e.g., their scores on tests, their past work history). Despite this fact, many personnel directors prefer to rely on their own judgment, choosing employees on the basis of brief, informal interviews (Arvey & Campion, 1982).

Can anything be done to reduce such overconfidence? Evidence gathered recently by Arkes, Christensen, and Blumer (1987) is encouraging. The researchers reasoned that if individuals learned that they had been overconfident in their own judgment in one experience, such overconfidence would later be reduced. To test this hypothesis, they asked subjects to provide answers to one of two sets of five questions. For one group of subjects, these items appeared to be very difficult (e.g., "The highest mountain in South America is: (a) Aconcagua, (b) Tormando"). For another group, the questions appeared to be relatively easy ("The state farthest north is: (a) Maine, (b) Minnesota"). In fact, both sets of questions were equally difficult, and subjects answered less than half of either set correctly. However, the first set seemed, subjectively, to be much more difficult than the second. After responding to the first set of items, and learning that they had missed many of them, subjects were given an additional thirty questions to answer. For each, they indicated their choice, and also their confidence that their answer was the correct one.

As you can see from Figure 7-13, results offered support for the view that overconfidence could be sharply reduced by a "humbling" experience. Subjects who learned

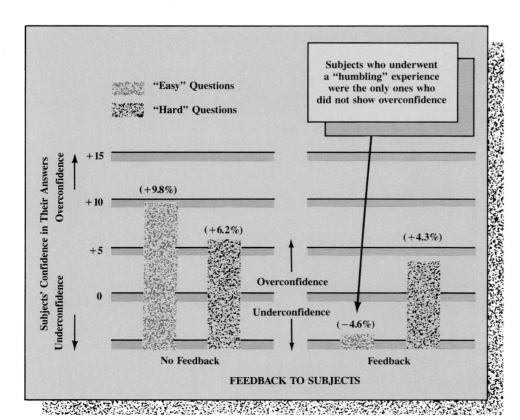

FIGURE 7-13. When individuals learned that they had done much worse on a seemingly easy task than they had believed, they did not demonstrate overconfidence on a subsequent related task. In contrast, individuals who learned that they had done worse than expected on a difficult task or who did not receive feedback on their performance continued to demonstrate overconfidence. *(Source: Based on data from Arkes et al., 1987.)*

Negative Feedback as a Technique for Reducing Overconfidence they had done much worse than they believed on the ''easy'' items showed far less overconfidence on the later test than other subjects; in fact, they actually demonstrated *underconfidence:* they felt that they did *worse* on the final thirty items than they really did. These findings suggest that our strong tendency towards overconfidence can be reduced. All that's needed, it appears, is an experience that brings us face to face with our unfounded optimism. (For a discussion of yet another factor that exerts surprisingly strong effects on our decisions, please see ''The Cutting Edge'' section below.)

FOCUS ON RESEARCH: The Cutting Edge

Ask and Ye Shall Receive: The Role of Arbitrary Anchors in Decision-Making

Suppose you were looking for a good used car and finally found one you wanted to buy. How would you decide what it was worth? The rational approach is to look in the ''Blue Book''—a publication which lists the average prices paid for various used cars in recent months. Perhaps you would proceed this way—*perhaps.* Another possibility, though, is that you would ask the seller what he or she wanted for the car, and would then counter with an offer somewhat below this figure. At first glance, this seems like a reasonable strategy, and, indeed, it is the one many people choose. But think carefully: what you have done in this case is to allow the seller to set a *reference point*—a figure from which your bargaining will proceed. If this price is close to the one in the ''Blue Book,'' all is well and good. If it is considerably higher, though, you may end up paying more for the car than it is worth.

Do such reference points (or *anchors,* as they are sometimes termed) really affect your judgments or decisions? Con-

Anchors and Judgments of Value: A ''Real'' Demonstration

FIGURE 7-14. The higher the asking price of a house, the more subjects thought it was worth. Moreover, such *anchoring* effects occurred among experienced realtors as well as students. Only the data for the more expensive house are shown here. *(Based on data from Northcraft & Neale, 1987.)*

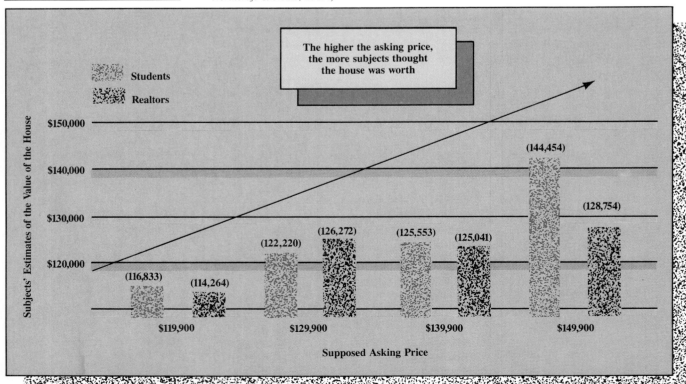

siderable evidence indicates that they do. Moreover, once an anchor is established, any adjustments you make tend to be insufficient—too small to counter the initial impact of the anchor (Tversky & Kahneman, 1974). A dramatic illustration of the power of such effects has recently been reported by Northcraft and Neale (1987).

These researchers hypothesized that the anchoring-and-adjustment phenomenon just described would occur even in a very important economic context—the price of real estate. To test this prediction, they conducted two studies in which individuals were given information about a house for sale, then were allowed actually to inspect it. In the first study the house was moderate in price (actual asking price: $74,900), while in the second it was considerably higher (asking price: $134,900). Some of the participants in each investigation were students, while others were real estate agents with considerable experience in the business. The independent variable in both investigations was the listed (asking) price of the house. In four different conditions this price was much lower, slightly lower, slightly higher, or much higher than the price actually being asked for the home. For example, for the higher-priced house, different groups of subjects were quoted the following prices: $119,900, $129,900, $139,900, and $149,900. (Remember: the actual asking price was $134,900.)

After inspecting a house, subjects were asked to indicate what they thought a reasonable price for it would be. Results indicated that the figure they suggested was strongly affected by the *anchor* they had received (the fictitious asking price). In general, the higher the anchor, the higher were subjects' estimates of the value of the house (please see Figure 7-14). Perhaps even more surprising, this was true for experienced real estate agents as well as for inexperienced students.

The practical message in these findings is clear: when trying to estimate the value of some item, beware of the asking price. If you accept it as a reference point, your judgment may be seriously affected; then, the bank account which suffers will almost certainly be your own!

Problem-Solving: Finding a Path to a Difficult Goal

Here's your dilemma: You have three roommates. Two of them are ''morning'' people like yourself, who like to go to sleep and arise fairly early. The third is a definite ''night person,'' who doesn't get sleepy until 2:00 A.M. You like him, but you really don't want him living with you next year. How can you handle this situation without hurting his feelings? After thinking about it for a while, you and your two friends come up with a solution: you'll move into an apartment on the opposite end of town from where he works evenings and weekends. You're sure that the twenty-five minute trip each way will cause him to look for other living arrangements. . . .

All of us encounter situations like this one frequently. We'd like to reach some goal, but there is no simple or direct way of doing so. Such situations involve **problem-solving,** another cognitive task which is very much a part of daily life and which has a wide range of practical implications.

Problem-Solving: An Overview

Granted that problem-solving is an important activity, just what does it involve? Psychologists are not totally in agreement on this basic issue, but many believe that three major aspects are central (Matlin, 1983a).

First, we must *understand* the problem—figure out just what issues, obstacles, and goals are involved. In the example described above, the problem boils down to this: you must find some way of avoiding the unwanted roommate without hurting his feelings. While this may seem obvious, understanding just what problem we face in a given situation is often more difficult than this. For example, imagine that you are involved in a serious romantic relationship, but lately you and your partner are not getting along well. What's the problem? Is it something you said or did? Has your partner found someone

Paying Attention to Relevant Information: First Step in Problem-Solving

TABLE 7-2

If you were asked to solve this problem, which of these sentences would you read most often? Subjects in a study by Simon and Hayes (1976) concentrated on sentences 5 and 3—the ones most directly relevant to solving the problem. These findings suggest that we are quite good at paying attention to the information that will be most useful to us, while ignoring information that is largely irrelevant.

(1) Three five-handed monsters from outer space were holding three crystal globes.

(2) Because of the strange properties of their home planet, both monsters and globes come in exactly three sizes: small, medium, large.

(3) The medium-sized monster was holding the small globe; the small monster was holding the large globe; the large monster was holding the medium-sized globe.

(4) Because this situation offended the monsters' sense of symmetry, they proceeded to transfer globes from one monster to another so that each would have a globe of its own size.

(5) Monster manners complicated the solution, since they require that: only one globe may be transferred at a time; if a monster is holding two globes, only the larger of the two may be transferred; a globe may not be transferred to a monster who is holding a larger globe.

(6) By what sequence of globe transfers can the monsters solve this problem?

(SOURCE: Adapted from materials used by Simon & Hayes, 1976.)

else? Are you simply incompatible? Identifying the precise problem in such cases can be difficult, to say the least.

One key step in understanding any problem seems to involve paying attention to important information about it, while weeding out information that is unimportant or irrelevant. Fortunately, we seem to be quite good at this task. That this is so is indicated by an intriguing study conducted by Simon and Hayes (1976). These researchers presented subjects with the ''five-handed monster'' problem shown in Table 7-2. Then, they asked them to describe their thoughts aloud as they worked on it. Simon and Hayes were primarily interested in how often subjects read and reread each sentence before they made their first move in the problem. As you can readily see, the sentences differ in terms of how relevant they are to solving the problem. Would subjects zero-in on the most relevant ones? In fact, they did. Sentence 5, which describes the rules to be followed in solving the problem, was reread fully thirty-two times. Sentence 3, which describes the current situation, was read an average of twenty-three times. In contrast, sentences 1 and 2, which contain largely irrelevant information, were read only a total of five times together.

A second basic step in dealing with problems is formulating possible solutions. Unfortunately, as we shall soon see, this is where we often fall down on the job. Because of certain tendencies and biases, we overlook useful solutions and get stuck, mentally, on ones that are less effective. Coming up with a wide range of possible solutions, therefore, is extremely useful in many contexts.

Third, we must evaluate each alternative and the outcomes it will produce. Will a given solution actually bring us to the goal we want? Are there any serious obstacles involved in its use? Are there hidden costs which make a potential solution less useful than first meets the eye? These are considerations which should be taken into account before we commit ourselves to a particular course of action.

Methods for Solving Problems: Trial-and-Error, Algorithms, and Heuristics

You are working on your friend's word processor to complete a term paper by Monday, and it's already Sunday. You're tired, so you decide to take a break—and then you panic. You don't remember how to save (put into memory) what you've written. What *was* that command? You think for a moment, then try hitting one of the keys, but nothing happens. You try another key; again, nothing happens. You hit a third key, and on the screen appears the question, ''Find what?'' That's not it, either. Now you decide to try combinations of keys—perhaps one of these will do it. You are still trying, still in a panic, when your friend arrives and rescues you.

FIGURE 7-15. Trial-and-error is one approach to solving problems, but often (e.g., in trying to figure out how to use a word processor), it doesn't work.

Almost certainly, you've used the problem-solving technique described here: **trial-and-error** (see Figure 7-15). This involves trying different responses until, perhaps, one works. Sometimes this is all you can do—you don't have enough information to adopt a more systematic approach. But, as you can readily see, such an approach is far from efficient, and it offers no guarantee that a useful solution will actually be found.

A second general approach to solving problems involves the use of **algorithms.** These are rules for a particular problem which will, sooner or later, yield a solution. For example, imagine that it's the day of a big exam, and you can't find your ''lucky'' pen. One way to locate it would be to search every possible nook and cranny of your room, home, or apartment. If the pen is there, you are sure to find it, but this may involve a lot of time. For another example, unscramble the following words: utonsilu, mlepobr, imtysatecs. Using an algorithm, you could proceed by taking each group of letters and working through every possible arrangement until words emerged. This algorithm would succeed, but you might not live long enough to complete the task! These two examples should make the major drawback of algorithms obvious: they work, but they are often highly inefficient. A more effective way of solving many problems is through the use of appropriate **heuristics.**

As you probably recall, these are rules of thumb which guide our cognition. With respect to problem-solving, heuristics involve strategies suggested by prior experience—ones we have found useful in the past. These may or may not work in the present case; a solution is not guaranteed. But what heuristics give up in terms of certainty they gain in terms of efficiency: they often provide useful shortcuts to workable solutions. Returning to the case of the missing pen, you might begin by trying to recall the last time you used the pen and where you left it. Alternatively, you might formulate a list of the places the pen is most likely to be, and search each of these in turn. In both cases, your strategy would be quite different from systematically searching your home or room from top to bottom. (Please see Table 7-3 on page 218 for a comparison of algorithms and heuristics.)

One heuristic we often employ is known as **means-ends analysis** (or *subgoals analysis*). This involves dividing the problem into a series of smaller pieces, or *subproblems*. Each of these is then solved, and the distance between our original state and the goal state we desire can then be reduced step by step. In short, we proceed by figuring out what ends we want to attain, and what means will be useful in reaching these. This

Algorithms and Heuristics: A Comparison

TABLE 7-3

Algorithms and *heuristics* **represent two different approaches to solving problems. Both offer advantages, and both involve certain drawbacks.**

	Basic Procedures	Advantages	Disadvantages
Algorithms	Exhaustive, systematic consideration of all possible solutions	Solution is guaranteed (provided one exists)	Can be highly inefficient, effortful
Heuristics	Strategies suggested by previous experience; rules of thumb which have worked in the past	Efficient, saves effort	Solution not guaranteed

may sound abstract but, in fact, we employ this approach in many contexts. For example, imagine once again that you are working on a term paper. How do you proceed? Basically, by breaking this project down into smaller parts. First, you work on selecting a specific topic. Once this is accomplished, you search for information about it in the library. Third, you read this material and try to understand it. Then you figure out how to organize it. Finally, you write (and probably re-write) the paper. Notice how you have applied means-ends analysis to this complex task. In each step, you first identified your present state and the goal you wanted to reach, and then you took steps to move in the "right" direction—toward the outcome you desired. (Please see Figure 7-16 for a summary of these steps.)

Another heuristic we often use in solving problems is **analogy.** Here, you reason that a problem you currently face is similar, in terms of underlying structure, to some you have encountered in the past. To the extent it is, then solutions that worked for these previous problems may also apply to the present one. For example, in one episode of *Star*

FIGURE 7-16. In solving many problems, we make use of *means-ends analysis*. That is, we divide the problem into smaller pieces, then work on each of these. For example, in writing a term paper you first decide on the topic. Next you search for information about it. Then you read this material and decide how it should be organized. Finally, you write and edit the paper.

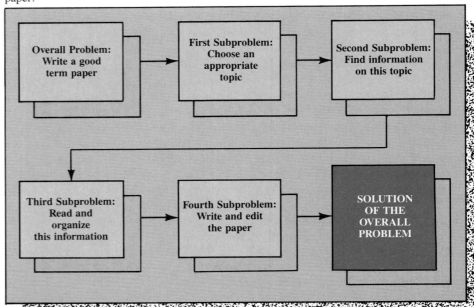

Solving Problems Through Means-Ends Analysis

Dr. McCoy: A Frequent User of Analogies

FIGURE 7-17. Dr. McCoy, in the television series *Star Trek,* often solved new medical problems by analogy. He would reason that a current problem was similar, in underlying structure, to others he had encountered—and solved—in the past. He would then adapt past solutions to the present situation.

Trek, Captain Kirk and his crew encounter a creature whose body is made out of various minerals. It is in great pain because of a wound inflicted by a group of miners who viewed it as a dangerous monster rather than the intelligent, sensitive being it really is. How can Dr. McCoy (the starship's medical officer) treat this new type of patient? By analogy, he decides to dress the wound with plaster of paris, a cement-like substance. This solution works, and the creature's wound is healed (refer to Figure 7-17).

People studying algebra use a similar approach. They soon learn that there are only a few basic types of problems teachers present on tests —for example, a *work problem* ("Mr. Smith takes 3 minutes less than Mr. Jones to assemble a machine when each works alone . . .") or a *river current problem* ("A river steamer goes 36 miles downstream in the same amount of time that it travels 24 miles upstream . . ."). Further, students learn that each type can be solved through one basic approach. When confronted with new problems on an exam, they apply these tactics and so solve the problems. Interestingly, it appears that individuals can very quickly recognize the type of problem being presented, even when nonsense words are substituted for standard English: "According to ferbent, the optimally fuselt grix of voipe umnolts five stens of volpe . . ." (Hinsley, Hayes, & Simon, 1977). These findings suggest that we do attempt to solve many problems by means of analogies—by noticing that they are similar to previous problems, and then applying similar solutions to them. Note, by the way, that while analogies are often useful, they are heuristics and do not guarantee workable solutions. Thus, a child who has learned to pronounce the word *though* will be correct when she applies the same pronunciation to *although,* but she'll be wrong for words such as *bough* or *through.*

Factors That Interfere with Effective Problem-Solving

Sometimes, despite your best efforts, you are unable to solve problems you face. In many cases, this is due to obvious causes such as lack of necessary information or experience. In

A Novel Way of Solving a
Complex Problem

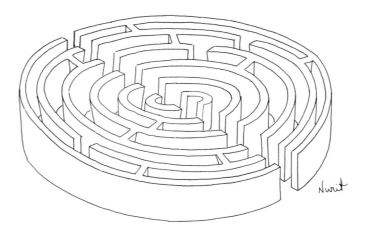

FIGURE 7-18. At one time or other we've all wished that we could solve a difficult problem with one bold stroke! *(Source:* The New Yorker.*)*

others, though, it seems to stem from more subtle factors relating to your own perceptions or past experience (Weisberg & Suls, 1973). In short, you may encounter difficulty with specific problems because you are unable to approach them in certain ways. (See Figure 7-18 for a novel way of dealing with one type of problem!)

Functional Fixedness: Prior Use Versus Present Solutions.   Suppose you were asked to use the objects shown in Figure 7-19 to attach the candle to a wall so that it can stand upright and burn properly. What solution(s) would you propose? If you are like most people, you would suggest such things as using the tacks to nail the candle to the wall, or attaching it with melted wax (Duncker, 1945). While these tactics may work, they overlook a much more elegant solution: emptying the box of tacks, nailing it to the wall, and placing the candle in it. Now that we've described it, this solution probably sounds obvious. Why, then, don't most people think of it? The answer involves **functional fixedness**—our strong tendency to think of using objects only in ways they have been used before. Since we've never used an empty box as a holder for a candle, we don't think

FIGURE 7-19. How can the candle be attached to the wall so that it stands upright using only the items shown? Because of *functional fixedness*—our tendency to think of using objects only as they have been used before—few persons hit on the solution of using the tacks to nail the box to the wall for a candle-holder.

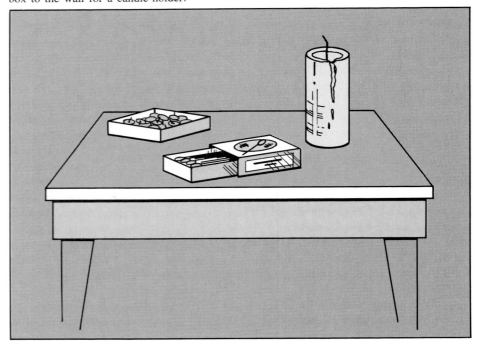

Functional Fixedness: It Interferes with Effective Problem-Solving

TABLE 7-4

How can you use three jars, A, B, and C, each holding the amounts shown to attain each goal listed in the right-hand column? Most individuals soon hit upon a workable solution: fill jar B, then use it to fill jar A once and jar C twice. The amount remaining is just what is wanted. Once problem-solvers hit upon this solution, they failed to perceive more direct solutions for items 6 and 7. This illustrates the effect of *mental set* on problem-solving.

	Amount Held by Each Jar			Goal (Amount of water desired)
Problem	Jar A	Jar B	Jar C	G
1	24	130	3	100
2	9	44	7	21
3	21	58	4	29
4	12	160	25	98
5	19	75	5	46
6	23	49	3	20
7	18	48	4	22

of it in these terms, so we fail to hit upon this solution. Interestingly, if the box of tacks is shown empty, people are much more likely to use it as a holder (Weisberg & Suls, 1973), so it doesn't take much to overcome such mental "blind spots." Unless we can avoid functional fixedness, though, our ability to solve many problems can be seriously reduced.

Mental Sets: Sticking to the Tried and True.   Another factor that often gets in the way of effective problem-solving is known as **mental set.** This refers to the fact that once we've solved a problem in a particular way, we tend to stick with this strategy even when more efficient approaches exist. The powerful impact of this factor was first demonstrated by Luchins (1942) in what is now a classic in the history of psychology. Luchins presented subjects with the problems shown in Table 7-4. As you can see, they involve using three jars, each a different size, to attain certain amounts of water. If you work through the first two or three items, you will soon discover that they can all be solved by the following simple formula: fill up jar B and from it fill jar A once and jar C twice.

This same formula works for all the items, so after they discovered it, subjects in Luchins' study stuck with it for all seven problems. But look at item 6: it can be solved in a simpler way. Just fill jar A, then from it, fill jar C; the amount remaining in jar A is precisely what's required (20 units). A simple solution exists for item 7, too. See if you can figure it out. Do you think most subjects noticed these solutions? Absolutely not—when they reached item 6, almost all continued to use their old tried-and-true formula. Thus, they stuck with an approach which worked before but was now relatively inefficient.

Similar effects occur in many other contexts. For example, people often continue to take the same crowded road to work each day because they have done so in the past; they never discover less-clogged routes they could travel. In these and numerous other cases, we seem to be trapped by past experience into sticking with approaches and solutions that are far from ideal. In this sense, slipping into "mental ruts" can prove costly. (Can individuals be trained to think more clearly and solve problems more effectively? For some comments on this issue, please see "The Point of It All" section below.)

THE POINT OF IT ALL

Teaching People to Think: Specific Knowledge or Metacognition?

Throughout this chapter, we have noted that human beings are far from perfect in their abilities to reason clearly, make decisions, and solve problems. Since one of psychology's ultimate goals is improving human welfare, many researchers have turned their attention to the following question: can anything be done to enhance our ability to think, reason, make decisions, and solve problems? The answer now emerging from ongoing projects seems to be "yes" (e.g., Bransford et al., 1987; Paris & Jacobs, 1987). Two approaches appear to be useful in this regard.

The first involves providing individuals with an increased *knowledge base*—increased information they can use in making decisions and solving various problems. Evidence for the value of such an approach is provided by many studies which have compared experts with beginners in various fields (e.g., chess masters, engineers, computer programmers). Results suggest that experts differ from beginners both in terms of the amount of specific knowledge at their disposal and in how this information is organized (Linn, 1985; Voss et al., 1983). So arming individuals with increased amounts of information and helping them organize such knowledge effectively may prove useful in enhancing their performance.

A sharply different approach involves the concept of *metacognition*. This refers to knowledge or awareness of our own cognitive processes. Presumably, if we understand how we are currently thinking about various problems and how we are attempting to solve them, we can experience major gains in both areas. In other words, increased understanding of our current cognitive processes can be an important first step to improving them. This principle has recently been applied in education, where efforts have been made to teach children how to reason clearly and how to use various mnemonic devices to improve their memory. The basic goal in all such procedures is enhancing youngsters' ability to acquire new information and then to apply it spontaneously to new situations. Does an approach focused on metacognition actually help? Growing evidence suggests that it does. For example, training focused on metacognition has been found to enhance children's ability to write clearly (Bereiter & Scardamalia, 1985) and to solve mathematical problems effectively (Schoenfeld, 1985).

Taking existing evidence into account, it seems reasonable to predict that through a combination of these approaches significant gains in key cognitive capacities can be attained. To the extent these are actually achieved, psychology—and basic research on cognition—will have contributed to human welfare in an important and lasting way.

Language: Cornerstone of Communication

In a best-selling book of the 1970s, Desmond Morris (1975) referred to the human species as the "naked ape." While this is an intriguing suggestion, it seems more appropriate to describe our species as the "talking ape," for it is our use of language, not our lack of a shaggy coat, that truly sets us apart from other primates. But what, precisely, is **language?** How do we use it? And what is its relationship to other aspects of cognition? It is on these questions that we now focus.

Language: Its Basic Nature

What do we mean by the term *language?* Most psychologists and *psycholinguists* (scientists who study the cognitive processes occurring during the acquisition and use of language) agree that it involves communication through sounds, written symbols, and, perhaps, gestures. Further, they suggest that before any set of sounds or symbols can be termed a language, three criteria must be met.

First, information must be transmitted by these sounds and symbols. That is, words and sentences must carry *meaning*. Second, although the number of separate sounds or words in a language may be limited, it must be possible to combine these into an essentially infinite number of sentences. Finally, the meaning of these combinations (sentences) must be independent of the settings in which they are used. In other words, they must be able to convey information about other places and other times. Only if all of these criteria are met does the term *language* apply to a system of communication. We will return to these criteria later, when we discuss the possibility of language in other species, so please keep them in mind for further use.

In actual use, language involves two major components: the *production* of speech or writing, and its *comprehension*. Intriguing evidence exists concerning both aspects.

The Production of Speech.   All spoken languages consists of *phonemes*, a set of basic sounds; *morphemes*, the smallest units of speech that convey some meaning; and *syntax*, rules about how these sounds can be combined into sentences.

English has forty-six separate phonemes, consisting of vowels, consonants, and blends. Other languages have more or fewer basic sounds. Further, all languages do not employ the same phonemes; sounds used in one language may be absent in another. (A good example is the clicking sounds used in several African languages, which are not found in European or Asian languages.) The number of morphemes is much greater than the number of phonemes—about 100,000 in English. Some morphemes are words, but others are not (e.g., the plural *s,* prefixes such as *un* or *sub*). The number of words is greater still—about 500,000 in English; and, as noted earlier, the number of sentences (combinations of these sounds) is, for all practical purposes, infinite.

We should add that at the present time most psycholinguists believe that the production of meaningful speech rests upon a speaker's knowledge of his or her language at three different levels: *phonological*—awareness of the sounds and sound combinations considered appropriate in the language; *syntactic*—understanding the ways these sounds can be combined; and *semantic*—understanding the meaning of the sounds and sound combinations. Only if all three forms of knowledge are at sufficient levels can meaningful, connected speech be produced (refer to Figure 7-20).

Speech Comprehension: Understanding What We Hear.   Have you ever listened to a conversation between two persons speaking a foreign language you didn't know? If so, you may recall that it seemed very confusing, like sounds without form or

FIGURE 7-20. In order to produce meaningful speech, individuals must have knowledge of (1) the sounds and sound combinations appropriate to their language, (2) the ways in which these sounds can be combined, and (3) the meaning of these sounds and sound combinations.

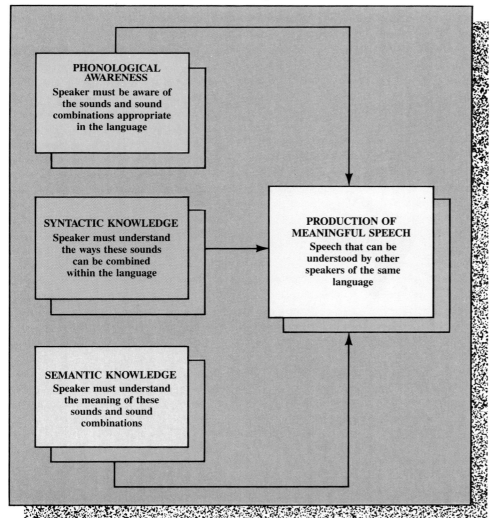

Knowledge Needed to Produce
Meaningful Speech

structure. In part, this is due to the fact that when you listen to a language you don't know, you can't even recognize the boundaries between words. But now consider what must occur when you listen to speech in your own language. The sounds you hear must be transformed into some kind of internal representation, which must be compared with corresponding information in memory; the meaning of each word must then be retrieved, and, finally, this information must be combined so that you can understand entire sentences. Clearly, our ability to perform these tasks quickly and effortlessly is impressive!

As you already know, however, not all speech is equally easy to interpret. Several factors determine the ease with which we comprehend spoken words. First, sentences containing *negatives* (not, no) are more difficult to understand than sentences without them (Clark & Chase, 1972). Second, sentences in the *passive voice* are harder to comprehend than those in the *active voice*. For example, it is easier to understand ''Bob ate the blackberry pie'' than ''The blackberry pie was eaten by Bob.'' Finally, as you might guess, ambiguous sentences—those with two or more possible meanings—are harder to understand than unambiguous sentences (Mistler-Lachman, 1975). Compare ''Last night I saw an alligator in my pyjamas'' with ''Last night I saw an alligator wearing my pyjamas.'' Which is easier to grasp? Clearly, the second. Incidentally, such ambiguity is far from rare; newspaper headlines often show this characteristics (e.g., ''Homeless Appeal to Mayor''; ''Amy Carter Found Drunk on White House Steps''; see Figure 7-21 for several more examples).

Not surprisingly, the ability to comprehend speech—or one's awareness of the sounds of one's own language—seems to play an important role in learning to read (Wagner & Torgesen, 1987). Children who are not effective at sound recognition tasks (e.g., determining which of four words contains different sounds than the others) tend to score lower on standard tests of achievement in reading and spelling. Further, when such youngsters are exposed to training designed to improve their *phonological awareness*

FIGURE 7-21. Many newspaper headlines are ambiguous in meaning. When you encounter them, you must pause to figure out just what they mean.

Ambiguity in the News

TABLE 7-5

Some milestones of language development. Please note: these are only *averages* for these ages, and each child departs from them to some degree.

Average Age	Language Behavior Demonstrated by Child
12 weeks	Smiles when talked to; makes cooing sounds
16 weeks	Turns head in response to human voice
20 weeks	Makes vowel and consonant sounds while cooing
6 months	Cooing changes to babbling, which contains all sounds of human speech
8 months	Certain syllables repeated (e.g., ''ma-ma'')
12 months	Understands some words; may say a few
18 months	Can produce up to fifty words
24 months	Has vocabulary of more than fifty words; uses some two-word phrases
30 months	Vocabulary increases to several hundred words; uses phrases of three to five words
36 months	Vocabulary of about a thousand words
48 months	Most basic aspects of language well established

(their ability to recognize the sounds of spoken speech), they show marked improvements in reading ability (Bradley & Bryant, 1985). In an important sense, then, the ability to understand spoken language may be basic to other important language-related skills.

The Development of Language

During the first few weeks of life, infants have only one major means of verbal communication at their disposal: crying. Within a few short years, however, children progress rapidly to speaking whole sentences and a vocabulary of hundreds or even thousands of words. Some of the milestones along this remarkable journey are summarized in Table 7-5. Since we'll consider the development of many cognitive skills, including language, in Chapter 8, we won't comment on this process in detail here. However, we should note that three contrasting explanations for the development of language have been proposed.

The first of these—the *social learning view*—suggests that speech is acquired through a combination of operant conditioning and imitation. Presumably, children are praised or otherwise rewarded by their parents for making sounds approximating those of their native language. Moreover, parents often model appropriate sounds, words, and sentences for them. Together, it is contended, these basic forms of learning contribute to the rapid acquisition of language skills (the abilities both to produce and to understand speech).

A sharply different view has been proposed by Noam Chomsky (1968), a noted linguist. According to Chomsky, language is at least partly innate. Human beings, he suggests, have a built-in neural system which provides them with an intuitive grasp of grammar. In other words, humans are *prepared* to acquire language skills, and that is why we rapidly do so.

Finally, a third approach suggests that the development of language is intimately linked to the growth of other cognitive capacities. As children gain greater understanding of themselves and the world around them and come to think in more and more sophisticated ways, their language skills, too, improve. Thus, shifts in their ability to produce and understand speech mirror underlying changes in general cognitive development.

Which of these theories is correct? At the present time each is supported by some evidence, but none seems sufficient by itself to account for all aspects of language development. A ''best guess,'' then, is that aspects of all three theories are probably essential for full understanding of the process through which we acquire the impressive communication skills that are such a basic part of our human heritage.

Language and Thought: Do We Think What We Say or Say What We Think?

Although we often have vivid mental images, most of our thinking seems to involve words. This fact raises an intriguing question: what is the precise relationship between language and thought? One possibility, known as the **linguistic-relativity hypothesis,** suggests that language actually shapes or determines thought (Whorf, 1956). According to this view, people who speak different languages may actually perceive the world in different ways because their thinking is determined, at least in part, by the words available to them. For example, it might be argued that Eskimos, who have many different words to describe snow, actually perceive this aspect of the physical world differently from English-speaking persons, who have only one word.

An opposing view is one you may find easier to accept: thought shapes language. This position suggests that language merely reflects the ways we think—how our minds work. Which of these two positions is more accurate? While the issue is far from totally resolved, current evidence seems to argue against the linguistic-relativity approach. If this view were correct, then differences in the vocabulary of various languages should be reflected in differences in the perceptions of persons who speak them. For example, if one language has few words to describe colors, but another language has more words of this type, then people who speak the first language should have greater difficulty in perceiving different colors than people who speak the second language. Research designed to examine such possibilities has generally yielded negative results (Rosch, 1975). For example, people from New Guinea, who have only two words for color—black and white—can recognize differences in hue as readily as other people. Such findings point to the following conclusions: while it may be easier to express a particular idea or concept in one language than in another, this does not imply that our thoughts or perceptions are greatly shaped by language. On the contrary, basic aspects of human perception and thought seem to be very much the same around the world.

Language in Other Species: Are Humans the Only "Talking Apes"?

That members of other species communicate with one another is obvious: bees do a complex "dance" upon returning to their hive to indicate the distance and direction of a new source of food; birds emit songs when trying to attract a mate; and we have discovered that porpoises, whales, and other sea-going mammals communicate with one another through complex patterns of sounds transmitted through water (see Figure 7-22). But what about language? Until quite recently, there seemed little question that humans were the only creatures on earth capable of using this elegant means of communication. Efforts to teach chimpanzees to speak failed miserably. For example, during the 1940s Keith and Cathy Hayes raised a chimp named Vicki from infancy in their home. Although they provided her with intensive speech training, she was finally able to utter only a few simple words such as "mama," "papa," and "cup." However, spoken words are not essential for the use of language. Persons who have lost the power of speech through accident or illness can still communicate by writing or other means, and clearly they retain language skills. The fact that chimps cannot learn to speak, then, does not rule out the possibility that they can learn to use *some* form of language. And in fact, the findings reported by several teams of researchers seem to support the view that they can.

First, Beatrice and Allen Gardner succeeded in teaching Washoe, a female chimp, to use and understand almost 200 words in American Sign Language, a means of communication based on hand gestures which is used by many deaf persons (Gardner & Gardner, 1975). After several years of practice with this system, Washoe became quite fluent in it. For example, when asked simple questions such as "Who are you?" she replies, "Me Washoe." She has learned to request actions (e.g., tickling) and objects (e.g., food) she desires. And she has even learned to describe her mood with signs for such words as "hurt," "sorry," and "funny." Perhaps most impressive of all, Washoe now lives with

FIGURE 7-22. Organisms from bees to porpoises communicate with other members of their own species. It does not appear, though, that such communication can appropriately be termed *language*.

Animal Communication

other chimps and seems to communicate with them by means of sign language, at least sometimes (Fouts, Hirsch, & Fouts, 1982).

In other research Ann and David Premack (1972) trained another chimp, Sarah, to read and write in a special language based on small pieces of colored plastic. Using standard conditioning techniques they taught Sarah to use 130 different words. For example in order to teach her the meaning of the symbol for "give," a tasty piece of banana or apple was placed outside her reach. Only after she placed the symbol for "give" on a magnetic board did she receive this reward. By means of such training, Sarah learned to read whole sentences placed on her word-board by her trainers. She then either followed the instructions presented or provided her own answers by means of the plastic "words."

In a third series of studies with chimpanzees, scientists at the Yerkes Primate Laboratory taught a young female named Lana to communicate by pushing various panels on a special keyboard. Each panel contains a different symbol, and Lana has learned to arrange these into what seem to be meaningful sentences. Thus, when shown several objects of different colors and asked, "What is the name of the object that is green?" she can reply correctly (Savage-Rumbaugh et al., 1983).

While research with chimps has been impressive, recent studies with gorillas have yielded results that seem even more dramatic. Francine Patterson (1978) has taught Koko, a female gorilla, to "speak" in sign language. To teach her these signs, Patterson used a technique known as *molding*. In this procedure she took Koko's hands and shaped them into the sign representing an activity or object while in its presence. Through such techniques, Patterson reports, Koko has acquired a vocabulary of several hundred signs (refer to Figure 7-23), and she shows great flexibility in their use. She constructs original sentences. She seems capable of remembering and describing past events, and she even creates her own signs for new objects and events. Thus, she terms zebras ''white tigers,'' and describes a Pinocchio doll with a large nose as ''elephant baby.'' Perhaps most surprising of all, she seems to use language in complex and all-too-human ways. Thus, she has learned to bend the truth to her own advantage when ''speaking'' in sign language. For example, in one incident she jumped on a sink and pulled it out from the wall. When asked if she had caused this damage, she accused one of the researchers of being responsible!

This research, plus more being conducted in over twenty different laboratories, has led some psychologists to conclude that we have already been removed from our throne as the only species capable of using a language. And many others believe that at the very least there are more similarities between our own use of language and that of other primates than was once believed (Premack, 1985). Other scientists remain skeptical, however (Limber, 1977; Terrace, 1979). There are several reasons behind these reservations.

First, some of the findings of such research—including the dramatic results reported by Patterson (1978)—have not been subjected to the kind of close scientific scrutiny that is the hallmark of modern psychology. Patterson's studies have been reported

Koko Using Sign Language

FIGURE 7-23. In the first photo, Koko is making the sign for ''on.'' In the second she is making the sign for ''mask'' (the object being held by her trainer, Dr. Francine Patterson). In the final photo, Koko is actually putting on the mask.

primarily in an informal manner in magazines and television shows rather than in the pages of carefully edited scientific journals. Second, critics have noted that the chimps and gorillas in several of these projects may merely have been imitating their trainers' signs and actions. Little if any evidence exists to suggest that they were demonstrating original thought. Such evidence is necessary before we can conclude that these animals are indeed using language in the same way as human beings do.

Third, and perhaps most important, although Washoe, Lana, Koko, and other animals have learned to use names for objects and actions, and even to combine these, they have not shown any grasp of the basic rules that underlie all human language (rules we described on page 222).

So, are we still the only "talking apes"? At present, this issue remains controversial. Some psychologists are convinced they have succeeded in teaching a true language to their chimpanzee or gorilla subjects, while others remain skeptical about such conclusions. Perhaps a clear answer will emerge in the near future, as additional research with these highly intelligent animals proceeds. At the moment, though, the jury is still out, and we remain uncertain as to whether language is, or is not, a uniquely human possession.

Summary and Review

Thinking

Thinking is strongly affected by *concepts*—mental categories in which nonidentical but related objects or events are grouped together. *Logical concepts,* those created for specific purposes such as classifying plants or animals, may be developed through a process of *hypothesis testing*. In contrast, *natural concepts,* those we use in everyday life, involve the development of *prototypes,* the best or clearest examples of the concept. New items are compared with our prototypes and are included in a concept if they share enough attributes with the prototypes. In addition, relationships between various attributes are important. Our experience tells us that certain events or characteristics tend to occur together, and this information, too, shapes natural concepts or categories.

Reasoning is the process through which we draw conclusions from given facts or assumptions. It is affected by several forms of bias. One of these, the *confirmation bias,* involves our tendency to test hypotheses by gathering information that confirms them. Another, *belief perseverance,* involves our tendency to cling to conclusions even when these are strongly refuted by additional evidence.

Making Decisions

In making decisions we employ several *heuristics,* rules of thumb which help us make reasonably good choices in an efficient manner. The *availability heuristic* leads us to judge events or objects we can readily bring to mind as more frequent or more likely than ones we cannot readily bring to mind. The *representativeness heuristic* leads us to judge the likelihood of events or objects in terms of how representative they seem to be of typical cases or prototypes. Because of a need to justify past actions we often become *entrapped* by our decisions—unable to admit that they were wrong. We often demonstrate *overconfidence* in our judgments. Finally, our decisions can be strongly affected by *reference points* or *anchors*—values setting floors or ceilings on our estimates of the true worth of some item.

Solving Problems

In solving problems we employ several different strategies. Using *trial-and-error* we try different solutions until one works. *Algorithms* involve exhaustive search procedures which will ultimately yield a solution. In contrast, *heuristics* are strategies suggested by prior experience. They do not guarantee a solution but can be much more efficient.

Sometimes, we attempt to solve current problems through *analogies*. Here, we reason that a problem we now face is similar, in underlying structure, to one we encountered in the past. We then adapt the prior solution to the current problem.

Language

Language involves communication through sounds, written symbols, and gestures. Different factors play a role in *speech production* and *speech comprehension*. Language development occurs at an impressive rate; it seems to involve basic forms of learning, cognitive development, and perhaps innate mechanisms as well. Language seems to reflect thought—the basic ways the mind works. In the past it was widely assumed that human beings are the only organisms on earth capable of using language. However, recent studies conducted with other primates suggest that chimpanzees and gorillas may be capable of such communication. Whether they can actually use language in the same manner as humans, though, remains an open question.

Key Terms

Algorithms Rules that guarantee solutions to appropriate problems.

Analogies Efforts to solve a problem by applying solutions that were previously successful with other problems which were different in content but similar in underlying structure.

Availability Heuristic A mental rule of thumb indicating that the more readily events or objects come to mind, the more frequent or likely we judge them to be.

Base Rates The frequency of some object or event in general (i.e., in a large population of events or objects).

Belief Perseverance The tendency to maintain established beliefs even in the face of evidence or information that contradicts them.

Concepts Mental categories for objects or events that are similar in enough respects to be grouped together.

Confirmation Bias The tendency to test beliefs or hypotheses by focusing on instances in which we expect them to be confirmed.

Decision-Making The process of choosing between various courses of action or alternatives.

Entrapment A process whereby individuals who have obtained negative results from a decision continue with the failed course of action in order to justify the time, efforts, and other costs they have already incurred.

Functional Fixedness The tendency to think of using an object only as it has been used in the past, which can interfere with effective problem-solving.

Heuristics Mental rules of thumb that permit us to make decisions and judgments in a rapid and efficient manner.

Language A system of communication employing sounds, written symbols, and gestures.

Linear Reasoning Reasoning in which we compare items to determine their relative order.

Linguistic-Relativity Hypothesis The view that language shapes thought.

Means-Ends Analysis A technique for solving problems in which the overall problem is divided into parts, and efforts are made to solve each part in turn.

Mental Set The impact of past experience on present problem-solving, specifically, our tendency to stick with methods that worked in the past, leading us sometimes to overlook more efficient means to a solution.

Natural Concepts Concepts used in everyday life that are not based on a concrete set of attributes. Natural concepts do not have clear-cut boundaries and often are defined by prototypes—the best or clearest examples of items or events the concept includes.

Overconfidence The tendency to overestimate one's own ability to make accurate judgments and decisions.

Positive Test Strategy Our tendency to test hypotheses by examining only instances in which we expect a positive result occurs.

Problem-Solving The process through which we attempt to determine the means for reaching a difficult goal.

Propositional Reasoning Reasoning in which we consider the truth of "If . . . then" statements.

Prototypes Best examples of natural concepts, for example, thinking of a chair or table for the natural concept "furniture."

Reasoning Thinking in which we attempt to draw conclusions from given facts or assumptions.

Representativeness Heuristic A mental rule of thumb suggesting that the more an event or object resembles what we consider to be ''typical,'' the more likely or frequent it is judged to be.

Syllogistic Reasoning Reasoning in which two premises are used to derive a logical conclusion.

Thinking The cognitive processes which take place as we process information from our senses and information already present in memory.

Trial-and-Error A strategy for solving problems in which all possible solutions are tried until one works.

For More Information

Bransford, J.D., & Stein, B.S. (1984). *The ideal problem solver: A guide for improving thinking, learning, and creativity*. New York: W.H. Freeman.

> This book presents specific strategies for solving problems, including some very complex ones. Many examples are included, so this is a good source to consult if you'd like to know more about this key process.

McWhinney, B., ed. (1987). *Mechanisms of language acquisition*. Hillsdale, NJ: Erlbaum.

> How do vocabulary, grammar, and the ability to produce and understand speech develop? Leading experts on these and related topics describe their views and the results of their recent research. The book is written primarily for professionals, but you can certainly understand some of the basic arguments presented if you read carefully.

Perkins, D.N., Lockhead, J., & Bishop, J.C., eds. (1987). *Thinking: The second international conference*. Hillsdale, NJ: Erlbaum.

> A collection of articles by noted researchers from several different fields (psychology, philosophy, education). Such topics as critical thinking, the development of thinking skills, and techniques for improving reasoning and problem-solving are examined. You may find some of the papers difficult to follow, but doing so is well worth the effort.

Weisberg, R. (1986). *Creativity: Genius and other myths*. New York: W.H. Freeman.

> What is creativity? What do we know about it? How is it related to problem-solving? These are only a few of the fascinating issues addressed in this book. Some of the views presented are controversial, but the author's comments are certain to stimulate your thinking.

CHAPTER

8

Human Development: Change Throughout Life

"So what's new in the old neighborhood?" Sharon McDonald asks her friend Karen Ettinger. "I haven't been around for . . . let's see, what is it, four years now. Has anything exciting happened?"

"Well, not exciting, maybe, but there's plenty going on," Karen replies.

"O.K., so don't keep me in suspense. Give!"

"Maybe the biggest surprise is what's happened to old Doc Pulaski."

"Really? What could happen to a dentist? A funny one, I'll admit, but a dentist all the same."

"Plenty. Last year he closed his office and went to Florida. You know how he always used to talk about buying a boat and running a charter business—taking people out to the Gulf to fish? Well, he actually did it. Named his boat *The Painless,* too!"

"No kidding!" Sharon says with a grin. "And I thought it was all just talk. He'd go on and on about it when your mouth was full and you couldn't answer. But isn't he pretty old for such a change? He must be over fifty, at least."

"Right. But he sure doesn't act it. The last couple of years before he left, he started wearing gold chains, even an earring. And after he got divorced, he started hanging out at bars. He's turned into a regular middle-aged swinger."

"You don't say! That really *is* a good one. But what else? No other boat captains, I guess."

"No, but there's other stuff, too. Remember Bud Kaufman, the big liberal? Well, after roaming around California for a while he got his act together and went to grad school. Got an MBA. Now you wouldn't know him. He cut his hair, wears three-piece suits, and, the last I heard, he was running for the state Assembly as a *Republican!*"

"What!" Sharon practically shouts. "I can't believe it! Bud Kaufman as a Yuppie? Whew! There really *have* been some changes around here."

"Yeah, I guess with people, you never know. Just when you think you've got 'em figured out, they up and change on you. . . ."

Change, it is often said, is the only constant. And where human beings are concerned, this statement is certainly true. Think about the many ways *you've* changed over the course of your life. From a cuddly infant unable to walk, talk, or do much besides endear yourself to surrounding adults, you've somehow been transformed into a complex adult capable of an impressive range of behaviors. Even if you consider only the past few years, major change may be apparent. Perhaps you've shifted your political views, modified your life goals, developed closer relationships with other persons. If you think carefully, the list will be a long one, for in a real sense, each of us does seem to be in a continuous state of flux—and while changing, we are not always aware of such shifts or of their ultimate impact upon us (refer to Figure 8-1 for an illustration of this fact).

It is on this basic process that the field of **developmental psychology** focuses. Briefly, it is concerned with how people change—physically, mentally, and socially—during the entire lifespan. Given the scope and importance of such shifts, it is not surprising that interest in *development* (all types of age-related change) is far from new. Philosophers, poets, and scholars have thought and written about this topic since the earliest days of human society. Yet it was not until the early twentieth century that systematic efforts to study it emerged. The primary reason for this delay is obvious: prior to the appearance of modern psychology, a scientific orientation on this topic was lacking. Once psychology took shape, however, efforts to apply its approach and tools to the study of human development were not far behind. Indeed, by the 1920s, at least one professional association concerned with the scientific study of development—the Society for Research in Child Development—had been formed. (This society still exists today and continues to play an active role in fostering basic research.)

FIGURE 8-1. We continue to change throughout life but, like the character in this cartoon, are not always aware of such shifts. *(Source:* The New Yorker, *1971.)*

"*It struck me all of a sudden. From being a Young Turk, I have passed by imperceptible degrees to being an Old Turk.*"

In the intervening years *developmental psychologists* have studied a dazzling array of topics: virtually every aspect of age-related change you might imagine. Thus, the scope of their work ranges from changes in physical structure and perception through changes in the capacity to reason, use language, or form friendships. Initially, much of this work focused on events occurring during our early years—infancy and adolescence. More recently, though, the scope of such research has expanded, so that it now considers important changes during our adult years, too.

In the remainder of this chapter we will summarize some of the fascinating findings uncovered by psychologists who focus on the process of *change.* While development itself is continuous (we go on changing throughout life), it is convenient for this discussion to divide the human life span into several distinct periods: the prenatal period, infancy, childhood, adolescence, and adulthood. Within each, we'll consider some of the important ways in which we change *physically, cognitively,* and *socially.*

◢ The Prenatal Period: The Origins of Life

When does human life begin? In one sense this is a philosophical or religious issue, outside the realm of science. From a purely biological point of view, your life as an individual begins when one of the millions of sperm released by your father during sexual intercourse reaches and fertilizes an *ovum* deep within your mother's body. The product of this union is barely $1/175$ of an inch in diameter—smaller than the period at the end of this sentence (see Figure 8-2). Yet packed within this tiny speck are the genetic ''blueprints'' (23 chromosomes from each parent) which guide all future growth.

Physical Growth and the Beginnings of Thought

After fertilization, the ovum moves through the mother's reproductive tract until it reaches the *uterus* (womb). This trip takes several days, and during this time the ovum divides again and again. By the time it reaches the uterus, it consists of several dozen cells arranged in two distinct layers. The inner one ultimately develops into the child, while the outer layer forms several protective and life-supporting structures we will soon discuss.

FIGURE 8-2. Life begins when a single sperm unites with an ovum.

The Beginnings of Life

Ten to fourteen days after fertilization, the ovum becomes implanted in the wall of the mother's uterus. For the next six weeks it is known as the **embryo** and develops at a rapid pace. By the third week a primitive heart has formed and begins to beat. By the fourth week the embryo is about one-fifth of an inch long (one-half centimeter) and the region of the head is clearly visible. Rapid growth continues, and by the end of the eighth week a face as well as arms and legs are present. By this time, too, all major internal organs have begun to form, and some (e.g., the sex glands) are already active. The nervous system develops rapidly, too and some reflexes appear during the eighth or ninth week.

During the next seven months the developing child—now known as the **fetus**—shows increasingly human form. Hair and nails appear by the end of the twentieth week. The eyes are completely formed by the end of the twenty-fourth to twenty-sixth week, and they begin to move when the eyelids are open. Physical growth, too, is impressive. At the end of the twelfth week the fetus is 3 inches long (7.6 centimeters) and weighs barely three-fourths of an ounce (21 grams). By the end of the twentieth week it is almost ten inches long (25 cm) and weighs 8 or 9 ounces (227–255 gm). During the last three months of pregnancy the fetus gains about eight ounces each week and grows rapidly. At birth, babies weigh more than 7 pounds (3.17 kilograms) on average, and are about 20 inches long (50.8 cm). (Please see Figure 8-3 for striking photos of development during the prenatal period.)

While physical growth clearly takes center stage during the prenatal period, growing evidence suggests that cognitive abilities, too, may be taking shape at this time. In a series of related studies DeCasper and his colleagues (e.g., DeCasper & Fifer, 1980;

FIGURE 8-3. The fetus develops rapidly. Notice the features visible in each photo.

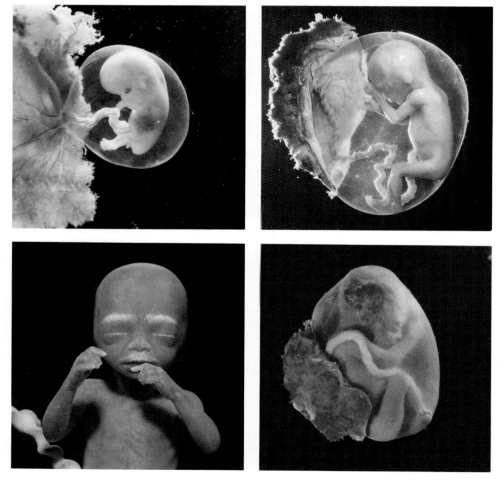

Spence & DeCasper, 1982) have uncovered evidence suggesting that the unborn fetus may already have the ability to learn and to distinguish familiar and unfamiliar stimuli. In one of these studies DeCasper asked women seven and a half months pregnant to read a story out loud three times each day for four weeks. At the end of that period the heart rate of each fetus was measured as recordings of the familiar story and of an unfamiliar one were played. Results indicated that the familiar story produced a slight decrease in fetal heart rate, while the unfamiliar one produced a slight increase. (A decrease in heart rate is often a sign of increased attention.) These and related findings suggest that even before we are born, our ability to process information and to benefit from our experience may already be operative.

Prenatal Influences on Development: When Trouble Starts Early

Under ideal conditions development during the prenatal period occurs in the orderly fashion described above, and the newborn child is well equipped at birth to survive outside its mother's body. Unfortunately, though, conditions are not always ideal. Many factors can interfere with the normal pattern of growth.

Mother's Diet.   One such factor is the diet eaten by expectant mothers. During the early months of pregnancy deficits in a mother's diet do not seem to cause any permanent harm. The relatively small fetus simply takes what it needs from its parent's resources—assuming these exist. In later months, however, poor nutrition can result in serious effects. Inadequate diet of mothers have been linked to premature births, increased frequency of disease, and even lowered intelligence among children. Even worse, such effects may be difficult or even impossible to reverse (Chow et al., 1971). Clearly, providing adequate nutrition for expectant mothers is a crucial task; failure to do so can have devastating effects on the coming generation.

Disease During Pregnancy.   The blood supply of the fetus and that of its mother come into close proximity in the **placenta,** a structure which protects and nourishes the growing child. As a result, disease-producing organisms present in the mother's blood can sometimes infect the developing child. Tragically, diseases that exert only minor effects upon mothers can be very serious for the fetus. For example, *rubella* (German measles) can cause blindness, deafness, or heart disease in the fetus if the mother contracts this illness during the first four weeks of pregnancy. Other diseases which can be transmitted to the fetus, and may thus interfere with the normal course of development, include influenza, mumps, smallpox, syphillis, and (perhaps) genital herpes.

Drugs.   A third factor which can exert important effects upon the developing fetus is the use of drugs by the mother. Many different substances seem harmful in this regard. Excessive use of aspirin, a drug most of us take without hesitation, can result in harm to the fetus's circulatory system (Kelsey, 1969). Smoking, a practice engaged in by millions of future mothers, also produces negative effects. Growing evidence points to a link between smoking by mothers and their infants' low birth weight, short body length, and higher than normal mortality at birth (Meredith, 1975).

Caffeine, the stimulating substance found in coffee, tea, and many soft drinks, can also exert adverse effects on the developing fetus. Some evidence suggests that caffeine may slow fetal growth and contribute to premature birth (Jacobson et al., 1984). In addition, a recent study by Hronsky and Emory (1987) indicates that during the first two days after birth the more caffeine consumed by mothers, the more irritable and less consolable their newborns tend to be. The potential importance of these findings is underscored by the fact that almost 95 percent of all new mothers report having used caffeine during their pregnancies (Hill, 1973).

The Fetal Alcohol Syndrome.   In some ways the harm produced by *alcohol* is even more unsettling. Children born to mothers who make heavy use of this drug some-

The Harmful Effects of Alcohol on a Fetus: Some Cause for Hope

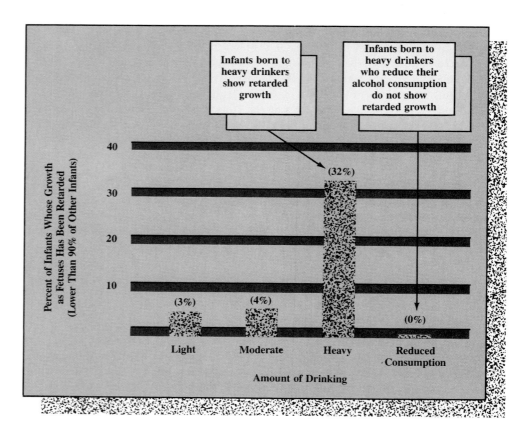

FIGURE 8-4. Women who are heavy drinkers have babies whose growth is retarded relative to the babies of women who are light or moderate drinkers. However, if mothers who are heavy drinkers reduce their consumption of alcohol during the last three months of pregnancy, such effects are reduced. *(Source: Based on data in Rosett & Weiner, 1985.)*

times suffer from a disorder known as the **fetal alcohol syndrome** (Rosett & Weiner, 1985). Included in this syndrome are severely retarded growth, damage to the nervous system, and distortions in the normal shape of the face. In many cases only some of these problems are present (e.g., an infant may show extremely low body weight and size, but not facial distortions). In such cases the infants are described as suffering from *fetal alcohol effects* but not from the fetal alcohol syndrome itself.

How much must a woman drink before such effects are produced? This is a difficult question to answer, for many factors probably play a role, such as susceptibility of the fetus to the impact of alcohol and other aspects of the mother's health. Careful studies suggest, though, that women who consume more than four ounces of alcohol per day (heavy drinkers) are much more likely to give birth to infants suffering from such effects than women who are light to moderate drinkers (one ounce of alcohol or less per day) (Rosett et al., 1983). Fortunately, there is some indication that alcohol's damage to the fetus can be readily prevented. When mothers who have been heavy drinkers reduce their consumption of alcohol during the last three months of pregnancy, their children are no more likely to suffer fetal alcohol effects than children born to moderate drinkers (Rosett & Weiner, 1985; refer to Figure 8-4).

Please note: these findings should *not* be taken as a license to drink while pregnant. Even small amounts of alcohol may affect the fetus in ways that are difficult to measure at birth. Thus, the safest course for prospective mothers seems to be, quite simply, to abstain.

Infancy and Childhood: The Early Years

In a sense, the course of human development is something like a ride on a roller coaster or, really, on several roller coasters at once. One aspect of development (e.g, physical growth) rushes ahead, while others progress more slowly. And this pattern may then reverse, so that rapid gains are made in cognitive abilities and social skills, while physical change is slower. When large differences among individuals are added to the picture, it becomes a confusing one indeed. Can we make any sense out of this complex pattern? The answer is definitely ''yes.'' Systematic studies have added greatly to our knowledge of each of these aspects of development (Flavell & Markman, 1983). Thus, we can now provide you with a good, working overview of how we change and grow during **infancy** (birth to age two) and **childhood** (age two to puberty). Before doing so, however, we will pause briefly to comment on another important issue: how developmental psychologists actually go about the task of acquiring information on various aspects of age-related change.

Developmental Research: Measures and Methods

Suppose that a developmental psychologist wishes to determine when infants can first detect various odors. How can she find out? Since infants can't talk, the simplest way of conducting this research—asking them what they can smell—isn't feasible. Instead, some indirect measure of perceptions and reactions is needed. Fortunately, several of these exist. For example, the researcher might measure changes in the infants' heart rate as she presents different odors; presumably, if they can smell one but not another, their heart rate will change in the presence of the first, but not the second. Alternatively, she may measure the extent to which they turn their heads toward or away from different odors. (Recall that Balogh and Porter [1986] actually used such procedures to determine if infants could recognize such smells as ginger and cherry. This study was described in Chapter 3.) Through indirect measures such as these, infants can tell us much about what they perceive and what they know, even if they can't talk.

Now, assume that the researcher has chosen a useful measure—one that reveals indirectly whether her subjects can or cannot detect various odors. How will she now proceed? Two basic methods are possible. In the first, known as **longitudinal research,** she may obtain the permission of parents to test a group of babies on several occasions. She might assess their ability to detect various odors at two months of age, then again at four months, and perhaps again at six and eight months. Presumably, changes in their reactions from one test to the other will reflect age-related changes in their ability to smell—in other words, in the *development* of their olfactory abilities.

Such research can provide valuable information about human development; indeed, it is the preferred method when this is practical. However, it suffers from several drawbacks. It requires repeated access to the same group of subjects, so there may be a substantial loss of participants (e.g., some families may move away and withdraw from the study). And it can be very time-consuming; indeed some longitudinal studies continue for years or even decades.

A second method, usually less time-consuming, is known as **cross-sectional research.** Instead of testing and re-testing the same infants at two-month intervals, the researcher merely tests one group of infants who are two months old, a different group who are four months old, and so on. Such a study could be conducted in a matter of days; there is no necessity to wait for subjects to grow older. But it, too, suffers from several problems. For example, if the various groups differ in some manner (e.g., family background, nutrition), differences in the babies' performance on the experimental task might stem from these factors, *not* from changes related to age. (See Figure 8-5 on page 240 for a comparison of these two basic methods of developmental research.)

Since both of these approaches offer a mixed pattern of advantages and disadvantages, the choice between them is far from simple. Thus, research employing both methods will be described throughout this chapter.

Physical and Perceptual Development: An Overview

Physical growth is rapid during infancy. Assuming good nutrition, infants almost triple in weight (to about 20 pounds or 9 kilograms) and increase in body length by about one-third (to 28 or 29 inches, 71 to 74 cm) during the first year alone.

Infants possess a number of simple reflexes at birth. They can follow a moving light with their eyes, suck on a finger or nipple placed in their mouth, and turn their head in the direction of a touch on the cheek. Their ability to move about or to reach for objects

Cross-Sectional and Longitudinal Research: A Comparison

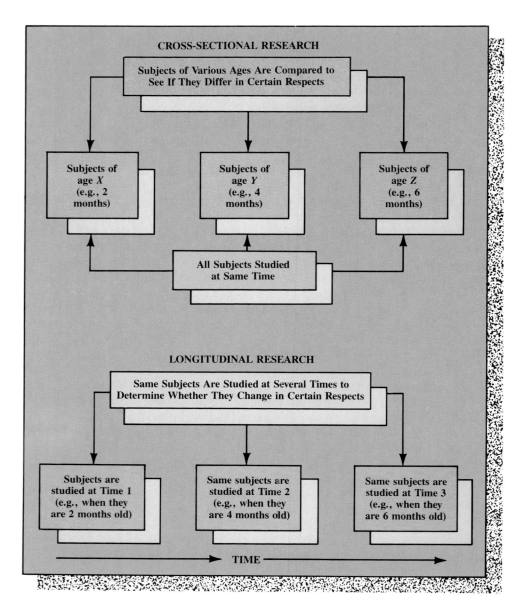

FIGURE 8-5. In *cross-sectional research* (upper panel) subjects of different ages are compared in order to determine if they differ in certain respects. In *longitudinal research* (lower panel) a single group of individuals is studied at different points in time to determine whether they change in various respects with the passage of time.

is quite limited, but this situation changes quickly. Within a few months they can sit and crawl, and, as harried parents quickly learn, most infants are quite mobile by the time they are fourteen or fifteen months old (refer to Figure 8-6). Several important milestones of motor development are summarized in Figure 8-7 on page 242. As you examine them, please keep the following point in mind: the ages indicated are *average* values. Departures from them are important only when they are quite extreme.

After the tremendous spurt during the first months of life, physical development slows considerably. Children usually grow only one-third as much between the ages of two and four as during the first years of life. Certain internal structures, though, continue to develop rapidly. For example, by the time children are three, their brains are almost 75 percent of adult size. And by age six, the brain has reached fully 90 percent of its ultimate size.

Perceptual Development.   How do infants perceive the world around them? Do they recognize form, see color, and perceive depth in the same manner as adults? As we have already noted, infants can't talk, so it is necessary to answer such questions through indirect methods (e.g., by observing changes in their heart rate, sucking responses, or the amount of time they spend gazing at various stimuli). Through such

FIGURE 8-6. Most infants can walk or even run by the time they are fourteen or fifteen months old—long before they are able to recognize (and react appropriately to) many dangers.

methods it has been determined that *neonates* (newborns) can distinguish between different colors (Adams, 1987), odors (Balogh & Porter, 1986), and tastes (Granchrow, Steiner, & Daher, 1983). The last of these facts has been revealed by studies in which infants just a few hours old were given small amounts of different liquids (e.g., water, a solution containing sugar, or quinine). Observation of their facial expressions indicates that they can indeed distinguish between these tastes: they show distinct expressions after each taste (refer to Figure 8-8 on page 243).

As we noted in Chapter 3, such findings suggest that some perceptual abilities are present at birth, or appear within a short period after birth. Thus, they appear to be innate—somehow built into our nervous system. In contrast, other abilities seem to require further physical growth (e.g., development of the nervous system), or experience with the external world, or both. For example, until they are about ten to twelve weeks old, infants do not seem to distinguish between visual stimuli that are equally complex but different in shape. Prior to this time, they do not prefer to gaze at a drawing of a human face with normally placed features rather than one in which the features have been "scrambled" (Fantz, Fagan, & Miranda, 1975). This suggests that certain types of form perception are not present at birth.

The ability to perceive depth, too, seems to develop gradually in the months after birth. Early studies of *depth perception* employed the *visual cliff* shown in Figure 8-9 on page 243 (Gibson & Walk, 1960). As you can see from this drawing, the patterned floor drops away on the deep side of the "cliff." Since a transparent surface actually continues across this chasm, though, there is no actual drop (and no real danger to subjects). Human infants six or seven months old refuse to crawl across the "deep" side to reach their mothers, thus indicating that they perceive depth by this time. Does this perceptual ability appear prior to this age? Since infants below this age aren't mobile enough to crawl across the cliff even if they wanted to, it is necessary to use other methods to find out.

One technique that has proven very useful in this regard is known as the *transfer-across-depth-cues* procedure. Here, infants are shown an object under conditions that provide one set of depth cues (e.g., the object moves through space). They are then shown the same object under conditions that provide a different set of cues (e.g., a drawing that contains monocular cues to depth; refer to our discussion in Chapter 3). At this time, they are also shown a novel stimulus. If they spend more time looking at this new stimulus than at the one they saw originally, this suggests that they can indeed perceive depth. If they

Some Milestones of Physical Development

BEHAVIOR	AVERAGE AGE AT WHICH ACTIVITY IS PERFORMED	
Child can raise chin from ground	1 month	
Child can sit with support	4 months	
Child can sit alone	7 months	
Child can stand by holding onto furniture	9 months	
Child can crawl	10 months	
Child can walk when held by hand and led	11 months	
Child can stand alone	14 months	
Child can walk alone	15 months	

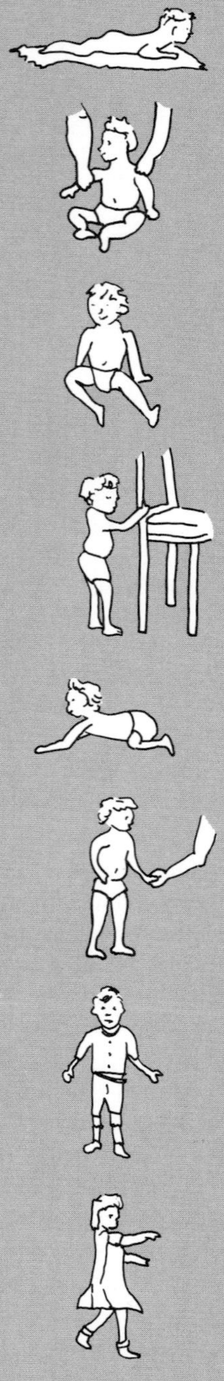

FIGURE 8-7. Physical development is rapid during infancy. (Please note: large individual differences exist with respect to this aspect of development. The values shown here are only averages, and many normal infants will depart from them substantially.)

could not, both stimuli would look equally unfamiliar, and the infants would spend equivalent amounts of time looking at both.

Studies using these procedures indicate that human infants can perceive depth when they are only four months old. For example, in one such study Yonas, Arterberry, and Granrud (1987) exposed four-month-olds to one stimulus (a triangle or tetrahedron) that rotated in space. This provided *kinetic* (motion) cues to depth. After they had seen

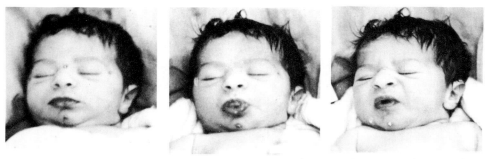

Taste Perception in Infants

FIGURE 8-8. Infants a few hours old show contrasting facial expressions when given small tastes of different substances. These photos illustrate an infant's expressions at rest (left) and after tasting sweet (center) and bitter (right) substances. *(Source: Courtesy J.R. Ganchrow. From Ganchrow, Steiner, & Daher, 1983.)*

this stimulus a number of times, the infants were shown this familiar item under conditions that provided different depth cues (they saw a stereoscopic projection of this stimulus that created the illusion of depth). During these testing sessions the infants also saw another, unfamiliar stimulus. Would they spend more time looking at the new one? As you can see from Figure 8-10 on page 244, they did. These findings suggest that even when the depth cues were changed, infants could still recognize the familiar object as the one they had seen before. In short, they could perceive depth (and three-dimensional object shape) on the basis of very different visual cues.

These findings, and those of many other studies concerned with additional aspects of perceptual development (e.g., Bertenthal et al., 1987), point to the following conclusion: many of our perceptual abilities develop after birth, but the process is a rapid one. In sum, recent research on perceptual development suggests that we can do more, at an earlier age, than was once widely believed.

FIGURE 8-9. Equipment like this "visual cliff" has been used to study depth perception in human infants and other organisms. Results indicate that by the time they are first mobile (at six or seven months of age), infants are reluctant to crawl out onto the "deep" side. This suggests that depth perception is present by that time. *(Source: Based on equipment first used by Gibson & Walk, 1960).*

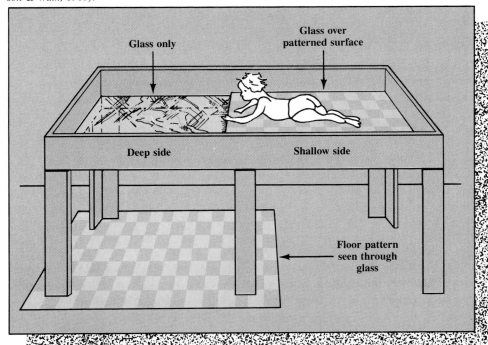

The Visual Cliff: One Technique for Studying Depth Perception

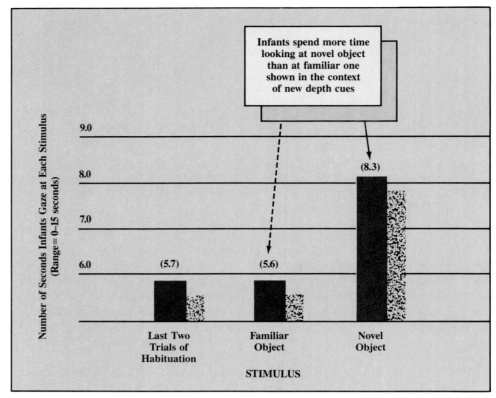

FIGURE 8-10. Four-month-old infants spent more time looking at a novel object (one they had not seen before) than at a familiar object which was presented under conditions that offered them different depth cues. These findings suggest that the ability to perceive depth (and three-dimensional object shape) is present even at this early stage of development. *(Source: Based on data from Yonas, Arterberry, & Granrud, 1987.)*

Breast-Fed versus Bottle-Fed Newborns: Some Recent Findings.   One question concerning infants' early development has been raised repeatedly, and sometimes heatedly, by parents as well as psychologists: Do newborns who are breast-fed obtain an advantage over those who are bottle-fed? Scientific evidence on this question is far from conclusive but generally suggests that this is indeed the case. Breast-fed infants *do* seem to score higher than bottle-fed infants on tests of development, and they even do better in later years in school (Taylor & Wadsworth, 1984). Why is this the case? A recent study by DiPietro, Larson, and Porges (1987) provides some intriguing answers.

These researchers studied one hundred healthy newborns (17 to 56 hours old) by measuring their heart action as they slept and by assessing their reactions to standard tests of behavior while awake. Sixty-one of the infants were breast-fed, while thirty-nine were bottle-fed. Results offered a mixed picture. On the one hand, breast-fed infants showed signs of better physiological functioning. Their heart rates were slower and more rhythmic. On the other hand, they were more irritable, showed greater and more sudden changes in reactions, and were harder to console than bottle-fed neonates (refer to Figure 8-11).

At first glance, these findings seem contradictory: breast-fed infants are in a better overall physiological state, yet they are more irritable than bottle-fed infants. In fact, though, it is possible that a high degree of irritability or behavioral activation may also be related to superior development (DePietro, Larsen, & Porges, 1987). After all, in many cases it is active, crying infants who receive attention and stimulation from their parents—not ones who are calmly sleeping. If this interpretation is correct, then breast-fed infants may indeed gain an important advantage over ones who are bottle-fed. However, there is one additional factor to consider. Many drugs and other chemicals consumed by mothers (e.g., various food additives) pass readily into their milk. Since the effects of such substances on newborns can be devastating, the benefits of breast-feeding mentioned earlier

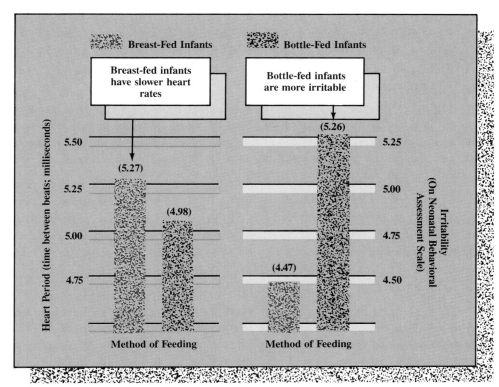

FIGURE 8-11. Breast-fed newborns showed slower and more rhythmic heart rate than bottle-fed newborns (left graph). In addition, breast-fed newborns were more irritable (e.g., easier to arouse) than their bottle-fed counterparts. Both findings can be interpreted as evidence for the benefits of breast-feeding. *(Source: Based on data from DePietro, Larson, & Porges, 1987.)*

may be totally offset by such factors among mothers who consume these substances. In view of this possibility, the most reasonable conclusion for new mothers seems to be: by all means, breast-feed your child if this is feasible, but if you do, take special care to make your diet as safe and wholesome as possible.

Cognitive Development: Piaget's View

Do children think, reason, and remember in the same manner as adults? Different societies have offered sharply contrasting answers to this question over the ages (Borstelmann, 1983). One view fairly popular through the centuries goes something like this: just as children are smaller and weaker than adults, their cognitive abilities, too, are less fully developed. But these are much the same, in basic form, as those of mature human beings.

Such ideas were vigorously challenged by the Swiss psychologist Jean Piaget. On the basis of careful observation of his own and many other children, Piaget concluded that in several respects children do *not* think like adults. We begin life with sharply different cognitive processes and only gradually come to think and reason like adults. Because Piaget's theory contains many valuable insights and has guided a great deal of research, we will summarize it here. But please note: it is no longer accepted by many psychologists as providing a fully accurate guide to the course of cognitive development. In particular, it appears that in many respects Piaget underestimated the cognitive abilities of young children (Gelman & Baillargeon, 1983; Kagan, 1984). After reviewing his theory, therefore, we'll comment on some important modifications in it suggested by recent research.

One more preliminary point: Piaget's theory is a **stage theory.** It proposes that human beings move through an orderly and predictable series of changes with respect to their cognitive functioning. Stage theories have always been popular in the study of development, and we will encounter others later in this chapter and in Chapter 12. For now, we simply wish to note that many psychologists currently question the ideas implicit in such theories that (1) all human beings move through a set series of stages, (2) they do so at certain ages, or (3) the order of such progress is fixed (Flavell, 1986). There simply seems to be too much variability among individuals to enable us to use such neat and orderly patterns.

Piaget's theory addresses the basic question: what mechanism underlies our cognitive development? In other words, what keeps us moving through the various stages the theory describes? According to Piaget, the answer involves tension between two basic processes: assimilation and accommodation. Put simply, **assimilation** refers to the tendency to fit new information into existing mental frameworks—to understand the world in terms of existing concepts and modes of thought. In contrast, **accommodation** involves the tendency to alter existing concepts or mental frameworks in response to new information. Perhaps a simple example will prove helpful.

Imagine that a three-year-old is taken to the zoo by his parents. There he sees porpoises swimming in a tank. Beacuse of his past experience and existing mental frameworks, he pronounces them "fish." This is an example of assimilation: new information is understood within existing concepts. Now, imagine that on another trip he sees the same porpoises breathing, watches them being petted by their trainer, and is also allowed to touch one himself. Here is information that doesn't fit readily with past experience: fish don't breathe, they don't feel warm, and they certainly don't like to be petted! Through accommodation, he now forms a new concept—one for animals that live in water but breathe air and are warm to the touch (refer to Figure 8-12). Piaget suggests that it is the constant interplay and tension between assimilation and accommodation that ultimately moves us toward cognitive maturity. Such movement, in turn, involves a very orderly passage through four major stages.

The Sensorimotor Stage. The first stage described by Piaget lasts from birth until about eighteen to twenty-four months. During this period, the **sensorimotor stage,** infants gradually learn that there is a relationship between their actions and the external world. They discover that they can manipulate objects and produce effects; in short, they acquire a basic understanding of the concept of *cause and effect.* During the sensorimotor period, though, infants seem to know the world only through motor activities and sensory impressions. They have not learned to use symbols or images to represent objects and events. This results in some interesting effects. For example, if an object is hidden from view, four-month-olds will not attempt to search for it. For such youngsters, the old

FIGURE 8-12. When a child first sees porpoises swimming in a large tank of water, he interprets this information within existing mental frameworks and labels them "fish." This illustrates the process of *assimilation.* Later, he learns that porpoises breathe air and like to be petted. As a result, he forms a new concept for air-breathing but water-living animals. This illustrates *accommodation.*

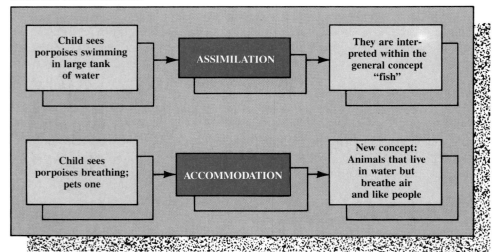

Assimilation and Accommodation: Key Processes in Cognitive Development

saying ''out of sight, out of mind'' seems to be true, at least under some conditions. By eight or nine months of age, however, the situation changes, and such infants *will* search for the hidden object. According to Piaget, emergence of **object permanence**—understanding that objects continue to exist even when they are removed from view—is a key attainment of the sensorimotor period.

The Preoperational Stage.   Sometime between the ages of eighteen and twenty-four months, infants acquire the ability to form mental images of objects and events. At the same time, language develops to the point at which they begin to think in terms of verbal symbols (words). According to Piaget, these developments mark the end of the sensorimotor period and the start of the **preoperational stage.**

During this period, which lasts until about age 7, children are capable of many actions they could not perform earlier. For example, they can imitate the words or actions of another person who has left the scene. They also begin to demonstrate what Piaget terms *intuitive thought*. For example, imagine that a four-year-old is shown three colored balls and a cardboard tube. The balls are placed inside one end of the tube, and the child is asked to predict which colored ball will emerge first, second, and third at the other end (refer to Figure 8-13). Youngsters in the preoperational stage can usually answer correctly; ones who have not yet attained this stage cannot.

While the thought processes of preoperational children are more advanced than those in the preceding stage, Piaget suggested that they are still immature in several

FIGURE 8-13. If children in the *preoperational stage* see three colored balls placed in one end of a tube, they can successfully predict the order in which they will emerge from the other end. Children younger than about four, who have not reached this stage of development, cannot perform this task. Piaget interpreted such findings as indicating that *intuitive thought* begins to emerge during the preoperational stage.

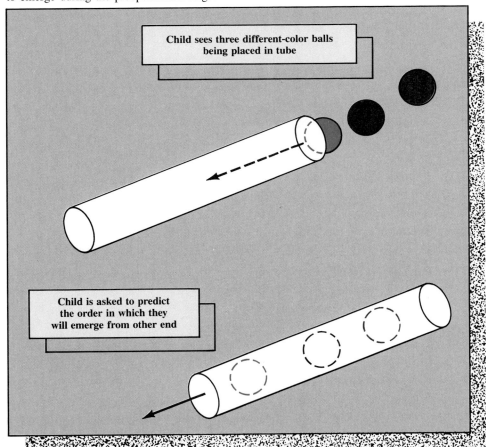

The Beginnings of Intuitive Thought: A Simple Demonstration

respects. First, they are **egocentric.** Children at this stage of cognitive development have great difficulty understanding that others may perceive the world differently than they do (Piaget, 1975). For example, consider the following demonstration (Flavell, 1973). Two-year-olds are shown a card with a picture of a dog on one side and a cat on the other (Flavell, 1973). The card is then placed between the child and the experimenter, so that each can see only one side. Now, the child is asked two questions: ''What do you see?'' and ''What do I see?'' Because of their tendency toward egocentric thought, many children indicated that the experimenter saw the same picture they did. As we'll soon note, however, the results obtained in such situations seem to depend strongly on how the questions are asked. Under some conditions, even two-year-olds seem capable of recognizing that what other people see may be quite different from what they see (Lempers, Flavell, & Flavell, 1977).

According to Piaget, preoperational children are also readily fooled or confused by appearances. For example, if a dog mask is placed on a cat, many three-year-olds will report that it has turned into a dog. Four-year-olds are uncertain in this situation but still say the cat is a dog. Six-year-olds, who are approaching the end of the preoperational period, however, will often report that the cat is still a cat.

Children in the preoperational stage also lack understanding of relational terms such as ''darker,'' ''larger,'' and ''bigger.'' Further, they lack *serialization*—the ability to arrange objects in order along some dimension. Finally, and perhaps most important, they lack what Piaget terms the principle of **conservation**—knowledge that an underlying physical dimension remains unchanged despite superficial shifts in its appearance. For example, imagine that two equal rows of nickels are placed in front of a four-year-old. She indicates that each row contains the same number of nickels. Now one row is adjusted so that the space between the nickels is greater. If the child is now asked whether that row has more nickels, she may well say ''yes.'' If the nickels are pushed back to their original position, she will again report that the two rows are equal (see Figure 8-14).

Similar effects can be observed with respect to length, area, and volume. Perhaps one more illustration will help. A three-year-old is shown two identical beakers of water. Then water from one of these is poured into a taller, thinner container. The child is asked whether this new container holds the same amount as that in the remaining beaker. Many

FIGURE 8-14. If two rows of nickels are equally spaced, four-year-olds will agree that the rows contain the same number (upper diagram). If the nickels in one row are then placed farther apart, many four-year-olds will state that this row now contains more nickels than the other. According to Piaget, this illustrates their lack of *conservation*.

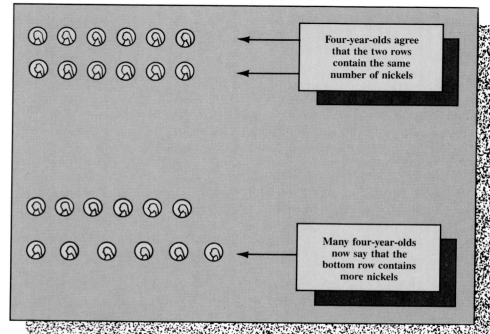

Four-year-olds agree that the two rows contain the same number of nickels

Many four-year-olds now say that the bottom row contains more nickels

Demonstrating the Absence of Conservation

children of this age will indicate that it does not hold the same amount and will go on to state that the tall container actually holds more. Piaget believes that errors of this type stem from children's tendency at this stage to focus on only one feature of an object or event. Since the water is higher in the thinner container, they conclude that it must hold more. If they also took the diameter of the two beakers (or the space between the nickels) into account, such errors could be avoided.

The Stage of Concrete Operations.   By the time they are six or seven years old (or even earlier, as we will see below), most children can solve the simple problems described above. According to Piaget, their mastery of conservation marks the beginning of a third major stage of cognitive development—the period of **concrete operations.** This lasts until the child is eleven or twelve, and it involves the emergence of many important skills. For example, during this stage youngsters gain understanding of relational terms and serialization. Further, they come to understand *reversibility*—the fact that many physical changes can be undone by reversing the original action. They also begin to make greater use of conceptual categories, such as fruit, toys, and furniture. Thus, if asked to sort various objects, four-year-olds will often do so in terms of color or size; older children will place the objects in other conceptual categories (e.g., all the fruits together, regardless of color or shape). Finally, children in the concrete operations stage of development begin to engage in logical thought. For example, if a child in the preoperational stage is asked, "Why did you go to the store?" he may reply, "Because afterwards, we came home." If a child in the concrete operations stage is asked the same question, she may answer, "Because my mother needed to buy some food."

The Stage of Formal Operations.   At about the age of twelve, Piaget suggests, most children enter the final stage of cognitive development—**formal operations.** During this period, major features of adult thought make their appearance. Individuals who have reached this stage become capable of *deductive reasoning*. They acquire the ability to think in abstract terms and to test hypotheses in a systematic manner (refer to our discussion in Chapter 7). They come to understand that words or statements can have several different meanings, depending on the context. And they are capable of taking many different factors into account. (Remember: younger children tend to focus on only one feature of a situation or problem at a time.) In sum, individuals at the formal operations stage are capable of advanced forms of thought and reasoning. The fact they *can* think in these ways, though, does not guarantee that they actually do so; even adults often slip back into less advanced modes of thought.

Piaget's Theory Revisited: Some Changes and a Look at Additional Cognitive Skills

While Piaget's theory has added greatly to our understanding of cognitive development, recent evidence suggests that it requires a number of modifications. The most important of these involve two points: (1) Piaget appears to have underestimated the cognitive abilities of infants and young children and (2) there are several aspects of cognitive growth Piaget did not consider which are also worthy of careful attention.

The Case of the Competent Preschooler: A Closer Look at the Cognitive Abilities of Infants and Young Children.   The picture of young children's cognitive abilities offered by Piaget is in some ways quite discouraging. According to his theory, children under the age of five lack many basic skills. They don't possess the concept of conservation and have difficulty in handling relationships such as *greater* or *lesser*. Further, they are egocentric and often do not realize that others often perceive objects or events differently than they do. Are these conclusions accurate, or are young children capable of somewhat more than Piaget believed? Evidence gathered in recent years points to an optimistic conclusion. When appropriate tasks and procedures are used—ones somewhat simpler in nature than those used in earlier studies—young children appear to be much more competent, cognitively, than was formerly assumed (Gelman & Baillargeon, 1983). First, consider Piaget's view that children below age of five are *egocen-*

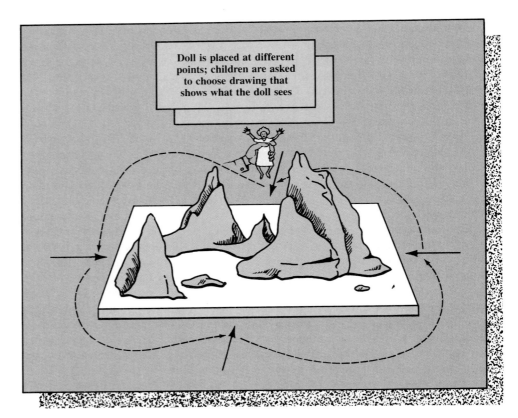

Doll is placed at different points; children are asked to choose drawing that shows what the doll sees

FIGURE 8-15. When children up to age six are shown a model similar to this one and are asked to indicate what a doll placed at different points would see, they often describe their own perspective. However, when situations more familiar to them are used (e.g., Grover driving a toy car), they *can* report this character's perspective accurately. Such findings indicate that young children are not as subject to *egocentrism* as Piaget believed.

tric—unable to realize that others may perceive the world very differently than they do themselves. Piaget based this suggestion on research in which children were shown a model of a mountain range and watched as the experimenter placed a doll at various locations in it. They were then shown drawings of the model from different perspectives, and asked to choose the one that showed the doll's point of view (Piaget & Inhelder, 1956). Results indicated that children four, five, or even six years old chose the drawing that represented their own view of the model (see Figure 8-15). Was this due to their inability to take another's perspective, or to the complexity and unfamiliarity of the task? Research findings support the latter conclusion. When more familiar situations are used (e.g., Grover, a *Sesame Street* character, driving a car along a toy road), children *can* accurately report on this character's perspective (Flavell, 1977).

Other findings, too, point to the conclusion that young children are not as egocentric as Piaget contended. For example, in a simple but revealing study Lempers, Flavell, and Flavell (1977) gave children one to three years old a hollow cube with a photograph of a familiar object glued to the inside bottom. Then they asked the youngsters to show the photograph to an observer sitting nearby. The results: virtually all of the children aged two or older turned the cube so that the observer could see inside. Clearly, they understood that this person saw the world from a different perspective than they did. (This does not mean, by the way, that young children understand precisely *how* an object or scene appears to others; the ability to accomplish this more complex task develops more gradually.) Finally, it has been noted that when four-year-olds talk to two-year-olds, they talk differently than when speaking to adults (Gelman & Shatz, 1977). This suggests that they are aware of the fact that different groups of people have different perspectives.

Second, let's consider *conservation*. Is appreciation of the fact that underlying physical dimensions don't change despite superficial shifts in appearance really lacking in young children, as Piaget contended? Here, too, recent findings offer an optimistic picture. When children who do not show evidence of conservation are exposed to others who do (*models* who demonstrate conservation while performing various tasks), they seem to quickly grasp this principle. For example, Botvin and Murray (1975) had one group of first-graders who had previously failed to conserve mass, weight, number, and amount watch other children who *had* previously shown such conservation. A second group of nonconservers merely watched these discussions. The results: when later tested for conservation, both groups now seemed to grasp this principle. Moreover, this was true not only with respect to the types of conservation they had witnessed (weight), but with others as well (number, length).

Additional research suggests that other, relatively simple training techniques can readily help young children grasp and use the principle of conservation (Gold, 1978). In one such study, Gelman (1982) had three- and four-year-olds count the number of items in two rows differing in length, but not in number. Then she tested them for conservation with rows containing different numbers of objects than the ones on which they were trained. Results failed to support Piaget's position: the children successfully applied conservation to these new problems.

Considered together, these and other findings indicate that Piaget did indeed underestimate the cognitive abilities of young children (Gelman & Baillargeon, 1983). Why? What factors led him to his conclusions? Perhaps the most important of these center around the specific methods used in his research. Piaget was certainly ingenious in devising situations in which to study the cognitive skills of young children. However, it now appears that some of the tasks he developed were ones in which the youngsters tested did not fully understand the questions being asked or the problems being posed. Under these conditions, of course, they could not answer correctly, and so they could not demonstrate skills they possessed. In sum, developmental psychologists now realize that in studying the ability of very young children to think and reason, a key task is devising appropriate methods—ones that will allow various capacities to appear, if they are present. In short, to determine what very young children can do, it is essential to use the right tasks and ask the right questions. When we do, even toddlers turn out to be considerably more competent than was once assumed.

Other Aspects of Cognitive Development. While Piaget examined many aspects of cognitive development, he did not consider several others which are also of great importance. For example, he did not directly examine children's knowledge of the **appearance-reality distinction.** This refers to the ability to distinguish the way something appears at the moment (right now) from what it is like in a permanent sense. For example, if a red car is placed under a green filter, it appears black. Yet its color is still red. As adults, we can readily make such distinctions; we know that things aren't always what they seem. But three-year-olds are often confused about this issue. If you ask them ''What is the color of the car now?'' they will say black. And if you ask ''What is its color, really and truly?'' they will also say black (refer to Figure 8-16). Four-year-olds do

FIGURE 8-16. When four-year-olds are shown a red car behind a green filter and asked ''What is its color, really and truly?'' they often say ''black.'' Six-year-olds, though, can distinguish between current appearance and enduring reality: they indicate that the car is still red.

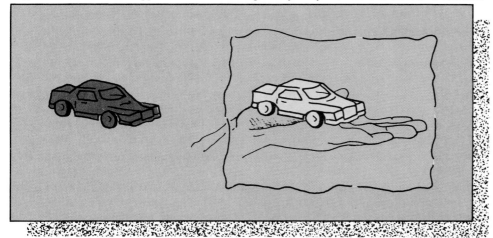

Distinguishing Appearance from Reality: Another Aspect of Cognitive Development

somewhat better; some can separate appearance from reality. And six- or seven-year-olds are quite good at this task. This suggests that they already understand a very important fact: our mental representations of objects and events are different from the things themselves, and can change over time. (Consistent with our discussion above, though, it may also be the case that four-year-olds don't completely understand what the question means, and thus are unable to answer correctly.)

Another facet of cognitive development not directly considered by Piaget's theory is *memory*. How does this central cognitive ability change with age? Recent evidence suggests that it does not merely increase in speed or capacity. Rather, as children grow older, they use different strategies for retaining information. For example, in one recent study, Weissberg-Benchell and Paris (1988) asked children ranging in age from three to six years old to memorize shopping lists containing six items. They observed that few three-year-olds rehearsed the items on the list, but many six-year-olds did. Thus, only the older children seemed aware of the usefulness of this tactic. And rehearsal was quite effective in this context: the three-year-olds who used it remembered about as many items on the list as did the six-year-olds.

In addition to changes in memory strategies, children also become increasingly aware of their own memory abilities as they grow older (Flavell, 1986). Children under the age of seven usually overestimate their ability to remember various items. By the time they are nine or ten, however, they can make such estimates as accurately as adults. Clearly, then, this important aspect of our cognitive functioning changes with age in important ways.

Language Development

In Chapter 7, we noted that the ability to use spoken and written language may be our most uniquely human characteristic. If this is indeed the case, then no discussion of cognitive development can be complete without some mention of this important topic.

The Beginnings of Speech. Until they are about three months old, infants have only two ways of communicating verbally: crying and cooing. At some point between three and six months, however, **babbling** appears. Babbling contains a rich mixture of sounds—in fact, virtually every sound used in human speech. By nine or ten months old, though, the range of babbling narrows and consists mainly of sounds used in the language of the child's culture. From this point to the production of the first spoken word is a relatively short step, and most children accomplish it prior to their first birthday. In most cases, early vocabulary consists mainly of words referring to objects that change or move (e.g., mama, papa, car, bow-wow). Few words referring to static objects (couch, house, table) are used. After the appearance of the first word, vocabulary grows rapidly. By the time children are two, they may already be using more than one hundred words. And at three, they have a working vocabulary of more than one thousand. The speed with which language develops is nothing short of amazing.

We should note, by the way, that large individual differences exist with respect to language development. Thus, any two youngsters the same age may differ tremendously in this respect. To take account of this fact, psychologists who study language often assess its development in terms of *mean length of utterance*—the average length of the sentences children use (Brown, 1973). By studying changes in this measure, the rates at which different children are acquiring language can be compared.

Some Characteristics of Early Speech. While they can usually make themselves understood, toddlers' speech is unusual in some respects. At first, it is *holophrastic:* single words are used to express complex meanings. For example, a fifteen-month-old may exclaim ''Eat!'' meaning ''I want to eat.'' On another occasion, she might see her mother sitting down to dinner and again say ''Eat.'' Now, though, the word means ''Mommy is eating.'' Such holophrastic speech does not last long and is replaced by simple sentences consisting of two words by the time most children are two. Even when other aspects of their speech are quite primitive, though, children show an impressive grasp of grammar. When forming their simple sentences, they combine the words in an appropriate order, not in a random manner. For example, a two-year-old seeing his older sister drop a glass might say, ''Carol drop.'' He would probably not say, ''Drop, Carol.''

During the preschool years children continue to make rapid verbal progress. By the time they are three, they add the letter *s* to nouns to make them plural (e.g., toy*s*, cookie*s*, shirt*s*). Further, they add the letters *ed* to verbs for past tense (e.g., walk*ed*, mix*ed*). (Of course, the examples we are using apply to English; equivalent developments in other languages occur.)

Such progress continues so that by the time they are four or five most children in all cultures studied to date can use complex sentences (e.g., *embedded sentences*, in which two sentences are combined into one: ''I heard what you said''). In just a few short years, then, they go from newborns unable to utter a single word to children who amaze us with their impressive communication skills. (Please refer to our discussion in Chapter 7 for contrasting views on how this rapid process of language development unfolds.)

Social Development: Forming Relationships and Interacting with Others

Cognitive development is one of the most important aspects of human growth, but it does not occur in a social vacuum. At the same time children are acquiring the capacity to think and reason, they are also gaining the basic mechanisms which allow them to form close relationships and to interact with others in a wide range of settings. We will now consider several aspects of such **social development.**

Attachment: The Beginnings of Love.   Do infants love their parents? They can't tell us directly, but by the time they are six or seven months old most appear to have a strong emotional bond toward these persons (Ainsworth, 1973; Lamb, 1977). They recognize their mother and father, smile at them more than at other persons, seek them out, and protest when separated from them. This emotional bond is known as **attachment,** and in an important sense it is the first form of love we experience toward another human being.

Until the late 1950s it was widely assumed that attachment was based largely on principles of conditioning. Since mothers, fathers, and other caregivers provided for infants' needs, they supplied many types of positive reinforcement and came to be associated with such rewards. Presumably, this led to the formation of the infants' strong emotional bond (refer to Figure 8-17 on page 254).

While conditioning probably plays a role in attachment, several other factors, too, are important. First, infants seem to be born with a strong inherited tendency to seek proximity to their caregivers (Bowlby, 1969). Moreover, they are equipped with several behaviors that help to attain this goal: crying, smiling, vocalizing in response to adults. If you've ever tried to ignore a crying baby, or one who is smiling at you, no further comment on the effectiveness of these actions is required.

Third, attachment seems to vary with the nature of the care received by infants. Those who receive warmth and affection seem to form stronger bonds to their caregivers than ones who experience rejection, coolness, or anger. It is not only the strength of attachment that varies with the quality of parental care; the nature of this bond, too, seems to differ. That this is the case is suggested by the reactions of infants in what developmental psychologists term the **strange situation.** Here, infants twelve to eighteen months of age are brought to an unfamiliar playroom by their mothers. They are then left alone in this room with a stranger for three minutes. Their behavior during their mother's absence and upon her reappearance is observed. When confronted with this set of circumstances, infants seem to react in three contrasting ways. About two-thirds actively seek contact with their mother and show more interest in her than in the stranger when she returns. They are said to be *securely attached.* Twenty-two percent ignore their mother on her return and even look away from her greeting. They are described as being *avoidant.*

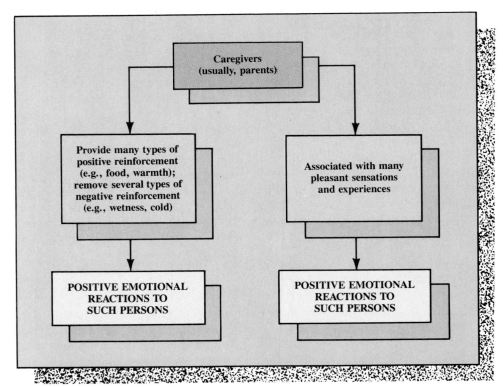

FIGURE 8-17. According to one explanation, *attachment* arises from the fact that caregivers both provide positive reinforcement and are associated with many pleasant sensations and experiences. In other words, such emotional bonds stem mainly from the operation of *classical* and *operant* conditioning.

Finally, about twelve percent become extremely upset when their mother leaves and are not readily consoled by her when she returns; they are labeled *insecurely attached* (Ainsworth & Wittig, 1969).

Such differences in pattern of attachment are of more than passing interest. Children showing these different patterns also differ in many other respects. For example, those who are securely attached are more sociable, are better at solving certain problems, and are more flexible and persistent than children who are avoidant or insecurely attached (Pastor, 1981). Moreover, securely attached children seem to experience fewer behavior problems during childhood (Clarke-Stewart, Friedman, & Koch, 1985).

A third factor that seems to play an important role in attachment is the *close physical contact* that occurs between infants and their caregivers. In short, attachment rests partly on the hugging, cuddling, and carresses babies receive from adults. The research that first established this fact was conducted by Harlow and his colleagues, and is among the most famous in the history of psychology. It is described in the "Classic Contribution" section below.

FOCUS ON RESEARCH: Classic Contributions

Attachment and Contact Comfort: The Soft Touch of Love

When Harlow began his research, infant attachment was the farthest thing from his mind. He was interested in studying the effects of brain damage on learning.

Since he could not perform such experiments with humans, he chose rhesus monkeys for his research. In order to prevent baby monkeys from catching various illnesses, Harlow raised them alone, away from their mothers. This practice led to a surprising observation. Many of the in-

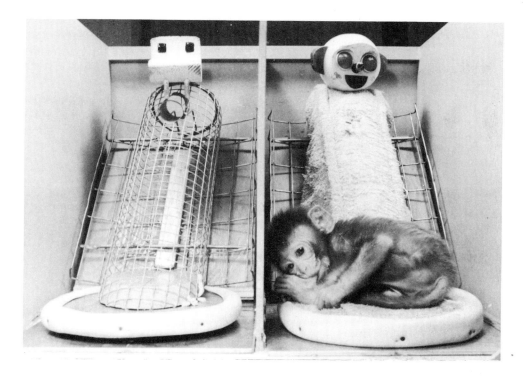

FIGURE 8-18. Although the wire "mother" on the left provided monkey babies with food, they spent most of their time clinging to the soft cloth "mother" on the right. *(Source: Harry Harlow, University of Wisconsin.)*

fants seemed to become quite attached to small scraps of cloth present in their cage. They would clutch these "security blankets" tightly and would protest strongly when clothes were removed for cleaning. This led Harlow to wonder whether the babies actually needed contact with soft, cuddly material.

To find out, he built the two artificial "mothers" shown in Figure 8-18. As you can see, one consisted of bare wire, while the other possessed a soft terrycloth cover. Conditions were then arranged so that the monkey babies could obtain milk only from the wire mother. According to the conditioning explanation of attachment outlined above, they should soon develop a strong bond to this cold wire mother. After all, she would be repeatedly paired with food. In fact, though, this was *not* the case. The infants spent almost all of their time clinging tightly to the soft cloth-covered mother. Only when driven by hunger did they venture onto the bare wire figure which supplied them with milk.

Additional evidence that the infants formed a strong bond to the soft mother was obtained in further research. For example, in one study the monkey babies were placed in an unfamiliar setting filled with strange—and for them terrifying—objects (Harlow & Zimmerman, 1958). When alone in this setting, the infants would cower in fear. The wire mother was little or no help in this regard; the babies

continued to show intense fear. When their cloth mother was present, however, the babies' reactions were very different. They would cling to her for a few moments and then, seemingly comforted, would begin to explore their new surroundings.

If you need further proof that the babies had developed a strong attachment to the cloth mother, consider the following: in still other studies, Harlow and Harlow (1966) exposed the babies to various forms of rejection by their "mothers." For example, some of the mothers blew their infants away with strong jets of air; others held metal spikes which suddenly appeared from within and drove the infants away. Surprisingly, none of these actions had any lasting effects upon the babies' love for their cloth mother. They merely waited until these periods of "rejection" were over and then clung to them as tightly as ever.

On the basis of these and related findings, Harlow has concluded that a monkey baby's attachment to its mother rests, at least in part, on her ability to satisfy its need for *contact comfort*—direct contact with soft objects. The satisfaction of other physical needs (e.g., food) is not, by itself, enough.

Harlow's results are fascinating, but they leave an important question unanswered: do similar effects occur among humans? Do human infants form strong emotional bonds to their mothers and fa-

Contact Comfort Among
Humans

For Better or For Worse®   **by Lynn Johnston**

FIGURE 8-19. Does contact comfort play a role in human attachment? Existing evidence does not provide a definite answer. There is little doubt about one fact, though: most people find some forms of contact comfort enjoyable throughout life. *(Source: Universal Press Syndicate, 1986.)*

thers because these persons cuddle, hug, and touch them? Some studies seem to support this possibility (Klaus & Kennell, 1976); they indicate that skin-to-skin contact between mother and child immediately after birth enhances the formation of attachment. However, such results have been difficult to replicate. Moreover, attachment develops more slowly in human infants and is not usually firmly established until six months after birth. Finally, only about 70 percent of one-year-olds are securely attached to adults (Sroufe, 1985). This is hard to explain if we assume that direct contact plays an important role, since virtually all parents hold and hug their offspring. At present, then, we can't offer firm conclusions. Given the fact that most persons enjoy at least certain forms of contact comfort throughout life, however, the possibility that it plays a role in our earliest and most basic form of love remains an intriguing one (refer to Figure 8-19).

The Development of Gender Identity.   In many cases, the first words spoken about newborns refer to their sex. And from the moment that parents hear a nurse or physician state, "It's a boy," or "It's a girl," they begin to think about and behave toward their child in ways that differ depending on its sex. Given this fact, it is hardly surprising that toddlers acquire **gender identity**—knowledge of their own sex—quite early. By age three most children refer to themselves as a "girl" or a "boy." However, many are still uncertain as to whether this is a permanent state. Thus, if a three-year-old girl is asked, "Would you still be a girl if you dressed in your brother's clothes?" there is some possibility that she will answer, "No—I'd be a boy." By age five such confusion is gone, and a large majority recognize their sexual identity as part of their basic self-concept. Moreover, they can readily classify other persons as being male or female from photos of them (Edwards, 1984).

Acquiring Gender Identity: Two Contrasting Views.   How do children acquire their gender identity? Two different theories have been suggested. According to the first, known as the **social learning view,** two forms of learning are important. One is *modeling* (or observational learning). Toddlers tend to imitate the persons around them, especially their parents. Further, they tend to imitate the actions of similar models more than those of dissimilar models (Perry & Bussey, 1979). As a result, they gradually come to demonstrate many of the behaviors of their same-sex parent. Second, parents often provide praise and other forms of reward to their children for imitating the "right" models—those of their own sex. They also often criticize or punish children for imitating members of the opposite sex. Through a combination of modeling and direct reinforcement, children come to behave more and more like their same-sex parent.

In contrast, the **cognitive view** suggests that the process starts with a child's recognition of his or her own gender. Supposedly, toddlers identify themselves as boy or girl on the basis of labels used by their parents and others. Then they adopt those behaviors which they view as appropriate for their own sex. In short, it is as if children begin by saying, ''I'm a girl (boy); therefore, I want to do girl (boy) things.''

Which explanation is correct? At the present time, some evidence supports both. Thus, it seems likely that modeling, direct reinforcement, and cognitive factors all play a role in the rapid development of gender identity.

Sex roles and Sex-Role Stereotypes.   At the same time that they are acquiring a firm gender identity, children are also learning what it means to be a male or a female. Specifically, they are learning cultural beliefs about the supposed traits of males and females, their roles in society, and even their relative worth. In many societies this package of beliefs is much more favorable to males than to females. For example, children in the United States, Canada, and Europe are exposed to stereotypes suggesting that males are aggressive, dominant, and strong, while females are passive, submissive, and weak (Deaux & Lewis, 1987). Similarly, until recently children in many nations rarely encountered females outside a few limited roles (e.g., homemaker, teacher, librarian). This situation has now changed greatly; in the United States more than half of all mothers work outside the home, females have moved into a much wider range of occupations (refer to Figure 8-20), and even the mass media have begun to portray women in roles and situations previously reserved mainly for males. Only time and additional research will reveal the ultimate impact of such shifts. Given their magnitude, however, the following conclusion seems reasonable: major change lies ahead.

Peer Relations: The Nature of Childhood Friendships.

While parents exert powerful effects upon their children's social development, *peers*—individuals of one's own age—also play an important role in this regard. Indeed, by the time they are approaching adolescence, children spend more time with peers than with parents or other adults (Cskszentmihalyi & Larson, 1984). While contact with classmates and casual acquaintances is important for normal social development, interaction with *friends*—those peers children seek out and prefer—is especially crucial in this regard. From such persons children acquire a wide range of beliefs, ideas about how to behave in various situations, and basic knowledge about their own characteristics (e.g., are they attractive or unattractive, bright or dull). What leads specific children to become friends? What are childhood friendships like? And what effects do they exert? Answers to such questions are beginning to emerge from current research.

The issue of which individuals become friends is perhaps the easiest to address. In general, *similarity* is the guiding rule where childhood friendships are concerned (Epstein, 1986). Thus, children who are similar in age, sex, race, and ethnic background are more likely to become friends than children who are dissimilar on these dimensions.

FIGURE 8-20. In recent years, women have moved into many occupations once filled solely by males.

Women in the Workforce: A
Current Perspective

The stability of childhood friendships, too, is easy to describe: they are quite stable—more so than most of us would guess. Even among fourth-graders (children about ten years old), more than three-fourths of friendships formed in the fall are still intact in the spring (Berndt & Hoyle, 1985).

Given the tremendous changes occurring during childhood, it might be expected that as children grow older the nature of their friendships, too, will change. To some extent, this is true. Older children stress the importance of loyalty and intimacy in friendship more than do younger children. They describe friends as people they can count on and as people to whom they can "bare their souls." However, children of all ages, including adolescents, describe many aspects of friendship in much the same terms: a friend is someone you spend time with, someone who will help you, and someone who is rarely, if ever, aggressive toward you (Berndt, 1988). Apparently, then, we seek the same basic qualities in friendship throughout much of childhood.

While children at different ages describe friendship in similar terms, they do seem to behave differently toward their friends at different ages. This point is demonstrated by a study conducted by Berndt, Hawkins, and Hoyle (1986). These researchers asked pairs of fourth- and eighth-graders to work on a task in which they could choose to cooperate or compete with their partner. The task involved coloring geometric designs, and in order to do a neat job each person needed a special "tracer." Since only one of the two children could use this at a time, subjects' tendencies to cooperate (by sharing the tracer) could be readily observed. The same pairs of children performed this task twice: in the fall and again in the spring. In the fall all pairs were close friends; in the spring some no longer described themselves in these terms. Drawing on previous research, Berndt and his colleagues predicted that because younger children are very concerned about being equal to their friends, the fourth-graders who remained friends in the spring would actually share *less* with their partners than those who were no longer friends. In contrast, among older children, the opposite would be true: subjects would share *more* with their partners if they still viewed them as close friends. As you can see from Figure 8-21, results offered support for these predictions. Fourth-graders shared less with close friends than with others; eighth-graders demonstrated the opposite pattern.

FIGURE 8-21. Fourth-graders shared *less* with partners who were close friends than with partners who were no longer close friends. The opposite was true for eighth-graders. These findings suggest that the nature of friendship changes as children grow older. *(Source: Berndt, Hawkins, & Hoyle, 1986.)*

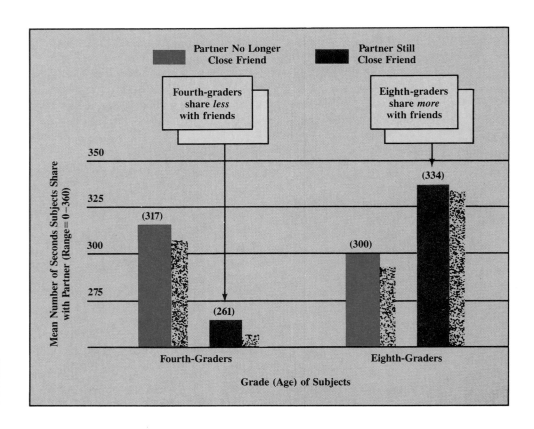

Friendship and Sharing

These findings and those of other research (Berndt, 1988) suggest that the nature of friendship does indeed change over the course of social development. We seem to expect different things from our friends at different ages, and in this aspect of life, as in many others, what we expect is often what we get.

Adolescence: Between Child and Adult

When does childhood end? When does adulthood start? Since development is a continuous process, there are no hard-and-fast answers to these questions. Rather, every culture decides for itself just where the dividing line falls. Many mark this passage with special rituals: individuals enter as children and emerge a few hours or days later as adults (see Figure 8-22). In the United States and many other countries, however, the transition from child to adult takes place during a period known as **adolescence,** which lasts for several years. Adolescence begins with the onset of *puberty,* a sudden spurt in physical development, and ends when individuals assume the responsibilities associated with adult life—marriage, entering military service, going to work (Rice, 1984). In this section we will describe some of the major changes that mark this transitional period of life.

Physical Growth During Adolescence

After the first two years of life, growth slows considerably. Sometime around the age of eleven or twelve for girls and thirteen or fourteen for boys, however, a dramatic shift occurs. At this time, the sex glands burst into increased activity. The period of sexual maturation which follows—**puberty**—involves many physical changes. Members of both sexes experience a rapid spurt of growth. Boys may gain as many as six inches and girls as many as five during a single year. Increasing signs of sexual maturity, too, begin to appear: breast enlargement in girls, growth of chest and facial hair in boys. Finally, some months after the onset of such changes, girls begin to menstruate and boys start to produce sperm. Usually these events take place by the time girls are thirteen and boys fifteen, but large individual differences exist. Thus, puberty can begin as early as seven or eight for some girls, and as late as sixteen for others (Faust, 1977). Environmental factors, such as nutrition, also play an important role. While the average age of first menstruation is slightly under thirteen in the United States, it is almost eighteen in New Guinea, where diets are often inadequate (Tanner, 1970).

Facial features, too, often change during puberty. Characteristics associated with childhood (e.g., large eyes, a high forehead, small chin, round cheeks) give way to a more adult appearance (Berry & McArthur, 1986). Recent studies suggest that such changes are of considerable importance. For example, individuals who retain childlike facial features (i.e., a "baby-face") are perceived as being weaker, more naive, and more submissive than persons who do not retain such features (Berry & McArthur, 1985). (Refer to Figure 8-23 on page 260.) Such "baby-facedness" is related to attractiveness in both sexes, but the direction of such effects is opposite in males and females. Males tend to find "baby-facedness" attractive in females, while females often react negatively to such facial appearance in males (McArthur & Apatow, 1984).

Cognitive and Moral Development

From our earlier discussion of cognitive development, you may have the impression that thinking and reasoning abilities are fully developed by the onset of puberty. In fact, this is not entirely true. First, while pre-adolescents (children of eleven or twelve) do demonstrate logical thought, they tend to reason in this manner only about objects with which they have had direct experience, and only about events or situations in the present. They are less successful in reasoning about purely abstract events. Adolescents can accomplish these tasks. In other words, they can reason not only about what *is,* but also about what *might be.* In addition, they can formulate hypotheses and test these systematically (Rice, 1984). In these respects, then, cognitive development continues during adolescence.

FIGURE 8-22. Many societies mark entry into adulthood with special rituals. In the United States and many other countries, however, this transition is accomplished gradually during *adolescence.*

Some Effects of "Babyfaced-ness"

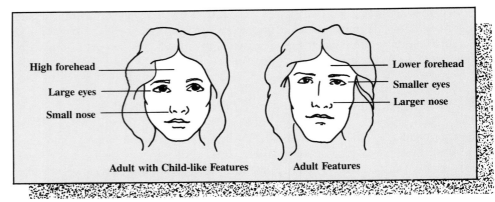

High forehead

Large eyes

Small nose

Lower forehead

Smaller eyes

Larger nose

Adult with Child-like Features   **Adult Features**

FIGURE 8-23. Individuals who retain childlike features as adults (left drawing) are perceived as more submissive, weaker, and more naive than persons who do not retain such features (right drawing). *(Source: Based on illustrations in Berry & McArthur, 1986.)*

Moral Development: Telling "Right" from "Wrong."   Another aspect of cognitive development that undergoes important change during our teen years is our capacity for *moral reasoning*—the way we evaluate the "rightness" or "wrongness" of our own and others' behavior. It seems natural to expect that, as our abilities to think and reason become more sophisticated, our moral judgments, too, will grow more complex. This seems to be the case. Research by Kohlberg and others (e.g., Kohlberg, 1976) indicates that our thinking about such matters does indeed change with age. In such research, subjects are presented with imaginary moral dilemmas (for example, should a husband steal a drug he cannot afford but which will save his wife's life?) and are then asked what they would do in these situations. Children younger than age nine tend to judge various behaviors in terms of the consequences they produce: those which yield positive outcomes or which help them reach their goals are judged to be "good." Those which produce harmful outcomes or which interfere with need satisfaction are "bad." Kohlberg terms this the *preconventional level*. (Thus, a person at this level might say that the husband should not steal the drug, because he'll be punished for this action.)

By age nine or ten, however, many individuals shift to another basis for evaluating their own and others' behavior. Actions which are consistent with conventional rules and

TABLE 8-1

According to Kohlberg (1976), individuals pass through several distinct stages of development with respect to moral reasoning. The nature of each stage is described here.

		What Is Viewed as "Right" in Each Stage
Preconventional Level	STAGE 1:	Obeying rules in order to avoid punishment; avoiding damage to persons or property
	STAGE 2:	Actions that satisfy the individual's own needs; what is fair in an agreement or exchange
Conventional Level	STAGE 3:	Doing what is expected by other people we care about
	STAGE 4:	Carrying out duties in fulfilling obligations; contributing to society, the group, or institutions
Postconventional Level	STAGE 5:	Being aware that people hold different values and opinions and that rules may vary from group to group; upholding certain values and rights (e.g., life, liberty)
	STAGE 6:	Following self-chosen ethical principles; respecting the rights and dignity of human beings

Kohlberg's Stages of Moral Development

laws or which will be approved of by others are judged to be ''good,'' while those which violate such rules or will be disapproved of are ''bad.'' This is known as the *conventional level* of moral judgment. (A child at this level might say that the husband should steal the drug because family members will approve of this action.)

Finally, as adolescents many individuals judge actions in terms of self-chosen moral principles. Behavior consistent with these principles is seen as ''right,'' while behavior that is not is viewed as ''wrong.'' Persons who reason in this manner are described by Kohlberg as having reached the *postconventional level* of moral judgment. (Returning to the drug example, an individual at this level might say that stealing the drug is justified because the right to life is more precious than the right to property.) A summary of the stages of moral development outlined by Kohlberg is presented in Table 8-1.

That many individuals do indeed pass through the stages described above is suggested by the findings of a longitudinal project which has continued for more than twenty years (Colby et al., 1983). Consistent with Kohlberg's predictions, the proportion of subjects who attain higher stages of moral reasoning has increased as they've grown older while the proportion at lower levels has decreased (refer to Figure 8-24). As you can see from Figure 8-24, though, no individuals actually reached the highest stage in Kohlberg's theory. It appears, then, that few if any individuals ever attain this lofty plateau. In addition, it is not clear that individuals in different cultures show the same progression, or even that men and women within the same culture show the same pattern of moral development (Gilligan, 1982). Finally, as you probably suspect, individuals often apply somewhat harsher moral standards to others' behavior than to their own (Weiss, 1982). Thus, we may judge actions acceptable when we perform them, but unacceptable when the same actions are carried out by someone else.

FIGURE 8-24. As individuals grow older, they seem to move from lower levels of moral development to higher levels. These findings are consistent with Kohlberg's theory. However, no persons in this study ever reached Stage 6. *(Source: Based on data from Kohlberg, Gibbs, & Lieberman, 1983.)*

Moral Development: Evidence from Longitudinal Research

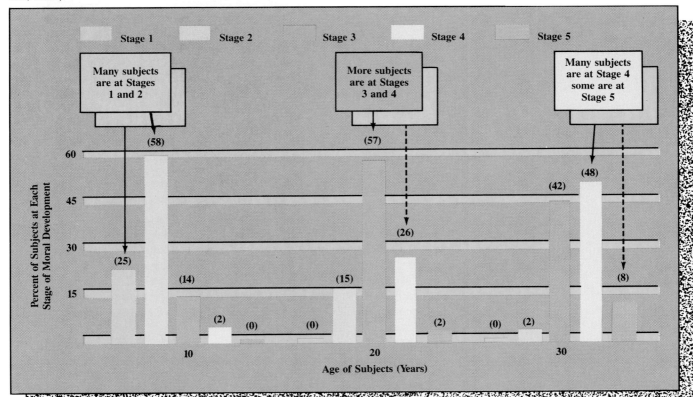

The "Generation Gap": Myth or Reality?

FIGURE 8-25. Contrary to the view represented in this cartoon, most adolescents do *not* seem to differ greatly from their parents in terms of attitudes or values. *(Source: King Features Syndicate.)*

In sum, there appear to be many subtle aspects to moral development, which greatly complicate the total picture. Still, one basic fact remains clear: our ability to reason about the "rightness" or "wrongness" of behaviors continues to change and develop throughout adolescence, and perhaps even into our adult years.

Social Development During Adolescence

Youth, it is often said, is given to extremes. If the word "adolescence" is substituted for "youth," this statement may hold much more than a grain of truth. Many reactions, from love to politics, seem to be more intense during adolescence than at any other time of life. That this is actually the case is suggested by the findings of an ingenious study by Cskszentmihalyi and Larson (1984). These researchers asked seventy-five high school students to wear electronic pagers for one week. When the pager signalled, they were to respond by writing down a description of what they were doing and how they were feeling. When the students' reports were compared with those of adults, several differences emerged. Perhaps the most impressive of these involved changes in emotions. Consistent with beliefs about the "moodiness" of teenagers, the young subjects in this study reported rapid shifts in their feelings. Often, they swung from extreme joy or happiness to deep sadness in a matter of minutes! In contrast, adults experienced smaller and slower shifts in reported moods.

While the heightened emotionality often attributed to teenagers appears to be real, another widespread belief about adolescence has turned out to be largely false. Contrary to many reports in the mass media (and the cartoon in Figure 8-25) there does not seem to be a large gap in attitudes or beliefs between teenagers and their parents. A majority share their parents' views on a wide range of issues (Lerner, 1975). Only with respect to fashion, music, and sexual behavior do sizable "generation gaps" appear.

The last of these differences, though, is one with important consequences. As you probably well know, many adolescents disagree sharply with their parents over sexual matters. While some parents continue to urge premarital chastity, most teenagers believe that sexual intimacy, at least within the context of stable, loving relationships, is acceptable (Glenn & Weaver, 1979). This portion of the generation gap has existed for several decades, but recent evidence suggests that it may now actually be decreasing. Several surveys have found that during the past ten years, college students (especially females) have grown increasingly conservative in their sexual attitudes (Gerrard, 1986). And these attitudes are reflected in actual behavior: a smaller proportion of students report being sexually active in the late 1980s than was true a decade ago (Gerrard, 1986). Why has this changed? One possibility lies in the rising incidence—and seriousness—of sexually-transmitted diseases. Young people are less and less willing to accept the risks involved in casual sexual encounters. Another is the general shift toward more conservative values that has occurred in United States and many other nations during the 1980s. Where will the pendulum move next? Your guess is as good as ours. But whatever direction it takes, these important shifts in attitudes and behavior illustrate the basic theme of this chapter once again: where human beings are concerned, *change* is indeed the only constant. (Is there any practical payoff to studying human development? For some comments on this issue, please see ''The Point of It All'' insert below.)

THE POINT OF IT ALL

Why Study Child Development? An International Perspective

Almost every culture has a saying equivalent to this one: ''Our children are our most precious natural resource.'' Given that today's youngsters will be tomorrow's leaders, this sentiment makes a great deal of sense. In developed countries, it has long been linked to actual practice: huge sums are spent each year to provide children with the best educational opportunities possible and to ensure their health and well-being. Moreover, experts on child development have often been consulted on the best ways to make these investments. Psychologists, physicians, nutritionists, educators—all have participated in planning and implementing programs designed to benefit children.

Unfortunately, the situation is quite different in many developing nations. Despite severe economic limitations, many third-world countries have invested large sums in efforts to improve the health, well-being, and education of children. Indeed, several now spend a higher proportion of their total income in this way than is true in their wealthier, developed neighbors (see Figure 8-26). What has been missing from such efforts, however, is the type of input mentioned above: the advice and guidance of scientists who have devoted their careers to the study of children's physical and psychological needs. How can such experts help? In many different ways (Wagner, 1986)—for example, with their knowledge of cognitive development, they can determine when various types of educational experiences will be most beneficial to children.

Further, they can assist in the design of educational programs, assuring that they neither overload recipients by asking them to do more than they can accomplish, nor bore them by underutilizing their cognitive skills. Similarly, experts in child development can help plan effective day-care centers, a growing need as the proportion of working mothers rises around the world. In sum, the advice and guidance of experts in child development appear to be a necessity—not a luxury—in any nation concerned about the welfare of its children.

Will the knowledge of such experts be utilized in the future? Some hopeful signs exist. For example, international lists of specialists in human development are currently being assembled. Identifying such persons is a useful first step; at least appropriate government officials in third-world nations will know where to find them! Second, efforts to apply existing knowledge about human development to the unique problems faced by third-world nations have also begun (Torney-Purta, 1984). These include projects concerned with the effects of nutrition on child development (Jelliffe & Jelliffe, 1982) and various programs for enhancing literacy (Wagner, 1986). Perhaps these initiatives will soon develop into an international network in which experts from developed nations share their skills and knowledge with colleagues in third-world nations, and so play a role in policy decisions about programs aimed at children. Should this come to pass, it will be of great benefit not just to the nations involved but, ultimately, to all humankind as well.

Concern with the Well-Being of Children is World-Wide

FIGURE 8-26. Many third-world countries now spend a higher proportion of their total government budgets on educational and health-related programs for children than developed countries do.

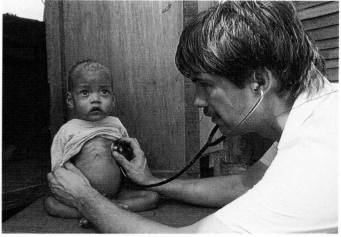

Adulthood and Aging

If you live for an average number of years, you will spend more than 70 percent of your life as an adult. (This assumes that the dividing line between adolescence and adulthood is about twenty years of age and that your life expectancy is greater than seventy years.) Will you continue to change during these long decades? By now, we're sure you know the answer: absolutely! Since human beings are affected by their experience, it could hardly be otherwise. Happy and unhappy love affairs, successes and failures in school or your career, marriage, divorce, parenthood: all these events leave their mark and assure that, in some ways, we *must* be different in our thirties than we were in our twenties, different in our forties than we were in our thirties, and so on. In this final section, we will examine some of the important ways in which human development proceeds during our adult years (Schaie & Willis, 1986).

Tasks and Stages of Adult Life

Many psychologists who study adult development have found it useful to divide this period of life into various stages. Some believe that entry into each of these stages is marked by definite, and sometimes stormy, transitions (Levinson, 1986). Others disagree and argue that unique, personal experiences are more important than age in determining adult behavior and lifestyles (Schlossberg, 1987). Both groups of researchers agree, however, that different periods in our lives are shaped by different tasks and activities.

The first question that arises about adult development is straightforward: when do we become adults? The answer seems to be: when we experience such important life events as graduation from school, taking a job, and setting up our own household (Levinson, 1986). These events usually take place in the years between our late teens and our middle twenties, depending on the career we have selected and the training it involves.

Early Adulthood: Getting Started. Once we are on our own, so to speak, we enter the period of *early adulthood*. This lasts through our twenties and thirties, and it is usually a very busy time of life. Careers are launched, most people marry, and many start families. Thus, responsibilities mount quickly, as individuals become full adult members of their society.

It is interesting to note that during recent decades, there have been important shifts in *when* individuals feel these key life events should take place. As you can see from Figure 8-27, large majorities now favor later marriage and parenthood and final selection of a career than was true earlier.

Middle Adulthood: Coming into One's Own. Sometime around age forty many persons seem to enter an important new period. During this *midlife transition* (Levinson, 1986) individuals begin to notice that their physical capabilities, while still adequate, are beginning to wane. At the same time, family obligations usually begin to decrease, as children near maturity. As a result, life becomes a bit less hectic, and many persons have more time to think about their lives, hopes, and goals. Many look back with satisfaction, pleased with what they have accomplished. But others must face the fact that some of their dreams will never be attained. The result, for some, is a *midlife crisis*, in which they experience emotional stress and ask themselves such questions as: "Has it all been worth it?" "Is this all there is?" We should hasten to note that many persons—perhaps most—do *not* experience such inner turmoil. They continue with their lives in much the same ways as before. But those who do sometimes react in ways that upset their families and friends. They may openly question the meaning of their lives, engage in numerous love affairs, or even quit their jobs and launch entirely new careers. (Do you recall the seafaring dentist mentioned in the opening story?)

For those who successfully traverse a midlife crisis, and for those who never experience one, the period of life that follows can be rewarding. Persons in their late forties and fifties tend to hold secure positions at work; indeed, they may fill top-level positions and have an important voice in key decisions. At the same time, family obligations decrease still further, thus allowing more time for hobbies, vacations, and the enjoyment of improved finances. For many, then, this is truly the "prime of life."

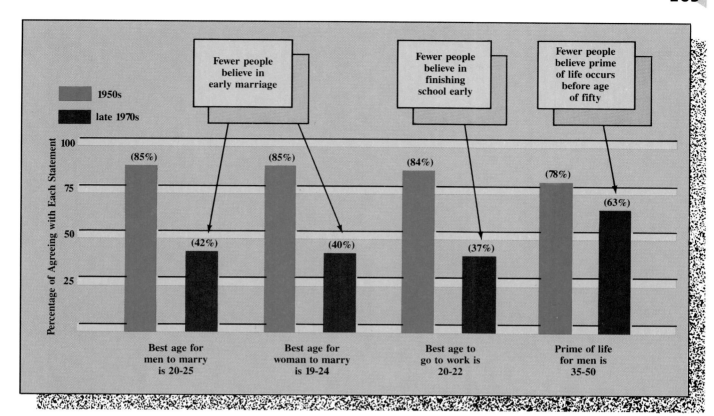

FIGURE 8-27. Between the 1950s and 1970s, major changes occurred in Americans' beliefs concerning *when* key life events should take place. For example, in the 1950s large majorities believed that the best time for women to marry was between the ages of nineteen and twenty-four. Now most people no longer hold this view. *(Source: Passath, Maines, & Neugarten, 1984.)*

The Timing of Key Life-Events: Changing Beliefs

At this point, we should note that the pattern of development we have been discussing is based largely on research with men. Recent studies suggest that women may experience a somewhat different pattern. Thus, while many men in their forties and fifties become increasingly mellow and relaxed, women show a different pattern, becoming more ambitious, self-disciplined, and independent. This is not due simply to the fact that with children grown many return to the work force. In a careful longitudinal project, Helson and Moan (1987) studied a group of women from the time they were college seniors (in the late 1950s) until they were in their early forties (in 1981). They divided these subjects into three categories: women who were mainly family-oriented, women who were mainly career-oriented, and those who fit neither pattern (they did not have children but did not pursue active careers). Despite major differences in life experiences, all three groups showed the trends described above: they became more assertive, confident, and independent as they approached midlife. Clearly, such differences between the sexes should be taken into careful account in any conclusions about changes in our adult years. (For information on another increasingly common aspect of middle adulthood, please see ''The Cutting Edge'' insert below.)

FOCUS ON RESEARCH: The Cutting Edge

Serial Marriage: An Emerging Life Style

Consider the following facts:

(1) From the 1960s through the early 1980s divorce rates rose continuously, so

that at present only about half of all marriages between young adults remain intact.

(2) A majority of individuals who divorce remarry—many within three years (Hetherington, 1986).

(3) The divorce rate among such

Serial Marriage: One Potential Consequence for Children

FIGURE 8-28. When their parents engage in *serial marriage*, children may be exposed to several periods of intense marital conflict.

couples is higher than that among couples marrying for the first time.

(4) Many persons who end their second marriage in divorce also remarry.

Together, these trends have combined to produce an emerging new life style, one sometimes described as *serial marriage*. It is estimated that at present more than two million persons in the United States alone have been married three or more times, and this figure increases each year (Brody, Neubaum, & Forehand, 1988). What are the causes of serial marriage? And what are its effects? Recent studies have begun to provide some answers.

With respect to causes, several factors seem to play a role. First, persons who engage in serial marriage tend to be somewhat more impulsive, nonconforming, and immature than persons who do not. In short, certain personality characteristics are related to having a series of different mates. Second, persons who have been married three or more times appear to hold different attitudes toward marriage than others. They more strongly endorse the idea of *conditional commitment*—the view that one should remain committed to a marriage only as long as one is happy in it. Similarly, they hold low expectations for marital success, coupled in many cases with unrealistic views of marriage as a cure-all for the many problems of life. Finally, they seem to carry

maladaptive patterns of behavior with them from marriage to marriage, including a tendency to repeatedly choose incompatible mates (Brody, Neubaum, & Forehand, 1988). Little wonder, then, that such persons tend to become quickly dissatisfied with each of their marriages and to seek new relationships.

The consequences of serial marriage are both complex and diverse. Perhaps the most severe effects, though, are those experienced by the children of parents who adopt this life-style. Such youngsters find themselves confronted with first one set of stepparents and then another. As a result, their patterns of *attachment* are repeatedly disrupted. Similarly, since their parents are under considerable strain prior to and soon after a divorce, such youngsters also experience prolonged periods of diminished parental care and attention. Finally, the children of parents with multiple successive mates are often exposed to recurrent periods of severe conflict between their biological parents and each successive stepparent (refer to Figure 8-28). Clearly, these experiences may combine to exert harmful effects on crucial aspects of a child's development. Unfortunately, such effects are already visible in recent surveys. For example, in one study focused on attitudes toward marriage and divorce (Kinnaird & Gerrard, 1986), fully 80 percent of single college women from families who had experienced repeated divorce and remarriage reported the belief that they, too, would some day be divorced. In contrast, only 40 percent of those from intact families held this view.

In sum, serial marriage, while satisfying in several respects to the persons who adopt it, appears to have important social consequences. Moreover, to a degree it may be self-perpetuating: the greater the number of persons who experience this pattern during childhood, the greater the number who may view it as acceptable or even inevitable for themselves as adults. Only further long-term research will fully reveal the impact of serial marriage on the fabric of modern society. At first glance, though, such effects appear to be somewhat unsettling.

Late Adulthood: Winding Down.   As individuals enter their sixties, many pass through another life transition. At this time, they must confront their coming retirement, an event many find disturbing. Further, family obligations, which have been low for years, often increase again as individuals find that they must take responsibility for their own aging parents. And when retirement actually occurs, it brings a mixed bag of gains and losses. Time for vacations, family visits, hobbies, and other leisure activities increases, but these pluses may be offset by a sharp drop in income, loss of contact with friends at work, and negative shifts in self-concept (from ''I'm a useful member of society,'' to ''I'm just a burden on others''). Thus, late adulthood, which has the potential to be one of the most enjoyable periods of life, becomes for some an unhappy prelude to despair.

Aging: Myths and Realities

You might not guess it from ads on television or in magazines, but at the present time the fastest growing segment of our population is people over the age of sixty-five. The number of such persons in the United States has risen from 18 million in 1965 to more than 28 million today; and projections indicate that they will constitute almost 20 percent of the total population by the year 2030! As the number of senior citizens has grown, so, too, has interest in the nature of aging. Research on this topic has expanded our knowledge of this final period of life and has countered many misconceptions about it.

Aging: The Physical Side.   If you are like most people, you probably hold a fairly negative view of old age. You may believe that, in general, people over sixty-five are ill, poor, unable to function in society, and perhaps mentally deficient, too. In fact, all of these ideas are false. A large majority of such persons are in at least moderately good health, and can continue to live rich, full lives. True, physical abilities *do* decline with increasing age. The surprising fact, however, is that they decrease more slowly, and to a smaller degree, than many persons believe. In fact, as you can see from Figure 8-29, many basic bodily functions retain much of their capacity into the seventies and beyond. Why, then, do we have the impression that older persons experience severe physical decline? In part because we confuse **primary aging**—changes produced by increasing age—with **secondary aging**—changes resulting from disease, disuse, or abuse of our bodies. When individuals remain active, and especially when they engage in regular physical exercise, they can be strong and vigorous for many years.

Aging: The Cognitive Side.   Do individuals lose part of their cognitive abilities as they age? For several decades psychologists believed that they do. Cross-sectional studies in which individuals of different ages completed standard tests of intelligence and other aspects of cognitive functioning indicated that older persons generally scored lower than younger ones (Doppelt & Wallace, 1955). These findings seemed to suggest that as people grow older they suffer declines in cognitive ability. More recent longitudinal research, however, points to more encouraging conclusions. In longitudinal studies the same individuals have been tested and re-tested across several decades. The results: they show little, if any, drop in mental ability with age (Schaie & Hertzog, 1985). While there is some slowing in the rate at which individuals process information, and some decline on

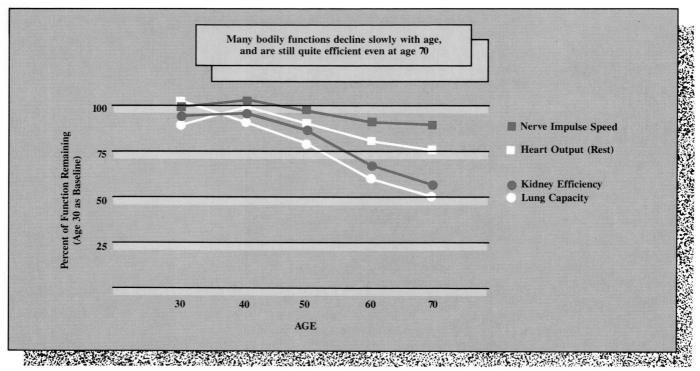

FIGURE 8-29. Physical decline with aging is actually more gradual and smaller than most people believe. *(Source: Based on data from Shock, 1962.)*

Physical Decline: Slower and Smaller Than You May Believe

tasks requiring speed, there is no sizable decline in memory, knowledge, or the ability to learn (Schaie & Willis, 1986). In fact, on some tests—ones that draw on experience and stored knowledge—older persons actually scored *higher* than young ones. For example, consider the items in Table 8-2; do you think old or young people would do better? The answer is clear: older persons attain higher scores than young ones on this *Test of Obscure Knowledge* (Kermis, 1984).

Why, then, did initial cross-sectional studies seem to reveal declines in intellectual functioning with age? One possibility involves *cohort differences*—differences in the background, experience, and education of various groups of subjects participating in such research. Remember: in cross-sectional studies, individuals of different ages are tested or compared at one point in time. This means, for example, that in a study involving persons who are twenty, fifty, and seventy years old, the latter two groups became adults many

TABLE 8-2

Older persons (those over sixty-five) actually score *higher* on items such as these (taken from the *Test of Obscure Knowledge*) than younger persons

(1) Deliticulate means:
   a. humble
   b. disturb
   c. bother
   d. faze
(2) The Greek writer Antigoras was noted for his:
   a. geometric proofs
   b. political influence
   c. philosophical paradoxes
   d. literary accomplishments
(3) What country has the largest deposits of marl?
   a. Lisbon
   b. Bulgaria
   c. Calcutta
   d. Bangkok

(SOURCE: Kermis, 1984.)

Congitive Abilities Do Not Necessarily Decline with Age

years before the twenty-year-olds were even born. Since persons born decades apart may experience sharply contrasting levels of education and nutrition, any differences between them in current performance may stem from these factors, *not* from simple differences in their age. Logitudinal research, in which the same individuals are studied across time, is not subject to such problems. The fact that studies using this approach indicate that intelligence and memory do not decrease greatly with age, then, is comforting. While our golden years may not be "golden" (problems of ill health and social isolation may well arise), we do, at least, seem to enter this final period with most of our cognitive abilities largely intact. To paraphrase a well-known saying: the mind remains willing (and capable) even if the flesh, in some respects, is weak.

Summary and Review

Development Before Birth

Developmental psychology studies the way human beings change physically, cognitively, and socially across the entire lifespan. Development during the prenatal period is rapid, but it can be adversely affected by inadequacies in mother's diet, by drugs, and by disease. The harmful effects of alcohol are visible in the *fetal alcohol syndrome,* a related series of disorders afflicting the newborns of mothers who abuse this drug.

Infancy and Childhood

Physical development is also rapid during *infancy*. Infants are born with several simple reflexes. Either at birth or soon afterwards they can perceive brightness, movement, and color and can distinguish different odors and tastes. Research using the *transfer across depth cues* technique indicates that depth perception is present by the time infants are four months old.

At one time, it was widely believed that children think and reason much like adults. According to Piaget, however, they attain such skills only gradually, after passing through several distinct phases of cognitive growth. While Piaget's theory of cognitive development remains influential, recent research indicates that it underestimated the abilities of young children. Contrary to what Piaget proposed, even two-year-olds seem to be aware of the fact that others see the world from a different perspective than they do. Moreover, four- or five-year-olds who show no evidence of *conservation* can acquire this principle through simple training techniques or merely from observing other children use it. Piaget's theory also failed to address several important aspects of cognitive development (e.g., memory, the appearance-reality distinction).

Language, a crucial cognitive skill, develops rapidly. Children move from *babbling* to uttering sentences in a few short years. *Mean length of utterance*—the average number of words in sentences they use—provides a useful measure of progress in acquiring language.

Social development begins in infancy with the formation of *attachment*—strong emotional bonds between infants and their caregivers. Attachment is affected by innate factors and by learning. In addition, close physical contact between infants and their caregivers seems to be important in its development.

Gender identity involves children's understanding of the fact that they are male or female. The formation of *friendships* is another important aspect of social development.

Adolescence

Adolescence begins with puberty, a period of rapid sexual maturation. Adolescents experience rapid physical growth and undergo important changes in facial features. Important advances in reasoning skills, including *moral reasoning,* occur during this period. Adolescents seem to experience wider and more intense swings in emotions than adults.

However, contrary to general belief, they do not differ sharply from their parents in terms of attitudes or values.

Adulthood: The Majority of Life

We spend more than 70 percent of our lives as adults. During *early adulthood* family and career responsibilities increase. In *middle adulthood* some persons question the meaning of their lives and may seek major change. Most, however, seem to avoid such a *midlife crisis*. During *late adulthood* individuals must make plans for retirement and many must care for their own aged parents.

While *old age* involves some decline in physical abilities, it is smaller and more gradual than most people believe. Also, contrary to popular belief, we do not seem to experience major declines in intelligence, memory, or other cognitive abilities during this final period of our life.

Key Terms

Accommodation According to Piaget, the modification of existing mental frameworks in order to take account of new information.

Adolescence The period between the onset of puberty and entry into adulthood.

Adulthood The period of life after individuals assume adult responsibilities (e.g., marriage, starting a career).

Appearance-Reality Distinction The ability to distinguish between the current appearance of an object and its enduring nature.

Assimilation According to Piaget, the tendency to understand new information in terms of existing mental frameworks.

Attachment A strong emotional bond between infants and their caregivers.

Babbling An early stage of speech development in which infants emit virtually all known sounds of human speech.

Childhood The period from age two until the onset of puberty.

Cognitive View (of Gender Identity) The view that gender identity is based on children's understanding that they are male or female and their subsequent tendency to acquire behaviors appropriate to this identity.

Concrete Operations According to Piaget, a stage of cognitive development between the ages of seven and eleven.

Conservation Understanding of the fact that basic physical dimensions (e.g., area, volume, number) remain constant despite superficial changes in appearance.

Cross-Sectional Research Research in which individuals of different ages are compared in order to determine whether they differ in specific, predicted ways.

Developmental Psychology The branch of

psychology that studies age-related changes in all aspects of behavior and cognition.

Egocentrism The inability of young children to realize that others may perceive the world differently than they do.

Embryo The developing child during the first eight weeks of life.

Fetal Alcohol Syndrome Severely retarded growth, nervous system damage, and distortions in facial shape among newborns, stemming from heavy use of alcohol by the mother during pregnancy.

Fetus The developing child during the last seven months of pregnancy.

Formal Operations According to Piaget, a stage of cognitive development during which individuals become capable of deductive reasoning.

Gender Identity Children's understanding of the fact that they are male or female.

Infancy The first two years of life.

Longitudinal Research Research in which the same individuals are studied at several points in time to determine whether some aspect of their behavior changes with age.

Object Permanence Understanding the fact that objects continue to exist even when they are removed from view.

Placenta A structure that surrounds, protects, and nourishes the developing fetus.

Prenatal Period The period prior to birth.

Preoperational Stage According to Piaget, a stage of cognitive development occurring between the ages of two and seven.

Primary Aging Physical or biological changes directly related to increasing age.

Puberty A period of rapid sexual maturation and growth.

Secondary Aging Physical or biological changes related to disease, injury, or abuse of our bodies.

Sensorimotor Stage According to Piaget, the earliest stage of cognitive development. During this period, infants gradually acquire a basic understanding of the concept of cause and effect.

Social Development Changes in social behavior and social relations occurring with age.

Social Learning View (of Gender Identity) The view that children acquire gender identity by imitating persons of their own sex (primarily their same-sex parents).

Stage Theory Any theory suggesting that all human beings pass through a set sequence of changes in an orderly and universal manner.

Strange Situation A procedure used to study attachment. Mothers leave their infants alone with a stranger for several minutes. The infants' reactions to this separation and later reappearance of their mothers are observed.

For More Information

Flavell, J.H. (1985). *Cognitive development,* 2nd ed. Englewood Cliffs, NJ: Prentice-Hall.
A highly respected researcher summarizes current knowledge about cognitive development in this book. Piaget's theory, language, memory, and many other aspects of cognitive development are discussed. This is an excellent source to consult if you'd like to know more about this important aspect of human development.

Fischer, K., & Lazerson, A. (1988). *Human development: From conception through adolescence.* New York: W.H. Freeman.
A clear and well presented overview of all aspects of human development. Separate chapters trace development in infancy, preschool years, school years, and adolescence. You can find information on virtually any aspect of development here.

Psychology Today. (May 1987). ''Special Report: Life Flow.''
This twentieth-anniversary issue contains a series of articles dealing with development throughout the entire lifespan. Interesting new findings concerning children, adolescents, and adults are described, and many intriguing statistics about birth rates, population trends, and related topics are included. A very readable source of additional information.

Schaie, K.W., & Willis, S.L. (1986). *Adult development and aging,* 2nd ed. New York: Wiley.
A broad introduction to the fields of adult development and aging written by two psychologists who have studied these topics for many years. If you'd like to know more about how we change during our adult years, and how we are affected by aging, this is a good place to start.

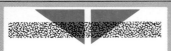

CHAPTER

Motivation: The Activation and Persistence of Behavior

''So I hear you have a new girlfriend,'' Mike Delaney says to his friend Barry Frankel as he joins him in the school cafeteria.

''News sure travels fast around here,'' Barry replies. ''I only met her three weeks ago.''

''Yeah, but Bev McCallum's telling everyone it's real serious. She says this woman's a dancer and that you're so nuts about her, you don't know what's happening anymore.''

At this comment, Barry turns slightly red. ''Well, I really *do* like her,'' he admits through his embarrassment. ''I never met anyone like her before. What beautiful eyes . . . and she's just so—different.''

''What do you mean?'' Mike asks.

''Well, for one thing, she's really wrapped up in her dancing—practices five or six hours every day. Sometimes I can hardly get to see her, she's so busy doing those exercises. And they're no fun. I've watched her, and some of them really *hurt,* even though she's been dancing since she was a kid. I don't know how she stands it.''

''Why does she do it, if it's so bad? Is she trying for the movies?''

''No, it's nothing like that. She's studying classical dance—ballet and all. I don't think she ever expects to go to Hollywood. What she really wants is just to qualify in this competition they have. Dancers like her from all over the country try out, and the best get chosen to work with this famous guy—someone who's trained the best dancers for years.''

''You mean she goes through all this stuff just for a chance to work even harder? Man, I can't understand it. I'd never torture myself like that unless there was big money in it—I mean *big* money!''

''Oh, I'm sure you wouldn't. You're always looking for the easy way. But I already told you, she's *different.* Dancing is everything to her; she'd do practically anything just to get a chance. You ought to see her when she talks about it.''

''Sounds weird to me,'' Mike says, shaking his head. Then, noticing the look of annoyance on Barry's face, he adds, ''Hey, don't get your blood pressure up—what do I know about this kind of thing? I guess maybe it's just that different people get excited about different things. . . .''

Why does Barry's girlfriend work so hard on her dancing? What led her to choose this activity early in life? And why does she continue to perform it, despite that it's painful, takes up most of her time, and doesn't offer the promise of huge riches? If you are like most persons, your answer probably goes something like this: ''She loves dancing and wants to do it as well as she can.'' This seems quite reasonable, but consider what it involves. On the basis of a description of her behavior, you have drawn some important *inferences* about this young woman. Specifically, you have inferred the presence of an internal process or state that *guides* her behavior (causes her to choose dancing over other activities), *activates* or energizes it (through all those long practice sessions), and causes it to *persist* over time (remember, she's been dancing since she was a child). Psychologists generally refer to such internal processes as **motivation.** More formally, they define motivation as an inferred internal process that activates, guides, and maintains behavior (Geen, Beatty, and Arkin, 1984).

Why do we need this concept? Quite simply, it is often difficult, if not impossible, to explain others' behavior solely in terms of external events or conditions. To see why this is so, consider the following situations:

An ambitious young executive comes to the office early, leaves late, and brings work home with him every weekend. (Refer to Figure 9-1.)

FIGURE 9-1. How can behaviors like these be explained? The concept of *motivation* is very useful in this respect.

Several people wake up at six every other morning, drive to a health center three miles away, and rigorously perform aerobics for an hour before going to work. They repeat this activity four times a week.

A young man places an ad in the "Personals" column of a newspaper, in which he lists his many charms and describes the traits he is seeking in potential lovers.

In these and countless other situations, the concept of *motivation* helps us understand *why* others behave as they do. We can't observe this hidden, internal process directly, but by inferring its existence we can often make sense out of actions which would otherwise seem confusing, puzzling, or bizarre.

In the remainder of this chapter we will examine several different aspects of human motivation. First, we'll consider several contrasting perspectives on this process. Next, we'll examine two motives with an important biological basis: hunger and thirst. Third, we'll turn to a topic most people find fascinating: sexual motivation. And finally, we'll discuss several motives that seem to be uniquely human in scope: needs for achievement, power, and affiliation.

Motivation: Some Contrasting Views

Why do people act the way they do? Over the centuries many different answers, providing different perspectives on motivation, have been offered. We will focus here on three of these views: instinct theory, drive theory, and expectancy (cognitive) theory.

Instinct Theory: A Biological Approach

In psychology, before there was *motivation* there was *instinct*. That is, before psychologists attempted to explain behavior in terms of motives, they sought to do so by means of **instincts**—innate patterns of behavior which are universal in a species, independent of experience, and elicited by specific stimuli or conditions. For a time, this approach was quite popular. Thus, William James (1890), one of the founders of American psychology, included pugnacity, acquisitiveness, sympathy, and even curiosity on his list of basic human instincts. And Sigmund Freud, one of the most influential psychologists of all time, suggested that many complex forms of behavior—everything from aggression to love—are heavily influenced by innate biological mechanisms.

To a large extent the origins of this instinct approach can be traced to Charles Darwin's *theory of evolution*. According to Darwin, human beings have evolved in the same manner, and in accordance with the same basic principles, as all other species on earth. Thus, the differences between us and other organisms are primarily ones of degree, not of kind. Since many other species possess instincts, he felt it was reasonable to suggest that human behavior, too, might be affected by built-in tendencies.

Whether this is true or not remains somewhat controversial even today. Most psychologists doubt that innate patterns or tendencies play an important role in complex forms of human behavior, but some scientists (especially sociobiologists) contend that they do (Lumsden & Wilson, 1981). Quite aside from the outcome of this ongoing debate, though, it soon became apparent to most psychologists that instincts were not very useful from the point of view of understanding motivation. The basic problem was this: in most cases, the existence of an instinct was inferred from the behavior it was supposed to explain. For example, take the case of James's *acquisitiveness*. The existence of this instinct was inferred from the fact most people seek various possessions and usually become strongly attached to them. This instinct was then used to explain the occurrence of such behavior. In short, how do we know that people possess an acquisitive instinct? Because we can see them working hard to gain homes, cars, and so on. Why do they engage in such behavior? Because they possess an acquisitive instinct! As you can readily see, this is a useless type of circular reasoning (refer to Figure 9-2 for another example). As realization of this fact grew, support for instinct theory waned, and it was soon replaced by a very different perspective in psychology—**drive theory.**

Drive Theory: Motivation and Homeostasis

What do being hungry, thirsty, too cold, or too hot have in common? One answer is: they're all unpleasant and make us want to do something to eliminate such feelings. This basic fact provides the basis for a second major approach to motivation: *drive theory*.

FIGURE 9-2. As illustrated here, *instincts* do not really explain various forms of behavior. In fact, if their existence is inferred from the occurrence of such behaviors, using them to ''explain'' these actions is a circular argument.

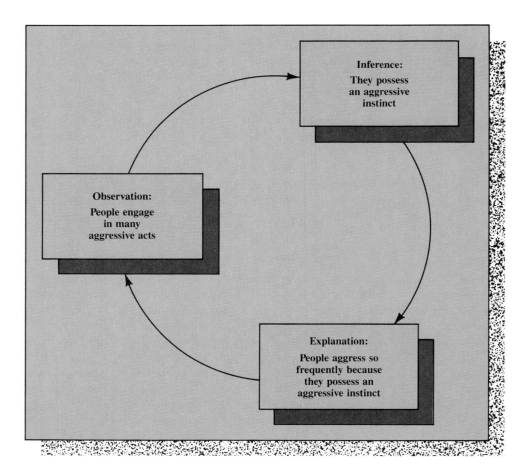

Using Instincts to Explain Human Behavior: Beware of Circular Reasoning

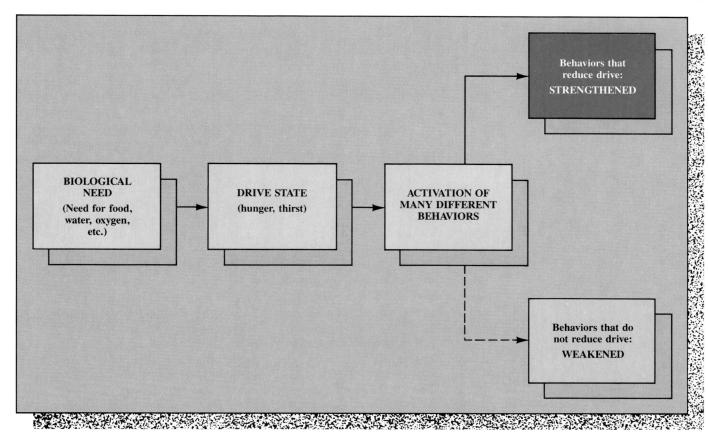

FIGURE 9-3. According to *drive theory,* biological needs lead to the arousal of appropriate *drives* which activate behavior. Behaviors that reduce these drives (by eliminating or reducing the underlying need) are strengthened and tend to be repeated. Behaviors that fail to produce such effects are weakened.

Drive Theory: An Overview

According to this view, biological needs arising within our bodies create unpleasant states of arousal—the feelings we usually describe as "hunger," "thirst," "fatigue," and so on. In order to eliminate such feelings and restore the body's physiological balance (a state known as *homeostasis*), we engage in certain activities. Thus, according to drive theory motivation is basically a process in which various biological needs push or *drive* us to actions designed to satisfy these needs (see Figure 9-3). Behaviors that work—that help reduce the appropriate drive—are strengthened and tend to be repeated. Those that fail to produce such effects are weakened and will not be repeated when the drive is present once again.

In its original form drive theory focused primarily on biological needs and the aroused states (or drives) they produce. Soon, though, psychologists extended this model to other forms of behavior not so clearly linked to basic needs. For example, consider the famous *frustration-aggression hypothesis* (Dollard et al., 1939). According to this theory, frustration—thwarting of our ongoing activities—leads to the arousal of an *aggressive drive* which can be satisfied only by some kind of assault against the source of frustration. Here, as in many other extensions of drive theory, a powerful drive is supposedly aroused by *external* events rather than by internal biological needs.

Drive theory persisted in psychology for several decades and has not been totally discarded even today. However, there is widespread recognition of the fact that it suffers from several serious drawbacks. The most important of these is this: contrary to what drive theory suggests, organisms (including human beings) often engage in actions that tend to *increase* rather than to reduce various drives. For example, have you ever delayed eating, even though you were hungry, in order to increase your enjoyment at the next meal? Have you ever increased your sexual excitement by watching an erotic film or reading an erotic story? And have you ever ridden on a roller coaster or gone to see a horror movie in order to experience fear, shock, or similar internal states (Zillmann et al., 1986)? If so, you already have first-hand evidence for the fact that we often seek to increase rather than to reduce various drives. Such effects are not restricted to human beings. For example, male rats learn to perform various responses that allow them to begin—but not complete—sexual intercourse with receptive females (Sheffield, Wulff, & Backer, 1951).

In the light of such evidence, most psychologists now believe that drive theory, by itself, does not provide a comprehensive framework for understanding human motivation. Thus, in recent years it has been largely replaced by a third view—one which places greater emphasis on the cognitive aspects of motivation.

Expectancy Theory: A Cognitive Approach

Why are you reading this book? It is not, we'd guess, to reduce some biological drive! Rather, the chances are good that you are reading it because you expect that by doing so you will (1) learn something useful or interesting, and (2) get a higher grade on the next exam. In other words, your behavior is determined by your *expectancies*—belief that your present actions will yield certain outcomes in the future. This basic point is the foundation for the third major theory of motivation we will consider, **expectancy theory.** This view suggests that motivation is *not* primarily a matter of being pushed from within by various urges; rather, it is more a question of being pulled from without by expectations of attaining desired outcomes or *positive incentives*. In short, while drive theory focuses mainly on the ''stick'' in the old carrot-and-stick notion, expectancy theory focuses directly on the ''carrot'' (see Figure 9-4 for an illustration of this point). So why do people engage in various behaviors such as reading this book, working too much, doing aerobics, or being videotaped at a dating service? Expectancy theory answers: they believe that doing so will yield outcomes they'd like to attain.

Expectancy theory has been applied to many different aspects of human motivation. Perhaps, though, it has found its most important use with respect to *work motivation*—the tendency to expend energy and effort on one's job (Mitchell & Larson, 1987). Research on this topic has consistently found that people will demonstrate a high level of work motivation only when (1) they believe that working hard will improve their performance, (2) they believe that good performance will yield various rewards (e.g., increases in pay, promotions), and (3) these rewards are ones they value. For example, offering extra time off to a workaholic wouldn't make much sense; for such persons, vacations are not a desirable outcome!

In sum, expectancy theory suggests that our motivation to engage in a given activity will be high only when we expect that performing it will somehow pay off—yield

---

How *Not* to Use Expectancy Theory

FIGURE 9-4. *Expectancy theory* suggests that behavior is motivated by *expectancies* of positive outcomes, not ''pushed'' from within by various drives.

HAGAR

outcomes or results we desire. In several respects, it is hard to imagine a more sensible statement about human motivation.

Hunger and Thirst: Motives with a Biological Basis

Why do we become hungry or thirsty? How do we know when we've had enough food or water to satisfy the needs from which these feelings arise? And why do some persons have so much difficulty regulating their intake of food, so that they gain or lose large amounts of weight? These are intriguing questions with important practical implications. Fortunately, research conducted by psychologists and others in the past few decades now allows us to offer partial answers. Since thirst has turned out to be the simpler of the two (although far from simple), we'll begin with this motive and then turn to hunger.

Thirst: Regulating Our Internal Fluid Balance

Both hunger and thirst involve the operation of *regulatory mechanisms* within our bodies. Both are affected by internal mechanisms that can (1) detect certain internal changes, (2) trigger corrective actions, and (3) bring these to a close when internal conditions return to optimal physiological values. If this sounds something like the operation of a thermostat in your home, you're on the right track. A thermostat detects departures from the temperature you've set, then turns on the furnace or air conditioning until the desired level is reached. But please note: the internal mechanisms regulating hunger and thirst are far more complex than this, so the comparison is a useful one only if you keep this limitation firmly in mind.

During the course of daily life, our bodies lose a large amount of water through evaporation from the skin and lungs and the elimination of bodily wastes. In addition, we can also lose water in less routine ways (e.g., through bleeding or vomiting). How are such losses detected so that we feel the urge to drink? Two separate mechanisms seem to be involved.

First, some evidence suggests that certain cells in the heart, in the kidneys, and in veins seem to detect changes in blood pressure produced by shifts in the volume of liquid outside the cells of the body (in the *extracellular fluid compartment*). When these **baroreceptors** are stimulated (primarily by a decrease in venous blood pressure), they trigger the secretion of *ADH* (antidiuretic hormone) by the pituitary glands. This hormone, in turn, causes the kidneys to reabsorb water which would otherwise be excreted as urine. In addition, other substances released by the kidneys in response to stimulation from the baroreceptors seem to stimulate receptors in the brain (especially in the hypothalamus), thus producing sensations of thirst.

Second, other neurons, located primarily in the hypothalamus, seem to respond to changes in the amount of water contained *within* cells of the body (in the *intracellular fluid compartment*). When the body's supplies of water are low, these **osmoreceptors,** along with many other cells, give up liquids to the blood and other bodily fluids. As they do, they shrink in size. This produces two effects: activity in the osmoreceptors stimulates the production of ADH, thus causing the kidneys to retain water, and it also generates sensations of thirst.

In sum, loss of water from our bodies is detected in two different ways. The sensations of thirst which result initiate drinking, and optimal physiological conditions are soon restored. (Please see Figure 9-5 on page 280 for a summary of these internal regulatory mechanisms.)

One final, interesting point: when we drink, sensations of thirst often cease long before the liquids we consume can reach either the extracellular or intracellular fluid compartments of our bodies. This suggests that receptors in the mouth and throat play a role in signaling satiety—telling us when we've had enough (Carlson, 1986). Moreover, it appears that we can learn to *anticipate* our future needs with respect to liquid intake. For example, when rats are switched from a diet consisting mainly of carbohydrates to one

Internal Mechanisms Regulating Thirst

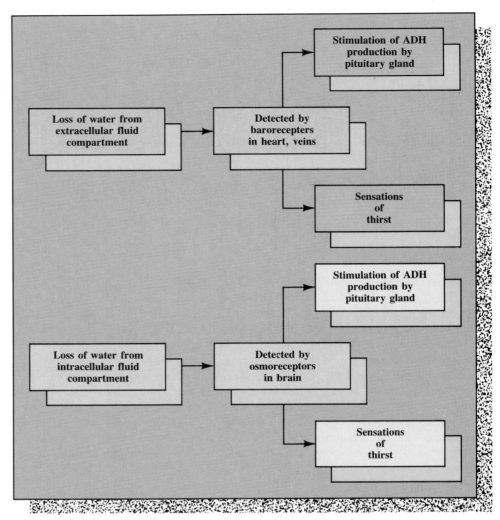

FIGURE 9-5. Loss of water from the body's two fluid compartments is detected by two sets of receptors. When stimulated, these *baroreceptors* and *osmoreceptors* stimulate internal mechanisms that conserve bodily fluids and arouse sensations of thirst.

rich in protein, which requires more water for digestion, they soon learn to drink more with their meals (Fitzsimmons & LeMagnen, 1969). Such findings suggest that, when coupled with the effects of learning, our internal mechanisms for regulating thirst can be effective indeed.

Hunger: Regulating Our Caloric Intake

Like Cathy in Figure 9-6, many persons find that the ''battle of the bulge'' is a hard one to win. Despite their best efforts, their weight creeps up, and up, and up. Yet most individuals don't experience such difficulties. They simply eat what they want, when they want, and the rest somehow takes care of itself. In this section, we'll focus on how most organisms (including most human beings) are able to regulate their intake of food so precisely that they neither gain nor lose weight over long periods of time.

Are There Discrete Hunger and Satiety Centers in the Brain? At first glance, hunger and the regulation of eating seem quite simple: we eat when our stomachs are empty, and we stop when they are full. Unfortunately, early studies designed to test these straightforward notions showed that they are false. While individuals often do report experiencing hunger when their stomachs are active (Cannon & Washburn, 1912), persons whose stomachs have been removed for medical reasons still report feeling hungry.

Maintaining Stable Weight: A Struggle Many Lose

FIGURE 9-6. Like Cathy, many persons experience difficulty in regulating their own weight. *(Source: Universal Press Syndicate, 1987.)*

This suggests that there is more to hunger than an empty stomach. Do brain mechanisms play a role? Intriguing hints that they might were provided by the medical histories of individuals who had suffered damage to the hypothalamus through surgery or accident. Such persons often experienced difficulty in regulating their weight, either gaining or losing large amounts.

These findings led some researchers to conduct systematic studies with animal subjects, studies in which portions of the hypothalamus were destroyed in order to observe the effects on eating. (We discussed such research briefly in Chapter 2.) Initial results were dramatic. In fact, they seemed to point to the conclusion that the hypothalamus contained discrete ''eating'' and ''satiety'' centers.

The first of these, the supposed eating center, was located in the **lateral hypothalamus.** Destruction of this region greatly reduced subjects' interest in food. Indeed, animals who had undergone this operation often refused to eat or drink and would actually starve if not forced to take food (see Figure 9-7). Further, they became quite finicky, refusing to eat any but the most palatable foods.

In contrast, destruction of a second region, the **ventromedial hypothalamus,** produced opposite effects. Animals who underwent this procedure became gluttons who consumed far more food than was true prior to the operation.

FIGURE 9-7. Destruction of the *lateral hypothalamus* often produces animal ''gourmets'' who will eat only very tasty foods. As a result, they lose large amounts of weight and may literally starve if not forced to eat. The location of the lesions (LH lesions) that produce such effects are shown in the photo of a rat brain below.

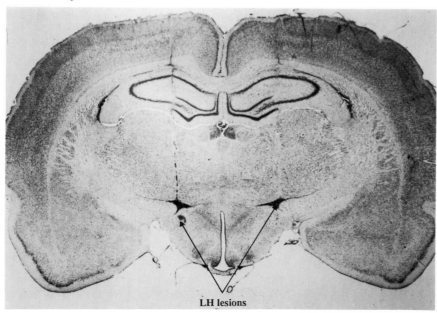

LH lesions

Destruction of the Lateral Hypothalamus: Some Dramatic Effects

Such findings quickly gripped the attention of psychologists and even of the mass media. After all, if there were indeed discrete eating and satiety centers in the hypothalamus, perhaps effective solutions to the dieter's dilemma were just around the corner. Unfortunately, such hopes were soon dashed by other findings, which served to muddy this seemingly clear picture. First, animals who suffered destruction of the lateral hypothalamus gradually regained their appetites, at least in part. This contradicted the notion that this region serves as a discrete eating center. Second, animals who have undergone this operation show many other changes in behavior aside from a loss of appetite. For example, they fail to groom themselves, have trouble recovering their balance after a fall, and demonstrate little interest in almost *any* stimuli—a phenomenon known as *sensory neglect*. In a similar manner, destruction of the ventromedial hypothalamus, too, produces a wide range of effects. Besides eliminating satiety, it appears to alter subjects' metabolism in basic ways, and these changes, not the elimination of a discrete satiety center, may account for their enormous appetites. In sum, the idea that the hypothalamus was a simple neurological key to understanding hunger and eating was soon discredited by additional research.

Detectors in the Liver and Elsewhere: A Less Dramatic but More Accurate Picture.   If the hypothalamus does not contain eating and satiety centers, then what accounts for the ability most of us have to regulate caloric intake so precisely? (That it *is* precise is indicated by the following fact: if you eat just ten more calories than you need each day—less than the amount in a carrot—you'll gain a pound every year.) The answer seems to involve several types of detectors located primarily in the liver, but existing elsewhere as well, which respond to different aspects of our diet (Stricker et al., 1977; Shimizu et al., 1983).

First, and perhaps most important, such detectors respond to the amount of *glucose* (sugar) in our blood, or perhaps they respond to its availability to our cells. When glucose levels are low (or when they are high but insulin levels are low, as is true for diabetics) feelings of hunger result. When, in contrast, glucose levels are high and sufficient insulin is also present, we experience satiety. Most of these glucose detectors are located in the liver, but some are present in the hypothalamus, too.

Second, some findings indicate that other detectors seem to respond to *protein*—more precisely, to amino acids. Thus, if we eat a meal high in protein (a thick, juicy steak, for example), we feel full even though the level of glucose in our blood may remain relatively low (refer to Figure 9-8). Finally, still other detectors respond to *lipids* (fats).

FIGURE 9-8. Most people feel quite full after eating a meal high in protein. This seems to stem from the fact that we have internal detectors which respond specifically to the amino acids of which proteins are composed.

Protein and Sensations of Satiety

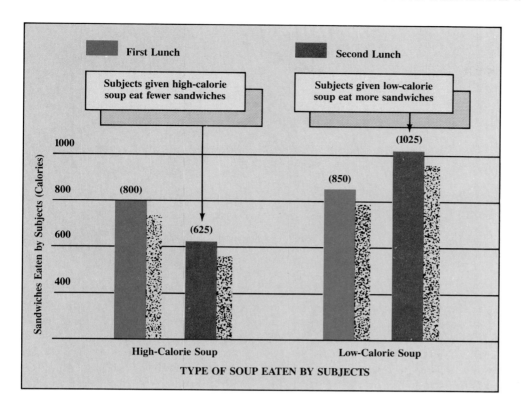

FIGURE 9-9. Subjects given a high-calorie soup ate the same number of sandwiches as subjects given a low-calorie soup during their first meal. It did not take many meals, however, before subjects in both groups adjusted to the number of calories they consumed. Those given the high-calorie soup ate less, while those given the low-calorie soup ate more. *(Source: Based on data from Booth, Mather, & Fuller, 1982.)*

Again, even if glucose levels are low, when the amount of lipids circulating in our blood is high, we do not feel hungry.

Complex as all this may sound, it is still only part of the total picture. In addition, eating and hunger are also affected by what are sometimes termed *head factors*—the sight, smell, and taste of food, as well as feedback produced by chewing and swallowing it. Such effects are illustrated by an interesting study conducted by Booth, Mather, and Fuller (1982). These researchers fed people three-course meals consisting of hot soup, small sandwiches, and a gelatin dessert. The number of calories in the soup could be varied by the addition of a tasteless but high-calorie starch. Subjects were not told about this difference, but spices were added so that the two versions were distinct in taste. On the first day subjects ate the same number of sandwiches with either kind of soup. Within a few days, however, they began eating fewer sandwiches after the high-calorie soup (see Figure 9-9). Remember: subjects were not told that one version of the soup was higher in calories than the other. Rather, they were able to associate later feelings of being full or hungry with the taste of each soup, and adjust their eating appropriately. In this way, the taste of relatively high and low calorie foods can affect how much we eat, even if we know nothing about the foods' nutritional content.

As you can see, feelings of hunger and satiety and their resulting impact upon eating are part of a complex internal system. Given such complexity, and the fact that several components of this regulatory system can be modified by learning, it is far from surprising that it sometimes gets out of whack. What happens when it does?

Obesity and Other Disorders in the Long-Term Regulation of Eating.   There can be little doubt that in the late 1980s thin is ''in.'' Each year millions of persons spend billions of dollars in a continuing quest for slimness (see Figure 9-10 on page 284). In most cases, their desire to shed excess pounds stems primarily from concern with their appearance. But growing evidence suggests that there is strong medical justification for these efforts to counter **obesity:** being overweight has been linked to high blood pressure, diabetes, arthritis, and several other illnesses (Kolata, 1985). Why do so many people have difficulty regulating their eating and hence their weight? Unfortunately, many factors seem to play a role.

Becoming and Staying Thin: A Modern Obsession

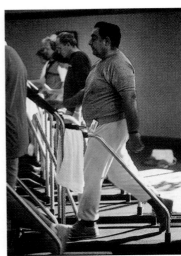

FIGURE 9-10. There seems to be almost no limit to what people will do (or how much they will spend) in the quest for slimness.

First, part of the problem seems to be learned. Many individuals acquire eating habits that are certain to generate excess pounds. They learn to prefer high-calorie meals (e.g., ones rich in protein and fats). Further, they learn to associate the act of eating with many different contexts and situations. If you feel a strong urge to eat every time you sit down in front of the television set or movie screen, you know about such learning at first hand. Apparently, the desire to eat can be classically conditioned, so that cues associated with eating when we are hungry acquire the capacity to elicit such behavior even when we are not hungry. Second, since eating often generates pleasant feelings, many persons learn to use this behavior as a means of coping with stress or unhappiness. Whenever they feel ''down'' or upset, they munch. Once again, such food intake is unrelated to bodily needs and can lead to unwanted pounds.

Genetic factors are important, too. As common sense suggests, individuals differ greatly in *basal metabolic rate*. In other words, they vary in terms of the number of calories their bodies require at rest. Indeed, persons of the same age and weight performing the same daily activities can differ by a factor of two in this regard: one may require almost twice as many calories as the other. As you can readily see, this is one area of life in which efficiency is *not* rewarded. Persons with a high metabolic rate can eat much more than those with a low metabolic rate without gaining any weight. And now for the most discouraging part: when an individual diets, his or her metabolic rate tends to decrease. Moreover, the longer the diet continues, the greater this drop. Thus, as many dieters soon note, the more weight they lose, the harder it becomes to lose still more because their bodies have adjusted to the apparent emergency (too few calories) by becoming more efficient!

Another inherited characteristic that may play a role in obesity is known as the **brown fat mechanism.** This system seems to provide a temporary means of storing extra calories. If they are not needed within a day after being consumed, they are released during periods of inactivity (e.g., during sleep) as heat. In contrast, white fat—the type dieters fervently wish to shed—stores excess calories in a more permanent manner.

That the brown fat mechanism can be very effective in maintaining fairly constant weight is shown by a study conducted by Rothwell and Stock (1979). Rats were fed a diet consisting of high calorie ''junk foods.'' (Like people, rats seem to enjoy such foods and happily gobble them down.) On this diet subjects' caloric intake went up fully 80 percent. Yet their weight increased only 27 percent. What happened to the rest? One possibility, suggested by the fact that their oxygen consumption rose sharply, is that it was simply released as heat by their brown fat mechanism. Since human beings, too, possess brown fat, it may play a similar role for us. Thus, those fortunate people you know who never seem to gain weight, no matter what they eat, may have a highly efficient brown fat mechanism. In contrast, those who seem to never lose weight, no matter what they eat, may lie at the opposite end of the scale in this respect. (We should hasten to note that this is largely informed speculation; such relationships have not yet been conclusively demonstrated among humans.)

A fourth factor that seems to play a role in the regulation of weight among humans involves contrasting effects of stress on eating by obese and nonobese individuals. How do *you* react to stress, for example, to a traffic ticket, a big exam, or negative feedback from your boss? If you are like most persons, your appetite probably decreases at such times; indeed, food may be the farthest thing from your mind. As we noted above, however, overweight persons often have a different reaction. They tend to eat *more* at times of stress, even if they do not feel hungry. Why is this the case? A *boundary model* of eating, suggested recently by Herman and Polivy (1984), provides one possible explanation. This theory suggests that among nonobese persons stress suppresses physiological reactions that accompany hunger (e.g., activity in the digestive system). The result: hunger and eating are reduced. Among persons who have difficulty regulating their own weight, however, stress has another effect: it interferes with the self-control required to restrict eating. When stressed, therefore, such persons actually *increase* their intake of food.

Evidence for these effects has been reported by Herman and his colleagues (Herman et al., 1987). In this study, women who indicated that they were or were not currently dieting were asked to participate in a market survey involving flavors of gourmet ice cream. Before tasting these products, one group was exposed to stress: they were told that after reporting their reactions, they would compose an advertising jingle for the ice cream and then sing it while being videotaped. The tape would then be shown to various marketing experts. In contrast, subjects in a second group were not exposed to such stress: they were told that after tasting the ice cream, they would merely be asked to list aspects of the product that should be stressed in future advertising. Both groups of participants were asked to refrain from eating for four hours prior to the study, so all were quite hungry.

Subjects were then given containers of chocolate, vanilla, and strawberry ice cream and were told to taste as much as they wished. The containers were weighed before and after subjects received them, so the amount they ate could be carefully measured. It was predicted that among nondieters stress would reduce the amount of ice cream consumed, while among dieters the opposite would be true. As you can see from Figure 9-11,

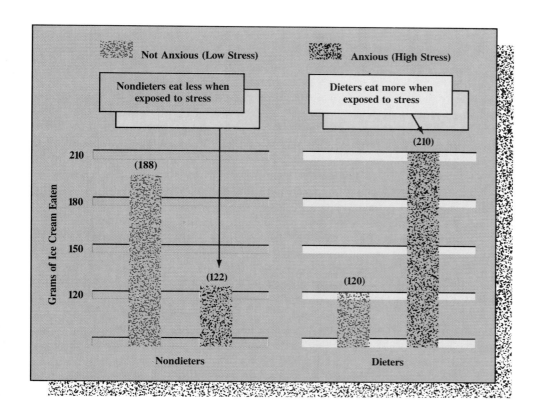

FIGURE 9-11. Nondieters ate less ice cream when exposed to stress than when not exposed to stress. In contrast, dieters ate *more* ice cream in the presence than in the absence of stress. These findings lend support to a boundary model of eating (Herman & Polivy, 1984). *(Source: Based on data from Herman et al., 1987.)*

Stress and Eating: Contrasting Effects for Dieters and Nondieters

Food Cues: There Seems to Be No Escape

FIGURE 9-12. We live in an environment that surrounds us with food-related cues. Little wonder, then, that so many people experience difficulty in regulating their weight.

results supported these hypotheses. Given these results and the frequency with which most of us encounter stress during our daily lives, it is not at all surprising that many persons experience great difficulty maintaining a stable weight. The conditions around them seem to disrupt the self-control needed to restrict caloric intake.

Fifth, individuals who suffer from obesity seem to differ from other persons in one more respect that seems quite relevant to their problem: they tend to respond more strongly to external cues relating to food. In other words, they are more readily stimulated to eat by the sight or smell of food (Rodin & Slochower, 1976). Given the frequency with which such cues appear in many societies, it is hardly surprising that concern with obesity is a growing problem in many nations (refer to Figure 9-12).

Finally, growing evidence points to the possibility that overeating, as well as several other ingestion-related disorders (e.g., alcoholism), may involve excess production of, or sensitivity to, morphine-like substances produced by our own bodies, known as *opioid peptides* or *endorphins*. (Recall that we mentioned these in our discussion of drugs and the nervous system in Chapter 2.) Several findings obtained in research with animals offer support for this hypothesis. First, small doses of morphine, which stimulate naturally occurring endorphin receptors in the brain, enhance the intake of several different substances (e.g., salt water, alcohol; Bertino et al., 1988). Second, the larger the dose of morphine administered, the larger such effects tend to be (Hubbell, Czirr, & Reid, 1987). Third, injections of drugs that counter the effects of morphine or endorphins (e.g., *naxolone*) reduce or even totally eliminate such results; rats receiving such drugs do *not* consume more of various substances (Hubbell et al., 1988).

Together, these results suggest that endorphins prolong ingestion once it has begun, perhaps by enhancing the pleasant aspects of various tastes. Thus, some overweight persons (and perhaps some alcoholics, too) may experience personal difficulties because their internal mechanism for generating or responding to opioid peptides (endorphins) is somehow overactive. If this is indeed the case, then treatment for such problems based on the administration of *opioid antagonists* (drugs that counter the effects of endorphins) may prove effective. Research designed to test this possibility is currently under way. (Please see Figure 9-13 for a summary of these suggestions.)

Before concluding, we should note that there is another, and perhaps even more disturbing side to long-term weight regulation. In contrast to persons who are obese, some individuals tend to eat less than they need—often far less. In this condition, known as **anorexia nervosa**, individuals literally starve themselves until they lose dangerous amounts of weight. Surprisingly, anorexia nervosa does not seem to stem from the fact that they dislike food or find it unappealing. On the contrary, such persons are often preoccupied with it and enjoy preparing it and serving it to others. Their unwillingness to

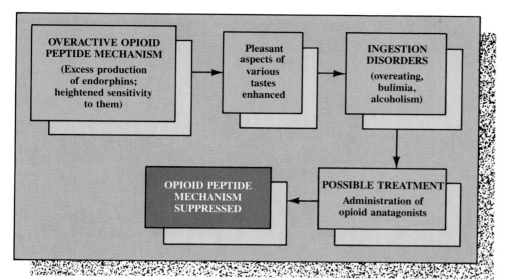

FIGURE 9-13. One possible cause of overeating and other ingestion disorders may be an over-active internal mechanism for the production of opioid peptides (endorphins). If this is actually the case, then one effective treatment for such disorders may involve the administration of *opioid antagonists*—drugs that counter the impact of opioid peptides (e.g. *naxolone*). *(Source: Based on suggestions by Hubbell et al., 1988.)*

eat appears to derive from an unreasonable fear of becoming obese. This disorder occurs primarily among young women, who, of course, are the primary target of all those ads to be slim and be attractive, but it is sometimes found among older persons, too. Whether true anorexia nervosa ever occurs among males is as yet uncertain.

Because individuals suffering from anorexia nervosa sometimes show decreased activity in areas of the brain concerned with eating (e.g., the hypothalamus), some scientists believe it may stem from biological disorders (Leibowitz, 1983). At present there is not sufficient evidence to reach firm conclusions in this respect. One point, though, is clear: the psychological and physical damage caused by anorexia nervosa may be even greater than that associated with obesity. (What steps can you take to help regulate your own weight? For some suggestions, see "The Point of It All" section below.)

THE POINT OF IT ALL

Winning the "Battle of the Bulge": Some Helpful Hints

If you want to stay slim (or become slim if you're not already), try following these steps. Regulating your weight is never easy in an environment filled with enticing foods, but these *can* help.

(1) *Avoid Temptation.* All of us—even persons who are obese—possess internal mechanisms designed to inhibit eating once we've had enough. Unfortunately, these can easily be overwhelmed by external cues: the sight or smell of attractive, delicious foods. Your first task, then, is to avoid such stimuli. Don't watch food commercials, and don't linger over beautiful food-related ads in magazines. Also, since we are often encouraged to eat when others are eating, try to consume at least some meals alone. The experience may not be pleasant, but the number of calories you save may be significant.

(2) *Eat Low-Calorie, High-Density Foods.* Earlier we noted that factors concerned with the taste and texture of food play

a role in the regulation of eating. You can put such effects to good use by eating foods which require lots of chewing but which contain relatively few calories (e.g., carrots, crusty bread *without butter*). There is some indication that such oral stimulation can actually reduce feelings of hunger.

(3) *Avoid Crash Diets.* When individuals diet, their metabolic rates decrease, thus making it harder to lose additional weight. Such reductions in metabolic rate are more likely to be triggered by crash diets, in which caloric intake is drastically reduced, than by diets that are more gradual in nature. So avoid the former; any short-term gains they yield will be more than offset by lowered metabolic rates (to say nothing of what they can do to your health).

(4) *Try to Keep Cool.* Here's a fact you may not know: most people use from 70 to 80 percent of the calories they consume in maintaining a constant body temperature. This figure can be increased by a cool external environment. (That's why many people report increased appetite in the winter.) Lower-

ing the thermostat in your home or apartment slightly or spending more time outdoors when it is cool can help tip the balance toward weight reduction rather than gain.

(5) *Make Exercise Part of Your Daily Life.* This last point is so obvious, we'll simply mention it in passing. Almost any type of exercise (walking, dancing, running, cycling, swimming) will increase your use of calories and may also raise your overall metabolic rate. When coupled with some of the other steps listed above, these effects can contribute substantially to reaching and maintaining your optimum weight.

Human Sexuality: The Most Intimate Motive

Are people in Western societies more preoccupied with food or with sex? A stroll through the streets of any major city suggests that this is something of a toss-up. Signs and ads relating to both motives are present just about everywhere, although establishments concentrating on one or the other may be located in somewhat different districts. And, as we noted in Chapter 4, most people report that thoughts and fantasies relating to sex are a frequent part of their daily lives (Lynn & Rhue, 1986). Since we're sure that you need no further convincing of the importance of sexual motivation, we'll turn at once to several of its key aspects.

Hormones and Sexual Behavior: Activation and Differentiation

As we noted in Chapter 8, puberty is marked by a tremendous increase in the activity of the sex glands or *gonads*—ovaries in women and testes in men. The hormones they produce (*estrogen* and *testosterone,* respectively) have many effects upon the body. The key question for purposes of this discussion, though, is this: do they influence sexual motivation? In most organisms other than human beings, the answer seems to be "yes." These hormones exert what are usually termed *activational effects;* in their absence, sexual behavior does not occur or occurs with a very low frequency (Geen et al., 1984). For example, removal of the ovaries (and the hormones they secrete) totally eliminates female sexual receptivity in many animals. Removal of the testes in males produces similar but somewhat less clear-cut results. Thus, for many species hormones play a key role in sexual motivation.

Human beings, though, are definitely the exception to this general pattern. Many women continue to engage in and enjoy sexual behavior after *menopause,* when the hormonal output of their ovaries drops sharply. Further, most do not report large changes in sexual desire over the course of their monthly cycle, despite major shifts in the concentration of various sexual hormones circulating in their blood. Thus, for humans hormones do not appear to be related to sexual drive or behavior in a simple or straightforward manner. This is not to say that they play no role, however. Some women do report peaks of sexual arousal in the middle of their cycle and again prior to menstruation (Udry & Morris, 1968). Among men there is some evidence that testosterone levels are associated with differences in sexual arousal. For example, in one intriguing study Lange and his colleagues (1980) measured the speed with which men became sexually aroused (experienced penile erections) while watching erotic videotapes. They found that men with high levels of testosterone in their blood became aroused more quickly than men with low levels. Of course, this in no ways implies that men in the former group have stronger motivation or that they engage in sexual behavior more frequently or more vigorously than those in the latter group. These findings merely suggest that testosterone may be related to certain aspects of sexual motivation.

In addition to affecting adult sexual behavior, hormones produced by the gonads play another important role: they exert apparently irreversible effects upon the developing fetus. Recall that in humans the gonads begin to function by the seventh or eighth week of life; thus, the substances they produce are present early in life. Such *organizational effects* are quite varied in scope. First, these hormones affect the development of the genitals, so that males and females develop structures appropriate to their gender. Second, they seem to affect development of the brain in subtle but important ways. The differences produced, in turn, seem to predispose males toward male patterns of sexual behavior and females toward female patterns (Carlson, 1986).

Perhaps the impact of sex hormones on the development and future behavior of the fetus is most dramatically illustrated by the **androgen insensitivity syndrome** (Money & Schwartz, 1978). In some individuals, a genetic defect prevents the cells of a genetic male from responding to *androgen* (a hormone found in both sexes but which is more abundant in males). As a result, they are born with what appear to be female sexual organs. Since they lack a fully formed female reproductive tract, they cannot become pregnant, but if such individuals are raised as girls, they develop in a seemingly normal manner. Indeed, most marry and report an average level of sexual motivation. If, instead, attempts are made to raise them as boys (their "true" genetic sex), serious problems can result. Administering testosterone to such persons when they reach puberty prevents the development of breasts, but it does not prevent them from remaining quite feminine in other ways (e.g., their voices stay high, they do not grow beards).

Opposite effects occur in a disorder known as the **adrenogenital syndrome.** Here, because of the presence of too much androgen, genetic females are born with what appear to be male reproductive organs. Many such persons undergo surgery shortly after birth to produce a more normal female appearance. When they reach puberty, they may also require injections of estrogen to counteract tendencies toward masculinization. (Their sex glands begin producing increased amounts of male hormone at this time.) Interestingly, although such individuals are raised as females, they show some behavioral characteristics of males. For example, they are often described as being tomboyish, and they often prefer wearing slacks to dresses. However, there is no indication that they are more likely to become homosexual than other persons (Money & Matthews, 1982). These findings call attention to an important point: although hormones affect the developing human fetus, social factors after birth are also extremely important. In sum, where human beings are concerned, hormones are only part of the total picture—perhaps a relatively small part—with respect to sexual behavior.

Human Sexual Behavior: Some Basic Facts

Until the 1960s the only source of scientific information about human sexual behavior was that provided by surveys. The most famous of these were the carefully conducted *Kinsey reports,* published in the 1940s and 1950s. These surveys, which were based on interviews with more than ten thousand women and men, yielded many surprising facts. Although they were conducted decades ago, most men and nearly half of the women reported having engaged in premarital sex (Kinsey, Pomeroy, & Martin, 1948; Kinsey et al., 1953). Further, they indicated that many couples engaged in practices which were considered at the time to be objectionable by society (e.g., oral sex, a wide variety of sexual positions). If there is one basic theme in the Kinsey data, though, it is this: where sexual behavior is concerned, individual variation is enormous. Thus, while some people reported remaining celibate for many years, others reported having engaged in sexual relations with a large number of partners. And while some reported that orgasms were a rarity, a few indicated that they typically experienced them several times each day.

Of course, the type of data reported by Kinsey and other researchers is always open to question. First, there is the question of who agrees to participate. Are such persons younger, less inhibited, and better educated than the persons who refuse? Some evidence suggests that they are (Hyde, 1986). Second, do people report their experiences accurately, or do they describe the types and frequency of sexual behavior they think will put them in a favorable light? This is harder to assess but the latter certainly seems possible.

Starting in the 1960s, another source of information about human sexual behavior became available: direct and systematic observation of actual sexual activities. The first and still the most famous project of this kind was conducted by Masters and Johnson in the mid-1960s (Masters & Johnson, 1966). These researchers observed, filmed, and monitored the reactions of several hundred volunteers of both sexes as they engaged in sexual intercourse or self-stimulation. All together, more than ten thousand cycles of sexual

Human Sexual Response: An Overview

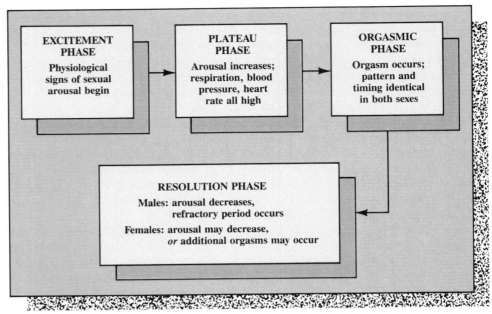

FIGURE 9-14. Human beings seem to move through four distinct stages during sexual relations: (1) the excitement phase, (2) the plateau phase, (3) the orgasm phase, and (4) the resolution phase. Note that males and females differ appreciably only in the last of these phases. (*Source: Based on data from Masters & Johnson, 1966.*)

arousal and satisfaction were studied. The results yielded important new insights into the nature of human sexuality. Perhaps the clearest finding was the fact that both males and females move through four distinct phases during sexual behavior (refer to Figure 9-14).

First, in response to a wide range of sexual stimuli, they enter the *excitement phase*. During this phase many physiological changes occur, such as enlargement of the penis and clitoris, vaginal lubrication, and nipple erection.

If sexual stimulation persists, members of both sexes enter the *plateau phase*. The penis increases in circumference, and the outer third of the vagina becomes engorged with blood, reducing its diameter. Some persons experience a light rash on their chests or thighs, and muscle tension, respiration, heart rate, and blood pressure all rise to high levels.

After a variable period of direct stimulation, both males and females approach the *orgasmic phase*. This consists of several contractions of the muscles of the genitals, along with intense sensations of pleasure. Interestingly, the pattern of contractions, and even their timing, is virtually identical in both males and females.

The biggest difference between the two sexes occurs during the final *resolution phase*. Among males, orgasm is followed by a reduction in sexual tension and a drop in respiration, blood pressure, and heart rate. In addition, males enter a *refractory period,* during which they cannot be sexually aroused or experience another orgasm. Among females, two different patterns are possible. First, they, too, may experience reductions in tension and return to an unaroused state. Second, if stimulation continues, they may experience additional orgasms before returning to this state.

The basic pattern we have just described seems to apply to all human beings, in all cultures. However, just about everything else seems to vary from one society to another. Different cultures accept widely different standards about such matters as (1) the age at which sexual behavior should begin, (2) the frequency with which it should occur, (3) physical characteristics considered attractive or ''sexy,'' (4) the particular positions and practices that are acceptable, (5) the proper time and setting for sexual relations, (6) which persons are appropriate partners, (7) how many marriage partners individuals should have at one time (see Figure 9-15). So, we repeat, where human sexuality is concerned, *variability* is definitely the key term.

How Many Marriage Partners
at Once? Different Cultures
Offer Contrasting Answers.

FIGURE 9-15. Different cultures hold sharply contrasting views about how many marriage partners individuals should have at a given time. Some permit multiple mates while others enforce (or at least recommend!) monogamy.

Human Sexual Behavior: What's Arousing and Why?

There can be little doubt that sexual motivation plays an important role in human behavior. Indeed, there is some indication that human beings engage in sexual activities much more frequently than the members of most other species, including primates. But what, precisely, stimulates such arousal? In some respects, human sexuality resembles that of other organisms. First, direct physical contact (e.g., kissing, touching, and other aspects of foreplay) produces such effects. Second, some researchers suggest that human beings, like other organisms, can be sexually stimulated by certain naturally occurring odors (Hassett, 1978). For example, in one study on this topic wives applied one of four perfumes at bedtime each night. One of these perfumes contained *copulins,* vaginal secretions that are presumably exciting to men. Results were mixed: some of the couples (about 20 percent) showed increased sexual activity on the nights when this perfume was worn; the others seemed unaffected. At present, then, we cannot conclude with any certainty that naturally occurring scents play a role in sexual arousal. The existence of a huge and flourishing perfume industry, however, suggests that many people believe in the potential benefits of *artificial* aromas.

One potential source of sexual motivation, however, does seem to set human beings apart from other species: real or imagined erotic stimuli and images. In contrast to other organisms, human beings possess the capacity to generate their own sexual arousal on the basis of erotic fantasies or images. And they respond strongly to a wide range of *erotic materials* containing either visual images or verbal descriptions of sexual behavior.

With respect to self-generated imagery, recent findings indicate that many persons can produce intense sexual arousal, even orgasm, through internally generated sexual images (Money, 1985). Further, many report using sexual thoughts or images to enhance their pleasure during sexual intercourse or masturbation (Sue, 1979) or to speed up or delay the occurrence of orgasms (Davidson & Hoffman, 1986). In these and other ways our impressive cognitive abilities can play a major role in sexual motivation.

Turning to external erotic stimuli, it has been found that virtually every physiological reaction and behavior recorded by Masters and Johnson during actual sexual activity can occur in response to erotic passages, movies, tapes, or slides (Kelley and Byrne, 1983). Of course, all persons do not find all materials of this type equally exciting. Given stimuli they find attractive, though, it appears that most persons can be highly sexually aroused by such materials. Moreover, such arousal seems to affect overt sexual behavior. For example, Bryant (1985) asked a large sample of young men and women whether they had wanted to imitate the actions shown in the first X-rated movie or magazine they had seen, and whether they actually did imitate these actions with a willing partner. As you can see from Figure 9-16, most of the men and almost half of the women reported a desire to imitate these actions. And one-fourth of the men and about 15 percent of the women actually *did* imitate them.

If increases in sexual arousal and sexual behavior were the only effects produced by erotic materials, we could end our discussion of them here. Actually, though, they seem to exert a wide range of additional effects on persons who view them. Since some of these have important implications, we would be remiss if we did not at least mention them here.

One of the most unsettling of these effects is as follows: repeated exposure to X-rated materials seems to produce undesirable shifts in the viewers' attitudes about several aspects of sexual behavior. For one thing, such experience leads individuals to overestimate the frequency of several unusual and widely disapproved sexual practices (e.g., sadomasochism, human-animal sexual contact; Zillmann & Bryant, 1984). It may also cause some persons to view actions which are generally deemed inappropriate by society (e.g., an adult male seducing a twelve-year-old girl, extramarital affairs) as somewhat less objectionable (Bryant, 1985). We should hasten to add that such effects seem to occur only after exposure to a large number of X-rated films. Still, their existence suggests that viewing such materials can produce important changes in the way many people think about, and evaluate, sexual behavior.

In addition, it appears that exposure to explicit sexual materials, especially to films containing scenes of *sexual violence* (e.g., rape and other types of sexual assaults), can weaken the restraints of at least some males against aggression toward females (Malamuth, 1984). Moreover, such materials may also stimulate sexually aggressive fantasies in some viewers, and so perhaps increase their willingness to use force in sexual encounters (Malamuth, Check, & Briere, 1986). Clearly, such effects are disturbing, to say the least.

In sum, our ability to become aroused by external erotic stimuli or by our self-generated erotic fantasies seems to be something of a mixed blessing. It can enhance sexual arousal and pleasure in some cases, but it may also lead to callous sexual attitudes

FIGURE 9-16. Most men and many women report that they wanted to imitate the activities shown in the first X-rated film or magazine they saw. In addition, sizable proportions of both sexes report that they actually *did* imitate these behaviors. *(Source: Based on data reported by Bryant, 1985.)*

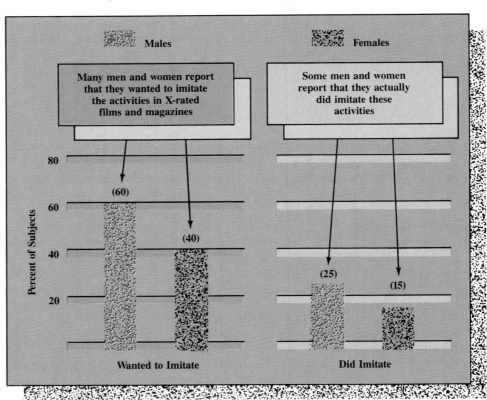

Effects of Erotic Materials on Sexual Intentions and Sexual Behavior

and perhaps to unacceptable sexual practices as well. Whether the latter risks are justified by the former benefits, of course, is largely a matter of personal values.

Sexual Orientation: An Unsolved Mystery

Estimates vary, but it appears that approximately 4 percent of all males and 2 or 3 percent of all females are exclusively *homosexual*—they engage in sexual relations only with members of their own sex. In addition, many other persons (perhaps another 2 or 3 percent of each sex) are *bisexual*—they seek out and enjoy sexual contact with members of both sexes. What factors are responsible for these departures from the majority pattern, which is exclusively *heterosexual*? Decades of research on this issue have failed to yield any clear-cut answers (Geen et al., 1984). In fact, all of the most obvious possibilities appear to be false. Male homosexuals do *not* have lower levels of male sex hormones (androgens) than other persons. Moreover, exposing them to injections of such hormones (testosterone) does *not* reduce their homosexual tendencies—if anything, these may be increased (Money, 1980). Similarly, careful study of the family background of homosexuals and heterosexuals has failed to yield any reliable differences between them (Hammersmith, 1982). Homosexuals do *not* have different kinds of relationships with their parents or different sexual experiences during childhood.

Evidence concerning yet another possible explanation for differences in sexual preference—one relating to prenatal hormones—is still inconclusive. According to this view, homosexual preferences stem from the fact that during the prenatal period male sexual hormones exert too little effect on some male fetuses and too much impact on some female fetuses. The result: their brains are not sufficiently "masculinized" or "feminized," and they develop homosexual preferences as adults (Dorner, 1976). Definitive evidence for such differences does not exist, so this remains an intriguing but as yet unverified possibility.

Finally, it has also been suggested that homosexual preferences may stem from experiences during puberty (Storms, 1981). According to this view, some individuals learn to associate their emerging sexual impulses with members of their own sex and so develop homosexual preferences. What might determine the nature of these associations? Perhaps the relative availability of members of each sex is the answer. For example, individuals attending schools that segregate the two sexes may be more likely to develop homosexual preferences than those attending schools containing both sexes. Is this view correct? At present no strong evidence for such effects exists. Moreover, many persons who are homosexual report that they had homosexual fantasies and thoughts long before puberty. Thus, this theory, too, is only food for thought and should not be viewed as proven.

In sum, the origins of homosexuality—for that matter, of *all* sexual preferences—remain something of a mystery even today. Some persons prefer partners of their own sex, but we don't yet know why this is so. What we do know, though, is this: once established, such preferences are not readily changed. Hence, efforts by family, friends, and others to "reform" homosexuals (to change their sexual preferences) are usually unlikely to succeed.

Achievement, Power, and Affiliation: Some Uniquely Human Motives

Consider the following incidents:

An artist, unhappy with the way in which a painting has turned out, destroys it rather than sell something that doesn't meet her standards.

An individual refuses to accept a transfer to a better job in his company because it will mean moving to another state and leaving many of his family and close friends behind.

A young woman gives up her high-paying law practice to run for public office, even though she has no real interest in the issues of the campaign.

High Achievement Motivation in Action

FIGURE 9-17. As shown here, some people are very high in achievement motivation—in their desire to accomplish difficult tasks and demonstrate excellent performance. (*Source:* The New Yorker.)

How can such actions be explained? Many psychologists would answer: through reference to important human motives. The first example illustrates the **achievement motive**—concern with meeting standards of excellence, "getting ahead," and accomplishing difficult tasks (McClelland, 1961). The second refers to the **affiliation motive**—the desire to maintain close, friendly relations with others (Hill, 1987; McAdams, 1982). The third involves the **power motive**—concern with being in charge, having status and prestige, and bending others to our will (Winter, 1973). Such motives do not derive directly from basic biological factors, as do hunger, thirst, and, to some degree, sexuality. Yet they exert powerful effects upon behavior in many different contexts.

Achievement Motivation: The Quest for Excellence

Everyone gets hungry and thirsty, but as you probably know from your own experience, individuals differ greatly in their desire for achievement. For some persons accomplishing difficult tasks and adhering to standards of excellence are important themes (see Figure 9-17). For others just "getting by" is usually enough. How can differences in this motive be measured? How do they arise? And what are their effects? These are the issues upon which researchers have focused most.

Measuring Achievement Motivation. The same basic method is used for measuring all three of the motives we will consider here (achievement, affiliation, and power). Originally, this consisted of showing individuals a series of ambiguous pictures, such as the one in Figure 9-18, and asking them to make up stories about them. This is known as the **TAT,** or **Thematic Apperception Test.** The content of the stories was then evaluated, by means of carefully developed keys, to yield scores for achievement and other important motives (McClelland, 1975). More recently, however, Winter (1983) has developed a technique for scoring such motives directly from any type of verbal material, without the need for ambiguous pictures or stories about them.

FIGURE 9-18. One method for measuring achievement motivation (and several other human motives) involves use of the *TAT (Thematic Apperception Test).* Individuals are shown ambiguous pictures such as the one shown here and are asked to construct a story about each one. These stories are then scored for the presence of achievement themes and imagery. (*Source: From McClelland et al., 1953.*)

Measuring Achievement Motivation: The TAT

One Family Known for High Achievement Motivation

FIGURE 9-19. Parents who place great emphasis on excellence and who reward success often instill high levels of achievement motivation in their children. The people shown here are all Kennedys—a family famous for its high-achieving members.

The Origins of Achievement Motivation.   Whatever measure is used, individuals are found to differ greatly in achievement motivation. How do such differences arise? Growing evidence suggests that they stem from certain differences in the child-rearing practices used by parents. First, as you might expect, parents who place great emphasis on excellence and competition tend to produce children who are higher in achievement motivation than parents who do not emphasize such factors (refer to Figure 9-19). Second, parents who praise their children for success tend to produce youngsters who are higher in achievement motivation than ones who are indifferent to such outcomes (Teevan & McGhee, 1972). Third, parents who encourage their children to take credit for successes (who attribute such outcomes to the child's own effort or abilities) often produce youngsters higher in achievement than parents who do not adopt this practice (Dweck & Elliott, 1983). Finally, parents also serve as models of achievement motivation for their children. Those holding jobs requiring independent action and decision-making often have children who are higher in such motivation than ones holding jobs of a more routine nature (Turner, 1970).

The Effects of Achievement Motivation.   Do individuals high and low in achievement motivation differ in other respects or in their life experiences? Existing evidence suggests that they do. First, as you might expect, individuals high in achievement motivation tend to get higher grades in school, earn more rapid promotions, and are more successful in running their own businesses than persons low in such motivation (Andrews, 1967; Raynor, 1970). Second, persons high in achievement motivation tend to prefer situations involving moderate levels of risk or difficulty; in contrast, those low in achievement motivation often prefer situations involving very low or very high levels of risk (Atkinson & Litwin, 1960). Why this difference? Because situations involving moderate risk or difficulty are ones with good chance of success, while also having sufficient challenge to make the effort worthwhile. Such situations are appealing to achievement-oriented people. In contrast, persons low in achievement motivation are more concerned about failure. Thus, they prefer situations in which either they are almost certain to succeed, or failure can be attributed to external causes (after all, the odds were so low, that almost *no one* succeeds). Finally, and perhaps most surprising, persons high in achievement motivation are *not* generally better managers than other persons. This seems to be true for the following reason: often, achievement-oriented people want to do everything themselves (so they can take full credit for success!). This is not an effective strategy in many work settings, where it is crucial to delegate tasks and responsibilities to others.

Sex Differences in Achievement Motivation: Do They Exist?   If you watch old films (ones made in the 1940s or 1950s), you may encounter the following situation: a teenage girl is brighter or more competent at some task than a teenage boy. However, she avoids making this fact known to him for fear that he will be threatened by this information and will, therefore, find her less attractive.

Is there any validity to this plot? In the past it appears there was. Traditional concepts of femininity seemed incompatible with high levels of competence, success, or achievement motivation. Taking note of this fact, Horner (1970, 1972) suggested that many women may actually fear success: they realize that striving for achievement can reduce their femininity in the eyes of others. And in fact, she found evidence for the widespread existence of such concerns (*fear of success*) among young women. More recent studies, though, have yielded a more encouraging pattern. At the present time clear differences between the sexes in this respect, or in overall achievement motivation, seem to be fading. Women still seem to have lower aspirations in some respects (e.g., they anticipate lower starting salaries than men in the same fields; Major & Konar, 1984), but the widespread fear of success reported by Horner seems to have all but disappeared (Terborg, 1977). Presumably, any remaining differences between the sexes with respect to achievement motivation will decrease further as traditional stereotypes of masculinity and femininity continue to shift.

Affiliation and Power Motivation: Two Sides of the Same Coin?

At first glance, the desire to be in charge (power motivation) and the desire to have close relationships with others (affiliation motivation) seem to be unrelated. After all, it's possible to imagine people high on both dimensions (people who want to ''run the show'' but who still like close ties with others), and people who are low on both (individuals who have little interest either in power *or* in friendly relations with others). In fact, however, research on these motives suggests that in several areas of life, they *do* seem to be related or, at least, are perceived as being linked (Mason & Blankenship, 1987; Winter, 1987b).

First, consider the question of managerial success, an issue we mentioned earlier in connection with achievement motivation. What kind of individuals are most successful in this role? One possibility, suggested by McClelland and Boyatzis (1982), is that persons *high* in power motivation and *low* in affiliation motivation might be more effective than others in achieving success as managers. This makes good sense: after all, persons concerned with gaining power will focus on influence and status and may be more successful in ''office politics.'' At the same time, their low concern with close interpersonal relations should permit them to avoid the kind of entangling ties that can prevent people from rising to the top (e.g., unwillingness to move from job to job or company to company). In fact, long-term studies suggest that individuals possessing this combination—known as the **leadership motivation pattern (LMP)**—who are high in power motivation but low in affiliation motivation—do rise to higher-level jobs than those not possessing it (McClelland & Boyatzis, 1982). Whether we'd want them for *our* boss, though, is quite another question.

Second, both motives seem to play a role in the occurrence of abuse in intimate relationships (Mason & Blankenship, 1987). Men high in power motivation report being more physically abusive toward their partners than men low in power motivation. And women high in affiliation motivation and who are experiencing high levels of stress report being more psychologically abusive toward their partners than others.

Finally, both motives may play a role in the escalation of conflicts. The reason for this is as follows: each side may perceive their opponent as higher in power motivation and lower in affiliation motivation than they actually are. Such bias may then make it easier for both sides to take a ''tough'' stance and to refrain from making concessions. That such effects actually occur is suggested by the results of an intriguing investigation by Winter (1987a).

In this study, the way newspapers portray candidates they support and candidates they oppose was compared. Two sets of data were used: debates from modern U.S. presidential elections or campaigns (e.g., Kennedy-Nixon debates in 1960; Reagan-Bush debates during the 1980 primaries), and speeches by Abraham Lincoln and Jefferson Davis at the start of the American Civil War. For both sets of data, the quotations and

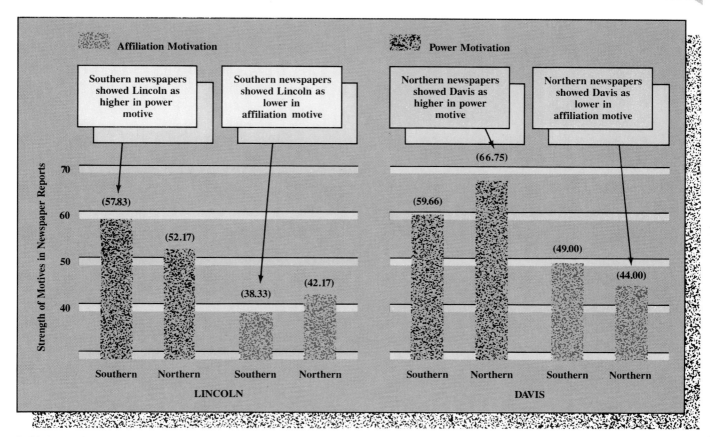

FIGURE 9-20. Northern and Southern newspapers presented different pictures of Abraham Lincoln and Jefferson Davis at the start of the American Civil War. Lincoln was shown as higher in power motivation and lower in affiliation motivation in Southern newspapers than in Northern ones. The opposite pattern was true for Davis. *(Source: Based on data from Winter, 1987a.)*

**Motives of Political Figures:
Distortion in the Mass Media**

paraphrases presented in various newspapers for each candidate were scored for achievement, affiliation, and power motivation. It was predicted that newspapers would quote the candidates in such a way that the apparent power motivation of their own candidates would be minimized, while that of the opponent would be enhanced. Actual power motivation was obtained by scoring copies of the speeches themselves. Results supported this prediction for both historical periods. Thus, as shown in Figure 9-20, Lincoln was portrayed as higher in power motivation in Southern newspapers than in Northern ones, while the reverse was true for Davis. Similarly, Lincoln was shown as having lower affiliation motivation in Southern newspapers, while Davis was portrayed in this manner in Northern ones. Such bias permits each side to a conflict to see itself as wanting only friendship and peace, while the other seeks power, domination, and war. Needless to add, such perceptions can contribute to the occurrence and escalation of many conflicts. (Do the motives of leaders play a role in their popularity and in their success? For evidence on this intriguing issue, see ''The Cutting Edge'' section below.)

FOCUS ON RESEARCH: The Cutting Edge

***Does Having the "Right" Motives
Make a Leader Great (or at Least
Popular)?***

Throughout history some leaders have been tremendously popular with their fol-

lowers, while others have not. And some are now widely viewed as having been ''great,'' while others are labeled as mediocre or worse. What accounts for these differences? Many possibilities exist, but one directly relevant to our discussion of

Achievement, Affiliation, and
Power Motivation of Some
American Presidents

TABLE 9-1

Careful analysis of their inaugural speeches suggests that American presidents have
differed considerably in terms of their achievement, affiliation, and power motivation.
Scores are the number of images relating to each motive per 1,000 words in each
president's inaugural speech. (Not all presidents are listed.)

| President | Scores on Each Motive | | |
	Achievement	Affiliation	Power
George Washington	3.85	3.86	4.62
Thomas Jefferson	5.65	3.30	6.59
Andrew Jackson	4.48	2.69	5.38
Abraham Lincoln	3.34	2.23	6.97
Theodore Roosevelt	8.14	1.02	4.07
Franklin Roosevelt	6.37	2.12	8.50
Harry Truman	6.91	5.99	11.98
Dwight Eisenhower	4.50	4.50	6.14
John Kennedy	5.90	9.59	11.81
Lyndon Johnson	6.77	4.74	6.09
Richard Nixon	8.94	8.00	7.06
Jimmy Carter	10.60	4.89	8.16
Ronald Reagan	7.78	3.28	9.01

(SOURCE: Based on data in Winter, 1987b.)

motivation is as follows: perhaps popular or great leaders are ones whose motives match those of their society. In other words, perhaps the closer the "fit" between a leader's motives and those of his or her followers, the more popular the leader will be and therefore the more able to accomplish major goals. That this may actually be the case is suggested by the results of another ingenious study conducted by Winter (1987b).

In this investigation the inaugural addresses of all thirty-four American presidents were subjected to careful analysis in order to obtain scores on three key motives: achievement, affiliation, and power. (See Table 9-1 for a sample of the findings.) In addition, the level of these motives prevailing in American society at the time of each president's election was also obtained. (This was derived from careful analysis of popular novels, children's readers, and hymns; McClelland, 1975). Obviously, there are many potential complications with respect to such data. For example, modern presidents don't usually write their own speeches. Thus, the content may reflect the motives of members of the president's staff as well as those of the president. Since presidents do choose their staffs and do approve their speeches, though, it

can be argued that the themes present in them still reflect their own underlying motives. In any case, Winter (1987b) was certainly aware of such problems and attempted to collect these data as carefully and systematically as possible.

The motive scores for presidents and for society were then correlated with an index of each president's popularity (e.g., the percent of the popular vote he received) and with ratings of "greatness" provided by more than five hundred historians. Results were revealing. First, as predicted, the closer the match between a president's motives and those of society, the greater his popularity. Second, and more surprisingly, ratings of greatness correlated *negatively* with such congruence. The closer the match between each president's motives and those of society, the lower the rating he received from historians. In sum, it appeared that popularity is indeed a function of leader-society match, while greatness may stem from being different in this respect. (Included among the leaders most discrepant from society at the time were Washington, Lincoln, Truman, and Kennedy.) These findings suggest that there may be some truth to the popular notion that in order to be great, leaders must truly lead and change their society in important ways.

Intrinsic Motivation: How (Sometimes) to Turn Play into Work

Before concluding, we should call your attention to the following fact: there are many activities individuals perform simply because they find them enjoyable. Actions ranging from hobbies through gourmet dining and lovemaking fit under this general heading. All may be described as stemming from **intrinsic motivation:** individuals perform them largely because of the pleasure they yield—*not* because of any hope of external reward. But what happens if such persons are paid for sipping vintage wines or for pursuing their favorite hobby? Some research findings suggest that they may actually experience a *drop* in their intrinsic motivation. In short, they may be less motivated to engage in such activities than they were before. Why? One answer is as follows. Overrewarded persons may conclude that they chose to engage in these activities partly to obtain external rewards. To the extent they do, they may then perceive their own interest as lower than was previously the case. In short, such persons may shift from explaining their behavior in terms of intrinsic motivation (''I engage in this activity simply because I enjoy it'') to explanations in terms of external rewards (''I engage in this activity partly to obtain some external reward''). (See Figure 9-21.)

Many studies support this explanation. In such research, subjects provided with extrinsic rewards for engaging in some task they initially enjoyed later demonstrated less interest in the task than subjects not given such rewards (Deci, 1975; Lepper & Greene, 1978). These results seem to have important implications for parents, teachers, managers, and anyone else seeking to motivate others by means of rewards (the promise of toys or treats, raises, promotions, and bonuses). Presumably, if the target persons already enjoy various activities, offering them rewards for performing them may reduce such intrinsic motivation and may counter any benefits provided. Fortunately, recent research suggests this is not always the case. External rewards *can* be offered or administered without necessarily reducing intrinsic motivation. In particular, if they are offered as a sign of competence or effectiveness, they may have positive rather than negative effects (Rosenfield, Folger, & Adelman, 1980). Further, if such rewards are large and satisfying, they can maintain rather than reduce intrinsic motivation (Fiske & Taylor, 1984). These results permit us to conclude on an optimistic note. While paying people for performing behaviors they enjoy can sometimes reduce their intrinsic motivation—turn play into work—this is not always the case. When delivered with care, and in accordance with the principles outlined here, such rewards can enhance rather than reduce motivation and performance.

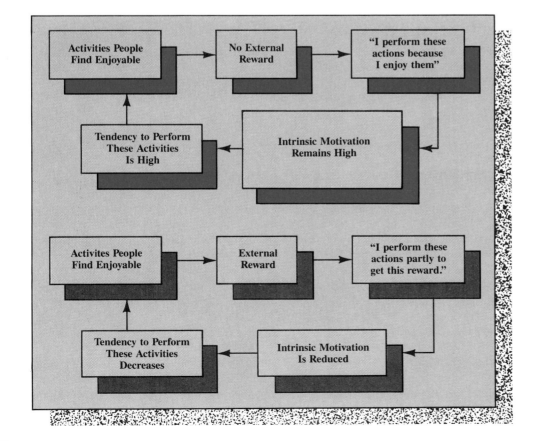

FIGURE 9-21. When individuals receive external rewards for performing activities they enjoy, their *intrinsic motivation* to engage in such behaviors may be reduced. This is because they shift from believing that they perform these activities simply because they enjoy them (top panel) to believing that they perform them partly to gain external rewards (bottom).

Why External Rewards Sometimes Reduce Intrinsic Motivation

Summary and Review

Theories of Motivation

Motivation refers to internal processes that activate, guide, and maintain behavior. *Instinct theory*, which is now rejected by most psychologists, suggests that many actions stem from innate urges or tendencies. It is often circular in nature, because specific forms of behavior are used as evidence for the existence of the instincts from which they supposedly stem. In contrast, *drive theory* contends that many forms of behavior are "pushed" from within by basic needs. Since people often engage in actions that increase rather than reduce various drives, however, this theory, too, seems inadequate. A third perspective on motivation, *expectancy theory,* suggests that behavior is often elicited by the belief that engaging in certain actions will yield desirable outcomes.

Hunger and Thirst

Hunger and *thirst* are regulated by internal mechanisms that detect departures from optimal physiological conditions and initiate actions (eating and drinking) to correct such imbalances. The internal need for water is detected by *baroreceptors* which respond to reductions in blood pressure produced by loss of water from the *extracellular fluid compartment,* and by *osmoreceptors* which respond to the loss of water from cells themselves (the *intracellular fluid compartment*).

Hunger is regulated by many different factors, including cells in the liver and elsewhere which respond to changes in the levels of glucose, proteins, and fats in the blood. Hunger is also affected by *head factors*—the sight, smell, and taste of food. Many factors contribute to *obesity*. Among the most important of these are a learned preference for high-calorie meals, association of eating with various external cues, differences in basal metabolism, and contrasting reactions to stress. Some people suffer from *anorexia nervosa* and eat far less than they need to remain healthy.

Sexual Motivation

In most mammals *sexual motivation* is strongly affected by *sex hormones*. These activate sexual behavior and affect the developing fetus in many ways. Hormones seem to play a smaller role in human sexual behavior, but they do affect development during the prenatal period. In addition, there is some indication that high testosterone levels in males may be associated with more rapid sexual arousal.

Among human beings sexual motivation can be elicited by self-generated fantasies and by a wide range of external erotic stimuli. Exposure to such stimuli produces other effects in addition to such arousal (e.g., it may contribute to "callous" sexual attitudes).

Achievement, Power, and Affiliation

Individuals differ greatly in terms of three important motives: *achievement, affiliation,* and *power*. Persons high in achievement motivation often attain greater levels of success than persons low in such motivation. However, they prefer situations involving moderate risk or difficulty. Females seemed at one time to be lower in achievement motivation than males, perhaps out of fear that success would be incompatible with traditional views of femininity. Such differences appear to have decreased sharply in recent years. Persons high in power motivation but low in affiliation motivation are more successful as managers than others, but may be more likely to abuse their partners in intimate relationships. Newspapers often portray candidates they favor as lower in power motivation and higher in affiliation motivation than candidates they oppose.

When individuals are rewarded for performing actions they enjoy, their *intrinsic motivation* for engaging in these activities may be reduced. However, this does not occur if such rewards are provided for success or competence, or if they are large and satisfying to the persons who receive them.

Key Terms

Achievement Motivation Concern with accomplishing difficult tasks and adhering to standards of excellence.

Adrenogenital Syndrome Occurs when genetic females are exposed to too much androgen during the prenatal period. Such females are born with what appear to be male reproductive organs.

Affiliation Motivation Concern with maintaining warm, friendly relations with others.

Androgen Insensitivity Syndrome Occurs when the cells of genetic males are insensitive to androgen. Such males are born with what appear to be female sexual organs.

Baroreceptors Cells in the heart and certain veins that detect changes in blood pressure produced by the loss of water from the body.

Brown Fat Mechanism A regulatory mechanism within the body that converts calories to heat rather than to permanent fat deposits.

Drive Theory A theory of motivation suggesting that behavior is ''pushed'' from within by drives stemming from basic biological needs.

Expectancy Theory A theory of motivation suggesting that behavior is induced by expectations that certain forms of behavior will yield valued outcomes.

Instinct Theory A theory of motivation suggesting that many forms of behavior stem from innate urges or tendencies.

Intrinsic Motivation The desire to perform certain activities because they are pleasant or rewarding in and of themselves.

Lateral Hypothalamus A portion of the hypothalamus that plays a role in the regulation of eating. It was once believed that this region serves as an eating center, but recent findings cast doubt on this suggestion.

Leadership Motive Pattern (LMP) A pattern consisting of high power motivation coupled with low affiliation motivation. Individuals showing this pattern are more successful as managers than others.

Motivation An inferred internal process that activates, guides, and maintains behavior.

Obesity A condition in which an individual's body weight exceeds optimal levels for his or her age, height, and build.

Osmoreceptors Receptors that detect the loss of liquid from cells of the body.

Power Motivation Concern with being in charge, having high status, and exerting influence over others.

Thematic Apperception Test (TAT) A test designed to measure the strength of several important human motives (achievement, affiliation, power).

Ventromedial Hypothalamus A portion of the hypothalamus that plays a role in the regulation of eating. It was once believed that this region serves as a discrete satiety center, but recent findings cast doubt on this suggestion.

For More Information

Geen, R.G., Beatty, W.W., & Arkin, R.M. (1984). *Human motivation: Physiological, behavioral, and social approaches*. Boston: Allyn and Bacon.

> A broad introduction to many facets of human motivation. The chapters on hunger and thirst, sexual behavior, and achievement motivation expand on coverage in the present chapter. A good place to start if you'd like to know more about any of these topics.

Malamuth, N.M., & Donnerstein, E., eds. (1984). *Pornography and sexual aggression*. New York: Academic Press.

> This book focuses on some of the disturbing effects that may result from repeated exposure to pornographic materials. Evidence concerning shifts in attitudes and changes in actual sexual behavior are summarized.

McClelland, D.C. (1985). *Human motivation*. Glenview, Ill.: Scott-Foresman.

> Prepared by a scientist who has studied various facets of human motivation for almost three decades, this book provides a great deal of fascinating information on topics covered in this chapter (e.g., achievement motivation, power motivation). It is well written and represents one important approach to the study of motivation in a clear and forceful manner.

CHAPTER

10

Emotions: Their Nature, Expression, and Impact

"Oh, oh," Joann Barton thinks to herself as her boss approaches her desk, "here comes even *more* trouble. You'd think that after that outburst this morning he'd quit for awhile. But oh no, not him! Just look at the way he's moving his mouth—that's always a dead give-away. He's ready to blow up again."

But when Dick Arnoff stops in front of her and clears his throat, Joann has a big surprise. "Joann," he begins, obviously very nervous, "I just wanted to . . . I mean, er . . . Look, I'm really sorry about the way I acted this morning. I didn't mean to lose my temper like that . . . I'm, uh . . . real embarrassed about it."

"Oh, that's O.K., Mr. Arnoff," Joann replies in her coolest manner. "You don't have to explain to *me*. After all, *you're* the boss." (And to herself she thinks: "Hmmph! I'm not going to let you off *that* easy, you miserable up-tight so-and-so. Yell at me in front of my friends, will you? We'll see about that!")

But Dick continues even in the face of this rejection. "I guess I deserve that . . . I know I've been tough to get along with lately. Too much pressure, I guess . . . My nerves are all on edge—but that's no reason to take it out on you. I'm really sorry. I've lost my temper three times this week already, and it's only Wednesday. That's not right."

("*Five* times, you creep, can't you count?" Joann thinks. But out loud, she says nothing—just continues to deliver one of her famous icy stares.)

"I guess I'm just too excitable," Dick continues, "always have been. But it seems to be getting worse. Everything's kind of coming apart here at work . . . and I've been having some problems at home, too. . . ."

("You're not kidding," Joann thinks. "I can imagine what having your wife run off with a guy half her age can do to a man!" But then, noticing the loose button on his cuff and the wrinkles on his shirt, Joann experiences a sudden shift in feelings. "Poor guy," she muses, "he really *is* on the thin edge. And after all, he's not such a bad sort, just kind of high-strung, like he says.")

"Honestly, I *do* understand, Mr. Arnoff," she says in a much softer voice. "Let's just forget all about it. Try to stay calm from now on. And smile, why don't you? Believe me, it'll make you feel better. The world's not coming to an end, you know."

And when Dick Arnoff follows her suggestion and forces a smile onto his lips, he finds that he really *does* feel a little better. "Thanks, Joann," he murmurs as he starts back into his office. "I really appreciate your being so understanding. Anyway, I promise to do better from here on—just see if I don't."

Emotions: we all have them, much of the time. Sorrow, joy, anger, excitement, fear, surprise—these are just a few of the subjective feelings we experience at different moments during a single day. But what, precisely, are such reactions? The closer we look, the more complex emotions appear to be, so there is no simple answer to this question. Psychologists generally agree, though, that they involve (1) subjective cognitive states (the personal experiences we label as "joy," "anger," "disgust," and the like); (2) physiological changes within our bodies (e.g., increases in heart rate when we are frightened or excited); and (3) expressive behaviors—outward signs of these internal states (Buck, 1984). (Refer to Figure 10-1.)

Whatever their basic nature, emotions clearly play a key role in our daily lives; indeed, it is hard to imagine life without them. For this and other reasons (e.g., their impact on many behavior disorders) emotions have long been an important topic of study in psychology. In the present chapter we will examine these complex clusters of internal and external reactions more closely. First, we'll describe several theories of emotion—contrasting perspectives on the nature of such reactions. Next, we'll consider the expression of emotions—how their internal components are reflected in external actions that we can recognize in ourselves and others. Third, we will consider the impact of emotions upon other aspects of behavior—how they influence the way we think and the way we act.

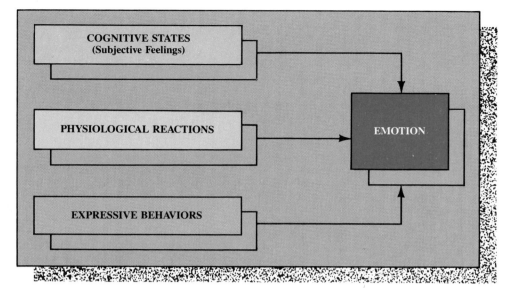

FIGURE 10-1. *Emotions* consist of cognitive states (subjective feelings), physiological reactions, and expressive behaviors.

Emotions: Their Basic Nature

Finally, we'll focus on one particular emotional experience that seems to be all too common in the late twentieth century: stress.

Theories of Emotion: Some Contrasting Views

Many different theories of emotion have been proposed, but three have been most influential in the history of psychology. These are known (after the scientists who proposed them) as the *James-Lange, Cannon-Bard,* and *Schachter-Singer* theories. Perhaps the most important difference among these views involves the relative importance they assign to physiological and cognitive factors in the occurrence of human emotions.

The James-Lange and Cannon-Bard Theories: Physiological Reactions and the Experience of Emotion

Imagine that as part of your new job you must make a brief presentation to a group of top executives. As you walk to the front of the room, your pulse races, your mouth feels dry, and you seem to have trouble breathing. In a word, you are *terrified*. What is the basis for this feeling? Sharply contrasting answers are offered by the **James-Lange** and **Cannon-Bard theories** of emotion.

Because it offers the "common sense" view—one consistent with our everyday experience—let's begin with the Cannon-Bard theory. This framework suggests that exposure to various emotion-provoking stimuli induces both the subjective experiences we label "emotions" and the physiological reactions which accompany them. Thus, in the situation above, the sight of the upturned expectant faces of the audience causes you to experience fear *and* a racing heart, dry mouth, and so on. In contrast, the James-Lange theory offers a more surprising view. It suggests that subjective emotional experiences are actually the *result* of various changes within our bodies. In other words, you feel frightened when making your speech *because* you notice that your heart is racing, your mouth is dry, and so on. As James himself put it (1890, p. 1066): "We feel sorry because we cry, angry because we strike, and afraid because we tremble." (Please refer to Figure 10-2 on page 306 for a summary of these two contrasting theories of emotion.)

Which of these theories is correct? Do we experience emotional states directly, as a result of exposure to various external stimuli, or indirectly, when we sense the physiological reactions these produce? Until recently, most psychologists believed that the first view (the Cannon-Bard framework) was more useful. This was so because several forms of evidence seemed to argue strongly against the James-Lange approach. For example,

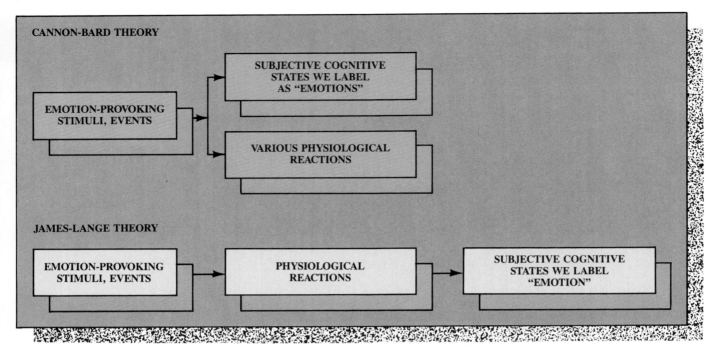

Cannon-Bard and James-Lange Theories of Emotion: A Comparison

FIGURE 10-2. According to the *Cannon-Bard* theory, emotion-provoking stimuli produce the subjective experience we label "emotions" and the physiological reactions which accompany them (upper panel). In contrast, the *James-Lange* theory contends that emotion-provoking stimuli induce physiological reactions, and our subjective emotional experiences *result* from our recognition of these (lower panel).

several experiments demonstrated that destruction of the sympathetic nervous system (which plays a key role in the type of physiological reactions mentioned by James) did *not* eliminate emotional reactions (Cannon, Lewis, & Britton, 1927). Similarly, it appeared that many, if not all, emotional states are accompanied by highly similar patterns of physiological activity. If this is the case, then physiological activities cannot readily serve as the basis for distinct emotional experiences such as anger, fear, joy, or sorrow. More recently, though, the pendulum of scientific opinion has begun to swing the other way. Two forms of evidence have contributed to this shift.

First, it now appears that different emotions *are* associated with different patterns of physiological activity. Not only do anger and sorrow *feel* different, they are reflected in somewhat different patterns of brain activity and in different outward expressions (e.g., contrasting patterns of electrical activity in various facial muscles; Panskepp, 1982). Second, support for at least some aspects of the James-Lange theory of emotion is provided by studies dealing with the **facial feedback hypothesis** (Laird, 1984). According to this proposal, changes in our facial expressions sometimes *produce* changes in our emotional experiences rather than mirror them. In other words, as James would suggest, we feel happier when we smile, sadder when we frown, and so on (refer to Figure 10-3). That this is actually the case is indicated by the results of several experiments (e.g., Zuckerman et al., 1981). In such research subjects were asked either to exaggerate or to suppress facial expressions while viewing emotion-provoking stimuli. Findings revealed that when they did, their emotional reactions to these stimuli were also altered. Exaggeration of facial expressions intensified reported emotions, while suppression of such expressions reduced these reactions. Perhaps even more surprising, such effects seem to occur even when subjects merely attempt to enhance or suppress tension in various facial muscles *without* changing their overt facial expressions.

This has been demonstrated recently by McCanne and Anderson (1987). These researchers asked female subjects to imagine positive and negative events (e.g., "you inherit a million dollars"; "you lose a really close friendship"). While imagining these events, they were told to either enhance or suppress tension in certain facial muscles. (One of these muscles is active when we smile or view happy scenes; the other is active when

FIGURE 10-3. Do changes in our facial expressions affect our emotional experiences? Some evidence suggests that they do. For example, skilled actors and actresses sometimes experience the emotions they portray while playing various roles.

we frown or view unhappy scenes.) Measurements of electrical activity in both muscles indicated that after a few practice trials most subjects could carry out this task successfully: they could enhance or suppress muscle tension when instructed to do so. Moreover, they could do this *without* any visible change in facial expression.

After imagining each scene, subjects rated their emotional experiences in terms of enjoyment or distress. If the facial feedback hypothesis is correct, these ratings should be affected by subjects' efforts to enhance or suppress muscle tension. For example, if subjects enhanced activity in muscles associated with smiling, they would report more enjoyment of the positive events; if they suppressed such activity, they would report less enjoyment. Similarly, if they enhanced tension in muscles associated with frowning, they would report more distress when imagining the unhappy events. Results offered partial support for these predictions. As shown in Figure 10-4 on page 308, subjects *did* report less enjoyment of the positive events when they suppressed activity in the appropriate muscle. In addition, they showed a slight tendency to report less distress to the negative events when they suppressed the muscle involved in frowning. Interestingly, subjects also reported less ability to imagine and experience scenes of both types when suppressing activity in their facial muscles.

These results and those of other studies on the facial feedback hypothesis suggest that there may be a substantial grain of truth in the James-Lange theory. Subjective emotional experiences do often arise directly, in reaction to specific external stimuli, as the Cannon-Bard view suggests. But they can also be affected by changes in (and awareness of) our own bodily state. Given current recognition of the intimate and subtle connections between conscious experience and physiological reactions, such conclusions are far from startling; indeed, they seem to make eminent good sense.

Schachter and Singer's Two-Factor Theory: Cognition, Arousal, and Emotion

Strong emotions are a common part of daily life, but how do we tell them apart? In short, how do we know if we are angry or frightened, sad or in love? The obvious answer is:

Tension in Facial Muscles and Experienced Emotions

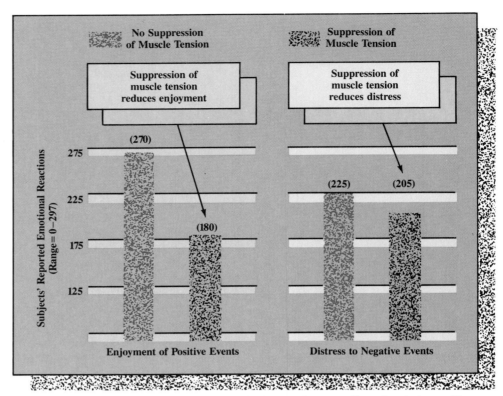

FIGURE 10-4. When subjects suppressed tension in muscles normally active during smiling, they reported less enjoyment of positive events they imagined. Similarly, if they suppressed tension in muscles active during frowning, they reported less distress to negative events they imagined. These findings offer support for the *facial feedback hypothesis*. (*Source: Based on data from McCanne & Anderson, 1987.*)

''we just know.'' By turning our attention inward and examining our internal state, we determine what particular emotion we are experiencing at a given moment. Is this actually the case? As we noted earlier, many strong emotions are associated with similar patterns of physiological reactions. Thus, this task may be somewhat more difficult than at first appears. For example, consider the following situation: while crossing a swaying suspension bridge high above a rocky gorge, you meet an attractive stranger. You realize that you are feeling excited, but why? Are you physically attracted to this person or just plain scared? As you can see, the task of separating these emotions might be far from simple.

Partly on the basis of such observations, Schachter and Singer (1962) proposed a third view of emotion that remains influential today. According to the **Schachter-Singer theory,** emotion-provoking events produce internal arousal. Sensing this excitement, we focus our attention on the external environment in order to discover the basis for its presence. The stimuli we then observe lead us to select a label for our arousal. And this, in turn, determines the precise emotion we experience. For example, if we feel aroused after a near-miss in traffic, we label our reaction ''fear.'' In contrast, if we experience a similar level of arousal after receiving an insult, we describe it as ''anger.'' The theory is described as a two-factor view because it considers both arousal and the cognitive processes through which such feelings are identified and labeled. (Refer to Figure 10-5 for a summary of these suggestions.)

Evidence for the accuracy of this intriguing theory has been obtained in many different studies. For example, in a famous experiment by Schachter and Singer (1962) subjects were given injections of a drug that increased their arousal (epinephrine). Then they were exposed to the actions of another person (an accomplice) who either behaved in a euphoric manner (he told jokes, shot papers at a wastebasket) or he demonstrated extreme anger while filling out a questionnaire. (His anger was understandable, for the questionnaire contained items such as, ''With how many men other than your father has your mother had extramarital relationships?'') Within each of these groups, some of the

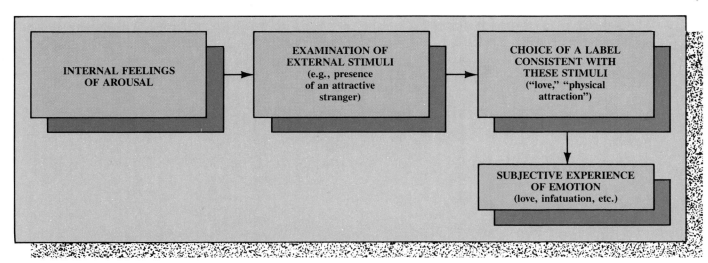

FIGURE 10-5. According to a *two-factor* theory proposed by Schachter and Singer (1962), we interpret internal arousal in a manner consistent with external cues. These labels, in turn, then determine the emotions we experience.

Cognitive Labels and the Experience of Emotion

subjects were provided with accurate information about the effects of the drug (they were told it would raise their heart rate); others were not given such information. Schachter and Singer predicted that because they had a ready explanation for their arousal, subjects given accurate information about the impact of the drug would *not* be affected by the accomplice's behavior. In contrast, those not provided with such information would use his actions as a basis for interpreting their own feelings. This was precisely what happened: subjects not informed about the effects of the drug reported feeling happier when they saw the accomplice behave euphorically and angrier when they saw him demonstrate signs of irritation than informed subjects did.

Other evidence, too, supports Schachter and Singer's theory. Remember the swaying suspension bridge? Dutton and Aron (1974) actually performed a study in which male hikers met a female accomplice in just this setting. Those who did so later indicated more sexual attraction to her and were more likely to call her for a date than subjects who met the same accomplice on solid ground. Again, subjects interpreted their internal arousal in terms of external cues. At this point, we should note that not all evidence is consistent with the two-factor theory. For example, individuals tend to label unexplained arousal negatively, as nervousness, even in the presence of cues suggesting that it is positive (Marshall & Zimbardo, 1979). Thus, there seem to be limits to the impact of cognitive labels on emotional states. In many cases, though, our subjective experiences *do* seem to derive from a complex interplay between physiological and cognitive factors. In other words, we don't know what emotion we are feeling until we name it and find a plausible explanation for its presence in the world around us. (Do individuals differ in the intensity of their emotions? For information on this intriguing question, please see "The Cutting Edge" section below.)

FOCUS ON RESEARCH: The Cutting Edge

Affect Intensity: Individual Differences in the Strength of Emotional Reactions

Do you know anyone you would describe as a "human volcano"—someone who reacts with powerful emotions to a wide range of events or situations? Similarly, do you know anyone you could describe as a placid "human lake"—an individual who reacts mildly even to strong emotion-provoking events? If so, you are already familiar with an important fact about emotions: individuals differ greatly in the intensity of their reactions (Larsen & Diener, 1987). Such differences in **affect**

Affect Intensity and Reactions to Live Events

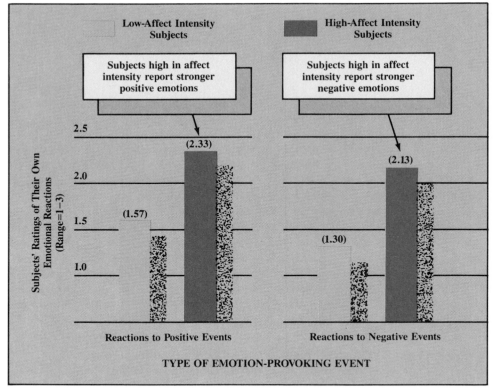

FIGURE 10-6. Individuals scoring high in *affect intensity* report more intense reactions to both positive and negative events than persons scoring low on this dimension. *(Source: Based on data from Larsen, Diener, & Emmons, 1986.)*

intensity have been the subject of growing interest in psychology, and intriguing evidence about their existence and impact now exists. For example, consider a recent study by Larsen, Diener, and Emmons (1986).

These researchers asked undergraduate students to imagine their own emotional reactions to a wide range of events (e.g., "you received a scholarship loan that you desperately needed"; "your bike got a flat"; "you saw your ex-boyfriend or ex-girlfriend with another person"). Subjects rated their reactions to each event on a scale ranging from "ecstatic, euphoric" to "despair, deep depression." In addition, they completed a brief questionnaire designed to measure individual differences in affect intensity (the *Affect Intensity Measure;* Larsen, 1984). When persons scoring high on this scale (those high in affect intensity) and persons scoring low were compared, clear differences emerged. As shown in Figure 10-6, the high-scorers reported more intense reactions to both positive and negative events than the low-scorers. Thus, as expected, persons high in affect intensity do seem to respond more strongly to a wide range of events or situations than do persons low on this dimension.

This is not the only way in which such individuals differ, however. First, as you might expect, persons high in affect intensity also seem to experience large swings of mood more frequently than persons low in affect intensity (Larsen, 1987). Not only are their emotional reactions more intense; they are more variable as well. Moreover, such differences in emotional style appear to be quite stable over time and across situations. College students' self-reports of their own affect intensity correlate positively with their parents' ratings of their emotional intensity as children. In other words, the more emotional they were as youngsters, the stronger their emotional reactions as adults (Thomas & Chess, 1984). Further, individuals who experience strong emotions in one type of situation (e.g., work settings) experience strong reactions in other situations, too (Diener & Larsen, 1984).

It is also interesting to note that affect intensity decreases with age, dropping most sharply between our young adult years and middle-age. Also, women tend to score higher on this dimension than men (Diener, Sandvik, & Larsen, 1985).

Does the tendency to experience strong emotions carry a high price in terms of psychological or physical health? Findings on this issue are somewhat mixed. On the one hand, persons high in affect intensity report a higher incidence of such symptoms as headaches, irritability, and nervousness (Larsen & Diener, 1987). On the other, they do not differ from persons low in this dimension in terms of their subjective well-being or happiness. Taken as a whole, such findings suggest that individuals high in affect intensity may in fact experience greater wear-and-tear on their bodies or nervous system than other persons, but they enjoy the stimulating, active lives they lead. In this sense, at least, they have no regrets.

In sum, large individual differences in emotional intensity seem to exist and are related to many other aspects of our psychological functioning. The pattern is complex, however, and it is not yet clear whether being high on this dimension should be viewed as a plus or as a minus where personal health and well-being are concerned.

Expression of Emotion: Expressions, Gazes, and Gestures

Emotions are a private affair. In an ultimate sense, no one, no matter how intimate, can share our subjective experiences. Yet we do recognize the presence of various emotions in others, and we manage to communicate our own feelings to them as well. How does such communication occur? A large part of the answer involves the transmission of **nonverbal cues:** external and observable signs of internal emotional states (Kleinke, 1986b).

Nonverbal Cues: The Basic Channels

How do you know that another person is angry, sad, happy, or frightened? And how do other persons recognize such emotional states in *you?* Several decades of research suggest that the answers involve information transmitted by facial expressions, eye contact and gazing, and a wide range of body movements.

Facial Expressions as Guides to the Emotions of Others.   Nearly 2,000 years ago the Roman orator Cicero stated: ''The face is the image of the soul.'' By this comment he meant that feelings and emotions are often exhibited on the face in the form of specific expressions. Systematic research indicates that Cicero was correct: facial expressions do indeed reveal much about emotional states (Buck, 1984). In fact, it appears that such expressions are something of a universal language. People all over the world demonstrate very similar facial expressions when experiencing such basic emotions as happiness, surprise, sadness, fear, anger, or disgust (Ekman & Friesen, 1975; Izard, 1977). (Refer to Figure 10-7 on page 312.) Moreover, such expressions are readily recognized, even by people from a very different culture. Thus, if you were to travel to a remote corner of the world, you would probably be able to interpret quite accurately the facial expressions shown by the people you'd meet there.

The importance of facial expressions in human communication, especially in the expression of emotions, is also indicated by another fact: they arise very early in life. As we noted in Chapter 8, infants only a few hours old seem to show distinct facial expressions when given small tastes of sweet, sour, and bitter substances (Granchrow, Steiner, & Daher, 1983). Other evidence for the early development of facial expressions has been gathered by Izard and his colleagues (Izard et al., 1980). They exposed infants one month to nine months old to various emotion-provoking situations (e.g., separation from their mothers, medical inoculations). The facial expressions shown by the infants were then videotaped and studied in a systematic manner. Results pointed to an intriguing conclusion: infants as young as one or two months could demonstrate discrete facial expressions for such emotions as interest, disgust, and distress. And a few months later, they could demonstrate clear facial signs of joy, sadness, anger, and surprise (refer to Figure 10-8 on page 312). Perhaps even more intriguing, differences in infants' facial expressions seem to be related to their later development and even to their budding personalities. For

Facial Expressions: A Language
Needing No Interpreter

FIGURE 10-7. Can you recognize the emotions shown in these photos? In all probability you can. Human beings from all cultures seem to show similar facial expressions when experiencing basic emotions such as happiness, anger, or sorrow.

example, the amount of anger infants show when two to seven months old predicts the amount of anger they will show in similar situations at later times.

Interestingly, infants are also able to recognize facial expressions in others at young age (Nelson, 1987). In one study on this issue, Kuchïk, Vibert, and Bornstein (1986) showed three-month-old infants photos of a woman demonstrating a neutral expression, as well as five other photos in which she demonstrated increasingly intense expressions of happiness. The infants preferred to look at the happy faces, and showed increasing preferences for the happier expressions. Similarly, in related research Nelson

Infant Facial Expressions: Early
Emotional Reactions

FIGURE 10-8. By the time they are a few months old, human infants show clear facial expressions reflecting joy, sadness, anger, and surprise. *(Source: Courtesy of Dr. Carroll Izard.)*

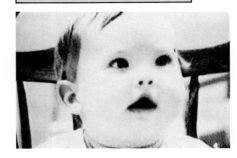

and Ludemann (1987) found that infants only three months old could distinguish between two degrees of fearfulness on the faces of adult models.

Together, such findings indicate that infants can recognize facial expressions within a few months after birth. But please note: this does not imply that they necessarily understand the *meaning* of such expressions (Nelson, 1987). Indeed, other research suggests that they may not be able to act in an appropriate manner in response to others' facial expressions until they are considerably older—perhaps not until age two (e.g., they may not refrain from some activity when their caregivers show signs of fear or distress).

What specific emotions are reflected in facial expressions? Six seem to be most basic: happiness, sadness, surprise, fear, anger, and disgust (Buck, 1977). But please note: this does not mean that we can demonstrate only six discrete facial expressions. Emotions occur in complex combinations (e.g., anger along with fear, surprise combined with happiness). Moreover, each of these reactions can vary in intensity. Thus, although there seem to be only a few basic themes in facial expressions, the number of variations upon them is almost limitless.

Eye Contact: Gazes and Stares.   Poets often refer to the eyes as "windows to the soul" (Stevenson, 1967) and with good reason: the pattern of others' eye contact with us (the extent to which they meet our gaze or look away) can reveal much about their emotional states (Kleinke, 1986a).

In general, a high level of eye contact is often a sign of positive feelings or attraction. In contrast, if others avoid our gaze and look away, this may suggest that they are experiencing negative feelings (e.g., guilt, shyness) or that they dislike us (Kleinke, Meeker, & LaFong, 1974). There is one important exception to this general rule, however. If another person gazes at us continuously, regardless of what we say or do, they may be said to be *staring*. And such eye contact is often a sign of hostility and anger, or an effort to dominate the situation (Carnevale & Isen, 1986).

In addition, a high level of eye contact can be a sign of confidence. For example, speakers who maintain a high level of such contact with their audience are often viewed as being more sure of themselves and at ease than speakers who look at their audiences infrequently (Kleinke, 1986a).

Finally, the way others look at us often provides a cue to their honesty. While you might guess that persons who are lying (and therefore are experiencing guilt and anxiety) would tend to avert their gaze, the opposite seems to be true: individuals telling lies or otherwise acting in a deceptive manner actually seem to gaze at their intended victims *more* than ones who are being truthful (Riggio & Friedman, 1986). As suggested by the cartoon in Figure 10-9, they may reveal such feelings through their eyes in other ways as well.

Body Language: Gestures and Movements.   Before going on, try this simple demonstration. First, think about some incident that made you angry (the angrier the better). Then, try to remember another incident that made you feel sad (again, the stronger the emotion, the better). Did you change your posture or move your hands, arms, or legs

FIGURE 10-9. As suggested by this cartoon, others' eyes often reveal much about their motives and feelings. *(Source: Universal Press Syndicate, 1986.)*

The Eyes: An Important Guide to Others' Emotions and Motives

Gestures: A Useful Source of Nonverbal Cues

FIGURE 10-10. Can you understand the gestures shown here? Specific body movements such as these often provide useful information about others' emotional reactions.

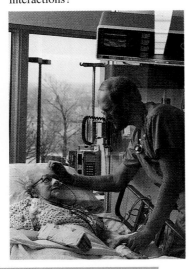

FIGURE 10-11. In certain occupations, a high level of *expressiveness*—demonstrating strong outward signs of emotion—can be beneficial. For example, would you rather be treated by a physician who showed signs of considerable concern for your well-being, or one who remained ''poker-faced'' throughout your interactions?

High Expressiveness: A Definite Plus in Some Fields

as you shifted your thoughts from the first event to the second? The chances are good that you did, for our current mood or emotion is often reflected in the posture, position, and movements of our bodies. Nonverbal cues from such sources are sometimes termed **body language,** and this term seems appropriate, for they often reveal much about private emotional experiences.

First, a high level of body movement (fidgeting, scratching, stroking one's hair) often reflects strong arousal or anxiety (Knapp, 1978). Such behavior is visible during important exams or job interviews: test-takers and applicants sometimes fidget unceasingly. Second, more specific information about others' emotions is provided by **gestures**—body movements conveying specific meanings in a given culture. For example, in many Western countries, holding out a closed hand with the thumb pointing up indicates a positive reaction or approval; the same gesture but with the thumb down signifies a negative reaction. Similarly, pounding one's fist into the other hand is generally a sign of anger. Several other gestures are shown in Figure 10-10; can you recognize their meaning? Remember: different cultures often have different gestures to convey the same meaning, so there's lots of room for confusion when people from different backgrounds meet.

Nonverbal Cues: Who Uses Them Best?

People differ greatly in their verbal skills. Some are eloquent and persuasive, while others find it difficult to express even simple thoughts clearly. Do such differences exist with respect to the unspoken language of nonverbal cues? Growing evidence suggests that they do. Here, we'll consider two factors that seem to play an important role in such differences: personal *expressiveness* and *sex*.

Expressiveness: A Definite Plus in Communicating Emotion. Earlier we noted that individuals differ greatly in the intensity of their emotions (Larsen & Diener, 1987). Given this fact, it seems only reasonable to expect that they will also differ in terms of the outward expression of such feelings. In fact, they do. Some persons—those high in *expressiveness*—show pronounced and clear nonverbal cues in emotion-provoking situations. Those low in expressiveness show fewer and less distinct nonverbal cues (Friedman et al., 1980). Even more important, such differences seem to be related to important outcomes in life. First, they may play a role in success in various occupations. For example, among a group of physicians in a family practice clinic, expressiveness was found to be closely linked to popularity among patients (refer to Figure 10-11). The more expressive each physician was, the more often he or she was chosen by people visiting the clinic (Friedman et al., 1980). Such evidence is far from conclusive, of course, but it does suggest that expressiveness can contribute to success in some occupations.

Second, a high level of nonverbal expressiveness seems to contribute to favorable first impressions. In one recent study, Riggio and Friedman (1986) showed subjects videotapes of other persons explaining an experiment in which they had just participated.

The more expressive these persons were, the more likable they were rated as being. In sum, existing evidence suggests that being high on the dimension of expressiveness may be an important plus in both work and social settings. Thus, this may be one personal characteristic worth developing.

Gender: Females Often Have an Edge.   Have you ever heard the phrase "feminine intuition"? If so, you probably know that it refers to the belief that women possess a special "sixth sense" that allows them to understand situations and events that seem quite mysterious to males. While such ideas sound slightly sexist as we enter the 1990s, they appear to have at least some basis in fact. A wide range of evidence suggests that females are generally superior to males in the use of nonverbal cues. They can both transmit and interpret such unspoken messages more effectively (e.g., May & Henley, 1981). (See Figure 10-12.) Thus, both males and females find the facial expressions of females easier to "read" than those of males. And females are more accurate than males in interpreting several types of nonverbal cues. In other words, they tend to be better at identifying the emotions that underlie such reactions (Rosenthal & DePaulo, 1979).

What factors are responsible for such differences? One possibility involves the operation of **sex-role stereotypes.** In most Western nations traditional views about masculinity and femininity suggest that the two sexes possess different characteristics. Males are assumed to be assertive, dominant, and logical, while females are thought to be expressive, sensitive, and passive. We should hasten to add that these stereotypes greatly exaggerate differences between males and females and may be false in several respects (Eagly & Crowley, 1986). Still, while they persist they may induce many parents to treat their male and female children differently. In particular, girls may be encouraged, to a much greater degree than boys, to pay careful attention to nonverbal cues. To the extent this is the case, it is hardly surprising that females develop a considerable edge in this respect.

Obtaining direct evidence on this explanation of sex differences in the use of nonverbal cues is difficult, to say the least. However, some evidence does support its accuracy. For example, in one intriguing study subjects completed questionnaires designed to assess their degree of masculinity and femininity (Zuckerman et al., 1982). Then their ability to transmit nonverbal cues to others was assessed (for example, they viewed pleasant or unpleasant scenes, and other persons tried to guess which of these they were seeing at a given moment). Results indicated that the higher subjects were on femininity, the better they were at sending nonverbal cues, while the higher they were on masculinity, the worse they were at this task. And, most important of all, this was true *regardless of whether the subjects were females or males.* In other words, the more feminine an individual was, regardless of his or her sex, the better he or she was at this task. These findings suggest that differences between women and men with respect to the use of nonverbal cues are probably not innate. Rather, they seem to stem from existing sex-role stereotypes and the differential child-rearing practices these encourage. Interpreted in this light, the phenomenon of "feminine intuition" certainly loses much of its seeming mystery.

FIGURE 10-12. While the differences may not be as great as this cartoon suggests, a large body of evidence indicates that in general, females are much better than males at both transmitting and interpreting nonverbal cues. *(Source: King Features Syndicate, 1985.)*

HAGAR

Nonverbal Cues: Females Have the Edge

The Impact of Emotion: Where Affect, Behavior, and Cognition Meet

Do emotions influence the way we behave and the way we think? The answer probably seems obvious: of course. If you've ever been paralyzed with fright or unable to concentrate on some task because of feelings of joy (or grief), you've already had first-hand experience with such effects. But, as psychologists have learned in recent years, being aware of their existence is one thing; understanding the precise nature of such effects is quite another (Isen, 1987; Zajonc, 1985). The relationships between emotions and behavior and between emotions and cognition have turned out to be more complex than anyone at first imagined.

Emotion and Behavior: From Helping to Harming

First, let's clarify a basic point. Most of the research concerned with the influence of emotions on behavior (and with the relationship between emotions and cognition) has focused mainly on relatively *mild* feelings. Thus, it has examined the impact of modest shifts in mood (or *affect*) rather than that of intense emotional reactions. We will consider some of the effects of more powerful emotions in a later part of this chapter (in the section dealing with stress) and in Chapters 13 and 14.

Do relatively mild shifts in current mood influence important forms of behavior? More than two decades of research on this topic leave little room for doubt: they do (Eisenberg & Miller, 1987). First, it has been found that positive feelings, induced by a wide range of experiences, increase the tendency of persons experiencing such feelings to offer help to others (Isen, 1987). In other words, the "milk of human kindness" seems to flow more freely when people are in a good mood than in a neutral or bad one. Among the experiences that have been found to produce such effects are finding a dime in a phone booth, thinking about happy past events, and receiving positive feedback on one's work. People even seem to be more helpful on bright sunny days than on cloudy or rainy ones (Cunningham, 1979). These results raise an intriguing question: why does being in a good mood increase our tendency to help others? One possibility is as follows: when we are in a positive emotional state, we don't want to do anything to disrupt such feelings. Since refusing to aid others may induce negative feelings, such as guilt, helping is increased (Manusia, Bauman, & Cialdini, 1985). Not all evidence supports this interpretation, so it should be viewed with some caution. Whatever the precise mechanism, though, it seems clear that even modest shifts in current moods can influence this aspect of our behavior.

Another important context in which affective states (mild emotions) seem to play a role is *negotiation*. Common sense suggests that when bargainers are in a good mood they may be more willing to cooperate in order to reach an acceptable agreement than when they are in a bad mood. This prediction, too, has been confirmed. In a recent study focused on this issue Carnevale and Isen (1986) had subjects play the roles of buyer and seller and bargain over the price of several items (television sets, typewriters, vacuum cleaners). Prior to the session some subjects were exposed to events designed to put them in a good mood (e.g., they rated some funny cartoons), while others were not exposed to these events. Carnevale and Isen (1986) predicted that those whose mood had been improved would engage in more effective bargaining than those in the control group, and as you can see from Figure 10-13, results confirmed this prediction. Subjects placed in a good mood attained higher joint outcomes in the bargaining session and used fewer threats and related tactics than those whose mood was not enhanced.

Finally, we should note that exposure to events or conditions that induce positive affect also seems to reduce anger and overt aggression against others (Baron, 1977; 1983a, b). For example, persons who have previously been angered (e.g., through unprovoked insults) and who are then exposed to various types of humor or mildly erotic stimuli (e.g., alluring photos of attractive members of the opposite sex) report less anger and show lower levels of overt aggression than angry persons who are not exposed to such materials. In sum, it appears that even relatively mild shifts in affective states can influence important forms of behavior.

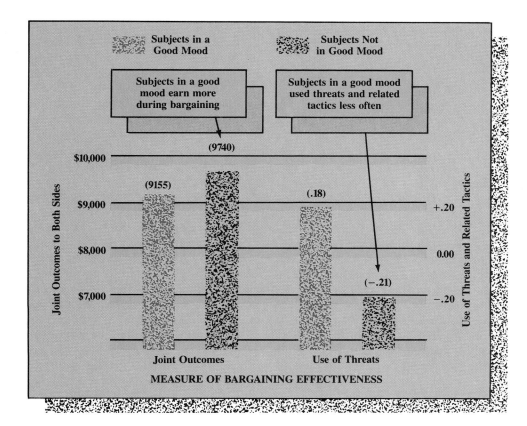

FIGURE 10-13. Individuals put in a good mood by examining funny cartoons bargained more effectively than individuals not placed in a good mood. *(Source: Based on data from Carnevale & Isen, 1986.)*

Emotion and Cognition: How Thought Shapes Feelings and Feelings Shape Thought

You are sitting quietly in your room when, without plan, your thoughts turn to the history exam you took on Tuesday. Although your instructor promised to give the class a multiple-choice test, she showed up that day with one that was entirely essay. As you think about how unfair this was, your pulse quickens, your blood pressure rises, and you experience mounting feelings of anger.

Incidents such as this suggest that cognitive processes—our current thoughts and memories—sometimes exert strong effects upon emotional states. This basic fact is so well established that it is used by clinical psychologists in the treatment of several types of behavior disorder. For example, as we will see in Chapter 14, individuals suffering from various *phobias* (strong, irrational fears) are sometimes asked to imagine the objects or events they fear in vivid detail. When they do, they experience strong emotional arousal. Reductions in such imagination-generated arousal, in turn, may then help eliminate their irrational fears (Stampfl & Levis, 1967).

Cognition can also affect our emotions through the type of labeling process described earlier in the context of the Schachter-Singer theory of emotion. As you may recall, that theory suggests that when we are physically aroused, we search the external environment for cues about the cause of such feelings, and then label our arousal accordingly. The label we choose may then exert strong effects upon our later behavior (Zillmann & Bryant, 1986).

While the effects of cognition on emotion are certainly important, the other side of the coin—the impact of emotion on cognition—has received somewhat more attention from psychologists in recent years. Research on this topic has yielded many interesting results.

First, it has been found that positive and negative affect exert a strong influence upon memory (Isen, 1987). In general, information consistent with our current mood or emotional state is easier to remember than information that is inconsistent with it (Isen,

1987). Moreover, mood seems to exert such effects both at the time of *encoding* (when information is first entered into memory) and at the time of *retrieval* (when it is remembered).

Turning first to effects at the time information is retrieved from memory, several studies indicate that if you are in a positive mood when trying to recall both positive and negative information, you will probably be more successful in remembering the former (e.g., Nasby & Yando, 1982). It is as if your current mood acts like a *retrieval cue* for positive information already stored in memory. (If you've forgotten what retrieval cues are, please refresh your memory by consulting Chapter 6.)

With respect to mood at the time information is first acquired (encoding), it has been found that, again, information consistent with your current emotional state is easier to remember. Thus, if you are in a good mood at the time you acquire both positive and negative information, you will be more likely to remember the positive items at a later time (Isen, 1987). For example, in one study on this process Bower, Gilligan, and Monteiro (1981) used hypnosis to place people in a happy or sad mood. Then, they exposed them to facts about strangers who were described as being happy or sad themselves. Later, subjects were more successful in recalling information consistent with their own mood during encoding; those made to feel happy remembered more about the happy strangers, while those made to feel sad remembered more about the unhappy persons. (Please see Figure 10-14 for a summary of these effects.)

One final point: although both positive and negative moods seem to influence memory, the findings for positive feelings have generally been more consistent (Isen,

FIGURE 10-14. Current mood or affective state plays a role in memory. Information that is consistent with our current mood is easier to encode and easier to remember at later times (upper panel). Similarly, we often find it easier to remember information consistent with our current mood than information inconsistent with it (lower panel).

LIVERPOOL JOHN MOORES UNIVERSITY
Aldham Roberts L.R.C.
TEL. 051 231 3701/3634

Affect and Memory

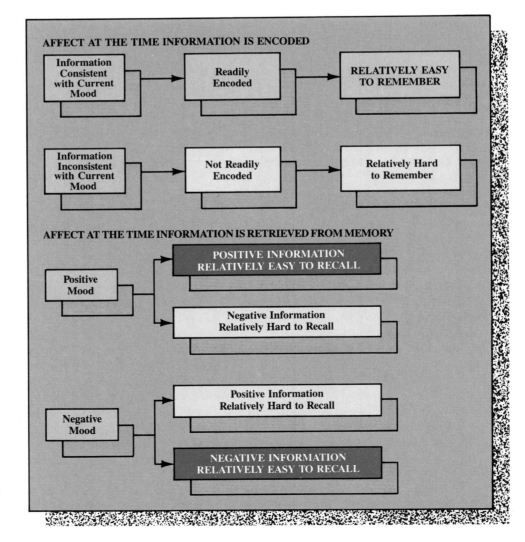

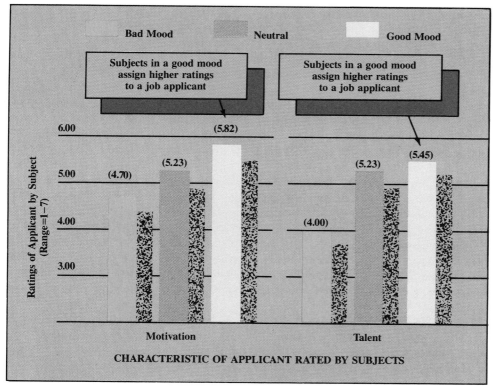

FIGURE 10-15. Interviewers who were in a positive mood rated a job applicant more favorably than interviewers who were in a negative mood. These findings indicate that our emotions often exert important effects upon our cognitive processes. *(Source: Based on data from Baron, 1987.)*

1987). Why is this so? One possibility is that positive material is better integrated or structured in memory than negative information. Thus, current mood can more easily influence its recall. Regardless of whether this is the case, one fact is clear: current emotional states can indeed affect memory in several different respects.

A second way in which emotion affects cognition involves its impact on judgments or decisions (Isen & Shalker, 1982). It appears that when we are in a good mood, we tend to evaluate a wide range of stimuli more favorably than when we are in a bad mood. In short, as one old song suggests, positive affect causes us to see the world through ''rose-colored'' glasses. That such effects can operate in important, practical contexts is indicated by a recent study conducted by the author (Baron, 1987c).

In this experiment subjects first worked on a task (solving some problems), then received feedback indicating that they had done well, average, or poorly. Following these procedures, which were designed to induce positive, neutral, or negative moods, subjects conducted a simulated interview with a stranger. This person was actually an accomplice, specially trained to provide standardized and relatively unrevealing answers to the questions asked by subjects during the interview. After the interview was concluded, subjects rated the accomplice on a number of different dimensions (e.g., motivation, talent, leadership potential). It was expected that those placed in a positive mood would rate this person higher than those placed in a negative mood, and, as shown in Figure 10-15, this was precisely what happened. Interestingly, though, the effects of current mood were stronger among males than females. Why? One possibility, suggested by other research (Baron, 1986), is as follows: perhaps females, who are more skilled in dealing with emotional reactions and emotional expression generally, find it easier to ignore their own feelings when evaluating others in a context where such reactions *should* be ignored (e.g., during a job interview). Further research is needed to determine if this is actually so, but these findings (Baron, 1987c) and those of other researchers point to the following conclusion: our emotional state can often color or distort our judgments even in important, practical contexts. In one sense, at least, it is hard to imagine a more unsettling demonstration of the complex interplay between emotions and cognition.

Stress: Its Causes, Effects, and Control

You have three exams in the next two days, all in important courses. On top of this, you've just learned that your car needs a new transmission. For the icing on the cake, you made a serious mistake at work last night, and had to listen to several minutes of angry, biting criticism from your boss. Now, you feel right at the end of your rope. One more thing, and you'll loose control. . . .

Have you ever felt this way—that you were right on the edge of being overwhelmed by negative events in your life? If so, you are already quite familiar with an especially unsettling type of emotional reaction: **stress.** Unfortunately, stress is a common part of life in the late twentieth century—something few if any of us can avoid. Partly for this reason, and partly because stress seems to exert negative effects upon both physical health and psychological well-being, it has recently become an important topic of research in psychology. We'll now examine the basic nature of stress, some of its major causes, its wide-ranging effects, and tactics for coping with its presence.

Stress: Its Basic Nature

A moment ago we indicated that stress is an emotional reaction. While this is certainly true, it is only part of the total picture. Stress involves several other components as well. First, when exposed to stressful conditions, we generally experience many *physiological reactions*. At first, our bodies become activated, as resources are mobilized to meet threats or dangers (Selye, 1976). If stress is prolonged, however, such reserves may become exhausted, with the result that we can no longer cope with the stress we are facing.

Second, in order to fully understand stress it is necessary to consider the external events or stimuli that induce it—the nature of **stressors.** What is it about these stimuli that induces stress? What do they have in common? While no final answers to such questions currently exist, it appears that many events we find stressful share the following characteristics: (1) they are so intense, in some respect, that they produce a state of *overload*—we can no longer adapt to them; (2) they evoke incompatible tendencies from us (e.g., tendencies both to approach and to avoid some object or activity); and (3) they are uncontrollable—beyond our limits of control.

Finally, and perhaps most important of all, it makes little sense to consider stress without at the same time considering several cognitive factors relating to it. The importance of these is made clear by the following fact: when confronted with the same potentially stress-inducing situation, some persons experience stress while others do not (refer to Figure 10-16). Why? One reason involves individuals' *cognitive appraisals*. In simple terms, stress occurs only to the extent that the persons involved perceive (1) that the situation is somehow threatening to their important goals and (2) that they will be unable to meet (cope with) these dangers or demands (Lazarus & Folkman, 1984; Lazarus et al., 1985). Perhaps a specific example will help clarify the nature of this approach.

Imagine that two teenagers are waiting to take their first driving test. Both want a driver's license very badly, so important goals are definitely at stake. One of the two persons was given lessons, grudgingly, by her older brother. She practiced only on back roads where no other traffic was present, and her brother shouted at her constantly throughout their sessions. The other teenager received her training from an excellent driving school and had lots of practice on busy streets. Her instructor was a real ''pro,'' who stayed calm throughout every lesson. How do the two persons now react to the test situation? The first, realizing that she is on pretty shaky ground, perceives it as an ordeal and fears she will be unable to cope. Her level of stress is probably high. The second is much more confident and perceives the situation more as one in which she will soon have the opportunity to demonstrate her polished driving skills to the examiner. Her level of stress is probably much lower (please see Figure 10-17 for a summary of this situation).

FIGURE 10-16. How much stress would you experience in this situation—moving to a new home. The answer depends, in part, on your *cognitive appraisals* of it—the extent to which you perceive the situation as threatening to your goals and perceive that you will be unable to cope with it.

In short, to understand the nature of stress, it is necessary to consider the emotional and physiological reactions it involves, the external conditions that produce it, and the cognitive processes that play a role in its occurrence (Lazarus et al., 1985). Taking all these factors into account, then, what *is* stress? A useful definition, which would be accepted by many experts on this topic, is that *stress* is a pattern of negative emotional states and physiological reactions occurring in situations where individuals perceive threats to their important goals which they may be unable to meet (Lazarus & Folkman, 1984). In short, stress occurs where individuals feel, rightly or wrongly, that they may soon be overwhelmed (Janis, 1982; McGrath, 1976).

FIGURE 10-17. When confronted with the same potentially stress-inducing situation, two individuals may have very different reactions. This is because they *appraise* the situation in contrasting terms.

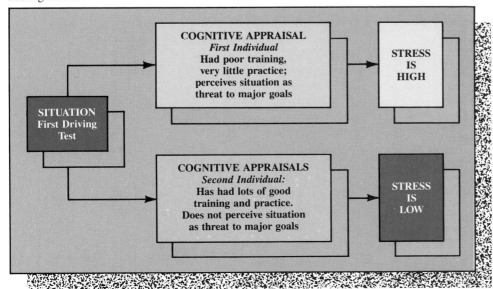

Stress: Some Major Causes

What factors contribute to stress? Unfortunately, the list is a long one. A wide range of conditions and events—many different *stressors*—seem capable of generating such feelings (Maslach, 1982). Among the most important of these are major *stressful life events* (e.g., the death of a loved one, divorce), the all-too-frequent minor *hassles* of everyday life, conditions and events relating to *work* (one's job or career), and certain aspects of the *physical environment*.

Stressful Life Events.   Death of a spouse, divorce, injury to one's child, a stock market crash, failure in school or at work, unwanted pregnancy—unless we lead truly charmed lives, most of us experience such traumatic events and changes at some time or other. What are their effects upon us? This question was first investigated by Holmes and Rahe (1967), who asked large groups of persons to assign arbitrary points (to a maximum of one hundred) to various life events according to how much readjustment each had required. It was reasoned that the greater the number of points assigned to a given event, the more stressful it was for the persons experiencing it.

As you can see from Table 10-1, participants in Holmes and Rahe's study assigned the greatest number of points to such serious events as death of a spouse, divorce, or marital separation. In contrast, they assigned much smaller values to such events as change in residence, vacation, or minor violations of the law (e.g., a parking ticket).

Holmes and Rahe (1967) then related the total number of points accumulated by individuals during a single year to changes in their personal health. When they did so, dramatic results were obtained—ones which did much to stir interest in the effects of stress among psychologists. The greater the number of ''stress points'' people accumulated, the greater was their likelihood of becoming seriously ill. For example, in one study on this topic, Holmes and Masuda (1974) asked patients at a university medical center to report all significant life changes (events) during the past eighteen months. Persons who experienced events totaling three hundred points or more showed a much higher incidence of illness during the next nine months than those with two hundred points or less (49 percent versus 9 percent).

We should hasten to add that this picture is complicated by the existence of large differences in individuals' ability to withstand the impact of stress (Oullette-Kobasa &

▨▨▨▨▨▨ TABLE 10-1 ▨▨▨▨▨▨

When individuals experience stressful life events, such as those near the top of this table, their health often suffers. The greater the number of points for each event, the more stressful it is perceived as being.

Event	Relative Stressfulness
Death of a spouse	100
Divorce	73
Marital separation	65
Jail term	63
Death of close family member	63
Personal injury or illness	53
Marriage	50
Fired from job	47
Retirement	45
Pregnancy	40
Death of close friend	37
Son or daughter leaving home	29
Trouble with in-laws	28
Trouble with boss	23
Change in residence	20
Vacation	13
Christmas	12

(SOURCE: Based on data from Holmes & Masuda, 1974.)

TABLE 10-2

Many everyday events are stressful. The categories shown here are ones in which most people report some degree of being "hassled."

Household Hassles	Preparing meals Shopping
Time Pressure Hassles	Too many things to do Too many responsibilities
Inner Concern Hassles	Being lonely Fear of confrontation
Environmental Hassles	Neighborhood deterioration Noise Crime
Financial Responsibility	Concerns about owing money Financial responsibility for someone who doesn't live with you
Work Hassles	Job dissatisfaction Concerns about job security Problems getting along with fellow workers

(SOURCE: Based on information in Lazarus et al., 1985.)

Puccetti, 1983). While some persons suffer ill effects after exposure to a few mildly stressful events, others remain healthy even after prolonged exposure to high levels of stress; they are described as being *stress-resistant* or *hardy*. We'll return to such differences below. For the moment, we merely wish to emphasize the fact that, in general, the greater the number of stressful life events experienced by an individual, the greater the likelihood that the person's subsequent health will be adversely affected.

The Hassles of Daily Life.   While traumatic life changes such as the one studied by Holmes and Rahe are clearly very stressful, they are relatively rare. Many persons live for years, or even decades, without experiencing any of them. Does this mean that they live out their days in a serene lake of tranquility? Hardly. As you know from your own existence, daily life is filled with countless minor sources of stress that seem to make up for their relatively low intensity by their much higher frequency. That such *daily hassles* are an important cause of stress is suggested by the findings of several studies by Lazarus and his colleagues (Kanner et al., 1981; Lazarus et al., 1985). These researchers have developed a *Hassles Scale* on which individuals indicate the extent to which they have been "hassled" by common events during the past month. As shown in Table 10-2, items included in this scale deal with a wide range of everyday events (e.g., having too many things to do at once, shopping, concerns over money). While such events may seem relatively minor when compared with the life changes studied by Holmes and Rahe (1967), they appear to be quite important. When scores on the Hassles Scale are related to reports of psychological symptoms, strong positive correlations are obtained (Lazarus et al., 1985). In short, the more stress people report as a result of such daily hassles, the poorer their psychological well-being. That such effects may also apply to physical health as well is indicated by a recent study conducted by Weinberger, Hiner, and Tierney (1987).

These researchers asked a group of elderly patients (all suffering from arthritis) to complete a modified version of the Hassles Scale. In addition, the subjects (whose average age was sixty-six, and who were mostly poor and black) reported on their current health by completing a questionnaire designed to assess the effects of their illness (arthritis), plus additional items to measure their general health (e.g., their current level of pain, difficulty in getting around, overall daily health). Finally, the same individuals also reported on major life events (changes) of the type studied by Holmes and Rahe (1967). The study continued for several months, beginning with an initial interview and proceeding with biweekly phone interviews. Thus, a substantial amount of information about the patients' lives and health was gathered.

Results indicated that scores of the Hassles Scale were indeed related to patients' health. The more hassles they reported experiencing, the more severe the effects of their

Daily Hassles, Major Life Events, and Health

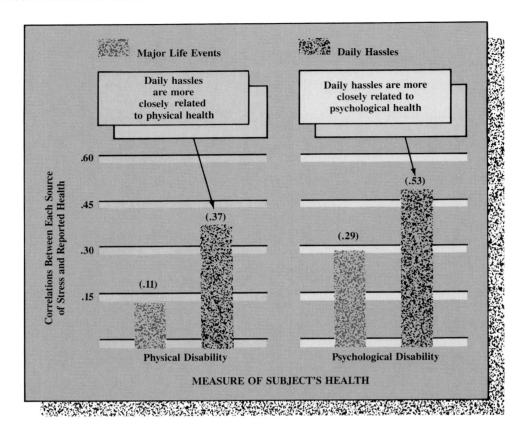

FIGURE 10-18. Among a group of elderly persons suffering from arthritis, scores on the Hassles Scale were more highly correlated with both physical and psychological health than were major life events. These findings suggest that daily hassles are often a more important source of health-related stress than major, traumatic change. *(Source: Based on data from Weinberger, Hiner, & Tierney, 1987.)*

arthritis. Similarly, the more hassles they experienced, the poorer their general health (e.g., the more pain they experienced, the greater their difficulty in getting around). Finally, scores on the Hassles Scale were actually a better predictor of subjects' health during the study than major life events (refer to Figure 10-18). When these results are combined with those of previous studies, the following possibility is suggested. Traumatic life events can indeed exert adverse effects on health. But for many persons, the more minor hassles of daily life—perhaps because of their frequent, repetitive nature—may actually prove even more important in this respect.

Work-Related Stress.   Most adults spend more time at work than in any other single activity. It is not surprising, then, that jobs or careers are an important source of stress (Mitchell & Larson, 1987). Some of the factors producing stress in work settings are obvious, for example, being asked to do too much in too short a period of time (work *overload*). Interestingly, being asked to do too little can also be quite stressful. Such *underload* produces intense feelings of boredom, and these, in turn, can be very stressful.

In contrast, several other factors that play a role in work-related stress may be less apparent. One of these involves *role conflict*—situations in which individuals find themselves the target of conflicting demands or expectations from different groups of people. For example, consider the plight of many first-line managers. Their subordinates often expect such persons to "go to bat" for them with the company, improving their work assignments, pay, and conditions. In contrast, the managers' own bosses often expect them to do the opposite: somehow to induce employees to work harder for fewer rewards. The result: a stressful situation for the managers.

A third factor that can sometimes generate intense levels of stress involves the procedures used for evaluating employees' performance (*performance appraisals*). If these are perceived as fair, stress tends to be low. If they are perceived as arbitrary or unfair, stress is almost certain to be high. After all, no one wants to feel that various rewards (raises, promotions, bonuses) are being distributed in a random manner. Addi-

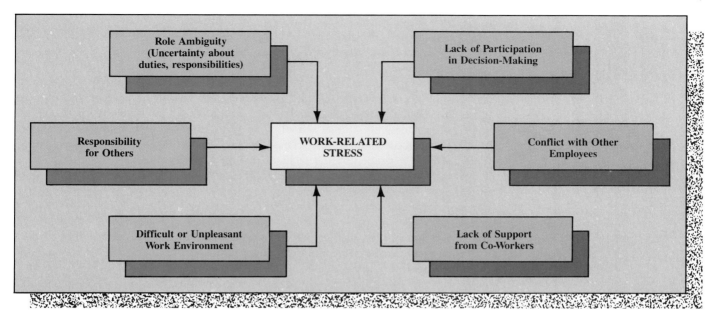

FIGURE 10-19. Many different factors contribute to stress at work. Several of the most important are summarized here.

Sources of Work-Related Stress

tional factors that have been found to contribute to stress at work are summarized in Figure 10-19. Please examine them carefully, for you are certain to encounter several in your own job and career.

Environmental Sources of Stress.   Have you ever seen a tornado? Lived through a hurricane? Experienced an earthquake? If so, you know that such natural events or disasters can be highly stressful. Human-produced events, too, can exert such effects. For example, when the nuclear reactor at Three-Mile Island in Pennsylvania released small amounts of radioactivity into the environment, people living nearby reported much higher levels of stress than ones living far away (Baum, Gatchel, & Schaeffer, 1983). (See Figure 10-20.)

But even far less dramatic aspects of the physical world can serve as important sources of stress. Air pollution, extreme temperatures, and perhaps even shifts in the concentration of negative and positive ions in the air we breathe (Baron, 1987a) can all serve as stressors, contributing to the feeling that we simply can't cope with the conditions around us. The factor that has received most attention in this respect, however, is *noise*. At present, most human beings are regularly exposed to levels of noise our ancestors

FIGURE 10-20.
Human-caused events are often highly stressful. When the nuclear reactor at Three-Mile Island failed, individuals living nearby reported high levels of stress.

Nuclear Accident: One Source of Environmental Stress

would probably have experienced only on rare occasions (e.g., during thunderstorms or volcanic eruptions). Trucks, machinery, jet planes, factories—all contribute to a high level of ambient (background) noise. Does the presence of such ''noise pollution'' produce the kinds of effects usually associated with stress? Growing evidence suggests that it does. For example, in an impressive series of field studies, Cohen and his associates (1986) studied children who attended a school located near a busy airport where a flight passed overhead about every two and a half minutes. Results were disturbing. Compared with children attending a quiet school, such youngsters had higher blood pressure and lower scores on standardized tests. These findings suggest that we may be paying a high price for noise generated by our technological civilization.

Before concluding, we should add that environmental stressors also affect other important forms of behavior. For example, people seem to be less likely to offer help to others in noisy than in quiet environments (Page, 1977). Further, the incidence of violent crime and riots seems to increase with higher temperatures, at least up to a point (Anderson, 1987; Baron & Ransberger, 1978). In sum, while stress produced by various aspects of the physical environment might not seem important, research findings indicate that quite the opposite is true.

Stress: Some Major Effects

By now, we're sure you are convinced that stress stems from many different sources and exerts important effects upon persons who experience it. What you may still not fully grasp, though, is just how powerful and far-reaching these effects can be. As we will now point out, stress can influence our physical and psychological well-being, our performance on many tasks, and even the ultimate course of our careers.

Stress and Health: The Silent Killer.

How strong is the link between stress and personal health? According to medical experts, it is very strong indeed. In fact, some authorities estimate that stress plays some role in anywhere from 50 to 70 percent of all physical illness (Frese, 1985). Moreover, included in these figures are some of the most serious and life-threatening ailments known to medical science. To list just a few, stress has been implicated in the occurrence of heart disease, high blood pressure, hardening of the arteries, ulcers, and even diabetes. How does it produce such effects? The mechanisms involved remain to be determined, but a good first guess goes something like this: by draining our resources and keeping us ''off balance'' physiologically, stress upsets our complex internal chemistry. In particular, it may interfere with efficient operation of our *immune system*—the complex internal mechanism through which our bodies recognize and destroy potentially harmful substances and intruders (e.g., bacteria, viruses, cancer cells).

Foreign substances that enter our bodies are known as *antigens*. When they appear, certain types of white blood cells (*lymphocytes*) begin to multiply. These attack the antigens, often destroying them by engulfing them. Other white blood cells produce *antibodies*, chemical substances which combine with antigens and so neutralize them. When functioning normally, the immune system is nothing short of amazing: each day it removes or destroys many potential threats to our health and well-being. Unfortunately, prolonged exposure to stress seems to disrupt this system. For example, in studies with animals, subjects exposed to inescapable shock demonstrated reduced production of lymphocytes relative to subjects exposed to shocks from which they can escape (Ader & Cohen, 1984). Remember: uncontrollability is one of the features shared by many stressors. Among human beings, persons experiencing high levels of stress (e.g., ones taking examinations, mourning widowers) show similar disruptions in their immune systems (Locke, 1982). Such findings are both unsettling and encouraging. On the one hand, they suggest that our complex, high-stress lifestyles may be undermining our ability to resist many serious forms of illness, at least to a degree. On the other hand, they indicate that reductions in such stress may be of major benefit to our overall health.

We should hasten to add that present evidence linking stress with impairment of the immune system is far from conclusive. More evidence is needed before any definite

cathy   by Cathy Guisewite

Stress and Task Performance:
An Over-Optimistic View

FIGURE 10-21. Contrary to what the character in this cartoon suggests, high levels of stress tend to interfere with task performance. *(Source: Universal Press Syndicate, 1984.)*

conclusions can be reached. Still, given the high stakes involved—health and well-being—this is one area in which many persons may decide to act (take steps to lessen their own exposure to stress) even before a final scientific verdict is reached.

Stress and Task Performance.   Is Cathy correct in Figure 10-21? Does stress improve performance on a wide range of tasks? At one time, many psychologists believed it did. They held that the relationship between stress and task performance takes the form of an upside-down *U*. At first, performance improves as stress increases, presumably because it is arousing or energizing. Beyond some point, though, stress becomes distracting, and performance actually drops.

While this relationship may hold true under some conditions, growing evidence suggests that stress exerts mainly adverse effects on task performance. In other words, performance can be disrupted even by low or moderate levels of stress. Evidence pointing to this conclusion is provided by a study conducted by Motowidlo, Packard, and Manning (1986). These researchers asked a large group of nurses to describe their own levels of work-related stress. Ratings of their actual job performance were then obtained from supervisors or co-workers. Results indicated that the higher the nurses' feelings of stress, the lower their job performance.

These results and those of several other studies indicate that in many real-life settings, performance may be reduced even by low or moderate levels of stress. Why? Shouldn't the activation produced by stress facilitate performance under these conditions? There are several reasons why even moderate levels of stress might interfere with task performance (Steers, 1984). First, even relatively mild stress can be distracting. Individuals experiencing stress may focus on the unpleasant feelings and emotions it involves, rather than on the task at hand. Second, prolonged or repeated exposure to even mild levels of stress may exert harmful effects on health, and this may interfere with effective performance. Finally, a large body of research indicates that as arousal increases, task performance may at first rise, but at some point it falls (Berlyne, 1967). The precise location of this turning or *inflection point* seems to depend, to an important extent, on the complexity of the task performed. The greater the complexity, the lower the levels of arousal at which the downturn in performance occurs. Are the tasks performed by today's working people more complex than those in the past? Many observers believe they are (Mitchell & Larson, 1987). For this reason, even relatively low levels of stress may interfere with performance in today's complex world of work.

Together, these factors help explain why stress may interfere with many types of performance, even when present at fairly moderate levels. We should note, though, that stress does not always produce adverse effects. For example, individuals sometimes *do* seem to "rise to the occasion," and turn in sterling performances at times when stress is intense (refer to Figure 10-22 on page 328). The most reasonable conclusion we can offer, then, goes something like this: in many situations, stress can indeed interfere with task performance. However, its precise effects depend on many different factors (e.g., complexity of the task being performed, personal characteristics of the individuals involved).

Excellent Performance under
High Levels of Stress

FIGURE 10-22. In many situations, high levels of stress interfere with task performance. When performance calls for highly practiced skills, however, stress sometimes appears to be beneficial. (In such cases, of course, it can be argued that stress is not really very high, since the persons involved have considerable confidence in their own ability.)

As a result, generalizations about its impact should be made with considerable caution. (For evidence that stress can also interfere with an especially important type of activity we must all perform—making decisions—please see "The Cutting Edge" section below.)

FOCUS ON RESEARCH: The Cutting Edge

Decision-Making under Stress: Bad Choices, Poor Strategies

Making decisions is one of the most important things we do. And the higher our status or power, the more crucial this process becomes. Unfortunately, as individuals rise to higher positions within a company or government, the level of stress they encounter, too, increases. As a result, many decisions—including ones with far-reaching implications—are made under stressful conditions. Does this affect the decisions that are reached or the

FIGURE 10-23. Individuals exposed to stress (the threat of painful electric shocks) were less effective in making decisions than individuals not exposed to stress. *(Source: Based on data from Keinan, 1987.)*

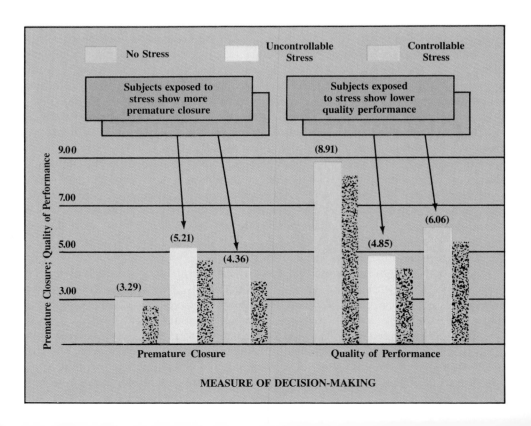

Stress and Decision-Making:
Evidence for Negative Effects

process by which they are formulated? Research by Keinan (1987) indicates that it does.

In a carefully planned study Keinan (1987) asked subjects to respond to a series of fifteen analogies, for example, "butter is to margarine as sugar is to . . ." (choices: beets, saccharine, honey, lemon, candy, chocolate). On each problem subjects could examine any of the six choices by pressing the appropriate key on a computer. The keys could be pressed in any order subjects wished, as often as they desired. After making their decision, subjects indicated their choice by pressing another key. Stress was introduced into the situation by informing two-thirds of the subjects that they might receive painful electric shocks during the session. One-third were told these shocks would be delivered at random and were uncontrollable. The others were told the shocks would occur whenever they made errors (presumably, then, they *were* controllable). Subjects in a third (control) group were never threatened with the shocks. Please note: *no shocks were ever delivered to subjects;* stress was produced merely by mentioning that shocks might occur.

Keinan predicted that subjects exposed to the threat of painful shocks (stress) would perform more poorly than those for whom stress was absent. In order to test this hypothesis, he examined

several key aspects of decision-making: *quality of subjects' performance* (did they choose the right answers?), *premature closure* (did they make decisions before examining all of the possible choices?), and *nonsystematic scanning* (did they examine the choice in a systematic way or in a disorganized manner?). Results were clear: on all three measures, subjects exposed to stress did more poorly (refer to Figure 10-23). The process through which they attempted to reach decisions was ineffective (e.g., they failed to examine all alternatives), and the decisions themselves tended to be wrong.

Surprisingly, the two stress groups (controllable and uncontrollable) did not differ significantly. Why didn't the threat of uncontrollable shocks produce stronger effects than the threat of controllable ones? Keinan offered one suggestion: perhaps subjects in the controllable condition were not confident of their ability to make the right decisions, and so to avoid the shocks. Whatever the reason for this result, the major implications of Keinan's study seem clear: individuals who must make decisions in the presence of high levels of stress should take special care to guard against "shooting from the hip" (making decisions without first carefully considering all of the possible choices). If they don't, the decisions they make may well prove ineffective.

Burnout: When Stress Consumes. Most jobs involve at least a degree of stress. Yet, somehow, the persons performing them manage to cope: they continue to function despite their daily encounters with various stressors. Some individuals, though, are not so lucky. Over time, they seem to be worn down (or out!) by repeated encounters with stress. Such persons are said to be suffering from **burnout,** and they show several distinct characteristics (Maslach, 1982; Pines, Aronson, & Kafry, 1981).

First, victims of burnout often suffer from *physical exhaustion*. They have low energy and always feel tired. In addition, they report many symptoms of physical strain, such as frequent headaches, nausea, poor sleep, and changes in eating habits. Second, they experience *emotional exhaustion*. Depression, feelings of hopelessness, and feelings of being trapped in one's job are all part of the picture. Third, persons suffering from burnout often show *mental or attitudinal exhaustion*. They become cynical about others, hold negative attitudes toward them, and tend to derogate themselves, their jobs, and life in general. To put it simply, they come to view the world around them through dark gray rather than rose-colored glasses. Finally, they often report feelings of *low personal accomplishment* (Maslach & Jackson, 1984). Persons suffering from burnout conclude that they haven't been able to accomplish much in the past, and they feel they probably won't succeed in the future, either. (Please see Figure 10-24 on page 330 for a summary of these components.)

What are the causes of burnout? The primary factor, of course, is prolonged exposure to stress. However, other factors, too, seem to play a role. Job conditions implying that one's efforts are useless, ineffective, or unappreciated seem to contribute to burnout (Jackson, Schwab, & Schuler, 1986). In particular, such conditions contribute to the feelings of low personal accomplishment which are an important part of burnout.

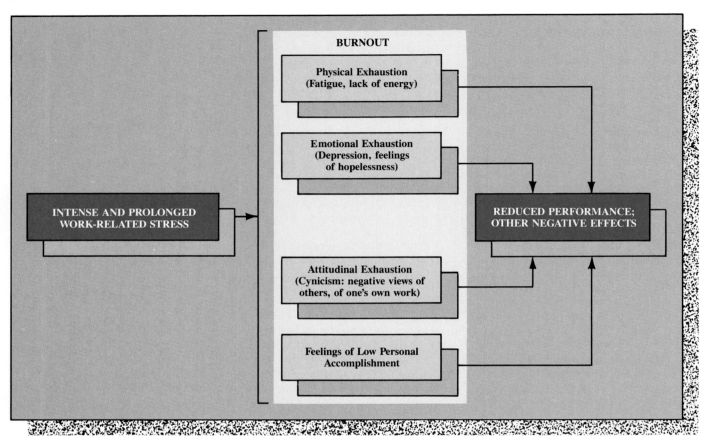

Burnout: An Overview

FIGURE 10-24. When individuals are exposed to high levels of stress for long periods of time, they may suffer from *burnout*. This state involves *physical, mental,* and *attitudinal exhaustion,* as well as feelings of *low personal accomplishment.*

Similarly, poor opportunities for promotion and the presence of inflexible rules and procedures lead individuals to feel that they are trapped in an unfair system and lead them to develop negative views of their jobs (Gaines & Jermier, 1983). Personal factors, too, play a role. People with satisfying lives outside work settings (e.g., happy marriages or love relationships) are less likely to experience burnout than ones without social buffers.

Whatever its precise causes, once burnout develops it has important consequences. First, it may lead individuals to seek a new job or career. In one recent study concerned with the effects of burnout, Jackson, Schwab, and Schuler (1986) asked several hundred teachers to complete a questionnaire designed to measure burnout and to report on the extent to which they would prefer to be in another job or career. As expected, the greater the teachers' degree of burnout, the more likely they were to prefer another job and to be actively considering leaving the field of education.

Second, persons suffering from burnout may seek administrative roles, where they can hide behind huge piles of forms from jobs they have grown to hate. While this pattern certainly occurs, recent evidence indicates it is relatively rare (Jackson, Schwab, & Schuler, 1986). Most victims of burnout seem either to change jobs or to withdraw psychologically and mark time until retirement.

One final question: is burnout a permanent condition, or can its effects be overcome? Fortunately, growing evidence suggests the latter is probably true. With appropriate help, victims of burnout *can* recover from their physical and psychological exhaustion. If ongoing stress is reduced, if individuals gain added support from friends and co-workers, and if they cultivate hobbies and other outside interests, at least some persons can return to positive attitudes and high levels of productivity. Such results are far from automatic, though, and can be gained only through active efforts to overcome burnout and the conditions that produce it.

Individual Differences in Resistance to Stress: Optimism, Pessimism, and Hardiness. Earlier we stated that individuals differ greatly in their resistance to stress. While some suffer ill effects from even mild levels of stress, others are able to function effectively even in the face of intense, ongoing stress. How do such persons differ? One answer involves the familiar dimension of *optimism-pessimism.* (Optimists are people who see the glass as half full; pessimists are ones who see it as half empty.) Recent studies indicate that optimists—persons who have general expectancies for good outcomes (Scheier & Carver, 1985)—seem to be much more stress-resistant than pessimists— persons who have general expectancies for poor outcomes. For example, optimists are much less likely than pessimists to report physical illness and symptoms during highly stressful periods such as final exams (Scheier & Carver, 1988). Additional evidence helps explain why this is the case. Briefly, optimists and pessimists seem to adopt different tactics for coping with stress. Optimists focus on *problem-focused coping*—making and enacting specific plans for dealing with sources of stress. They also seek to obtain *social support*—the advice and help of others. In contrast, pessimists tend to adopt different strategies, such as giving up the goal with which stress is interfering, and denying that the stressful events have occurred (Scheier, Weintraub, & Carver, 1986). Needless to say, the former strategies are often more effective than the latter. (See Table 10-3 for a summary of the different strategies adopted by optimists and pessimists.)

Another characteristic that seems to distinguish stress-resistant people from ones who are more susceptible to its harmful effects is **hardiness** (Kobasa, 1979). Actually, this term refers to a cluster of characteristics, rather than just one. Hardy persons (those who are relatively stress-resistant) seem to differ from others in three respects. First, they show higher levels of *commitment*—deeper involvement in whatever they do and stronger tendencies to perceive such activities as meaningful. Second, they tend to view change as a *challenge*—an opportunity for growth and development—rather than as a threat or a burden. Third, hardy persons have a stronger sense of *control* over events in their lives and over the outcomes they experience.

Together, these characteristics seem to arm hardy persons with high resistance to stress. For example, in one study on this topic, Oullette-Kobasa and Pucetti (1983) asked executives at a large public utility to complete questionnaires designed to measure their level of hardiness, the number of stressful life events they had recently experienced, and their current health. Results indicated that persons classified as high in hardiness did in fact report better health than those low in hardiness, even when they had recently encoun-

---

TABLE 10-3

Optimists and pessimists employ different strategies in coping with stress. Those used by optimists seem to be more effective than those adopted by pessimists.

Strategies Preferred by Optimists	Description
Problem-focused coping	Making specific plans for dealing with the source of stress; implementing such plans
Suppressing competing activities	Refraining from other activities until the problem is solved and stress is reduced
Seeking social support	Obtaining the advice of others; talking the problem over with others

Strategies Preferred by Pessimists	Description
Denial/distancing	Ignoring the problem or source of stress; refusing to believe that it exists or is important
Disengagement from the goal	Giving up with respect to reaching the goal that is being blocked by stress
Focusing on the expression of feelings	"Letting off steam" instead of working on the problem directly

(SOURCE: Based on suggestions by Scheier, Weintraub, & Carver, 1986.)

Optimists and Pessimists: Contrasting Strategies for Coping with Stress

tered major stressful life changes. Similar results have been reported by Pines (1984) in a study of executives during the breakup of AT&T into several regional companies. Here, hardy persons suffered fewer personal difficulties as a result of these stressful events than persons low in hardiness. These and other findings indicate that individuals differ greatly in terms of their ability to deal with stress, and that understanding the reasons for such differences can be of considerable practical value.

Managing Stress: Some Useful Tactics

Stress stems from so many different factors and conditions that it is probably impossible to eliminate it from our lives. What we *can* do, though, is apply several tactics to lessen its potentially harmful effects. Several of these are described below.

Improving Physical Fitness. If you needed one more inducement for getting into shape, here it is: individuals who exercise regularly are better able than those who do not to withstand prolonged exposure to stress (McLean, 1980). Further, it doesn't seem to matter how such fitness is attained: jogging, swimming, aerobic dancing, team sports—all are equally effective in reducing the incidence of stress-related illnesses such as heart disease and high blood pressure. So, expend the effort needed to improve your physical fitness: the benefits to your career, as well as your health, may be pronounced.

Learn to Relax. Stress is inevitable; most of us confront it every day. Growing evidence suggests, though, that it doesn't have to play havoc with our physical and psychological health. If we learn how to *relax* following exposure to stress, its harmful effects can be substantially reduced. Many different techniques for reducing tension and attaining a relaxed state exist. One of the most effective involves learning to reduce the tension in your own muscles. People using this procedure begin by relaxing muscles in their feet, then gradually move upwards toward the head. Such procedures seem effective in reducing emotional as well as physical tension.

A related tactic is **meditation.** Individuals assume a comfortable position, close their eyes, and clear all disturbing thoughts from their mind. Then they silently repeat a single syllable, or *mantra,* over and over. While meditation remains somewhat controversial, many persons report that it helps them feel relaxed. Further, some research findings indicate that it reduces oxygen consumption and induces brain-wave patterns indicative of a calm mental state (Wallace & Benson, 1972; Wallace & Fisher, 1987).

Don't Bring Stress Home with You. When the day ends, some people manage to leave their stress at the office or factory. Others bring it home with them, so that they continue to be exposed to stress even in the peace and quiet of their own home. Guess which group suffers more ill effects from work-related stress. The latter, of course. In fact, persons who bring their stress home with them (ones described as low in *tension discharge rate*) report greater use of tranquilizers and alcohol, as well as more visits to physicians, than persons who leave their cares at work (Matteson & Ivancevich, 1983). The moral of such findings is clear: try to divide your life into high-stress and low-stress compartments, and don't bring tension from the first into the second.

Seek Help and Support from Others. Do you have a friend, lover, or relative in whom you can confide freely, to whom you can turn for support and advice at times of stress? If so, you are already familiar with another important tactic for coping with the occurrence of stress: seeking *social support.* Growing evidence indicates that having one or preferably several persons who can provide such help is quite beneficial (Bruhn & Phillips, 1987; Lieberman, 1983). First, these persons can help you to perceive stressful events as less threatening and more under your control than might otherwise be the case. As you may recall, such *cognitive appraisal* plays a crucial role in the experience of stress. Second, they can suggest strategies for dealing with the sources of stress that you might not generate yourself. Third, they can help reduce the negative feelings which often accompany exposure to stressful events or situations. Evidence for this last benefit has

Social Support: One Tactic for Coping with Stress

FIGURE 10-25. Under some conditions contact with others can help reduce the anxiety produced by stressful situations. To the extent this occurs, an individual's ability to cope with stress can be enhanced.

recently been obtained in an experiment conducted by Costanza, Derlega, and Winstead (1988).

These researchers asked subjects to perform a highly stressful task: guiding a live tarantula through a maze after watching the experimenter do so. (The tarantula was inside a fishing net from which it could not escape, but through which it could potentially extend its legs.) Subjects signed up for the study with a friend, and before performing this stressful task, some were given an opportunity to have a brief conversation with this person. One group was told to discuss their feelings concerning the situation, another was told to discuss how they expected to handle the guidance task, while a third was told to talk only about topics unrelated to the study. A fourth (control) group was not given any opportunity to talk with a friend; each participant waited alone for the start of the task. Costanza and his colleagues predicted that talking about their feelings with another person might actually intensify subjects' fears; after all, in this condition they would dwell on their concerns and anxieties. In contrast, talking about how they would perform the task or about topics unrelated to it would reduce such feelings. This would be so because in the first case subjects' confidence in their abilities would be enhanced, and in the second they would be distracted from thinking about what lay ahead (refer to Figure 10-25). All these predictions were confirmed. When subjects completed a questionnaire designed to measure their anxiety, those permitted to discuss unrelated topics or how they would handle the task reported lower anxiety than those who waited alone. In short, certain types of social contact or support did indeed help participants cope with a stressful situation. (Incidentally, subjects never actually guided the spider through the maze; they merely expected to perform this stress-inducing task.)

 Summary and Review

Emotions: Contrasting Views on Their Nature

Emotions are complex reactions involving subjective cognitive states, physiological changes, and expressive behaviors. Contrasting theories of emotion emphasize the role of physiological reactions, cognitive factors, or both in the occurrence of human emotions.

The *Cannon-Bard theory* is closest to our common sense view of emotion. It suggests that exposure to emotion-provoking stimuli induces both the subjective experiences we label "emotions" and the physiological reactions which accompany them. In contrast, the *James-Lange theory* suggests that our subjective experiences of emotion are the result of physiological changes occurring within our body when we are exposed to various external stimuli. At present, some evidence for both views exists. Thus, it appears that our emotions are the result of both external stimuli and changes in (and awareness of) our own bodily states.

A third view of emotion, *Schachter and Singer's two-factor theory,* suggests that emotion-provoking events induce generalized arousal and that we then attempt to understand or interpret such arousal by searching the external world for likely causes. Once we identify such a cause, we label our arousal accordingly and experience a specific emotion. This theory, too, is supported by some evidence. Thus, in one sense, it seems, we don't know what emotion we are experiencing until we label it.

Large individual differences in the intensity of emotions exist. Persons high in *affect intensity* experience larger swings in mood than those low in affect intensity. Persons high in affect intensity report more symptoms such as headache and nervousness than do others, but they do not report lower levels of happiness or subjective well-being.

Emotions: Their Communication to Others

Information about others' emotions is often transmitted by various *nonverbal cues*. Facial expressions arise early in life and reveal much about emotional states. Patterns of eye contact can reveal others' liking or disliking for us, as well as whether they are being honest in their verbal statements. Finally, much information about others' emotions is revealed by *body language*—the movement, position, or posture of a person's body or body parts.

Large individual differences in the effective use of such cues exist. Persons high in *expressiveness* are more effective transmitters and interpreters of nonverbal cues. In addition, females are better at both of these tasks than males.

Emotions and Behavior

Emotional states affect a wide range of behaviors. People in a good mood are more willing to offer help to others and engage in more effective negotiations than persons in a bad mood. Similarly, persons in a good mood are less likely to demonstrate anger and aggression. Emotions are often strongly affected by cognitive processes.

Emotions exert important effects upon cognitive processes. In general, we find it easier to recall information consistent with our current mood than information inconsistent with it. Similarly, emotions often color our judgments or decisions. When we are in a good mood, we evaluate many stimuli (including other persons) more favorably than when we are in a bad mood.

Stress: Its Nature, Causes, and Management

Stress involves a complex pattern of negative emotions and physiological reactions occurring in situations where individuals perceive threats to their major goals which they may be unable to meet. To understand stress fully we must take account of reactions to it, stimuli that produce it (*stressors*), and *cognitive appraisal* (individuals' perceptions that events pose a threat to their important goals or beliefs).

Many factors contribute to stress. Major life changes (e.g., divorce, death of a close relative) are often highly stressful and can exert adverse effects upon physical and psychological health. Recent evidence, though, suggests that the minor *daily hassles* of everyday life may be even more important in this regard. Many aspects of jobs (e.g., work overload, responsibility for others, role conflict) contribute to stress. Finally, certain features of the physical environment (e.g., noise, extreme temperatures) can be highly stressful.

Prolonged exposure to high levels of stress exerts adverse effects upon individuals' physical health and psychological well-being. Stress also interferes with the performance of many tasks and with effective decision-making. Job-related stress can sometimes lead to *burnout,* a psychological state characterized by physical, mental, and emotional exhaustion, as well as feelings of low personal accomplishment.

Large individual differences exist in the ability to resist the adverse effects of stress. *Optimists* are more successful in this regard than *pessimists,* largely because they adopt more effective tactics for coping with stress. Persons high in *hardiness*—ones who have a strong sense of commitment and personal control and who perceive change as a challenge—are more resistant to the adverse effects of stress than persons low in hardiness.

The harmful effects of stress can be reduced by physical fitness, relaxation techniques, learning to leave job-related stress at the office, and developing networks of social support (persons in whom one can confide, and to whom one can turn for help and guidance).

 Key Terms

Affect Intensity Individual differences in the degree to which people experience emotional reactions.

Body Language Movements in various parts of the body reflecting various emotional reactions.

Burnout A psychological state that sometimes follows prolonged exposure to intense stress. Burnout involves physical, mental, and attitudinal exhaustion, as well as feelings of low personal accomplishment.

Cannon-Bard Theory A theory of emotion suggesting that various emotion-provoking events simultaneously produce the subjective reactions we label as emotions *and* the physiological changes which accompany them.

Emotions Reactions consisting of subjective cognitive states, physiological responses, and expressive behaviors.

Facial Feedback Hypothesis The suggestion that changes in facial expressions can influence as well as convey underlying emotions.

Gestures Movements of various parts of the body that convey a specific meaning to others.

Hardiness A characteristic (or cluster of characteristics) that helps individuals resist the adverse effects of stress. Persons high in hardiness have a sense of commitment and of personal control and view change as a challenge rather than a burden.

James-Lange Theory A theory of emotion suggesting that emotion-provoking events produce various physiological reactions and that these, in turn, give rise to our subjective experiences of emotion.

Meditation A relaxation technique for countering the effects of stress in which individuals clear their minds of disturbing thoughts and then repeat a single syllable (*mantra*) over and over.

Nonverbal Cues Outward signs of others' emotional states. Important nonverbal cues are communicated by facial expressions, eye contact, and body language.

Schachter-Singer Theory A theory of emotion suggesting that our subjective emotional states are determined, at least in part, by the labels we attach to internal feelings of arousal.

Sex-Role Stereotypes Beliefs within a given culture about the supposed characteristics of persons of each gender and patterns of behavior that are considered appropriate for each to demonstrate.

Stress An unpleasant emotional state in which individuals feel that their capacity to cope with the demands upon them will soon be overwhelmed.

Stressors Various conditions and factors in the external environment that induce feelings of stress.

 For More Information

Buck, R.W. (1984). *The communication of emotion*. New York: Guilford.
This well-written text presents a great deal of intriguing information about the nature of emotion and the ways in which emotional experiences are communicated. The chapters on nonverbal communication are especially interesting.
Isen, A.M. (1987). Positive affect, cognitive organization, and social behavior. In L. Berkowitz, ed., *Advances in experimental social psychology*, vol. 21. New York: Academic Press.
Although this chapter is intended primarily for a professional audience, it is clearly written and well organized. If you'd like to know more about the many ways in which our emotions shape our behavior and our cognitive processes, this is a valuable source.
Maslach, C. (1982). *Burnout: The cost of caring*. Englewood Cliffs, NJ: Prentice-Hall.
What is burnout? Why does it occur? How can it be measured or recognized? These are among the questions considered by this insightful text. An excellent source to consult if you'd like to know more about this important effect of stress.
Mitchell, T.R., & Larson, J.R., Jr. (1987). *People in organizations*, 3rd ed. New York: McGraw-Hill.
The chapter on stress provides an excellent, up-to-date summary of our current knowledge about the causes and effects of work-related stress.

C H A P T E R

11

Measuring Individual Differences: The Nature of Psychological Testing

"Did you enjoy the fair?" Carrie Miller asks her friend Jo Sandvik.

"Yeah!" Jo replies with enthusiasm. "Bill won a big stuffed animal at the sharp-shooting booth, and I ate cotton candy until it came out my ears. It was like turning the clock back ten years. We acted like little kids all day."

"He really won a prize? I always thought those things were rigged so you couldn't win no matter what."

"Not at this fair. It was sponsored by the Hospital Committee, so it was all legit." Then, after a brief pause, Jo continues: "But you know what I enjoyed the most? The gypsy fortune-teller. She read my palm, and it was really weird—it was like she could see right inside my head."

At this comment, Carrie begins to laugh. "Aw, come off it! You don't take that stuff seriously, do you? I mean, it's just a big put-on."

"That's what *you* think!" Jo replies testily. "I'm not kidding. She really *could* kind of read my mind." When Carrie continues to giggle and shake her head, Jo continues. "O.K., see this? It's my heart-line, and it shows I'm easy to get along with, and 100 percent faithful. It's long and even-colored, just like she said. Let's see yours." She grabs Carrie's hand and looks at the palm. "Hmmph! Just what I thought. Short and pale: that means you're self-centered, don't care much about anyone except yourself."

"You know, I'd get mad if I took you seriously," Carrie answers. But the fact that she's stopped smiling indicates that she *has* been affected by Jo's remark. "How can you tell anything about someone from their palm? It's just silly."

But Jo is not convinced. "Oh yeah?" she shoots back, "Well, listen to *this*. See that other line? It's my head line. Look how wavy it is. That means that I'm real moody—you know *that's* true. You're always saying so yourself. And another thing. See these little marks? Those are my marriage lines. They mean that I'll probably get married twice."

"Well, since your mother's on her third, you'd better add some more lines."

At this remark, Jo *really* looks angry, so Carrie backs off a little. "Come on, don't get so excited. If you want to believe in it, that's O.K. by me. I just don't see how an intelligent person like you can really believe those little lines have any meaning. I've heard all that stuff about 'Ze gypsy sees all,' but it's *so* hokey. Next, you'll be telling me that she read a crystal ball, too."

"Well, now that you mention it. . . ."

Variety, it is often said, is the spice of life. If this is true, then other persons certainly provide us with lots of spice. Individuals differ in a seemingly countless number of ways—in their physical traits, abilities, and personalities, to mention just a few. Differences in the physical traits are fairly easy to measure. For example, if we want to identify the tallest person in a group, we can use a ruler to compare their heights. Differences with respect to psychological characteristics, though, are somewhat harder to assess. How can we tell whether one person is brighter than another, possesses more musical talent, or has greater potential to master the complexities of computer programming? Until the present century, no satisfactory answers to such questions existed. Many techniques for measuring individual differences were used, but most, like palm-reading, were of questionable value (refer to Figure 11-1).

Fortunately, modern psychology has come to the rescue in this respect. Over a period of several decades our field has developed special procedures for measuring individual differences in a scientific (or at least science-based) manner. Such procedures take several forms, ranging from systematic (structured) *interviews* through direct *observations* of behavior in various situations. The most important of these, however, are **psychological tests**—special devices for evaluating and comparing the characteristics of individuals.

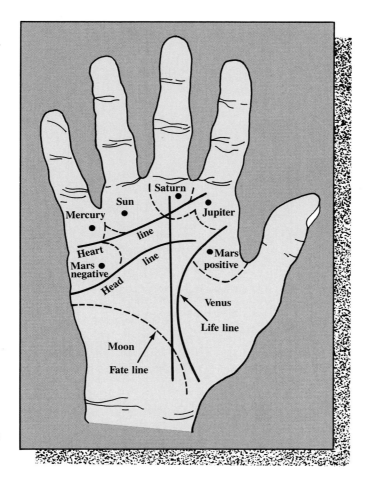

FIGURE 11-1. Do lines on the palm reveal the character and future of individuals? No scientific evidence for such claims exists.

Because they are used to measure a wide range of human abilities and traits, and because the information they yield is put to many important uses, such tests will serve as the focus of the present chapter.

Our discussion of psychological tests, and the assessment of individual differences generally, will proceed as follows. First, we'll examine some basic requirements of all tests—ones that must be met if they are to be of any practical value. Next, we'll consider the use of such tests in the measurement of a crucial human trait: **intelligence.** As will soon be apparent, efforts to measure individual differences in this respect have sparked several heated controversies in recent years. Finally, we'll touch briefly on the use of psychological tests in the measurement of a wide range of *interests, aptitudes,* and *achievements.* (We'll consider methods for assessing other individual differences, especially ones relating to *personality,* in Chapter 12.)

One final point before beginning: why is there all this fuss about individual differences? Why do we want to measure such differences accurately in the first place? There are two basic reasons. First, knowledge about individuals' relative standing on various psychological traits often allows us to make useful *predictions* about them. For example, knowing how specific persons compare with others in intelligence or other abilities can help us predict their chances of success in various jobs and the probability that they'll do well in college or other educational settings (refer to Figure 11-2 on page 340). Second, knowledge about individual differences is crucial in many *clinical settings,* where psychologists attempt to use their special skills and knowledge to help specific persons. For example, being able to measure an individual's degree of *mental retardation* (impairment in thinking or reasoning abilities) is crucial in choosing the best techniques for assisting this person. Similarly, identification of an individual's emotional problems, and assessment of their severity, are often essential first steps to selecting the most effective therapy.

Individual Differences: Useful in Predicting Occupational Success

FIGURE 11-2. Different jobs or careers require contrasting skills and abilities. Knowledge about *individual differences*—the extent to which specific persons possess such characteristics—can help predict whether they are likely to be successful or unsuccessful in these jobs. This information, in turn, can be useful both to the individuals themselves and to organizations which might hire or train them.

In sum, being able to measure individual differences with respect to psychological characteristics is of great practical value in several different ways.

Psychological Tests: Some Basic Requirements

At the present time many persons seem to view psychological tests with something bordering on awe. Indeed, in the public mind such devices are often assigned almost magical powers. Through their use, it is widely believed, psychologists can probe the deepest corners of your mind and uncover amazing facts about your traits and abilities (see Figure 11-3). Are such beliefs justified? Only to a degree: in the hands of trained psychologists, various tests *can* yield useful information about specific persons. Like any other type of measuring device, however, they are far from perfect. Psychological tests are subject to numerous forms of error and are only useful to the extent that they meet several basic requirements. The most important of these involve a given test's reliability, validity, and standardization.

Reliability: Why Consistency Counts

Suppose that after a winter of overeating you decide to go on a diet so you can look your best on the beach. Your goal is to lose 12 pounds, and your current weight is 135. For two weeks you deny yourself your favorite treats, and you engage in strenuous exercise. Then you step onto your bathroom scale to see how much progress you've made. To your horror, the needle reads 138; you've actually *gained* three pounds. How can this be? For a moment, you're crushed. Then you step back onto the scale. This time it reads 130. You'd like to believe the second number, but is it correct? To find out, you weigh yourself once again. Now the scale reads 135. At this point, you give up in disgust. It's obvious that you'll need another scale to keep track of your progress.

This simple situation calls attention to a very important point. In order to be of any use, measuring devices must be *reliable*. They must yield the same result each time they are applied to the same quantity. If they don't, like the scale just described, they are unreliable—and therefore essentially useless.

The same principle applies to psychological tests or any other device used to measure human traits or characteristics. They, too, must be reliable to be of any value. In other words, they must yield the same (or very similar) scores when taken by the same person on different occasions, or when taken by persons known to be similar on the trait

FIGURE 11-3. Many people seem to believe that psychological tests have an almost magical power to reveal important facts about them.

being measured. How can we tell if this is the case? Several different methods for assessing **reliability** exist.

Internal Consistency: Do the Items on a Test Measure the Same Thing?
Perhaps the first question we should ask about a test is this: Do the items on it all measure the same trait or characteristic? In order to answer this question, we can examine its **split-half reliability.** This involves dividing the test into two equivalent parts, such as odd-numbered and even-numbered items, and then comparing the scores on each. Obviously, these should be similar; if they are not, then some items in the two halves may be measuring different things, and the test, in one important sense, is unreliable.

We should add that there are also special statistical formulas for assessing internal consistency (e.g., *coefficient alpha*). Essentially, these formulas indicate how similar the scores on two halves of the test would be if we divided the test in half in every possible way and then compared each pair. Since this is done mathematically, on high-speed computers, the process is very efficient, and such formulas have become the standard means used by psychologists for measuring this aspect of reliability.

Consistency Across Time: Test-Retest Reliability. As we have already noted, a test that yields very different scores when taken by the same persons on different occasions is of little value. Thus, another aspect of reliability, **test-retest reliability,** is usually also assessed. This involves giving the test to the same group of persons on more than one occasion and comparing the scores. The more similar these are, the higher the test's reliability. The scale in the example above, of course, showed low test-retest reliability: it yielded different results when the same person stepped on it repeatedly, with only a few seconds between each measurement.

Of course, test-retest reliability often decreases as the interval between successive administrations of the test increases. Psychological characteristics, like height or weight, do not fluctuate greatly from moment to moment but may change appreciably over a period of months or years. Thus, this factor must be taken into account when considering a test's reliability. In general, though, only tests that yield similar scores for the same persons when taken on different occasions are useful for measuring important individual differences. (Please refer to Figure 11-4 on page 342 for a summary of the two aspects of reliability we have just discussed.)

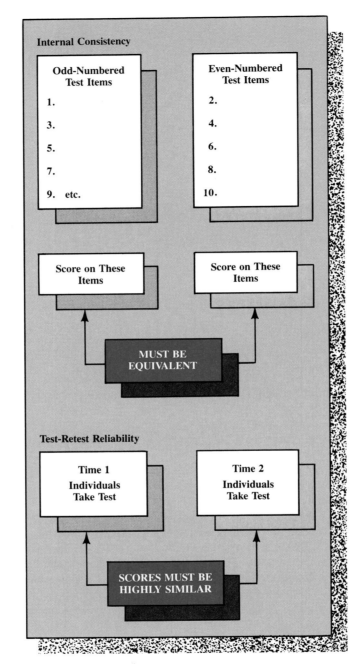

Reliability: An Essential Requirement of Useful Psychological Tests

FIGURE 11-4. In order to be useful, psychological tests must be *reliable*. All the items they contain must measure the same trait or characteristic *(internal consistency)*, as shown in the upper panel, and scores must be stable over time *(test-retest reliability;* lower panel).

Validity: Do Tests Measure What They Claim to Measure?

When the author was a little boy, his mother often sat him on her lap and recited the following poem: "Tickle, tickle on the chin, if you laugh you don't love me." While uttering these words, she would smile at him and tickle him under the chin. Although he tried his best not to laugh, on most occasions he failed. Did this mean that he didn't love his mother? Hardly—as you can readily see, this "test" probably had nothing whatsoever to do with love, affection, or attachment. In short, there are strong grounds for questioning its **validity**—its ability to measure what it was supposed to measure.

Admittedly, this example is a trivial one: no one would take this poem seriously as a test of anything (except perhaps the ability to refrain from laughing when tickled). But the principle it illustrates is an important one, and applies to *any* technique for measuring human characteristics. To be useful, such techniques (including psychological tests) must

"Sorry. Next!"

FIGURE 11-5. The "test" shown here is probably unrelated to performance on the job in question. Hence, it is *invalid* for choosing the best future employee. *(Source:* The New Yorker.*)*

measure what they claim to measure. Only to the extent they do are they *valid* and therefore useful. (Refer to Figure 11-5 for an amusing illustration of this fact.) How can we determine whether this is the case? Again, several methods for answering this basic question exist.

Content Validity: Covering the Right Ground.   Suppose that a group of dentists faces the following task: develop a test for licensing new members of their field. What kind of items would the test include? Probably, items dealing with the proper way of filling a tooth, the correct use of X-ray machines, and so on. In other words, the test would consist of items that this group of experts agrees are closely related to good performance as a practicing dentist. To the extent the items were selected in this manner, the test would possess **content validity:** the items on it would be ones drawn from the types of activities actually performed by dentists.

But now imagine that this group of dentists, faced with a rising glut of practitioners in their field, decides to restrict the number of new dentists. To do so, they include test items dealing with nuclear physics, famous dates in history, and the names of different kinds of trees. From a practical point of view, the test might work: fewer candidates would pass and be licensed. As we're sure you can see, though, it would probably evoke howls of protest from new graduates of dental schools, and for good reason: it would no longer possess a high degree of content validity. The items on it are *not* ones that a group of experts would identify as closely related to the activities dentists actually perform.

Criterion-Related Validity: Where (Hopefully) Test Scores and Behavior Meet. A second important form of validity is based on the following reasonable assumption: if a test actually measures what it claims to measure, then persons attaining different scores on it should also differ in terms of their behavior. Specifically, they should differ in terms of some *criterion* or standard relating to the trait or characteristic being measured. For example, if a test measures academic potential or aptitude, persons scoring high on it should attain better grades than those scoring low. Similarly, if a test measures a need for stimulation or excitement, persons scoring high on it should be more likely to engage in such activities as sky-diving, mountain climbing, or gambling than persons scoring lower.

Two different methods exist for assessing such criterion validity. In the first, **predictive validity,** scores on a test are used to predict later performance on some criterion. For example, if a test really measures academic potential, we would predict that a higher proportion of individuals scoring high on it would go on to earn advanced degrees than persons scoring lower. And scores on a test measuring need for stimulation should predict the frequency of accidents: people high on this dimension should experience such events more often than ones low on this dimension.

A second type of criterion-related validity, **concurrent validity,** relates test scores to present performance or behavior. Thus, we might expect persons scoring high on academic aptitude to have higher grades at the present time than persons scoring low.

Both predictive and concurrent validity are crucial in evaluating the usefulness of psychological tests. Indeed, if evidence for either type of criterion-related validity is lacking, a test should probably be discarded as useless (Aiken, 1985).

Construct Validity: Psychological Theory and the Meaning of Test Scores. A third important type of validity, which some psychologists feel is *the* most important type, refers to the following issue: does a test actually measure a *construct* (concept, process) described by a psychological theory? In other words, does it measure something identified by a specific theory as important or worthy of attention? Perhaps a concrete example will help illustrate this type of validity.

Imagine that a psychologist develops a test to measure *abrasiveness*—a tendency to rub others the wrong way. A theory dealing with this characteristic suggests that (1) it derives from certain types of early experience (e.g., rejection by one's father), (2) it involves a low level of sensitivity to others' feelings (abrasive people can't tell when they are annoying or irritating the persons around them), and (3) it is related to loneliness (abrasive people are disliked by others and are avoided by them). In order to determine

FIGURE 11.6. *Construct validity* refers to the extent to which a psychological test measures a *construct* (concept or process) described by a psychological theory. If persons scoring high and low on the test differ in ways predicted by the theory, the test can be described as possessing a high degree of construct validity. If such persons do not differ in the predicted ways, the test's construct validity is low.

Construct Validity: An Overview

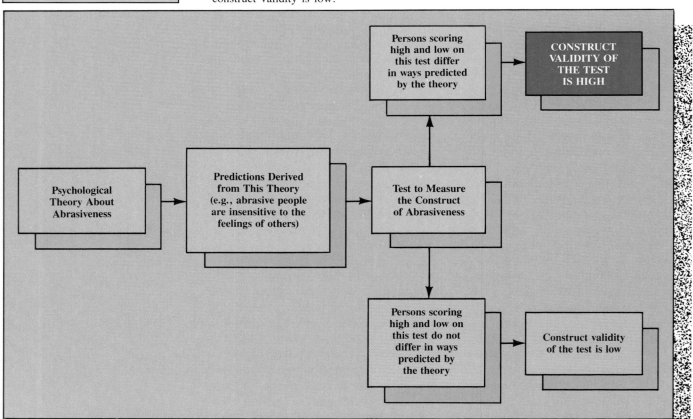

whether his test of *abrasiveness* is really measuring this construct, the psychologist now relates scores on it to such things as (1) the kind of relationship individuals had with their father, (2) their ability to recognize nonverbal signs of anger in others, and (3) their reported loneliness. To the extent the scores on the test of abrasiveness correlate with these measures, evidence for construct validity is obtained: the test of *abrasiveness* does really seem to measure the construct specified by the underlying theory. (Please see Figure 11-6 for an overview of the nature of construct validity.) In sum, construct validity relates to the question of whether a test designed to measure a construct described by a psychological theory really measures this construct.

Standardization: A Basis for Interpreting Test Scores

Suppose that a psychologist develops a test to measure an important characteristic: the *need for power*—the desire to influence others and to tell them what to do. Further, assume that the test is reliable and that evidence for its validity exists (for example, the presidents of large companies score higher on this test than college professors or farmers). This information suggests that the test is a useful one; it allows us to measure differences between individuals on an important psychological dimension. What it does not tell us, though, is how to interpret specific scores. What, precisely, defines a high score? What is a low one? And what level can be described as average? In order to answer such questions, the test must be carefully **standardized.**

This involves administering it to a large number of persons who are representative of the population for which it is designed, and then examining their scores. The main goal is straightforward: determining how these scores are distributed. In other words, we wish to know such things as the *range* of scores (what are the highest and lowest) and the *mean* or average score. Once such information is available, *test norms* can be formulated. These tell us what proportion of individuals taking the test will score at or below each level. Thus, after test norms have been established, we can readily interpret the score attained by any individual. (Please see the Appendix at the end of this book for more information on score distributions and other aspects of *statistics*.)

For example, suppose that after we administer our test of need for power to several thousand persons, we find that the range is 40 points (scores vary from 10 to 50), and that the mean is 30. Now we give the test to two persons who have applied for a job as a top executive. One attains a score of 34 and the other a score of 42. Obviously, the two persons differ, but by how much? By examining test norms, we determine that about 75 percent of the people taking this test attain a score below 34; only 25 percent score at or above this level. So, the first individual is fairly high in the need for power. However, test norms also reveal that fully 95 percent of all people taking the test score below 42. This means that only 5 percent attain a score as high as that received by the second person (refer to Figure 11-7 on page 346). Clearly, this individual is considerably higher than the first in the need for power.

Needless to say, psychologists usually direct careful attention to the task of developing test norms. When such information is available, scores on the test can be readily interpreted; without them, direct comparisons between individuals are difficult, and the terms ''high,'' ''average,'' and ''low'' with respect to test scores remain subjective and ill-defined.

Uniform Test Conditions: Eliminating Sources of ''Noise'' in Test Scores. Before concluding, we should call your attention to one final point: the way in which tests are administered is important, too. If the kind of norms described above are to be useful, each time a test is given it must be administered under uniform conditions—preferably, ones as similar to those used with the standardization group as possible. If this is not the case, it is inappropriate to interpret the scores in terms of existing test norms. To see why this is so, consider the following example: when a test is standardized, one set of instructions is used. Later, when it is given to other persons, a different set is employed; for example, test-takers are allowed less time to complete the test. Can the scores obtained by this second group be interpreted in terms of those obtained by the first (standardization)

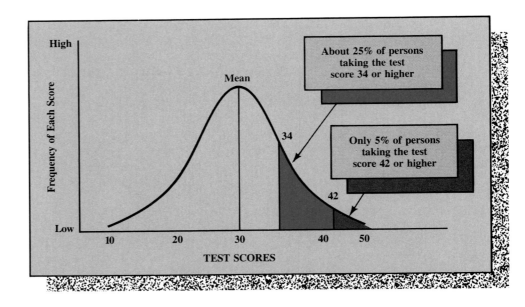

FIGURE 11-7. *Test norms* indicate how scores on a particular psychological test are distributed. This information, in turn, permits us to compare specific persons on the characteristic measured by the test. The norms shown here indicate that about 25 percent of persons taking this test attain a score of 34. However, only about 5 percent attain a score of 42.

group? Obviously they cannot. The contrasting instructions may affect performance and make it inappropriate to use existing test norms in this manner.

In a similar manner, other differences between present test conditions and those prevailing when a test was standardized can cloud the issue. For example, if a test is standardized in one kind of setting (e.g., neat and quiet classrooms at a major university), but this is then administered under other conditions (e.g., a run-down auditorium in a noisy public building), the scores may be difficult to interpret. For this reason, it is crucial that psychological tests be administered under conditions that are as uniform as possible (see Figure 11-8).

FIGURE 11-8. If a test is standardized under one set of conditions (left photo), but then administered to new test-takers under a different set of conditions (right photo), accurate interpretation of scores may be difficult.

The Nature and Measurement of Human Intelligence

Psychological tests have been used to measure a tremendous range of human characteristics—everything from highly specific skills to complex and intriguing aspects of personality. (We'll consider this last topic in detail in Chapter 12.) Perhaps the single characteristic that has received most attention, though, is **intelligence.** Efforts to measure individual differences in this respect have long been a part of modern psychology; indeed, they were one of the first tasks psychologists addressed when our field emerged. Any discussion of psychological testing, then, should include consideration of this important topic. In the present section we'll first examine the nature of human intelligence, describing several contrasting views of what it is. Then, we'll consider efforts to measure individual differences in intelligence and some of the complex issues these raise. Finally, we'll return to the *nature-nurture* controversy we've addressed previously, and consider the following question: what are the relative contributions of environmental and genetic factors to human intelligence?

Human Intelligence: Some Contrasting Views

What is intelligence? Most of us think we know—until we are asked to define it precisely! To illustrate this point, think of two good friends. Which is brighter or more intelligent? You can probably answer quite readily, for we make informal judgments about others' intelligence on a regular basis. But just what is it about one of these persons that causes you to perceive him or her as smarter? Here, you may experience some difficulty. The reason for this is simple: for many of us, intelligence is similar to ''sex appeal'' in our cognitive map of the world: we can recognize it when we see it, but we can't define it precisely. Psychologists, too, have found the task of defining intelligence a difficult one, and even today they are not in full agreement about its basic nature (Sternberg, 1986a). Traditionally, it has been defined as the ability to think abstractly (Flynn, 1987) or to learn readily from experience. While these definitions seem to make sense and are still widely accepted, they do not address an important issue: is intelligence a unitary characteristic, or one composed of many parts?

Intelligence: Unified or Multifaceted?   The question we have just posed is one that has generated wide swings in the pendulum of scientific opinion in psychology. Initially, researchers such as Spearman (1927) felt that performance on any cognitive task depended on a major general factor (which he labeled g) and one or more specific factors relating to that particular task. Thus, in his view intelligence could be understood largely in terms of a general ability to solve problems and perform well on a wide range of cognitive tasks.

In later decades contrasting views of intelligence, stressing the fact that it consisted of many different components, rose to prominence. For example, Thurstone (1938) suggested that intelligence actually consists of several distinct *primary mental abilities*. Included in his list were such factors as *verbal meaning*—understanding ideas and word meanings; *number*—speed and accuracy in dealing with numbers; and *space*—the ability to visualize objects in three dimensions (see Table 11-1 on page 348 for a summary of Thurstone's suggestions.)

More recently, a somewhat different view proposed by Cattell (1963) has received considerable attention. According to this theory, intelligence consists of two major components: *fluid intelligence,* which is similar to Spearman's general factor and is largely inherited, and *crystallized intelligence,* which represents the results of applying fluid intelligence to experiences—especially those at school. Cattell suggests that while fluid intelligence reaches a peak during our teen years, crystallized intelligence continues to grow well into adulthood.

Where is the pendulum located at present? It is now somewhere in the middle of this range of views. At present most psychologists believe that intelligence involves both a general ability to handle a wide range of cognitive tasks and problems as well as a number

---

Thurstone's Primary Mental Abilities

TABLE 11-1

Thurstone proposed that intelligence involves a number of distinct *primary mental abilities*.

Primary Mental Ability	Description
Verbal meaning	Understanding ideas and word meanings
Number	Speed and accuracy in performing arithmetical computations
Space	Ability to visualize form relationships in three dimensions
Perceptual speed	Ability to quickly distinguish visual details and similarities and differences between objects
Word fluency	Speed in thinking of words
Memory	Ability to memorize words, numbers, etc.
Inductive reasoning	Ability to derive a rule from given information

of more specific abilities (refer to Figure 11-9). Perhaps it can be represented, in our mind's eye, as a large and beautiful jewel which, while reflecting light as a whole, also glistens from separate facets. Having said this, however, we should add that efforts to understand the nature of intelligence have recently taken a very different turn. Within the past dozen years, many researchers have attempted to relate human intelligence to our growing knowledge about cognitive processes generally. As an example of this newer, and perhaps more sophisticated approach, we'll consider a theory proposed by Sternberg (1986a).

Sternberg's Triarchic Theory: Three Kinds of Intelligence. As a cognitive psychologist, Sternberg began with a view of intelligence emphasizing the ability to think critically (Trotter, 1986). In short, he concentrated on what happens inside peoples' heads when they reason and process information effectively. Soon, though, he noticed an interesting fact: some people who are good at critical thinking are not very creative—they rarely have good, original ideas of their own. He then came to the realization that some people who are not high on either of these dimensions seem to be "street smart"—they are able to adapt to changing situations in ways that enhance their intellectual strengths and compensate for their weaknesses.

Intelligence: A Multifaceted Jewel

FIGURE 11-9. Intelligence seems to involve both a general ability to deal with a wide range of cognitive tasks and problems, plus specific abilities most useful in particular contexts.

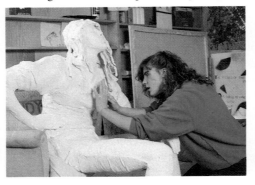

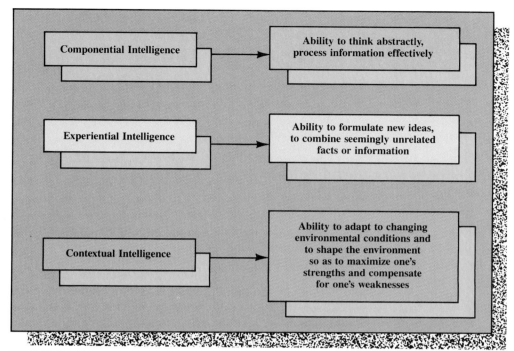

FIGURE 11-10. According to Sternberg's *triarchic theory,* there are three distinct types of intelligence: *componential, experiential,* and *contextual.*

On the basis of such observations, Sternberg (1985, 1986a) reached the conclusion that there are really three distinct types of human intelligence. The first, known as **componential intelligence,** emphasizes effectiveness in information processing. Persons high on this dimension are able to think critically and analytically. Thus, they usually shine on standard tests of academic potential and make excellent students. In contrast, the second type, which Sternberg labels **experiential intelligence,** emphasizes insight and the ability to formulate new ideas. Persons high on this dimension excel at zeroing in on information that is critical and at combining seemingly unrelated facts. For example, William Fleming, the discoverer of penicillin, was high in these respects. He quickly recognized the significance of the fact that bacteria would not grow where an unknown mold was present and so provided the first of our many ''wonder drugs.''

Finally, there is what Sternberg terms **contextual intelligence.** Persons high on this dimension are intelligent in a *practical* sense. They quickly recognize what factors influence success on various tasks and are adept at both adapting to and shaping their environment so that they can accomplish various goals. Successful people in many fields, from psychology to the world of business, seem to excel in this regard. (See Figure 11-10 for a summary of these three types of intelligence.)

Is Sternberg's **triarchic theory** correct? Since it is so new, little direct evidence about it is yet available. However, some findings support its accuracy (Sternberg, 1985, 1986a), and it does seem to ring true with respect to our own life experiences: almost everyone has known people who seem to be high on one of these dimensions without being high on the others. Until it is confirmed by additional research findings, though, Sternberg's theory should be viewed with a degree of caution. Still, it offers an intriguing new approach to the mystery of human intelligence and seems worthy of careful attention for this reason alone.

Measuring Human Intelligence

In 1904, when psychology was just emerging as an independent field, members of the Paris school board approached Alfred Binet with an interesting request: could he develop an objective method for identifying children who were mentally retarded and so could not

Sample Items from the First Successful Test of Intelligence

TABLE 11-2

Items such as these appeared on the first version of the intelligence test designed by Binet and Simon.

A child is asked to:
  Recognize the difference between a square of chocolate and a square of wood.
  Execute simple commands or imitate simple gestures.
  Name objects shown in pictures.
  Repeat a sentence of 15 words.
  Tell how two common objects are different.
  Make a rhyme. (''What rhymes with _____?'')
  Complete sentences begun by the examiner.
  Use three nouns mentioned by the examiner in a sentence.
  Define abstract terms (e.g., ''What is the difference between esteem and friendship?'')

benefit from regular classes? Binet was already at work on related topics, so, enlisting the aid of his colleague Theodore Simon, he readily agreed.

In designing their test, Binet and Simon were guided by the following belief: the items used should be ones children could answer without special training or study. He felt this was important because the test was designed to measure the ability to handle intellectual tasks—*not* specific knowledge acquired in school. In order to reach this goal, Binet and Simon decided to use items of two basic types: ones which were so new or unusual none of the children would have prior exposure to them, and ones which were so familiar almost all the youngsters would have been exposed to them in the past.

The first version of their test was published in 1905 and contained thirty items (refer to Table 11-2). Much to Binet and Simon's pleasure, it was quite effective in attaining its major goal. With its aid, children in need of special assistance could be readily identified. Encouraged by this early success, Binet and Simon broadened the scope of their test so that it could measure variations in intelligence among normal children. This revision, published in 1908, grouped items by age, with six items at each level between three and thirteen years. Items were placed at a particular age level if about 75 percent of the children of that age could pass it correctly.

Binet's tests were soon revised and adapted for use in the United States by Lewis Terman, a psychologist at Stanford University. The **Stanford-Binet test,** as it came to be known, gained rapid acceptance and was soon put to use in many settings. Indeed, over the years it has been revised several times and remained a highly popular tool for measuring intelligence for several decades. One of the features of the Stanford-Binet which its users found attractive and which contributed to its popularity was that it yielded a single score assumed to reflect an individual's level of intelligence—the now famous **IQ.**

IQ: Its Meaning Then and Now.   Originally, the letters *IQ* stood for *intelligence quotient,* and, in fact, this is precisely what such scores represented. They were obtained by dividing an individual's *mental age* by his or her *chronological age,* and multiplying by 100. Mental age referred to an individual's level of intellectual development; it was determined by adding the items he or she passed correctly on the test (test-takers were awarded two months for each item answered correctly). If an individual's mental and chronological age were equal, an IQ of 100 was obtained. Numbers above this level indicated that the person's intellectual age was greater than his or her chronological age; in other words, such persons were ''smarter'' than typical youngsters their own age. In contrast, numbers below 100 indicated that an individual was less intelligent than his or her peers.

While an IQ based on a ratio of mental to chronological age seems reasonable, it suffers from one obvious flaw: at some point, mental development ceases while chronological age continues to mount. Thus, we are left facing a situation in which IQ scores begin to decline after the early teen years! Partly because of this problem, IQ scores now have a different meaning. They simply reflect an individual's performance on an intelligence test relative to that of persons the same age. In other words, an individual's score is interpreted in terms of norms for his or her own age, as described on page 345. The mean for each age is arbitrarily set at 100, so once again scores above this value indicate that an individual is brighter than average, while scores below it indicate lower-than-average intelligence. In short, an individual's IQ score simply expresses the extent to which his or her performance on the test departs from average; the concept of mental age no longer enters the picture. Interestingly, it has been necessary to adjust the norms for various intelligence tests *upwards* in recent decades, to reflect the fact that more and more people attain high scores. Even with such adjustments, though, average IQ scores have risen substantially around the world. Why is this so? For one interpretation see ''The Cutting Edge'' section below.

FOCUS ON RESEARCH: The Cutting Edge

Worldwide Gains in IQ Scores: Are We All Getting Smarter?

Intelligence tests are popular. Millions of persons in many different countries complete them each year. Moreover, this has been the case for several decades. Now for the surprise: recent examination of this massive store of data reveals a puzzling trend. IQ scores have risen significantly over time all over the world (refer to Figure 11-11). Such changes seem to have occurred at all age levels, from children through young adults. And, perhaps even

more surprisingly, they have actually been somewhat larger on tests of intelligence especially designed to minimize the impact of cultural factors (e.g., amount and quality of schooling) than on more traditional measures (Flynn, 1987). What accounts for these changes? According to Flynn (1987), a researcher who has studied this problem for several years, two possibilities exist.

Either we are in fact becoming smarter as a species, or intelligence tests measure something other than intelligence. The first possibility seems unlikely.

The Worldwide Rise in IQ Scores

FIGURE 11-11. As shown here, IQ scores have risen significantly in many different countries in recent decades. *(Source: Based on data from Flynn, 1987.)*

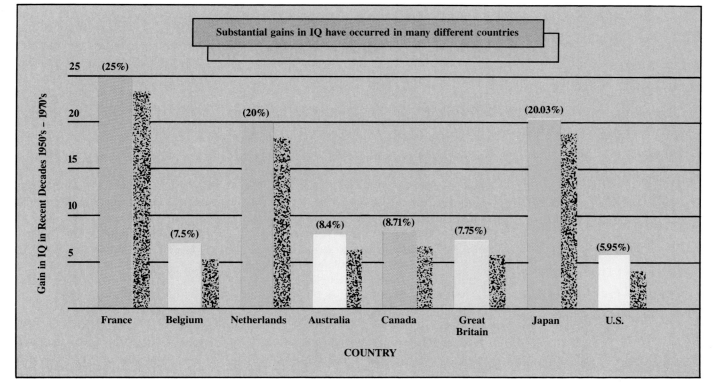

If intelligence were actually increasing, the present generation should be far outpacing previous ones in terms of inventions, scientific breakthroughs, and other achievements. Allowing for the sharp rise in world population, this does not seem to be the case. For example, in the Netherlands the number of people with an IQ of 150 or greater has increased more than *sixty times* in recent decades. Yet, no corresponding rise in tangible signs of genius are visible. The second interpretation seems far more plausible. Perhaps intelligence tests do not measure intelligence itself, but some factor that is only modestly linked to it. Flynn suggests that what such tests actually measure is the ability to solve abstract problems. Since this is only part of the total picture where intelligence is concerned (recall Sternberg's triarchic theory), it is not surprising that a rise in IQ scores has failed to produce a corresponding rise in human achievement.

But what factors are responsible for the sharp increase in measured IQ? Improved education, enhanced standards of living, and the worldwide information explosion probably all play a role. As yet it is impossible to point to a small list of environmental changes and conclude that these are the central ones (Flynn, 1987).

In sum, the worldwide rise in IQ observed in recent decades has two major implications. First, it calls attention to the fact that intelligence is an extremely complex phenomenon and that existing tests may be tapping only part of its basic structure. Second, it suggests that at least some components of human intelligence can be strongly affected by environmental factors—by the lives we lead and the experiences we encounter. Rising IQ scores, then, do not suggest that we must abandon existing tests of intelligence as useless; however, they do suggest that we interpret their results with extra caution.

The Wechsler Scales.   As we noted above, the tests developed by Binet and later adapted by Terman and others remained popular for many years. Indeed, they have been repeatedly revised and updated, and modern versions are in use today. They did suffer from one major drawback, however: all were predominantly verbal in content. As a result, they paid relatively little attention to the fact that intelligence can be revealed in nonverbal as well as verbal activities. For example, an expert mechanic capable of repairing complex pieces of equipment is obviously demonstrating intelligence. Yet, no means of assessing such abilities was included in early versions of the Stanford-Binet test.

To overcome this and other problems, David Wechsler devised a set of tests for both children and adults which include nonverbal *(performance)* as well as verbal items and which yielded scores for two components of intelligence: verbal and performance. Included in the performance section of the Wechsler Adult Intelligence Scale-Revised (WAIS-R) are such tasks as: (1) *picture arrangement*—examinees must arrange cards containing small pictures so that they tell a sensible story; (2) *block design*—red and white geometric designs are shown on cards, and subjects are asked to duplicate each with a series of blocks; (3) *digit symbol*—test-takers are asked to fill in ninety-three boxes with the appropriate coded symbols standing for numbers printed above the boxes. Included in the verbal section are such tasks as these: (1) *digit span*—examinees try to recall series of digits read to them by the examiner; (2) *vocabulary*—subjects are asked to define thirty-seven words of increasing difficulty; (3) *information*—individuals are asked to answer a wide range of questions which tap general knowledge, such as, ''Who was Shakespeare?''. Wechsler believed that each subtest would measure a different aspect of intelligence. However, so far, no convincing evidence that this is the case has as yet been uncovered. (Recall our discussion of the various components of intelligence.)

Different versions of the Wechsler tests exist for children and adults, and both continue in widespread use today.

Individual Tests of Intelligence: A Note on Their Uses.   Over the years, various versions of the Stanford-Binet and Wechsler tests have been administered to many millions of persons. Since these tests should only be given by a trained psychologist or other professional, and since completing them can require several hours, they involve considerable effort and expense. Why, then, are they used? One major answer (more true in the past than at present) is for purposes of *educational intervention*.

Specifically, such tests were often used to identify children at the extremes with respect to intelligence: those who suffer from some degree of **mental retardation**—intellectual functioning that is considerably below average (Kail & Pellegrino, 1985), and those who are *intellectually gifted*—persons whose intelligence is far above average (Terman, 1954; Goleman, 1980). Once such persons were identified, it was suggested, appropriate steps could be taken to enrich their educational experiences. Children in need of extra help because of impaired intellectual functioning could be assigned to special classes for special attention. And those whose unusually high level of intelligence might cause them to be bored by the regular curriculum could be provided with extra stimulation (e.g., Stanley & Benbow, 1983).

At first glance these certainly seem like reasonable goals. Why, then, have we phrased our comments largely in the past tense or in hypothetical terms (''children *could be*'')? The answer involves the following fact: in the United States, a large proportion of the children labeled as mentally retarded on the basis of such test scores turned out to be members of minority groups (such as Blacks and Hispanics). This led to charges that the tests were being used to assign such students to educational dead-ends—that they were, in fact, one more form of racial or ethnic prejudice. As we'll soon note, considerable evidence suggests that such tests are indeed *culturally biased*. Since they were developed primarily for use with white, middle-class children, they place youngsters from minority backgrounds at a serious disadvantage. We'll return to this issue as it applies to *group* tests of intelligence on page 354.

Taking note of such potential problems, a federal District Court in California banned the use of intelligence tests for purposes of identifying black children as mentally retarded (Larry P. *v* Riles, 1979). Many school systems in other states took similar actions, even in the absence of comparable court decisions. Thus, at the present time the use of individual tests of intelligence for purposes of diagnosis and educational intervention has been greatly reduced. Will there be a return to large-scale testing in the future? The controversy over the tests continues, so only time will tell (Prasse & Reschley, 1986). One point *is* clear, however: such tests must be used and interpreted with great care. Individual tests of intelligence are, after all, primarily a *tool*—one means for measuring an important human characteristic. As such, they can be used for beneficial or harmful ends. The key is to make certain they fit the task in hand and are used only in an appropriate and unbiased way.

Group Tests of Intelligence.   As we've already noted, the Stanford-Binet and Wechsler scales are *individual* tests of intelligence: they are designed for use with one person at a time. Obviously, it would be much more efficient if *group tests* existed which would be administered to large numbers of people at once. The need for such tests was driven home at the start of World War I, when the armed forces in the United States were suddenly faced with the task of screening several million recruits (see Figure 11-12 on page 354). In response to this challenge, psychologists such as Arthur Otis developed two tests: the *Army Alpha* (for persons who could read) and *Army Beta* (for persons who could not read or who did not speak English). These early group tests proved highly useful; for example, they were used to choose candidates for officer training school. Thus, they did much to boost the public image of psychology at a time when it was first getting started.

In the succeeding decades many other group tests of intelligence were developed. Among the more popular of these are the *Otis Tests,* such as the Otis-Lennon School Ability Test (Otis & Lennon, 1967); the *Henmon-Nelson Tests* (Nelson, Lamke, & French, 1973); and the *Cognitive Abilities Test (CAT)* (Thorndike & Hagen, 1982). All are available in versions which can be administered to different age groups, and all have been administered to large numbers of persons. In fact, during the 1950s and 1960s intelligence testing became so popular and so routine that the motto in education seemed to be ''test, test, and test again.'' For a long time, no one seemed to object to this activity. During the 1970s, though, criticism of the widespread, and often careless, use of group tests of

The "Great War" and Group
Tests of Intelligence

FIGURE 11-12. When the U.S. Army suddenly faced the task of screening several million recruits for service during World War I—for instance, determining which persons should be assigned to various duties—the need for group tests of intelligence became apparent.

intelligence emerged. We will now examine some of the complex issues raised in this continuing debate.

Intelligence Testing and Public Policy: Are Intelligence Tests Fair?

Objections to the widespread use of group tests of intelligence have touched on many different points. Perhaps the most important, though, involves the possibility that such tests are biased against certain groups. The basis for such concerns is obvious: in the United States (and elsewhere) individuals belonging to some ethnic or racial minorities score lower on group tests of intelligence than other persons. Such differences were first noted in the 1920s, when these tests had their initial widespread use. For example, Scandinavian, German, and Jewish immigrants attained higher scores than immigrants from other backgrounds (Hirsch, 1926). These differences have persisted until the present time. Even now, blacks, Native Americans, and persons of Hispanic descent score lower than whites of European ancestry (Aiken, 1985). What factors are responsible for such differences? Many critics of group intelligence tests contend that they stem mainly from strong **cultural bias** built into these tests. (Recall that we mentioned this problem in our discussion of the uses of individual tests of intelligence.)

Specifically, it has been suggested that because they were developed for use with white, middle-class children, many tests of intelligence place youngsters (and even adults) from other backgrounds at a severe disadvantage. Careful examination of the items used on such tests lends support to this suggestion. Many of these assume that all children have had the opportunity to acquire certain kinds of information. If they fail to demonstrate such knowledge, it is suggested they must be behind others of their own age in intellectual ability. The basic problem with such reasoning is clear: children from minority group backgrounds may never have had the chance to gain the knowledge being tested. Thus, they cannot answer correctly, no matter how high their intelligence. In addition, such youngsters may also suffer from language barriers that tend to reduce their scores.

The importance of such factors is dramatically illustrated by tests such as the one shown in Table 11-3. Here, the items have been specially prepared so as to give black

TABLE 11-3

Cultural Bias in Reverse

These questions are designed to give blacks the same cultural advantage afforded to whites on standard tests of intelligence. Can you answer them correctly?

Instructions: Circle the letter indicating the correct answer for each item.

1. Which word is out of place here?
   a. gray
   b. splib
   c. black
   d. spook

2. T-Bone Walker got famous for playing what?
   a. ''Hambone''
   b. trombone
   c. guitar
   d. piano

3. ''Bo Diddley'' is a:
   a. cheap wine
   b. down-home singer
   c. children's game
   d. dance

4. Running a game is:
   a. writing a bad check
   b. looking at something
   c. running a contest
   d. getting what one wants from another person

5. To cop an attitude is to:
   a. become angry
   b. sit down
   c. leave
   d. change one's mind

(Answers: a,c,b,d,a.)
(SOURCE: Adapted from tests devised by Williams (1974) and Dove (1968).

children the same type of advantage provided to whites on many standard tests. Can you answer the items correctly? Many black children would find this test quite easy.

While the arguments just summarized seem convincing, we should note that other groups who have recently entered the United States (primarily from Asia) score as high as, or even higher than, persons of European ancestry (Aiken, 1985). Since these individuals come from cultures very different from that experienced by white, middle-class Americans and can often barely speak English, their high scores are somewhat puzzling. Perhaps part of the answer involves the fact that these recent immigrants place an extremely high value on education. Thus, they may possess certain test-taking skills that children from various other minority groups have not had the opportunity to master. Further, most recent immigrants to the United States are part of intact families (ones with both parents present). In contrast, children of some other minority groups often grow up in single-parent homes. For example, at the present time almost 80 percent of all black children in the United States are born to single mothers (Hacker, 1983; Read, 1988). Given the potential negative impact of such conditions upon their development, it is hardly surprising that such youngsters are at a severe disadvantage on intelligence tests.

Whatever the basis for such group differences in test scores, their existence has led to efforts to develop *culture-fair* tests of intelligence. In such tests, the items are ones to which all groups, regardless of ethnic or racial background, have been exposed. One of these is the **Raven Progressive Matrices** (Raven, 1977). Sample items from one such test (The Culture Fair Intelligence Test) are shown in Figure 11-13 on page 356. As you can see, they require test-takers to work with abstract figures or relations between various objects. Presumably, specific cultural knowledge is not required for answering such items.

Another test, which has gained increasing popularity in recent years, is the *Kaufman Assessment Battery for Children*—the *K-ABC* for short (Kaufman, 1983). This test,

Sample Items from One Cul-ture-Fair Test of Intelligence

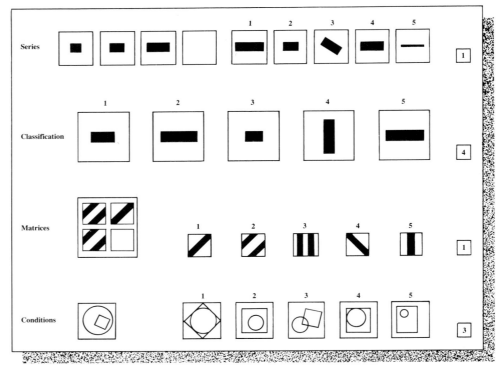

FIGURE 11-13. *Culture-fair tests* of intelligence (e.g., the *Raven Progressive Matrices,* the *Culture Fair Intelligence Test*) include items designed to be unaffected by specific cultural knowledge or experience. Unfortunately, it has proven impossible to devise a test that is totally independent of such factors. The items shown here are similar to those in one such test. *(Source: Based on items from the Culture Fair Intelligence Test, Institute for Personality and Ability Testing, Inc. Copyright © 1949, 1960, by the Institute for Personality and Ability Testing, Inc. All rights reserved. Reproduced by permission.)*

which is individually administered, is specifically designed to measure an individual's ability to process information. In other words, it focuses on effectiveness in handling new information; the role of language and previously acquired information or skills is minimized. Tasks that require *sequential processing* (e.g., repeating a series of digits in the same order in which they were presented) and ones that require *simultaneous processing* (integrating many stimuli at once) are included. An example of the latter is remembering the placement of various pictures on a page following a brief exposure to it. Early results with this test have been promising. Differences between blacks, Hispanics, and whites are much smaller than those on other tests, and the K-ABC is relatively easy to administer. Further evidence is needed before the test can be accepted as one that is genuinely free of cultural bias. Still, the fact that it focuses on the ability to process information rather than specific facts or knowledge is encouraging, and this may indeed be a useful approach to solving a difficult and complex problem.

Taking all of the above into account, we feel that the following conclusions are reasonable ones. Differences between various ethnic or racial groups in scores on many standard tests of intelligence *do* exist. Moreover, efforts to eliminate them through the development of culture-fair tests have not been entirely successful. The precise basis for such differences, however, remains unknown. Since all groups from different cultural backgrounds do not score low on such tests, it seems likely that other factors, aside from cultural bias, play a role. Among these, family structure and early childhood development may be crucial, but this remains to be determined. In any case, given the uncertain meaning of scores on standard intelligence tests (Flynn, 1987), the existence of group differences should definitely *not* be interpreted as evidence that some groups are more or less intelligent than others. So many factors probably contribute to such differences that any conclusions along these lines would be premature, to say the least.

Human Intelligence: The Role of Heredity and the Role of Environment

That people differ in intelligence is obvious. Indeed, we rarely need test scores to remind us of this fact. The causes behind these differences, though, are much less obvious. Are they largely a matter of heredity—differences in the genetic materials and codes we inherit from our parents? Or are they primarily the result of environmental factors—conditions favorable or unfavorable to intellectual growth? By this time we're sure you know the answer: both types of factors are involved. Human intelligence (and individual differences on this dimension) appears to be the product of an extremely complex interplay between genetic factors and environmental conditions. We'll now review some of the evidence pointing to this conclusion.

Evidence for the Influence of Heredity

Several lines of research offer support for the view that heredity plays at least some role in human intelligence. First, consider findings with respect to family relationship and measured IQ. If intelligence is indeed determined by heredity, we would expect that the more closely two persons are related, the more similar their IQs will be. As shown in Figure 11-14, this prediction has generally been confirmed (Bouchard & McGue, 1981; Erlenmeyer-Kimling & Jarvik, 1963). For example, the IQs of identical twins raised together correlate almost +.90, those of brothers and sisters about +.50, and those of cousins about +.15. (Remember: higher correlations indicate closer relationships between variables.)

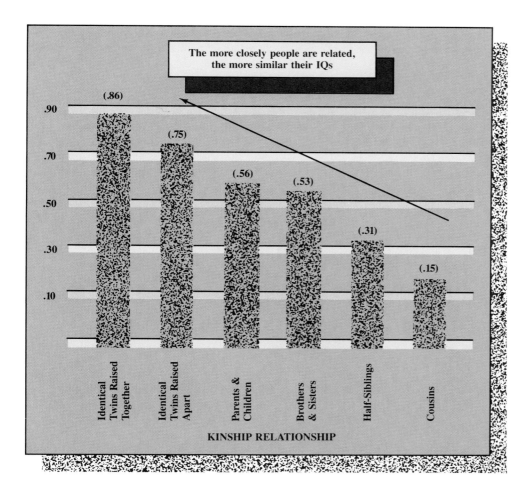

FIGURE 11-14. The closer the kinship relationship between individuals, the more similar their IQ scores tend to be. This finding provides support for the view that genetic factors play an important role in shaping human intelligence. *(Source: Based on data from Bouchard & McGue, 1981; & Erlenmeyer-Kimling & Jarvis, 1963.)*

Kinship and IQ Scores

Additional support for the impact of heredity upon intelligence is provided by studies involving adopted children. If intelligence is strongly affected by genetic factors, the IQs of adopted children should resemble those of their biological parents more closely than those of their adoptive parents. In short, they should be more similar in IQ to the persons from whom they received their genes than to the persons who raised them. This prediction, too, has been confirmed. While the IQs of adopted children correlate about +.40 to +.50 with those of their biological parents, they correlate only about +.10' to +.20 with those of their adoptive parents (Jencks, 1972; Munsinger, 1978). We should add, though, that not all studies have yielded such results. Further, in some investigations, the IQs of adopted children have been observed to become increasingly similar to those of their foster parents over time (Scarr & Weinberg, 1977). Such findings, of course, suggest that environmental factors, too, play a role.

Perhaps the most intriguing evidence for the role of genetic factors in intelligence, though, has been provided by Bouchard and his colleagues (Bouchard, 1984, 1987). In an ongoing project these researchers have located a number of pairs of identical twins who were separated early in life and were raised in different homes. Since such persons have been exposed to different environmental conditions (in some cases, sharply contrasting ones), a high correlation between their IQs would suggest that heredity plays a key role in human intelligence. In fact, this is what has been found. The IQs of identical twins reared apart (in many cases, from the time they were only a few days old) correlate almost as highly as those of identical twins reared together. Moreover, such persons are also amazingly similar in many other characteristics, such as physical appearance, dress, mannerisms, and even personality (see Figure 11-15). Clearly, such findings point to an important role of heredity in intelligence and in many other aspects of psychological functioning.

Before concluding, we should briefly mention one additional finding that might be interpreted as support for the view that human intelligence stems, at least in part, from genetic factors. In recent research employing Positron Emission Tomography (PET)—a technique which permits researchers to study the intact human brain during various activi-

Identical Twins Reared Apart: Similar in IQ and Many Other Respects

FIGURE 11-15. Identical twins raised in different homes have very similar IQs. In addition, they are remarkably similar in other respects, too. These findings offer support for the view that genetic factors play an important role in many human characteristics. *(Source: Photo courtesy Dr. Thomas J. Bouchard Jr.)*

ties—Haier and his colleagues (Haier, et al., 1988) have noted a relationship between level of brain activity and scores on one well-known test of intelligence (Raven's Advanced Progressive Matrices). Surprisingly, this relationship is an inverse one: the higher people score on this test, the lower their brain activity while taking it. Indeed, activity was twice as high in some parts of the brains of low scorers as in the brains of high scorers.

One interpretation of these findings is that intelligent people have efficient brains: they can accomplish the same amount of cognitive work with less physical effort. And since the physical structure of the brain, like that of other parts of our bodies, is strongly determined by genetic factors, it seems possible that intelligence, too, is shaped at least partly by such factors. Needless to add, such suggestions are mainly speculative at the present time; much additional evidence is necessary before firm conclusions can be reached concerning the relationship between brain activity, the brain's physical structure, and intelligence. Still, Haier et al.'s (1988) findings are suggestive and point to an intriguing new technique for studying human intelligence, and for linking important psychological characteristics to basic biological processes.

Evidence for the Influence of Environmental Factors

Genetic factors are definitely *not* the total picture where human intelligence is concerned, however. Other findings point to the conclusion that environmental factors, too, are of great importance. We have already mentioned one of these: worldwide gains in IQ in recent decades. Unless one assumes that massive shifts in human heredity have occurred during this period, such findings can only be interpreted as stemming from environmental factors—changes in living standards and educational opportunities for millions of human beings.

Second, studies of environmental deprivation and of environmental enrichment offer support for the important role of such factors. With respect to deprivation, it has been found that intelligence can be reduced by the absence of certain forms of environmental stimulation early in life (Gottfried, 1984). In terms of enrichment, removing children from sterile, restricted environments and placing them in more favorable settings seems to enhance their intellectual growth (Skeels, 1966). In addition, special programs designed to enrich the educational experiences of children from disadvantaged backgrounds (e.g., Project Headstart and others) have been found to produce sizable increases in the IQ scores of participants (Royce, Darlington, & Murray, 1983). Such gains seem to fade with the passage of time (Gray, Ramsey, & Klaus, 1982), but children who have participated in such programs continue to do better in academic achievement. Together, these findings underscore the importance of environmental factors in shaping human intelligence or skills closely related to it.

Additional evidence is provided by the type of kinship studies described earlier. Such research indicates that for a given degree of kinship (family relationship), individuals raised in the same environment have more similar IQs than persons raised apart, in different environments. For example, the IQs of brothers and sisters raised together correlate about +.50, while those of brothers and sisters raised apart correlate about +.45. Similarly, the IQs of unrelated persons raised together correlate about +.23, while those of unrelated persons raised apart show virtually no correlation whatsoever (a value of 0.00).

A fourth source of evidence for the influence of environmental factors is provided by research on birth order and intelligence. Several studies on this topic report that first-borns tend to have higher IQs than second-borns, who tend to have higher IQs than third-borns, and so on (Zajonc & Markus, 1975). The differences are not large—only a few IQ points at most—but they do seem to be real. Why do such differences exist? One possibility is suggested by the **confluence theory** proposed by Zajonc (1976, 1986). According to this theory, each individual's intellectual growth depends, to an important degree, upon the intellectual environment in which he or she develops. A first-born child benefits from the fact that for some period of time (until the birth of another child), he or she lives with two adults who provide a relatively ''advantaged'' intellectual environment

One Reason First-Borns May Have an Edge in Intelligence

FIGURE 11-16. According to *confluence theory,* first-born children benefit, intellectually, from spending part of their lives only in the presence of adults. In contrast, later-born children grow up in the presence of both adults and other children.

(refer to Figure 11-16). A second-born child, in contrast, lives with two adults who divide their attention with another child; thus the average level of his or her intellectual environment is somewhat lower. Such effects become even stronger for third-borns, and continue to grow as the number of children in a family rises (refer to Figure 11-17).

Regardless of whether Zajonc's interpretation proves accurate, the fact that first-borns tend to have higher IQs than later-borns cannot readily be explained in terms of heredity; the genes contributed by parents should remain fairly constant across the entire birth order. Thus, the impact of environmental factors is suggested once again.

One final point relating to such research: since a woman's egg cells are formed early in her life (before her birth), the ova from which second-borns develop are older than those for first-borns, and so on. Thus, it might be argued that it is this factor—not the intellectual environment in which the children are raised—that contributes to the higher IQ of first-borns. Even if this argument is accepted, though, the importance of environmental factors in shaping intelligence is still suggested. After all, why would ''younger'' ova differ from ''older'' ones? In all likelihood, it would be because of the impact of many environmental factors (e.g., changes in the mother's diet or life style, exposure to harmful chemical substances.)

Finally, we should note that a wide range of other environmental factors have been found to be related to IQ scores. These include nutrition, family background (e.g., parents' education and income), and quality of education, to mention just a few (Bouchard & Segal, 1985). Such effects are small, but, again, they appear to be real.

Environment, Heredity, and Intelligence: Summing Up

Taking all this evidence into account, what can we conclude? In our view the following suggestion seems justified: both heredity and environment contribute to human intelligence, so neither should be ignored. While this may strike you as an eminently reasonable middle ground, we must admit that it ignores a related issue that has been the subject of heated (sometimes passionate!) debate: what is the *relative* contribution of these factors? In other words, do environmental factors play a stronger role than genetic factors in shaping intelligence, or are they of roughly equal importance? To date, efforts to answer this question have failed to yield a clear reply. However, growing evidence does seem to point to the possibility that genetic factors are quite important—perhaps more important in some respects than environmental ones. As you can probably guess, many psychologists are made uneasy by such conclusions (Kamin, 1978). Being concerned with human welfare, they would strongly prefer to be in a position to intervene—to help enhance the intellectual capacity of all human beings. An important genetic basis for intelligence

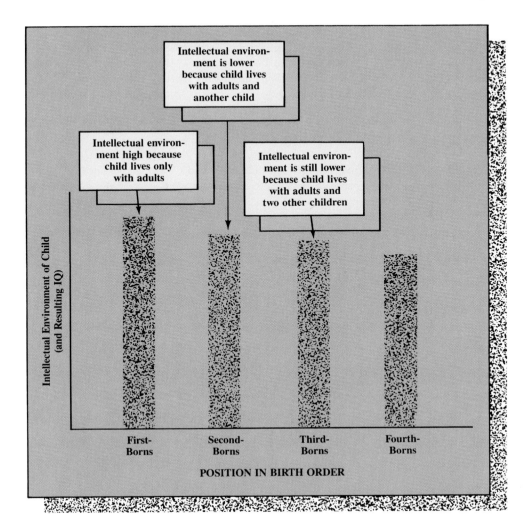

FIGURE 11-17. According to *confluence theory*, the intellectual environment in which children develop becomes less and less favorable as the number of previous children born in the family increases. As a result, the IQ of first-borns is higher than that of second-borns; the IQ of second-borns is higher than that of third-borns; and so on. *(Source: Based on suggestions by Zajonc, 1976.)*

seems, at first glance, to rule out such possibilities. Two comments about such reactions seem appropriate.

First, even if intelligence is indeed strongly affected by genetic factors, this in no way implies that it cannot be altered. Many physical conditions with a large genetic component (e.g., near-sightedness, high blood pressure) can be corrected through appropriate treatment, and there are no grounds for assuming that the same could not be true for intelligence. Second, scientists must always be on guard against the possibility that their own political views, or political pressures around them, will influence their interpretation of scientific data (Baron, 1987c). Unfortunately, such pressures abound where the study of human intelligence is concerned. Thus, psychologists should take great care to assure that the findings they uncover are interpreted in the cold light of reason—not through the perspective of either conservative or liberal ideologies. Only then will progress toward our ultimate goal—fuller understanding of the nature of human intelligence—be assured.

Other Uses of Psychological Tests: Measuring Interests, Aptitudes, and Achievement

At the start of this chapter we indicated that people differ in an almost limitless number of ways. Information about many of these differences can be intriguing but is of little practical value. After all, there is little use for information about differences among people in the size of their ears, the strength of their preference for mushroom over sausage pizza, or their ability to construct sand castles on the beach. Information about differences on other dimensions, though, *is* highly useful. In particular, knowing something about a person's *interests, aptitudes,* and *achievement* can be of value both to the individual and to organizations with which he or she comes into contact (e.g., colleges which must decide whether to admit the person, businesses which must decide whether to hire her or him). In this final section we'll consider how individual differences in these areas are measured, and how such knowledge can then be put to practical use.

Measuring Interests: Choosing the Right Career

Choosing the right job or career is a difficult task. How can we tell, in advance, whether we'll enjoy the work or be able to perform it effectively? While no simple or perfect solution to this dilemma exists, psychological tests designed to measure **interests**—preferences for certain types of activities—can help (Aiken, 1985). Such tests indicate how your preferences compare with those of other persons, and this information, in turn, can help you choose career paths that are right for you.

While many tests for measuring interests exist, the one that is most widely used is the *Strong-Campbell Interest Inventory* or *SCII* (The Psychological Corporation, 1974). On this test an examinee indicates whether she or he likes, dislikes, or is indifferent to each of a wide range of activities. Replies are then compared to the answers which have been given by individuals who are already working in various occupations. The more

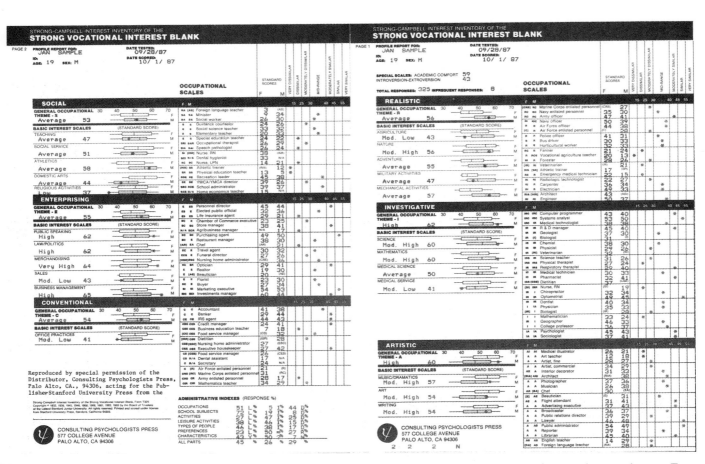

FIGURE 11-18. The individual who took this test shows strong interests in several areas. Together, these suggest he might be happy as a public administrator or a systems analyst. *(Reproduced by special permission of the Distributor, Consulting Psychologists Press, Palo Alto, CA., 94306, acting for the Publisher Stanford University Press from the Strong-Campbell Interest Inventory of the Strong Vocational Interest Blank, Form T325. Copyright © 1933, 1938, 1945, 1946, 1966, 1968, 1981, 1983, 1985 by the Board of Trustees of the Leland Stanford Junior University. All rights reserved. Printed and scored under license from Stanford University Press, Stanford, California 94305.)*

A Sample Profile on the Strong-Campbell Interest Inventory

similar an examinee's replies to those given by people in each field, the greater the examinee's interest in that field is assumed to be. An individual's relative standing on certain basic interest themes is reported, as well as his or her similarity to persons in specific occupations. For example, the scores shown in Figure 11-18 suggest that the person who completed the SCII has strong interests in the investigative and artistic areas. Not surprisingly, this person shares interests with persons whose careers reflect the characteristics of both fields.

Of course, scores on the SCII or other interest tests are not the only basis for making career choices. Individuals should also consider their abilities in relation to the requirements of various jobs, and even whether they possess personality traits that suit them for a given career. Thus, the information yielded by interest tests can be helpful in narrowing the field, but it is by no means the entire story where career or job choice is concerned.

Measuring Aptitudes: In Search of Hidden Talents

No one finds all activities equally easy to master. Some people easily master mechanical tasks; others can hardly hold a hammer or screwdriver. Some persons learn to play musical instruments with ease; others seem incapable of keeping time or finding the right notes. And some find typing to be a snap, while others seem doomed to hunt and peck throughout life. In short, individuals vary greatly in terms of various **aptitudes**—their capacity to profit from specific types of training. Since different jobs require different skills, information about individual differences in this respect can be helpful; indeed, such information can save organizations and teachers a great deal of wasted effort, and the persons involved considerable frustration. Recognizing this fact, psychologists have developed many tests for assessing specific aptitudes. So many of these exist that it would be impossible to describe them all here. Among the most important and most widely used, though, are tests designed to measure mechanical, clerical, musical, and artistic aptitudes. Sample items from one such test, designed to measure aptitude for art, are presented in Figure 11-19. Persons taking this test indicate which of two or three versions of an

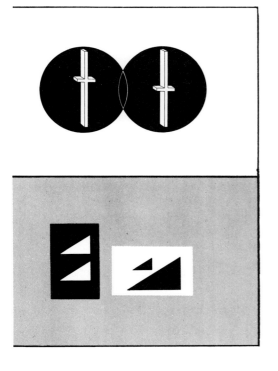

FIGURE 11-19. Persons taking this test of art aptitude indicate which designs they find most pleasing. The more closely their choices agree with those of practicing artists, the higher the score they receive. *(Source: Graves Design Judgment Test. Copyright © 1946, 1948, renewed 1974 by The Psychological Corporation. Reproduced by permission. All rights reserved.)*

Sample Items from a Test of Art Aptitude

abstract design they find most pleasing. Their answers are then compared with those given by a large number of practicing artists. The more similar their preferences to those of such persons, the higher their aptitude for art training is assumed to be.

Other aptitude tests are designed to measure several different types of potential at once. One of these, the *General Aptitude Test Battery (GATB)* is often used for vocational counseling and for selecting employees. The entire test requires more than two hours to administer and involves both paper-and-pencil tasks and ones requiring the use of apparatus. It yields scores on several different factors, including Verbal Aptitude, Numerical Aptitude, Spatial Aptitude, Clerical Perception, Motor Coordination, and Manual Dexterity. An individual's scores on these factors can be compared with those of people currently performing a given job successfully; the closer the match, the better the chances that this person, too, will be successful at the job. Alternatively, for purposes of counseling, an individual's score profile can be compared with those of people in many different occupations. Where close matches occur, a possible career is indicated.

With rapid changes in the nature of many jobs, there has been a growing tendency for large companies to develop their own tests for screening job applicants. Regardless of whether aptitude tests or specially created tests are used, though, the major goal remains the same: selecting employees who are most likely to benefit from various forms of training and who are likely to go on to become valuable members of the organization.

One final point about aptitude tests such as the GATB. In the past, substantial sex differences on them were often noted. For example, males scored higher than females on measures of mechanical aptitude and spatial visualization (visualizing and moving objects in three-dimensional space). In contrast, females scored higher than males on measures of verbal ability (e.g., spelling, language) and perceptual speed. Although such differences were reported for several decades, they now appear to be vanishing (Feingold, 1988). By the early 1980s males had cut the gap in perceptual speed in half, while females had made similar gains with respect to mechanical reasoning and spatial relations. Presumably, these changes reflect more equal opportunities for both sexes in a wide range of educational experiences. Given current efforts in many societies to eliminate any remaining vestiges of inequality in this respect, it seems likely that such differences between the sexes will continue to fade in the years ahead. (Can individuals improve their scores on standardized tests through practice or special coaching? See "The Cutting Edge" section below for information on this issue.)

FIGURE 11-20. Can practice or special coaching increase scores on standardized tests such as the SAT? Recent evidence suggests this is the case.

Coaching, Practice, and Scores on Standardized Tests

FOCUS ON RESEARCH: The Cutting Edge

Coaching and Practice: Reducing Their Impact on Standardized Tests

If they can get it, most persons dearly love to hold an edge. They prefer to be in a situation where they have an advantage over others with whom they must compete. Getting into college, graduate programs, medical school, or law school is no exception to this rule. Each year millions of persons spend vast sums of money on special courses, books, and tutoring programs that promise to raise their scores on entrance tests such as the SAT, the LSAT (Law School Admissions Test), the GRE (Graduate Record Examination), and so on (refer to Figure 11-20). Do such procedures work? The answer seems to be "yes," at least to a degree (Messick & Jungeblut, 1981). Practice and special types of coaching do seem to raise scores on such tests, although the size of such gains seems to decrease as more and more time is spent on such tasks. (At first, practice yields large gains. Later, the rate of gain decreases.) Since they are used to select future leaders in many fields, it seems important that these standardized tests be as fair as possible—that such advantages be eliminated or at least reduced. How can this be accomplished? One approach is to ensure that all test-takers are familiar with the test and the strategies needed to take it. Presumably, this will reduce the impact of special coaching or practice. Another tactic is to construct the tests in such a way that the items they contain are relatively immune to special preparation. How can this be accomplished? A study by Powers (1986) offers some suggestions.

In this investigation Powers examined the results of several previous studies in order to determine whether certain types of items are affected by coaching and practice to a greater extent than others. Results indicated that this was indeed the case. Tests with more options per item (e.g., five choices) were less susceptible to such effects than tests with fewer options (e.g., four choices). Second, the greater the time allotted to each item, the smaller the effects of coaching and practice. Finally, and strongest of all, the longer and more complex the directions for each test, the more readily it was affected by coaching and practice.

Together, these results suggest that it may be possible to design standardized tests that are relatively unaffected by special preparation by some test-takers. In order to do so, though, it will be necessary to construct them using only certain types of items and instructions. Unfortunately, many standardized tests have been in use for many years and employ norms based on the scores of hundreds of thousands of persons. Changing their content or format, therefore, is a formidable task. But precisely such change may be necessary if the validity of these tests is to be maintained—if they are to remain useful in selecting the best candidates for college or advanced study.

Measuring Achievement: Assessing Current Knowledge

The last type of test we'll consider is one with which you've already had lots of experience: **achievement tests.** These are designed to measure current knowledge in some chosen area—how much a test-taker knows about some subject or task. Classroom exams in high school and college fall under this general heading, although, as you well know, students taking them often complain about their validity! (Some students state that the tests don't provide a fair evaluation of what they know; hence, they are invalid.)

Other achievement tests, designed to measure basic skills in such areas as reading, vocabulary, spelling, and arithmetic, are administered to millions of children each year. These include the well-known *Iowa Tests of Basic Skills* and the *Stanford Achievement Series*. The results on such tests are used to counsel individual students—to identify those in need of special assistance in certain subjects. In addition, they are used to assess the extent to which schools are attaining their major goals: teaching students the skills they need to function in an increasingly complex and demanding technology-based society.

Summary and Review

Psychological Tests: Some Basics

Psychological tests are special devices for measuring the characteristics of individuals. In order to be useful they must be *reliable:* a test must yield the same (or similar) scores each time it is taken by the same persons. In addition, tests must possess *internal consistency*—all items on them should measure the same thing.

Validity is another major requirement of psychological tests. It refers to whether the test actually measures what it claims to measure. Several types of validity exist (e.g., concurrent validity, predictive validity). However, the most important may be *construct validity*—the extent to which a test measures a concept which is part of a psychological theory.

Tests must also be carefully *standardized* through administration to a large group of appropriate persons. Standardization yields information on the total range of scores and the average score attained by people taking the test. A given person's score can be compared with these figures to determine his or her relative standing on the characteristics being measured.

Intelligence

Intelligence has traditionally been defined as the ability to think abstractly or to learn readily from experience. It seems to involve several different components. A theory proposed by Sternberg (1985) suggests that there may actually be three distinct types of intelligence: *componential, experiential,* and *contextual.* Many tests designed to measure intelligence exist. The IQ scores they yield describe an individual's performance relative to that of others of the same age. The members of some minority groups tend to score lower on standard intelligence tests than other persons. This has led to efforts to develop tests that are entirely *culture-fair.* Such efforts have not been totally successful, but one test developed in recent years (the K-ABC) attempts to assess information processing abilities. Some studies suggest that scores on this test may reflect individual differences in such abilities rather than differences in previously acquired facts or knowledge.

Recent years have witnessed large worldwide gains in IQ scores. Since it is unlikely that all people are becoming more intelligent, this pattern suggests that intelligence tests probably measure some factor that is moderately related to intelligence, rather than intelligence itself.

Intelligence and the Nature-Nurture Controversy

Several forms of evidence suggest that heredity plays an important role in human intelligence. For example, the IQs of adopted children correlate more closely with their biological parents than with those of their natural parents. Further, identical twins separated early in life often show striking similarities in intelligence and personality, despite being reared apart. Other evidence points to the importance of environmental factors. Programs designed to provide children with intellectually enriched environments (e.g., Project Headstart) have succeeded in raising IQ scores and academic achievement. Similarly, children born early in the birth sequence tend to have higher IQs than those born later (e.g., first-borns have higher IQs than second-borns). This seems to stem from advantages gained by living only with adults, rather than with both adults and younger siblings.

Interests, Aptitudes, and Achievement

Psychological tests are also used to measure *interests*—preferences for various activities. Understanding one's pattern of interests can aid in the selection of an appropriate job or career. *Aptitude tests* measure the capacity to profit from specific types of training. They are widely used in vocational counseling and in the selection of employees. *Achievement tests* are used to assess knowledge of some subject or task. Scores on standard aptitude tests (e.g., the SAT) can be enhanced through practice and special coaching. However, it may be possible to reduce such effects through the use of certain types of test items.

 **Key Terms**

Achievement Tests Tests designed to measure knowledge of a specific subject or task.

Aptitude Tests Tests designed to measure the capacity to profit from specific types of training.

Componential Intelligence The ability to think analytically.

Concurrent Validity The relationship between test scores and current performance on some criterion.

Confluence Theory A theory suggesting that IQ tends to decrease across the birth order within a family (first-borns tend to have a higher IQ than second-borns, and so on).

Construct Validity The extent to which a test measures a construct described by a psychological theory.

Content Validity The extent to which the items on a test sample the skills or knowledge needed for achievement in a given field or task.

Contextual Intelligence The ability to adapt to a changing environment.

Cultural Bias Occurs when answering the items on a test of intelligence requires specific cultural experience or knowledge.

Experiential Intelligence The ability to formulate new ideas or combine seemingly unrelated information.

Intelligence Traditionally, the ability to think analytically or to learn readily from experience.

Interests Preferences for participation in certain activities.

IQ A numerical value that reflects the extent to which an individual's score on an intelligence test departs from the average for other people of the same age.

Predictive Validity The relationship between scores on a test and later performance on a criterion.

Psychological Tests Special devices for assessing the traits or characteristics of individuals.

Raven Progressive Matrices One popular "culture-free" test of intelligence.

Reliability The extent to which any measuring device yields the same results when applied to the same quantity.

Split-Half Reliability The extent to which individuals attain equivalent scores on two halves of a psychological test.

Standardization Administration of a psychological test to a large group of people who are representative of the population for which the test is intended.

Stanford-Binet Test A popular test for measuring individual intelligence.

Test-Retest Reliability The extent to which a psychological test yields similar scores when taken by the same persons on different occasions.

Triarchic Theory A theory suggesting that there are actually three distinct kinds of intelligence.

Validity The extent to which psychological tests actually measure what they claim to measure.

For More Information

Aiken, L.R. (1988). *Psychological testing and assessment,* 6th ed. Boston: Allyn and Bacon.
A clearly written introduction to all aspects of psychological testing. The chapters on intelligence and on ethics in testing are of special interest.

Eysenck, H.J., and Kamin, L. (1981). *The intelligence controversy*. New York: Wiley.
In this book two researchers with sharply opposing views about the relative importance of genetic and environmental factors in intelligence debate their beliefs. You could hardly find a better illustration of the impact of political views and pressures on the course of scientific inquiry.

Sternberg, R.J. (1986). *Intelligence applied*. New York: Harcourt Brace Jovanovich.
A relatively brief and well-written description of the author's *triarchic theory* of intelligence. The main point is that there are really three types of intelligence rather than only one. Sternberg's views promise to become quite influential in psychology, so this is an excellent source to consult for the latest word on our understanding of human intelligence.

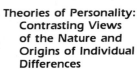

CHAPTER

12

Personality: The Uniqueness and Consistency of Individual Behavior

It's the twentieth reunion of James Madison High School's Class of '68, and two old friends, Rick Kravetz and Bob Flynn, have run into each other in front of the registration desk.

"Rick—is that really you?" Bob asks, staring at his old friend. "You bet!" Bob replies, grasping Rick's hand and shaking it warmly. "Man, it's great to see you. It's been too long!"

"You're a sight for sore eyes yourself," Rick exclaims. "But you sure have changed. I wouldn't have recognized you without the name tag. Gray at the temples—whew! Who'd ever have thought it."

"Well, it *has* been a long time. What is it, fifteen years? Anyway, I'm not complaining. At least I've still got hair to turn gray!"

At this comment, Rick laughs and runs his hand over his rapidly thinning locks. "You've got me there. I guess that by the time we hit the thirtieth reunion I'll look like my dad, shiny as a bowling ball."

"So how's life treating you? I heard you were living in Texas. Do you like it down there?"

"Love it, just love it. You know how I hated winter? Well, we don't have any in Houston, or not much, anyway. Some people are bothered by the heat, but not me. You know how I always liked it warm—I don't even feel alive until it hits 85. How about you? Still up there in the frigid north country?"

"Yep, and I wouldn't trade—I hate heat more now than when we were kids. Ugh! I never could figure out how you could stand it. But tell me, how do you like living in a big city? Doesn't the traffic drive you nuts?"

"Naw, it's not so bad. Besides, I'm where I always wanted to be, right in the middle of things. There's so much going on, and so much to do; it's great!"

"Well, I see that you still love excitement! But that's not for me. The older I get, the more I need peace and quiet. Woods, fields. . . ."

"Well, you sure must get plenty up there in Plainfield. Living there would wipe me out! But, hey, let's make some dinner plans. We've got a lot of catching up to do. I hear that there's a great French restaurant out on Route 32. What do you say we get a group together and hit it?"

Bob looks hesitant. "Well, er, it would be great to spend some time together, but, um, I hear it's pretty fancy. Can't we find someplace that's a little more, um, down-to-earth?"

At this remark, Rick breaks out in a laugh. "You mean *cheap*, don't you? Same old Bob, still pinching those pennies. And you say *I* haven't changed! O.K., we'll find someplace more 'down-to-earth'—I wouldn't want to ruin a great occasion by straining your budget."

If our experience with other people tells us anything, it is this. First, they are all *unique*; each possesses a pattern of traits and characteristics not fully duplicated in any other person (refer to Figure 12-1). Second, these traits or characteristics are fairly *stable* over time. As the two friends in our opening story observed, the traits people possess at one time are often visible months, years, or even decades later—although perhaps in somewhat altered form. These two observations form the basis of a definition of **personality** currently accepted by many psychologists: the unique but stable set of characteristics and behaviors that sets each individual apart from others (Carver & Scheier, 1988). In short, it refers to the lasting ways in which a given person is different from all others.

Do you find this definition reasonable? In all probability you do. Most people accept the view that human beings possess specific traits (tendencies to think and act in certain ways) and that these traits are fairly constant over time. In other words, we assume that if one of our friends is ambitious, energetic, and humorous today, she or he will also

FIGURE 12-1. As suggested by this cartoon, human beings differ from one another in an almost infinite number of respects. *(Source:* The New Yorker.*)*

"For Willard, life is a ball. For me, it isn't."

The Uniqueness of Human Behavior

behave in these ways tomorrow, next month, or next year. You may be surprised to learn, therefore, that until quite recently a heated controversy existed in psychology concerning the accuracy of these beliefs.

On one side of this debate were scientists who contended that people do *not* possess lasting traits (Mischel, 1977, 1985). According to these researchers (whom we might term the "anti-personality" camp), behavior is shaped largely by external factors or conditions. Thus, we should not expect people to behave consistently in different periods or settings. Our belief that they do is largely an illusion stemming from the fact that we *want* to perceive such consistency: after all, it makes our task of predicting others' actions easier (Schweder, 1975).

On the other side of the controversy were scientists who held, equally strongly, that stable traits *do* exist, and these lead individuals to behave consistently at different times and in a wide range of settings. Which of these opposing views has prevailed? As you can guess from the presence of this chapter, the latter one has. At present the weight of scientific opinion has swung toward the view that individual behavior *is* often shaped by stable traits or characteristics. Several lines of evidence offer support for this conclusion.

First, in a number of large-scale projects the behavior of many individuals has been studied for extended periods of time (weeks or even months) in many different contexts. The result: a considerable amount of consistency has in fact emerged (Moskowitz, 1982). People who are energetic at one time are also energetic at others; those who react strongly to emotion-provoking events in one setting also do so in others, and so on (Larsen, 1987). Why was such consistency not observed in many earlier studies? Because, quite simply, only brief intervals of time (two or three hours) and a restricted range of situations were examined. Apparently, a larger sample of behavior is needed before the type of consistency our informal experience tells us exists can be observed.

Second, other research indicates that individuals' behavior does indeed reflect their stable traits whenever this is feasible—in situations where these personal tendencies are not overwhelmed by powerful situational factors (Monson, Hesley, & Chernick, 1982). As an illustration of this point, consider the following fact. When stopped by a state trooper, most motorists—even people who are highly aggressive—tend to act in a fairly polite manner. Why? Because situational pressures are so strong that little room for expressing individual preferences is present. In other contexts (e.g., at a neighborhood bar, in their own home), such pressures are absent, and large differences in behavior,

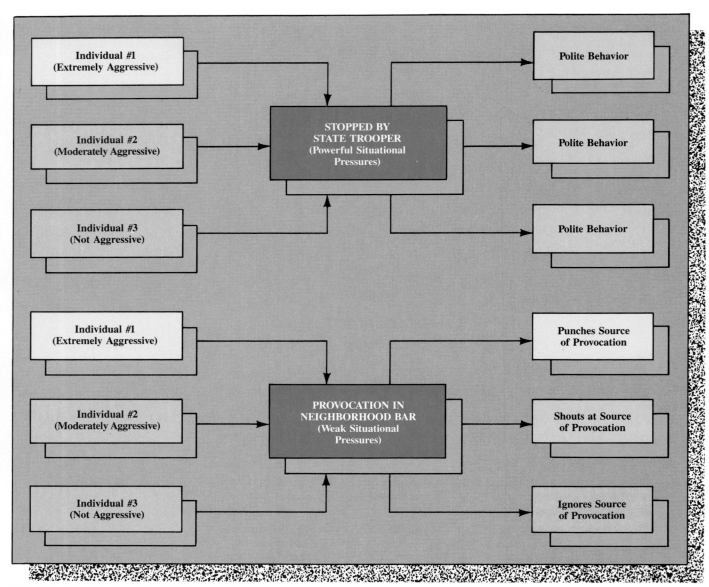

Situational Pressures and Individual Differences

FIGURE 12-2. When stopped by a state trooper (upper panel), most persons—even ones who are highly aggressive—behave politely. This is because strong situational pressures outweigh individual differences in underlying traits (e.g., level of aggressiveness). When provoked in a neighborhood bar (lower panel), situational pressures are weaker, and differences among individuals may be more readily visible.

reflecting underlying traits, may appear (refer to Figure 12-2). Please note, by the way, that large individual differences sometimes appear even in situations that might at first seem even more powerful than ones involving state troopers. For example, during earthquakes or other natural disasters some people react calmly, others panic and rush madly about, while still others become literally paralyzed with fear. Such differences indicate that differences among individuals may be visible even in contexts where we might expect almost everyone to behave in very much the same way.

Third, and probably most surprising, people seem to differ in the extent to which they are consistent (Kenrick & Stringfield, 1980). In other words, consistency itself is an aspect of personality! At one extreme on this dimension, which is known as **self-monitoring,** are persons whose actions stem largely from their underlying traits or preferences. As you can probably guess, they show a high degree of consistency across situations and over time. At the other extreme are individuals whose behavior is shaped mainly by external factors; they often behave very differently in different situations and show little consistency (Snyder, 1987). Because of such differences, the fact that specific individuals do not show similar patterns of behavior in all settings does not, in itself, argue against the existence of lasting traits. On the contrary, individual differences in consistency may actually reflect the impact of one such trait or characteristic.

On the basis of such evidence, many psychologists have concluded that it does make sense to talk about—and to study—personality. But please keep the following point in mind: the fact that various traits exist and influence behavior does not suggest that the impact of situational factors is weak or unimportant. On the contrary, most psychologists believe that human behavior stems from a complex interplay between situational *and* personal variables. To understand it fully, therefore, both must be taken carefully into account. Having said this, we should note that our attention in the present chapter will be focused primarily on *personality*—consistent differences among individuals in the ways they think, feel, and behave. To provide you with a broad introduction to this important topic, we'll first examine several *theories of personality*—contrasting views about the nature and origins of such differences. Next, we'll consider different ways of *measuring* or assessing personality. Finally, we'll review several *key dimensions* of personality identified by recent research.

Theories of Personality: Contrasting Views of the Nature and Origins of Individual Differences

What is personality? How does it develop? What are its major components? Efforts to answer such questions have often taken the form of grand, sweeping theories of personality. Literally hundreds of these have been proposed, but here we will focus on a few that have proven most influential within our field.

Psychoanalytic Theories of Personality: Freud, His Disciples, and Dissenters

Perhaps the most dramatic, and in many ways most unsettling, theory of personality is the **psychoanalytic** view proposed by Sigmund Freud. Freud, who spent most of his life in Vienna (hence the German accents of many film psychiatrists), was trained as a physician and planned to enter medical research (see Figure 12-3). During the course of his practice,

FIGURE 12-3. Sigmund Freud, one of the most influential figures in the history of psychology, in the office where he developed much of his intriguing theory of personality.

Sigmund Freud

however, he encountered several puzzling cases: patients whose symptoms (e.g., blindness, deafness, paralysis in one arm) seemed to have no underlying physical ailment. As he attempted to help such persons, Freud gradually formulated a theory of human behavior and mental illness. His ideas were complex and touched on many issues. Freud's ideas about personality, though, involve three related topics: *levels of consciousness*, the major *structures of personality*, and *psychosexual stages of development*.

Levels of Consciousness: Beneath the Iceberg's Tip.　　As the captain of the ill-fated ocean liner *Titanic* discovered, most of an iceberg lies beneath the surface. According to Freud, the same holds true for the human mind (refer to Figure 12-4). Above the surface, readily available to our mental inspection, is the realm of the *conscious*. This includes our current thoughts—whatever we are thinking about at a given moment. Beneath the conscious realm is the much larger *preconscious*. This contains memories which are not part of current thoughts but can readily be brought to mind. Finally, beneath the preconscious, and forming the bulk of the human mind, is the *unconscious*—thoughts, desires, and impulses of which we remain largely unaware. Although some of this material was always unconscious, Freud believed that much of it had been conscious but was *repressed*—it was thrust out of consciousness because it was too anxiety-provoking (e.g., shameful experiences, unacceptable sexual or aggressive urges). The fact that we are not aware of the unconscious, though, in no way prevents it from affecting our behavior. Indeed, Freud believed that many of his patients' symptoms were disguised reflections of repressed thoughts and desires present in the unconscious. This is why one major goal of **psychoanalysis**—the method of treating mental illness devised by Freud—involves bringing unconscious, repressed material back into consciousness.

The Structure of Personality: Id, Ego, and Superego.　　Do you know the story of *Dr. Jekyll and Mr. Hyde*? If so, you already have a basic idea of some of the key structures of personality described by Freud. He suggested that personality consists largely of three parts: the *id, ego,* and *superego* which roughly correspond to the words *desire, reason,* and *conscience*.

FIGURE 12-4. Freud believed that the human mind operates at three distinct levels: *conscious, preconscious,* and *unconscious*.

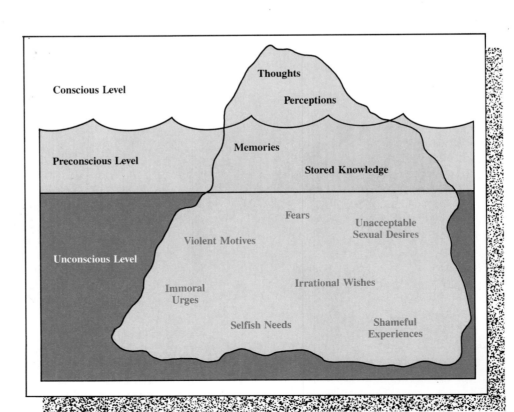

Conscious Level

Thoughts

Perceptions

Preconscious Level

Memories

Stored Knowledge

Unconscious Level

Fears

Unacceptable Sexual Desires

Violent Motives

Irrational Wishes

Immoral Urges

Selfish Needs

Shameful Experiences

Freud's View of the Human Mind: The Mental Iceberg

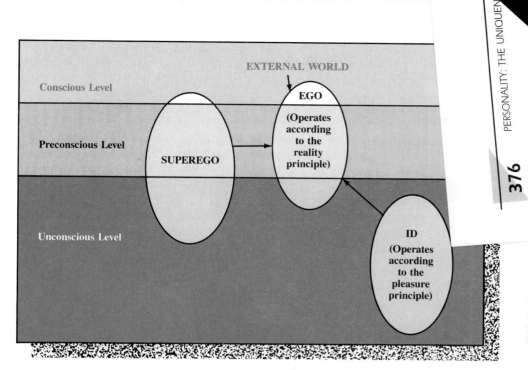

EXTERNAL WORLD

Conscious Level

Preconscious Level

EGO
(Operates according to the reality principle)

SUPEREGO

Unconscious Level

ID
(Operates according to the pleasure principle)

...ponents: *id, ego,* and *super-ego.* The id is largely unconscious and operates in terms of the *pleasure principle*. The ego is partly conscious and operates in terms of the *reality principle*. Finally, the superego, too, is located only partly in the realm of consciousness.

In a sense, the **id** (desire) is the ''motor'' or source of energy for human personality. It consists of all of our primitive, innate urges. These include various bodily needs, sexual desire, and aggressive impulses. According to Freud, the id is totally unconscious and operates in accordance with what he termed the *pleasure principle*—the desire for immediate, total gratification. In short, it is the Mr. Hyde of our personality (refer to Figure 12-5).

Unfortunately, the world offers few opportunities for instant pleasure. Moreover, attempting to gratify many of our innate urges would soon get us into serious trouble. It is in response to these facts that the second structure of personality—the **ego**—develops. The ego's task is to hold the id in check until conditions appropriate for satisfaction of its impulses exist. Thus, the ego operates in accordance with the *reality principle*; it takes account of the external world and directs behavior so as to maximize pleasure and minimize pain. The ego is partly conscious but not entirely so; thus, some of its actions, too, are outside our conscious understanding.

The final structure described by Freud is the **superego.** It, too, controls the satisfaction of id impulses, permitting their gratification only under certain conditions. In contrast to the ego, though, the superego is concerned with morality: it can tell right from wrong. It permits gratification of id impulses only when it is morally correct to do so—not simply when it is safe or feasible, as required by the ego. The superego is acquired through experience, from our parents, and represents our internalization of their moral teachings and the norms of our society. Unfortunately, such teachings are often quite inflexible and leave little room for gratification of our basic desires: they require us to be good all the time, like Dr. Jekyll. Because of this fact, the ego faces another difficult task: it must mediate between the id and superego, striking a balance between our primitive urges and our learned moral constraints. Freud felt that this constant struggle between the id, ego, and superego plays a key role in the development of personality—the topic to which we turn next.

Psychosexual Stages of Development.   When is personality formed? Freud's answer was: ''very early.'' In fact, he believed that the personality we will possess as adults is largely determined by events occurring during the first few years of life. Between birth and age seven, he proposed, all human beings pass through a series of distinct *psychosexual stages*. These reflect the fact that, as we grow, different parts of the body serve as the focus of the id's constant quest for pleasure. First, we seek pleasure primarily through the mouth (the *oral stage*). Next, in response to efforts by parents or others to institute toilet training, the id focuses on the process of elimination (the *anal stage*). At about age four, our genitals become the primary source of pleasure and we enter the *phallic stage*. Freud speculated that at this time, we fantasize about sexual relations with our opposite-sex parent. Fear of punishment for such desires initiates the *Oedipal conflict*.

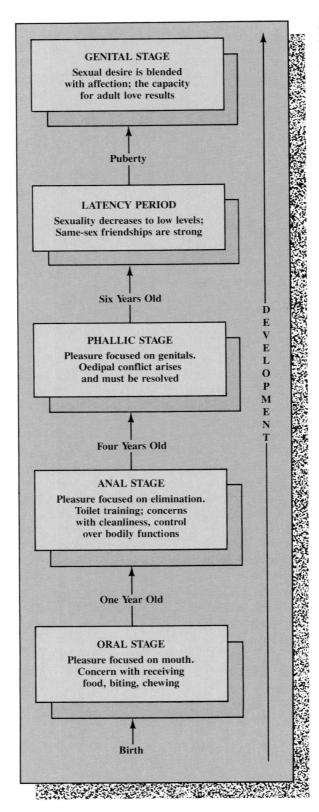

FIGURE 12-6. According to Freud, all human beings pass through a series of discrete *psychosexual stages* of development.

Freud's Psychosexual Stages of Development

In boys the punishment feared is castration; in girls it is loss of parental love. Since the former struck Freud as being far more vivid and threatening than the latter, he concluded that girls don't resolve the Oedipal conflict as firmly or completely as boys. The result: they have a weaker conscience (superego). If this sounds somewhat negative toward females, don't be surprised. In several respects, Freud held views that would be described today as sexist. Please remember, though, that he was writing in the nineteenth century, a time when few scholars questioned the view that females were inferior to males in many ways.

However the Oedipal conflict is resolved, most of us give up our sexual desire for our parents. When this occurs, Freud contended, sexual urges are largely repressed and we enter the *latency period*, when sexual urges appear to be largely ''on hold.'' This lasts until puberty, when lust is blended with affection, and we enter the final *genital stage*. (Please see Figure 12-6 for a summary of these stages.)

Freud believed that normal personality development can be derailed at any of these stages by either too much or too little gratification. In either case, we may suffer *fixation* and fail to proceed to the normal, adult pattern. For example, too much gratification of id impulses during the oral stage can result in a personality that is overly dependent, conforming, and trusting (refer to Figure 12-7), while too little gratification can produce a personality in which verbal aggression and hostility predominate. Similarly, too much gratification during the anal stage can produce an adult who is excessively neat, while too little can have the opposite effect: an adult who is sloppy and disorganized.

Freud's Theory of Personality: Summing Up.

By now, you are probably convinced that Freud's theory of personality is intriguing, to say the least. But what, you may be wondering, does it have to do with *uniqueness* and *consistency*—the central aspects of our definition of personality? While Freud did not address these issues directly, his theory seems relevant to both. First, it can explain our uniqueness by pointing to the fact that during psychosexual development all individuals experience different patterns of gratification and frustration. The result: each possesses a different pattern of fixations, as well as a unique balance of the id, ego, and superego. Turning to consistency (the existence of stable traits), Freud's theory suggests that personality is formed during the first few years of life and remains stable thereafter—unless altered by psychoanalysis! So, consistency should be the rule rather than the exception where human beings are concerned. In sum, Freud's theory offers ready explanations for both the uniqueness and the consistency of human behavior. As such, it qualifies as a theory of personality. We will comment on its value in this respect below.

The Neo-Freudians: Disciples and Dissenters.

Freud himself was a dynamic personality who had a powerful impact on many persons who came in contact with him. Thus, over the years he had many students who later went on to famous careers themselves. In general, these **neo-Freudians** accepted Freud's ideas about the importance of the unconscious and the basic components of personality (id, ego, and superego). However, they disagreed with him—sometimes angrily—over certain issues. For example, they tended to place greater emphasis on the role of *social experience*—our early interactions with the people around us. Similarly, they tended to de-emphasize the importance of sexual and aggressive impulses. In other words, they felt that human behavior stems from a somewhat wider range of motives than did Freud. And several of them—Karen Horney in particular—disagreed with several of Freud's assumptions about females and their supposed psychological inferiority to males. A summary of the major ideas and concepts introduced by several neo-Freudians (Freud's disciples and dissenters) is presented in Table 12-1 on page 378. Please examine it carefully, for their views, especially those of Erikson and Fromm, remain influential even today.

Psychoanalytic Theory in Perspective: Assessing Its Value.

When asked to name the persons whose ideas have been most influential in shaping the twentieth century, many historians respond without hesitation: Karl Marx, Albert Einstein, and Sigmund Freud. In one sense, then, Freud's impact on modern thought is obvious. But what about

Early Experience: An Important Determinant of Personality?

FIGURE 12-7. Can experiences such as this early in life affect the nature of one's adult personality? Freud believed that this is so. He suggested that too much oral gratification during the first years of life might result in a personality characterized by dependence on others. (Note: while most psychologists agree that early experiences can indeed shape personality, they also believe that such relationships are far more complex than the ones proposed by Freud.)

Views of Several Neo-Freudians: A Summary

TABLE 12-1

Neo-Freudians adopted many of Freud's basic ideas about human personality but suggested changes in others, and they added new concepts of their own. The views of some of the most prominent theorists in this group are summarized briefly here.

Theorist	Major Ideas, Concepts
Alfred Adler	Experiences in early childhood are important, but social experiences and the need for power or superiority are more crucial than sexual motives.
Erik Erikson	Human beings pass through a series of eight stages, each involving a different "crisis." These are psychosocial, not mainly sexual, stages. The way in which each crisis is resolved shapes the person's adult personality.
Erich Fromm	The ego is more than a mediator between the id and superego: it actively strives for unity, love, freedom. Adult behavior is more than just the appropriate handling of basic sexual and aggressive motives.
Karen Horney	The primary human need is for security. This stems from feeling alone and threatened during childhood. Sexual and aggressive drives are of less importance. Women do not have weaker consciences than men.
Carl Jung	The unconscious contains more than repressed thoughts, impulses, and feelings. It also holds the *collective unconscious*—memories and symbols shared by all human beings. These play an important role in our behavior.

his theory of personality; is it accepted by modern psychology as accurate or useful? The answer, in general, is "no." Criticisms of Freud's views have occurred at two distinct levels.

First, many critics have noted that his "theory" is not really a theory at all, at least in the scientific sense of this term. Several of the concepts it contains cannot be measured, even indirectly. How, for example, does one go about observing an id, fixation, or the Oedipal conflict? Similarly, it offers few, if any, testable hypotheses about human behavior. As you will recall, a theory is essentially useless unless it can be tested.

Second, several of Freud's proposals are not consistent with the results of modern research. For example, he suggested that dreams contain messages from the unconscious— disguised wishes or impulses. As we noted in Chapter 4, this does not seem to be the case; dreams appear to be the result of random activity in the sleeping nervous system and our cognitive systems' efforts to make sense out of such activity (Foulkes, 1985); they do not seem to possess the significance Freud believed. Similarly, he contended that forgetting is largely a function of *repression*: we push information we find threatening or painful out of consciousness. While this may sometimes be the case, decades of research on memory suggest that forgetting actually stems from many different factors, several of which are more important than repression (refer to Chapter 6).

For these and other reasons, Freud's theory of personality is not currently accepted by most psychologists (refer to Figure 12-8). Having said this, though, we should note that several of Freud's ideas or insights *have* contributed to our understanding of human behavior in general, and of personality in particular. The most important of these seem to be the following:

(1) Many of the thoughts, motives, and memories that affect human behavior are unconscious; individuals are not always aware of the basis for their own thoughts or actions.

(2) Important aspects of personality can indeed be affected by events occurring early in life. These are not as permanent as Freud believed, but they may be relatively difficult to change.

(3) Balance is indeed a key ingredient in personality development. Too much gratification or too much frustration early in life may lead to serious problems at later times.

In sum, while Freud's theory itself is primarily of historical rather than practical or scientific interest, several of his ideas are now part of the intellectual heritage of psychology. In this respect, at least, his continued, honored place in our field seems assured.

FIGURE 12-8. At present, few psychologists accept Freud's theory of personality as accurate. *(Source: Universal Press Syndicate, 1983.)*

Freud's Theory of Personality: A Comment on Its Current Status

Humanistic Theories of Personality: Emphasis on Growth

Id versus ego, Jekyll versus Hyde—on the whole, psychoanalytic theories of personality take a dim view of human nature. They contend that we must constantly struggle to control our own brutish impulses if we are to function as healthy, rational adults. Is this picture accurate? *Humanistic psychologists* disagree. They feel that human beings are basically good and that our strivings for growth, dignity, and self-determination are just as strong, if not stronger, than the wild sexual and aggressive impulses Freud described. Only when negative environmental conditions block our positive tendencies do problems arise. Such views have been incorporated into several **humanistic theories of personality** (Engler, 1985). We will now describe two such theories: Maslow's *self-actualization* approach (Maslow, 1970) and Rogers' *self theory* (Rogers, 1954, 1977).

Human Needs and Self-Actualization.   Central to Abraham Maslow's theory is the suggestion that human beings have five distinct types of needs they strive to satisfy. These are arranged in a hierarchy so that satisfaction of lower-order needs is necessary before higher-order ones arise. As you can see from Figure 12-9, at the bottom of this hierarchy are basic biological drives (e.g., the need for food and water) and the desire to be secure both physically and psychologically. Above these are the need to be loved and accepted by others and the need to enhance one's self-esteem. Finally, at the very top is the need for *self-actualization*. This involves our desire to develop to our fullest potential— to become the best person we can be, with the fullest range of skills and satisfactions we are capable of developing.

Maslow based his conception of the mature, self-actualizing person on careful study of individuals known to have lived exceptionally full and productive lives (e.g.,

FIGURE 12-9. According to Maslow, human beings have five basic types of needs. More basic needs (e.g., physiological, safety needs) must be satisfied before higher level needs can arise. At the top of this hierarchy is the *need for self-actualization*—strivings to become the best and most fully developed person we can be.

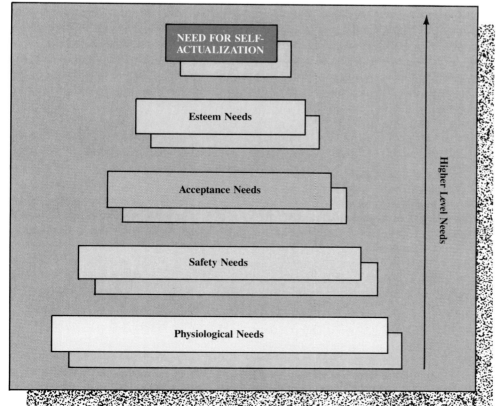

NEED FOR SELF-ACTUALIZATION

Esteem Needs

Acceptance Needs

Safety Needs

Physiological Needs

Higher Level Needs

Maslow's Need Hierarchy

Abraham Lincoln, Thomas Jefferson, Eleanor Roosevelt). He concluded that such persons were all self-accepting, spontaneous, loving, secure, and open in their dealings with others. In addition, they focused their energies on specific tasks—and usually accomplished them! Presumably, all human beings have the capacity to attain this healthy, self-actualized state; it is only restrictive environments, which force us to spend our energy meeting lower-level needs, which prevent such development.

Rogers' Self Theory: "To Thine Own Self Be True."   Another well-known humanistic psychologist, Carl Rogers, agrees with several of Maslow's points. He, too, suggests that left to their own devices human beings show many positive traits, such as openness, honesty, and strong tendencies toward personal growth. Unfortunately, though, the external environment often places major obstacles in the path of such development. For example, instead of providing us with **unconditional positive regard**—assurance that we will be loved and accepted despite our failings—such acceptance is often conditional on our acting in certain ways or meeting specific standards. Similarly, instead of sharing their feelings with us, and recognizing ours, other persons conceal their emotions behind a social mask and pay little attention to the ones *we* are experiencing. Under such conditions, Rogers suggests, we may form a distorted *self-concept*, one which does not fit with our feelings or experience. When this occurs, growth is blocked, and serious personality problems can result. How do distortions in the self-concept arise? Consider the following example.

A little girl is jealous of her new baby brother and demonstrates this in her actions: she grabs one of his toys and makes him cry. Her parents, observing this, say, "Good girls *love* their brothers; they don't act like that." The implication, of course, is that if the child continues to feel this way, and to torment her brother, she will lose her parents' love. In other words, unconditional positive regard is *not* present. Now the little girl faces a dilemma: she knows that she has negative feelings about her brother, and she *does* want to upset him. To please her parents and to avoid losing their love, however, she denies the presence of these feelings. Since she is now out of touch with some of her own feelings, her self-concept is distorted, and serious psychological harm may result. The basic message in Rogers' theory, then, is this: human beings will develop in healthy ways and show many positive traits if they live in the right kind of environment—one that offers acceptance and empathy, among other things. The task of parents, schools, and psychologists is to assure that such conditions exist; the rest will presumably take care of itself. (Is there any scientific evidence for Rogers' views? In fact, there is. For a description of such research, please see "The Cutting Edge" section below.)

FOCUS ON RESEARCH: The Cutting Edge

Creative Environments and Creative Potential: One Test of Rogers' Theory

According to Rogers (1954, 1977), individuals develop many desirable traits if allowed to grow in positive environments. One such characteristic is *creativity*—the ability to generate new and useful ideas, often by combining existing information in novel or unusual ways (Barron & Harrington, 1981). What kind of environment will encourage this trait? According to Rogers (1954), one that provides *safety* (the feeling that one has unconditional per-

sonal worth) and one that offers *psychological freedom* to engage in unrestrained expression of ideas and thoughts. That such conditions actually do foster creativity is indicated by a recent study conducted by Harrington, Block, and Block (1987).

These researchers obtained information about the child-rearing practices of more than one hundred parents with preschool children 3.5 to 4.5 years old. Of special interest, of course, was the extent to which these practices supplied the conditions described by Rogers. As part of a larger longitudinal study, Harrington

TABLE 12-2

Items similar to the ones shown here were used by Harrington, Block, and Block (1987) to assess the use by parents of child-rearing practices Rogers believed would foster creativity (upper list) and to measure children's creativity (lower list).

Items Used to Assess Parents' Child-Rearing Practices

I respect my child's opinions and encourage their expression.
I let my child make many decisions by himself/herself.
I encourage my child to be curious.
I make sure my child knows that I appreciate what he or she tries to accomplish.

Items Used to Assess Children's Creative Potential

Is proud of his/her own accomplishments.
Is curious, eager for new experiences.
Has high standards for judging his/her own performance.
Appears to have high intellectual capacity.
Seeks to be independent.
Is self-reliant and confident.

(SOURCE: Adapted from Harrington, Block, Block, 1987.)

and his colleagues then obtained ratings of the children's creativity several years later, when they were in the sixth and ninth grades (11.5 and 13.5 years old, respectively). These ratings were provided by the children's teachers and by psychologists who interacted with them. Some of the items used to assess parents' child-rearing practices and children's creativity are shown in Table 12-2.

Results offered clear support for Rogers' proposals. The greater the extent to which parents provided their child with safety and psychological freedom, the higher the child's rated creativity. In fact, the correlations between these variables were quite substantial (+.46, on average). These findings suggest that providing children with the kind of environment humanistic psychologists feel is important for personal growth may in fact prove beneficial. As Rogers, Maslow, and others believe, our potential for developing positive traits may indeed be strong. However, various situational factors (aspects of the environment in which we spend our early years) may be crucial in determining whether, and to what extent, they actually appear.

Trait Theories: Identifying the Key Dimensions of Personality

When we describe other persons, we often do so in terms of specific **traits**—stable aspects of their behavior. For example, we may state that one of our friends is *sharp, energetic,* and *sexy,* while another is *calm, happy,* and *naive.* This same general approach is reflected in **trait theories of personality.** Such theories focus on the task of identifying key dimensions of personality—the most important ways in which people differ. The basic idea behind this approach is as follows: once we know *how* people differ, we can measure how *much* they differ, and then go on to relate such differences to behavior in a wide range of settings.

Unfortunately, this task sounds easier than it actually is. As we noted in Chapter 11, human beings differ in an almost countless number of ways. How can we determine which of these are most important? The scope of the problem was first suggested by a famous study conducted more than fifty years ago by Allport and Odbert (1936). By consulting a standard dictionary, these researchers identified 17,953 words in English that referred to specific traits. Even when words with similar meanings were combined, 171 traits remained.

How can we cope with this multitude of potential traits? One solution is to search for *clusters*—traits that seem to go together. Statistical techniques for identifying such clusters in subjects' responses to psychological tests exist and have been put to such use.

Cattell's Sixteen Basic Dimensions of Personality

TABLE 12-3

Through analysis of the responses of thousands of persons to many different items, Cattell has identified sixteen basic dimensions of human personality. The extremes on these dimensions are listed here.

End-Points on Sixteen Dimensions of Personality

Cool, reserved	Warm, easygoing
Concrete thinking	Abstract thinking
Easily upset	Calm, stable
Not assertive	Dominant
Sober, serious	Happy-go-lucky
Expedient	Conscientious
Shy, timid	Venturesome
Tough-minded	Tender-minded
Trusting	Suspicious
Practical	Imaginative
Forthright	Shrewd
Self-assured	Apprehensive
Conservative	Experimenting
Group-oriented	Self-sufficient
Undisciplined	Self-disciplined
Relaxed	Tense, driven

(SOURCE: Adapted from the 16 Personality Factor Questionnaire; Cattell and the Institute for Personality and Ability Testing, 1983.)

On the basis of extensive research of this type, Cattell and others (Cattell & Dreger, 1977) have identified sixteen basic personality dimensions (refer to Table 12-3). Presumably, differences on these basic dimensions, which Cattell terms *source traits*, underlie differences on many others. Whether this is actually the case is not yet clear (Aiken, 1985).

We might add that Cattell's theory can be described as *biosocial* in nature: it suggests that important individual differences stem, at least in part, from biological as well as environmental factors. In other words, Cattell and others contend that our major traits may reflect genetic factors as well as the influence of learning and experience. We have already reviewed some evidence that supports this contention. As you may recall from our discussion in Chapter 11, recent studies of identical twins who were separated early in life and raised in very different environments indicate that, despite their contrasting experiences, such individuals often show striking similarities in personality (Bouchard, 1984, 1987) and even in certain attitudes (e.g., satisfaction with their jobs; Arvey, et al, 1989).

Additional support for the role of genetic factors in at least some aspects of personality is provided by research on infant *temperament*—patterns of behavior characteristic of specific individuals. Shortly after birth infants differ in such factors as overall activity level, intensity of reactions, and typical mood—whether they are happy or fuss most of the day (Thomas & Chess, 1981). Further, some of these differences seem to persist throughout childhood and even into the adult years (Buss & Plomin, 1975, 1984). In view of such evidence, we are left once more with the following general conclusion: all aspects of human behavior—even those as complex as personality—are shaped both by our experience and by our genetic inheritance. Where human beings are concerned, in short, there is no escape from the nature-nurture issue we confronted in the earliest chapters of this book.

A second approach to understanding traits involves efforts to identify those traits that distinguish groups of persons already known to differ in important ways. For example, the **MMPI** (*Minnesota Multiphasic Personality Inventory*) was developed in this manner—through *empirical keying*. Hundreds of statements were given to groups of patients suffering from different psychological disorders (see Chapter 13). Items answered differently by these groups than by persons who were not patients (so-called "normals") were retained for use in the test. The results of these procedures was the identification of ten dimensions of personality closely related to psychological problems (e.g., *hypochon-*

driasis—abnormal concern with bodily functions and symptoms; *paranoia*—suspiciousness and delusions of persecution; *hypomania*—intense excitement, overactivity). We'll return to the MMPI in Chapter 13; for now, we simply wish to note that comparing persons known to differ in important respects is another useful strategy for identifying some of the key dimensions of personality.

While efforts to identify key dimensions of personality in these two ways continue, many psychologists interested in personality adopt a different approach: they focus on particular traits that, for theoretical or practical reasons, seem to be of special interest. No claim that these are *the* key dimensions is made; rather, efforts to understand such traits, and to relate them to important forms of behavior, are of central concern. Research of this type does not, by itself, contribute to the formulation of a grand theory of personality. However, it does often yield fascinating evidence about the nature and impact of individual differences. Thus, as we will see in a later section, it has proven to be a valuable way of studying this fascinating topic.

Reciprocal Causality: The Social Cognitive Approach

Consider two people: one is sociable and outgoing; she loves interacting with others and enjoys being the center of attention. The other is shy and reserved; social situations make her nervous, and the very idea of being in the limelight gives her the chills. Will these individuals lead different kinds of lives? In all likelihood, they will. The first may join lots of clubs, go to many parties, and perhaps seek a career that puts her in contact with many people. The second will probably stay at home much of the time, avoid social gatherings, and will choose a career that allows her to work alone. In short, their contrasting traits may well lead them to choose to spend their time in different situations or *environments*, ones consistent with their own personalities (Diener, Larsen, & Emmons, 1984).

Will these differences in their traits also *shape* these environments? Again, the answer is "yes." Because they demonstrate contrasting patterns of behavior, these individuals will probably be treated in different ways by people they meet. For example, the first may receive more invitations, will attract different kinds of friends, and may even get different types of job offers than the second. The result: the two persons may live in very different social worlds which, to an important extent, *are of their own making*. Finally, will these contrasting patterns of experience then affect their underlying traits? Once again, the answer seems clear: they will. It seems reasonable to predict that unless something changes, the first person will become more and more sociable as time passes, while the second may become more shy and withdrawn.

What we have just described, in essence, is a modern perspective on personality (and human behavior generally) known as **social cognitive theory** (Bandura, 1986). It suggests that behavior, environmental conditions, and cognitive or personal factors (including various traits) interact in complex ways as determinants of one another. Our traits or characteristic ways of thinking influence our behavior. This, in turn, affects the external environment, which then shapes our cognitive processes and our behavior. We could continue, but we would simply be repeating the same theme: the environment, our behavior, and our underlying cognitions and traits all influence one another, hence the term *reciprocal causality* (refer to Figure 12-10 on page 384).

As we noted above, this social cognitive view is actually more than a theory of personality; indeed, with certain extensions (e.g., attention to various *self-regulatory* processes), it applies to all aspects of human behavior (Baron, 1987b). Despite this fact, however, it can readily deal with the two key aspects contained in our definition (uniqueness and consistency). With respect to uniqueness, it is apparent that, since we all have different patterns of life experience and live in contrasting environments, differences in our characteristic patterns of thought and action are to be expected. Similarly, since our traits shape our behavior and this, in turn, shapes our environment, reciprocal causality assures that current modes of thought and action will tend to persist, other factors being equal. In a word, a degree of consistency is built into the system.

In sum, the social cognitive perspective is not a theory of personality in the traditional sense. As a sophisticated framework for understanding all aspects of human behav-

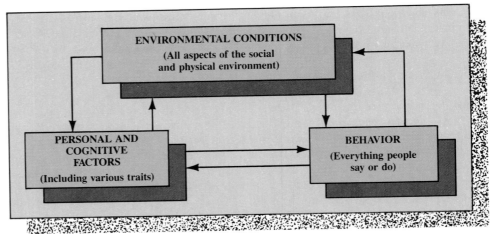

FIGURE 12-10. According to *social cognitive theory,* environmental conditions, cognitive and personal factors (including various traits), and behavior interact as determinants of one another. In short, each influences, and is influenced, by the others. *(Source: Based on suggestions by Bandura, 1986.)*

ior, though, it permits us to bring many findings of modern psychology to bear on this intriguing subject. The result, we believe, may well be a more comprehensive grasp of the nature of personality than has ever before been available.

Measuring Personality: Some Basic Methods

As we noted in Chapter 11, physical traits such as height and weight can be measured directly. Various aspects of personality, though, cannot be assessed in a similar manner. There are no rulers for measuring competitiveness and no scales for weighing self-esteem. How can such differences among individuals be quantified? The answer, of course, is through adaptations of the methods described in Chapter 11: various types of *psychological tests.* Several of these will now be described.

Inventories and Questionnaires: Assessing Personality Through Self-Report

By far the most widely used method for assessing personality involves the use of *inventories* or *questionnaires.* These consist of a series of questions or statements to which individuals respond in various ways. For example, subjects may be asked to indicate whether various statements are true or false about themselves, or to report on whether, and how often, they experience certain feelings. Their answers to these items are then scored by means of special keys and are compared with those obtained by hundreds or even thousands of other persons (the *norm group* for the test; refer to Chapter 11). In this way, a specific person's relative standing on the trait or traits being measured can be determined.

For example, an individual taking a test designed to measure *expressiveness* (a characteristic we discussed in Chapter 10), might obtain a score higher than that received by 75 percent of other people who have taken the test. This would indicate that she is relatively high on this dimension. Similarly, someone taking a test that measures the need for excitement or new experiences might receive a score lower than that of 80 percent of other persons; such an individual would be quite low in this trait. (See Table 12-4 for sample items from a test designed to measure this characteristic.) Of course, as is true for all psychological tests, personality inventories or questionnaires are useful only to the extent that they are *reliable* (yield scores that are stable) and *valid* (measure what they purport to measure). For example, if the individual shown in Figure 12-11 did not score high on a test designed to measure *self-consciousness* (awareness of one's own thoughts

::::: **TABLE 12-4** :::::

These items are similar to those on a questionnaire used to measure individual differences in *sensation-seeking*: the tendency to seek new experiences, excitement, and high levels of risk.

For each item below, circle the letter (a or b) of the choice that best describes your preferences or the way you feel.

1. (a) I often wish I could be a mountain climber.
   (b) I can't understand people who risk their necks climbing mountains.

2. (a) A sensible person avoids activities that are dangerous.
   (b) I sometimes like to do things that are a little frightening.

3. (a) I would like to take up the sport of water-skiing.
   (b) I would not like to take up water-skiing.

4. (a) I would not like to learn to fly an airplane.
   (b) I would like to learn to fly an airplane.

5. (a) I enjoy spending time in the familiar surroundings of home.
   (b) I get very restless if I have to stay around home for any length of time.

(SOURCE: Adapted from a test developed by Zuckerman, 1979.)

and feelings), we might wonder whether this test is, in fact, a valid measure of this important characteristic.

Projective Techniques: Ambiguous Stimuli and Personality Assessment

Look at the illustration in Figure 12-12 on page 386—what do you see? If you don't see anything at first, take a moment to consider whether it reminds you of anything.

You have just examined an example of another approach to measuring personality: **projective techniques.** These are based on the following assumptions: if different persons are exposed to ambiguous stimuli and then asked what they see, each will report some-

FIGURE 12-11. The person shown here would be expected to score high on a test designed to measure *self-consciousness* (awareness of one's own feelings and thoughts). If he did not, we might question the *validity* of this test. *(Source:* The New Yorker.)

KOREN

"Oh, there's Freddie. He knows the best places to suffer."

Projective Techniques: A Controversial Method for Assessing Personality

FIGURE 12-12. What do you see when you look at this ink blot? Some psychologists believe that the answer an individual provides in response to such ambiguous stimuli can reveal much about his or her personality. Many others, however, have serious doubts about the validity of such *projective techniques*.

thing different. The differences in their reactions, in turn, can reveal much about important aspects of their personalities.

These are intriguing suggestions, but are they true? For some projective tests, such as the one shown in Figure 12-12, which resembles the famous **Rorschach Ink Blot Test,** the issue is still in doubt. Several ways of scoring this test to yield information about various aspects of personality exist. Unfortunately, they often point to different conclusions (Holley, 1973). Thus, it is uncertain whether this test and several techniques related to it are actually useful. In contrast, other projective techniques, such as the *TAT* (which we described in Chapter 9), appear to be both reliable and valid. Scores on such tests do seem to be related to important aspects of behavior (e.g., striving for achievement, effectiveness as a leader; Winter, 1987b).

In sum, individuals' interpretations of ambiguous stimuli can sometimes yield useful information about their personality. This is by no means assured, though, and the intriguing nature of these tests should not be accepted as a substitute for convincing evidence of their reliability and validity. (Is the availability of various techniques for measuring personality of any practical use? For some comments on this issue, please see ''The Point of It All'' section below.)

THE POINT OF IT ALL

Putting Personality Measures to Work: Assessment Centers and the Identification of Managerial Talent

A key task faced by organizations is identifying talented persons—people suited for leadership roles. Many techniques for accomplishing this task have been developed, but among the most successful to date are **assessment centers** (Thornton & Byham, 1982). Such procedures are based on the following suggestion: certain traits or characteristics are closely

related to success as a manager. Thus, careful measurement of these characteristics should help us to predict the performance of specific persons in this role.

Assessment centers are much more elaborate, and therefore more expensive, than other techniques for measuring personality. (They are paid for by large corporations.) Typically, they require two or three days rather than one or two hours of an individual's time. During this period, the persons

Assessment Centers: One Practical Use of Measures of Personality

FIGURE 12-13. Many large organizations attempt to identify individuals suited for managerial or other leadership roles through *assessment centers*. These involve careful study of the persons in question during a two- or three-day period.

being assessed are asked to perform a wide range of tasks previously found to be related to managerial success. Many of these tasks simulate activities and conditions managers confront in their actual jobs (e.g., interviews, decision-making tasks), but several personality inventories are also usually included. The overall goal is to acquire information relating to many different characteristics believed to be related to later success: work motivation, administrative skills, creativity, maturity, and independence, to mention just a few (see Figure 12-13).

Assessment centers have been used for many years by a number of large companies, (such as AT&T). This raises an important question: do they really work? Do they yield information helpful in predicting future success? Some evidence suggests that they do. For example, in one study (Ritchie & Moses, 1983) more than 1,600 female managers employed by the Bell System took part in two-day assessment centers. On the basis of their scores on many tasks, each person was as-

signed an overall rating of future management potential. When these ratings were correlated with later success (the positions these persons held in the company six or seven years later), a significant relationship (a correlation of + .47) was observed. The higher the assessment center ratings, the more successful the employees had been at a later time. Further, those who received high ratings seven years earlier were now rated higher than others by current supervisors on such key dimensions as work standards, leadership, and communication skills.

Such findings suggest that assessment centers really work: they help organizations identify persons who are most suited for various leadership roles. Of course, they are far from perfect, so great care must be taken to guard against errors that can damage promising careers. When used with caution, though, assessment centers constitute one potent and practical answer to the question: why bother to measure personality?

Key Dimensions of Personality: A Sample of Recent Research

All psychologists who study personality agree that it is a multi-faceted phenomenon; they realize that people differ from one another in a large number of ways, and many of these are worthy of careful study. We have already considered two basic approaches to dealing with this problem: (1) the formulation of sweeping theories which seek to account for all aspects of personality, and (2) efforts to identify all of the key dimensions at once. While both strategies have sometimes proven useful, most researchers currently follow a different tactic. They focus on one or perhaps a few aspects of personality at a time. Presumably, once we know enough about many such dimensions, a comprehensive picture of human personality can be constructed. Consistent with this approach, a wide range of traits or characteristics is now actively being studied. We will consider three which have received a great deal of research attention: the Type A behavior pattern, self-monitoring, and shyness.

The Type A Behavior Pattern: Who Succeeds and Who Survives?

Think about all the persons you know. Can you name one who always seems to be in a hurry, is extremely competitive, and is often hostile and irritable? Now, in contrast, can you name one who shows the opposite pattern—someone who is relaxed, not very competitive, and easy-going in relations with others? If you succeeded, you now have in mind two people who could be described as showing *Type A* and *Type B behavior patterns*, respectively. In other words, you have generated personal examples of the extremes on one key dimension of personality (Glass, 1983). Type As are described as showing high levels of competitiveness, irritability, and time urgency (they are always in a hurry). Type Bs are the opposite in each of these respects (Jenkins, Zyzanski, & Rosenman, 1979). (Refer to Figure 12-14.) As we will now see, these contrasting patterns of behavior have important implications for personal health, performance on many tasks, and interpersonal relations.

The Type A Pattern and Health.   Interest in the **Type A behavior pattern** was first stimulated by medical research. Several physicians (Jenkins, Zyzanski, Rosenman, 1979; and their colleagues) noticed that many patients who had suffered heart attacks seemed to share certain personality traits—they tended to be competitive, driven, and irritable people. In order to examine this observation more systematically, they developed a personality inventory and a structured interview to measure these characteristics. When such measures were applied to a large number of persons, results were dramatic: Type As were more than twice as likely as Type Bs to experience serious heart disease (Siegel, 1984). While the strength of this relationship has been weaker in subsequent research (Booth-Kewley & Friedman, 1987), its existence has generally been confirmed. Thus, Type As definitely seem to pay a high price for their hard-driving, overstimulated life style.

Additional research suggests just why Type As are so much more at risk for heart disease than Type Bs. Briefly, they seem to respond to stress with greater physiological arousal. For example, when performing stressful tasks, Type As have higher blood pressure and pulse rates than Type Bs (Holmes, McGilley, & Houston, 1984). Given such reactions, and the frequency of stress in modern life, it is far from surprising that Type As suffer more heart attacks than Type Bs.

The Type A Pattern and Task Performance.   Given their competitiveness and hard-driving style, it seems reasonable to expect that Type As will perform better than

FIGURE 12-14. Persons (or other entities!) classified as Type A are highly competitive and assertive. *(Source: NEA, 1987.)*

Type A Behavior Pattern
in Action

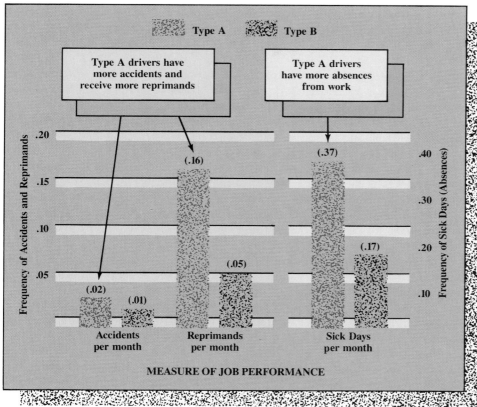

Type A Behavior Pattern
and Job Performance

FIGURE 12-15. Bus drivers classified as Type A had more accidents, were absent from work more frequently, and received more official reprimands than drivers classified as Type B. These findings indicate the relevance of this particular aspect of personality to on-the-job performance. *(Source: Based on data from Evans, Palsane, & Carrere, 1987.)*

Type Bs on many tasks. In fact, the situation turns out to be more complex than this. Type As *do* work faster on many tasks than Type Bs, even when no pressure or deadline is involved. Similarly, they are able to get more done in the presence of distractions (Fazio et al., 1981). Also, Type As often seek more challenge in their work and daily lives than Type Bs. For example, when given a choice, they select more difficult tasks than Type Bs (Ortega & Pipal, 1984). The Type A behavior pattern is even related to success in academic careers. Type A professors publish more articles and have higher salaries than those who are Type B (Taylor et al., 1984).

Surprisingly, though, Type As do not *always* perform better then Type Bs. For example, Type As frequently do poorly on tasks requiring patience or careful, considered judgment. They are simply in too much of a hurry to complete such work in an effective manner (Glass, Snyder, & Hollis, 1974). Further, as you might guess, Type As perform worse than Type Bs under high levels of stress. This fact is clearly illustrated by the results of study conducted by Evans, Palsane, and Carrere (1987).

These researchers examined the performance of bus drivers in both the United States and India. They predicted that in this often stressful job, Type As would show poorer performance in several respects. To test this hypothesis, they examined each driver's past work record (the number of accidents experienced, the number of absences from work). In addition, they actually observed the drivers' performance while at work. Results offered support for the major predictions. Type As did have more accidents and absences, and they had received more official reprimands (refer to Figure 12-15). In addition, observations of on-the-job behavior indicated that such drivers blew their horns and passed other vehicles more frequently (these latter findings were obtained in India, but not in the United States).

In sum, existing evidence suggests that Type As do better than Type Bs on some tasks, especially ones involving meeting deadlines or working alone. However, they may actually do *worse* than Type Bs on tasks involving complex judgments, accuracy rather than speed, and high levels of stress. Neither pattern, then, appears to have an overall edge.

The Type A Pattern and Interpersonal Relations.   Are Type As harder to get along with than Type Bs? Research findings offer a clear conclusion: yes. Because they are always in a hurry, Type As tend to become impatient with other persons, and they become angry if delayed in any manner. Similarly, they lose their temper more frequently and are more irritable and aggressive than Type Bs (Holmes & Will, 1985). As a result of these tendencies, Type As report becoming involved in more conflicts at work than do Type Bs (Baron, 1988c). Perhaps more surprising, Type As even report engaging in sexual relations with their spouses less frequently and for shorter periods of time than Type Bs (Becker & Byrne, 1984). In short, their time urgency extends to areas of life aside from work. Combining these diverse findings, it seems clear that Type A persons experience more difficulties in their interpersonal relations than Type B persons.

The Type A Pattern: A Note on Its Origins.   Before concluding, we should comment briefly on one other issue: what factors encourage development of the Type A behavior pattern? While this question has not yet been totally answered, comparisons of Type A and Type B persons point to one important difference in their early home lives. In many cases, Type As were encouraged to attain high goals by their parents but received ambiguous feedback on whether they had actually met these standards (Strube et al., 1987). Thus, it is the combination of being urged to achieve while not receiving any clear response after such efforts that seems to generate the Type A pattern. Since such conditions are open to change, parents may have it in their power to affect where their children fall on this dimension. The choice they make, of course, is largely a matter of personal values and preferences—*not* scientific judgment.

Self-Monitoring: Public Appearance or Private Reality?

Answer honestly: do you usually tell other people what they want to hear (what will cause them to react favorably to you?) or what you really believe and feel? This is a difficult question, for most of us know that at different times we do both. Despite this fact, a growing body of research evidence indicates that large and important individual differences exist in this respect (Snyder, 1987). At one end of this dimension, known as **self-monitoring**, are persons who usually adjust their own behavior so as to produce positive reactions in others. They are known as *high self-monitors*, and their actions are usually guided by the requirements of a given situation. As high self-monitors themselves note, they are often "different with different persons and in different situations" (Shaffer, Smith, & Tomarelli, 1982; Snyder & Monson, 1975). At the other end of the self-monitoring dimension are individuals who seem less aware of their impact on others or who are less concerned with producing positive impressions of themselves. Their behavior usually reflects their inner feelings and attitudes, and they are less likely to adjust it to each new context they encounter.

At this point, we should add that self-monitoring may involve more than a single characteristic or aspect of personality. Recent evidence suggests, in fact, that scores on tests designed to measure self-monitoring may actually reflect two distinct factors (Briggs & Cheek, 1986, 1988). One of these involves willingness to be the center of attention—a tendency to be outgoing (*extraverted*) in social situations. The other involves concern with the reactions and evaluations of others—desires to please and be liked by them. Regardless of whether self-monitoring involves two factors or a single one, this trait is related to several important forms of behavior.

First, consider liking for others and choice of friends. Low self-monitors are often closely attuned to their own attitudes and values. Thus, it seems reasonable to expect that they will often like others who resemble themselves in these ways—persons who share their views and beliefs. In contrast, high self-monitors realize that they often act differently in different situations. As a result, they may like and choose as friends others who share their preferences for various activities—people who enjoy doing the same things

Friendship Choice and Self-Monitoring

FIGURE 12-16. Do you perform different activities with different friends? If so, you may be relatively high in *self-monitoring*. Persons high in this characteristic often choose friends who enjoy the same activities they enjoy, even if such persons don't share their values and beliefs.

they enjoy (see Figure 12-16). Both predictions have recently been confirmed (Jamiesen, Lydon, & Zanna, 1987). Attitude similarity is a stronger determinant of liking for others among low self-monitors, while shared activity preferences is a stronger basis for attraction among high self-monitors.

Second, consider dating and sexual relationships. Do you think high self-monitors or low self-monitors will have a larger number of different partners? The answer is provided by a study by Snyder, Simpson, and Gangestad (1987). These researchers asked male and female students to complete a personality inventory designed to measure self-monitoring, and to provide information on their dating and sexual behavior. As predicted, high self-monitors reported having more different partners, expected to have more partners in the future, and even had more ''one-night stands'' than low self-monitors (refer to Figure 12-17 on page 392). Snyder and his colleagues interpret these findings as evidence that high self-monitors tend to adopt an *uncommitted* orientation toward social relationships: they are more willing than low self-monitors to change partners and seek variety.

Differences in self-monitoring are related to other types of behavior as well. For example, who should be more popular as teachers—high or low self-monitors? Since high self-monitors seem more sensitive to the reactions of others, or at least are more willing to adjust their behavior to please their audience, they should be superior. In fact, this seems to be the case. College professors who are high in self-monitoring receive higher ratings from students than ones who are low in self-monitoring (Larkin, 1987). We should hasten to add that this does not necessarily indicate that they are more effective in this role—they may not communicate more information in a more organized manner. Still, since more students tend to take courses with popular instructors, differences in self-monitoring may have important practical effects.

Finally, we should note that self-monitoring is related to the performance of certain jobs. Persons high in self-monitoring are more successful than persons low in self-monitoring in positions requiring contact with different groups—ones who, because of contrasting goals, training, or skills, ''speak different languages'' (Caldwell & O'Reilly, 1982). Since they can readily adjust to each of these groups, high self-monitors are more effective in communicating with them, and this enhances their performance.

Shyness: Feeling Anxious in Social Situations

Have you ever felt awkward or tense at a party or in other contexts when meeting strangers for the first time? If so, you are like most persons; indeed, few individuals report that they have *never* experienced feelings of **shyness** (Zimbardo, 1977). While shyness is a com-

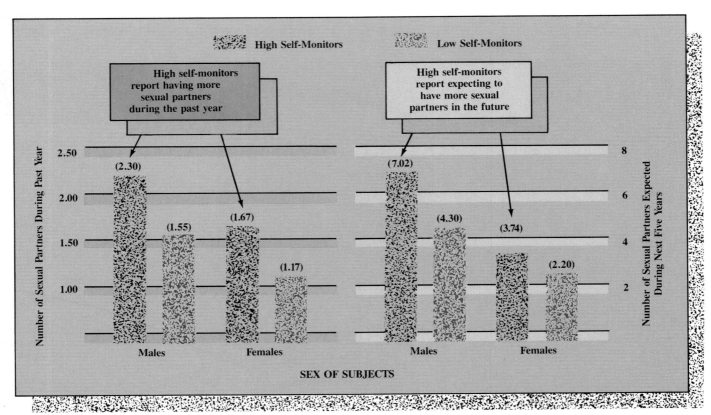

FIGURE 12-17. High self-monitors report having a larger number of different sexual partners and expect to have more sexual partners in the future than low self-monitors. Thus, they seem to be less committed to current romantic relationships. *(Source: Based on data from Snyder, Simpson, and Gangestad, 1986.)*

Self-Monitoring and Sexual Relationships

mon experience for most of us, at least occasionally, large individual differences exist in this dimension. For most persons, feelings of shyness are both temporary and mild. For some, however, they are so intense that they pose a serious personal problem. Just what is shyness? How does it develop? And what are its effects? These are some of the intriguing questions addressed in recent research on this topic.

Shyness: Its Basic Nature.   Try to remember times when you felt shy. What were your reactions like? One widely accepted view of shyness suggests that they probably involved three distinct components (Buss & Plomin, 1984). First, you experienced signs of *emotional arousal*, such as a pounding heart, sweating, or blushing. Second, you experienced *cognitive reactions*, such as acute feelings of self-consciousness, worries about being evaluated negatively by others, and self-deprecating thoughts ("I'm just no good with other people"). Finally, you may have acted in an awkward, inhibited manner; this is the *behavioral component* of shyness. (Please refer to Figure 12-18 for a summary of these reactions.) In sum, shyness seems to consist of a cluster of reactions which, together, leave individuals feeling tense, worried, or awkward during social interactions (Cheek, Melchior, & Carpentieri, 1986).

The Roots of Shyness: Distortions in the Self-Concept.   Now that we've described the nature of shyness, let's turn to an even more complex question: Why do such reactions occur? In other words, why do individuals experience shyness in the first place? One unsettling possibility, suggested by some research findings, is that the tendency to be shy is at least partly inherited. For example, in one recent study, Kagan, Resnick, & Snidman (1988) found that youngsters who were shy very early in life (at the age of eighteen months) remained shy for several years (until they were eight), despite efforts to alter this tendency. Another, somewhat less controversial explanation for shyness centers around the development of distorted *self-concepts*.

The *self-concept*, of course, is our subjective picture of who we are as individuals— our beliefs about our own traits, motives, and abilities. For most persons, the self-concept is quite positive: they generally like themselves and see themselves in a favorable light.

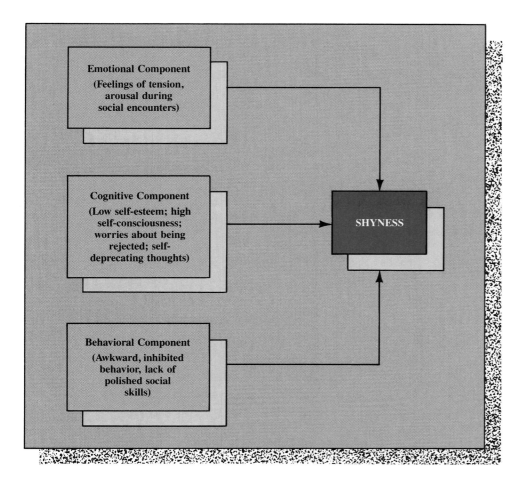

FIGURE 12-18. *Shyness* consists of three basic components. These involve feelings of arousal or tension (emotional component), distortions in the self-concept (cognitive component), and behavior lacking in social skills (behavioral component).

This is *not* the case for persons who suffer from intense shyness. First, they tend to have low self-esteem: they perceive themselves as falling short in important, desirable traits (e.g., academic ability, physical beauty). Second, in a pattern directly opposite that shown by most persons, they tend to attribute their successes to external causes, such as lucky breaks, but their failures to internal causes, such as their own lack of desirable traits (Tegliasi & Fagin, 1984). Third, they tend to focus on themselves—especially on their real or imagined shortcomings—during social encounters. This tendency was clearly demonstrated in a study conducted by Melchior and Cheek (1985). They asked pairs of previously unacquainted college women to hold brief conversations. After these were over, Melchior and Cheek (1985) asked these subjects to report how much of the time they spent thinking about themselves and what they said. Women previously identified as being shy reported that they thought about themselves more, and in more negative terms, than women who were not shy.

Finally, shy individuals perceive themselves as having poorer social skills and as making a more negative impression on others than is actually the case. In other words, after meeting strangers they evaluate their own social performance more unfavorably than these other persons do (Lord & Zimbardo, 1985).

Combining these results, a disturbing picture of shy individuals emerges. Such persons seem to think, feel, and act in ways that almost guarantee repeated failure in social encounters. In a sense, their actions are self-defeating, trapping them in a vicious circle in which distortions in their self-concept produce social failures, which in turn intensify such distortions (refer to Figure 12-19 on page 394). When viewed in these terms, shyness appears to be more serious a problem than many individuals (especially those who are not shy!) might suppose.

Loneliness: A Major Cost of Shyness.   Shyness has many negative effects. For example, shy persons often adopt an overly cautious interpersonal style. Being afraid of

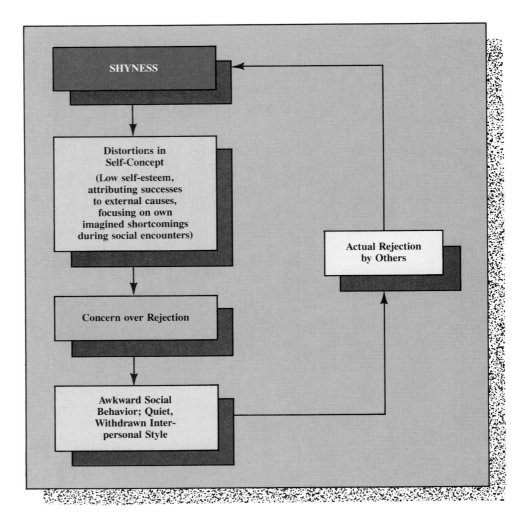

Shyness and Social Behavior:
Another Vicious Circle

FIGURE 12-19. Because of distortions in their self-concept, shy persons fear and expect rejection from others. This leads them to adopt a quiet, withdrawn interpersonal style which is interpreted by the people around them as arrogance or aloofness. The result: they really *are* rejected, and their shyness is confirmed or even intensified.

rejection (and convinced of its inevitability) they often remain quiet and withdrawn in social gatherings. The result: others perceive them as arrogant or unfriendly and *do* in fact reject them (see Figure 12-20). Similarly, shy persons tend to conform to the majority opinion (whatever it may be), and refrain from expressing their own point of view (Arkin, Lake, & Baumgardner, 1986). As Cheek (1987, p. 500) has put it, shy persons "do not 'play to win'—they play not to lose."

Second, shyness can interfere with an individual's career. Shy persons often perform more poorly in job interviews, in making contact with customers, and in many other contexts than persons who are not shy (Cheek, 1987). Perhaps the most harmful effect of shyness, however, is the **loneliness** it often produces (Cheek, 1987).

Loneliness is not the same thing as being alone, of course; it occurs only when individuals desire close social contact with others but are unable to attain it (Peplau & Perlman, 1982). Needless to say, this is precisely the plight of many shy individuals. They have fewer dates, fewer friends, and fewer social contacts generally than persons who are not shy (Cheek, 1987).

While shyness is one cause of loneliness, it is not necessarily true that all lonely people are shy. Some may experience loneliness because of other factors: divorce, multiple moves in pursuit of career opportunities, decreasing family size. However, research which has focused on the causes and effects of loneliness suggests that shyness contributes to its occurrence in many cases—particularly when individuals find themselves in new social situations. For example, in one intriguing study on this relationship Cheek and Busch (1981) had students at a large university complete the *Shyness Scale*, a psychological test designed to measure individual differences in shyness, at the start of a new semester. In addition, the same subjects completed a second questionnaire, one designed to measure loneliness (Russell, Peplau, & Cutrona, 1980). This second scale was admin-

FIGURE 12-20. Shy persons often stay on the sidelines in social situations. This may lead others to perceive them as cold or unfriendly, with the result that they remain isolated and lonely.

Shyness: One Cause of Loneliness

istered twice: one week after the start of the semester and again two weeks before its end. Cheek and Busch predicted that shy individuals (those scoring high on the Shyness Scale) would report being more lonely at both times than persons who were not shy. As you can see from Figure 12-21, this is precisely what they found. While both shy and unshy students reported being less lonely at the end of the semester, the difference between the two groups in this respect persisted: shy persons did *not* overcome their high level of loneliness with the passage of time.

Additional research focused on lonely individuals suggests that they share many characteristics with persons who are shy. Like those who are shy, lonely persons report spending more time by themselves, and they date less often than persons who are not lonely (Russell, Peplau, & Cutrona, 1980). Second, lonely people appear to behave in

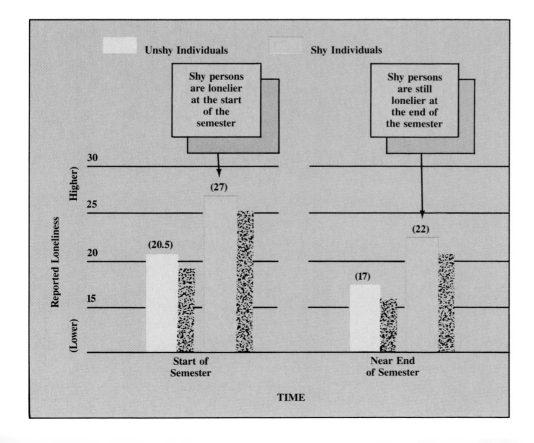

FIGURE 12-21. Shy individuals reported being lonelier both at the beginning of the semester and several months later. These findings suggest that shyness is indeed one major cause of loneliness. *(Source: Based on data from Cheek & Busch, 1981.)*

awkward ways during social interactions. For example, when they have a brief conversation with a stranger, they refer to the other person less often, don't pick up on topics of conversation he or she introduces, and ask fewer questions (Jones, Hobbs, & Hockenbury, 1982). In short, they are less adept at interacting with others.

Third, and perhaps most unsettling of all, lonely people tend to have negative perceptions of themselves and their own personalities. As a result, they (like shy persons) *expect* failure in social situations. And since expectations are often translated into reality, they get just what they fear: rejection by others. The existence of this self-defeating pattern of expectations and behavior has recently been confirmed in a study conducted by Vitkus and Horwitz (1987).

These researchers asked male and female students previously identified as lonely or nonlonely to interact with a stranger who was actually an accomplice of the researchers. Subjects performed one of two tasks: either they listened while their partner described his or her reactions to several interpersonal problems, or they described these problems and their own reactions to them. (An example of a problem: Imagine that you are approached by a stranger at a party and have difficulty conversing with this person.) Subjects' comments during the session were recorded, so that the actual behavior of lonely and nonlonely people could be compared. In addition, they rated various aspects of their own performance (e.g., how good they were at solving the problems, the quality of their solutions).

Results indicated that subjects did act differently when serving as a listener or as a presenter. They made more unsolicited remarks and more direct references to their partner when listening than when they were busy presenting. Interestingly, lonely and nonlonely people did *not* differ in such respects; their actual behavior during the conversation was quite similar. As shown in Figure 12-22, though, these two groups *did* differ in evaluating their own performance. Lonely subjects rated their solutions as lower in quality than nonlonely subjects. Most important, this was true even though a large group rated written descriptions of these solutions as equal in quality. In sum, lonely persons perceived that their solutions were worse, but this was not actually the case.

FIGURE 12-22. Lonely persons did not differ from nonlonely persons in their behavior during a brief conversation with a stranger. However, as shown here, they rated their own performance significantly lower than did nonlonely individuals. These findings suggest that lonely persons expect failure in social situations, and they then may act in ways that cause these fears to be confirmed. (*Source: Based on data from Vitkus & Horwitz, 1987.*)

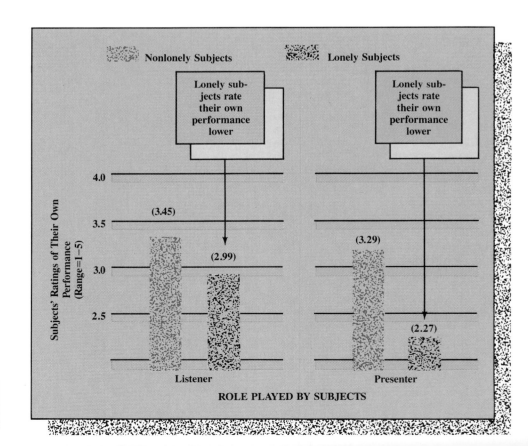

These findings and those of other studies (deJong-Gierveld, 1987) point to the following conclusion: while lonely people may differ from others in some aspects of social skills, the most important differences between them lie in their contrasting perceptions. Like shy individuals, lonely people *expect* rejection and failure when interacting with others. These expectations, in turn, lead them to act in ways that cause such fears to be confirmed.

To repeat: not all lonely persons are shy; other factors, too, can contribute to this state. However, the fact that lonely persons share many characteristics with those who are shy suggests that the distorted self-concept this characteristic involves often plays an important role in being unable to maintain close social contacts with others, even when such contact is strongly desired.

Overcoming Shyness: Some Grounds for Hope. The discomfort produced by shyness is all too real. Can such reactions be overcome, or at least reduced? Fortunately, this seems to be the case. Specific therapies, each aimed at alleviating one of the major components of shyness described above, currently exist and seem effective (Cheek, 1987). With respect to the emotional component, *relaxation training* can be helpful. In such procedures shy persons learn to induce feelings of relaxation as they imagine scenes ranging from saying hello to a casual acquaintance to asking an attractive stranger for a date. As such training proceeds, the feelings of tension induced by such an encounter are reduced, and shy individuals learn to remain calm in situations that once "drove them up the walls."

Other forms of therapy are designed to change the ways in which shy people think about themselves. These help them to view themselves in more positive terms, and to realize that they are often their own worst critic. As distortions in their self-concept fade, they become more confident in a wide range of social situations. Finally, to overcome the behavioral aspects of shyness, shy persons can receive training in specific *social skills*—how to hold conversations with others, appropriate ways of making requests or saying "no."

Through a combination of such procedures, shy individuals can break the vicious cycle described above: shyness—panic—fear or rejection—social awkwardness—actual rejection. When they do, they can go on to enjoy the kind of full, active social life they once thought was beyond their reach.

Summary and Review

Personality: Some Contrasting Views

Personality is the unique but stable set of characteristics and behaviors that sets each individual apart from others. In the past the question of whether such stable traits actually exist was hotly debated by psychologists. In the light of recent findings, however, most now accept the view that such stable (cross-situational) individual differences do indeed exist.

Theories of personality attempt to account for the nature and origins of such stable differences. The most famous of these is Freud's *psychoanalytic theory*. Freud suggested that most of the human mind is unconscious and proposed the existence of three major components of personality: *id, ego,* and *superego*. These refer, respectively, to what may be termed "desire," "reason," and "conscience." According to Freud, it is the continuing struggle between these components of personality, plus our experiences during *psychosexual stages* of development, that shapes our personality as adults. At present, few psychologists accept Freud's theory as valid. However, several of his ideas (e.g., the view that many of the thoughts and motives affecting human behavior are unconscious) remain influential today.

Humanistic theories of personality emphasize the capacity of human beings for growth. Maslow suggests that once our more basic needs are met, we strive for *self-actualization*. In another influential humanistic theory, Rogers proposes that people show many positive traits if they are permitted to develop in a favorable environment—one that provides them with *unconditional positive regard*.

Trait theories of personality attempt to identify the key dimensions of personality. Several of these theories (e.g., one proposed by Cattell) adopt a *biosocial perspective*: they suggest that many of our most important traits stem from genetic factors or predispositions as well as learning and experience.

At present, many psychologists view personality from the perspective of *reciprocal causality*—the suggestion that cognitive or personal factors, environmental conditions, and behavior influence one another in complex ways. It is out of such interactions that personality arises.

Measuring Personality

Several techniques for measuring personality exist. *Personality inventories* or *questionnaires* consist of a series of questions or statements to which individuals respond. *Projective techniques* attempt to assess personality through individuals' responses to ambiguous stimuli. *Assessment centers* are used to determine individuals' potential for leadership (managerial) roles. They measure many kinds of behavior during a two- or three-day period. In order to be useful in the study of personality, all such measures must meet the basic standards applied to all psychological tests: they must be *reliable* (yield scores that are internally consistent and stable) and *valid* (measure what they purport to measure).

Personality: Some Key Dimensions

Much current research on personality focuses on specific traits. Among the ones receiving most attention are the *Type A* behavior pattern, *self-monitoring*, and *loneliness*.

Type A individuals demonstrate such characteristics as a high level of competitiveness, time urgency (they are always in a hurry), and tendencies to be irritable and aggressive. Type As experience heart attacks much more frequently than Type Bs (persons who do not show such characteristics). Type As are better at performing some tasks (e.g., ones involving deadlines) than Type Bs, but do more poorly on other tasks (e.g., ones involving high levels of stress).

Persons high in *self-monitoring* adjust their behavior readily to each new situation they enter. In contrast, persons low in self-monitoring behave consistently, in accordance with internal standards or values, across many situations. Self-monitoring may actually involve two distinct factors: willingness to be the center of attention, and concern with the reactions of others. High self-monitors have more dating and sexual partners than low self-monitors, and college instructors who are high on this dimension tend to be more popular with their students.

Shyness, the tendency to feel awkward in social situations, involves three major components: emotional reactions (feelings of tension or arousal), cognitive reactions (negative self-concepts), and behavioral reactions (acting in an awkward or socially unskilled manner). The most central of these seems to be the distorted self-concepts held by shy persons. They tend to be low in self-esteem, blame themselves for failures, and expect rejection from others. Shy persons are often *lonely*—they are unable to attain close social contact with others even though they strongly desire such relations. All lonely persons are not shy, but studies of individuals suffering from loneliness indicate they share many characteristics with those who are shy. Fortunately, shyness can be overcome through forms of therapy that focus on relieving each of its major components (feelings of tension, negative self-concept, a lack of social skills).

 **Key Terms**

Assessment Centers Procedures for measuring a wide range of traits and characteristics, often used for identifying individuals with leadership or management potential.

Ego In Freud's theory of personality, the structure that holds primitive biological impulses in check until they can be satisfied in a safe and appropriate manner.

Humanistic Theories of Personality Theories emphasizing human potential for growth and development.

Id In Freud's theory of personality, the structure containing our primitive urges.

Loneliness Refers to the inability to attain close social contacts with others when these are desired.

MMPI (Minnesota Multiphasic Personality Inventory) A widely used test designed to measure individual differences on several traits related to psychological disorders.

Neo-Freudians Personality theorists who accepted many of Freud's basic ideas but modified his theory in important ways and added several new concepts of their own.

Personality The unique but stable set of characteristics that sets each individual apart from all others.

Projective Techniques Procedures for measuring personality in which individuals are asked to interpret ambiguous stimuli.

Psychoanalysis The method of therapy devised by Freud for the treatment of mental disorders.

Psychoanalytic Theory of Personality Freud's theory of personality. It includes Freud's ideas about the nature of the human mind, basic structures of personality, and psychosexual stages of development.

Rorschach Ink Blot Test A famous projective test of personality in which individuals are asked to interpret a set of ambiguous figures created by ink blots.

Self-Actualization The need to become the most fully developed person you can be.

Self-Monitoring A personality dimension relating to the extent to which individuals adapt their behavior to current circumstances or act in accordance with stable attitudes, values, and beliefs.

Shyness The tendency to feel tense or awkward during social interactions, especially ones involving strangers.

Social Cognitive Theory A sophisticated theory of human behavior suggesting that environmental conditions, personal and cognitive factors, and behavior interact as determinants of one another.

Superego In Freud's theory of personality, the structure representing conscience.

Traits Specific behavioral or psychological dimensions along which individuals differ.

Trait Theories of Personality Theories that seek to identify the key dimensions of human personality.

Type A Behavior Pattern A cluster of traits (competitiveness, time urgency, hostility) related to important aspects of health, social behavior, and task performance.

Unconditional Positive Regard Acceptance of another person, despite her or his failings or shortcomings.

For More Information

Engler, B. (1985). *Personality theories: An introduction,* 2nd ed. Boston: Houghton Mifflin.
An excellent overview of many different theories of personality. All of the theories considered in this chapter are summarized, and many others not described here (e.g., existential theories, social learning theories) are included, as well.

Peplau, L. A., & Perlman, D. (1982). *Loneliness: A sourcebook of current theory, research, and therapy.* New York: Wiley.
This book contains a number of chapters prepared by experts on various aspects of loneliness. The origins of this characteristic, its effects, and techniques for overcoming it are all considered.

Snyder, M. (1987). *Public appearances/Private realities: The psychology of self-monitoring.* New York: Freeman.
An excellent overview of research and theory concerning one important aspect of personality. The author is the foremost expert on self-monitoring, and the book itself is well written and thought-provoking.

Siegel, J. M. (1984). Type A behavior: Epidemiologic foundations and public health implications. In L. Breslow, J. E. Fielding, & L. B. Lave (eds.), *Annual review of public health* (pp. 343–367). Palo Alto: Annual Reviews.
A comprehensive summary of the effects of the Type A behavior pattern on personal health. If you'd like to know more about how this aspect of personality can influence heart disease and many other ailments, this is an excellent source to consult.

LIVERPOOL JOHN MOORES UNIVERSITY Aldham Robarts L.R.C. TEL. 051 231 3701/3634

CHAPTER 13

Psychological Disorders: When Being Different Hurts

"I've got a bad feeling about this," Cheryl Brophy says to her husband Vic as they cross their livingroom toward the front door, "a really bad feeling."

"Oh come on, Cheryl!" Vic answers, a note of annoyance in his voice. "What can happen at a party? Gee!"

"Well, we could have an accident on the way for one thing. And Barb and Frank might be there—we sure don't want to run into them after last week. And I'm worried about the smoke: you know how it irritates my eyes when I've worn my contacts all day."

"And I suppose that the moon might be full, and Joe could turn into a werewolf. Stop worrying; once we're there you'll have a good time."

"That's easy for you to say!" Cheryl answers, with mounting emotion. "What if the house is broken into while we're gone? There's been so much of that in the neighborhood lately—I just *knew* we should have had that alarm system installed, but I couldn't make up my mind to do it. Now we're sitting ducks. What if they get in while we're gone and take Grandma Thompson's crystal? I'd never be able to face her!"

Trying to remain calm, Vic answers, "Look, most of these break-ins happened when people were away on vacation, not when they stepped out for a few hours. Stop worrying; everything'll be fine." Then, after a brief pause, he continues: "O.K., if it'll make you feel any better, I'll hook up the timers. Then there'll be lights on all over the house. O.K.?"

"I don't know, I just feel so nervous," Cheryl answers, breathing heavily. Then she begins to tremble. "No! I just can't go! Don't ask me to! I can't face people tonight—I'm too upset, . . ." and with these words, she breaks into tears and rushes from the room.

After Cheryl leaves, Vic sits down in the nearest chair. "No, I'm not going after her this time," he thinks to himself. "It never does any good. Besides, she's probably locked herself in the bathroom by now." Then, shaking his head, he utters a long, loud sigh. "What's happening to her? I don't understand it. We used to be so happy, but now Cheryl's so nervous it's like living with a wound-up spring. All she does is worry. . . . What am I going to do? I love her, but I can't take much more—it's driving me up the wall! We've got to get some help; I can't handle it by myself. . . ."

Pain. In a word, that's what this chapter is all about—not the physical pain produced by injuries or illness, but psychological pain, the distress experienced by individuals when they suffer from various **psychological disorders.** What, precisely, are such disorders? Psychologists have debated this question for decades, for there appears to be no simple way of distinguishing "abnormal" behavior from "normal" behavior. At present, though, most agree that psychological disturbances involve the following major features.

First, as we have just noted, such disorders generate *distress* in the people involved. Like Cheryl, the character in our opening story, individuals suffering from such problems generally *do* suffer: they experience anxiety, internal conflict, and many other negative feelings (see Figure 13-1 on page 403). Second, such disorders involve patterns of behavior or thought that are relatively *atypical*. The persons involved do not think and act like most others; rather, they show unusual, often surprising, reactions to ordinary life events. Most people, after all, don't burst into tears and demonstrate signs of panic at the thought of going to a party with their spouse. Finally, the behavior indicative of a psychological disorder is evaluated negatively by members of a particular society; it is perceived as somehow objectionable or unacceptable. Combining these points, we can define *psychological disorders* as patterns of behavior and thought which are atypical, are viewed as undesirable within a given culture, and cause the persons who demonstrate them considerable distress.

FIGURE 13-1. *Psychological disorders* usually involve anxiety, internal conflicts, and other negative feelings. *(Source:* The New Yorker.)

Psychological Disorders: A Source of Personal Distress

Are such problems common? Absolutely: recent surveys indicate that almost 20 percent of the adult population in the United States suffers from at least one psychological disorder (Myers et al., 1984). Thus, the chances are high that during the course of your life you or someone close to you will experience one or more psychological problems. This is *not* cause for alarm. As we will see in Chapter 14, many effective procedures for dealing with such difficulties exist, and can lessen their negative impact.

In the present chapter we'll focus on the task of describing a number of different psychological disorders. To do so effectively we'll begin with two preliminary tasks: an overview of several contrasting perspectives on such disorders and a brief description of one widely used system for identifying their presence, the DSM-III-R. After that, we'll examine several important types of disorders that cause individuals considerable pain but leave them capable of functioning in everyday life, at least part of the time (e.g., anxiety disorders, dissociative disorders, mood disorders). We'll turn next to *schizophrenia*—an extremely serious condition involving major disturbances of thought and behavior. Such disturbances are often so pronounced, and the behavior of such persons so bizarre, that they must often be removed from ordinary society for their own protection. Finally, we'll consider several different *personality disorders*—clusters of traits that cause serious problems for the persons who possess them and for society as well.

The Nature of Psychological Disorders: Demons, Illness, or Behavior?

While it is tempting to assume that many psychological problems stem from the stress of modern life, it appears that they have always been present in human society. Indeed, some evidence suggests that such disorders existed long before the dawn of civilization: Ancient skulls containing neatly cut or drilled holes have been found by archaeologists. One explanation for these holes which seems to make sense is that they were produced to permit the escape of evil spirits which were causing the person to act in strange and unacceptable ways. Over the centuries, ideas about the nature of such disorders have altered radically. We'll now consider several of these contrasting views.

The Supernatural Perspective: Demons, Witches, and Devils

As we have just suggested, the earliest perspective on psychological disorders seems to have involved the view that they were produced by supernatural forces. Possession by

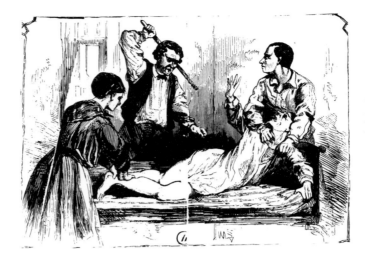

FIGURE 13-2. As late as the seventeenth century unusual patterns of behavior and thought were attributed to possession by demons or other evil spirits. Various forms of torture were then used to drive these spirits out of the people they had presumably attacked.

demons, gods and goddesses, or evil spirits—this was the explanation accepted for bizarre forms of behavior and thought. And such ideas did not disappear with the days of antiquity. During the Middle Ages many episodes of *animal possession* (supposed possession by the spirits of animals, especially wolves) were recorded. Even during the sixteenth and seventeenth centuries unusual patterns of behavior were often attributed to the influence of witchcraft. Indeed, from the mid-fifteenth to the mid-seventeenth century more than 100,000 people in Europe and North America (mostly women) were convicted of being witches and were executed for their ''crimes'' (Deutsch, 1949). (This early form of sex discrimination was partly based on religious grounds; church authorities reasoned that since Jesus was a man, males were largely protected from direct dealings with the devil.) How could one tell whether an accused person was actually a witch? Some of the tests were chilling, to say the least. For example, any birthmark, scar, or mole on a woman's body could be interpreted as a sign that she had formed a pact with the Devil and was therefore a witch.

Efforts to drive evil demons out of the bodies of possessed persons were often extreme, too. Various forms of torture were deemed appropriate in this respect (see Figure 13-2). And when such tactics failed (i.e., when the possessed persons failed to change their bizarre behavior), the ultimate solution was often applied: they were proclaimed to be tools of the devil and were executed.

The Medical Perspective: Psychological Disorders as Treatable Diseases

By the eighteenth century—the Age of Enlightenment—Western societies were ready for a change. Appalled by the horrible living conditions and harsh treatment used in publicly supported ''mad houses,'' where patients were typically chained to the walls and given severe whippings to ''beat reason into them,'' reformers such as Chiarugi in Italy and Philippe Pinel in France called for a radically new approach. They suggested that madness was *not* the result of supernatural forces but is, rather, a kind of illness—one which can be treated with appropriate medical techniques. This view implies that there are biological causes of psychological disorders (or ''mental illness,'' as it was often termed), just as there are biological causes of other types of illness. As this view gained acceptance, the chains were struck from the arms and legs of persons who, because of their unusual behavior, had been committed to public asylums, and efforts were begun to help bring about their ''cure'' (see Figure 13-3).

At this point, we should note that the idea of physical causes for psychological disorders was, in one sense, far from new. It had been suggested during the second century by Galen, a famous Greek physician (130–201 A.D.). Galen proposed that *hysteria,* a condition mainly afflicting women and involving such symptoms as headaches, paralysis, dizziness, and epileptic-like fits, stemmed from a malfunctioning sexual organ

FIGURE 13-3. By the eighteenth century psychological disorders were viewed as a form of illness. This shift led to more humane treatment for the unfortunate victims of such disorders.

(the uterus). Specifically, he felt that hysteria was brought about by sexual abstinence and could perhaps be cured by sexual satisfaction. Unfortunately, Galen's ideas—along with other science and knowledge of the Ancient World—disappeared from view for many centuries. It is interesting to speculate about how many lives might have been saved had his views (and the data he marshaled for them) remained well known during the centuries that followed.

In any case, the view Galen proposed—that mental disorders stem from physical causes and should be viewed as instances of disease—is represented today in the field of *psychiatry,* a branch of medicine specializing in the treatment of such disorders. As we'll soon see, many psychologists, too, accept this medical model, at least to a degree. However, they have also suggested a somewhat expanded view that takes account of the role of learning, environmental conditions, and cognitive processes. We'll return to this perspective shortly. First, though, we'll consider another influential approach: the **psychodynamic perspective.**

The Psychodynamic Perspective: Freud's View of Mental Illness

When we examined Freud's theory of personality, we described some of his views about mental illness. As you may recall, he suggested that serious problems result when individuals become *fixated* at some point during their psychosexual development. Too much or too little gratification at any of these stages may interrupt normal growth and may result in serious problems that continue to haunt us throughout life—or at least until we undergo psychoanalysis! This is only part of Freud's proposals, however. He also called attention to the importance of *anxiety* arising out of the continuous struggle between the id, ego, and superego.

Such anxiety occurs when the ego feels that it may be overwhelmed by demands of the id—intense and unacceptable sexual and aggressive impulses. To protect itself from such anxiety, the ego adopts a number of different **defense mechanisms.** Several of these are described in Table 13-1 on page 406. As you can see, they all serve to disguise the nature of unacceptable impulses, and so reduce the anxiety experienced by the ego.

As we noted in Chapter 12, few psychologists currently accept Freud's views about the origins of psychological disorders. However, the defense mechanisms he de-

TABLE 13-1

When the ego feels it may be unable to control impulses from the id, it resorts to various defense mechanisms. These permit the ego to disguise the nature of such unacceptable urges while partially satisfying them.

Defense Mechanism	Its Basic Nature	Example
Repression	Unacceptable thoughts or impulses are "forgotten"—pushed from consciousness into unconsciousness	A woman fails to recognize her attraction to her handsome new son-in-law
Reaction Formation	The opposite of a wish or impulse one finds unacceptable is expressed	A man who is strongly drawn to gambling claims that he views it as repulsive
Rationalization	Socially acceptable reasons are provided for thoughts or actions based on unacceptable motives	A young woman explains that she ate an entire chocolate cake so that it wouldn't spoil in the summer heat
Displacement	An emotional response is redirected from a dangerous object to a safe one	Anger is redirected from one's boss to one's child
Projection	Unacceptable motives or impulses are transferred to others	A person sexually attracted to a neighbor perceives the neighbor as being sexually attracted to him
Regression	Responding to a threatening situation in a way appropriate to an earlier age or level of development	A student asks a professor to raise her grade; when she refuses, the student throws a temper tantrum

scribed do seem to be ones most of us use, from time to time, to cope with the stress and pressures of daily life. Only when they are used excessively, so that they seriously distort our perceptions of reality, are they a sign of serious psychological disorder.

The Psychological Perspective: Behavior, Cognition, and Environment

"Mental illness," "abnormal behavior"—these terms make some psychologists uneasy. Why? The answer centers around the fact that these terms imply acceptance of the medical perspective described above. They suggest that psychological problems are illnesses which can be cured through appropriate treatment. In one respect, this view makes eminent sense: many behavioral problems *do* seem to have a biological basis. They arise, at least in part, from disturbances in body chemistry, from the functioning of our brain, or from the impact of various drugs or microorganisms.

In another sense, though, the medical view seems to miss the mark. Several decades of research suggest that many behavioral problems are better understood in terms of psychological processes (e.g., learning, perception, cognition) and the impact of environmental conditions. In other words, many of the disorders we'll soon consider seem to spring from faulty learning, from exposure to damaging external conditions, and from key aspects of the ways some people think about the world around them—*not* from diseases that have "infected" their minds. Having said this, we should add the following caution: this psychological perspective does *not* imply that all behavioral problems stem from such factors, nor does it suggest that biological factors play no role. It simply notes that considering all behavioral problems from the perspective of illness can cause us to ignore psychological processes which also play a key role in their occurrence.

This expanded, psychological perspective has important implications for helping people deal with such disorders. It suggests that such efforts should concentrate, not on

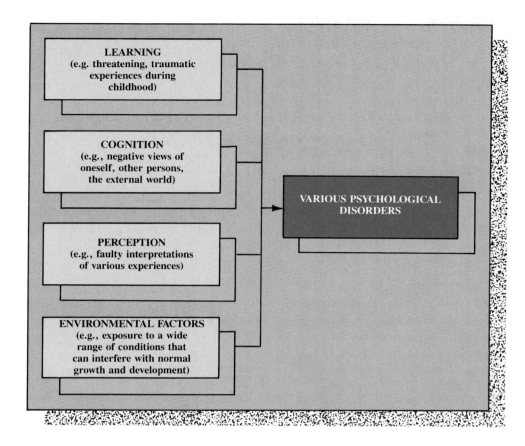

FIGURE 13-4. The *psychological perspective* suggests that many behavioral disorders are better understood in terms of basic processes such as learning and cognition than as "mental illness."

curing mental illness, but on altering maladaptive ways of thinking, perceiving, and behaving. As we'll see in Chapter 14, techniques based on this suggestion have proven highly successful. Thus, the psychological perspective has already made important contributions to human welfare and promises to offer many more in the years ahead. For these and other reasons it will form the background for our discussion in the remainder of this chapter. (Please see Figure 13-4 for a summary of the psychological perspective.)

Identifying Psychological Disorders: A Basic System of Classification

No physician would attempt to treat a common cold through surgery or internal injuries with a Band-Aid. The first and most crucial step in medical practice is *diagnosis:* determining the nature of the ailment which brought the patient to the doctor's office in the first place. Even if we do not accept a medical model of psychological disorders, the need for identifying such problems in a clear and reliable manner remains. In the absence of such a system of classification, different psychologists (or psychiatrists) might describe the same problems in different terms and could not then share information or methods for dealing with them. Similarly, without a uniform system for classifying various psychological problems systematic research on them would be almost impossible; different teams of investigators might use the same terms for different problems, or different terms for the same problems.

Fortunately, a widely accepted system for identifying psychological disorders does exist: the *Diagnostic and Statistical Manual of Mental Disorders* (Third Edition—Revised) or **DSM-III-R.** Because it is published by the American Psychiatric Association (1987), the DSM-III-R often adopts terms more popular in medicine than in psychology. However, psychologists, too, were involved in its development, so it also reflects the psychological approach, to a degree.

The DSM-III-R: An Overview

TABLE 13-2

The DSM-III-R is used to identify a wide range of psychological disorders. As shown here, an individual is classified on five different dimensions, or axes.

Axis I: Clinical Syndromes (Major Mental Disorders)

Disorders usually first evident in infancy, childhood, or adolescence
Organic Mental Disorders (e.g., Senility, Psychoactive Substance-Induced Organic Mental Disorders)
Psychoactive Substance Use Disorders (e.g., Alcohol Abuse, Cocaine Dependence)
Schizophrenia
Mood Disorders (e.g., Major Depression)
Anxiety Disorders (e.g., Simple Phobia)
Somatoform Disorders (e.g., Hypochondriasis)
Dissociative Disorders (e.g., Multiple Personality Disorder)
Sexual Disorders (e.g., Exhibitionism, Sexual Aversion Disorders)
Sleep Disorders (e.g., Insomnia)

Axis II: Developmental Disorders and Personality Disorders

Developmental Disorders (e.g., Mental Retardation, Autistic Disorder)
Personality Disorders (e.g., Paranoid, Antisocial, Avoidant)

Axis III: Physical Disorders and Conditions

Axis IV: Severity of Psychosocial Stressors (Acute events and enduring life circumstances are distinguished)

Axis V: Highest Level of Adaptive Functioning (Current psychological, social, and occupational functioning are rated. In addition, the highest level of functioning in these categories during the past year is also assessed.)

(SOURCE: Based on the DSM-III-R, American Psychiatric Association, 1987.)

The DSM-III-R divides psychological disorders into nineteen major categories, and within these further identifies more than two hundred specific problems. One important plus of the DSM-III-R is that it describes specific criteria that must be met before the presence of any of these problems is assumed (diagnosed). In other words, only when individuals show specific, clearly defined patterns of behavior (symptoms) are they described as suffering from certain disorders (forms of mental illness). This feature has helped increase the *reliability* of the DSM-III-R—the probability that different psychologists or psychiatrists will agree on the identification of specific problems shown by individuals (Wakefield, 1987). However, it is still far from perfect in this respect.

Another important feature of the DSM-III-R is that it uses a *multiaxial* approach. Individuals are classified on five separate dimensions (axes) rather than simply labeled as suffering from a particular problem. Two of these axes refer to specific major disorders and their development. Others relate to physical conditions that may affect psychological functioning; the severity of stress occurring in the person's life; and his or her current level of functioning in social, occupational, and leisure activities during the past year (refer to Table 13-2). In sum, the DSM-III-R offers a fuller and more sophisticated picture of persons to whom it is applied than earlier schemes.

Because of the features just described, plus several other factors, the DSM-III-R has become a standard guide for identifying psychological disorders and is currently in widespread use. While it represents an advance over earlier techniques, it still suffers from a major drawback we should mention here: its end product is a *label* assigned to each person to whom it is applied. As we noted earlier, such labels are often useful; without them, we would be at a loss as to how to help people cope with their problems. Yet they also carry a high price tag, so to speak. Once such labels are attached to specific persons, we may begin to think about them in certain ways. Indeed, in extreme cases the label may become more powerful in shaping our perceptions than the words or actions of the persons themselves! For a dramatic illustration of this process, please see the ''Classic Contributions'' section below.

FOCUS ON RESEARCH: Classic Contributions

Effects of Labeling Others: The Vicious Circle Strikes Again

Suppose that, after interviewing a troubled person, a psychologist using the DSM-III-R decides that this individual has a particular disorder: depression. Presumably, she can now go on to choose an effective means of dealing with this problem. So far, so good. Imagine, though, that she has made a mistake: the person is not really depressed and is actually suffering from some other problem. Will the psychologist quickly notice this mistake and change strategies in order to help this person more effectively? Perhaps not: A large body of research findings indicate that once we have labeled a person as showing some trait or characteristic, we are quite reluctant to alter our judgment. Behaviors inconsistent with our label are viewed as exceptions to the rule, and actions that would normally be open to multiple interpretations are readily viewed as supporting our initial decision. In short, labels may soon take on a life of their own and may shape—rather than be shaped by—our perceptions (Ross & Fletcher, 1985).

Perhaps the most dramatic demonstration of such effects—certainly the most relevant to our discussion of classifying psychological disorders—is one provided by David Rosenhan and his colleagues (Rosenhan, 1973). In a bold and ingenious study, Rosenhan and seven others (mostly graduate students in clinical psychology) pretended to have certain symptoms of serious psychological disorders: they claimed to hear voices which repeated such words as "empty," "hollow," and "thud." When each of the researchers described these symptoms to various professionals at twelve mental hospitals, each was quickly diagnosed as *schizophrenic* and admitted for treatment.

Once admitted as patients, Rosenhan and his accomplices dropped all pretense of mental problems and acted in a completely normal manner. Despite this, they all found it extemely difficult to convince members of the staff that they were not seriously disturbed. Psychiatrists, nurses, orderlies—all continued to view the false patients as ill. Indeed, the trained staff persons frequently interpreted ordinary actions by Rosenhan and the others as proof of illness! For example, while in the hospital all members of the research team took detailed notes on their experiences. Other patients soon recognized that each researcher was not a real inmate. Members of the hospital staff, however, reached strikingly different conclusions: they viewed such note-taking behavior as a clear sign of disturbed behavior! Indeed, one nurse even went so far as to describe note-taking as a sign of *compulsion*, one form of neurotic disorder. In short, once they had been labeled as mentally ill, all actions by the researchers were interpreted as consistent with this label (refer to Figure 13-5 on page 410). In fact, when they were finally released, Rosenhan and his assistants were described as "recovered schizophrenics" rather than as normal persons who had been admitted by error.

Perhaps another example of the powerful effects of labels is in order. In a closely related study, Langer and Abelson (1974) had mental health professionals watch a videotape in which a young man discussed his experiences on various jobs with an older, bearded man. Some of the subjects were informed that the young man was a job applicant, while others were told he was a patient. After watching the videotape, individuals in both groups were asked to describe this individual. As you can probably guess, those in the latter group described him as showing more signs of psychological disturbance than did those in the former. For example, they noted that he seemed to be a "tight, defensive person" or one "frightened of his own aggressive impulses." In contrast, subjects told that the young man was a job applicant described him as an "upstanding middle-class citizen" and as "candid and innovative." Clearly, the label assigned to this person strongly altered their perceptions of him.

We do not offer these results as evidence of the evils of mental hospitals. As noted earlier, it *is* important to identify specific problems if we are to help individuals effectively. Rather, we present Rosenhan's research to call your attention to the following fact: while labels are certainly useful, they involve dangers we should both recognize and take active steps to resist.

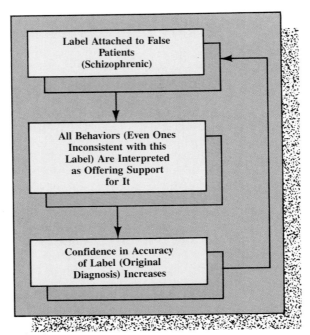

FIGURE 13-5. Once an individual is labeled as showing some psychological disorder, all actions by this person tend to be perceived as consistent with this diagnosis. As a result, confidence in the accuracy of the original diagnosis increases, even if it was false.

The Self-Confirming Nature of Labels

Some Major Psychological Disorders

Earlier we noted that psychological disorders are common; many persons experience at least one of them at some point during their lives. In most cases, such disorders are painful and disturbing but do not prevent individuals from continuing their everyday lives. They stay in touch with reality most of the time, and they demonstrate behavior that, by and large, is acceptable or at least tolerable to those around them. In the past, disturbances of this type were often termed *neurotic disorders* (or neuroses). Since the DSM-III-R does not include a special category of this type, however, we'll refrain from using this term here.

Many different psychological disorders exist—far more than we could possibly consider within the scope of this chapter. Among the most important, though, are the following: *anxiety disorders, dissociative disorders* (disturbances in self-identity or memory), *somatoform disorders* (physical symptoms in the absence of underlying physical causes), and *sexual disorders* (disturbances in sexual functioning or behavior). A fifth type—*mood disorders*—involves disturbances of emotional state. Because mood disorders have been the subject of so much recent research, we'll consider them separately in a later section of this chapter.

Anxiety Disorders: When Dread Debilitates

At one time or another, we all experience **anxiety**—feelings of fear, tension, or dread. If such feelings become very intense, and if they persist for long periods of time, though, they can produce harmful effects. Such **anxiety disorders** take a number of different forms. We'll discuss several of them under the following headings: generalized anxiety, phobias, and obsessive-compulsive reactions.

Generalized Anxiety Disorder. For some people, the anxieties they experience are unfocused: they do not center around a specific event, situation, or object. Rather, such persons are filled with dread much of the time, in a wide range of settings.

They are jittery and spend a great deal of time worrying. Further, their worries go beyond the normal concerns we all experience as part of daily life. They fret for hours about past mistakes and possible future calamities. They may also become incapable of reaching decisions because of the fear that they will make mistakes.

Closely related to generalized anxiety is *panic disorder*. In this case an individual experiences relatively brief but intense periods of panic, rather than continuous, but somewhat milder, feelings of anxiety. Such **panic attacks** do not seem to be triggered by a specific object or event; rather, they appear (at least subjectively) to come from nowhere—out of the blue, so to speak. Whatever their origins, they involve intense feelings of dread or terror; physical symptoms such as a pounding heart, dizziness, or trembling; and frightening thoughts (e.g., the belief that death is imminent, or that the individual may go completely out of control). Cheryl, the young woman in our opening story, provides a vivid example of such reactions.

What is the origin of such problems? According to psychoanalytic theory, anxiety occurs when the ego seems incapable of dealing with unacceptable impulses from the id. In contrast, a more modern psychological perspective suggests that anxiety may be one response to situations in which individuals feel incapable of dealing with unpredictable, and perhaps uncontrollable, events. Under such conditions, stress is intense, and prolonged anxiety may be the result (Schwartz, 1984). Whatever its precise origins, one fact is clear: generalized anxiety can be a serious and distressing problem for those who face it.

Phobias: Fear That Is Focused.   Most people express some fear of snakes, heights, and violent storms. Since all of these can pose real threats to our safety and well-being, such reactions are adaptive, up to a point. Some persons, though, experience intense anxiety when in the presence of these or other objects, or merely when they think about them. Such **phobias** can be so strong as to interfere with everyday activities. For example, the author once knew a young woman who was so afraid of snakes—or even of the thought of seeing one—that she refused to go on picnics in the country, to walk through woods, or to approach a wood pile. She was even reluctant to look at stuffed snakes mounted behind glass in museums! (Please refer to Figure 13-6). Other common phobias focus on insects, open spaces, mice, and flying.

FIGURE 13-6. Individuals suffering from *phobias* experience extreme anxiety when they see or even think about the objects they fear.

One Common Phobia

As we noted in Chapter 5, *classical conditioning,* a basic form of learning, seems to be involved in such disorders. Recall, though, that individuals do not acquire phobias to *any* stimuli. Phobias directed toward pencils, rabbits, or palm trees are virtually nonexistent. Thus, we seem to be *prepared* by our biological nature to acquire some fears but not others. Fortunately, as we shall see in Chapter 14, phobic disorders can often be readily eliminated through certain types of therapy. Recent evidence indicates, though, that they may sometimes reappear when individuals are exposed to stressful conditions (Jacobs & Nadel, 1985). This suggests that they may involve an even more basic type of learning, the kind that occurs during early infancy, before many of our cognitive mechanisms are well developed. Whatever their precise basis, phobias produce considerable distress among persons who develop them.

Obsessive-Compulsive Disorders: Behaviors and Thoughts Outside One's Control.   Have you ever left your home, gotten halfway down the street, and then returned to see if you really locked the door or turned off the oven? Most of us have had such experiences. But, again, for some persons such anxieties are so intense that they become trapped in repetitive behaviors *(compulsions)* or recurrent modes of thought *(obsessions)*. For example, a person suffering from an **obsessive-compulsive disorder** may feel that he has to tie his tie over and over again before delivering a speech. Only if the knot is *just right* will he succeed at making the speech. Similarly, a mother may be so afraid of germs that she washes her hands many times each day, in order to avoid infecting her young son. What is the basis for such reactions? One intriguing possibility is as follows (Rachman & Hodgson, 1980).

We all have obsessional (repetitive) thoughts at some times. For example, after watching a film containing disturbing scenes of violence, we may find ourselves thinking about these events over and over again. Most persons soon manage to distract themselves from such unpleasant thoughts. In contrast, individuals who develop an obsessive-compulsive disorder are unable to do so. They are made anxious by their obsessional thoughts and can't dismiss them readily from their minds. This is due in part to the fact that (1) they have elevated levels of arousal (they are more activated most of the time than other persons), and (2) they tend to overreact to emotion-provoking stimuli (Turner, Beidel, & Nathan, 1985). Their inability to avoid obsessional thoughts then causes such persons to become even more anxious, and the cycle builds from there (refer to Figure 13-7). This same theory also explains the ritualistic behaviors that are often part of such

FIGURE 13-7. Individuals who develop an *obsessive-compulsive disorder* tend to have elevated levels of arousal and to overreact to emotion-provoking stimuli. As a result, they experience anxiety in response to recurrent (obsessional) thoughts and are unable to terminate them. These thoughts tend to persist and may lead such persons to adopt compulsive rituals which help reduce their anxiety.

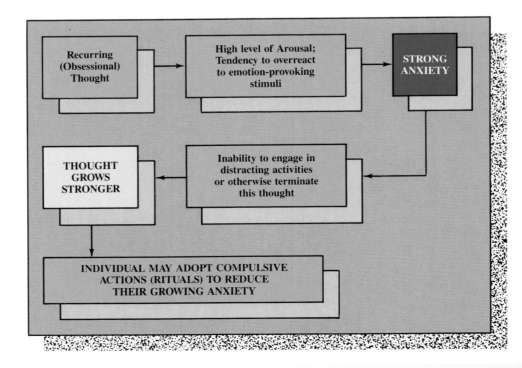

Obsessive-Compulsive Disorders: One Interpretation

disorders. Since the people suffering from such problems can't dismiss obsessive thoughts from their minds, they use other tactics. Specifically, they attempt to neutralize such "threats" by engaging in actions that ensure their safety: they tie their tie over and over, check their front door dozens of times, and so on. Such behavior is reinforced by the temporary relief they experience each time it is performed. Thus, the behavior tends to grow stronger over time, and unless outside help is obtained, individuals suffering from this disorder become locked into it ever more deeply.

Dissociative Disorders: When Memory Fails

Have you ever awakened during the night and, just for a moment, been uncertain about where you were? Such temporary disruptions in our normal cognitive functions are far from rare; many persons experience them from time to time as a result of fatigue, illness, or over-indulgence in alcohol or other psychoactive substances. Some individuals, however, experience much more profound and lengthy losses of identity or memory. These are known as **dissociative disorders,** and they constitute one of the most intriguing subjects we will consider.

Psychogenic Amnesia: Forgetting as a Means of Escape.   From time to time, newspapers print accounts of the following type:

> TOLEDO, OHIO. One day in 1983 Herman Slade, owner of a local hardware store, simply vanished. He stepped outside for a breath of fresh air and was never heard from again. Efforts by police and state authorities to locate him failed, and his disappearance remained a total mystery. The mystery was finally solved today, when Herman picked up the phone and called his wife Sally from Elkhart, Nebraska, where he was working as manager of a large motel. "I just woke up this morning and remembered everything," Slade reported. "Until then, I had no idea who I was or where I came from." Apparently, Slade was under considerable stress at the time of his memory loss. His daughter had been badly injured in an auto accident, and his personal finances were near collapse. "I just want to go home and pick up the pieces," Slade told reporters. "Those four years are gone, and I guess I'll never get them back. . . ."

Are such accounts accurate? Do people suddenly lose their memory, only to recover it months or even years later? In fact, they do. Such persons are victims of **psychogenic amnesia**—a sudden disruption of memory that seems to occur in response to unbearable stress. Such reactions are accurately described by the term *dissociative,* for they seem to represent disorders in which some portion of memory is split off (dissociated) from conscious awareness. Needless to say, such experiences can be extremely unsettling for the persons who have them.

Multiple Personality: Two (or Several) Minds in One Body?   Even more bizarre than psychogenic amnesia is **multiple personality,** a rare disorder in which a single individual seems to possess two, or even several, distinct personalities (refer to Figure 13-8). The most famous example of this disorder involved Chris Sizemore, a young

FIGURE 13-8. Contrary to what this cartoon suggests, different personalities aren't present at the same time in *multiple personality disorders*. *(Source: NEA, 1987.)*

FRANK and ERNEST   **By Bob Thaves**

Multiple Personality: A Humorous View

FIGURE 13-9. The photo on the left shows Eve White—Chris Sizemore's virtuous personality. The photo on the right shows Eve Black—her seductive, bold, and reckless personality. (Please note: these are photos of an actress in the movie, *The Three Faces of Eve;* they don't actually show Ms. Sizemore.)

homemaker whose story was portrayed in the movie *The Three Faces of Eve* (Thigpen & Cleckley, 1954). At first, Ms. Sizemore seemed to possess two distinct personalities: Eve White—a mild, meek, and virtuous wife and mother; and Eve Black—a bold, seductive, fun-loving woman who rejected the responsibilities of marriage and family (see Figure 13-9). After intensive therapy, however, a third personality emerged, which seemed to blend some of the traits of the other two.

In the years since Chris Sizemore's case first came to light many other instances of multiple personality have been reported (e.g., Davis & Osherson, 1977). Their appearance has sparked a heated controversy within psychology: is this a real phenomenon—a real form of psychological disorder? Or are the persons involved merely faking? On one side are skeptics who contend that many cases of multiple personality are faked and that other cases merely reflect unconscious efforts by the persons involved to play various roles (Spanos, 1984). On the other side are psychologists who accept the validity of multiple personality and who explain it in the following terms.

Individuals differ greatly in their ability to enter self-induced hypnotic states. A few who are especially good at such self-hypnosis are exposed to traumatic events during early childhood. They cope with these events by generating a second personality to endure the trauma for them. Since this strategy relieves emotional stress, the "alternate self" is retained and used as the need arises (Rosenhan & Seligman, 1984). Some support for this explanation is found in the fact that persons reporting multiple personality show different patterns of brain waves when each "individual" appears (Goleman, 1985). At present, though, the issue is far from resolved, and the existence of multiple personality remains an open question.

Somatoform Disorders: Physical Symptoms Without Physical Causes

Several of Freud's early cases, ones which played an important role in his developing theory of personality, involved the following, puzzling situation. An individual would show some physical symptom (e.g., deafness, paralysis of some part of the body, persistent pain), yet careful examination would reveal no underlying physical cause for this problem. Such disorders, known as **somatoform disorders,** still occur today. In addition to the physical symptoms just mentioned, they also usually involve an absence of anxiety (the persons involved are not very upset by their physical problems), and a lack of voluntary control (such persons cannot simply "will" their physical difficulties away).

Somatoform disorders take several distinct forms. The most common type is *conversion*. Here, some form of psychological stress seems to be converted into a physical problem. For example, an individual who feels extreme guilt because he caused an accident that left another paralyzed may suddenly experience paralysis of the arm or leg responsible for the accident. In a second type, *Briquet's syndrome,* many different physical symptoms, rather than only one, occur. As a result, persons who develop this type of disorder have a long history of medical treatment. They go from physician to physician, often receiving unnecessary drugs, examinations, and even surgery in the process. Finally, in a third type *(psychalgia),* individuals experience intense pain that has no physical cause.

Freud explained such disorders as involving defenses against anxiety. Presumably, the persons involved convert unacceptable impulses or conflicts into various symptoms. Doing so reduces the anxiety generated by such impulses, and so the condition persists. An alternative view, more consistent with modern psychological principles, suggests that persons suffering from somatoform disorders use their symptoms as a form of *communication*—to inform others that they are experiencing intense distress (Rosenhan & Seligman, 1984). Such persons may not be fully conscious of this purpose, but they seem to be aware of it at some level. In any case, the specific symptoms they choose seem to depend upon their perceptions (conscious or otherwise) of what others will recognize as an important problem. Consistent with this view, the symptoms involved in conversion disorders have changed over the decades since Freud's early work. Paralysis, blindness, and deafness were common among his patients in late nineteenth-century Vienna. At present, though, pain, dizziness, headache, and weakness are much more common.

Sexual Disorders: Disturbances in Desire and Behavior

What is "normal" and what is "abnormal" where sexual behavior is concerned? As we're sure you can appreciate, this is a complex matter. Beliefs and expectations about sexual matters vary greatly in different societies and across time. How often should sexual relations occur? What forms should they take? At what age should they begin? Are they enjoyed equally by men and women? These are just a few of the matters on which various societies have held sharply different views at different times.

In recent decades there has been a shift toward a broader definition of what is sexually acceptable in many Western nations. Correspondingly, our conception of what is *not* acceptable has narrowed. Despite such changes, though, the DSM-III-R and the vast majority of psychologists recognize the existence of many **sexual disorders**—disturbances in sexual behavior or functioning which cause emotional stress to the persons who experience them. These fall into two major categories: sexual dysfunctions, and paraphilias.

Sexual Dysfunctions: Disturbances in Arousal and Desire.   Sexual dysfunctions involve disturbances in sexual desire, sexual arousal, or the ability to attain orgasm. Persons suffering from such problems do not become aroused sexually in situations where most people would view arousal as appropriate (e.g., during lovemaking with their mate), and they are not able to maintain such arousal and fail to achieve orgasm. In women, lack of sexual desire or arousal is termed *female sexual arousal disorder* and involves failure to have sexual fantasies or to experience reactions such as vaginal lubrication or clitoral enlargement. In men, it often takes the form of *male erectile disorder*—inability to have or maintain an erection. Problems relating to orgasm include the inability to experience sexual climax (primarily in women) and premature or delayed ejaculation in men. Needless to say, all of these dysfunctions are usually very disturbing to the persons who experience them, and any of them can exert adverse effects on self-esteem.

Paraphilias: Disturbances in Sexual Object or Behavior.   What is sexually arousing? For most persons, the answer involves the sight or touch of another human being—one they find sexually attractive. Many persons, however, become sexually aroused by other stimuli, too. For example, many men find certain types of women's lingerie arousing; and some members of both sexes are aroused by specific scents—

Sexual Arousal to Inanimate
Objects Is Not Necessarily a
Psychological Disturbance

FIGURE 13-10. Many persons find stimuli aside from other human beings to be sexually arousing. This is not a sign of psychological disturbance unless such reactions take precedence over, or interfere with, the capacity for affectionate erotic relations.

seductive perfumes or other aromas they associate with past sexual encounters (Levine & McBurney, 1982). (Refer to Figure 13-10.) Others find that either inflicting or receiving pain during sexual relations adds to their arousal and pleasure. Such reactions do not necessarily constitute a sexual disorder. A disorder is present only when such reactions interfere with the capacity for affectionate erotic relations (Rosenham & Seligman, 1984). Several types of such disorders, known collectively as the *paraphilias,* exist.

First, individuals may become aroused exclusively by inanimate objects or *fetishes.* Often these are articles of clothing, but in unusual cases they can involve human waste, dirt, animals, or even dead bodies. Second, there is *transvestic fetishism*—arousal among males produced by dressing in women's clothing. Two other sexual disorders are *sexual sadism* and *sexual masochism.* In the former, individuals become sexually aroused by inflicting pain or humiliation on others. In the latter, they are aroused by receiving such treatment. Another paraphilia involves becoming aroused by nonconsenting partners. This can take the form of *exhibitionism*—exposing one's genitals to unsuspecting strangers, or *voyeurism*—arousal through looking at others who do not know they are being observed. Most objectionable of all is *pedophilia,* a disturbance in which an individual prefers sexual activity with children.

Problems of Gender Identity: Transsexualism.   Have you ever read a newspaper or magazine article describing a man who altered his gender to become a woman or vice versa? Such accounts describe *transsexuals*—individuals who feel, often from an early age, that somehow they were born with the wrong sexual equipment. Such individuals are often disgusted by their own body and the prospect of living their entire life within it. Because such problems invariably begin during childhood, they are classified with other childhood disorders in the DSM-III-R. However, since they relate to sexual behavior and functioning, it seems reasonable to mention them here.

In the past, persons suffering from a gender identity disorder would often dress as members of the opposite sex and would do everything they could to assume their preferred sexual identity. Advances in surgery have now made it possible for such persons to undergo a *sex-change operation,* in which their sexual organs are actually altered in the manner they desire. Following such an operation, the person changes to a new name and goes on to live as a member of the new gender (see Figure 13-11). Many transsexuals who have adopted this drastic course of action report being happier than they were before the sex-change operation. Whether they are actually less psychologically disturbed, however, remains somewhat controversial (Hunt & Hampson, 1980).

Tennis Player, Renee Richards, A Transsexual Who Has Undergone a Sex-Change Operation

FIGURE 13-11. *Transsexuals* feel that they have been born into the wrong gender. Some persons who suffer from this disorder undergo an operation to alter their sexual organs so that they can live the remainder of their life as a member of the opposite sex.

Mood Disorders: The Downs and Ups of Life

Everyone experiences wide swings in mood or emotional state at least occasionally. We all have days when we feel unusually happy, energetic, and cheerful. And we all have days when we feel sad, incapable of effort, and miserable. Such extremes are usually short-lived, and most of the time we are somewhere in between, in a range we define as ''normal.'' In contrast to this typical pattern, some persons experience disturbances in mood that are both extreme and prolonged. Their highs are higher, their lows are lower, and the periods they spend at these emotional heights and depths are prolonged. In short, such persons suffer from what are termed **mood disorders.** The DSM-III-R recognizes two major types: *depressive disorders* and *bipolar disorders.*

The most common depressive disorder is **major depression,** in which an individual moves between deep emotional despair and a state most of us would describe as relatively normal. In **bipolar disorders,** in contrast, the person's mood swings between deep despair and **mania**—a state in which the person feels extremely elated and energetic, and often experiences feelings of being all-powerful and invulnerable to harm (refer to Figure 13-12 on page 418).

Major Depression: The Emotional Black Hole of Life

Unless we lead a truly charmed existence, our daily lives bring some events that make us feel sad or disappointed. When do such reactions constitute depression? While there is no definite point where we can draw a line and say ''beyond this lies depression,'' most psychologists agree that several criteria are useful for making this distinction. First, persons suffering from depression are sad for prolonged periods of time. Moreover, such sadness is intense and blots out all the usual pleasures of life (eating, sex, sports, hobbies). Second, depressed persons usually have a lasting negative view of themselves and the world around them. They feel they are inferior and inadequate, and they view the future as hopeless. ''Things are bad and they can't possibly change''—this summarizes the thoughts such persons often hold. Third, individuals suffering from depression seem to suffer from a paralysis of will: they are unable to get going and find doing anything to be a great effort. Finally, they may show a variety of physical symptoms. Weight loss, sleeplessness, and physical weakness may all be present. When such reactions occur and persist for prolonged periods of time, it is reasonable to describe the persons involved as suffering from depression.

Two Mood Disorders

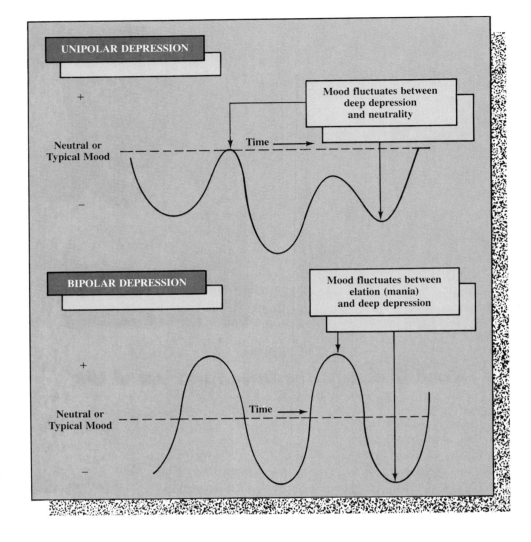

FIGURE 13-12. In *major depression* an individual swings between emotional despair and a fairly neutral state. In *bipolar disorders* the mood swings from despair through mania.

Unfortunately, depression is all too common; it is by far the most frequent type of psychological disorder. Interestingly, it is much more common among women than men. About 25 percent of all women experience an episode of serious depression during their lives, while for men the corresponding figure is only 10 percent. What accounts for this difference? One possibility suggested by recent research (Nolen-Hoeksema, 1987) is as follows. When they experience depression, men and women adopt different strategies for dealing with such reactions. Men seem to engage in activities designed to distract them and to generate positive emotions. For example, they avoid thinking about why they're depressed, engage in sports, or turn to drugs. In contrast, women tend to focus on their own depression: they think about the reasons for such feelings, talk to others about their problems, and cry to relieve their tension. Given these different strategies, it is not surprising that men experience depression far less often, and for shorter periods of time, than women. (Please see Figure 13-13 for a summary of this explanation.)

But why do the two sexes react to negative emotions in these contrasting ways? Nolen-Hoeksema (1987) suggests that *sex-role stereotypes* may hold the answer. Traditional views of masculinity imply that men are active and ignore their feelings and moods. Corresponding views of femininity, however, often emphasize passivity, resignation, and staying in close touch with one's feelings. Whatever the reason, though, women are more than twice as likely as men to suffer from serious depression.

Suicide: The Ultimate Cost of Depression. Depression is a painful disorder. Sadness, feelings of inadequacy, lack of energy—these are reactions that few of us care to experience. Little wonder, then, that large numbers of depressed individuals, filled with

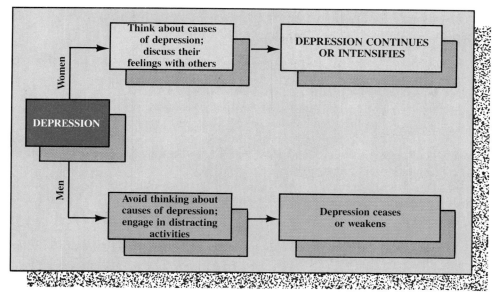

Reactions to Depression:
How the Sexes Differ

FIGURE 13-13. Men and women seem to adopt different strategies in response to depression. Women tend to think about the causes for their depression, or they discuss their feelings with others. This may prolong or intensify their depression. Men try to avoid thinking about the reasons for their depression and engage in distracting activities. As a result, such feelings may soon weaken.

despair, adopt a drastic means of dealing with their problems: suicide. A person suffering from depression is twenty-five times more likely to attempt to take his or her own life than a nondepressed person (Goodstein & Calhoun, 1982). Again, some intriguing sex differences appear. While more women attempt suicide, a greater proportion of men actually complete the act. Apparently this stems from the fact that the two sexes adopt different methods for ending their own lives. Men are more likely to use a gun or jump off a building, while women tend to prefer less certain methods (e.g., an overdose of sleeping pills, slashing their wrists). Men and women also differ in their reported motives for suicide. Men often mention failure at work or financial problems; women frequently refer to the unhappy end of love affairs or other interpersonal problems (Linden & Breed, 1976).

While many suicides seem to stem from the desire to escape from emotional pain and distress (such persons have literally given up), others involve a different motive. Some persons end their lives in order to have some effect upon the world—to make a final point in a continuing argument, to gain revenge by inducing guilt in another person, or even to express their ultimate rejection of a lover. (The evidence for such motives is provided by notes left behind, or by the persons themselves, if their attempt at suicide failed.) Two final, and somewhat surprising, facts: contrary to popular belief, suicide is *not* more common among rich than among poor persons—it is equally frequent in both groups; and suicide is *not* most likely to occur when individuals are in the depths of depression. Its incidence actually rises as improvement occurs and an individual regains the will and energy to take drastic action.

The Causes of Depression: Its Biological and Psychological Roots

Depression and other mood disorders tend to run in families. Thus, if one identical twin develops such a problem, the other does, too, more than 70 percent of the time. This and related findings suggest that there is an important genetic component in depression and related disorders (Allen, 1976). But what is it that is inherited? Growing evidence suggests that mood disorders in general, and depression in particular, may involve abnormalities in brain biochemistry. For example, it has been found that levels of two neurotransmitters—*norepinephrine* and *serotonin*—are lower in the brains of depressed than nondepressed persons. Similarly, levels of such substances are *higher* in the brains of persons demonstrating mania. Further evidence for the role of these neurotransmitters in affective disorders is provided by the fact that drugs that produce depression (e.g., reserpine, used in the treatment of high blood pressure) tend to reduce concentrations of norepinephrine (Rosenhan & Seligman, 1984). Similarly, drugs that reduce depression act to increase brain levels of norepinephrine. Unfortunately, this relatively neat picture is somewhat muddied by the following facts: not all persons suffering from depression show reduced levels of norepinephrine or serotonin; and not all persons demonstrating mania have increased levels of these substances. In addition, drugs used to treat both mood disorders produce many effects in addition to changing the presence or activity of various neurotransmitters. At present, then, it is clear that *some* biological factors (including ones that may be affected by genetic factors) influence depression. The nature of these factors, though, remains to be determined.

Psychological Factors and Depression.   While the biochemical roots of depression remain uncertain, significant progress has been made in recent years in understanding the psychological mechanisms that underlie this damaging disorder. Two models have proven extremely useful in this respect.

The first, sometimes known as the *control perspective,* relates depression to feelings of **helplessness** (Seligman, 1975). It suggests that when individuals are exposed to situations in which they cannot control their own outcomes, they develop negative expectancies: they conclude that nothing they do really matters and that no actions on their part will permit them to avoid the occurrence of unpleasant events. Obviously, it is a relatively short step from such beliefs to serious depression.

An important addition to this framework involves attention to an individual's *attributions* about the causes behind such lack of control (Abramson, Seligman, & Teasdale, 1978; Sweeney, Anderson, & Bailey, 1986). According to this modified learned helplessness model, depression is related not simply to the belief that one cannot influence one's outcomes but is linked more specifically to the tendency to attribute bad events to internal, stable causes. In short, when negative events befall depressed persons, they take the blame for their occurrence and attribute these events to their own lasting characteristics (e.g., lack of intelligence, laziness, poor judgment, and so on). Clear evidence for the role of such attributions in depression has recently been reported by Seligman and his colleagues (Seligman et al., 1988). These researchers found that depressed individuals were much more likely than nondepressed persons to attribute negative events to lasting internal causes. Further, as they underwent therapy for their depression, these self-defeating attributions and the depression itself decreased.

A second important framework for understanding the psychological causes of depression emphasizes the role of additional *cognitive* factors (e.g., Beck, 1976; Beck et al., 1979). According to this perspective, the roots of depression lie in negative beliefs and cognitive sets (tendencies to think in certain ways). Depressed people, it is suggested, hold negative views about themselves—they have low self-esteem. They tend to blame themselves for failures or negative experiences. (Nondepressed persons tend to give themselves the benefit of the doubt in this respect. In fact, as we'll see in Chapter 15, they often fail to take responsibility for negative outcomes even when they deserve it!) Depressed persons hold negative views about the future, other persons, and the world around them. Finally, they are prone to several types of faulty thinking. For example, they often draw conclusions without sufficient supporting evidence, they overgeneralize, and, perhaps most important of all, they magnify the importance of negative events while minimizing the importance of positive ones. In sum, according to this approach, depression stems primarily from certain ways of thinking about oneself, one's experiences, and the external world. (Please see Figure 13-14 for a summary of the control and cognitive perspectives.)

Both of these frameworks are supported by a large amount of research evidence. Depressed persons *do* often feel helpless and adopt self-defeating attributions: they blame themselves for lack of control over the world around them. And they *do* often tend to see the world through cognitive frameworks that seem almost guaranteed to crush any rays of

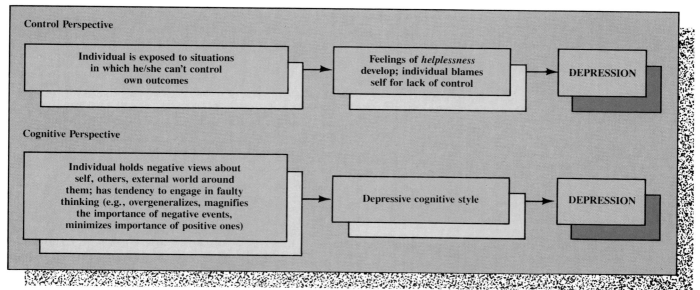

FIGURE 13-14. According to the *control perspective*, exposure to situations in which individuals cannot control their own outcomes leads to feelings of helplessness which generalize to a wide range of situations. Such feelings, in turn, contribute to depression. The *cognitive perspective* suggests that depression results from negative views about oneself, others, and the external world, plus certain faulty types of thinking.

Depression: Two Psychological Perspectives

hope or optimism. Thus, by calling our attention to the importance of these factors, the control and cognitive perspectives have increased our knowledge of depression. As we will see in Chapter 14, such knowledge has been put to practical use in several useful techniques for combating affective disorders. (For another intriguing explanation of depression, please read ''The Cutting Edge'' section below.)

FOCUS ON RESEARCH: The Cutting Edge

Self-focused Attention and Depression: Getting Trapped in No-Win Situations

In a classic book entitled *Mourning and Melancholia* Freud (1917) explained depression as follows. When individuals experience a loss (e.g., death of a loved one), they feel both sorrow and anger—they are saddened by their loss and angry at the lost object or person. Since such hostility can produce intense guilt (after all, how can one be angry at someone for dying?), they redirect their anger inward, toward themselves, and so become depressed. Does this colorful interpretation have any bearing on our modern conception of depression? In one sense, it does. A recent theory proposed by Pyszczynski and Greenberg (1987) also assumes that depression has its origins in some loss an individual experiences. From that point on, though, the theory moves in direc-

tions that would have been quite unfamiliar to Freud.

Following a loss, Pyszczynski and Greenberg (1987) reason, individuals turn their attention inward. They engage in *self-focused attention* in order to understand the reasons for this loss, whether they could have prevented it, and how they can best deal with it. This, in turn, initiates a process in which the individuals compare their present state with desired states. If the loss is one that can be regained, corrective behaviors are then taken. When these succeed, the process stops, and self-focus terminates. For example, if you receive a poor grade on an exam (a serious blow to your self-esteem), you compare this grade with the one you desire, and then perhaps increase your studying.

Unfortunately, though, some losses are irreversible: no corrective actions will restore them. When faced with such

Self-Focused Attention and Depression

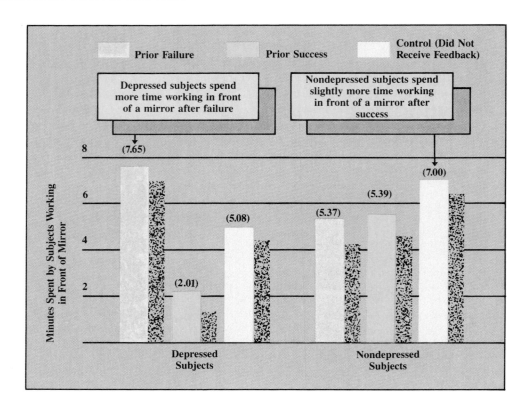

FIGURE 13-15. Depressed persons chose to work on a puzzle located in front of a mirror after failure, but avoided this task after success. Nondepressed persons did not show the same pattern; they demonstrated a slight preference for working in front of a mirror after success. These findings support the view that depressed persons often become trapped in a pointless cycle of self-regulatory behavior. *(Source: Based on data from Pyszczynski & Greenberg, 1986.)*

losses, it is adaptive to terminate self-focus and concentrate on other matters. Most people manage to accomplish this task. This is not so for persons who become depressed, however. They tend to get trapped in an endless *self-regulatory cycle* in which they continue to dwell on the irreversible loss. This, in turn, generates negative feelings and initiates self-criticism and blame. As these reactions continue, such persons experience further drops in self-esteem, and develop what Pyszczynski and Greenberg (1987) term a *depressive self-focusing style.* They turn their attention inward after failures, but they avoid doing so after successes or other positive outcomes. The ultimate result: they become trapped in a situation in which they absolutely can't win. No matter what happens from this point on, they remain negative about themselves and the world around them, and, of course, they remain depressed.

Support for these suggestions has been obtained in several recent studies. For example, in one investigation (Pyszczynski and Greenberg, 1986) depressed and nondepressed individuals worked on an anagrams (scrambled-letter) task, and were then informed that

they had done quite well or very poorly. (A third group never worked on the anagrams and received no feedback.) They were then asked to work on two additional puzzles. One puzzle was located in front of a mirror, while the other was not. Since working in front of a mirror increases self-focused attention, it was predicted that depressed individuals would spend more time working on the puzzle in front of the mirror after failure than after success. In contrast, nondepressed subjects would show the opposite pattern. As you can see from Figure 13-15, these predictions were confirmed. In short, after failure, depressed persons did, in a sense, pour salt into their own wounds: they focused on themselves and their loss of self-esteem. Nondepressed subjects, in contrast, tended to avoid this cycle.

In conclusion, it appears that depression may sometimes involve the tendency to get trapped in endless, and largely useless self-regulatory activity. To the extent this is the case, there may be more truth than we once suspected to the old saying that thinking about oneself too much can prove harmful.

Schizophrenia: Out of Touch with Reality

All of the psychological disorders we have considered so far are serious ones: they induce considerable distress in the persons who experience them, and they interfere to some degree with the persons' ability to function effectively. In a sense, they are like lead weights some persons carry with them as they go about their daily activities. Yet most sufferers *can* still function. Individuals who experience **schizophrenia** are a very different story. Such persons are usually not capable of living ordinary lives. Indeed, in many cases their ability to cope is so limited that they must be removed from society for their own protection. What is the nature of the disorder we call schizophrenia? What different forms does it take? How does it arise? These are the questions we will now address.

The Nature of Schizophrenia: Its Major Symptoms

Persons suffering from schizophrenia may demonstrate a wide range of symptoms. Indeed, their patterns of behavior and thought are often as varied as they are bizarre. The most important problems they face, though, involve *disorganized modes of thought, distorted perceptions*, and *inappropriate emotions*.

Disturbances of Thought.   Individuals identified as schizophrenic do not think like other persons. Perhaps this is revealed most dramatically in their speech, which often jumps about in a fragmented and disorganized manner. They may use words of their own invention and may be unable to complete sentences. Indeed, their speech is so jumbled and meaningless that it is sometimes described as ''verbal salad''—a hodgepodge of unconnected words and phrases.

These problems, and several others, seem to stem from a breakdown in the capacity for *selective attention*. Normally, we can focus our attention on certain stimuli while largely ignoring others. This is not the case among schizophrenics. They are easily distracted by anything and everything. Even the sound of their own words may disrupt their train of thought and send them far off the point.

Finally, schizophrenics often suffer from *delusions*—strange beliefs that cannot be refuted even in the face of strong contradictory evidence. Delusions take many different forms. One common type is termed *delusions of grandeur*. Here, an individual believes that he or she is extremely important—perhaps the President, a queen, a famous star, or even a saint. In contrast, *delusions of control* involve beliefs that one's thoughts or behaviors are being controlled from without—by special ''rays,'' psychic energy, or some other unseen force. A third common form is *delusions of persecution*—the belief that others are plotting one's downfall and are ''out to get me.'' (Refer to Figure 13-16.)

FIGURE 13-16. Captain Queeg, played by Humphrey Bogart in *The Caine Mutiny,* suffered from delusions of persecution. While it's not clear that he was schizophrenic, his behavior certainly bordered on this condition.

Delusions of Persecution: One Example

Disturbances of Perception. Another symptom shown by schizophrenics is even more dramatic than the ones we have been discussing: **hallucinations.** These are sensory experiences, often intense and vivid, that have no basis in physical reality. Auditory hallucinations, in which individuals ''hear'' voices, music, or other sounds that aren't actually present, are the most common. However, visual ones also occur, and occasionally smells and tastes are reported.

Disturbances of Emotion. A third category of symptom often shown by schizophrenics involves inappropriate or unusual emotional reactions. Some show virtually no emotion at all; they remain impassive in the face of events that evoke strong reaction from others. For example, on being told that her mother is seriously ill, such a person may make no comment or simply remark: ''Is that so?'' This split, or separation between thought and emotion, reflects the meaning of the term *schizo* (split) *phrenia* (mind) as envisioned by its originator, Eugen Bleuler. Please note, by the way, that Bleuler (1924) did *not* mean to imply that schizophrenia involves a Dr. Jekyll/Mr. Hyde split *personality;* rather, he suggested only that certain psychological functions—thought and emotion, thought and perception—were somehow split or separated.

In other cases, schizophrenics *do* demonstrate emotion, but their reactions are inappropriate. They may smile when experiencing pain or fly into a rage when someone offers them a gift. In sum, their disturbed patterns of thought, perception, and emotion weaken schizophrenics' grip on reality, and virtually assure that they live in a private world largely of their own creation.

Types of Schizophrenia

Although all schizophrenics show some of the problems outlined above, the pattern of these symptoms differs greatly. Largely on the basis of such differences, schizophrenia is divided into five distinct types. We'll describe several of these here.

Disorganized Schizophrenia. The most striking characteristic of persons in this group is their silliness and incoherence. They burst into laughter or tears for no apparent reason and babble on meaninglessly for hours. Such persons sometimes have delusions and hallucinations, but these are fuzzy and poorly developed.

Paranoid Schizophrenia. As its name suggests, persons in this category have delusions of persecution—they see plots to harm them everywhere. In addition, they may experience delusions of grandeur. In both cases, these delusions are detailed and systematic, to the point where they might almost form the plot of a complex novel.

Catatonic Schizophrenia. In some respects this is the most bizarre form of all. Persons suffering from catatonic schizophrenia show behavior that is either totally ''frozen'' or wildly excitable. Moreover, they often swing between these two states, sitting totally paralyzed in some unusual posture for a long period, then suddenly erupting into activity (see Figure 13-17). At present, this type of schizophrenic disorder is quite rare, probably because it is prevented by some powerful drugs now routinely administered to patients in mental hospitals.

Undifferentiated Schizophrenia. This is the catchall category, to which all persons who do not fit neatly under the other headings are assigned. It includes schizophrenics who demonstrate disturbances of thought, perception, and emotion, but not the features peculiar to the other types.

Schizophrenia: Its Causes

That schizophrenia is an important, serious, and fascinating type of psychological disorder is clear. But what are its origins? What factors contribute to its occurrence among

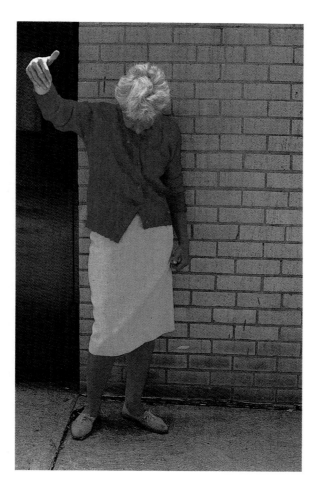

Catatonic Schizophrenia:
A Rare and Serious Disorder

FIGURE 13-17. Persons suffering from *catatonic schizophrenia* often remain immobile in unusual positions for long periods of time. Then, unpredictably, they burst into frenzied activity.

specific persons? Early investigators of this disorder, such as Bleuler and Emil Kraepelin, believed that it was primarily biological in origin. For example, Kraepelin (1919) suggested that it stemmed from a chemical imbalance produced by malfunctioning sex glands, an imbalance which somehow interfered with normal operation of the nervous system. Interest in the origins of schizophrenia has continued for many decades, and much research has been focused on this issue in recent years. As yet, no definitive answers have been obtained, but such research points to the following conclusion: schizophrenia has its origins in a complex pattern of genetic, biochemical, and psychological factors.

Genetic Factors: Does Schizophrenia Run in Families?   The answer to this question appears to be ''yes.'' In fact, the closer the family relationship between two individuals, the higher the odds that if one develops schizophrenia, the other will show this disorder, too (Gottesman & Shields, 1972). Among identical twins, this figure is about 40 percent; if one develops schizophrenia, the other stands a 40 percent chance of doing so, too. Among non-identical twins, this figure drops to about 10 percent. It is about five percent (or slightly higher) for parents and children. Since the rate of schizophrenia in the population as a whole is less than one percent, it seems clear that genetic factors do play a role in this disorder.

Additional support for this conclusion is provided by a famous study conducted by Heston (1966). His subjects were forty-seven children with schizophrenic mothers who had been placed for adoption before the age of one month. As a comparison group he also studied fifty additional children raised in the same homes (these children, of course, did *not* have schizophrenic mothers). When the two groups were examined by psychiatrists who knew nothing about the children's backgrounds, large differences emerged. More

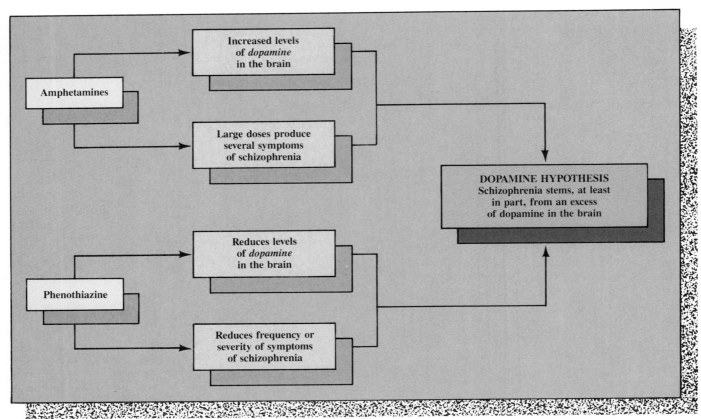

The Dopamine Hypothesis

FIGURE 13-18. Large doses of *amphetamines* induce schizophrenia-like symptoms and increase levels of *dopamine* in the brain. Certain drugs (e.g., phenothiazine) reduce such symptoms and also lower brain levels of dopamine. Together, such findings suggest that schizophrenia may stem, at least in some instances, from an excess of dopamine in the brain.

than 10 percent of the youngsters with schizophrenic mothers were diagnosed as schizophrenic; none of the control children were. Again, an important role for genetic factors is suggested.

The Neurochemistry of Schizophrenia. What, precisely, is inherited? One possibility is suggested by the following findings. The behaviors produced by large doses of *amphetamines* are highly similar to those observed in some types of schizophrenia (e.g., delusions of persecution, hallucinations). Amphetamines seem to produce such effects by increasing levels of, or sensitivity to, the neurotransmitter *dopamine*. Second, drugs effective in treating schizophrenia (e.g., *chlorpromazine*) reduce levels of dopamine in the brain. When these results are combined, it seems reasonable to suggest that schizophrenia may stem, at least in part, from an excess of dopamine in the brain; this is the **dopamine hypothesis.** It may be the case that individuals who develop schizophrenia have an inherited disposition to produce too much of this neurotransmitter. (See Figure 13-18 for a summary of the evidence bearing on this hypothesis.)

We should hasten to add that while some evidence supports the dopamine hypothesis, not all findings are consistent with it. Further, many other factors seem to contribute to the occurrence of schizophrenia, and it is difficult to see how several of these could relate to dopamine and its effects. To mention just one, children born in winter months are more likely to develop schizophrenia than children born at other times of the year, perhaps because their mothers experience more complications and poorer health at the time of birth (Bradbury & Miller, 1985). Until we know how such factors interact with individual differences in dopamine production, the need for caution is suggested. Dopamine may well offer a key to the puzzle of schizophrenia. At present, though, our knowledge is too incomplete to offer firm conclusions.

Psychological Factors in Schizophrenia: Families That Place Children at Risk. The fact that schizophrenia seems to run in families offers evidence for a contribution of genetic factors to this disorder. It also raises the possibility that some families create certain types of environments, ones that increase the likelihood of schizophrenic disorders among their members. Careful study of families in which schizophrenia occurs with higher than expected frequency indicates that this may be so.

First, such families seem to adopt styles of communication that lead children to doubt their own feelings and perceptions. For example, parents often refuse to recognize the meaning of a word or phrase their children are saying and, instead, may substitute one of their own (Wynn et al., 1977). This can be quite confusing to children, especially if they are very young, and may play a role in the children's later problems. Second, families with a high incidence of schizophrenic disorders tend to be ones in which the parents treat each other with contempt and vie openly for the support of the children (Lidz, 1975). Alternatively, a pattern in which one parent (usually the psychologically disturbed one) is highly dominant may be present. Additional factors that seem to be important are frequent absence of either parent and complications during birth (Watt et al., 1984).

In sum, it appears that certain types of home environments—especially ones that are *unstable*—seem to interact with genetic factors to predispose certain persons toward schizophrenic disorders. To the extent we can identify such *high-risk* persons, the possibility of intervening to protect their welfare exists. Whether such interventions will actually be attempted, however, is a social and political decision largely outside the realm of science.

Personality Disorders: Traits That Prove Costly

Have you ever known someone who lied frequently, even when there was no real need for doing so? Have you known someone who was highly suspicious and distrustful of others in virtually all situations (see Figure 13-19)? Or can you think of someone who required constant admiration from others and seemed to be deeply in love—with himself? If so, you have already met people suffering from **personality disorders.** These are collections of strong, inflexible traits that interfere with personal adjustment and cause distress both for the persons who possess them and for others with whom they interact. Many such

A Personality Disorder, Perhaps?

FIGURE 13-19. Some persons are suspicious and distrustful of others in almost all situations. They may be suffering from a *paranoid personality disorder. (Source: NEA, 1986.)*

FRANK and ERNEST   **By Bob Thaves**

patterns exist, but the one that has received the most attention is the antisocial personality disorder.

The Antisocial Personality Disorder: People Without a Conscience

We live in violent times. Our daily newspapers are filled with accounts of murders, assaults, and other crimes of violence. While the crimes themselves are often shocking, even more disturbing are the reactions of the persons who have performed them, when apprehended. Often such persons show absolutely no remorse or regret. ''O.K., I killed them—so what? It's no big deal,'' seems to be the sentiment they express, even during trial (see Figure 13-20). Moreover, it is often found that such persons have a long history of criminal activity, often extending back to childhood.

These traits, plus several others, constitute the **antisocial personality disorder.** Individuals are described as showing this pattern when they demonstrate:

(1) A total lack of conscience—they can lie, cheat, steal, and even kill without any sign of remorse;

(2) High impulsiveness, often coupled with recklessness—when they have an urge or desire, they act on it, regardless of the consequences or dangers it may involve;

(3) An absence of close ties to others; they have little interest in other people except as a means for reaching their own ends—love, affection, loyalty are all beyond their comprehension;

(4) A long history of antisocial behavior, beginning in adolescence and extending through the adult years;

(5) Relatively good social skills—often such persons make a good first impression; indeed, many are charming, witty, and attractive.

FIGURE 13-20. Persons like Theodore Bundy who have committed shocking crimes (Bundy is a multiple murderer of young women) often express no regrets or remorse for their behavior. They may be suffering from the *antisocial personality disorder*.

The Antisocial Personality Disorder: Crime without Guilt

When these traits are combined, the result is often an individual who is quite dangerous to others. Confidence artists, accomplished thieves, prostitutes, pimps, and mass murderers—all frequently show at least some of this pattern. Certainly, then, the antisocial personality disorder is one of great significance for society.

Origins of the Antisocial Personality Disorder. What factors cause individuals to develop this disturbing pattern of traits? Again, the answer seems to involve both genetic factors and aspects of early development. Turning first to genetic factors, a large-scale study by Hutchings and Mednick (1977) is of interest. These researchers studied the behavior of a large group of men who had been adopted within a few months of birth. Some had biological parents with criminal records, while others did not. Moreover, some had been placed in homes where their foster parents had such records, while others had been placed in homes where this was not the case. Results indicated that subjects whose own biological parents had a record of criminal behavior were much more likely to engage in such actions themselves. Moreover, this was true even if they had been raised by foster parents who had no record of criminal offense (refer to Figure 13-21.) These findings indicate that genetic factors may play at least some role in antisocial behavior.

In terms of psychological factors, it appears that children raised in poor homes, in single-parent families, in families where their needs are neglected, and in environments where they are exposed to a high incidence of criminal behavior are at risk. Such youngsters are much more likely to develop the antisocial personality disorder than children raised under more favorable circumstances. If these conditions sound to you like a de-

FIGURE 13-21. Adopted children whose biological parents had criminal records were more likely to commit such offenses themselves than were adopted children whose biological parents did not have such records. This was true even when the foster parents had no history of criminal behavior. These findings suggest that genetic factors may play a role in the antisocial personality disorder. *(Source: Based on data from Hutchings & Mednick, 1977.)*

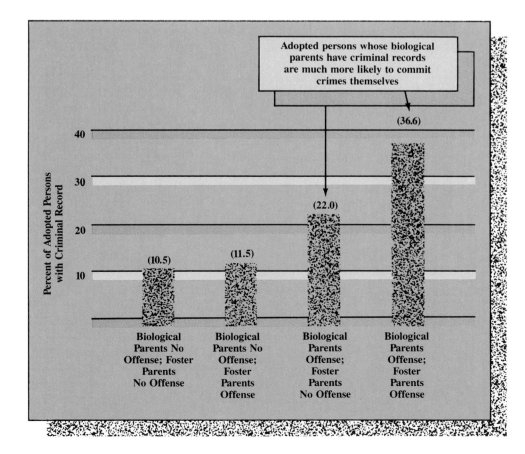

Adopted persons whose biological parents have criminal records are much more likely to commit crimes themselves

Evidence for Genetic Factors in Antisocial Behavior

scription of those faced by many minority children in urban areas of the United States, you're correct. Such youngsters *do* seem to face a devastating combination of poor economic opportunities, welfare policies which economically punish stable family relationships, and the presence of many persons who have succeeded financially by means of criminal activities. Since these conditions may foster development of at least some aspects of the antisocial personality disorder, it seems clear that such children—and society as a whole—risk serious problems in the years ahead unless these conditions are somehow altered.

Other Personality Disorders: A Sampling

Famous actors and actresses are sometimes described by those who know them in unflattering terms. Charming on the outside, they are highly excitable, insincere, and express a powerful desire to be the center of attention at all times and in all settings. They are demanding in their relationships and often ignore the needs and wishes of others, even their own children. Such persons—and many others not on the stage—demonstrate what has been termed the **histrionic personality disorder.** It seems to be more common among women than men but can be found in both sexes (Kass, Spitzer, & Williams, 1983). A very different pattern of traits is seen among persons with the **avoidant personality disorder.** Such individuals are shy, and although they wish to enter social relations with others, they are often reluctant to do so unless certain of total approval and acceptance. They tend to withdraw at the slightest hint of criticism, for it threatens their already shaky self-esteem. Many persons suffering from *loneliness* seem to possess this pattern of traits, and, as we noted in Chapter 12, it may cause them considerable distress.

Persons demonstrating the **dependent personality disorder** present yet another pattern of maladjustment. Such individuals seem incapable of running their own lives. They allow others to make decisions for them and let others tell them how to act. They subordinate their own needs to those of the people (or person) on whom they are dependent in order to please them. They lack self-confidence and will often put up with very negative treatment in order to maintain relationships with key people in their lives. Persons with the dependent personality disorder can be relatively happy when feeling secure, but experience great distress if abandoned or rejected by the person who literally controls their life.

Looking back over these descriptions, and this entire chapter, it is easy to get discouraged. ''Just think of how many ways there are to become disturbed,'' you may be thinking. In closing, then, we should emphasize two points. First, despite the stress and strain of modern life, most people—a large majority—manage to cope with their problems and are free from debilitating psychological disorders. Second, as we'll see in the next chapter, many effective techniques exist for dealing with such problems if they *do* arise. Thus, when individuals experience anxiety, depression, or another form of psychological distress, they do not have to accept such feelings as a normal and inescapable part of life. On the contrary, help is readily available. All they have to do is seek it out!

Summary and Review

Contrasting Views about Psychological Disorders

Psychological disorders involve patterns of behavior and thought that are unusual, are disapproved of within a given culture, and cause distress to the persons who experience them. Such disorders were once viewed as stemming from supernatural forces but are now seen either as forms of illness or as disturbed patterns of behavior and thought produced by a complex interplay between genetic, biochemical, and environmental factors. One widely used framework for identifying various psychological disorders is provided by the *DSM-III-R.*

Some Major Psychological Disorders

Many psychological disorders cause much personal distress but allow the sufferers to function in society. *Anxiety disorders* involve intense feelings of fear or dread. They can be unfocused *(generalized anxiety)* or focused on specific objects *(phobias)*. They may occur in a chronic manner or in relatively short-lived *panic attacks*. *Obsessive-compulsive disorders* involve repetitive thoughts (obsessions) or behaviors (compulsions) which seem to occur whether the individual wants them to or not.

    Dissociative disorders involve disturbances in memory or self-identity. Individuals who have *psychogenic amnesia* forget events that disturb them. In some cases, they may lose all memory for who they are or what type of life they have led up to a point in time when the amnesia began. In *multiple personality* disorders, an individual actually seems to possess two or more distinct personalities, that alternate in occurrence.

    Somatoform disorders involve the occurrence of various physical symptoms in the absence of underlying physical causes. The symptoms of such disorders serve as a form of communication—an indication to others that the person experiencing them is undergoing intense stress and needs assistance.

Sexual Disorders

Sexual disorders involve disturbances in sexual behavior or sexual functioning. They are generally divided into two major categories: *sexual dysfunctions* and *paraphilias*. Sexual dysfunctions involve low desire, low arousal, or the inability to attain orgasm. Paraphilias center around experiencing sexual arousal to inappropriate objects or events. These include fetishism (sexual arousal in response to inanimate objects), transvestism (arousal among males from dressing in women's clothes), and sadomasochism (sexual arousal from inflicting or receiving pain). Other sexual disorders involve arousal from contact with nonconsenting persons (e.g., voyeurism, exhibitionism, pedophilia).

    Disorders of gender identity occur when individuals who are genetically and biologically members of one sex feel strongly that they should have been born as members of the opposite sex.

Mood Disorders

Mood disorders involve major disturbances of mood and emotion. The most important of these is *major depression,* a prolonged negative emotional state. Biochemical factors play a role in this disorder, as do several important psychological processes. Depression seems to result when individuals believe that they cannot control their own outcomes and when they adopt a cognitive perspective involving negative views of themselves, the world around them, and the future. It may also stem from an inability to terminate *self-focus* following some personal loss. If depression persists and is intense, it may result in *suicide,* an effective if drastic means of escape from such feelings.

    In some cases, deep depression alternates with periods of *mania*—elation and high levels of energy. This pattern is known as *bipolar depression*.

Schizophrenia

Many persons suffering from *schizophrenia* show such disturbed patterns of thought, perceptions, and emotion that they are unable to function in society. For example, schizophrenics may suffer from various delusions—strange beliefs with little connection to reality. They may also demonstrate a separation between thought and emotion, such as reporting no emotion on learning that someone they love has died. This type of split between psychological functions was the original basis for the term *schizo* (split) *phrenia* (function).

    Biochemical factors (e.g., an excess of dopamine in the brain) may play a role in schizophrenia. Since schizophrenia seems to occur more frequently among some families, a genetic component, too, is indicated. Finally, certain experiences during childhood are also important. For example, schizophrenia occurs at a higher than expected rate in families where parents struggle with each other for the children's support and in families in which one parent totally dominates the other.

Personality Disorders

Persons suffering from *personality disorders* possess inflexible traits which interfere with their effective functioning. The most important type is the *antisocial personality disorder*. Such persons have little or no conscience, do not form close ties to others, and are impulsive and reckless. They often show a pattern of criminal behavior extending from an early age. Other personality disorders include the *histrionic, paranoid,* and *avoidant* patterns. Such persons, respectively, (1) constantly seek to be the center of attention, (2) are uniformly suspicious and distrustful of others, and (3) are too afraid of rejection to establish satisfying social contacts.

 **Key Terms**

Antisocial Personality Disorder A disorder involving lack of conscience, inability to form close ties to others, and high impulsiveness.

Anxiety Fear involving the expectation of some unspecified danger.

Anxiety Disorders Psychological disorders centering around the occurrence of anxiety, including phobias and obsessive-compulsive disorders.

Avoidant Personality Disorder A disorder in which individuals cannot form adequate social relations with others because of a profound fear of rejection.

Bipolar Depression A mood disorder involving swings of emotion between deep despair and extreme elation.

Defense Mechanisms Efforts by the ego to disguise unacceptable impulses or wishes and so to allow their partial gratification.

Dependent Personality Disorder A disorder in which individuals allow others to make decisions for them and tell them how to act.

Dissociative Disorders Psychological disorders involving profound and lengthy losses of identity and memory.

Dopamine Hypothesis The hypothesis that schizophrenia stems, at least in part, from an excess of dopamine in the brain.

DSM-III-R A framework for identifying (diagnosing) a wide range of psychological disorders.

Generalized Anxiety A disorder in which individuals experience intense anxiety which is not directed toward any specific object.

Helplessness The belief that one cannot exert any influence over one's own life outcomes.

Histrionic Personality Disorder A disorder in which an individual desires to be the center of attention at all times and cannot bear even the slightest criticism.

Major Depression A mood disorder in which an individual's moods swing between deep despair (depression) and a relatively neutral state.

Mania A state of extreme elation and activity.

Mood Disorders Psychological disorders involving major disturbances in mood or emotional state (e.g., depression).

Multiple Personality A psychological disorder in which an individual appears to have two or more distinct personalities.

Neurotic Disorders A wide range of psychological disorders which are both serious and stressful but which usually permit their victims to function in society.

Obsessive-Compulsive Disorders Psychological disorders in which, because of extreme anxiety, individuals repeat the same thoughts and actions over and over again.

Panic Attack Periods (usually relatively brief) during which individuals experience extreme feelings of anxiety and a wide range of physical symptoms (e.g., shortness of breath, trembling).

Personality Disorders Psychological disorders involving strong and inflexible traits that interfere with the individuals' personal adjustment.

Phobias Disorders in which individuals experience intense anxiety toward specific objects.

Psychodynamic Perspective Freud's views concerning the nature and origin of mental illness.

Psychogenic Amnesia: Sudden disruptions of

memory that seem to occur in response to unbearable stress.

Psychological Disorders Patterns of behavior and thought that are atypical, undesirable within a given culture, and cause the persons involved considerable distress.

Psychological Perspective The view that psychological disorders are better understood as the result of basic processes such as learning and cognition than as forms of illness.

Schizophrenic Disorders Very serious disorders in which, because of disturbed thought, perceptions, and emotions, individuals lose contact with reality.

Sexual Disorders Psychological disturbances in sexual arousal, sexual behavior, or gender identity.

Somatoform Disorders Psychological disorders in which various physical symptoms (e.g., numbness, deafness, pain) do not stem from physical causes.

For More Information

Argas, S. (1985). *Facing fears, phobias, and anxiety.* New York: Freeman.
> This relatively brief book explores the causes and treatment of panic and related reactions (e.g., phobias). If you'd like to know more about these problems (which affect more than one percent of all adults), this is a good source to consult.

Holmes, R. M., & DeBurger, J. (1987). *Serial murder.* Newbury Park, CA: Sage.
> What kind of individuals are capable of killing many strangers—persons who have done them no harm? This excellent book examines factors that may contribute to this pattern, including traits associated with the antisocial personality disorder. An insightful, if chilling, analysis.

Carson, R. C., Butcher, J. N., & Coleman, J. C. (1988). *Abnormal psychology and modern life,* 8th ed. Glenview, IL: Scott, Foresman.
> If you'd like more information on virtually any of the topics covered in this chapter, this book will provide it. It presents a broad introduction to current knowledge about many psychological disorders. The authors are well-known researchers, and the book is easy to read and understand.

CHAPTER 14

Therapy: Easing the Pain of Psychological Disorders

"Look," Bev Whalen says to her friend Sally Gorski, "don't talk about it if you don't want to. But you know that I care and want to help."

"Thanks, Sally," Bev replies, squeezing her friend's hand. "I know you do. You're the best friend I've got. But I don't mind telling you—in fact, Dr. Neff said it might be a good idea."

"So what happens when you go to see him? Do you lie on a couch, like in the movies, and say whatever comes into your mind?"

At this comment Bev smiles and shakes her head. "No, that's what I expected, too, but it's nothing like that at all. We just sit facing each other. And he doesn't have a beard or an accent, either!"

"Well, what do you talk about? Your dreams? Your childhood?"

"No. Mainly we discuss what he calls my 'confused thinking.'"

Bev looks puzzled. "I don't get it. Why would you pay someone seventy bucks an hour to tell you you're confused?"

"Well, Dr. Neff believes that most people's problems come from irrational thinking. Somehow, we get weird ideas into our heads, and then try to live according to them. *That's* what gets us into trouble."

"Give me a for-instance," Bev answers.

"O.K.: one of the main reasons I finally decided to go for help is that I'm tired of being pushed around. Everyone seems to take advantage of me."

"I'll say!" Bev interjects. "I've been telling you that for years."

"And I appreciate it. But I didn't think there was anything I could do about it. Every time I tried saying "no" to someone, I'd get real nervous—like if I didn't do what they wanted, they wouldn't like me."

"So what? Who says everyone has to like you?"

"No one. I just had this idea that if some people didn't like me, no one would, and I'd be a worthless human being."

"Whew! No wonder you've been unhappy. You thought you *had* to act like a door mat." Then Bev adds, "I'm beginning to see what you mean. Talking about some of the strange ideas we get really *could* help. . . ."

"Yeah, it does," Sally answers. "Once I know what the ideas are, it's easy to see how silly they are, and I can stop doing things that only make me unhappy. Anyway, I feel a lot better. And just yesterday I told Helen Rosenberg I couldn't take her to the airport after work. She was annoyed, but so what? If she doesn't like it, too bad."

"That's great!" Bev replies warmly. "I hated to see the way she took advantage of you—acted like you were her own private chauffeur. Gee, whatever this stuff is, it seems to work. Just four sessions and you're able to put the pushiest person in the office in her place. Don't stop now—I think you're onto something!"

In Chapter 13 we noted that psychological disorders, and the pain they induce, are *not* unavoidable aspects of the human condition. On the contrary, many techniques exist for relieving such disorders and easing the distress they generate. In this chapter we will examine several of these procedures. First, we'll describe contrasting forms of *psychotherapy*—procedures for dealing with psychological disorders through psychological means (e.g., changing the ways in which individuals think or act). After summarizing these methods, we'll consider several key questions about them: Do they really work? Are some techniques more effective than others? How can they be adapted for use with people from different cultures? Finally, we'll examine several *biotherapies*—efforts to relieve psychological disorders through biological means (e.g., by somehow altering the structure or function of the brain). After reading this material, we're confident you'll share our conviction that (1) psychological pain is *not* something that has to be endured, and (2) help is available to those who need it and decide to seek it out.

Psychotherapy: Psychological Approaches to Psychological Disorders

Say the word **psychotherapy** to most persons, and they conjure up images similar to those reported by Bev in our opening story. They imagine a dim room in which the ''patient'' lies on a couch and reveals hidden fears or secrets to a therapist, seated in a nearby chair (refer to Figure 14-1).

As we'll soon see, this popular image has little to do with many modern forms of *psychotherapy;* in fact, it applies to only one specific type: Freud's **psychoanalysis.** Psychotherapy, as currently practiced by psychologists and other professionals, actually occurs in many different settings, can involve several persons or only one, and includes an amazingly wide range of procedures (Price & Lynn, 1986). What do all these methods have in common? In short, just what *is* psychotherapy? Most psychologists agree that two features are crucial: (1) establishment of a special type of relationship between a person suffering psychological distress and a trained therapist—one in which the distressed person feels free to reveal important, and often embarrassing, facts; and (2) efforts by the therapist to bring about beneficial changes in the client's behavior, feelings, or thoughts. In short, whatever form it takes, psychotherapy strives to place disturbed individuals in an environment where they feel free to confide in another human being who is specially trained to help them change in beneficial ways (Strupp, 1986).

One additional point: despite its name, *psych*otherapy is performed by the members of several professions, not solely by psychologists. *Psychiatrists* (physicians with special training in psychological disorders), *psychiatric social workers,* and *psychiatric nurses* all regularly conduct such activities. Do such persons differ in their approach to psychotherapy? Intriguing insights into this question have recently been provided by Steven Kingsbury, who holds both a Ph.D. in *clinical psychology* and an M.D. with special training in *psychiatry*. According to Kingsbury (1987), the two fields differ in several important respects. First, psychologists tend to view science as an ongoing process in which theories and empirical findings are modified or even discarded in the light of new

FIGURE 14-1. This is what most people imagine when they hear the word ''psychotherapy.'' (*Source:* The New Yorker, 1982.)

Psychotherapy: A Popular View

evidence. In contrast, psychiatrists tend to view science as an established body of facts—information unlikely to change much in the future. The result: psychologists tend to be somewhat more cautious in interpreting the information at their disposal than psychiatrists. They realize that today's ''facts'' may be altered by tomorrow's research.

Second, as we've noted previously, psychologists are well aware of the potential dangers of labeling others. They realize that once an individual has been described as suffering from a particular disorder, it may be difficult to perceive this person in other terms. In short, psychologists have reservations about the usefulness of the *medical model,* which suggests that accurate *diagnosis* (identifying an individual's problem) is the heart of the entire process. In contrast, psychiatrists accept this model as a tried-and-true method for dealing with all health-related problems, including psychological disorders.

Please note: we do not offer these comments as a means of boosting our own field or criticizing others. Each field offers its own pattern of strengths and weaknesses, and none can be described as best. Having said this, we wish to add that, in our view, psychology—with its strong commitment to science and the scientific method—has played a unique role in the development of effective methods of psychotherapy. Several forms of therapy we'll consider derive directly from basic research on human behavior, and it is safe to say that they would probably not have been developed in the absence of a scientific field of psychology (Leary & Maddux, 1987). In sum, while our field is certainly not alone in helping to reduce the pain of psychological disorders, it continues to play a unique and especially valuable role in this respect.

Psychoanalysis: Insight in Place of Repression

If Freud had known how many movies, television shows, and even cartoons would be based on his method of psychotherapy, it seems possible—just possible—that he might have changed it in several respects. He was a serious scholar and might well have found such representations of his work highly distasteful. In any case, as shown in Figure 14-2, he *did* use a couch and several other procedures which have entered the ''collective consciousness'' of Western culture.

FIGURE 14-2. Freud developed this famous form of psychotherapy *(psychoanalysis)* in an office in Vienna.

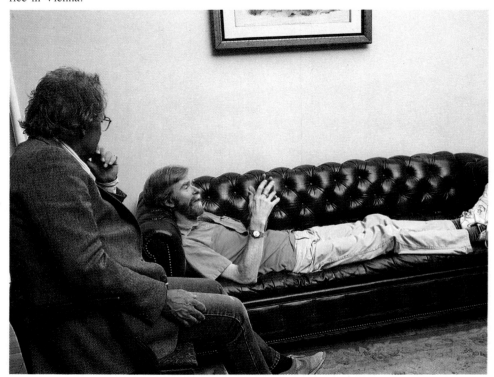

Freud's Method of Therapy

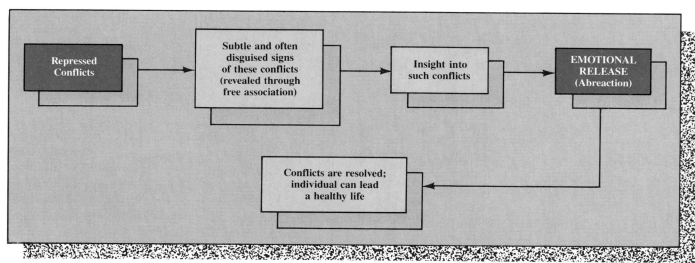

FIGURE 14-3. The main goal of psychoanalysis is providing an individual with insight into repressed inner conflicts. Once these are recognized, an emotional release occurs, and the person can attain ''mental health.''

Psychoanalysis: Its Primary Goals

Psychoanalysis: Its Theoretical Foundations.   What reasoning lay behind Freud's methods? To a large extent, the answer is provided by his theories of personality and the origins of psychological disorders. To review briefly, Freud believed that personality consists of three major components: the *id, ego,* and *superego,* which correspond, roughly, to the words ''desire,'' ''reason,'' and ''conscience.'' He suggested that many psychological disorders arise out of the fact that some impulses of the id are unacceptable to the ego or superego and are therefore *repressed*—pushed from consciousness into the unconscious. Many of these conflicts between the components of personality first appear during childhood and, if left unresolved, interfere with normal psychosexual development. This, in turn, produces the psychological disorders individuals carry with them into their adult years.

How can such problems be relieved? Freud felt that the crucial task is overcoming repression, so that patients can come face to face with their own hidden feelings and wishes. Having gained such *insight* and an accompanying release of emotion, known as *abreaction,* they become capable of a healthy life, one based on Freud's basic prescription for happiness: ''work and love'' (please see Figure 14-3). All of the now-famous aspects of psychoanalysis were directed toward this central goal: replacing repression with insight.

Psychoanalysis: Its Basic Methods.   What actually happens during psychoanalysis? Most of the procedures are ones you will probably find familiar. The patient lies on a couch in a partly darkened room and engages in **free association.** This involves reporting everything that passes through his or her mind, no matter how trivial or irrelevant it seems. Presumably, the repressed wishes and conflicts present in the unconscious are evident in these mental wanderings, at least to the trained ear of the analyst. (Freud considered dreams to be an excellent source for free association since in his view they contained repressed urges and conflicts in disguised form.) As therapy progresses and the analyst gains understanding of the patient's problems, he or she asks questions or offers suggestions designed to enhance the patient's awareness of inner conflicts. It is through this process of *interpretation* that the increased insight, which Freud felt was crucial, is ultimately gained.

During the course of treatment, several interesting phenomena often occur. First, a patient may demonstrate **resistance**—refusal to report certain thoughts during free association, or rejection of the analyst's interpretations. Presumably, resistance occurs because of the wish to escape from the anxiety produced as the individual comes closer and closer to recognizing hidden impulses. Second, many patients show **transference**—intense feelings of love or hate toward the analyst. According to Freud, these stem from unresolved inner conflicts and represent a re-direction of the powerful emotions released as these conflicts approach consciousness during analysis. As insight increases, such feelings tend to decrease in intensity and gradually fade away.

Psychoanalysis: Is It Useful?   As we have already noted, psychoanalysis is by far the best-known form of psychotherapy. Does its effectiveness match its fame? Sadly, the answer is "no." In the form proposed by Freud, often known as *classical psychoanalysis,* it suffers from several major drawbacks which lessen its value as a form of psychotherapy. First, psychoanalysis is a costly and time-consuming process. Several years and many thousands of dollars are required for its completion. Second, it is based largely on Freud's theories of personality and development. As we noted in Chapter 12, these are difficult to study scientifically. Thus, it is also difficult to assess the usefulness of psychoanalysis. Third, Freud designed psychoanalysis for use with educated persons who had highly developed verbal skills. For this reason, it is unsuitable for a large proportion of the general population. Finally, and perhaps most important, it is very much a closed system: a critic who raises questions about its validity is described as suffering from resistance— psychological problems which prevent the critic from recognizing the "obvious" value of psychoanalysis!

Because of such problems, classical psychoanalysis is a relatively rare type of therapy today. However, modified versions of psychoanalysis introduced by Freud's students and disciples (the neo-Freudians we mentioned in Chapter 12) are much more common. Such *psychoanalytic psychotherapy* is usually briefer than the procedures Freud used. In addition, it puts less emphasis on the role of unconscious inner conflicts and more weight on the impact of social factors (the environment in which patients live) and the rational, problem-solving capacities of the ego. Despite these differences, however, important features suggested by Freud are retained: an emphasis on free expression by patients, and the importance of insight into one's own motives and conflicts. In these respects, certainly, Freud's ideas have found their way into several modern forms of therapy and remain influential even today.

Humanistic Therapies: Encouraging Self-Fulfillment

In a sense, Freud was a pessimist about human nature. He felt that we must constantly struggle with brutish impulses from the id. As we noted in Chapter 12, many psychologists reject this view. They contend that people are basically good and that our strivings for growth, dignity, and self-determination are just as strong as the powerful aggressive and sexual impulses Freud described. According to such *humanistic* psychologists, people do not become disturbed because of unresolved inner conflicts. Rather, they suffer from psychological disorders because their environment somehow blocks their personal growth.

Needless to add, such views suggest forms of psychotherapy very different from those proposed by Freud. Such **humanistic therapies** focus on the tasks of increasing individuals' self-awareness—helping them recognize and get in touch with their own feelings—and enhancing their self-concept. Many variations on these basic themes exist, but here we will consider only two: Rogers' *person-centered therapy* (Rogers, 1980) and Perls's (1969) *Gestalt therapy.*

Person-Centered Therapy: The Benefits of Being Accepted.   According to Carl Rogers (1970, 1980), perhaps the most famous advocate of the humanistic view, people experience psychological problems when they (1) lose contact with their own feelings, and (2) form a distorted self-concept. In other words, problems arise when individuals do not understand what emotions they are experiencing, and when they come to perceive themselves in distorted (usually negative) ways. The central task of **person-centered therapy,** then, involves correcting these imbalances or distortions.

How can this be accomplished? Rogers suggests that the key ingredient is a therapist who can provide three things: *unconditional acceptance* of the client and his or her

FIGURE 14-4. No psychologist using person-centered therapy (or any other form of psychotherapy, for that matter) would ever act this way toward a person seeking help. (Please note the diploma on the wall!) *(Source: NEA, 1978.)*

feelings, a high level of *empathy* (accurate understanding of the client's feelings and perceptions), and *genuine* interest in and concern for this person (see Figure 14-4). In the context of this warm, caring relationship, freed from the threat of rejection, individuals can come to understand their own feelings and accept even previously unwanted aspects of their own personality. In short, they can come to see themselves as unique human beings with many desirable characteristics, and stop criticizing themselves for falling short of perfection which they can never attain. To the extent such changes occur, Rogers contends, many psychological disorders disappear, and individuals can resume their normal progress toward full self-actualization.

Gestalt Therapy: Becoming Whole.   As we have already noted, Rogers and other humanistic therapists tend to emphasize the present. They are concerned with the feelings people are experiencing *now* rather than with the possible origins of such feelings in the distant past.

One exception to this general rule is provided by **Gestalt therapy,** developed by Fritz Perls (1969). Such therapy focuses attention largely on helping individuals become aware of themselves and their true, current feelings. To accomplish this task, Gestalt therapists use many different tactics. They may challenge their clients to give up their "phony games," ask them to act out their dreams, and encourage them to recognize and release their current feelings by translating them into physical actions (e.g., tapping on a table in proportion to their experienced anger).

When the past arises, it is quickly made the focus of therapy. The individual is asked to re-enact the original scene that caused the feelings in question, so that the initial (and now partly repressed) conflict can become fully conscious. Clients are urged to re-experience such emotions vividly and are told to swear, scream, or weep as the need arises. Presumably, once such feelings are recognized and released, the person will become "whole" and resume normal growth. In sum, Gestalt therapy combines certain aspects of psychoanalysis (emphasis on the importance of unconscious feelings and conflicts) with those of the humanistic approach (concern with current feelings and accurate understanding of one's own characteristics).

Some of the techniques developed by Gestalt therapists for helping individuals recognize their own feelings are quite ingenious. For example, in the *two-chair* exercise, clients move back and forth between two chairs. In one they play themselves, while in the other they assume the role of some important person in their life (e.g., wife, husband, father, mother). The ultimate goal, of course, is to increase their understanding of their own feelings and relations with others.

Existential Therapy: The Fear of Nonbeing.   Does life have any meaning? Why are we born? Why do we die? These are questions most of us ponder at least occasionally. Some persons, however, seem to get "stuck" on such issues; they think about them frequently and reach largely negative conclusions (e.g., "life is meaningless"). Moreover, they dwell on the finality of death—ceasing to exist and being totally forgotten. These thoughts, of course, confirm their conclusions about the essential point-

Existential Therapy: Its Basis

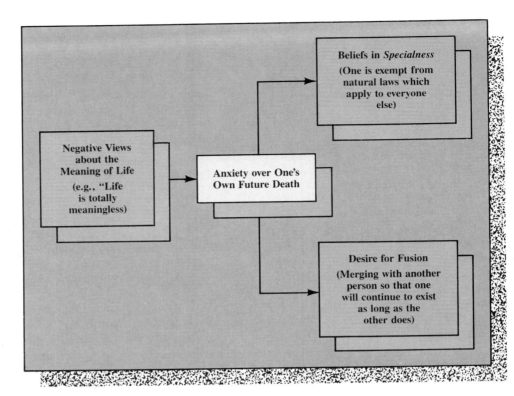

FIGURE 14-5. *Existential therapists* believe that when individuals hold pessimistic views about the meaning of life, they experience anxiety over their own future death. This leads them to adopt unrealistic views about their own *specialness* or to seek *fusion* with others. Existential therapy seeks to counter these tendencies.

lessness of life. Their anxiety over death (their own nonbeing) then leads such persons to adopt certain maladaptive strategies. Some accept the notion of *specialness*—the view that they possess unique qualities which set them apart from the rest of humanity and which will allow them to avoid the inevitability of death. Clearly, such confused thinking is detrimental to psychological health.

Alternatively, they may seek *fusion* with other persons. Presumably, if one merges one's own identity with other persons, one will continue to live as long as they do. This, in turn, can lead to strong anxiety over being separated from or rejected by others. (Please see Figure 14-5 for a summary of these reactions.)

To combat such feelings and reactions, Rollo May (1977) and others have devised **existential analysis** or **therapy.** One goal of such procedures is getting people to surrender their pessimistic views and to think about life in more positive terms—as an ongoing, challenging process in which we continue to change and grow. Existential therapy also focuses on helping clients recognize that they can indeed control the course of their lives and can endow life with meaning if they so desire (Frankl, 1975). As individuals adopt such conclusions, they feel less threatened by the thought of their own future death and are better able to go about the business of leading a fuller, richer, and more satisfying life.

Cognitive Therapies: Changing Disordered Thought

A major theme in modern psychology—and in this book—is as follows: cognitive processes exert powerful effects both on emotions and on behavior. In other words, what we *think* strongly affects how we *feel* and what we *do.* This basic fact forms the foundation for a third major approach to psychotherapy: **cognitive therapy.** The basic idea behind such therapy is simple: many psychological disorders stem from faulty or distorted modes of thought. Change these, it is reasoned, and the disorders, too, can be alleviated. We have already considered such an approach in our discussion of *depression* (see Chapter 13). As you may recall, this serious problem has been related to faulty negative views held by individuals about themselves and the external world (e.g., Beck, 1976) or to the maladaptive tendency to focus attention *inward* after failure, while avoiding self-focused attention after success (Pyszczynski & Greenberg, 1987). (See Figure 14-6.) The cogni-

FIGURE 14-6. *Cognitive therapies* attempt to alter the confused or faulty thinking that often lies behind serious psychological disorders (e.g., unduly blaming oneself for failures while failing to take credit for successes).

tive approach has been applied to many other psychological problems as well. Perhaps its most popular form is **rational-emotive therapy (RET),** a technique devised by Albert Ellis (1977, 1987a).

Rational-Emotive Therapy: Eliminating Irrational Beliefs.   According to Ellis (1987b), many psychological disorders have a common root: they spring from powerful *irrational beliefs* held by most human beings. Ellis suggests that these, in turn, can be understood as part of what he terms the *ABC model*. The model begins with the fact that most people have strong desires for success, love, and a safe, comfortable existence. Life, however, often fails to gratify such desires; some *activating event (A)* occurs which blocks progress toward these goals. At that point, two categories of beliefs can be initiated. Many of these are *rational*. For example, following a failure at work, an individual may conclude, "I don't like failing, but it's not the end of the world, and I can still reach many of my other goals." Unfortunately, though, people seem to have strong built-in tendencies toward *irrational beliefs* as well (part *B* of the model).

Such beliefs take many different forms, but most seem to involve escalating reasonable desires into "musts" and what Ellis describes as "awfulizing" or "catastrophizing." An example of the "must" tendency is provided by the following idea: Because I strongly desire to succeed, I *must* perform well *at all times*. An example of "awfulizing" is contained in this statement: I absolutely *cannot stand it* if my lover rejects me. Once such beliefs develop, Ellis argues, individuals essentially cause their own disturbances. They worry about their inability to reach impossible goals, convince themselves that they cannot tolerate the normal frustrations and disappointments of life, and experience many other negative cognitive, behavioral, and emotional consequences (part *C* of the model). To add insult to injury, once negative feelings and behaviors develop, these tend to perpetuate the irrational beliefs which caused them in the first place. As Ellis notes (1987b, p. 367), this is the "Catch-22 of human neurosis"—unrealistic ideas create disruptive feelings and behaviors which tend to sustain and even intensify such "crazy" beliefs! (Please refer to Figure 14-7 on page 444 for a summary of the ABC model.)

How can this self-defeating cycle be broken? Ellis suggests that the answer involves forcing disturbed individuals to recognize the irrationality of their views. Thus, the

Ellis's ABC Model of Psychological Disorders

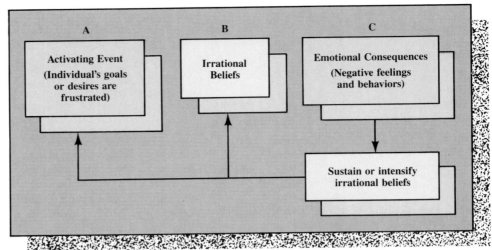

FIGURE 14-7. According to Ellis (1987b), individuals often experience frustrations and disappointments *(A)*. These may activate irrational beliefs *(B)*. Such beliefs produce negative feelings and behaviors *(C)* which then sustain or intensify the beliefs. The result: people are trapped in an especially damaging type of vicious circle.

therapist's task is to identify such beliefs and then to induce the person to recognize them for what they are: distorted views of reality. Unfortunately, this task is more difficult than it seems. Many irrational beliefs are not as obvious as the ones described above (Ellis, 1987b). For example, consider the following ideas:

Because I *really try hard* at various tasks, I *deserve* to do well on them.
Because I have failed *so many times in the past,* I absolutely must succeed now.
Because I only want *a little approval from others,* I absolutely must have it.
Because I *haven't had much love and approval for a long period of time,* I absolutely must have it now.

Such beliefs are illogical, but it may be difficult for many persons to recognize this fact. As Ellis puts it (1987b, p. 365), humans have a strong "tendency to needlessly and severely disturb themselves . . . and they are powerfully predisposed to prolong their mental dysfunction and to fight like h__l against giving it up." It is the job of the therapist to combat such tendencies and induce patients—even ones who are strongly resisting—to recognize that their problems are largely self-inflicted. In a sense, then, therapists using RET often act in an opposite manner from those employing the person-centered approach. Rather than expressing warm understanding and acceptance of a client's thoughts, they strongly and mercilessly reject these. Only by doing so, Ellis suggests, can the irrational beliefs be overcome and unnecessary psychological pain be eliminated.

Attributional Therapy: Changing Distorted Views about the Causes of Behavior and Outcomes. Another cognitive therapy, one which has yielded promising results, focuses on *attributions*—individuals' beliefs about the causes of their own and others' behavior (Forsterling, 1986). The basic idea behind such therapy is this: in many cases, individuals engage in unrealistic or faulty attributions (Leary & Maddux, 1987). These, in turn, can cause them considerable distress and can contribute to important forms of psychological disorder. As an example of such problems, consider persons suffering from low self-esteem (in Rogers' terms, a negative self-concept).

Such individuals seem to attribute failures to internal causes—their own lack of ability or effort—even when this is *not* the case. Similarly, they attribute successes to external causes—lucky breaks or an easy task, again, even when it was their own skill or effort that yielded positive results. Persons high in self-esteem show the opposite pattern: they tend to take credit for positive outcomes and to blame failures on external factors.

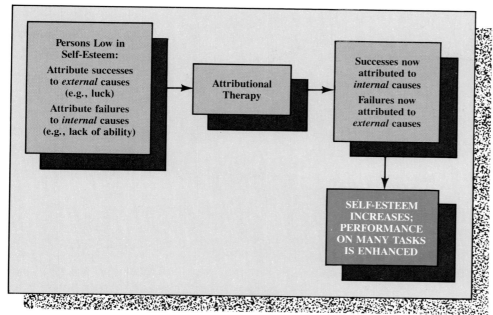

Attributional Therapy: An Overview

FIGURE 14-8. Persons low in self-esteem tend to attribute their successes to external causes (e.g., luck) but their failures to internal causes (e.g., a lack of ability). *Attributional therapy* attempts to reverse this pattern. When such efforts are successful, self-esteem and task performance both improve.

Cognitive therapy based on attributions attempts to break the vicious circle endured by low self-esteem persons. During therapy they are trained to perceive successes as resulting from *internal* causes (their own ability or efforts), and failure as resulting, at least sometimes, from *external* factors beyond their control. When such efforts succeed, the persons involved show increased self-esteem, greater confidence, and better performance on many tasks (e.g., Brockner & Guare, 1983; Wilson & Linville, 1982). (Refer to Figure 14-8.) Since such *attributional therapy* requires only a small number of sessions, it seems to be a very promising way of combating several psychological disorders.

Behavior Therapies: Psychological Disorders as Bad Habits

In Chapter 5 we indicated that all organisms, including human beings, are strongly affected by experience. In a word, they all *learn*. Does this basic process play a role in psychological disorders? Many researchers believe that it does. They assume that several psychological problems, including ones responsible for intense distress, involve some type of faulty learning. In short, such disorders involve learning that results in maladaptive rather than adaptive patterns of behavior (Rosenhan & Seligman, 1984). Since learned behaviors can generally be eliminated (extinguished) and replaced by others, yet another approach to therapy is suggested, one derived from basic principles of learning. In fact, several such **behavior therapies** have been developed and put to actual use. Since they have proven remarkably effective in eliminating at least some behavioral problems, they are worthy of our careful attention.

Therapies Based on Classical Conditioning.   Two important forms of behavior therapy are based on *classical conditioning*. As you may recall, such learning occurs when one stimulus comes to serve as a signal for the occurrence of another stimulus. (If you don't remember how this process operates, just refer, right now, to the cartoon on page 140.) The first of these behavior therapies, **systematic desensitization,** is used in the treatment of anxiety disorders such as *phobias*—strong fears of relatively harmless objects or events (Wolpe, 1958, 1982). This form of therapy is based on the following simple principle: it is generally impossible to experience two opposite emotions at once to the same stimulus.

Systematic Desensitization: How It Works

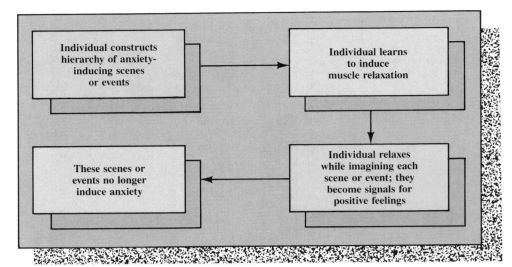

FIGURE 14-9. In *systematic desensitization* an individual practices feeling relaxed while imagining scenes or events which initially produced anxiety. Because it is impossible to experience two opposite emotional states at once, these stimuli gradually lose their capacity to evoke anxiety.

In actual use, systematic desensitization proceeds as follows. First, the person suffering from such problems constructs an *anxiety hierarchy*—a series of scenes or events that produces higher and higher levels of fear. For example, if an individual suffers from fear of open spaces, he might begin with a scene in which he looks out a window toward a small, fenced garden. Next, he might imagine walking out into this area. A third scene in the hierarchy might consist of looking out, in his imagination, from the garden into a large busy street. After the anxiety hierarchy has been constructed, the individual next receives *relaxation training*. He learns to relax various muscles so that he experiences pleasant feelings of calmness and well-being. Now, the crucial phase begins. The individual is asked to imagine each anxiety-provoking scene, one at a time, while practicing relaxation. As therapy proceeds, this is repeated for scenes which cause higher and higher levels of anxiety. When the process is complete, feelings of anxiety have been replaced with positive ones of relaxation, and the person's fears may have entirely vanished (refer to Figure 14-9 for a summary of these procedures). In terms of classical conditioning, what has happened is this: each imaginary scene was previously a signal for anxiety. Now, each becomes a signal for feelings of relaxation and well-being. Thus, the person no longer experiences fear or anxiety in such situations.

A second procedure based on classical conditioning is known as *aversive conditioning*. Here, stimuli that have previously been associated with positive feelings are linked, instead, with negative ones. Why would we wish to accomplish this substitution? Perhaps a concrete example will help. Imagine that an individual is sexually aroused by the sight of young children and finds it difficult to resist making advances to them. Disturbed by these feelings, she seeks the help of a psychologist. To counter such feelings, the individual is shown slides of attractive young children. Each is quickly followed by a painful (but safe) electric shock. As the process continues, the individual's emotional reactions to these stimuli change. Initially, such actions were positive (the person became sexually aroused at the sight of the children). Later such responses are negative; after all, the photos of attractive children have been paired with painful electric shocks. If such treatment is successful, as it has been in several studies (Rosenhan & Seligman, 1984), the individual may find that she is no longer sexually excited by children and can seek more appropriate partners. (For a humorous example of aversion therapy, please see Figure 14-10.)

Therapies Based on Operant Conditioning.   Behavior is often shaped by its consequences: actions are repeated if they yield positive outcomes or if they permit us to

BLOOM COUNTY
by Berke Breathed

FIGURE 14-10. In therapy based on *aversive conditioning*, stimuli that induce positive feelings or reactions are paired with unpleasant outcomes. In this cartoon (which shows procedures no therapist would ever use!) a sweet dessert is associated with strong physical pain. Presumably the ''patient'' would lose his desire to eat such foods as a result of this experience. *(Source: Washington Post Co., 1987.)*

avoid negative ones. In contrast, actions that lead to negative results are suppressed (we avoid them). These basic principles are incorporated in several forms of therapy based on *operant conditioning*. Several forms of *operant therapy* exist, but all involve the following basic steps:

1. Undesirable or maladaptive behaviors currently shown by patients are identified.

2. Reinforcers that currently maintain such responses are identified.

3. Environmental changes that will alter these patterns of reinforcement are devised and put into practice. This can involve providing positive reinforcers for the performance of adaptive behaviors or withholding rewards when maladaptive actions occur.

Initially, operant principles were used in hospital settings, where a large degree of control over a patient's reinforcements could be obtained (Kazdin, 1982). For example, several projects involved establishment of **token economies**—conditions under which a patient could earn tokens which could be exchanged for various rewards (e.g., television-watching privileges, candy, trips to town). Tokens were awarded for various forms of adaptive behavior which would help an individual to function effectively after leaving the hospital (e.g., keeping one's room neat, participating in group meetings or therapy sessions). The results of such programs were impressive. When individuals learned that they could acquire various rewards by behaving in certain ways, they often did so, with important benefits to them as well as to the hospital staff (refer to Figure 14-11 on page 448).

More recently, operant principles have been used in the treatment of a wide range of behavioral problems among persons not confined to mental hospitals. For example, as we noted in Chapter 5, selective delivery of positive reinforcers has been used to treat *anorexia nervosa*, a disorder in which individuals eat so little that their physical health is endangered (Stunkard, 1976). In such cases, persons undergoing operant therapy are provided with various rewards (e.g., the opportunity to watch television or engage in conversation with friends) only when they eat specified amounts.

In a similar manner, operant principles have been successfully used in the alleviation of shyness. (Refer to our discussion of this topic in Chapter 12.) Here, a technique known as *behavioral contracting* is often useful. This involves an agreement between therapist and client that if the client manages to perform certain tasks, a specific reward will occur or a penalty will be avoided. (A concrete example: the client gives the therapist some money to hold, with the understanding that if he or she manages to talk to two strangers during the next week, the money will be returned. If the client fails to accomplish this agreed-upon goal, the money will be forfeited.)

We should add that punishment, too, can be used in operant-based therapy, although it is generally reserved for dealing with harmful or dangerous behavior. For example, some seriously disturbed children harm themselves; they bang their heads against the

Token Economies: Applying Operant Procedures in Mental Hospitals

FIGURE 14-11. In *token economies* patients in mental hospitals are given tokens which can be exchanged for desired rewards when they behave in certain ways considered desirable by the hospital staff. The result: such operant procedures work, and the patients often show an increase in the frequency of desired behaviors.

wall or bite themselves severely. Mild but unpleasant electric shocks following such actions have been found to reduce the frequency of such actions (Lovaas, 1973, 1977). While some persons may object to delivering shocks or other unpleasant consequences to children, such procedures seem justified by virtue of protecting these youngsters from much greater harm.

Modeling: When Seeing Is Doing.   Have you ever been afraid to taste some new food but then gathered up your courage and did so after watching other persons eat it? If so, you are already familiar with the basis for yet another approach to therapy: **modeling.** In Chapter 5 we noted that individuals often acquire new forms of behavior from others simply by observing their actions (through *observational learning*). This is not the only effect in such situations, however. In addition, observing the actions of others—and the consequences they then experience—can strengthen or reduce our inhibitions against engaging in similar actions. If we see others perform some behavior and then experience positive outcomes as a result of doing so, our internal restraints against performing it, too, may be reduced. If, instead, we see others perform an action and then experience negative consequences, our inhibitions against similar behavior may be strengthened. Eating new foods we have seen others enjoy provides an example of the first kind of effect (known as *response disinhibition*). Slowing down after seeing another motorist stopped for speeding by a police officer is an example of the second (*response inhibition*). (See Figure 14-12 for examples of both types.)

What do such effects have to do with therapy? Quite a bit: when individuals suffering from anxiety disorders are exposed to appropriate *models*—persons who perform the actions they are afraid to perform or who venture into situations they strongly fear—their levels of anxiety are sometimes reduced. In short, exposure to models who do *not* demonstrate anxiety can help individuals overcome their own fears (Bandura, 1986). In order for such procedures to work, the models must approach the feared objects or situations in a gradual manner; if they are too bold too soon, high levels of anxiety are produced among observers, and therapy may fail. Further, live models, who actually guide individuals in the actions they perform, seem to be superior to filmed or videotaped models. When such factors are taken into account, therapy based on modeling can be

FIGURE 14-12. When we see others enjoying positive consequences as a result of certain actions, we may be encouraged to perform them ourselves (left photo). In contrast, if we see others receiving negative consequences for some behavior, our inhibitions against performing similar actions may increase (right photo). These are *response disinhibitory* and *response inhibitory* effects, respectively.

Some Effects of Observing Others

highly effective. Indeed, it has been used successfully (1) to help children who are socially isolated learn how to interact with others, (2) to teach juvenile offenders the basic social skills they need to stay out of trouble, (3) to assist individuals in becoming more assertive, and (4) to help persons addicted to alcohol or drugs resist such temptations (Bandura, 1986; Gotestam & Melin, 1974; McFall & Twentyman, 1973). Clearly, modeling has proven to be a useful addition to psychology's repertoire of therapies. (For a dramatic illustration of the effectiveness of such treatment, please see the "Classic Contributions" section below.)

FOCUS ON RESEARCH: Classic Contributions

Vicarious Courage: Modeling and the Elimination of Phobias

Persons suffering from a phobia often lead restricted lives. They are afraid to visit locations where the object of their fears may be encountered and as a result may be prevented from carrying out normal business or social activities. Surprising as it may seem, one common phobia involves dogs. Many persons are afraid to interact with even obviously friendly canines. Can such fears be reduced through modeling? A well-known study by Bandura and Menlove (1968) indicates that this is the case.

In this experiment, all children in a nursery school were first given a behavioral test for fear of dogs. This involved fourteen graded acts requiring increasingly intimate contact with a live dog. The easiest behaviors required each child to approach the dog and pet it; later acts involved walking the dog on a leash,

scratching it on its stomach, and feeding it. The final act in the series required the child to enter a playpen with the dog and remain with it while the experimenter left the room. (The more acts the children were willing to perform, the *lower* their fear of dogs.) On the basis of this test, youngsters with a strong fear of dogs were chosen for the study to receive modeling therapy. They were then divided into three groups. Those in the first (the *single-model* condition) watched eight brief (three-minute) films—two a day for four days. These films showed a five-year-old boy engaging in progressively bolder and bolder interactions with a live dog. Subjects assigned to a second, *multiple-model* condition watched similar films, but in this case several different models of both sexes were shown interacting with several different dogs. Finally, those in a *control* condition viewed an equal number of films showing Disneyland and Marine-

Modeling and the Reduction of Phobic Reactions

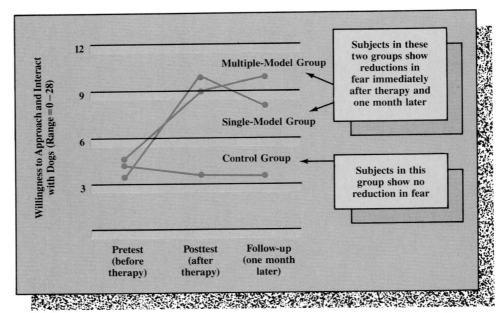

FIGURE 14-13. Children who were initially afraid of dogs showed an increase in willingness to interact with dogs after watching one or several fearless models. Moreover, their reduction in fear was still apparent when the children were tested again one month later. *(Source: Based on data from Bandura & Menlove, 1968.)*

land of the Pacific; they were never exposed to fearless models during the study.

Following the last film, the behavioral test for fear of dogs was given to all subjects once again. As you can see from Figure 14-13, children exposed to the fearless models (those in the single- and multiple-model conditions) showed a marked reduction in fear: they were able to complete many more of the items on the test than was true initially. In contrast, and as expected, subjects in the control group showed no change in behavior. When it is recalled that the children saw a total of only twenty-four minutes of film, these findings become even more impressive. This and other research results (Bandura, Blanchard, & Ritter, 1969; Bandura, Jeffery, & Wright, 1974) suggest that even long-standing phobic reactions can be readily extinguished by a few moments' exposure to fearless models.

We should hasten to add that therapy based on modeling is *not* suitable for all psychological disorders; for example, it may not be helpful in eliminating personality disorders or in treating serious depression. When applied to disorders related to anxiety, however, it seems to be one of the most effective and efficient types of therapy currently available.

Group and Family Therapies: Seeking Help Together

All forms of therapy we have considered so far (except perhaps operant techniques) were originally designed for use with one person: they are *individual* forms of treatment. While such procedures can be highly effective, they do raise practical problems: they are costly, and there may simply not be enough trained therapists available to assist all of the persons in need of help. Partly for this reason, several of these therapies (e.g., rational-emotive therapy, Gestalt therapy) have been adapted for use with groups. In addition, several other forms of *group therapy* have also been developed. In such procedures, groups of individuals who are not seriously disturbed meet under the guidance of a psychologist or other professional and work together to overcome their personal problems. Many types of group therapy exist, but here we'll concentrate on three: transactional analysis, humanistic growth groups (sensitivity training or encounter groups), and family therapy.

Transactional Analysis: Parent, Child, or Adult?   Over twenty years ago Eric Berne (1964) published a book entitled *Games People Play*, which became a best-seller. It described an intriguing view of the basis of many of our interpersonal problems—difficulties centering around our relations with other persons. According to Berne, our behavior at any given time is determined by one of three basic aspects of personality: the *Child, Parent,* or *Adult.* The Child aspect is demanding, dependent, and impulsive, seeking gratification of all wishes *now.* The Parent aspect represents internal restraints—rules and prohibitions we learned from our own parents. Finally, the Adult is the mature, rational aspect of personality; it is flexible and adapts to new situations as they arise.

What does all this have to do with interpersonal relations and psychological disorders? According to Berne, a great deal: He suggested that many interactions between individuals are *complementary*—aspects of their personalities are matched. For example, one person's Adult communicates to another's Adult; their interaction is rational and mature (e.g., Bill: "These data don't make sense." Lucy: "I agree. Let's run them through the computer again.") Trouble arises when such interactions are *crossed*—the aspects of personality operating do *not* match. For example, a person operating in the Child mode says, "Whee! Come on, go faster, faster!" The other, whose Adult is in charge, answers, "No way; I saw a state trooper back there, and I'm not taking any chances on a ticket." Another example: one person, adopting the Parent role, comments, "I'm not spending any money on that kind of thing: it's wrong to waste." The other, in the Child mode, responds, "Aw c'mon; please? Pretty please? You *never* want to have any fun!" (Refer to Figure 14-14 on page 452.)

Berne contended that such crossed interactions often take the form of *games*—repeated patterns of interactions which leave both persons feeling upset or angry. For example, in one of these patterns, "uproar," one person baits another. The second responds in kind, and the exchange escalates until one individual storms off in anger. It is the endless repetition of such games, Berne and other transactional therapists contend, that produces many personal difficulties (Altrocchi, 1980).

Transactional analysis therapy seeks to lessen such problems. Groups of individuals focus on increasing each other's awareness of the three basic aspects of personality (Child, Adult, Parent) and the role these play in social relations. This involves participation in various exercises, such as playing one role after the other in a given situation. Through group experiences, individuals come to recognize their usual style of interacting with key persons in their lives. Adaptive changes can then be instituted. For example, a wife may come to realize that she is adopting the Parent role in many interactions with her husband, thus encouraging him to behave in the Child mode and be dependent upon her. By changing her own behavior, she may alter his, and so help make their marriage more satisfying for both persons.

Humanistic Growth Groups: Increasing Self-Awareness.   As you certainly realize by now, individuals seek psychological help for many different reasons. One of the most common, though, involves an inability to get along well with others. Continuous and intense friction with family, spouse, and co-workers—this unpleasant state of affairs is experienced by all too many individuals. How can such difficulties be reduced? One approach is through the use of **humanistic growth groups,** also known as *sensitivity training*.

This form of group therapy derives from the humanistic approach described earlier in this chapter. It assumes that one of the main reasons individuals experience difficulties with others is that they lack accurate insight into their own feelings and those of others. One of the key tasks of such groups, then, is to increase self-awareness among the participants. This is accomplished by creating conditions which emphasize openness and honesty. Group members are encouraged, at first by the *trainer* (the person directing the group), but later by other members, to express their feelings directly and openly (refer to Figure 14-15 on page 453). They then receive immediate and honest feedback on these feelings from others. Under such conditions, it is reasoned, participants can learn a great deal about themselves, their impact on others, and interpreting other persons' reactions

Complementary and Crossed Interactions in Transactional Analysis

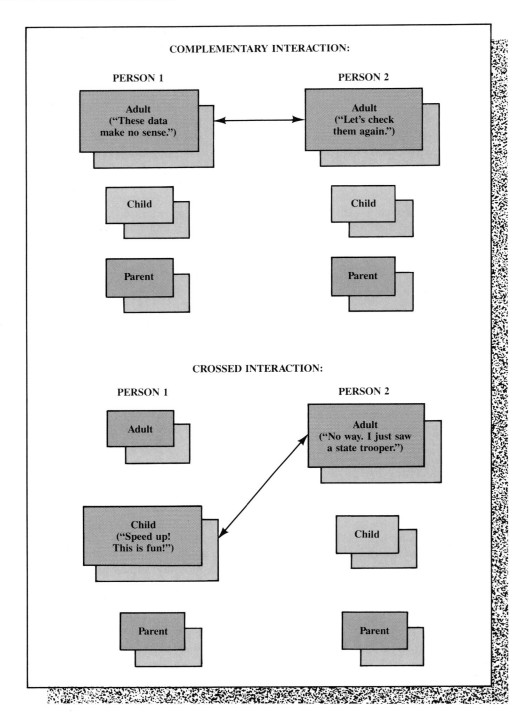

COMPLEMENTARY INTERACTION:

PERSON 1

PERSON 2

Adult ("These data make no sense.")

Adult ("Let's check them again.")

Child

Child

Parent

Parent

CROSSED INTERACTION:

PERSON 1

PERSON 2

Adult

Adult ("No way. I just saw a state trooper.")

Child ("Speed up! This is fun!")

Child

Parent

Parent

FIGURE 14-14. According to *transactional analysis,* three aspects of personality govern our behavior: Adult, Child, Parent. *Complementary interactions* occur between two individuals when they are both operating in the same aspect. *Crossed interactions* occur when these aspects do not coincide.

(Daft, 1986). This process is carried even further in *encounter groups*. Here, efforts are made to generate strong emotions so that these can be experienced, shared, and understood by group members. Specific exercises are often used for this purpose. For example, one member is lifted overhead by the others and carried around the room; all members close their eyes and touch each other's faces with their fingers.

Do such groups work? Unfortunately, their outcomes are difficult to assess. How do we measure a person's insight into her or his own feelings or personality, or improvements in ability to accurately ''read'' the feelings of others? Also, it is not clear that skills and insights acquired in such groups transfer readily to other contexts, where open and direct communication is not always encouraged. For this reason, sensitivity training and encounter groups are not as popular as they were in the past. Some evidence does suggest,

Sensitivity Training: A Popular Form of Group Therapy

FIGURE 14-15. In *humanistic growth groups* (also known as *sensitivity training*) individuals acquire greater self-awareness by sharing their feelings with others. In such groups, openness and honesty are emphasized.

though, that when directed by skilled and experienced trainers, some important benefits (e.g., improved relations with others) can be obtained (Campbell & Dunnette, 1968).

Family Therapy: The Most Intimate Group.   Why do psychological disorders arise? Different theorists offer different interpretations. Freud suggested that they spring from unresolved inner conflicts. Rogers and other humanistic psychologists contend that they involve a lack of self-awareness. Behavior therapists emphasize the role of faulty learning. In recent years, yet another intriguing perspective has been suggested. This approach, known as **family therapy,** argues that many psychological problems can be traced to relations within a family—to the patterns of interaction among various family members (Hazelrigg, Cooper, & Borduin, 1987). Attempting to treat one member of a family, this approach suggests, often makes little sense. After all, this individual continues to live in the same social context that contributed to his or her problems in the first place (refer to Figure 14-16 on page 454). Unless this context is changed, the benefits of therapy may be short-lived; indeed, they may be akin to throwing a person who has just been saved from drowning back into deep, icy waters (Goldenberg & Goldenberg, 1985; Minuchin, 1974).

Interest in family therapy has grown rapidly in recent years (Hazelrigg, Cooper, & Borduin, 1987), and several different procedures based on this general approach have been developed. In one, sometimes described as *experiential family therapy,* attention is focused primarily on current maladaptive patterns of behavior. While the causes of such difficulties are viewed as important, they are put aside until current problems are recognized by family members and new patterns of interaction can be established. For example, consider a family in which a child often becomes nauseated during meals. Sessions with the entire family may reveal that this is due to tension introduced at mealtime by both parents, who, concerned that their youngster isn't eating enough, constantly urge food upon him. Getting the parents to refrain from such behavior may change the entire situation and eliminate the child's nausea. Moreover, this may occur even before the reasons for the parents' anxiety become clear.

A second approach is known as *structural family therapy*. In this procedure efforts are concentrated on understanding various sets of relationships within the family (e.g., parent-child interactions, child-child interactions). Analysis of such relations may reveal

Family Therapy: Help in a Broader Social Context

FIGURE 14-16. *Family therapy* is based on the reasonable assumption that psychological problems often stem from disturbed relations among family members. In order to help individual family members, then, it is often necessary to change the pattern of relationships existing within the entire family group.

important causes of distress within the family. In one pattern, a mother and child may form a close relationship or *subsystem* that all but excludes the father. This, in turn, may strain the relationship between the two parents to the point at which the child, sensing this anger, develops various symptoms (e.g., disruptive behavior at school, symptoms of illness without any apparent physical cause). Similarly, anger or hostility of one parent toward the other may be reflected in rivalry between siblings who take sides in the parental dispute. This may result in considerable psychological distress for several family members.

Family Therapy: Evidence for Its Effectiveness

FIGURE 14-17. Family members who have participated in *family therapy* show more adaptive behavior and describe their relations more favorably than family members who have not received such therapy. *(Source: Based on data from Hazelrigg, Cooper, & Borduin, 1987.)*

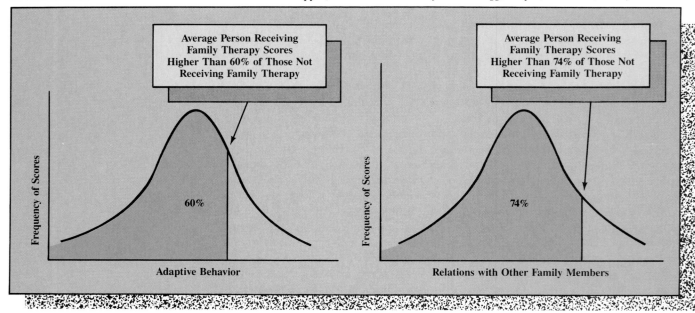

Many specific procedures are used in both types of family therapy, which is quite eclectic in this respect. Often these involve the application of principles discussed under the heading of *behavior therapies* (Gurman, Kniskern, & Pinsof, 1986; Patterson, 1982). Attention is focused primarily on changing specific patterns of behavior and on dealing with current problems; somewhat less emphasis is placed on uncovering the roots of present difficulties in the distant past, or on altering the personalities of the people involved.

Does family therapy work? Although it is relatively new, encouraging findings have already been reported. For example, in one recent review Hazelrigg, Cooper, and Borduin (1987) found that family therapy seems to be better than no therapy at all, and better than some other forms of therapy (e.g., individual therapy, training in problem-solving skills). Specifically, families receiving such therapy are rated by therapists, teachers, and others as showing more adaptive behavior and better relations with each other than families receiving other forms of treatment. In addition, family members describe their relations with one another in more favorable terms (refer to Figure 14-17). In view of such findings, it appears that family therapy may indeed provide a useful and relatively efficient alternative to individual therapy with each family member.

 ## Psychotherapy: Some Current Issues

In the late 1980s psychotherapy has come into its own. While some people continue to view it with a mixture of skepticism and fear, increasing numbers of distressed individuals have chosen to seek it out. Perhaps this shift is best illustrated by the following fact: in the 1950s only one percent of the population in the United States and other Western nations had ever had contact with a psychologist or other therapist. Currently, this figure is approaching ten percent. If you need further proof of the growing popularity of psychotherapy, just pick up any phone book and turn to listings under "Psychologists." Thirty or even twenty years ago, you might have found few entries; now, you are likely to find many.

What accounts for this rapid growth? In part, the answer seems to involve increasing sophistication on the part of the public: many more people now realize that there is no reason to go on suffering the pain and distress of psychological disorders when expert help is readily available. In addition, it reflects the growing interest among psychologists in *application*—using their knowledge and skills in practical ways. Whatever the causes, psychotherapy has certainly enjoyed something of a boom in recent years. This is not to suggest, however, that important questions about it no longer exist. In fact, as therapy has grown in popularity, these questions have become ever more pressing and have received increased attention within our field. In this section we'll focus on several of the most important of these questions: Does psychotherapy really work? Are some types better than others? And how should psychotherapy take account of cultural differences in a diverse society such as the United States?

Does Psychotherapy Work? Some Grounds for Optimism

In 1952 Hans Eysenck, a prominent psychologist, dropped a bombshell on his colleagues: he published a paper indicating that psychotherapy is ineffective. Specifically, Eysenck (1952) reported that 67 percent of patients with neurotic disorders improved after therapy, but that about the same proportion of persons receiving no treatment also improved. As you can guess, this led to a great deal of soul-searching—and research—in psychology. Fortunately, the findings of additional studies soon pointed to a different conclusion: psychotherapy *is* indeed helpful (Bergin & Lambert, 1978; Shapiro & Shapiro, 1982; Smith, Glass & Miller, 1980). Apparently Eysenck overestimated the proportion of persons who get better spontaneously, without therapy. And he also underestimated the proportion who improve as a result of therapy. For example, in a major review of the evidence on this issue, Smith, Glass, and Miller (1980) found that in almost five hundred separate studies, the average person receiving therapy showed fewer symptoms or difficulties than 80 percent of those who had not yet received therapy (who were still on waiting lists for such help).

Additional support for the effectiveness of therapy is provided by recent studies indicating that, as we might expect, the more treatment individuals receive, the greater the benefits they receive. In other words, as therapy progresses, individuals continue to improve and experience fewer symptoms and less distress (Orlinsky & Howard, 1987). Many studies support this conclusion, but perhaps the clearest evidence to data has been provided by Howard, Kopta, Krause, and Orlinsky (1986). Please see the "Cutting Edge" section below for a summary of their findings.

FOCUS ON RESEARCH: The Cutting Edge

The Dose-Effect Relationship in Psychotherapy: When More (Up to a Point) Is Better

If psychotherapy is truly effective, we would expect that the more therapy individuals receive, the greater the benefits they experience. Is this actually the case? In order to provide a reasonably clear an-

swer, Howard and his colleagues (1986) examined data from almost 2,500 patients, collected over a thirty-year period. All of these persons had undergone individual therapy, and all were treated for depression, anxiety, or borderline psychotic states. Two different measures of change in their behavior were employed: ratings by clinical psychologists or other profes-

The Dose-Effect Relationship: Evidence for the Effectiveness of Psychotherapy

FIGURE 14-18. The longer individuals receive psychotherapy, the higher the proportion who show improvements. Indeed, most persons suffering from anxiety or depression benefit after only a few months. These findings lend support to the view that psychotherapy is indeed effective. (*Source: Based on data from Howard et al., 1986.*)

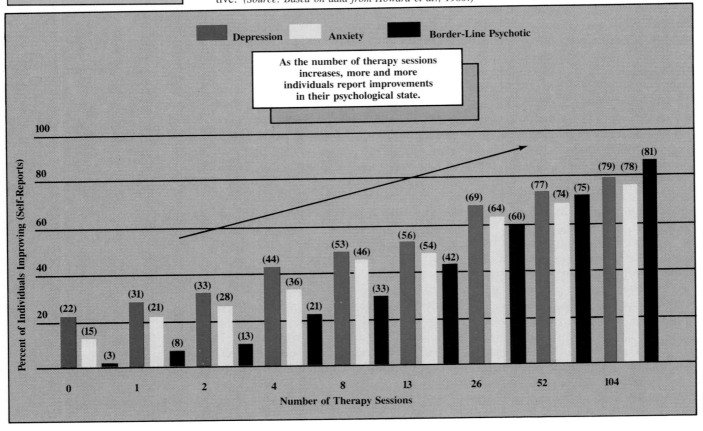

sionals and the persons' ratings of their own well-being. Results provided convincing evidence for the value of psychotherapy. As the number of sessions increased, the proportion of individuals in all three groups showing improvements rose (see Figure 14-18). Indeed, more than half of those suffering from depression or anxiety improved by the time they had participated in only thirteen weekly sessions. Not surprisingly, those suffering from more severe disorders (borderline psychotic) improved more slowly; still,

almost three-quarters of these persons were helped within a year. Interestingly, some individuals experienced benefits even before their first therapy session, presumably because the act of making an appointment provided grounds for hope.

These findings and similar results in other studies (Orlinsky & Howard, 1987) suggest that psychotherapy really works. As we've noted repeatedly, then, there's no reason for individuals to go on suffering the pain of psychological disorders. Effective forms of help *are* available. ◣

Are Some Forms of Therapy More Effective Than Others? A Persistent Puzzle

Psychoanalysis, person-centered therapy, systematic desensitization—the procedures used in these and many other forms of therapy differ sharply. It seems only reasonable, then, to expect that some types will be more effective than others. But now brace yourself for one of those surprises you have probably come to expect from psychology: efforts to demonstrate such differences have generally failed. Despite contrasting procedures (Luborsky et al., 1982), various forms of therapy seem to yield equal benefits (Kiesler, 1985; Luborsky, Singer, & Luborsky, 1975). How can this be? Several potential answers have been proposed.

Differences Between Various Therapies Exist, but We Have to Search for Them in the Right Places. First, it is possible that some forms of therapy *are* more effective than others, but only with respect to certain types of disorders. As Kiesler (1966) suggested, in comparing various psychotherapies we should not ask, "Which is better?" Rather we should inquire, "What type of treatment by what type of therapist is most effective in dealing with what specific problems among specific persons?" In other words, we should not expect to find that one type of psychotherapy is superior to others in all cases and in all respects. It is much more likely that some types will prove to be more useful in dealing with certain types of psychological disorders, and when administered by certain therapists. Many psychologists accept this view, although they realize that from a practical point of view, comparing the effectiveness of many types of therapy in overcoming a wide range of psychological disorders is a huge task, to say the least (Stiles, Shapiro, & Elliott, 1986).

Differences Among Various Therapies Exist, but We Have to Measure Them in Appropriate Ways. Different therapies focus on different goals. For example, behavior therapies seek to change overt behavior; cognitive therapies focus on altering patterns of thought; and humanistic therapies seek to enhance self-awareness and the self-concept. Given these different goals, it may make little sense to compare these diverse procedures on the same global measures (e.g., the proportion of patients rated as improved, or patient reports of their own well-being). Each type of therapy should be judged in terms of the extent to which it attains its own stated goals and the degree to which reaching its ends helps relieve distress among the persons seeking aid. In sum, the issue is a complex one and may not permit us the luxury of simple answers (Garfield & Bergin, 1986).

Various Types of Psychotherapy Yield Equivalent Benefits Because They Share a Common Core. In some respects this statement is the most intriguing possibility of all. It contends that the differences among various forms of psychotherapy are superficial ones; under the surface, all share common features, and for this reason all yield roughly

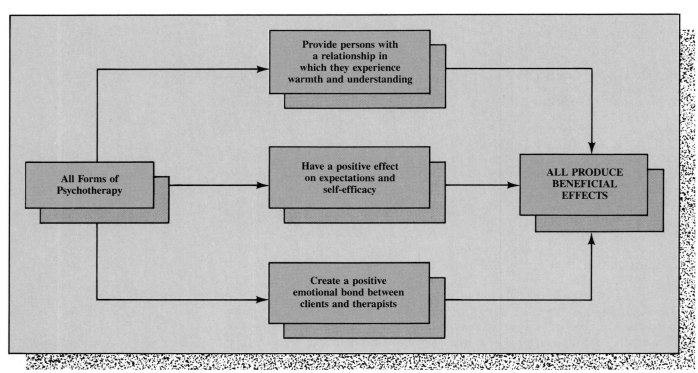

Psychotherapy: Why Many Different Types Succeed

FIGURE 14-19. Many different forms of psychotherapy may produce beneficial effects because all forms (1) provide individuals with warmth and understanding, (2) enhance expectations and self-efficacy, and (3) create positive emotional bonds between client and therapist.

equal benefits. What might constitute this common core? One possibility is that all effective therapists—whatever their perspective—provide individuals with personal warmth, understanding, and a new perspective on their problems. Perhaps, it is reasoned, major benefits flow from this factor.

Another possibility is that all forms of therapy have a positive effect on *expectations*. Participating in therapy offers the hope that things will get better. Further, as the process unfolds, individuals often experience enhancement of their own *self-efficacy*— their confidence in their own ability to accomplish various tasks. Such factors, which seem to be common to all major forms of therapy, may also contribute to positive change.

Third, it may be the mutual involvement between therapists and clients that is central—the *therapeutic alliance,* as it is often termed (Luborsky, 1984). The positive emotional bonds a client feels toward the therapist and the belief that they are working together to solve problems may be central to the benefits achieved. Specific tasks, techniques, and theories underlying therapy may be relatively unimportant. (Please see Figure 14-19 for a summary of these suggestions.)

The Paradox Revisited: Some Concluding Words. Where does all this leave us with respect to our central question: are some forms of therapy more effective than others? It leaves us, we believe, with the following conclusions. Differences among various psychotherapies may exist; however, these probably take the form ''*some* therapies are better for dealing with *some* types of disorders among *some* types of people,'' *not* ''one specific therapy is better than the others in all cases.'' Also, many, if not all, forms of therapy probably share some basic characteristics that contribute to their success. What is needed, then, is not a head-on battle between opposing camps, but rather more detailed efforts to determine when each therapy is most effective, and what, precisely, all types have in common.

Cultural Differences and Psychotherapy

In Chapter 11 we noted that many persons object to standard tests of intelligence because they may be culturally biased. Since such tests were first designed for use with white, middle-class children, they may place minority youngsters at a disadvantage. Similar criticisms have recently been leveled against psychotherapy. It, too, must take account of large differences in persons from contrasting ethnic or cultural backgrounds. In short, it must be *culturally sensitive*. What does this mean? Rogler and his colleagues (1987) believe that three points are most important.

First, efforts must be made to make psychotherapy accessible to members of various ethnic groups, especially groups that are economically disadvantaged. This implies that language barriers must be overcome and that government-sponsored programs and centers should be placed in minority communities where they will be available to persons who often lack personal means of transportation and large amounts of leisure time (refer to Figure 14-20).

Second, the types of therapy employed should be consistent with the culture of the group and its members' economic and educational background. For example, it would probably be inappropriate to employ psychoanalysis or other techniques requiring a high level of verbal skill in a poor community where most of the people have completed only a few years of school. Other types of psychotherapy (e.g., behavior therapies) might be more useful.

Finally, efforts should be made to adapt existing forms of therapy or develop new ones to take account of established values and traditions within a minority culture, values and traditions which may not be identical to those of the majority. For example, in working with persons of Hispanic descent it is essential to take account of widely held views about the roles of males and females which may differ from those of society in general (Rogler et al., 1987). Further, types of therapy should be devised that make use of traditional cultural forms, such as the use of folktales to present social models (Constantino, Malgady, & Rogler, 1986).

In sum, in psychotherapy, as in the assessment of individual differences, efforts to aid specific persons should occur against a backdrop of cultural sensitivity. If such differences are overlooked, much effort may be wasted, and even dedicated, talented therapists may fail to accomplish their major goal: easing the pain of psychological disorders.

FIGURE 14-20. Psychotherapy should be made available to members of all groups, including those of established values and traditions within a minority culture. This may require the establishment of *community mental health centers* in a wide range of neighborhoods.

Making Psychotherapy Accessible to All Groups

Biological Forms of Therapy: Shocks, Drugs, and Surgery

Ultimately, everything we think, feel, perceive, or do reflects activity in the central nervous system, especially in the brain. Attempts to modify the function or structure of these organs, then, offer another potential means of dealing with psychological disorders. Psychologists themselves have rarely been involved in such efforts, but other professionals (e.g., physicians, psychiatrists) have devoted considerable attention to such procedures. We will now briefly examine several of these **biological therapies.**

Electroconvulsive Therapy: Changing the Brain Through Powerful Electric Shocks

In the 1930s physicians noted that schizophrenics rarely had epileptic seizures. This observation (which, by the way, was not entirely correct) led the Hungarian psychiatrist Meduna to propose that artificially inducing such seizures might be effective in treating this serious psychological disorder. At first, such seizures or convulsions were produced by injection of a drug (e.g., camphor), but this was soon replaced by a method employing strong electric shocks—**electroconvulsive therapy (ECT).** This technique remains popular, especially in treating severe depression; more than 90,000 patients receive ECT each year in the United States alone (Weiner, 1985).

In actual use, ECT involves placing electrodes on the patient's temples, then delivering shocks of more than 100 volts for brief intervals (less than one second). These are continued until the patient has a seizure (body-wide muscle contraction) lasting at least thirty seconds. In order to prevent broken bones and other injuries, a muscle relaxant and a mild anesthetic are usually administered prior to the start of the shocks (please see Figure 14-21). Patients typically receive three treatments a week for several weeks.

Surprisingly, ECT seems to work, at least with certain disorders. It is especially effective with severe depression and appears to help many depressed persons who have failed to respond to other forms of therapy. It is less effective with schizophrenia, leading to improvements in about 15 to 20 percent of such cases. Although the mechanism by which ECT produces its effects has not yet been established, it appears to influence neural transmission deep within the brain, especially in the hypothalamus and limbic regions. Since these are areas intimately related to emotion, ECT's impact on depression may arise

FIGURE 14-21. When electroconvulsive therapy is administered under safe conditions, it can sometimes help combat depression and related psychological disorders.

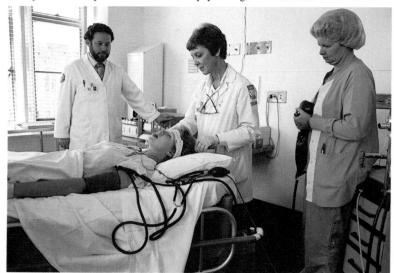

Electroconvulsive Therapy (ECT)

in this manner. Because modern procedures have rendered ECT much less dangerous than was true in the past, and because it does seem effective in some cases where other treatments fail, its continued use by psychiatrists seems likely.

Psychosurgery: From Lobotomy to Tractotomy

In 1936 a Portuguese psychiatrist, Egas Moniz, attempted to reduce aggressive behavior in psychotic patients by severing neural connections between the prefrontal lobes and the remainder of the brain. The operation (known as *prefrontal lobotomy*) seemed to be successful: aggressive behavior by unmanageable patients did decrease, and Moniz received the 1949 Nobel Prize in Medicine for his work. Encouraged by these findings, psychiatrists all over the world rushed to treat a wide range of disorders through **psychosurgery.** Unfortunately, results were not always positive. While some forms of objectionable or dangerous behavior did decrease, important side-effects occurred. Some patients became highly excitable and impulsive, while others slipped into profound apathy. A few became "living vegetables," requiring permanent care after the operation.

In view of such harmful outcomes, most physicians stopped performing prefrontal lobotomies, and by the 1950s this procedure had all but faded from the scene. It was replaced by a much more limited type of psychosurgery focused on the limbic system and hypothalamus. Such *tractotomies* interrupt neural pathways believed to play a role in emotion (Donnelly, 1985) and are used mainly to treat depression. Some reports indicate success with these procedures: from 50 to 90 percent of the patients improve (Donnelly, 1985). However, findings have been variable, and no firm conclusions can yet be reached.

Psychosurgery, even in its more limited modern form, raises important ethical questions. Is it right to destroy healthy tissue in a person's brain? And, since the benefits are uncertain, should such irreversible procedures be performed? These and related issues have led many psychiatrists to view psychosurgery as a "treatment of last resort," to be used only when everything else has failed. As a result, fewer than one hundred such operations are now performed in the United States each year, and psychosurgery is no longer an important form of treatment for psychological disorders.

Drug Therapy: The Chemical Revolution

In 1955 almost 600,000 persons were resident patients in psychiatric hospitals in the United States. Twenty years later, this number had dropped below 175,000. Were Americans achieving mental health at a dizzying pace? As you can probably guess, the answer is "no." What happened in the intervening years was something we might describe as the "chemical revolution." A wide range of drugs effective in treating many serious psychological disorders was developed. Indeed, so successful were these drugs in relieving major symptoms that hundreds of thousands of persons who previously were hospitalized for their own safety (and that of others) could now be sent home for treatment as out-patients. Please note: the fact that these drugs are successful in relieving major symptoms does not mean that they eliminate the problems that underlie them. Many persons released from mental institutions are still seriously disturbed and do *not* go on to live well-adjusted lives. Indeed, some add to the growing ranks of homeless "street people" in the United States and elsewhere (refer to Figure 14-22 on page 462).

Anti-anxiety Drugs (Minor Tranquilizers). Alcohol, a substance used by many persons to combat anxiety, has been available since antiquity. However, as we're sure you know, it has important negative side-effects. Synthetic drugs with anti-anxiety effects—*barbiturates* such as phenobarbital—were first manufactured in the early twentieth century. They, too, proved to have unfortunate side-effects (e.g., people often became dependent on them). The situation improved greatly in 1957 when a new group of anti-anxiety drugs, the *benzodiazepines* (e.g., Valium, Librium, Dalmane), was developed. These drugs were highly effective and could reduce feelings of anxiety and tension without producing sleepiness or physiological dependence. Unfortunately, they, too, involve

Psychoactive Drugs: A Plus, but No Panacea

FIGURE 14-22. Psychoactive drugs often relieve major symptoms of schizophrenia and other serious psychological disorders. When such persons are released from mental hospitals, however, the underlying causes of their disorders are still present. The result: they continue to experience considerable distress and at least some may join the growing ranks of ''street people.''

various side-effects. Some persons who use them complain of drowsiness and lethargy. Even more important, combining any of these drugs with alcohol can be quite dangerous. Finally, some persons do seem to become psychologically dependent upon them, especially when they are used for long periods of time (Davis, 1985a). Thus, although these drugs have attained widespread use and are effective in controlling even intense anxiety, they do not provide such benefits without associated risks.

The benzodiazepines seem to produce their effects by depressing activity in the central nervous system, perhaps binding to sites in the brain that would otherwise be occupied by certain neural transmitters.

Antidepressants.   A wide range of drugs, having a number of different chemical formulas, are effective in reducing depression (e.g., imipramine). Many are fast-acting and can produce major shifts in mood within a few days. Side-effects vary greatly and seem to depend on the chemical structure of each drug; they include agitation, difficulty in elimination of bodily wastes, and irritability. Such effects are relatively rare and seem to occur mainly when an overdose is consumed. Antidepressants seem to exert their effects by altering the activity of neurotransmitters and receptivity to these within the brain.

Antipsychotics (Major Tranquilizers).   Perhaps the most dramatic effects of all are produced by the *antipsychotics* (e.g., chlorpromazine). These drugs are highly effective, producing major improvements in many severely disturbed patients within a few weeks (Davis, 1985c). They relieve a wide range of symptoms, including hallucinations, thought disorders, anxiety, and extreme hostility. As noted earlier, the availability of such drugs has produced dramatic changes in psychiatry. In a few short decades, mental hospitals which had provided custodial care for large numbers of patients who were almost totally out of touch with reality became places in which cooperative residents could be treated with many forms of psychotherapy (please see Figure 14-23). Perhaps this change is best summarized by the following fact: in the mid-1950s 70 percent of all persons diagnosed as suffering from schizophrenia spent most of their lives in mental hospitals; at present, this figure is under 5 percent.

How do antipsychotics produce such remarkable effects? Current theory suggests that they may block brain receptors for *dopamine,* one neural transmitter. As we noted in Chapter 13, the presence of an excess of this transmitter, or a person's increased sensitivity to it, may play a role in the development of schizophrenia. Whatever the precise mechanism involved, there can be little doubt that the development of antipsychotic drugs has helped transform many previously hopeless patients into ones responsive to psychotherapy. In such cases, a biological therapy paves the way for later psychological interventions.

Anti-Psychotic Drugs: Paving
the Way for Psychotherapy

FIGURE 14-23. *Antipsychotic drugs* help eliminate severely disturbed patterns of behavior among schizophrenics (left photo). As a result, it may become possible to treat such persons by means of psychotherapy (right photo).

Summary and Review

Psychotherapy: Some Major Forms

Psychotherapy involves establishment of a special relationship between a *therapist* and an individual experiencing psychological distress—a relationship designed to facilitate beneficial changes in the client's feelings, behavior, or thought. Psychotherapy is performed by members of several different professions (psychologists, psychiatrists, psychiatric nurses).

Many forms of psychotherapy exist. The goal of *psychoanalysis* is to bring repressed inner conflicts into consciousness. It employs *free association* by the client and *interpretations* by the analyst as means of attaining these ends. Modern adaptations of psychoanalysis devote less attention to inner conflicts concerning sexual and aggressive impulses, but more attention to the social causes of psychological disorders.

Humanistic therapies focus on increasing an individual's awareness of her or his own feelings and enhancing the self-concept. In Rogers' *person-centered therapy,* this is accomplished by providing clients with *unconditional acceptance*. In another humanistic therapy, *Gestalt therapy,* much emphasis is placed on making individuals aware of their own feelings.

Cognitive therapies focus on the task of altering irrational beliefs and other faulty cognitions. In one popular form, *rational-emotive therapy,* strenuous efforts are made to induce individuals to surrender irrational beliefs which cause them to experience intense psychological stress. This is accomplished by making these beliefs explicit and by pointing out the extent to which they distort the individual's view of reality.

Attributional therapy is primarily concerned with changing a person's faulty attributions—unrealistic or inaccurate beliefs about the causes of behavior and outcomes. One major goal of such therapy is inducing individuals to attribute successes to internal causes but failure to external ones.

In *behavior therapies,* basic principles of learning are used to change maladaptive patterns of behavior. *Systematic desensitization* is based upon classical conditioning. It involves teaching an individual how to relax and then to use the relaxation technique in the presence of stimuli that initially induced feelings of anxiety. As desensitization proceeds, feelings of anxiety are reduced. In *aversive conditioning* stimuli previously associated with positive feelings are linked with negative ones, instead. Forms of therapy based on principles of operant conditioning are effective, too. Such *operant therapies* provide individuals with positive reinforcers for desired, adaptive behaviors or administer mild punishment for engaging in maladaptive behaviors.

Several individuals work together to overcome their problems in *group therapy*. Such therapy often focuses on the tasks of increasing individuals' awareness of their own impact on others. In *family therapy* efforts are made to change the pattern of relations among family members in order to help one or more persons overcome psychological disorders. This approach assumes that psychological problems experienced by any members of a family derive, at least in part, from interactions among family members and the nature of the interpersonal relationships within the family.

Psychotherapy: Is It Effective?

Growing evidence suggests that psychotherapy is effective: it reduces psychological distress among at least some persons. However, comparisons of various forms of therapy suggest that none is uniformly superior to the others. This may stem from the fact that each kind of therapy is most effective in dealing with certain disorders. It may also be the case that all forms of therapy share common elements that contribute to their effectiveness. In addition, psychotherapy should take careful account of cultural differences among various groups.

Biological Therapies

Biological therapies attempt to deal with psychological disorders by changing the structure or function of the brain. In *electroconvulsive therapy* (ECT) strong electric shocks are delivered to a patient's head. Such procedures appear to be effective in relieving severe depression. *Psychosurgery* employs operations on the brain to eliminate dangerous or harmful forms of behavior. *Prefrontal lobotomies* were once common but have now been replaced by *tractotomies*—smaller-scale operations which interrupt neural pathways related to emotion. Few such operations are performed today.

Many drugs are effective in relieving the symptoms of psychological disorders. They reduce anxiety, counter depression, and reduce psychotic symptoms. Unfortunately, many drugs have important side-effects and can induce psychological dependence among persons who take them for long periods of time. Antipsychotic drugs are effective in relieving major symptoms of schizophrenia and other disorders, but they do not remove the underlying causes of such disorders. As a result, persons who can now be released from a mental hospital because of such drugs often continue to suffer considerable distress.

Key Terms

Behavior Therapies Forms of psychotherapy derived from basic principles of learning.

Biological Therapies Efforts to alleviate psychological disorders by changing the structure or function of the brain.

Cognitive Therapies Forms of psychotherapy that focus on changing disordered or faulty patterns of thought.

Electroconvulsive Therapy (ECT) A biological therapy which delivers strong electric shocks to the patient's head in order to alleviate major depression or other forms of psychological disorder.

Existential Therapy Therapy that attempts to change a patient's cognitions, especially the belief that life is meaningless.

Family Therapy Therapy that focuses on changing interactions among family members.

Free Association A procedure in psychoanalysis in which the individual spontaneously reports all thoughts passing through his or her mind.

Gestalt Therapy A form of therapy designed to increase an individual's awareness and understanding of her or his own feelings.

Humanistic Growth Groups A form of group therapy that focuses upon increasing individuals' awareness of their own feelings and their impact upon others.

Humanistic Therapies Therapies that seek to increase self-awareness and enhance the self-concept.

Modeling A form of behavior therapy in which individuals are shown others who perform actions they are unable to perform themselves.

Person-Centered Therapy A humanistic therapy which seeks to enhance an individual's self-awareness and induce a more realistic self-concept.

Psychoanalysis A form of therapy, devised by Freud, that attempts to provide individuals with insight into repressed inner conflicts.

Psychosurgery A biological therapy that attempts to alleviate psychological disorders by performing medical operations upon the brain.

Psychotherapy Efforts to produce beneficial changes in an individual's behavior, feelings, or thoughts through establishment of a special type of relationship between the person seeking help and a trained professional.

Rational-Emotive Therapy A cognitive therapy that focuses on the task of eliminating irrational beliefs.

Resistance Efforts by individuals undergoing psychoanalysis to prevent repressed conflicts from entering consciousness.

Systematic Desensitization A form of behavior therapy in which an individual learns to relax in the presence of imagined stimuli or events which initially caused feelings of anxiety. As such stimuli become associated with feelings of relaxation, they gradually lose the capacity to evoke anxiety.

Token Economies A form of therapy based on operant conditioning. Patients at mental hospitals are given tokens that can be exchanged for valued rewards when they behave in specific desirable ways.

Transactional Analysis Therapy Focuses on how individual interacts with key persons in life by role playing situations in group therapy.

Transference Strong positive or negative feelings toward the therapist experienced by many individuals undergoing psychoanalysis.

For More Information

Bentovim, A., Barnes, G. G., & Cooklin, A. (1987). *Family therapy,* 2nd ed. New York: Academic Press.

> A comprehensive overview of one of the newest and most popular forms of psychotherapy. The causes of strain within families and techniques for dealing with these are covered clearly and in detail.

Goldstein, A. P., & Krasner, L. (1987). *Modern applied psychology.* New York: Pergamon Press.

> This text surveys developments and contributions in all fields of applied psychology. The chapter on clinical applications provides an excellent summary of major forms of psychotherapy. All of the therapies considered in this chapter, plus several others, are fully described.

Rickel, A. U., & Allen, L. R. (1987). *Preventing maladjustment from infancy through adolescence.* New York: Sage.

> Much attention has been focused in recent years on the possibility of preventing psychological disorders. This text summarizes the findings of research concerned with this issue. It also describes practical techniques which may prove useful in preventing various problems, especially among children and adolescents.

CHAPTER

15

Social Behavior and Social Thought: How We Think about and Interact with Others

"Well what the heck are they up to *now*?" Jan Taylor remarks, flinging her hands into the air in disgust.

"Darned if I know," replies Tom Wallace, another member of Standex Corporation's contract team. "They really pulled the rug out from under me. I've been negotiating construction deals for twenty years, but I've never heard an offer as good as that one. I mean thirty percent under the next lowest bid! And they actually *suggested* a penalty if they fail to meet the schedule. It's weird, really weird."

"Maybe they're just setting us up for a big cost overrun," Jan muses. "John Stoner operates like that sometimes. He's reasonable until he's got you on the hook and the project's under way—then he lets you have it from all directions at once."

"Maybe that's it," Tom answers, "but who knows? They really *do* need this project. Things have been slow for them this year and they've got a lot of people on the payroll. Could be that we've just got 'em at a time when they want our business so bad they'll do practically anything to get it."

Bev Andrews, who has been listening intently, shakes her head. "If it were anyone else, I'd agree. But that Lou Collins . . . she's so slippery—I don't think she'd tell you what she's really thinking if you held a gun on her. I don't like her, and I don't like dealing with her. I wish they hadn't brought her along!" With this, she pounds her fist on the table in front of her.

"Take it easy," Jan replies in a soothing voice. "I don't like her much either, but she's here and we've got to put up with it. Anyway, maybe we're all being too sensitive. After what we went through with the people at Highland Industries last month, we're all a little jumpy. We shouldn't let the fact that *they* were trying to pull a fast one make us think everyone is out to do the same."

"Good point," Tom replies. "Anyway, let's get our act together and come up with a counter-proposal. The sooner we wrap things up, the better."

Of one fact there can be no doubt: other people play a central role in our lives. We work with them, live with them, and depend upon them for satisfaction of many of our most important needs (refer to Figure 15-1). We are in contact with other people almost continuously and spend a large portion of our day either thinking about or interacting with them. It is for these reasons that one active branch of our field, **social psychology,** focuses entirely on the topics mentioned in the title of this chapter: *social thought* and *social behavior*.

As you can probably guess, social psychology is tremendously diverse in scope: how could it be otherwise, when it focuses on virtually all aspects of social relations plus the ways in which we think about others and our efforts to understand their traits and motives? We'll try to represent this diversity in the present chapter by considering a number of key topics investigated by social psychologists.

First, we'll examine several aspects of social thought. Included here will be discussions of *attribution*—the process through which we attempt to understand the causes behind others' actions; and *social cognition*—the ways in which we sort, combine, and store information about other persons. (Both processes were visible in our opening story; members of Standex's contract-negotiating team attempted to guess the motives behind their opponents' latest offer, and in this respect their thinking was influenced by their recent experiences in other negotiations.)

Next we'll turn to key aspects of *interpersonal behavior*. Here, we'll consider *social influence*—efforts by one or more persons to change the behavior of one or more others—and *attraction* and *love*. Finally, we'll examine some key *applications* of social psychology—ways in which its principles and findings help us understand several aspects of the *legal process* and the impact of the physical *environment* on our behavior.

FIGURE 15-1. Thinking about others and interacting with them are among the most important activities in our daily lives.

> **Other Persons: Central to Our Lives**

Thinking about Others: Attribution and Social Cognition

How many times have you thought about other people today? If you are like most persons, your answer might well be "Who's counting?" Other people play such an important role in our lives that we think about them all the time. In fact, there are few periods when they are *not* in our thoughts, directly or indirectly. What form does such thinking take? Does it follow the same principles that govern other forms of thought? Intriguing evidence on these issues is provided by research on *attribution* and *social cognition*.

Attribution: How We Answer the Question "Why?"

Imagine the following situation. At a party you are introduced to a stranger of the opposite sex. As this person greets you, he or she turns bright red, stammers, and generally gives every sign of being highly embarrassed. How do you react? The answer depends partly on your conclusions about *why* this person shows such signs of embarrassment. Is it because he or she finds you highly attractive? Or is this person simply very shy and acts in much the same manner when meeting practically anyone? This question—*why* others act the way they do—is one we address every day in a wide range of contexts. For example, in the opening story of this chapter, negotiators from one company faced the task of trying to determine just why negotiators from another company had made a surprisingly generous offer. Was it a trap—some sort of set-up? Or was it a genuine desire to reach an agreement? As you can see, **attribution** is a basic aspect of social life and plays an important role in our relations with others.

Causal Attributions: One Influential Framework.
Our efforts to understand the causes behind others' behavior takes many forms. One of the most important questions we ask, however, is this: Do their actions stem mainly from *internal* causes (e.g., their own traits, motives, and intentions) or largely from *external* causes (factors in the world around them)? In a sense, this was the question raised in the party example above: was the other person's embarrassment a sign of shyness (an internal cause) or a reaction to your appearance and charm (an external cause)? How do we go about reaching such conclusions? A theory proposed by Kelley (1972; Kelley & Michela, 1980) provides one useful answer.

According to Kelley, we seek to determine whether another's actions stem mainly from internal or external causes by focusing on three types of information. First, we consider *consistency*—the extent to which this person reacts in the same way to a given stimulus or event at other times (if the person does, consistency is high). Second, we consider *distinctiveness*—the extent to which this person reacts in the same way to other events or stimuli (if this is the case, distinctiveness is low, but if the person reacts differently, distinctiveness is high). Finally, we consider *consensus*—the extent to which other people react in the same way as this person to a given stimulus or situation (if they do, consensus is high).

Now let's apply this theory to our party example. If consistency is *high* (this person reacts with embarrassment when seeing you at other times), consensus is *low* (few people react with embarrassment when meeting you), and distinctiveness is *low* (the

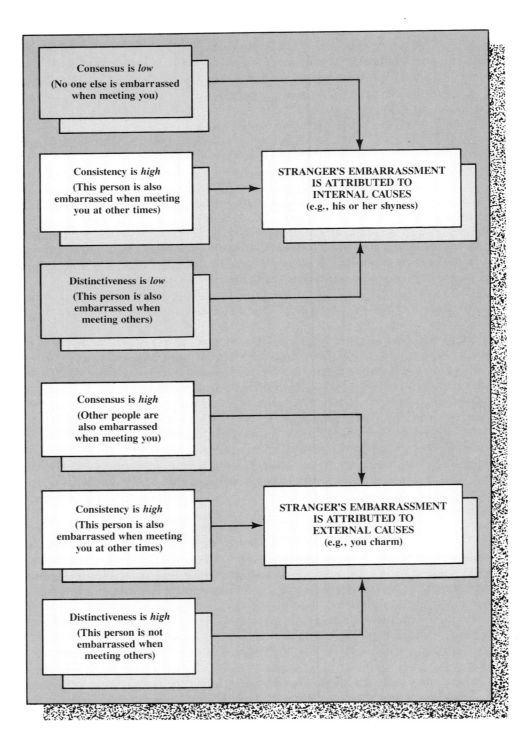

How We Answer the Question "Why?"

FIGURE 15-2. In determining whether others' behavior stems mainly from internal or external causes, we pay attention to information about *consensus, consistency,* and *distinctiveness.*

stranger also shows embarrassment when meeting other people), you would probably conclude that he or she is shy. In other words, you would attribute his or her behavior to internal causes. In contrast, if consistency is high (this person is embarrassed when meeting you at other times), consensus is high (other people, too, show embarrassment when meeting you), and distinctiveness is high (the person is *not* embarrassed when meeting others), you would probably attribute his or her embarrassment to external causes—your own charm or good looks! (Please refer to Figure 15-2 for a summary of these suggestions.)

Do we really think about others, and the causes behind their actions, in this manner? A large body of research evidence suggests that we do. So in general terms Kelley's theory appears to be correct (Harvey & Weary, 1984). However, it has also been modified in two important respects. First, as you might guess, we don't engage in this kind of effortful cognitive work (careful attention to consensus, consistency, and distinctiveness) unless we have to—unless we are faced with unexpected events we can't readily explain (Hansen, 1980).

Second, in thinking about why other people act as they do, we often consider two other dimensions in addition to the internal-external one: whether such actions are controllable or uncontrollable, and whether they stem from stable (lasting) or unstable (temporary) causes (B. Weiner, 1985). An intriguing illustration of the importance of our social thinking in such respects is provided by a study conducted by Weiner and his colleagues (Weiner et al., 1987).

This study was concerned with a practical question: what kind of excuses work best in situations where one person has annoyed or inconvenienced another? To gain information on this issue, Weiner and his co-workers first asked students to describe the kind of excuses they gave or did not give to others when they came late for an appointment or failed to do something that was expected of them. In addition, subjects described the effects of such excuses—how the other persons reacted and how such excuses affected their relations. Careful analysis indicated that, in general, subjects tended to use excuses that focused on external, uncontrollable causes (e.g., ''I was stuck in traffic and couldn't get here'') and avoided excuses that focused on internal, controllable causes (e.g., ''I just forgot all about it''). As you might guess, subjects also reported that excuses of the first type were much more successful in preventing others from becoming angry.

Encouraged by these results, the same researchers conducted a follow-up study in which an accomplice of subjects' own gender kept them waiting fifteen minutes (he or she was late for the study). In one condition the accomplice offered a good excuse when he or she finally showed up—an excuse based on uncontrollable, external causes (''The professor in my class gave an exam that ran way over time''). In another condition, the accomplice offered a weak excuse (''I was talking to some friends in the hall''). As expected, subjects in the latter condition reported more negative feelings toward the accomplice (greater anger and irritation), described this person in more negative terms (e.g., as being less dependable), and reported less desire to see him or her again. (Please see Figure 15-3.) Such findings suggest that attribution is often closely related to social behavior: our conclusions about the causes behind others' behavior can strongly shape our relations with them.

Attribution: Some Major Sources of Bias. Our comments so far seem to imply that attribution is a highly rational process, one in which we employ all the clues at our disposal to identify the causes behind others' behavior. In general, this is the case; attribution *is* logical in many respects. However, it is also subject to several forms of bias that can lead us to serious errors in our thinking about other persons.

One of these is so basic that it is sometimes described as the **fundamental attribution error.** It involves our tendency to explain others' actions in terms of internal causes rather than external ones. In other words, we seem to perceive others as acting the way they do because they are ''that kind of person''—they are individuals with certain traits or dispositions. The many external factors which may also affect their behavior tend to be ignored or at least downplayed. For example, if you approach a ticket counter at an airport and see a customer shouting angrily at the clerk on duty, you may jump to the conclusion

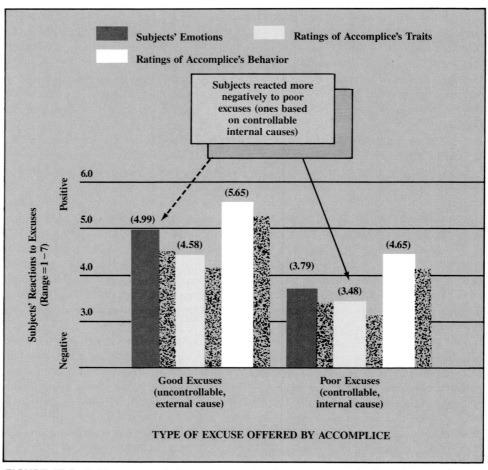

FIGURE 15-3. Subjects responded more negatively when a stranger who kept them waiting offered a weak excuse (one based on controllable, internal causes) than when this person offered a good excuse (one based on uncontrollable, external causes). *(Source: Based on data from Weiner et al., 1987.)*

that the customer is a rude, hostile individual. You are likely to overlook the possibility that he had been delayed for several hours, had his luggage shipped to the wrong city, and has been overcharged for his ticket.

Why does the fundamental error occur? One possibility is that when we focus on others' actions, we simply don't pay much attention to the context in which the actions occur. Another possibility is that we do pay attention to the context, but we give it less weight than it deserves (Gilbert & Jones, 1986). Whatever its precise basis, the fundamental attribution error seems to be quite strong and represents one way in which our thinking about others can sometimes go astray.

A second type of attributional bias is illustrated by the following situation. Imagine that you do extremely well on an exam. How will you explain this performance? Probably you will attribute this success to internal causes: your own intelligence, hard work, and effort. Now, in contrast, imagine that you do extremely poorly on an exam. How will you explain *this* outcome? The odds are good that you will attribute it to external causes: the unfairness of the test, the poor quality of lectures provided by your instructor, and so on.

This tendency to attribute successes to internal causes but failures to external ones is known as the **self-serving bias** (Baumgardner, Heppner, & Arkin, 1986; Miller & Ross, 1975). More generally, it refers to our strong tendency to interpret our own behavior and its causes in positive, flattering terms—often more favorably than we deserve (refer to Figure 15-4). It seems to stem from two tendencies: (1) a desire to protect or enhance our self-esteem, and (2) a desire to ''look good'' in the eyes of others—to make a

FIGURE 15-4. As shown here, individuals often interpret their own behavior (and the causes behind it) more favorably than others' behavior. This is known as the *self-serving bias*. (Source: The New Yorker.)

"Now, I'm a reasonable fellow, but it seems to me that in case after case and time after time in these labor disputes the fairer, more enlightened position has always been held by management."

favorable impression upon them. In both respects, it often works: if we are responsible for positive outcomes but are not to blame for negative ones, our beliefs in our own self-worth may be bolstered (Greenberg, Pyszczynski, & Solomon, 1982). Similarly, taking credit for positive results, but avoiding blame for negative ones, does enhance our "social image." Although it represents a distortion in our attributions, therefore, the self-serving bias may have adaptive value. Indeed, as you may recall from our discussion in Chapter 14, one problem faced by persons suffering from low self-esteem is that they *don't* show this bias. On the contrary, they tend to attribute successes to external causes (e.g., luck), and failures to their own shortcomings. So the self-serving bias, like other types of errors we make in processing social information, may be beneficial in at least some respects.

We'll have more to say about this point in our discussion of social cognition. At the moment, though, we wish to turn briefly to another issue: is information about attribution of practical value? Our answer is simple: absolutely! For some indication of why this is so, please see "The Point of It All" insert.

THE POINT OF IT ALL

Putting Attribution Theory to Work: When Answering the Question "Why?" Can Be of Practical Help
In a sense, we have already replied to the question, "Is knowledge about attributions of practical use?" In earlier discussions we noted that attributions play a role in effective forms of therapy used to treat such problems as depression (Pyszczynski & Greenberg, 1987). Here, we'd like to add that knowledge about attribution has also been applied to understanding several other important topics.

First, attributions have proven helpful in understanding the nature of conflict and aggression. For example, attribution theory suggests that individuals will be made much angrier by provocations they view as intentional than by provocation they view as unintentional. This prediction has been confirmed in several studies (e.g., Johnson & Rule, 1986). Similarly, attribution theory helps explain several aspects of negotiation, an important means of resolving conflicts. One tactic frequently used by bargainers is the "my hands are tied" strategy. Persons adopting this tactic claim that they'd gladly make concessions but are prevented from doing so by external factors (e.g., orders to "be tough" from their superiors). Attribution theory predicts that such tactics may be helpful as long as they are believed by the persons receiving them, but they may backfire and actually *intensify* conflicts if they are viewed as false. Such predictions have been confirmed in recent research (Baron, 1989). The moral for negotiators is clear: treat the "my hands are tied" tactic with care!

Second, knowledge about attributions has been used to understand marital distress (Holtzworth-Munroe & Jacobson, 1985). Apparently, many marriages get into serious difficulties when the partners begin attributing negative actions by their spouse to internal causes (e.g., his or her lasting traits) but positive actions to external factors. Furthermore, happy, well-adjusted couples seem to show an intriguing reversal of the

usual self-serving bias: they view the causes of their spouse's actions more favorably than those of their own. For example, they attribute positive behaviors by their mates to such internal causes as unselfish motives and positive intentions, and they make such attributions more strongly about their mate's positive actions than about their own! Unhappy couples, in contrast, show the opposite pattern. Counseling based on shifting such attributional patterns offers new hope to couples who wish to save their relationship but who have not been aided by more traditional techniques.

In these and several other ways, knowledge about attributions has already proven to be of considerable practical value. In short, understanding how people go about explaining others' behavior seems to provide a useful new perspective on important social problems.

Social Cognition: How We Process Social Information

Identifying the causes behind others' behavior is an important part of social thought, yet it is far from the entire process. In thinking about other persons, we perform many additional tasks: we must determine which information about them is most important; we must enter this input into long-term memory; and we must retrieve it at later times in order to make judgments and decisions about them (Wyer & Srull, 1986). How do we perform such tasks? Are we effective at them? Research on **social cognition** has yielded a mixed picture.

On the one hand, we *do* seem to be highly efficient in sorting, combining, and remembering a wealth of information about others (Wyer & Srull, 1984). Considering the amount of input provided by people's words and deeds, this is no simple feat. On the other hand, our social thought seems to be subject to a number of intriguing forms of bias and error. Most of these involve what might be termed *mental short-cuts*—strategies we use to extract the maximum value from the widest range of information, with the least amount of mental work. Since much research on social cognition has focused on these short-cuts and their effects, we'll consider several here.

Heuristics: Rules-of-Thumb for Making Social Judgments.   We have already considered heuristics in our discussion of decision-making (Chapter 7). At that time, we described two of these rules-of-thumb for making decisions or judgments in some detail: the availability and representativeness heuristics. As you may recall, the *availability heuristic* refers to our tendency to judge the frequency of an event in terms of how readily we can bring examples of it to mind (Kahneman & Tversky, 1982). The more easily we can think of an instance, the more frequent we view such an event as being. This principle also plays an important role in our thinking about others. For example, imagine that one of your friends asks you whether a professor, whose course she plans to take, is fair. How do you answer? Probably you do so by a quick scan of your memory for instances when the professor acted in a fair or unfair manner. The more readily you can think of instances of one type or the other, the more likely you will be to judge this instructor as fitting into that category.

We also use the availability heuristic in judging the frequency of various events. During 1986 a series of near-misses and tragic accidents involving commercial airlines took place—even one which threatened President Reagan (refer to Figure 15-5). As a result of these events, which are dramatic and easily brought to mind, many persons concluded that flying is very dangerous—more dangerous than other forms of transportation. In fact, such conclusions are false: accidents involving airplanes are extremely rare, and the chances of being hurt are actually much lower than the chances of being harmed in

FIGURE 15-5. Because the mass media provide detailed coverage of accidents and near-accidents involving airplanes, such information is readily available in memory. The result: many persons overestimate the frequency of such events. This illustrates the operation of the *availability heuristic.*

an automobile or bus. Because of the availability heuristic, though, many persons overestimate the relative frequency of airplane accidents.

The *representativeness heuristic,* too, influences our thinking about other persons. If another person seems to possess traits that are ''typical'' of persons belonging to some category, we assume that this person, too, belongs to this group. Thus, if we meet a young man dressed in a business suit and carrying a leather briefcase, we quickly assume that he is a lawyer or executive. When he pulls a gun out of the case and says, ''This is a stick-up,'' we are dumbfounded; our mental short-cut which works in most cases has led us seriously astray! This is an important point: the reason we use such heuristics is that they usually *do* work. They permit us to reach valid conclusions about others with a minimum of cognitive work. They are far from infallible, though, and can sometimes generate false judgments or decisions.

Other Forms of Error in Social Thought: The False Consensus Effect, Priming, and Illusory Correlation.   Heuristics are not the only mental short-cuts that sometimes lead us into error. Several others also exist. One of the most intriguing of these is the **false consensus effect**—our tendency to believe that others share our views and think very much as we do. When asked to estimate the proportion of other persons who agree with them about such diverse issues as abortion, drugs, President Reagan's record, hamburgers, and Brooke Shields, most persons badly overestimate the numbers; they think that others share their views to a much greater extent than they actually do (Nisbett & Kunda, 1985). What accounts for this tendency? One possibility is that we tend to associate with people who *do* share our attitudes. As a result, instances of agreement are more readily available in our memory and are judged (according to the availability heuristic) as more frequent than they really are. Another possibility is that we perceive others as agreeing with us because we want to be correct—we want to hold the ''right'' or popular views (Marks & Miller, 1987). Whatever the mechanism involved, one fact is clear: we often overestimate the degree of similarity between our own views and those of others.

A second type of bias in our thinking about others is illustrated by the following incident. Imagine that you have just watched a spy film in which betrayal and treachery were the central themes: double and triple-agents lied, cheated, and tricked one another repeatedly. After this, you go shopping for new clothes. When you try on an outfit and are not sure how it looks, you ask the clerk. She's enthusiastic and tells you it looks great. Do you believe her? Or do you conclude that she's just trying to make a quick sale? Because you have just seen a movie about treachery, ideas about misleading others may be present in your mind, and you are more likely to perceive the clerk as dishonest than if you had *not* seen the movie. Such effects, in which recent experiences activate certain categories of memory, are known as **priming,** and they are quite common. For example, many first-year medical students, hearing frequent lectures about various diseases, often perceive the symptoms of common colds and other minor illnesses they experience as signs of serious illness—an effect known as the *medical student syndrome*. As you can see, this tendency to interpret new information or situations in terms of recent experiences can sharply reduce the accuracy of our social thought. (Please see Figure 15-6 for a summary of priming and how it operates.)

Finally, we should mention a third potential error, known as *illusory correlation* (Hamilton, Dugan, & Trolier, 1985). This refers to our tendency to perceive associations (correlations) between variables when in fact these associations don't exist. One example: many people believe that there is a correlation between high levels of intelligence and psychological disorders, so that the higher one's IQ, the greater the chances of being eccentric—or worse. Moreover, they believe in this relationship despite the total absence of scientific evidence for it. Illusory correlations also play an important role in *stereotypes* and the prejudice that often accompanies them. In such cases, individuals perceive differences between two or more social groups in terms of the strength of the correlations between membership in one of the groups and certain characteristics. Moreover, they perceive these differences when they actually don't exist (Sanbonmatsu et al., 1987). For example, we may hold the view that persons of Cuban descent are more violent than persons of European descent when, in fact, being Cuban or European is equally unrelated to this characteristic.

FIGURE 15-6. Prior experiences can sometimes activate specific categories of memory. Such activation, in turn, may strongly affect the interpretation of later events or experiences. This is known as *priming*.

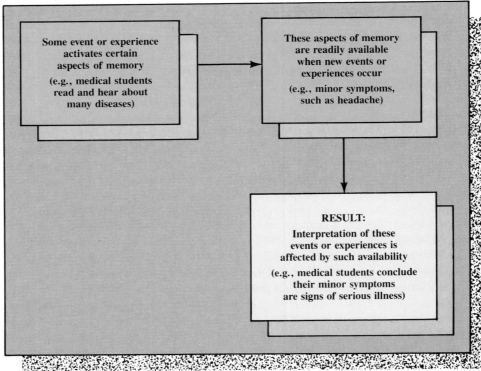

Priming: An Overview

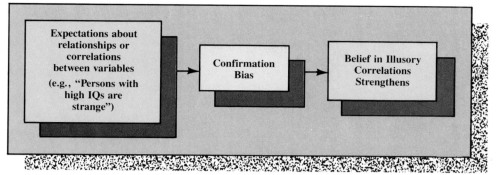

FIGURE 15-7. Once we believe that a correlation exists between two variables, we tend to notice or seek out information consistent with such beliefs, even if they are not correct. The result: our confidence in the existence of such *illusory correlations* grows stronger.

Illusory correlations seem to occur because our expectations about certain events or characteristics distort the ways in which we process information about them. In other words, once we believe that extremely high intelligence is related to madness, or that members of a minority group possess certain negative traits, we tend to seek out, notice, and remember information that supports our belief, a tendency known as the *confirmation bias*. The result: belief in nonexistent correlations grows stronger, even without real evidence (refer to Figure 15-7). Clearly, this type of distortion in social cognition can prove costly.

Heuristics, Biases, and Errors: Some Words of Encouragement. Looking back, our comments about social cognition seem to paint a discouraging picture. In our efforts to make sense out of the social world—to understand the persons and events around us—we use many mental short-cuts. And these, it appears, can lead us into serious error. While this is certainly true in some instances, growing evidence permits us to conclude on a much more positive note. First, while the tendencies we've described do sometimes result in false conclusions and erroneous judgments, this seems to be the *exception,* not the rule. More typically, our mental short-cuts allow us ''to have our cake and eat it too''—to process more information than we could otherwise handle in an efficient and generally accurate manner. In this sense, biases in social thought may not constitute errors at all—just useful working compromises we adopt in the face of persistent *information overload* (Funder, 1987).

Second, the impact of such tendencies can be readily overcome in many cases. For example, when individuals are asked to imagine views opposite their own, the false consensus effect decreases sharply. In short, just considering the fact that others may hold views quite different from ours is sufficient to overcome this otherwise powerful effect (Goethals, 1986). Such findings suggest that errors in social cognition are not the result of faults or weaknesses in our information-processing abilities. Rather, they may often be the result of our functioning on ''automatic pilot.'' When we halt the rapid flow of social thought and consider matters carefully, the potential sources of error tend to disappear. In short, thinking about others is a difficult task, but it is one we *can* accomplish successfully.

Social Behavior: Interacting with Others

Thinking about others is an important activity, but it represents only one aspect of our total social experience. In addition, we also *interact* with the persons around us in many different ways. Such *social behavior* ranges from cooperation and mutual approval through conflict and open hostility (Baron & Byrne, 1987). Since we can't possibly consider all forms of interpersonal behavior here, we'll focus on two that seem especially important: social influence (including persuasion, conformity, and compliance) and attraction and love.

Social Influence: One Interesting Tactic

FIGURE 15-8. As shown here, individuals attempt to influence others in many different ways. *(Source: King Features Syndicate, 1981.)*

Social Influence: Changing Others' Attitudes and Behavior

Have you ever had the following daydream? One morning you wake up with a special skill or power—one that permits you to control all the people you meet. Through this power, you can get them to do, think, or feel anything you wish. This is an enticing fantasy and for good reason: if you possessed such a power, you could satisfy your every wish instantly, with little or no effort.

Fortunately (or unfortunately!), such powers do not exist. Bending others totally to our will must remain only a daydream. This does not mean that we cannot affect other people at all, however. On the contrary, several techniques do exist for exerting **social influence**—for changing others' behavior, attitudes, or feelings. As suggested by Figure 15-8, these take many different (and sometimes unexpected) forms. Some of the most important, and successful, are considered below (Cialdini, 1985).

Attitudes and Attitude Change: The Process of Persuasion. Television commercials, paid political announcements, giant billboards, mailings from charitable organizations: what do these seemingly disparate items have in common? In a word, *persuasion*—all are designed to change our reactions with respect to specific targets (products, candidates, charities) and in this way to alter our overt behavior as well (refer to Figure 15-9).

FIGURE 15-9. Each day, we are exposed to many forms of *persuasion*—efforts to change our attitudes in some way.

Persuasion: Big Business in the 1980s

Purchasing the advertised products, voting for the candidates, contributing to certain charities—these are the actions desired by those who pay for these efforts to persuade us.

The reactions such tactics hope to change are generally termed **attitudes.** These are our lasting, general evaluations of people, objects or issues—in a sense, our cognitive reactions to virtually any aspect of the social world around us (Petty & Cacioppo, 1986). While attitudes certainly involve an evaluative dimension (feelings of liking or disliking for specific objects, events, or people), they also include two other aspects as well. First, they generally involve a cognitive component—various *beliefs* about the attitude object. (For example, you may like pizza and believe that it is nutritious but also fattening.) Second, attitudes involve a behavioral component—intentions to act in certain ways relative to the items or persons involved. (For example, you may dislike a political candidate and decide to vote for his opponent mainly for this reason.)

How are attitudes acquired? Partly from others, who either model certain views, or reinforce us for expressing attitudes similar to their own (or punish us for attitudes different from theirs). Parents, teachers, friends, and associates all play a role in this process. In addition, attitudes are acquired directly, from experience with various aspects of the social world (Fazio, Lenn, & Effrein, 1984). Thus, we learn from direct experience that we don't like the taste of certain foods, do like certain types of music, and positively hate getting stuck in traffic during rush hour.

The Process of Persuasion: Some Major Findings.   Regardless of the nature of attitudes or the way they are formed, one fact is clear: the business of changing them is a big one in the late twentieth century. Many companies spend more on advertising various products than they do on manufacturing them. Similarly, the huge cost of political campaigns (at least in the United States) now means that raising large sums is a necessity for anyone seeking public office. Given the practical importance of changing attitudes, a great deal of attention has been directed to this issue. Such research has continued for several decades, so we can't possibly summarize its many (often complex) conclusions here. We can, however, mention a few of the factors that seem to play a key role in the success or failure of efforts at persuasion.

First, *experts* are generally much more persuasive (more successful in changing attitudes) than nonexperts (Hovland & Weiss, 1952). Arguments delivered by someone with established expertise in a given area carry more weight than identical arguments presented by someone lacking in such expertise. Second, *intentions* of the would-be persuader are important. Individuals are more likely to change their attitudes in response to appeals from persons who seem to have no ''axe to grind'' than from ones who stand to profit from such shifts. For example, you would probably be influenced to a greater degree by an appeal for energy conservation from an electric company, which stands to lose profits from efforts at conservation, than from a company that manufactures home insulation and other energy-saving products. Third, and contrary to popular belief, persuaders who speak rapidly are usually more successful in changing attitudes than ones who speak more slowly (Miller et al., 1976). This apparently stems from the fact that we view fast-talkers as more knowledgeable and more deeply committed to their views than slow-talkers. Fourth, it is sometimes possible to frighten people into changing their attitudes: messages designed to induce fear or anxiety in the persons who hear them can often be effective in changing attitudes—more effective than messages that are more neutral in content (refer to Figure 15-10 on page 480). However, this is only the case if the level of fear induced is not extreme. When exposed to truly frightening appeals, individuals seem to shut them out by rejecting the message as unbelievable and extreme (Mewborn & Rogers, 1979).

We could go on and on with this list, for many different factors seem to affect the process of persuasion. Instead, though, we'd like to note that recently, research on this process has taken a somewhat different path. Rather than asking, ''What kinds of messages produce the most attitude change?'' (a very practical issue), recent studies have focused on the question, ''What cognitive processes determine whether someone is or is not persuaded?'' In other words, efforts have been made to tie the process of persuasion more closely to what we know about human cognition generally, and to social cognition in particular.

Changing Attitudes Through Fear

Lady Killer

Smoking is deadly. For help in quitting, please call us.

AMERICAN
CANCER
SOCIETY

FIGURE 15-10. Persuasive appeals that induce fear among recipients can be effective in changing attitudes as long as they are not too extreme in content.

One intriguing finding which has emerged from such research is this: there seem to be two distinct ways in which persuasion or attitude change occurs (Petty & Cacioppo, 1985). In the first, we think about the arguments presented in a careful, rational manner. They remain at the center of our attention, and we are persuaded because, logically, they make sense. This is known as the *central route* to persuasion. In the second, *peripheral route,* we do not give the arguments presented our full attention. Rather, we are distracted by other events, or perhaps by thoughts about the style or appearance of the would-be persuader. Here, persuasion occurs in a kind of automatic manner. If you have ever accepted the views presented by another person merely because you liked him or her, or you believed that this person had much more expertise than you, you are familiar with this less direct process. (Please see Figure 15-11 for a comparison of these two routes to persuasion.)

The practical message for would-be persuaders in these findings is as follows: if you have strong, logical arguments for the views you are recommending or the products you wish to sell, then concentrate on these. If you don't, then by all means distract your audience so that they focus on other matters. In both cases, you'll maximize the degree of attitude change you produce.

Changing Our Own Attitudes: The Role of Cognitive Dissonance. Suppose that as the time of graduation approaches, you receive two job offers. After much agonizing, you select one. After you do, will your attitudes toward the two companies change? If you are like most people, they may. After you accept one of the two jobs, you may find your evaluation of this position, and the company that offered it, improving: the job now seems better than it did initially, before you reached your decision. Conversely, you may find your attitude toward the job you rejected becoming less favorable. The same process occurs after other kinds of decisions, too. Whether we choose among cars, schools, or lovers, we often experience a positive shift in our attitude toward the chosen alternative, and a negative shift in our attitudes toward the others. Why? The answer seems to lie in a process known as **cognitive dissonance** (Festinger, 1957).

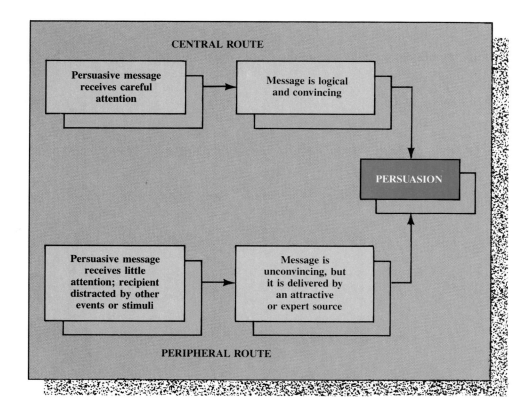

CENTRAL ROUTE

Persuasive message receives careful attention

Message is logical and convincing

PERSUASION

Persuasive message receives little attention; recipient distracted by other events or stimuli

Message is unconvincing, but it is delivered by an attractive or expert source

PERIPHERAL ROUTE

Persuasion: Two Possible Mechanisms

FIGURE 15-11. Persuasion can occur through two distinct processes. In the first (*central* route), it is based on careful attention to logical and convincing messages. In the second (*peripheral* route), it occurs in a seemingly automatic manner because individuals are distracted by other stimuli (e.g., the appearance or expertise of the source). (*Based on suggestions by Petty & Cacioppo, 1985.*)

In one sense, dissonance refers to the fact that human beings dislike inconsistency. When we say one thing but do another, or we discover that one attitude we hold is inconsistent with another that we also accept, an unpleasant state of *dissonance* arises. We notice the inconsistency between our words and deeds, or among our various attitudes, and we react negatively to this inconsistency. As the above examples suggest, dissonance is also generated by many decisions. When we choose one alternative, we must necessarily forego the benefits of the others. The result: post-decision dissonance.

Many factors determine the magnitude of dissonance and the precise ways in which we choose to reduce it (Baumeister & Tice, 1984). Since it is usually easier to change our attitudes than our overt behavior, however, cognitive dissonance often leads to attitude change. We've already noted how this occurs following decisions: chosen alternatives are enhanced, while rejected ones are derogated. In other cases we may change our attitudes to bring them into line with our overt actions, or alter one attitude to make it more consistent with others. For example, suppose that you believe strongly in affirmative action (special efforts to hire and promote members of minority groups who have previously been victimized by discrimination). Simultaneously, you also believe in promotion on the basis of merit. No problems arise until one day a person from a minority group is promoted over one of your close friends, despite the fact that your friend has more experience and seems better qualified in several ways. Confronted with this situation, you experience dissonance: your two attitudes seem inconsistent. What will happen? There is a good chance that one or the other attitude will shift; you may become less favorable toward affirmative action or less supportive of promotions by merit (please see Figure 15-12 on page 482).

Because it is an unpleasant state most persons wish to reduce, dissonance can be an important entering wedge for persuasion (Croyle & Cooper, 1983). If would-be persuaders can place individuals in a situation where they will experience dissonance unless they alter their attitudes (or their behavior) in the direction desired, considerable success can be obtained. Such tactics are actually used in many contexts, but perhaps their most dramatic application occurs in some *cults*—religious groups whose members hold views

Cognitive Dissonance: A Source of Attitude Change

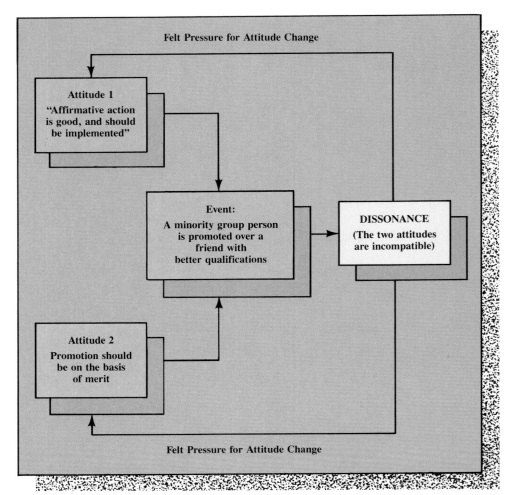

FIGURE 15-12. When individuals find that two attitudes that they hold are inconsistent, an unpleasant state of *cognitive dissonance* results. As a result, it is likely that one (or perhaps both) of the attitudes will change.

quite different from those of most other people in their society. Cults often require severe initiations from their new members. While this may be used partly to weed out those lacking in conviction, it is also an effective means for strengthening acceptance of the cult's views and positive attitudes toward it. Once an individual has passed through a painful initiation, any doubts about the cult may generate considerable dissonance: after all, such reactions are inconsistent with the individual's knowledge that he or she has suffered to join it (Baumeister, 1986). So, in sum, the induction of dissonance can be a powerful tactic of persuasion. In fact, under the right conditions, persons experiencing dissonance become virtual allies of the persuader: they generate internal pressures to change their own attitudes!

Conformity: Going Along with the Group.   Have you ever been in a situation where you felt that you stuck out like a sore thumb? If so, you know how unpleasant such experiences can be. In these situations we experience powerful pressures to get ''back in line'' and act or think like the others around us. Such forces toward **conformity**—behaving or thinking like most other persons—stem from a multitude of rules or *norms* about how we are supposed to behave in certain situations. Some, such as the rules governing athletic contests, government constitutions, and traffic regulations, are explicit: they are written down for all to see or read. Others are implicit, such as ''Don't stare at others'' and ''Never come to parties exactly on time,'' yet they still exert powerful effects on behavior. Whatever form they take, social norms are obeyed by most persons most of the time. Is this necessarily bad? Not at all: if most people didn't follow such rules on most occasions, we'd live in total chaos. Crowds outside movie theaters and sports arenas would fail to form lines; motorists would drive wherever and however they pleased—this would greatly endanger life and limb. And employees would show up for work any time they chose. Obviously, norms, and the conformity they produce, are a necessary part of social life. Only when they enforce uniformity in situations where this seems unnecessary are norms objectionable and open to serious question.

Factors Affecting Conformity: Number, Support, and Gender.   We have already noted that most people conform most of the time. This fact was first called to the attention of psychologists several decades ago by Solomon Asch (1951). He asked subjects to respond to a series of simple perceptual problems, such as the one in Figure 15-13. Unknown to each participant, all of the other persons present were accomplices, instructed to give wrong answers. For example, the accomplices reported that line *A*, instead of line *B*, matched the standard. A subject would state a choice after hearing the false judgments of the others. What should the subject do? Follow the evidence of his or her own senses or go along with the opinions of others? Sadly—but not surprisingly—most subjects chose to conform and gave the false answers (please refer to Figure 15-13). They did not yield in this fashion on all occasions, though. Sometimes, they stuck to their guns and gave the correct choice. This finding points to an important fact: while most people conform most of the time, they don't always do so. What factors determine whether conformity occurs? Several play a role.

First, as you might guess, the more persons around us who obey a specific norm, and so exert implicit influence on us to conform, the greater our tendency to "go along." Interestingly, though, this seems to be true only up to a point. Beyond three or four influencing persons, individuals begin to suspect collusion—they assume that the persons

FIGURE 15-13. When subjects heard other people (actually accomplices) give wrong answers to problems such as the one on the left, many went along with these persons and also gave incorrect answers (graph on the right). *(Source: Based on materials and findings reported by Asch, 1951.)*

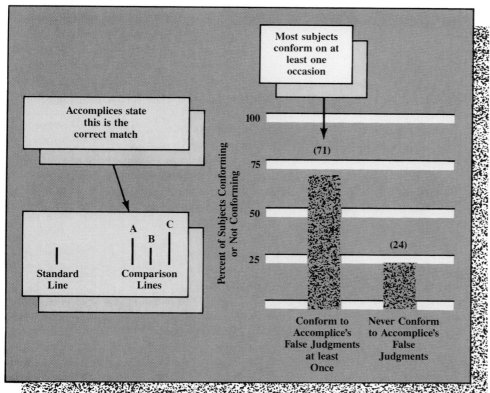

involved have joined forces to affect them (Wilder, 1977). Then, they may "dig in their heels" and resist.

Second, conformity is often reduced by support from others—from allies who also depart in some manner from expected or standard patterns of behavior (Morris, Miller, & Spangenberg, 1977). Knowing that one is not alone greatly lessens pressures to conform. This is one reason why small but deeply committed minorities in a group or society can sometimes succeed in changing the views of an initially overwhelming majority. In a sense, they turn the tables on conformity and change existing norms rather than adhere to them (Moscovici, 1985). A good illustration of such effects is provided by the success of the environmental movement during the 1970s. An initially small group of activists gradually changed the attitude of entire societies about the dangers of uncontrolled pollution.

A third factor once assumed to play a key role in conformity is gender. Early research indicated that females are more susceptible to this form of influence than males (Crutchfield, 1955). More recent findings, though, have failed to confirm such results (Sistrunk & McDavid, 1971). Why this difference? One possibility has been suggested by Eagly and her colleagues (Eagly & Wood, 1982; Steffen & Eagly, 1985). They note that differences between males and females with respect to conformity may actually reflect differences in status between the sexes—*not* differences in their susceptibility to social influence. In the past, females generally had lower status in society than males. Little wonder, then, that they were found to show greater conformity. As this pattern has changed, apparent differences between males and females in this respect have decreased until they now seem nonexistent (see Figure 15-14). Whatever the precise explanation, it

FIGURE 15-14. Early studies indicated that females show higher levels of conformity than males. More recent research has failed to observe such differences. This probably reflects the fact that females and males are now much more equal in overall social status.

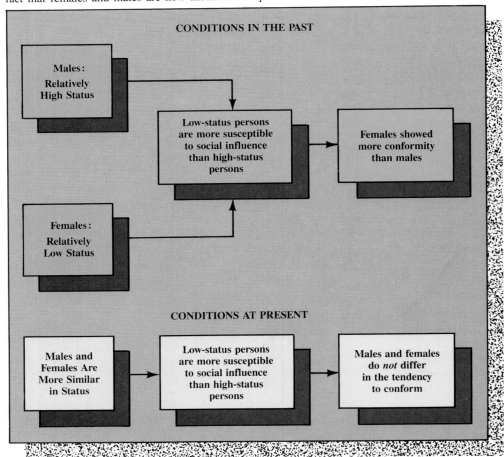

cathy®   **by Cathy Guisewite**

FIGURE 15-15. As Cathy's boss has just discovered, praise, flattery, and related techniques of *ingratiation* can succeed—unless they are overdone! *(Source: Universal Press Syndicate, 1985.)*

The Limits of Ingratiation

now seems safe to conclude that gender alone is *not* an important determinant of conformity. Males and females seem about equal in their tendency to go along with the group.

Compliance: To Ask Is (Sometimes) to Receive.   How can we get others to do what we want—to say "yes" to various requests? We face this practical question over and over again in daily life. While no single method seems assured of success in this regard, several do seem helpful in tipping the odds in our favor.

Ingratiation: Liking as a Key to Compliance.   One effective way of inducing others to say "yes" is by somehow getting them to like us. This is the basis of **ingratiation,** an extremely common tactic for gaining compliance. How do individuals attempt to induce positive feelings or reactions in others? The list of specific tactics is a long one. Flattery—undeserved praise or compliments—is one common technique. As long as it is not overdone (not recognized as false by the recipients), it seems to be effective (Cialdini, 1985). (Please see Figure 15-15.) Agreeing with target persons, or expressing similarity to them, is another. As we'll see in the next section, we usually like persons who agree with us more than ones who don't. Other techniques include showing interest in the target persons, giving them gifts, getting them to talk about themselves, offering them help, and showing friendliness and positive reactions to them (e.g., smiling, maintaining a high level of eye-contact). When blended in a skillful manner, such tactics really do work: they induce positive reactions on the part of the persons who receive them and so increase the likelihood that they'll comply with requests from the ingratiator (Godfrey, Jones, & Lord, 1986).

Multiple Requests: The "Foot-in-the-Door" and the "Door-in-the-Face."   The phone rings. When you answer, a woman indicates that she is conducting a survey and asks if you'll reply to a few simple questions. You agree, and she asks you three brief questions about your home and background. Then she moves on to the real purpose of the call: a larger request (e.g., will you purchase some product, subscribe to some magazine). If you say "yes," you may be the victim of another common tactic for gaining compliance: the **foot-in-the-door** approach. This refers to the strategy of beginning with a relatively small request and, once this is accepted, escalating to a larger one.

While common sense seems to suggest that such efforts are transparent and will fail, they actually succeed in many cases. For example, in one well-known demonstration of this effect, homemakers were called by phone and asked to answer a few questions about the kind of soap they used at home; almost all agreed to be interviewed. A few days later the same person called again and made a much larger request: would the homemakers allow a crew of five or six persons to visit their home and make a full inventory of all products on hand? Subjects in a control (one-contact) condition were called only once and were presented with the large request "cold." Results were dramatic: while only about 20 percent of those in the control group agreed, more than 50 percent of those in the two-contact "foot-in-the-door" group consented (Freedman & Fraser, 1966). While the effect has not been as strong in many later studies, it has usually been confirmed: the foot-in-the-door tactic does often work.

What is the secret of its success? Growing evidence points to the following mechanism. After agreeing to a small request, individuals experience subtle shifts in self-perception. They come to see themselves, more than before, as *helpful*—as the kind of person who does favors for others when requested. In order to be consistent with such self-perceptions, they then feel compelled to consent to the second, larger request (DeJong & Musilli, 1982). Support for this interpretation is provided by the results of a study conducted by Eisenberg and her colleagues (Eisenberg et al., 1987).

In this study, children in three age groups—five to six, seven to eight, and ten to eleven—were exposed to the foot-in-the-door procedure. Since youngsters below about the age of seven do not have a clear grasp of the nature of lasting traits and don't seem concerned with being consistent, it was predicted that the foot-in-the-door tactic would have little impact upon them. Thus, it was hypothesized that this tactic for gaining compliance would succeed only with the two older groups. In order to test this prediction, all subjects first worked on a task requiring them to judge which of two sounds in several pairs was louder. They were then given two prize coupons for their performance. At this point, children in the foot-in-the-door condition were asked to donate one of their coupons to poor children who had no prizes. To assure that all agreed, the experimenter repeated this request several times. Subjects in the control group were never asked to make such donations.

In a second phase, both groups of youngsters were given a choice between playing with attractive toys or helping sick children in a hospital by working on a dull task (sorting papers). It was predicted that among the two older groups subjects exposed to the previous request (those in the foot-in-the-door condition) would sort more papers for the sick children than those in the control group. As you can see from Figure 15-16, this was actually the case. In addition, it was found that in the two older groups the stronger subjects' expressed desire to be consistent, the more they helped.

FIGURE 15-16. Children older than age seven are concerned about being consistent. Thus, they are susceptible to the foot-in-the-door effect. Children of five or six, however, show little concern with being consistent and therefore are not readily affected by this tactic. *(Source: Based on data from Eisenberg et al., 1987.)*

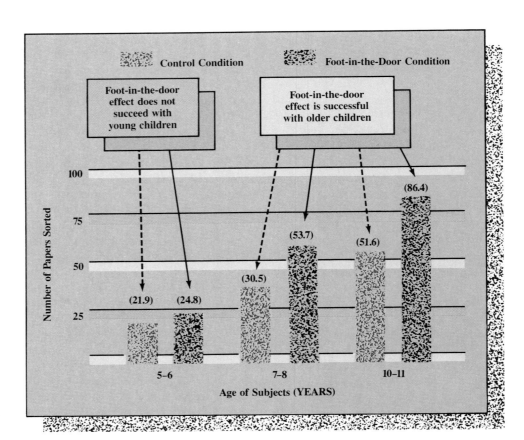

Age, Concern with Being Consistent, and the Foot-in-the-Door Effect

Of course, children change in many ways as they grow older, so it is impossible to be certain that these differences stem from shifts in concern over being consistent. However, these results certainly fit with the view that the success of the foot-in-the-door technique derives, at least in part, from shifts in self-perception. In a sense, then, this tactic may succeed because target persons *help* it succeed: internal pressures to be consistent and maintain their image of helpfulness combine to make them say ''yes.''

While the foot-in-the-door tactic is often effective, so, too, is an opposite approach: beginning with a large request and then, when this is rejected, retreating to a smaller one. This strategy, known as the **door-in-the-face,** seems to work for somewhat different reasons (Cialdini, 1985). When persons reduce the size of their request, this puts pressure on the recipient to make similar concessions. After all, the requester has retreated; now it's the recipient's turn to do so, too! The result: people may become more willing to comply with the second, smaller request, which just happens to be the one the requester wanted all along.

Multiple Requests: A Note of Caution.   Before you rush right out and begin using these two tactics on your friends, relatives, and anyone else you encounter, please consider the following facts. First, neither is likely to succeed if the target persons recognize them for what they are: techniques for exerting social influence. Second, both have specific limitations. The foot-in-the-door is more effective if considerable time has elapsed between the first and second request, while the door-in-the-face usually succeeds only if the second request follows the first almost at once (Cialdini, 1985). Third, both require considerable fine-tuning of the requests employed. If the second request is too large, in the case of the foot-in-the-door tactic, or if the first seems outlandish, in the door-in-the-face procedure, *less* rather than more compliance may result (Schwarzwald, Raz, & Zvibel, 1979).

Finally, both tactics, like all other techniques for attaining compliance, raise important ethical issues. Is it right to manipulate others in such a way that they agree to requests they'd normally refuse? Only *you* can decide whether, and to what extent, this is the case. At the very least, though, you should think carefully about such questions. (Just how powerful can social influence be? For some unsettling evidence on this issue, please see the ''Classic Contributions'' section below.)

FOCUS ON RESEARCH: Classic Contributions

Obedience: Social Influence by Demand

Would you harm an innocent victim—someone who had never harmed you—simply because you were ordered to do so? And would you do this even if the person who commanded such actions had no real authority to do so? Your immediate answers are probably "No!" and "Of course not!" Unfortunately, such conclusions are not supported by the results of relevant research (Bushman, 1984). On the contrary, it appears that under some conditions many or most individuals can readily be induced by orders from a source of authority to engage in actions they would otherwise never choose. This fact was first uncovered by Stanley Milgram (1963, 1974) in a series of studies that

are now among the best known in psychology.

In his research, Milgram told subjects that they were taking part in a study of the effects of punishment on learning. Their task was that of delivering an electric shock to another person (actually an accomplice) each time he made an error in a simple learning task. The shocks were to be delivered by switches on the apparatus shown in Figure 15-17 on page 488, and the subject was told that each time the learner made an error, the next higher switch was to be used. The first switch was labeled as delivering a shock of 15 volts, while the last one was labeled as delivering 450 volts. During the session the learner (accomplice) made many errors. Thus, the subject soon faced a painful dilemma: should he or she continue to

Studying Obedience: Milgram's Technique

FIGURE 15-17. The photo on the left shows the equipment used by Milgram in his famous studies of obedience. The photo on the right shows the experimenter (wearing a lab coat) and a subject attaching the shock electrodes to the learner's wrists (this person was actually an accomplice who never received any shocks). *(Source: From the film* Obedience, *distributed by the New York University Film Library.)*

punish this person with what seemed to be painful and dangerous shocks? Or should he or she refuse to go on? The experimenter urged the subject to continue, uttering such remarks as "Please go on," and "It is absolutely essential that you continue." Since subjects were volunteers, and they had been paid prior to the study, you might predict that they would resist these orders. In fact, fully *65 percent showed total obedience*, continuing right to the final 450-volt shock. *(Please note: no shocks were ever delivered to the accomplice; subjects were simply led to believe that shocks were being administered.)* Of course, many persons protested and asked that the session be ended. When ordered to proceed, however, a majority yielded to social pressure and continued to obey.

In further studies Milgram (1965, 1974) found that similar results could be obtained even under conditions that might be expected to reduce **obedience.** For example, when the study was moved from its original location at Yale University to a run-down office building in a nearby city, subjects level of obedience was virtually unchanged. Similarly, a large proportion continued to obey even when the accomplice groaned and complained about the pain he was experiencing and begged to be released. Perhaps most surprising, fully 30 percent continued to obey even when this required them to force the victim's hand down upon the shock plate! Similar results have been reported in several different countries (Jordan, Germany, Australia), so they appear to be alarmingly general in scope (Shanab & Yahya, 1977).

What accounts for such findings, and for parallel events outside the laboratory, in which armed police or military follow orders to fire upon unarmed civilians? Several factors seem to play a role. First, in Milgram's research—and in many real-life tragedies—the persons in authority relieve those who obey of all responsibility for their own actions. (Milgram's subjects were explicitly told that no harm would befall the learner, and that the experimenter would assume all responsibility for his welfare.) This may greatly reduce internal restraints against performing harmful actions. Second, obedience is often demanded in a gradual manner. Initial requests are small; only later do they increase to the point where they involve dangerous or harmful actions. In a sense, therefore, the foot-in-the-door effect, as well as pressures to be consistent with one's own past actions, plays a role. Third, persons wishing to resist face a difficult decision: just where should they draw the line? Since the process often moves quickly, they have little time to reflect on such matters.

For these and other reasons, demands from sources of authority are often difficult to resist. This doesn't mean that they are all-powerful, however. Some evidence suggests that this type of social influence *can* be overcome (1) if individuals realize that they *will* be held morally responsible for their own actions; (2) if they witness others refusing to obey; and (3) if they question the wisdom, power, or motives of those in authority (Cialdini, 1985; Powers & Geen, 1972). Even then, the task is a difficult one. Thus, here, as in many other cases, *prevention* seems to be the byword: the best protection from the potentially harmful effects of obedience is assuring that persons in positions of authority are ones who will not abuse it.

Attraction and Love

"Love makes the world go 'round," an old song contends. While you may never have heard these lyrics, we doubt that you'll object to their message: **love** (intense positive feelings between individuals) exerts a profound impact upon society. Social psychologists agree. In fact, their research suggests that even much weaker positive or negative reactions toward others can strongly affect social relationships (Berscheid, 1985; Duck, 1986). What are the causes of feelings of liking or disliking? And what is the nature of love itself? It is on these questions that we'll focus next.

Interpersonal Attraction: Some Major Causes. Pause for a moment, and think of three different persons: someone you like very much, someone you dislike quite strongly, and someone you'd place in the middle on this dimension. What factors contribute to such feelings—to high, moderate, or low interpersonal attraction? As we'll now see, many play a role.

Propinquity: Nearness Makes the Heart Grow Fonder. The first, and in some ways most basic, of these factors is *propinquity*—the physical distance between individuals. Many studies indicate that people are generally much more likely to form friendships and even romantic relationships with persons living nearby than with persons living farther away (Ebbesen, Kjos, & Konecni, 1976; Festinger, Schachter, & Back, 1950). Why is this the case? The answer seems to involve increased frequency of contact. All other factors being equal, the more often we are exposed to almost any stimulus—people included—the more we tend to like it (Moreland & Zajonc, 1982). Propinquity increases contact with specific persons, so liking for them increases. We should hasten to add that this is true only if these individuals do not act in ways that irritate or annoy us; repeated contact with someone who behaves unpleasantly can *reduce* rather than enhance interpersonal attraction. In most cases, though, familiarity seems to breed attraction—*not* contempt, as the old saying suggests (Dixit, 1985). It is partly for this reason that many life-long friendships and romances begin when two persons are assigned to the same dormitory or even to nearby seats in class (see Figure 15-18).

FIGURE 15-18. Frequent contact with another person, even if this occurs at first by chance, is often the basis for friendship or romance.

Propinquity and Attraction:
Repeated Contact as a Basis
for Liking

Similarity: An Important Basis for Attraction

"*We had a hunch they'd be perfect for each other.*"

FIGURE 15-19. The more similar individuals are in attitudes, values, interests, or personality, the more they tend to like one another. (*Source:* The New Yorker.)

Similarity: Liking Others Who Resemble Ourselves. At some point, you've probably heard both of the following adages: birds of a feather flock together; opposites attract. Which is true? Do we like others who resemble ourselves, or others who are quite different—perhaps opposite? A large amount of evidence, gathered over several decades and in many different countries, leaves little room for doubt: in general, the more similar others are to us in several respects (e.g., their attitudes and beliefs, personality traits, values), the more we tend to like them (Byrne, 1971; Byrne, Clore, & Smeaton, 1986). (See Figure 15-19 for an amusing illustration of this fact.)

The powerful effect of similarity on attraction has been observed in many studies employing the following strategy. Subjects are provided with information about a stranger which suggests that this person either shares or does not share their attitudes to varying degrees. (For example, some subjects learn that the stranger shares almost all of their views, others that she or he shares about half, and so on.) Results are generally clear: the greater the degree of similarity between subjects and the stranger, the more they report liking this person (Byrne, 1971). One final point: some recent findings (Rosenbaum, 1986) suggest that dissimilarity may play a stronger role in repulsion than similarity does in initial attraction. In other words, in choosing friends and associates, the process may go something like this. First, we eliminate all persons who are quite dissimilar to ourselves. Then among those remaining we concentrate on the ones who are most similar to us (Byrne, Clore, & Smeaton, 1986). Whether or not the acquaintance process actually proceeds in this fashion, however, it is clear that similarity often plays an important role in interpersonal attraction.

Physical Attractiveness: Is Beauty only Skin Deep? On the basis of television commercials and ads in magazines, one could easily conclude that physical beauty is an obsession in modern society. Cosmetics, perfumes and other grooming aids, new fashions, diet soft drinks—all are promoted as means for enhancing one's physical appeal. The implication, of course, is that once physical beauty is attained, many benefits—including enhanced appeal to the opposite sex—will follow. Does physical attractiveness actually yield such effects? Systematic research on this topic suggests that it generally does.

First, physically attractive persons are indeed more popular and more sought after as dates than ones who are less attractive (Hatfield & Sprecher, 1986). Second, they are assumed to be higher in various positive traits (e.g., social poise, charm, intelligence) than unattractive persons (Hatfield & Walster, 1985). (At the same time, though, they are also perceived as being higher on several *undesirable* traits such as conceit and insincerity.) Third, physically attractive persons are often viewed more favorably even in situations where their physical charms seem irrelevant. For example, they tend to receive higher ratings in job interviews and are more likely to be hired than relatively unattractive

FIGURE 15-20. As shown here, what is considered to be physically attractive varies greatly from culture to culture and from one time to another.

Physical Attractiveness: Very Much in the Eye of the Beholder

persons (Baron, 1986b; Cash, 1985). Finally, and perhaps most surprising of all, physically attractive individuals actually seem to experience greater success in their careers than unattractive ones (Dickey-Bryant, Lautenschlager, & Mendoza, 1986). Given such results, it is little wonder that millions of copies of books indicating how to dress and groom for success are sold each year.

By now, you're probably convinced that physical attractiveness is indeed one powerful source of interpersonal attraction. But what precisely is it? What specific characteristics lead us to view other persons as attractive or unattractive? This has proven to be a difficult question to answer, partly because what is considered attractive varies greatly from culture to culture and over time (refer to Figure 15-20) and because individuals, too, differ greatly in what they find attractive. However, some systematic findings have begun to emerge.

With respect to facial features, we have already noted (in Chapter 8) that the retention of certain aspects of a "baby face" (e.g., a high forehead, large eyes) by females is generally viewed as attractive by males (Berry & McArthur, 1987). The opposite is true when females judge males: they generally find such features unappealing. Turning to other aspects of physical appearance, the results of a study conducted by Franzoi and Herzog (1987) are informative. These researchers asked male and female students to rate the importance of various parts of the body (and other aspects of physical appearance) in determining the attractiveness of members of the opposite sex. Results indicated that men and women generally rated the same items as being most important. These included body build, chest or breasts, legs, appearance of eyes, buttocks, hips, and overall figure or physique. However, as shown in Figure 15-21 on page 492, some interesting differences between the sexes did emerge. Men viewed women's sex drive and sexual activities as important aspects of physical attractiveness, while females did not share such reactions. And females rated health and physical stamina as more important aspects of attractiveness than did males.

In sum, many aspects of physical appearance seem to contribute to judgments of attractiveness. When the range of such features, differences between males and females, and differences among individuals are taken into account, it is hardly surprising that no simple formula for physical beauty can be derived. Attractiveness is simply too much in the eye of the beholder for there to be a single, ideal pattern.

Love: The Most Intimate Emotion.   Love: it is the subject of countless songs, poems, and novels and has been pondered for thousands of years by thoughtful persons without number. Can psychology add anything to this vast store of informal knowledge? While some skeptics have questioned this possibility, they appear to be wrong. Through systematic (and often ingenious!) research, social psychologists have uncovered much about this fascinating topic. Here we'll focus primarily on two aspects of their work: the nature of love—just what is it?—and its role in long-term relationships. (Please note: our comments will be concerned primarily with *romantic* or *passionate* love. Other types of love certainly exist, but they have received somewhat less attention in recent studies.)

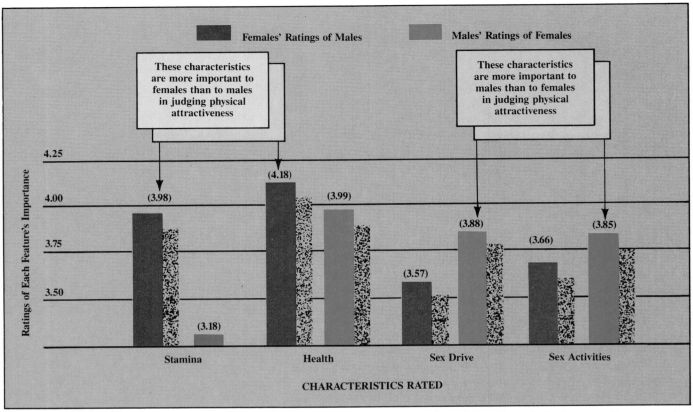

Females' Ratings of Males   Males' Ratings of Females

These characteristics are more important to females than to males in judging physical attractiveness

These characteristics are more important to males than to females in judging physical attractiveness

FIGURE 15-21. Men and women generally base their ratings of physical attractiveness on similar parts of the body. However, men view sex drive and sexual activities as more important in judging the attractiveness of women, and women view health and stamina as more important in judging the attractiveness of men. *(Source: Based on data from Franzoi & Herzog, 1987.)*

Physical Attractiveness: How Males and Females Judge It

The Nature of Love: A Psychological Perspective. One way of determining the nature of love is to ask, "What conditions are necessary before individuals say "I'm in love"? Research on this process indicates that three conditions are required before people reach this conclusion (Hatfield & Walster, 1985). First, the persons involved must experience strong emotional arousal; love, after all, is a very "hot" emotional state. Second, they must experience such feelings in the presence of an appropriate love object—someone defined by their culture as a suitable object of such love. (For example, in most Western countries, this would be a member of the opposite sex of about one's own age.) Third, the notion of romantic love must be present in the individual's culture. (Actually, the idea of romantic love is fairly new. It did not arise in Europe until the Middle Ages and is still unfamiliar in many places even today.) In sum, individuals seem to conclude that they are in love only when certain conditions are met. If one or more of these elements is missing, an individual might experience strong emotions but would probably *not* label such feelings as love.

Now let's take our examination of love one step further. Assuming people report being in love, what, precisely, will they experience? While love obviously means different things to different people, a theory proposed by Sternberg (1986b) suggests that for most persons three components will be central. First, persons in love experience *intimacy*—feelings of closeness to their lover. Second, they feel *passion*—physical attraction to their lover and the desire for sexual union with him or her. Third, they experience *decision* and *commitment*—recognition of the fact that they are in love and a desire to maintain that love.

The three components just described can exist in different patterns and to different degrees. According to Sternberg, such variations yield different types of love, or at least different experiences of it. For example, if only the intimacy component is present, the experience is one of *liking*. If only passion is present (without intimacy or commitment), we are dealing with *infatuation*. If intimacy and commitment exist, but passion is absent, individuals experience *companionate love*—the kind often seen in happy couples who have been married for many years. If both passion and commitment exist but intimacy is lacking, the pattern is described by Sternberg as *fatuous love,* in which one person worships another from afar. Only if all three components are present does *consummate love*— the fullest form of romantic attachment—exist. (Please see Figure 15-22 for a summary of these suggestions.)

The Course of Love: How It Changes over Time.   Romantic novels and old movies often end with the hero and heroine riding off into a blissful future in which their love will remain bright and unchanged forever. Unfortunately, real life often fails to live up to this picture. People fall *out* of love as well into it. Why? What accounts for relationships that begin in a burst of joyful emotion and end in bitterness and anger, or at least boredom? Sternberg's theory offers one possibility. It suggests that over time the passion component of love generally decreases. This is hardly surprising; most persons know that such strong feelings simmer down over time. More surprising is the possibility that intimacy, too, sometimes decreases. Over the years, many couples stop communicating with one another, since they feel that ''they've said it all already.'' Further, they may be pulled by different careers into different patterns of experience, and each may come to feel there is little to discuss with their mate. If the third component—the couple's decision that they are still in love and are committed to maintaining their relationship—does not increase, the result may be a gradual erosion of love and a deterioration of their relationship.

These suggestions are supported by research on the course of actual romantic relationships. Over time, many couples (especially ones who have divorced or are considering this action) report that they talk less and less about their positive feelings for one

FIGURE 15-22. According to a theory proposed by Sternberg (1986b), love involves three basic components: intimacy, passion, and commitment. When these are present in different patterns, different types of love (or the absence of love) result. For example, intimacy without passion or commitment produces liking, while passion without intimacy or commitment yields infatuation. *(Source: Based on suggestions by Sternberg, 1986b.)*

Love: Some Basic Patterns

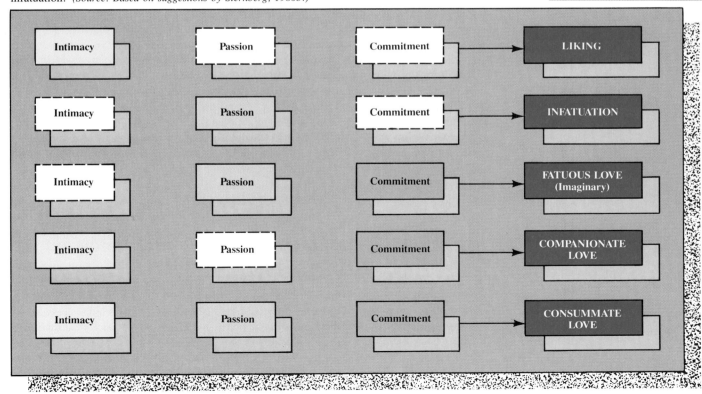

Love That Lasts

FIGURE 15-23. Love does not have to fade with the passage of time. When two individuals work at maintaining their relationship, life-long happiness can result.

another. Instead, their communication comes to focus on negative evaluations—criticism and nagging (Byrne & Murnen, 1987). Similarly, many indicate increasing boredom with one another and their relationship; indeed, this is the most frequent cause of break-ups in dating couples (Hill, Rubin, & Peplau, 1976). Finally, as time passes many couples discover that they have more areas of dissimilarity than they originally realized. This may be the result of changes occurring over the life-span (refer to Chapter 8), or it may stem from the fact that individuals don't consider these differences important early in their relationship when love is in full bloom.

Do such developments indicate that love is doomed to failure? *Definitely not.* Many couples remain happily married for several decades and report that although their love has changed (from passionate to companionate), it is as strong as or stronger than ever (refer to Figure 15-23). Maintaining lasting, loving relationships is indeed possible, even in the modern world. Such happy endings do not occur by chance, however. Rather, they are the result of strenuous efforts by two deeply committed persons who actively choose to keep their love alive.

Applying Social Psychology: Putting Knowledge of Social Behavior to Practical Use

Throughout this text, we've noted that psychological knowledge can be, and often is, *used:* it is applied to the solution of important practical problems. Knowledge about social behavior is no exception to this rule. In fact, increasing efforts to use such information in practical ways have been one of the major themes of social psychology in recent decades (Baron, 1986a). In this final section we'll consider two topics which have received considerable attention in this respect: social aspects of the *legal system* and the impact of the *physical environment* on social behavior.

Social Psychology and the Legal System: Where Law and Social Behavior Meet

The legal system now existing in the United States and many other nations is the result of centuries of thought and tradition. It seems only reasonable, then, to assume that it works—that it yields the kind of objective, unbiased decisions we desire. Is this actually the case? Is justice really blind—fair and impartial in all cases and for all persons? Unfortunately, growing evidence suggests the following answer: "Not always." Because trials and other legal proceedings are *social situations,* involving such things as attempts by attorneys to persuade juries, there is ample room for social factors to play a role. And, often, the effects of such factors are not the ones we might wish.

Sources of Bias in Legal Proceedings: Characteristics of Defendants. One basic principle of our legal system is this: defendants should be judged in terms of the evidence, *not* by their backgrounds or personal characteristics. Having read earlier sections of this chapter, you may now realize that this principle faces formidable obstacles. Jurors, and even judges, cannot help but notice, and be affected by defendants' physical appearance—their attractiveness, their gender, their race, and so on. Further, certain aspects of social thought, too, may play a role (e.g., *stereotypes* about the members of various groups). The overall result is that many factors other than available evidence may enter into jurors' decisions concerning guilt or innocence. That this is actually the case is indicated by the results of many different studies. For example, attractive defendants are acquitted more often than unattractive ones (Michelini & Snodgrass, 1980), and some evidence suggests that persons belonging to various minority groups may be at a disadvantage relative to others (Stewart, 1980). Evidence on this point, however, is mixed; other studies indicate that in the United States blacks and other minorities are *not* convicted more frequently or sentenced more harshly than whites (Welch, Gruhl, & Spohn, 1984).

That other characteristics of defendants may play a role, too, is suggested by a study conducted by Stephan and Stephan (1986). These researchers examined the impact of a male defendant's ability to speak English on his treatment by simulated juries. Subjects listened to tapes based on actual trials. In one condition, the defendant spoke in accented but correct English. In another, he could speak only Spanish, and his testimony was translated as he spoke. Finally, in a third condition, the defendant spoke only Spanish, but subjects were told (as they might be by a judge) to disregard the fact that his answers were translated and to base their verdict solely on the evidence. Some of the subjects in each of these conditions were of Hispanic descent themselves, while others were not. After hearing the tapes, subjects rated the defendant's guilt on a ten-point scale. Results indicated that subjects of Hispanic descent were not affected by the defendant's ability to speak English: they rated him equally in all three conditions. Subjects who were not of Hispanic descent, however, did react negatively when the defendant could not speak English: they rated him as more guilty in this condition (refer to Figure 15-24 on page 496). Encouragingly, those warned to ignore this language barrier did *not* demonstrate a similar pattern. Thus, although a bias against non-English-speaking defendants appeared, it could easily be overcome by instructions. Similar findings have been obtained in several other studies, so there seem to be grounds for some optimism. Jurors are not as fair and unbiased as we might wish, but they can readily be induced to behave in this manner by appropriate procedures.

Sources of Bias in Legal Proceedings: Procedures Themselves. As we noted earlier, current legal procedures are based on centuries of practical experience. This does not guarantee that they are infallible. On the contrary, it appears that in some cases they may shape jurors' verdicts in ways that were never intended.

First, during many trials judges give instructions to jurors before they leave the courtroom to deliberate the defendant's fate. The judge's comments at that time, or even his or her facial expressions and other nonverbal cues, may reveal personal feelings which can, in turn, affect the final outcome (Goleman, 1986).

Language: One Potential Source of Bias in the Courtroom

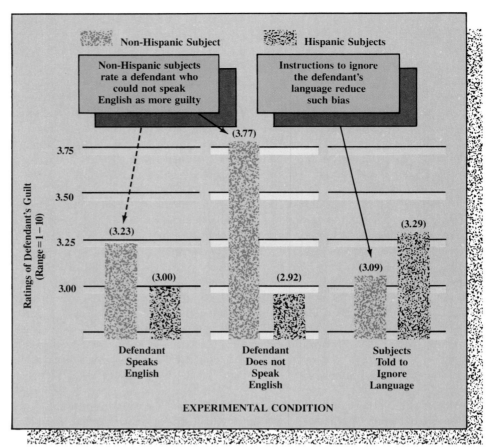

FIGURE 15-24. Subjects who were not of Hispanic descent rated a defendant who could not speak English as more guilty than one who could speak English. Such bias was eliminated by urging subjects to ignore such factors and to concentrate on the evidence. *(Source: Based on data from Stephan & Stephan, 1986.)*

Second, in many states juries are instructed to begin by considering the harshest verdict—guilty of the most serious charge. Only if they fail to reach agreement should they move on to lesser charges or verdicts. Recent studies indicate that following this standard procedure tends to yield harsher decisions than an opposite one, in which jurors begin by discussing the mildest verdict first (Greenberg, Williams, & O'Brien, 1986).

Finally, the range of possible verdicts also seems to exert a strong effect on the outcome. In one study on this topic (Savitsky & Lindblom, 1986) some jurors were given only two verdicts to choose between: guilty or innocent. Others were given a third choice: not guilty by reason of insanity. Still others had all of these plus a fourth: guilty but mentally insane. Subjects then watched a tape of a trial in which the evidence suggested that the defendant was innocent. Results were somewhat unsettling: subjects given the extra potential verdicts used them with a high frequency. In short, they tended to convict an individual who was viewed as innocent by subjects who had only the standard choice between innocent and guilty. These and related findings indicate that even procedures designed to *increase* the fairness of legal proceedings can have unexpected, and unfortunate, effects. As research by social psychologists has uncovered such potential problems, efforts to guard against them have been started in at least some states. In this respect, certainly, psychological knowledge has begun to have important beneficial effects.

Environmental Psychology: The Physical Environment and Social Behavior

It is difficult, these days, to pick up a newspaper or listen to the evening news without learning something upsetting about the environment: mysterious holes in the ozone layer,

FIGURE 15-25. Human activities are changing the physical environment in many different ways. Unfortunately, most of these are harmful.

Human Impact on the Physical Environment: Danger Ahead

the greenhouse effect, nuclear near-disasters. Confronted with such stories, most of us are keenly aware of the fact that human activities are affecting the physical world in many harmful ways (see Figure 15-25). The fact that the equation works in the opposite direction, however, may not be as obvious. Not only do we affect the physical environment— it affects *us,* as well. We are influenced by weather, noise, crowding, and many other aspects of the world around us (Fisher, Bell, & Baum, 1984). Such effects are the focus of **environmental psychology.** While environmental psychologists have studied many topics, one that has received a great deal of attention is the impact of various forms of *environmental stress* on human behavior. We'll briefly consider the impact of two sources of such stress: *noise* and *heat.*

Noise: Sound That Harms.   Each day we are exposed to higher levels of noise than our ancestors probably experienced in a lifetime. Does this auditory pollution affect us adversely? The answer seems to be ''Yes.''

First, growing evidence suggests that exposure to noise—especially the high levels encountered in most large cities—can harm our health. Persons who live near large factories or airports show higher blood pressure than others and a higher incidence of strokes (Cohen et al., 1981). Apparently the high levels of arousal produced by such noise take a heavy toll on our bodies. Such effects don't seem to stem from the fact that persons living in such areas are poorer than those living elsewhere, for they occur even when level of income and several other factors are taken into account (Cohen et al., 1986).

Second, prolonged exposure to loud noise also seems to interfere with the performance of at least some tasks. Cohen and his colleagues (1986) spent several years studying children who attend school near a busy airport. One finding: such youngsters have lower scores on some standard achievement tests and solve puzzles less successfully than children from schools in quiet areas. That adults, too, may suffer such effects is indicated by a recent study carried out by Nagar and Pandey (1987). They exposed male subjects to three different levels of noise while performing two cognitive tasks: (1) reading a story and then answering questions about it, and (2) unscrambling anagrams. Results indicated that the higher the level of noise, the poorer was the subjects' performance.

Finally, noise seems to influence social behavior as well. Individuals exposed to loud, irritating noise lose their temper more easily and are less willing to help others than persons not exposed to such noise (Donnerstein & Wilson, 1976). In sum, we may be paying a heavy price for the noisy environment we have created, in which most of us now live.

Temperature: Is the Long, Hot Summer Really Hot? Despite the fact that millions of persons have moved to the Sunbelt in the United States, many people strongly dislike high temperatures (or high temperatures coupled with humidity). If forced to spend long periods in such conditions, they report feeling tired and irritable. Moreover, many people believe that as the temperature climbs, the likelihood of losing their temper, too, increases. Such beliefs have been confirmed, at least in part. The frequency of violent crimes does seem to increase with rising temperatures, so that more assaults, rapes, and murders take place on hot days than on cool ones (Cotton, 1986). Moreover, cities with hot climates tend to have higher rates of violent crime than cities with cooler climates, at least in the United States (Anderson, 1987).

Such findings point to the conclusion that the "long, hot summer" really *is* hot—that many types of violence are more likely in the presence of high temperatures. Unfortunately, the picture is somewhat complicated by the fact that all of this research, excellent though it is, is *correlational* in nature: it is based on observing the incidence of various crimes on days with different temperatures. It is possible, therefore, that high temperatures do not *cause* increased violence or aggression. Perhaps as temperatures increase, there are more people out on the street, or a higher consumption of alcohol. These factors, not temperature itself, may contribute to higher levels of violence. In addition, laboratory studies in which subjects have been exposed to different levels of heat (e.g., temperatures in the 70s, 80s, 90s, *F*) point to the possibility that beyond some level aggression may actually *decrease* as temperature continues to rise. This may be the case because individuals become so uncomfortable that they lose all interest in virtually *any* type of vigorous activity, including violence (Baron, 1978; Bell & Fusco, 1986). (See Figure 15-26.)

FIGURE 15-26. As temperatures rise from comfortable levels, individuals become more and more irritable. Thus, aggression and violent crimes increase. Beyond some point, however, individuals experience so much discomfort that they avoid all forms of vigorous activity. The result: aggression actually decreases. Findings consistent with this model have been obtained in several laboratory studies (Baron, 1978), but it has not yet been fully confirmed.

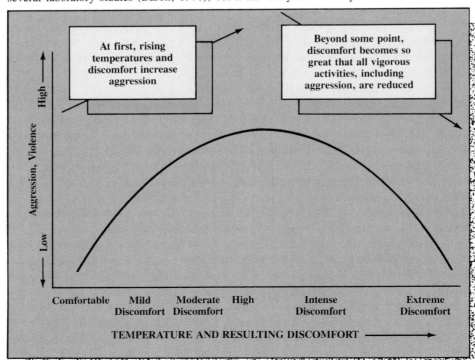

LIVERPOOL JOHN MOORES UNIVERSITY
Aldham Roberts L.R.C.
TEL. 051 231 3701/3634

Heat and Violence: One Possible Pattern

Taking all these diverse findings into account, what can we conclude? On the basis of the data collected so far, it seems clear that uncomfortably high temperatures are indeed one of the many different factors contributing to human aggression. These unpleasant environmental conditions seem capable of shortening tempers and setting the stage for individual or collective outbursts of violence. Yet there may also be certain limits to this relationship: beyond some point, discomfort may be so intense that the likelihood of aggression drops rather than increases. We realize that you might prefer more definite conclusions—we would too! This, however, is where current research leaves us: face to face, once again, with the complexities of human behavior.

Actually, we have purposely chosen to end on this note, mainly because we wish to emphasize the following point: psychology, like other branches of science—and like human knowledge generally—is never final or complete. Rather, it is a continuing adventure, in which each week, month, and year brings new information and insight. We know quite a bit today, but it is certain that we will know even more tomorrow. So, as newscasters often remark, stay tuned for further developments. They are sure to come and are certain to be of practical as well as scientific value.

Summary and Review

Social Thought

Social psychology studies the ways in which we think about and interact with other persons. One key aspect of social thought is *attribution,* our efforts to understand the causes behind others' behavior. We often seek to determine whether their actions stemmed from internal causes (e.g., their own traits and motives) or external causes (conditions in the world around them). Attribution is subject to several forms of error and bias. The most basic of these is the *fundamental attribution error,* our general tendency to explain others' actions in terms of internal causes rather than external ones. Another is the *self-serving bias,* a tendency to take credit for positive outcomes but to attribute negative outcomes to external causes. Attribution theory has been put to many practical uses. For example, it has contributed to our understanding of aggression and conflict and the causes of marital distress.

Social cognition refers to the ways in which we sort, process, store, and recall information about others and how we make judgments or decisions about them. In accomplishing these tasks, we often make use of mental short-cuts known as *heuristics.* One of these, the *availability heuristic,* leads us to judge the frequency of various events in terms of how readily we can bring them to mind. Another, the *representativeness heuristic,* leads us to judge others in terms of the extent to which they are typical of some social group or category. Social cognition is subject to several forms of bias or error. Among the most important of these are the *false consensus effect,* a tendency to assume that others are more similar to us than they really are; *priming,* the tendency to perceive current stimuli in terms of mental categories that have recently been activated; and *illusory correlation,* perceiving correlations or relationships between variables that don't actually exist.

Interpersonal Behavior

Social (or *interpersonal*) *behavior* ranges from cooperation and attraction through conflict and aggression. One especially important form is *social influence*—efforts by one or more individuals to change the behavior or attitudes of one or more others. Attempts to change others' *attitudes* often take the form of *persuasion*—written or spoken messages designed to alter views about various objects, persons, or issues. Many factors determine the success of persuasion. These include the expertise of the would-be influencers, their apparent intentions, and even the speed of their speech. Attitude change can also result from the impact of *cognitive dissonance,* an unpleasant state resulting from our recognition of inconsistency between our attitudes and our behavior, or between various attitudes that we hold. Dissonance follows many decisions and can be reduced by changes in relevant attitudes.

Individuals often experience strong pressures to act like others—pressures toward *conformity*. The tendency to yield to such forces increases as the number of persons exerting influence rises, at least up to a point. It is reduced by the presence of one or more allies—other persons who resist group pressure.

In seeking to influence other persons we use many techniques for gaining *compliance*—agreement to our requests. These include *ingratiation* and several strategies based on the use of multiple requests (e.g., the *foot-in-the-door* and the *door-in-the-face* tactics). A third form of influence, *obedience,* occurs when a source of authority orders individuals to act in ways they would not otherwise choose. Research findings suggest that even relatively powerless authority figures can sometimes induce high levels of obedience.

Interpersonal attraction derives from many sources. *Propinquity*—being near others and in contact with them—often increases attraction. *Similarity* also enhances attraction, as does *physical attractiveness*. *Love* seems to involve three basic components: intimacy, passion, and commitment. These components can be present to different degrees, thus yielding different patterns of love (e.g., passion without intimacy or commitment without infatuation). Passion, and sometimes intimacy, seem to decrease over time in many relationships. However, such declines can be avoided and many couples enjoy decades of deep companionate love.

Applying Social Psychology

The findings and principles of social psychology have been applied to many practical problems. With respect to the legal system, several types of bias that may interfere with fair and impartial verdicts have been uncovered (e.g., positive or negative reactions to defendants' appearance or background). Certain legal procedures, too, can affect jurors' decisions in unintended ways. For example, permitting jurors to choose such verdicts as "guilty but mentally ill" may increase the likelihood that they will convict persons who would otherwise be found innocent.

Our behavior and emotional states are strongly affected by the physical environment. Prolonged exposure to excessive noise may harm our health and can interfere with task performance. Exposure to uncomfortable levels of heat can produce feelings of irritability and so contribute to the occurrence of violent crimes.

 ## Key Terms

Attitudes Our lasting, general evaluations of people, objects or issues.

Attraction The extent to which we evaluate others in a positive or negative manner.

Attribution The process through which we determine the causes of others' behavior.

Cognitive Dissonance An unpleasant affective state that results when an individual notices that his or her attitudes and behaviors are inconsistent.

Compliance A form of social influence in which individuals change their behavior in response to direct requests from others.

Conformity A type of social influence in which individuals change their attitudes or behavior in order to adhere to the expectations of others or the norms of groups to which they belong or wish to belong.

Door-in-the-Face A technique for gaining compliance in which a large request is followed by a smaller one.

Environmental Psychology A field that studies the impact of the physical environment on human behavior.

False Consensus Effect Our tendency to believe that others share our attitudes to a greater extent than is actually the case.

Foot-in-the-Door A technique for gaining compliance in which a small request is followed by a larger one.

Fundamental Attribution Error Our tendency to explain others' behavior in terms of internal causes (e.g., their traits or motives) when such conclusions are not really justified.

Ingratiation A technique for gaining compliance based on first inducing others to like us and then making various requests.

Love An intense form of attraction involving

feelings of intimacy, passion, and commitment.

Obedience A form of social influence in which one individual simply orders another to behave in some manner.

Priming Refers to the fact that recent experiences which have activated certain aspects of memory may affect our current interpretation of events or stimuli.

Self-Serving Bias The tendency to view positive outcomes as stemming primarily from internal causes (e.g., our own effort or ability) but negative outcomes as stemming largely from external causes.

Social Cognition The processes through which we sort, store, and retrieve social information, often to make decisions or judgments about others.

Social Influence Efforts by one or more persons to change the behavior, feelings, or thoughts of one or more others.

Social Psychology The branch of psychology that studies all aspects of social behavior and social thought.

For More Information

Baron, R. A., & Byrne, D. (1987). *Social psychology: Understanding human interaction,* 5th ed. Boston: Allyn and Bacon.

> A broad and up-to-date introduction to the field of social psychology. All of the topics included in this chapter are covered in more detail, and many others, too, are examined. If you'd like to know more about social behavior or social thought, this is an excellent place to begin.

Cialdini, R. B. (1985). *Influence: Science and practice.* New York: Random House.

> A witty and insightful account of the many tactics people use to influence others. The findings both of systematic research and of informal observations made by the author in a wide range of settings (e.g., sales, public relations, fund-raising campaigns) are included. An exceptionally interesting and informative book.

Fiske, S. T., & Taylor, S. E. (1984). *Social cognition.* Reading, MA: Addison-Wesley.

> This book provides a well-written and thorough review of our current knowledge about social cognition. Many examples are provided, and a wide range of topics is included.

Perlman, D. S., & Duck, S., eds. (1986). *Intimate relationships: Development, dynamics, and deterioration.* Newbury Park, CA: Sage.

> This intriguing text examines the initiation, development, and ending of intimate relationships. Such fascinating topics as jealousy and relations between former spouses are included.

CHAPTER

16

Using the Essential Science: Making Psychology Part of Your Life

All good things, it is often said, must come to an end. We hope that during the past few months, this book and your first course in psychology have been among the good things in your life. Whether you view them in these terms or not, though, we're quite sure of one fact: when most college courses come to an end, that really *is* the end. The book is closed, and the information presented between its covers is quickly lost in the press of other matters. This should *not* be the case where psychology is concerned. Instead of leaving its information in the dustbin of discarded knowledge, you should take it with you into the years ahead. Why? Because, as we noted at the beginning, psychology really *is* essential. Its principles and findings will be of great value to you—if you decide to use them.

"O.K.," we can practically hear you saying, "enough with the hype. Sure, psychology is interesting; I always knew it would be. But how can *I* ever use it? I don't want to be a psychologist." In a sense, it is correct to have such concerns. One course in psychology does not qualify you to engage in research, therapy, or the other tasks performed by professional psychologists (refer to Figure 16-1). What it *can* do, though, is provide you with a new perspective—a new way of thinking about yourself and other people. As we now hope to demonstrate, this in itself can be useful.

What, then, should you take with you from this book and course? What information will prove most useful to you in the years ahead? Our answer has three parts. First, as we just noted, we hope you have acquired a new way of thinking about human behavior—a new approach to the many questions about yourself and others that arise as part of daily life. Second, we think you should retain a set of *basic principles* about human beings and human behavior—generalizations suggested by decades of research and the growing sophistication of modern psychology. Third, you should take with you a willingness to

FIGURE 16-1. One course in psychology (or even several) certainly doesn't make you an expert on human behavior. Yet, it *can* provide you with a valuable new perspective on this fascinating subject. *(Source: King Features Syndicate, Inc., 1983.)*

How *Not* to Use Psychology

apply these principles to yourself and many aspects of your life. In other words, you should be able to recognize their relevance to many situations and problems you encounter, and to actually *use* them when this seems appropriate. In the remainder of this chapter, we'll elaborate on each of these major themes.

Using Psychology: Thinking Like a Psychologist

In one sense, psychology can be viewed as a body of knowledge: facts, principles, and theories about many aspects of behavior. Yet it is more than this; it also involves an *approach* to the study of these topics—a set of methods for obtaining information and thinking about them. We described the methods used by psychology in Chapter 1. Here we wish to comment on how psychologists think about human behavior and how you, too, can adopt these techniques and develop your own capacity for critical thinking.

Common Sense Is Useful, but It Is No Substitute for Empirical Evidence or Critical Thinking

At many points in this book, we have described gaps between common sense (informal beliefs about human behavior) and the results of careful research. When common sense and scientific data clash, which do we accept? We're sure you know our answer: the latter. To the extent you adopt this point of view, you will be thinking like a psychologist, for concern with sound empirical evidence is a guiding principle of our field.

But placing one's faith in scientific data rather than untested assumptions is only part of the total picture. If you wish to operate like a psychologist, and benefit fully from your first exposure to our field, you must also be willing to think about behavior—and research focused on it—in the same way that psychologists do. In short, you must be willing to do the hard work involved in *critical thinking*. Just what does such thinking involve? Primarily, maintaining a healthy degree of skepticism, even where the findings of systematic research are concerned. In short, thinking critically implies evaluating all statements—including ones based on research—very carefully. What are the assumptions behind such statements? How were they tested? What is the precise evidence on which they are based? Was the research conducted carefully and in an objective manner free from political or other forms of bias? These are just a few of the questions you should ask when confronted with statements about behavior.

Psychologists, of course, are well aware of the importance of such skepticism, and of thinking critically about all aspects of human behavior. Indeed, training in such thinking is a basic part of their scientific training, so they usually subject all research projects to very careful scrutiny before accepting them as informative or valid. You should adopt the same approach, for unquestioning acceptance of research findings can be just as dangerous or misleading as unquestioning acceptance of the "wisdom" of common sense. In sum, never assume that conclusions about human behavior are accurate until you have examined (1) the assumptions behind them, and (2) the methods and data on which they are based.

Where Human Behavior Is Concerned, Beware of Simple Answers

Psychologists are often accused of being overly cautious: when asked some question about human behavior, their answers tend to contain such phrases as "under some conditions," or "all other factors being constant. . . ." Some people find this annoying: can't psychologists give a straight answer to a simple question? Our reply is of course they can, but they realize that the questions *themselves* are complex—often far more complex than first meets the eye. In other words, psychologists are aware of the fact that, where human behavior is concerned, it's all too easy to jump to false conclusions. *This,* not a desire to hedge or waffle, lies behind their caution.

Simple Answers to Complex
Problems: Buyer Beware

FIGURE 16-2. Each year millions of books promising simple routes to success, happiness, or confidence are sold. Beware: they may promise more than they actually deliver.

As we've noted at many points in this book, human behavior is complex—in most cases too complex to afford us the luxury of simple answers. Our feelings, behavior, and thought are affected by too many different factors, interacting in complex ways, for it to be otherwise. We hope you'll keep this fact in mind. To the extent you do, you—like psychologists—will be skeptical of simple answers about human behavior (refer to Figure 16-2).

Remember That Today's "Facts" May Be Tomorrow's Curiosities

Fewer than thirty years ago many physicists believed that they had uncovered most of the atom's major mysteries. They knew which particles existed, and they could describe their major properties. Then came the 1960s and 1970s with discovery after discovery: quarks, muons, gluons, charm, "strangeness"—the list of new particles and new properties began to seem endless. Why do we mention these events? To illustrate an important point: where scientific knowledge is concerned, *there are no guarantees*. Today's "facts" often turn into tomorrow's curiosities—beliefs that make a new generation of scientists shake their heads and smile.

Psychologists are well aware of such swings in the scientific pendulum, of the rise and fall of established "truths." We hope you will be, too. This is not to say that much of our current knowledge about human behavior will soon be found to be false—far from it. As our sophistication about many topics grows, however, *some* of our ideas and concepts are certain to change (Benjamin, 1988). If you want to think like a psychologist, keep an open mind in this respect and realize that what we know is definitely *not* set in stone.

Naming Is Not Necessarily Explaining

PATIENT: "What's this spot on my arm?"
DOCTOR: "Oh, that's probably a virus."
PATIENT: "What caused it?"
DOCTOR: "I just told you, it's a virus."
PATIENT: "Yes, but why does it look like that?"
DOCTOR (annoyed): "That's the way viruses are. Just rub this cream on it and it'll go away."

What accounts for this failure to communicate? In part, the distinction mentioned in the heading of this section. The patient (who happens to be the author) was asking for an explanation—an account of *why* something existed or had occurred. The physician was answering with a *label*—a name for the object or event in question. He was not interested in why viruses (or their effects) look like this, why they happen to invade particular patches of skin, or related matters. From the point of view of the practicing physician, this makes good sense: his (or her) task is to recognize illnesses and treat them. Interest in their underlying causes is of secondary concern.

As we're sure you realize, this is *not* the approach taken by psychology. As a science, it focuses on the task of *explanation*—understanding *why* people act, feel, or think in certain ways. Simply describing their behavior or labeling it is not the major goal. For example, merely describing individuals as ''aggressive,'' or ''driven'' is not sufficient from psychology's perspective: psychologists want to know why they show these characteristics (how they got to be that way) and how, perhaps, they may change. If you want to think like a psychologist, you will not be satisfied with merely labeling human behavior; you will try to *understand* it, as well.

Always Ask "How?"

''Why'' is not the only question psychologists ask. In addition, they often focus on ''How?'' When presented with information about human behavior, they ask such questions as: ''How were these data obtained?'' ''What methods were used?'' and ''Were alternative explanations carefully ruled out?'' In the years ahead, you will encounter many articles about human behavior in magazines and newspapers, as well as many statements about it on television (see Figure 16-3). If you want to think like a psychologist, *never* accept such accounts as valid until you know something about their basis. In short, remain skeptical until, through careful, critical thinking, you have answered the question, ''how.''

FIGURE 16-3. Whenever you encounter statements about human behavior (even ones far less lurid than these), you should stop and ask, ''How was this information obtained?'' To the extent you do, you will be thinking like a psychologist.

''How?'' A Question You Should Always Ask about Statements Concerning Human Behavior

Using Psychology: Some Basic Principles

If psychology is anything, it is diverse. Consistent with this fact, we've covered a tremendous range of topics in the preceding chapters. Unless you are blessed with a truly superhuman memory, there is no way you could possibly retain all the facts, findings, and definitions presented earlier; nor is there any reason for doing so. If you decide to keep this book, such knowledge will always be available for your use. And even if you don't, you can recover it by a visit to any library. What we think you *should* try to retain, therefore, is the "big picture"—basic principles that, together, capture the essence of our field in the late twentieth century. Please note: we're not suggesting that these points provide a complete summary or overview of psychology. *That* task just required an entire book! Rather, we simply feel that the principles described below (together with the modes of thought outlined earlier) are ones you should carry away from your first formal encounter with our field. All are important, and, as we'll soon point out, all can be of considerable practical value.

There Are No Simple Answers, but This Doesn't Mean That There Are **No** Answers

In the preceding section we cautioned you to beware of simple answers about human behavior. Here, we wish to turn to the other, and more optimistic, side of the coin: the fact that there are no simple answers about human behavior in no way implies that there are *no* answers at all. On the contrary, as previous chapters of this text suggest, psychologists have acquired valuable information about virtually all aspects of human behavior through systematic research. Can newborns perceive depth or different tastes or smells? Is stress an important factor in illness? Do persons suffering from depression think about themselves differently from persons not suffering from depression? We already are beginning to know the answers to these and countless other questions about human behavior. These answers, though, reflect the complexity of the subject they address: human beings. In sum, if you want simple answers, psychology is *not* the place to look. If you want accurate and useful ones, though, you've come to the right field.

We Sometimes Think We Know More Than We Do (or Can)

Our abilities to think, reason, decide, and remember are impressive—of this there can be no doubt. Indeed, we are in a class by ourselves in these respects (at least on Planet Earth). Yet, as we've seen repeatedly, our cognitive skills are far from perfect. Information is sometimes lost very quickly—in a matter of seconds. In other cases, it cannot be retrieved from long-term memory, even though we know that it is "in there" somewhere. And even when information *is* retained, it is frequently distorted or changed in important ways, so that the "facts" we remember fail to reflect reality. We overestimate our ability to make accurate judgments, and our decisions are often influenced by factors that, from a totally rational perspective, should have little bearing upon them (e.g., a desire to justify our previous actions; Dawes, 1988). Even fluctuations in our current mood can strongly affect what we perceive and remember, our judgment, and the strategies we adopt in solving various problems. Finally, our thinking about other persons, too, seems to be subject to a wide range of biases—tendencies which can lead us into serious error in such important tasks as identifying the causes behind people's actions.

The point of all this is not to convince you that we are cognitively incompetent. On the contrary, as noted above, our abilities are, in many respects, nothing short of amazing. We simply wish to emphasize the limits of our cognitive abilities, because they are often overlooked in daily life. Most of us have the impression that our memory is highly reliable, that we can separate our feelings from our judgment, and that our decisions are usually accurate. It is important to realize that we are often somewhat over-optimistic in such respects—that in many cases, we really *do* know less than we think we do. Keeping this fact firmly in mind can help counter such unfounded confidence. And this, in turn, can be a preliminary step toward enhanced accuracy and validity.

FIGURE 16-4. Because perception is strongly affected by our unique experience, there's a lot of truth to the old saying that everyone sees the world through different eyes. *(Source:* The New Yorker, *1977.)*

The World Isn't Always What It Seems

Most persons would agree that beauty is in the eye of the beholder. In other words, we realize that what one person finds appealing, another may find repulsive. Further, we understand that this applies to judgments about art, furniture, foods, and even other human beings. Somehow, though, we often lose sight of this fact in our daily lives. We tend to assume that the way in which *we* perceive the world around us is the way it actually *is,* and we overlook the fact that others may perceive it in very different terms (refer to Figure 16-4).

Psychology, of course, cautions us against such assumptions. Perception is an *active* process, in which we construct a meaningful picture of reality from the information brought to us by our senses. Since all human beings have unique experiences, their interpretations of the same external stimuli can differ radically (Heuer & Sanders, 1987). For example, persons trained in different fields often see the world differently, and this, in turn, may hinder communication between them. Similarly, persons from different cultures often interpret events or objects in sharply contrasting ways—a fact that has been driven home to many businesses as they have expanded operations outside their home country (Harris & Moran, 1987).

When various errors in perception (e.g., illusions, misperceptions) are added to the picture, an important conclusion follows: where perception is involved, there are no absolutes. Our picture of the world around us may range from a highly accurate to a quite inaccurate one, and it may be shared by others to a greater or lesser degree. Keeping these points in mind may encourage you to check frequently on the accuracy of your own perceptions, perhaps by comparing them with those of other persons. As we're sure you can see, doing so can be useful in several different respects.

Where People Are Concerned, Change Really Is the Only Constant

Everyone realizes that we all change radically during the early years of our lives. Infancy, childhood, adolescence: each period is known to bring major shifts in the way we look, think, and act. For some reason, though, many people seem to assume that once we reach our early twenties, most of these processes stop. They realize that physical change continues throughout life (aging, after all, is too evident to ignore!), but they tend to view psychological development as virtually complete.

Such ideas seem to stem, in part, from Freud's influential suggestion that most, if not all, aspects of personality are determined during the first few years of life. As Freud put it, "The child is father to the man." As we noted in chapters 8 and 12, this assumption is questionable to say the least. It is not at all clear that early experiences shape our personalities in the ways Freud suggested. Further, and even more important, evidence gathered by psychologists indicates that we continue to change in many ways throughout life. Ideas, goals, motives, values—all may alter during the several decades we spend as adults. Specific traits or characteristics, and even personality as a whole, are also subject to change. Thus, individuals may be quite different in their thirties than they were in their twenties, different in their forties than they were in their thirties, and so on . . . and on! (Refer to Figure 16-5.)

Such internal change, in turn, can radically affect the lives of persons who experience it. They may seek new careers, new mates, or even entirely new life styles in a new locale. In such cases, the impact of change during our adult years is certainly as dramatic as that occurring during childhood or adolescence.

One word of caution: we do not mean to imply that all persons experience such major shifts. On the contrary, people differ greatly in this respect. Some remain quite stable in many ways, while others undergo radical change. The major point to keep in mind is this: development definitely does *not* stop with physical maturity. So while it may be unsettling to observe change in our parents and other important persons in our lives, it is best to expect it; it is almost certain to occur, at least to some degree.

We Are Shaped—and Reshaped—by Our Experience

"O.K.," you may now be thinking, "that makes sense. We *do* go on changing throughout life. But what makes this happen? Why do we change in so many ways?" Part of the

FIGURE 16-5. Development does not stop when we reach physical maturity; it continues throughout life. *(Source: The New Yorker, 1985.)*

answer involves biological clocks built into our body. These regulate early growth, puberty, and even aging. Another major cause of change centers around *experience*. As we've noted throughout this text, human beings are shaped and re-shaped by their experiences with the world around them. In a word, we *learn*. We learn to repeat actions that yield positive outcomes and to avoid ones that yield negative results (refer to Chapter 5). We learn to anticipate various events because they are "signaled" by certain stimuli. And we acquire new information and forms of behavior simply by observing the actions of others and the consequences *they* experience. Little wonder, then, that we change in many ways over time; indeed, it is hard to imagine how it could be otherwise.

It's important to note that learning often occurs without direct attention to this process and in the absence of conscious awareness of it. In other words, we are changed by our experiences even when we are not seeking such effects and don't recognize that they are occurring. If you take a step back from your own actions and view them from this perspective, you will soon see that this is so. For example, you may discover that your taste in food or wine has changed considerably over the years, even though you never set out to alter it. For many persons, such shifts seem to take place in a relatively automatic manner merely as a function of having been exposed, repeatedly, to new tastes and combinations of tastes. Similarly, you may find that you have acquired a new accent or various mannerisms merely as a result of meeting other persons who show them. In these and many other instances, we are changed by experience, even if we don't realize that such change is occurring. It is partly for this reason that most of us really *are* different persons today than we were last month or last year, and we will probably also be different next month and next year as well.

Individual Differences Exist and Matter—but They Aren't Set in Stone

Now that we've offered strong arguments for the view that change plays a central role in human life, we should balance the scales by noting that stability, too, exists. People *do* possess lasting traits, abilities, and characteristics which they carry with them from situation to situation over long periods of time. Moreover, individuals differ greatly in their relative standing on many of these dimensions (e.g., intelligence, interests, personality traits, specific aptitudes). Ignoring such differences or pretending they don't exist is both foolish and wasteful. Because individuals differ, some are better suited than others for certain jobs or types of training, and some persons enjoy activities others find unappealing. By taking such differences into account, both wasted expense (for companies and schools) and needless frustration (for employees and students) can be avoided. Thus, recognizing and accurately measuring individual differences is often well worth the effort.

On the other hand, the fact that such differences exist in no way implies that they are permanent or unalterable. On the contrary, growing evidence suggests that many are readily open to modification. Are some people more irritable than others? They can be taught social skills that help them control such reactions (Goldstein et al., 1981). Are some so lacking in motivation that they seem doomed to failure? Their willingness to work hard can be greatly increased through appropriate interventions, such as giving them more control over their own jobs (Tjosvold, 1986). Do certain groups or individuals score low on scholastic aptitude? Their relative standing can be greatly improved through special educational programs.

In sum, individual differences do exist and do matter—they affect behavior in many ways. However, they, too, are open to change, and psychology has already devised practical techniques for attaining such goals.

Simple Answers Revisited: Behavior Is Multiply Determined

Why do people behave in the ways they do? As we noted in Chapter 9, this question involves *motivation,* an inferred internal process that activates, guides, and maintains behavior. Most persons who have never had any contact with principles of psychology tend to perceive motivation in fairly simple terms. In seeking to explain their own and

Behavior Is Determined
by Many Factors

FIGURE 16-6. Why did these famous people choose to follow certain careers? An appropriate answer is that each did so for many different reasons.

others' actions, they search for explanations based on a single, dominant cause: Fred went out looking for trouble because he had a fight with his boss this morning; Jill took the job because it paid more than the others; Pam bought the car because the salesperson was such a smooth-talker. These are the kinds of explanations they offer and ones they accept.

As you probably already realize, such single-factor accounts are rarely correct. People adopt certain courses of action, experience various emotions, and reason to various conclusions because of many factors, not just one or two. In short, behavior is *multiply determined*—it springs from many different causes. In trying to understand others and ourselves, therefore, it is useful to keep this point in mind. True, in any given situation, one factor or motive can be the most important cause behind an individual's behavior. Even in such cases, though, many other motives probably also play a role. For example, consider the individuals shown in Figure 16-6. What made them choose the careers they followed: a desire for fame? approval from others? power? money? love of the activities involved? Obviously, all of these motives, plus several others, may well have been involved (Winter, 1988). In trying to understand other persons, then, keep the following point in mind: explaining behavior in terms of one motive, or even a few, is merely a special type of simple answer. And to re-echo a point we've made before, simple answers really don't work where human beings are concerned.

Beauty May Be Only Skin Deep, but the World Pays Lots of Attention to Skin

From our earliest days, we are warned about the dangers of placing too much emphasis on outward appearance. ''True beauty comes from within,'' we are told; ''never judge a book by its cover.'' Unfortunately, a large amount of evidence from several different lines of research in psychology suggests that such warnings have little effect. Throughout life (especially when we are young), we *do* pay attention to the way others look. We are affected by their physical attractiveness, gender, style of dress, use of cosmetics and other grooming aids, and many other aspects of their outward appearance (Heilman, Martell, & Simon, 1988). (See Figure 16-7.) Moreover, such effects are not restricted solely to our liking for, or attraction to, such persons. Research findings indicate that attractive persons receive higher ratings as job applicants than unattractive persons (Arvey & Campion, 1982). Their actual work is evaluated more favorably, and they receive more rapid promotions (Dickey-Bryant, Lautenschlager, & Mendoza, 1986). Juries, too, are susceptible

FIGURE 16-7. As suggested by this cartoon, individuals' physical appearance often exerts powerful effects upon their careers. *(Source: The New Yorker.)*

"Let's take the next one, Stoddard. These people aren't going anywhere."

to the impact of physical beauty: attractive defendants are acquitted more frequently than unattractive ones. Finally, to add icing to the cake, attractive persons are often perceived as possessing more favorable traits and characteristics than unattractive persons (e.g., high intelligence, a pleasant personality). In sum, the world really *does* pay lots of attention to skin. (Review Chapter 15 for more detailed coverage of this topic.)

What are the practical implications of such findings? Two seem most important. First, as objectionable as this may seem, it probably *is* worthwhile to do everything in your power to enhance your own appearance in many situations. The right clothing and grooming can make a difference in both your career and other aspects of your life (Baron, 1986b). Second, you should be on guard against making such judgments yourself. In some contexts (e.g., purely social ones), being affected by others' physical attractiveness seems reasonable. In many others, though, (e.g., judging others' work) it is not. In both cases, keep the message in the heading of this section in mind: it may help you avoid certain problems.

Suffering May or May Not Be Good for the Soul, but It Certainly Isn't Necessary

By its very nature life brings a certain amount of pain. Disappointments, frustrations, the death of loved ones—all are unavoidable parts of being alive. In contrast, psychological distress is *not* inevitable. As we noted in chapters 13 and 14, the problems it involves are extremely common; indeed, it is a rare individual who has never experienced *some* symptoms of psychological distress or of specific psychological disorders (Carson, Butcher, & Coleman, 1988). Does this mean that the vast majority of human beings are doomed to suffer from needless fears, anxieties, depression, and other difficulties? To repeat comments we made earlier in this book: *absolutely not.* Effective help is readily available. All that's necessary is the will to seek it out.

Where should you, your friends, family, or acquaintances look for such aid? There are several ways to proceed. Many departments of psychology are actively involved in providing such services to students. You can start by asking your instructor for the names of people to contact. In addition, your college or university almost certainly has a student health center. The staff of such facilities can provide the names of qualified psychologists.

Similar information can sometimes also be obtained from local physicians and clergy. Finally, if none of these sources is available, you can check your local phone book for an appropriate referral service (under the heading "Psychologist Information and Referral Service") for listings of individual psychologists or for local mental health or counseling services. Be certain that any therapist you see is licensed by your state; if he or she is also certified by the American Psychological Association and holds a Ph.D. degree in clinical psychology or a related field, so much the better. In any case, don't be shy about seeking appropriate help. Clinical psychologists and other professionals *want* to help—this is one reason why they chose such work in the first place. But they can only do so if you give them the chance, so the first step *must* be yours.

Using Psychology: Some Concrete Examples

The principles and approaches described above are important ones; in a sense, they capture the spirit of psychology in the late twentieth century. But are they really as useful as we claim? Can thinking like a psychologist, or applying the basic methods and findings of our field, really contribute to the solution of major problems? We trust that the preceding chapters of this book have offered at least a partial answer. In each chapter we've attempted to stress the practical as well as the scientific value of psychology. To close on an even more positive note, we will now describe a few additional examples of the benefits that often follow when psychologists turn their attention, skills, and knowledge to solving practical problems.

Psychology and Safety: Interventions That Save Lives

Each year millions of persons are injured and tens of thousands are killed in traffic accidents (refer to Figure 16-8). For example, in 1979, 51,900 Americans died as a result of injuries sustained in such accidents; another two million experienced serious injuries (Sleet, 1984). Many of these deaths and injuries can be prevented by a simple action: wearing a safety belt. It has been estimated that at least half of accident-related injuries and fatalities could have been prevented if all drivers had buckled up. Yet, less than 20 percent of motorists in the United States do so, despite laws requiring safety belt use. Can

FIGURE 16-8. Many injuries or deaths resulting from traffic accidents could be prevented if all drivers wore safety belts.

SAFETY BELT CAMPAIGN
NEWSPAPER AD NO. SB-88-1324—2 COL.

Traffic-Related Injuries: An Avoidable Tragedy

anything be done to change this situation? Recent research projects suggest that the answer is "Yes." In several ingenious studies, Geller and his colleagues (e.g., Geller, 1984) have employed basic principles of operant conditioning to produce such results. For example, in one project (Geller, Paterson, & Talbot, 1982) drivers in a metropolitan area learned from newspapers and television announcements that if they were observed wearing safety belts, they might receive small rewards donated by local merchants (lottery tickets or coupons good for a free hamburger). The result: safety belt use rose from 26 percent to 46 percent while the rewards were available.

In a related study, drivers not wearing safety belts were exposed to a sign saying, "Please Buckle Up. I Care." This sign was flashed at them by a passenger in an adjacent automobile when both vehicles were stopped at a traffic signal (Geller, Bruff, & Nimmer, 1985). If the driver buckled up, the sign was flipped over, so that the message, "Thank You!" was visible. Amazingly, almost 22 percent of the drivers exposed to these stimuli complied and buckled up.

Finally, in still another strategy, small signs stating "Safety Belt Use Required in This Vehicle" were placed on the dashboards of twenty-four automobiles (Thyer & Geller, 1987). Observations revealed that this simple action, too, greatly increased safety belt use by passengers. As shown in Figure 16-9, it rose from 32 percent to fully 70 percent. When the signs were removed usage fell, and when they were installed once more, safety belt use rose again. Together, the results reported by Geller and his colleagues suggest that straightforward interventions derived from basic principles of psychology (operant conditioning, modeling) can be quite effective in increasing safety belt use. Given the fact that even modest increments in such behavior by drivers may translate into hundreds or even thousands of lives saved, the benefits of such research are too obvious to require further comment.

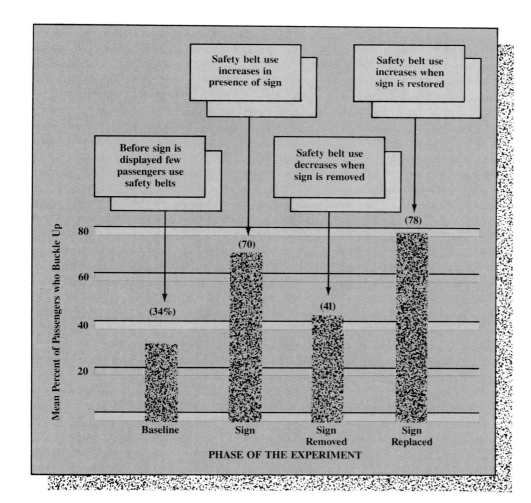

FIGURE 16-9. When a small sign reading "Safety Belt Use Required in This Vehicle" was placed on the dashboard of private automobiles, most passengers complied. Safety belt use dropped when the sign was removed, but it rose once more when the sign was again displayed. *(Source: Based on data from Thyer & Geller, 1987.)*

Increasing Safety Belt Use: One Effective Technique

The Case of the Missing Voters

FIGURE 16-10. Only a small proportion of eligible voters make it to the polls in most local elections. Psychological research suggests several ways of reducing this problem.

Psychology and the Political Process: Getting Out the Vote

Only slightly more than half of all eligible voters have gone to the polls in recent presidential elections in the United States. This figure is even lower in off-year campaigns and falls to truly distressing levels in primaries and purely local elections (refer to Figure 16-10). Most individuals would agree that this is a negative state of affairs: we do, after all, have a responsibility to participate in a democracy and to make our views known. Can psychology offer any means for changing this state of affairs? Some intriguing possibilities are suggested by recent research on one aspect of our cognitive processes (Sherman, 1980). Such research has focused on the following question: when we make predictions about our own future behavior, do these predictions become self-confirming? In other words, once we have made such predictions, do we then act in ways that serve to confirm them? The answer appears to be "Yes." Apparently, when we predict our future behavior, we form an image of it and associate such mental representations with reasons supporting the action (Sherman, 1980).

Can this self-confirming process be used to increase voting behavior? The results of a recent study by Greenwald and his colleagues (Greenwald et al., 1987) indicate that it can. In this experiment two groups of students at a large state university were phoned and asked simple questions about the voting process (did they know the location of their voting precinct and the hours when it was open). For one group, that was the end of the interview. For the other, subjects were also asked whether they expected to vote, and those answering "Yes" were asked what was the most important reason for doing so.

The actual voting behavior of both groups was later assessed by public records from the Board of Elections which listed the names of persons who actually voted. Results were clear: almost 87 percent of those asked to predict their behavior voted, while less than 62 percent of those not asked to predict their behavior did so. Since participants were phoned at random, it seems reasonable to conclude that what produced this difference was the act of making a prediction about their own behavior. Of course, the study was conducted only with students in a single location; it must be repeated with other populations and in other places before definite conclusions can be reached. When it is realized that this simple procedure increased voting by fully 25 percent, however, the potential value of such interventions, which were suggested by basic psychological research, is readily apparent.

Psychology and Work: Enhancing Effort on the Job

As the United States and many other industrialized countries have learned, there is little room in the 1980s for weak economic performers. Only nations whose industries are highly efficient can survive in today's competitive global economy. One factor that contributes to such efficiency is employee motivation. Committed and motivated workers turn out better products at lower cost than workers who are less committed or motivated. These facts, in turn, raise the following crucial question: what steps can be taken to increase such motivation? While no final or complete answer yet exists, one technique suggested by basic psychological research has proven highly effective. This technique is known as **goal-setting,** and it involves the establishment of specific levels of performance or output toward which employees (or others) are expected to work.

While it might strike you as being too simple to actually work, goal-setting has been found to exert powerful effects on performance in many different settings. For example, consider an early study on this topic by Latham and Baldes (1975). The setting for the investigation was a large logging company in the Pacific Northwest. Giant trucks are used to move the cut trees to the mill. Much to the dismay of the company involved, loggers were loading the trucks only to about 60 percent of capacity. This resulted in wasted time and wasted fuel, as the half-empty trucks were driven from the forest to the sawmill. To change this situation, Latham and Baldes established a specific, concrete goal: fill the trucks to 94 percent of capacity before driving to the mill. Amazingly, this simple procedure produced a dramatic change in the loggers' behavior (refer to Figure 16-11). In fact, after only a few weeks the trucks were being consistently filled to the new level, even though employees were told that they would not receive any special rewards for meeting the goal nor punishments for failing to meet it.

Similar results have been obtained in many other studies. Indeed, goal-setting also seems to enhance performance in settings unrelated to work. For example, in one intriguing study Anderson and his colleagues (Anderson et al., 1988) had coaches set performance goals for college hockey players. The players responded to these goals and actually improved their play, with the result that their teams won more games! Additional findings suggest that goal-setting works best when the goals are chosen participatively by the

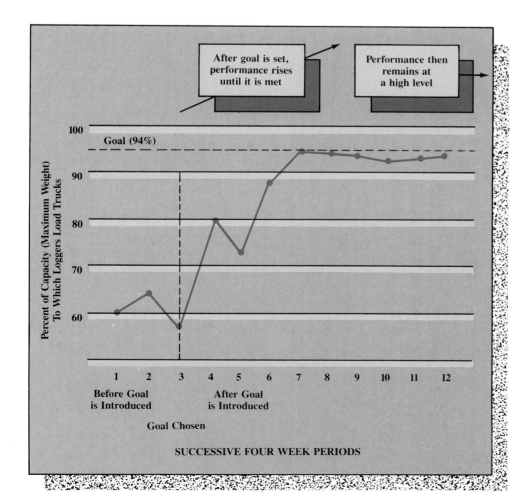

FIGURE 16-11. Loggers began loading their trucks more fully after a specific, challenging goal was set. This resulted in considerable economic savings for their company. *(Source: Based on data from Latham & Baldes, 1975.)*

Benefits of Goal-Setting: A Concrete Example

persons involved rather than when they are simply assigned (Erez & Earley, 1987). And goal-setting seems to be more effective with simple rather than complex tasks (Wood, Mento, & Locke, 1987). Finally, this technique is most valuable when the individuals involved become committed to the goal—when they decide to attempt to reach it. If they merely accept it as a frame of reference, weaker effects are produced (Hollenbeck & Klein, 1987).

Why does goal-setting work? The answer seems to involve at least three factors. First, concrete, challenging goals seem to increase motivation. Second, establishing concrete goals lets employees know just what is expected of them (ambiguity in this respect is often a serious problem in work settings). Third, such goals affect the nature of the strategies adopted by individuals working on various tasks (Locke et al., 1984). Apparently, such strategies are chosen more carefully in the presence of concrete goals than in their absence, so they tend to be more effective. Whatever the precise mechanisms involved, however, there can be no doubt that knowledge about goal-setting and its impact represents a major contribution by psychology—specifically by **industrial/organizational psychology**—to the key task of enhancing productivity.

Psychology and the Design of Equipment: Where Engineering and Behavior Meet

Have you ever witnessed the following scene? One of your instructors has ordered a film and is about to show it in class. He or she approaches the array of switches that control the room lights and tries to turn them off and start the projector. The result: a good laugh for the entire class, since try as he or she may, the instructor seems unable to attain the right combination.

What's responsible for this humorous outcome: a total lack of mechanical skill on the part of the instructor? A desire to entertain the class? The chances are good that the problem is a more basic one: the switches are poorly designed. All are identical in appearance, and they contain no clear markings indicating their function. Further, they do not control the lights and projector in a consistent manner. Flipping some to the ''up'' position turns on various lights; pushing others to the same position actually turns other lights off. The problem, then, is one of design: the controls are not presented in a way that is most effective for human use.

Unfortunately, this type of problem—a gap between the design of equipment or controls and human capacities or expectations—is a very common one. Partly for this reason, an active area of research in psychology known as **human factors** has developed (e.g., Kantowitz & Sorkin, 1983). Human factors, which derives in large part from basic

FIGURE 16-12. Where should crucial warning devices or signals be placed in the cockpit of modern jet airliners? Research by *human factors* psychologists provides the answer to this and many other questions about the design of various types of equipment.

Designing Effective Controls and Equipment: One Task for Human Factors Psychologists

areas of experimental and cognitive psychology, is concerned with the interface between human beings and the systems or equipment they must use. It attempts to assure that our basic perceptual and information-processing capacities are taken into account when such equipment is designed.

The importance of devoting careful attention to this task is readily illustrated. Several years ago, a malfunction occurred in a nuclear power plant in Pennsylvania. This potentially dangerous problem (a drop in coolant level) was indicated by a gauge, but no one noticed its warning for several hours—by which time considerable damage had been done to the entire plant. Why was this the case? Apparently, part of the answer involved the type of gauge used, and its placement in the control room. The crucial gauge was very similar in appearance to many others, and it was placed in a position where employees rarely focused their attention. Little wonder, then, that it was ignored for several hours! A more attention-getting device, placed in a more central location, might well have been noticed sooner, thus avoiding the dangerous situation that soon developed.

Research by human factors psychologists often addresses just this type of practical issue. For example, consider the following question: Where should warning or signaling devices be placed within the visual field of operators (e.g., pilots, people running complex equipment)? In short, should such devices be placed so that they stimulate the left or right visual field? (Refer to Figure 16-12.) Recent studies by Boles (1987) and others suggest a clear answer: the left visual field is best. People respond more quickly to stimuli in this location. Since stimuli in the left visual field ultimately reach the right cerebral hemisphere, these findings imply an interesting fact: some types of visual information are processed more rapidly in the right than left cerebral hemisphere.

By helping to assure that controls and equipment take full account of our perceptual and information-processing capacities, human factors psychologists can substantially improve the design of such devices. Clearly, this is a very valuable application of basic knowledge about key psychological processes.

Psychology and Public Health: Coping with AIDS

One word that sends chills up and down our spine in the late 1980s is *AIDS* (an abbreviation for Acquired Immune Deficiency Syndrome). The mere mention of this disease causes many individuals to turn pale. Such reactions are understandable: there is currently no known cure for this disease. Contracting it amounts to a death sentence—and one that often involves prolonged suffering. Unfortunately, despite the best efforts of public health authorities, AIDS is on the rise. Indeed, it has already reached epidemic proportions in some countries. For example in the war-ravaged African nation of Uganda, up to 40 percent of the medical patients at several large hospitals test positively for the AIDS virus (Caputo, 1988). If these figures are indicative of the numbers of people who will ultimately contract the disease, they foretell a disaster of staggering proportions.

Until a cure or vaccine for AIDS exists, it is clear that prevention must be the only defense (Temoshok, 1987). This, in turn, requires that we have accurate knowledge about such issues as: (1) How much information about the disease do various groups (e.g., adolescents, hospital workers) possess? (2) How accurate is this information? (3) To what extent do various high-risk groups (e.g., homosexuals, intravenous drug users) recognize their risk of contracting AIDS? (4) Are such persons willing to modify their behavior in order to reduce the probability of contracting AIDS? Research on all of these issues, plus many others, is proceeding at a rapid pace, and some of the findings are unsettling.

First, there appears to be considerable confusion among many persons concerning the nature and causes of AIDS. In a sample of adolescents in the San Francisco area, almost 42 percent believed that AIDS can be contracted by kissing someone with the disease, and fully 30 percent believed that it can be cured if treated early enough (DiClemente, Zorn, & Temoshok, 1987). That such false beliefs are not restricted to adolescents is suggested by research with hospital workers. Even among these trained individuals, 38 percent believe that AIDS can be transmitted on eating utensils, and more than 26 percent think that it can be spread through the air, like a common cold (O'Donnell et al., 1987). Together, such views often lead to angry confrontations, such as the one shown in Figure 16-13, in which concerned citizens seek to isolate AIDS victims from all

False Beliefs about AIDS: One Consequence

FIGURE 16-13. Scenes such as this one stem from false beliefs about the nature and spread of AIDS. They may be prevented by large-scale programs designed to provide the general public with accurate information about this frightening disease.

contact with others. The fears of such persons are certainly understandable, but they appear to be out of proportion to the risks involved.

Second, other findings suggest that persons who are especially at risk for contracting AIDS (e.g., male homosexuals) tend to underestimate the danger of behaviors that are involved in its transmission, such as various sexual practices (Bauman & Siegel, 1987). Such false optimism may lead people to continue actions that place them at a high risk for AIDS, and so may contribute to its spread. Finally, and perhaps most unsettling, individuals in high-risk groups who do perceive themselves as being in danger of contracting AIDS sometimes report greater resistance to changing their behavior than persons who do not perceive such risk. Some persons in high-risk groups report that they reason as follows: "There is little hope of escaping the disease, so why shouldn't I live the way I wish?" (Joseph et al., 1987). Clearly, such views may increase the incidence of this frightening illness and so confirm their own accuracy!

AIDS is a complex disease, and medical authorities are not optimistic about the possibility of developing an effective treatment or vaccine for it in the near future. The major hope of slowing the spread of this deadly illness, then, rests on shifts in the attitudes and behavior of hundreds of millions of human beings (see Figure 16-14). It is in this arena that psychology, with its special knowledge about changing human behavior, must play an active role. Doing so in an effective and timely manner is just one of many challenges currently facing the *essential* science.

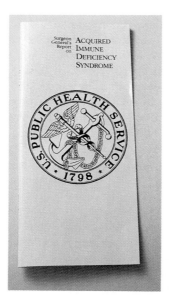

Providing the Public with Accurate Information about AIDS: A Recent Effort

FIGURE 16-14. The leaflet shown here was mailed during 1988 to every household in the United States. It is designed to enhance the public's knowledge of this disease, and to dispell several inaccurate beliefs about it.

The Essential Science Revisited: Some Final Words

Now we really *have* come to the end. In the preceding chapters we've summarized many of the key findings of our field, and we have suggested in this chapter why you should make psychology part of your life. Do we have any final words? Of course! As you close this book, please keep three thoughts in mind: (1) you don't have to be a psychologist to think like one—to approach human behavior in a systematic, scientific manner with the aid of critical thought; (2) you don't have to be a psychologist to retain a working knowledge of several key principles of the essential science; and (3) doing (1) and (2) can be of practical value to you in a wide range of situations. To echo the theme we presented at the start of this book, we haven't chosen to describe our field as the *essential* science without good reason.

Summary and Review

Thinking Like a Psychologist

You don't have to be a psychologist to think like one. All that's necessary is that you adopt a special kind of perspective on human behavior. Key aspects of this perspective include recognizing that scientific data are generally more accurate than common sense, relying on critical thinking, understanding that there are few (if any) simple answers where human beings are concerned, and realizing that naming an object or event is not the same thing as explaining it. Adopting a psychological perspective also involves realizing that scientific facts may well change in the future as new evidence is acquired.

Basic Principles of Psychology

You can't possibly retain every fact, definition, and finding presented in this text. However, you *can* try to remember several basic principles about human behavior. These include the following: the world isn't always what it seems (perception reflects past experience and is open to several forms of distortion and error); change is the only constant (development continues throughout life); we are shaped by our experience (we continue to learn throughout life); our cognitive abilities are limited in important ways; and behavior is multiply determined—it often stems from several motives and a wide range of interacting factors.

Psychology in Action

In recent years, psychologists have turned their attention to a number of practical problems. They have developed effective techniques for inducing individuals to wear safety belts, based upon principles of operant conditioning and modeling. They have devised strategies useful for increasing the percentage of persons who vote in political elections. Efforts to increase employee motivation and productivity, too, have been common. One procedure that has proven highly effective in this regard is *goal-setting*. Finally, psychologists have also applied basic knowledge about perception and human cognition to the task of designing better equipment and controls. In the area of public health, they have attempted to develop procedures for slowing the spread of AIDS. Such efforts have focused on providing accurate information about this disease and on modifying behaviors that increase the risk of contracting it.

Key Terms

Critical Thinking Systematic thinking in which all assumptions underlying conclusions or ideas are subjected to careful, detailed analysis.

Goal-Setting A technique for enhancing motivation (especially work motivation) in which specific, challenging performance goals are established.

Human Factors The interface between human beings and the systems or equipment they must use.

Industrial/Organizational Psychology A

subfield of psychology that focuses upon aspects of behavior in work settings. Topics studied by industrial/organizational psychologists are the selection and training of employees, work-related attitudes (e.g., job satisfaction), performance appraisal, motivation, and leadership.

 ## For More Information

Goldstein, A.P., & Krasner, L. (1987). *Modern applied psychology*. New York: Pergamon.
This text provides an up-to-date summary of the many ways in which knowledge uncovered by psychologists is currently being put to practical use. A wide range of applications in education, industry, health, sports, and the law are described. This is a good source to consult if you'd like to know more about practical applications of psychology.

Hothersall, D. (1984). *History of psychology*. New York: Random House.
A well-written discussion of the history and development of psychology. Special attention is directed to advances that have shaped the development of our field, and these are linked to the careers of several famous psychologists.

Appendix

Thinking Like a Psychologist Revisited: The Use— and Abuse— of Statistics

In Chapter 16 we noted that one benefit you should gain from your first course in psychology is the ability to think about human behavior in a new way. More concretely, we voiced the hope that in at least some respects you would begin to think like a psychologist. Here, we will expand upon that theme by offering a basic introduction to one essential aspect of psychological thinking: **statistics.**

What does this special form of mathematics have to do with psychology or thinking like a psychologist? The answer involves the fact that all fields of science require two major types of tools. First, scientists need various kinds of equipment to gather the data they seek. Obviously, this equipment differs from field to field, so that, for example, biologists use microscopes, astronomers employ telescopes, and geologists wield hammers (or even dynamite!) in their work (refer to Figure A-1).

Second, all scientists need some means for interpreting the findings of their research—for determining the *meaning* of the information they have acquired and its relationship to important theories in their field. Again, this varies from one science to another. In most cases, though, some type of mathematics is involved. Psychology is no exception to this general rule: to understand the findings of *their* research (and, hence, important aspects of human behavior), psychologists make use of *statistics*—or, more accurately, *statistical analysis* of the data they collect.

As we'll soon point out, statistics are a flexible tool and can be used for many different purposes. In psychology, however, they are usually employed to accomplish one or more of the following tasks: (1) *summarizing* or *describing* large amounts of data, (2) *comparing* individuals or groups of individuals in various ways, (3) determining whether certain aspects of behavior are *related* (whether they vary together in a systematic manner), and (4) *predicting* future behavior from current information. In the pages that follow we'll consider each of these major uses of statistics by psychologists. After doing so, we'll illustrate several ways in which statistics can be abused—how they can be employed to disguise or conceal important facts rather than to clarify them.

Descriptive Statistics: Summarizing Data

Suppose that a psychologist conducts an experiment concerned with the following topic: the effects of staring at others in public places. The procedures of the study are simple. He stares at people in stores, airports, and a variety of other locations, and records the number of seconds until they look away—or until they approach to make him stop! After carrying out these procedures twenty times, he obtains the data shown in Table A-1. Presented in this form, the scores seem meaningless. If they are grouped together in the manner shown in Figure A-2, however, a much clearer picture emerges. Now, we can now see at a

Tools for Research

FIGURE A-1. Scientists in different fields use different types of equipment to conduct research.

glance that most people look away after about 4 seconds, that fewer look away after 3 or 5 seconds, and that even fewer look away very quickly (after 2 seconds) or after a longer delay (6 seconds). This graph presents a **frequency distribution:** it indicates the number of times each score occurs within an entire set of scores. Here, the frequency distribution indicates how many times scores of 1, 2, 3, 4, 5, or 6 seconds were recorded in the study of staring.

Examining a graph such as the one in Figure A-2 provides a rough idea of the way a set of scores is distributed. In science, however, a rough idea is not sufficient: more precision is required. In particular, it would be useful to have an index of (1) the middle score of the distribution of scores (their **central tendency**) and (2) the extent to which the scores spread out around this point (their **dispersion**). Such measures are provided by **descriptive statistics.**

Measures of Central Tendency: Finding the Center

You are already familiar with one important measure of central tendency: the **mean,** or average. It is calculated by adding all scores and then dividing by the total number of scores. The mean represents the typical score in a distribution and in this respect is often quite useful. Sometimes, though, it can be misleading. This is because the mean can be strongly affected by one or a few extreme scores. To see why this is so, consider the following example. Ten families live on a block. The number of children in each family is shown in Table A-2. Adding these numbers together and dividing by ten yields a mean of 4. Yet, as you can see, *not one family actually has four children*. Most have none or two, but one has eight and another has nineteen.

In cases such as this, it is better to refer to other measures of central tendency. One of these is the **mode**—the most frequently occurring score. As you can see, the mode of the data in Table A-2 is 2: more families have two children than any other number.

FIGURE A-2. Scores are grouped together according to the number of times each occurs in a *frequency distribution*. This one suggests that most persons react to being stared at within about four seconds.

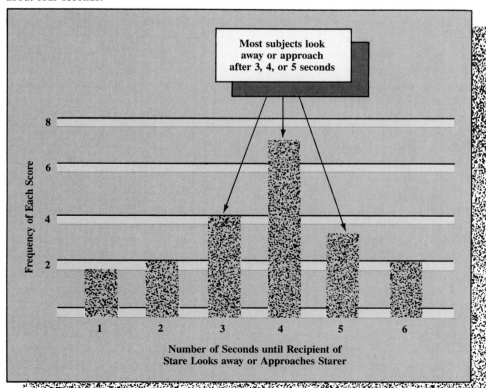

Raw Data from a Simple Experiment

TABLE A-1

When a psychologist stares at strangers in a public place, these persons either look away or approach him in the number of seconds shown. Note that more people look away or approach after 4 seconds than any other value.

	Number of Seconds Until Subject Either Looks Away or Approaches
Subject 1	4
Subject 2	4
Subject 3	1
Subject 4	4
Subject 5	3
Subject 6	2
Subject 7	5
Subject 8	3
Subject 9	6
Subject 10	5
Subject 11	4
Subject 12	4
Subject 13	3
Subject 14	3
Subject 16	5
Subject 17	4
Subject 18	4
Subject 19	2
Subject 20	6

A Frequency Distribution

TABLE A-2

Ten families have a total of forty
children among them. The mean
is 4.0, but, as you can see, not
one family has this number of
children. This illustrates the fact
that the *mean*, while a useful
measure of central tendency, can
be distorted by a few extreme
scores.

	Number of Children
Family 1	0
Family 2	0
Family 3	2
Family 4	2
Family 5	2
Family 6	2
Family 7	2
Family 8	3
Family 9	19
Family 10	8
Total = 40 children	
Mean = 40/10 = 4.0	

Another useful measure of central tendency is the **median**—the midpoint of the distribution. Fifty percent of the scores fall at or above the median, while fifty percent fall at or below this value. Returning to the data in Table A-2, the median also happens to be 2: half the scores fall at or below this value, while half fall at or above it.

As you can readily see, both the mode and median provide more accurate descriptions of the data than does the mean in this particular example. But please note: this is *not* always, or even usually, the case. It is only true in instances where extreme scores distort the mean. In fact, there is no simple rule for choosing among these measures. The decision to employ one over the others should be made only after careful study of frequency distributions such as the one shown in Figure A-2.

Measures of Dispersion: Assessing the Spread

The mean, median, and mode each tell us something about the center of a distribution, but they provide no indication of its shape. Are the scores bunched together? Do they spread out over a wide range? This issue is addressed by measures of *dispersion*.

The simplest measure of dispersion is the *range*—the difference between the highest and lowest scores. For example, the range for the data on number of children per family in Table A-2 is 19 ($19 - 0 = 19$). Although the range provides some idea of the extent to which scores vary, it suffers from one key drawback: it does not indicate how much the scores spread out around the center. Information on this important issue is provided by the **variance** and **standard deviation.**

The variance provides a measure of the average distance between scores in a distribution and the mean. It indicates the extent to which, on average, the scores depart from (vary around) the mean. Actually, the variance refers to the average *squared* distance of the scores from the mean (squaring eliminates negative numbers). The *standard deviation* then takes account of this operation of squaring by calculating the square root of the variance. So, the standard deviation, which is widely used in psychology, represents the average distance between scores and the mean in any distribution. The larger the standard deviation, the more the scores are spread out around the center of the distribution.

The Normal Curve: Putting Descriptive Statistics to Work

Despite the inclusion of several examples, our discussion so far has been a bit abstract. As a result, it may have left you wondering about the following question: Just what do descriptive statistics have to do with understanding human behavior or thinking like a psychologist? One important answer involves their relationship to a special type of frequency distribution known as the **normal curve.**

While you may never have seen this term before, you are probably quite familiar with the concept it describes. Consider the following characteristics: height, size of vocabulary, strength of sexual drive. Suppose you obtained measurements of each among thousands of persons. What would be the shape of each of these distributions? If you guessed that they would all take the form shown in Figure A-3, you are correct. In fact, on each dimension most scores would pile up in the middle, and fewer and fewer scores would occur farther away from this value. In short, most people would be found to be average height, would have average vocabularies, and would show average sexual drive; very few would be extremely high or low on these characteristics. We should add, by the way, that the normal curve applies to an amazingly wide range of human characteristics— everything from personality traits to cognitive abilities and physical attributes.

What does the normal curve have to do with the use of descriptive statistics? A great deal: one key property of the normal curve is as follows. Specific proportions of the scores within it are contained in certain areas of the curve; moreover, these portions can be defined in terms of the standard deviation of all of the scores. These facts suggest an important point: once we know the mean of a normal distribution and its standard deviation, we can determine the relative standing of any specific score within it. Perhaps a concrete example will help clarify both the nature and value of this relationship.

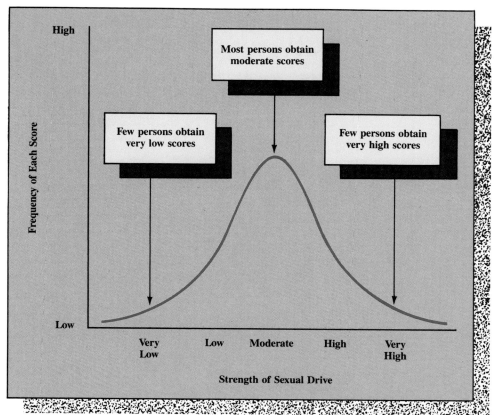

FIGURE A-3. On many dimensions relating to behavior, scores show the kind of frequency distribution illustrated here: the *normal curve*. Most scores pile up in the middle, and fewer and fewer occur toward the extremes. For example, if you administered a test of sexual drive to thousands of persons, most would fall near the middle, and only a few would show very high or very low scores.

Figure A-4 on page 530 presents a normal distribution with a mean of 5.0 and a standard deviation of 1.0. Let's assume that the scores shown are those on a test of desire for power. Suppose that we now encounter an individual with a score of 7.0. We know that she is high on this characteristic, but *how* high? On the basis of descriptive statistics (the mean and standard deviation), plus the properties of the normal curve, we can tell. Statisticians have found that 68 percent of the scores in a normal distribution fall within one standard deviation of the mean (either above or below it). Similarly, fully 96 percent of the scores fall within two standard deviations of the mean. Given this information, we can conclude that a score of 7 on this test is very high indeed: only 2 percent of persons taking the test attain a score equal to or higher than this one (refer to Figure A-4).

In a similar manner, descriptive statistics can be used to interpret scores in any other distribution, providing it approaches the normal curve in form. As we noted above, a vast array of psychological characteristics and behaviors do seem to be distributed in this manner. The result: we can readily determine an individual's relative standing on any of these dimensions from just two pieces of information: the mean of all scores in the distribution and the standard deviation. Little wonder, then, that the normal curve has sometimes been described as a statistician's or psychologist's delight.

Now, imagine that your first psychology test contains fifty multiple-choice items. You obtain a score of 40. Did you do well or poorly? If your instructor provides two additional pieces of information—the mean of all the scores in the class and the standard deviation—you can tell. Suppose the mean is 35, and the standard deviation is 2.50. The mean indicates that most people got a lower score than you did. The relatively small standard deviation indicates that most scores were quite close to the mean—only about 2.5 points away, on average. This, too, suggests that you did quite well: your own score is

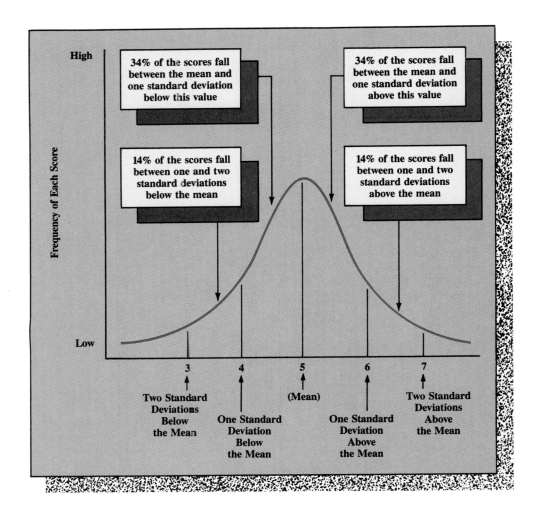

FIGURE A-4. Sixty-eight percent of the scores in a normal distribution fall within one standard deviation of the mean (above or below it). Similarly, fully 96 percent of the scores fall within two standard deviations of the mean. Thus, on a test with a mean of 5.0 and a standard deviation of 1.0, only two percent of persons attain a score of 7.0 or higher.

twice this distance *above* the mean. Further—and here is a key point—this conclusion would be accurate whether there were thirty, one hundred, or five hundred students in the class, assuming the mean and standard deviation remain unchanged. It is precisely this type of efficiency that makes descriptive statistics so useful for summarizing even large amounts of information.

Inferential Statistics: Determining Whether Differences Are or Are Not Real

Throughout this book, we have reported the results of many different experiments. When we discussed these studies, we often referred to differences between various conditions or groups. We noted, for example, that subjects exposed to one set of conditions or one level of an independent variable behaved differently from subjects exposed to another set of conditions or another level of an independent variable. How did we know that such differences were real ones rather than ones that might have occurred by chance alone? The answer involves the use of **inferential statistics.** These methods allow us to reach conclusions about just this issue: whether a difference we have actually observed is large enough for us to conclude (to *infer*) that it is indeed a real or *significant* one. The logic behind inferential statistics is complex, but some of its key points can be illustrated by the following example.

Suppose that a psychologist conducts an experiment to examine the impact of mood upon memory. (As you may recall, we discussed such research in Chapter 6.) To do so, he exposes one group of subjects to conditions designed to place them in a good mood (e.g., they watch a very funny videotape). A second group, in contrast, is exposed to a neutral tape—one that has little impact upon their mood. Both groups are then asked to memorize lists of words, some of which refer to happy events (e.g., "party," "success"). Later, both groups are tested for recall of these words. Results indicate that those who watched the funny tape remember more happy words than those who watched the neutral tape; in fact, those in the first group remember twelve happy words, while those in the second remember only eight. Is this difference a real one?

One way of answering this question would be to repeat the study over and over again. If a difference in favor of the happy group was obtained consistently, our confidence that it is indeed real (and perhaps due to differences in subjects' mood) would increase. As you can see, however, this would be a costly procedure. Is there any way of avoiding it? One answer is provided by *inferential statistics*. These methods assume that if we repeated the study over and over again, the size of the difference between the two groups obtained each time would vary; moreover, these differences would be normally distributed. Most would fall near the mean, and only a few would be quite large. When applying inferential statistics to the interpretation of psychological research, a very conservative assumption is made: we begin with the view that there is no difference between the groups—that the mean of this distribution is zero. Through methods that are beyond the scope of this discussion, we then estimate the size of the standard deviation. Once we do, we can readily evaluate the difference obtained in an actual study. For example, assume that in the study we have been discussing, this standard deviation (a standard deviation of mean differences) is 2.0. This indicates that the difference we observed (4.0) is two standard deviations above the expected mean of zero (please refer to Figure A-5). As you should recall from our discussion of the normal curve, this means that the difference is quite large and would occur by chance fewer than two times in a hundred. Our conclusion: the difference between the two groups in our study is *probably* real. Thus, mood does indeed seem to affect memory.

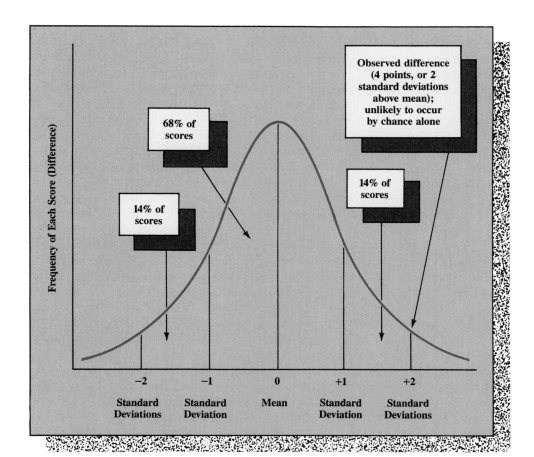

FIGURE A-5. Two groups in a study concerned with the effects of mood on memory attain mean scores of 12.0 and 8.0, respectively. Is this difference *significant* (real)? Through inferential statistics, we can tell. If the study were repeated over and over, and the two groups did not really differ, the mean difference in their scores would be zero. Assuming that the standard deviation is 2.0, we know that the probability of a difference this large is very small—less than two percent. In view of this fact, we conclude that this finding is indeed significant.

Using Inferential Statistics to Determine Whether an Observed Difference Is a Real One

Please note the word *probably* above. Since the tails of the normal curve never entirely level off, there is always some chance—no matter how slight—that even a huge difference we have observed is due to chance. In general, though, psychologists assume that when a difference is large enough that it would occur by chance less than 5 percent of the time, it is also large enough to be viewed as real or *significant*. (The term significant is not a synonym for "important"; it merely means that we have considerable confidence that the same findings would be obtained again if we repeated the study.)

Correlation and Prediction

Does crime increase as temperatures rise? Does the chance of winning election increase with a candidate's height? Does our ability to solve certain kinds of problems change with age? Psychologists are often interested in such questions. In short, they are concerned with whether two or more variables are *related*, so that changes in one are associated with changes in the other. (Remember: this is quite different from the issue of whether changes in one variable *cause* changes in another. If you're unclear about this distinction, refresh your memory by referring to Chapter 1.)

In order to answer such questions, we must gather information on each variable. For example, assume that we wanted to find out if political fortunes are indeed related to height. To do so, we might obtain information on (1) the height of hundreds of candidates and (2) the percentage of votes they obtained in recent elections. Then we'd plot these two variables (height against votes) by entering a single point for each candidate on a graph such as those in Figure A-6. As you can see, the first graph in this figure indicates that tallness is positively associated with political success. The second points to the opposite conclusion, and the third suggests that there is no relationship at all between height and political popularity.

While such graphs (known as *scatterplots*) are useful, they don't, by themselves, provide a precise index of the strength of the relationship between two or more variables. To obtain such an index, a statistic known as a **correlation coefficient** is often calculated. Such coefficients can range from -1.00 to $+1.00$. Positive numbers indicate that as one variable increases, so does the other. Negative numbers indicate that as one factor increases, the other decreases. The greater the departure from 0.00 in either direction, the stronger the relationship between the two variables. Thus, a correlation of $+.80$ is stronger than one of $+.39$ Similarly, a correlation of $-.76$ is stronger than one of $-.51$.

Once a correlation coefficient is computed, its significance can be tested: we can determine whether it is large enough to be viewed as unlikely to occur by chance alone. Further, correlations can also be compared to determine if, in fact, one is significantly larger (or smaller) than another. The methods used for completing these tasks are somewhat different than those used for comparing means, but the logic is much the same.

In addition to determining the extent to which two or more variables are related, statistical procedures also exist for determining the degree to which a specific variable can be *predicted* from one or more others. These methods of *regression analysis* are complex, but they are of great practical value. Knowing the extent to which performance can be predicted from currently available information (e.g., grades, past performance, scores on psychological tests) can aid companies, schools, and many other organizations in selecting the best persons for employment or educational opportunities.

The Misuse of Statistics: Numbers Don't Lie . . . or Do They?

A public figure once remarked, "There are lies, damned lies, and statistics!" By this he meant that statistics are often used for purposes quite different from the ones we've described. Instead of serving as a valuable basis for understanding scientific data, interpreting test scores, or making predictions about behavior, they are employed to confuse, deceive, or mislead their intended victims. To make matters worse, in the wrong hands,

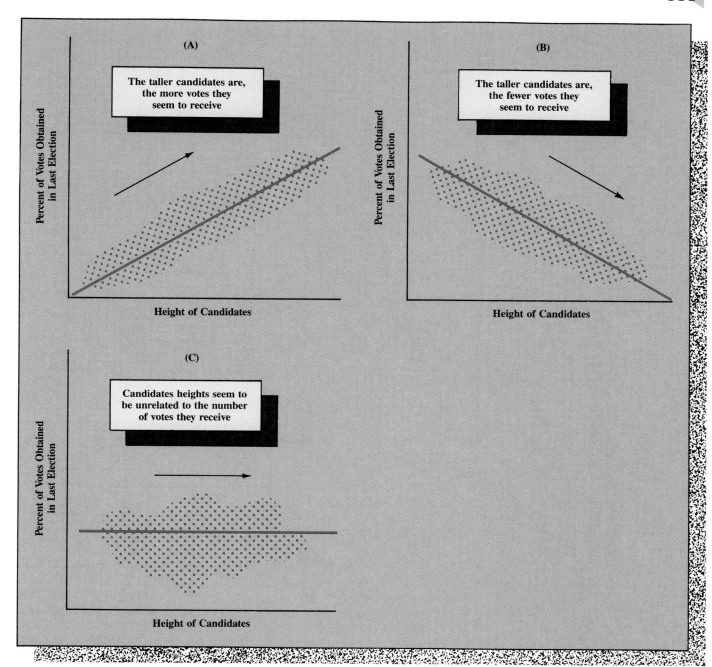

FIGURE A-6. Is height related to success in politics? To find out, we measure the height of many candidates and obtain records of the percent of votes they obtained. We then plot height against votes in a *scatterplot*. Chart A indicates a positive relationship between height and political success: the taller candidates are, the more votes they get. Plot B indicates a negative relationship between these variables. The third (plot C) suggests that there is no relationship between these variables.

Illustrating Relationships Through Scatterplots

statistics can be quite effective in this role. The reason for such success lies in the fact that most of us firmly accept another popular saying: "Numbers don't lie" (refer to Figure A-7 on page 534). Thus, when confronted with what appear to be mathematical data and facts, we surrender our usual skepticism and readily accept what we are told. Since the costs of doing so can be quite high, we'll conclude this brief discussion of statistics by pointing out some of the more common—and blatant—*mis*uses of statistics. Here, too, thinking like a psychologist can be of considerable practical value. If you keep the princi-

"Tonight, we're going to let the statistics speak for themselves."

FIGURE A-7. Contrary to what common sense suggests, numbers (or at least *statistical* presentation of them), can indeed be made to lie. *(Source: The New Yorker.)*

ples outlined here firmly in mind, you'll often be able to spot such statistical abuses and can avoid being deceived by them.

Random Events Don't Always Seem Random

You pick up the paper and read an account of a young woman who won more than one million dollars at a gambling casino. She placed sixteen bets in a row at a roulette table and won on every spin of the wheel. Why? Was she incredibly lucky? Did she have a system? If you are like many people, you may jump to the conclusion that there is indeed something special about her. After all, how else can this incredible series of events be explained?

If you do jump to such conclusions, you are probably making a serious mistake. Here's why. For any single player, the odds on winning so many times in succession are indeed slight. But consider the vast number of players, and the number of occasions on which they play. (Some casinos remain open around the clock.) Also, remember the shape of the normal curve. The mean number of wins in a series of sixteen bets is indeed low—perhaps one or two. But the tails of the curve never level off, so there is some probability, however slight, of even sixteen wins occurring in a row. In short, even events that would be expected to occur by chance very rarely *do* occur. The moral is clear: don't overinterpret events that seem, at first glance, to border on impossible. They may actually be rare chance occurrences with no special significance of their own.

Large Samples Provide a Better Basis for Reaching Conclusions Than Small Ones

Many television commercials take the following form. A single consumer is asked to compare three unlabeled brands of facial tissue or to compare the whiteness of three loads of wash. She then makes the "right" choice, selecting the sponsor's product as softest, brightest, or whitest. The commercial ends with a statement of the following type: "Here's proof. Our brand is the one most shoppers prefer." Should you take such evidence seriously? We doubt it. In most cases, it is not possible to reach firm statistical conclusions on the basis of the reactions of a single individual, or even of several individuals. Rather, a much larger number of cooperative participants is necessary. After watching such a commercial, then, you should ask what would happen if the same procedures were repeated with 20, 50, or 500 shoppers. Would the sponsor's brand actually be chosen significantly more often than the others? The commercials leave the impression that it would but, as we're sure you now realize, jumping to such conclusions is risky. So, be skeptical of claims based on very small samples: they are on shaky grounds, at best, and may well be designed to be purposely misleading.

Unbiased Samples Provide a Better Basis for Reaching Conclusions Than Biased Ones

Here's another popular type of commercial, and another common misuse of statistics. An announcer (usually dressed in a white coat) states: "Three out of four dentists surveyed recommend *Jawbreak* sugarless gum." At first glance, the meaning of this message seems clear: most dentists prefer that their patients chew a specific brand of gum. But look more closely: there's an important catch. Notice that the announcer says: "Three out of four dentists *surveyed* . . ." Who were these people? A fair and representative sample of all dentists? Major stockholders in the *Jawbreak* company? Close relatives of the person holding the patent on this product? From the information given, it's impossible to tell. To the extent these or many other possibilities are true, the dentists surveyed represent a *biased* sample: they are *not* representative of the population to which the sponsor wishes us to generalize: all dentists. So whenever you encounter claims about the results of a survey, ask two questions: (1) who were the persons surveyed? (2) how were they chosen? If they can't be answered to your satisfaction, be on guard: someone may be trying to mislead you.

Beware of Unexpressed Comparisons

Another all-too-common misuse of statistics involves what might be described as "errors of omission." Persons using this tactic mention a comparison but then fail to specify all of the groups or items involved. For example, consider the following statement: "In recent laboratory tests, *Plasti-spred* was found to contain fully 82 percent less cholesterol! So, if you care about your family's health, buy *Plasti-spred,* the margarine for modern life." Impressive, right? After all, *Plasti-spred* seems to contain much less of a dangerous substance than—what? There, in fact, is the rub: we have no idea as to the identity of the other substances in the comparison. Were they other brands of margarine? Butter? A jar of bacon drippings? A beaker full of cholesterol? The lesson offered by such claims is clear. Whenever you are told that a product, candidate, or anything else is better or superior in some way, always ask the following question: better than *what?*

Ignoring Differences That Aren't Really There

Here's yet another type of commercial you've probably seen before. An announcer points to lines on a graph that diverge before your eyes and states, "Here's proof! *Gasaway* neutralizes stomach acid twice as fast as the other leading brand." And in fact, the line labeled *Gasaway* does seem to rise more quickly, leaving its poor competitor in the dust. Should you take such claims seriously? Again, our answer is "No." First, such graphs are usually unlabeled. As a result, we have no idea as to what measure of neutralizing acids or how much time is involved. It is quite possible that the curves illustrate only the first few seconds after taking the medicine, and that beyond that period the advantage for the sponsor's product disappears.

Second, and even more important, there are no grounds for assuming that the differences shown are *significant*—that they could not have occurred by chance. Perhaps there is no difference whatsoever in the speed with which the two products neutralize acid, but the comparison was run over and over again until—by chance—a seemingly large difference in favor of the sponsor's brand occurred. We're not suggesting that all advertisers (or even most) engage in such practices. Perhaps the differences shown in some commercials are indeed real. Still, given the strong temptation to stress the benefits of one's own product, the following policy is probably best: assume that all differences reported in ads and similar sources are *not* significant (i.e., real) unless specific information to the contrary is provided.

Graphs That Distort (or at Least Bend) Reality

It is often said that a picture is worth a thousand words. Consistent with this view, the results of psychological research are often represented in graphs. When used in this manner, such illustrations are helpful. Major findings can be communicated efficiently, and complex relationships, difficult to describe verbally, can be more readily presented. Unfortunately, however, graphs are often used for another purpose: to alter the conclusions drawn from a given set of data. This can be accomplished in many ways, but the most common of these involves alterations in the meaning of the axes—the horizontal or vertical boundaries of the graph. Perhaps a specific example will help clarify the nature of this process.

Consider how two political candidates (a Democrat and a Republican) might choose to represent the budget deficit in the United States in recent years. The Democrat, eager to convince voters that the deficit has risen alarmingly under Republican rule, might choose the graph shown on the left in Figure A-8. In contrast, the Republican might prefer to use the graph shown on right. Notice that in both the same numbers are represented: the deficit rose from $65 billion in 1982 to almost $200 billion in 1986. Yet this rise seems

Misleading Graphs: One Common Technique

FIGURE A-8. By altering the scale of the vertical axis, graphs representing the same data can be made to appear very different. They may then seem to point to sharply contrasting conclusions. Here, the growth in the deficit looks huge in the left-hand graph but modest in the right-hand one.

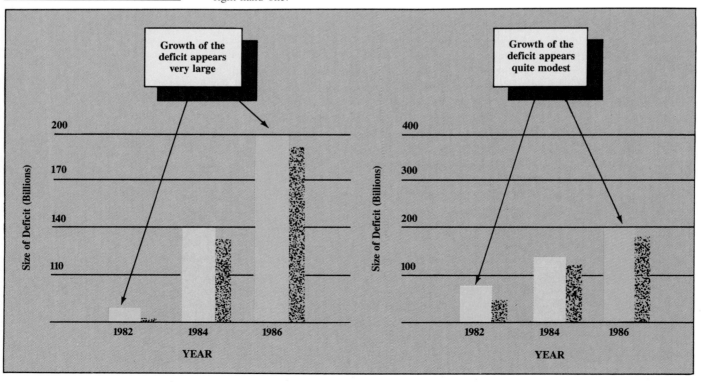

larger and more dramatic in the left-hand graph. As you can readily see, these contrasting patterns are produced by shifts in the size of the units along the vertical axis. These are small in the left-hand graph, but very large in the right-hand one. Would you reach different conclusions about the growth in the deficit if you were exposed to one or the other? If you are like most persons, the answer is "Yes," especially if the graph was accompanied by appropriate verbal commentary. (Democrat: "The growth in the deficit under Republican rule has been nothing short of *alarming!*" Republican: "There has, indeed, been a modest increase in the deficit. But weighed against the economic benefits obtained, this is a small price to pay.")

Sad to relate, such "fine-tuning" of graphs is common and can be noted in magazines, political mailings, and many other sources. For this reason, it is important to pay careful attention to the scale employed in any graph, the precise quantities being measured, and all labels employed. If you overlook such factors, you may be a "sitting duck" for those who wish to lead you to false conclusions.

Summary and Review

Descriptive Statistics

All scientists require two types of tools in their research: equipment for collecting data and some means of interpreting their findings. In psychology, *statistics* are often used for the latter purpose.

Large amounts of data can be grouped into *frequency distributions*, indicating the number of times each score occurs. Two important facts about any frequency distribution are its *central tendency*—its center—and its *dispersion*—the extent to which scores spread out around this value. Common measures of central tendency include the *mean, mode,* and *median.* Dispersion is often measured in terms of *variance* and the *standard deviation.* The last-named refers to the average distance of each score from the mean.

The frequency distributions for many behavioral characteristics show a distinct bell-shaped form known as the **normal curve.** Most scores fall somewhere near the middle, and fewer occur at increasing distances from this value. One property of the normal curve which makes it very useful to psychologists is that specific proportions of the scores are found under certain parts of the curve. Moreover, these portions can be defined in terms of the standard deviation. For example, 68 percent of the scores occur in the region between the mean and one standard deviation above or below this value. Because of these facts, the relative standing of specific scores can be readily interpreted if we know the mean and standard deviation.

Inferential Statistics

Psychologists often use *inferential statistics* to determine whether differences between individuals or groups are *significant* (real). Inferential statistics assume that the mean difference in question is zero, and that observed differences are distributed normally around this value. If an observed difference is large enough that it would be expected to occur by chance alone only five percent of the time, it is viewed as being significant.

Correlation and Prediction

To determine whether two or more variables are related, psychologists compute *correlation coefficients*. These range from -1.00 to $+1.00$. The larger the departure from 0.00, the stronger the correlation between the variables in question. Correlations (and other statistics derived from them) can be used to predict future behavior from currently available information. Such predictions are of great practical benefit to schools, companies, and other organizations that wish to predict the future performance of individuals who may be hired or admitted as students.

Misuse of Statistics

Although statistics have many beneficial uses, they are often employed to deceive or mislead large numbers of persons. This can involve the use of extremely small or biased samples, unexpressed comparisons, and misleading graphs and presentations. In addition, we must be on guard against assuming that rare but chance-produced events have some special meaning or significance.

Key Terms

Central Tendency Refers to the middle (center) of a distribution of scores.

Correlation Coefficient A statistic indicating the degree of relationship between two or more variables.

Descriptive Statistics Statistics that summarize the major characteristics of an array of scores.

Dispersion The extent to which scores in a distribution spread out or vary around the center.

Frequency Distribution The frequency with which each score occurs within an entire distribution of scores.

Inferential Statistics Statistical procedures that permit us to determine whether differences between individuals or groups are ones that are likely or unlikely to have occurred by chance.

Mean A measure of central tendency derived by adding all scores and dividing by the number of scores.

Median A measure of central tendency indicating the midpoint of an array of scores.

Mode A measure of central tendency indicating the most frequent score in an array of scores.

Normal Curve A symmetrical, bell-shaped frequency distribution. Most scores are found near the middle, and fewer and fewer occur toward the extremes. Many psychological characteristics are distributed in this manner.

Range The difference between the highest and lowest scores in a distribution of scores.

Standard Deviation A measure of dispersion reflecting the average distance between each score and the mean.

Statistics Mathematical procedures used to describe data and draw inferences from them.

Variance A measure of dispersion reflecting the average squared distance between each score and the mean.

Glossary

Absolute Threshold The smallest amount of a stimulus that we can detect 50 percent of the time.

Accommodation According to Piaget, the modification of existing mental frameworks in order to take account of new information.

Acetylcholine An important transmitter substance found in the brain and other parts of the nervous system. The death of cells normally sensitive to this substance seems to play a role in *Alzheimer's disease*.

Achievement Motivation Concern with accomplishing difficult tasks and adhering to standards of excellence.

Achievement Tests Tests designed to measure knowledge of a specific subject or task.

Action Potential A rapid shift in the electrical charge across the cell membrane of neurons. It is through the rapid movement of this disturbance along the membrane that information is communicated within neurons.

Active Touch Our ability to detect and recognize objects we touch with our hands or other body parts.

Acuity The visual ability to see fine details.

Adolescence The period between the onset of puberty and entry into adulthood.

Adrenogenital Syndrome A disorder in which the adrenal glands of a female fetus produce too much androgen. As a result, such infants are born with sexual organs resembling those of males, and even after corrective surgery these individuals may continue to show masculine characteristics in their behavior.

Adulthood The period of life after individuals assume adult responsibilities (e.g., marriage, starting a career).

Affect Intensity Individual differences in the degree to which people experience emotional reactions.

Affiliation Motivation Concern with maintaining warm, friendly relations with others.

Algorithms Rules that guarantee solutions to appropriate problems.

Amnesia A disorder involving loss of memory.

Analogies Efforts to solve a problem by applying solutions that were previously successful with other problems which were different in content but similar in underlying structure.

Androgen Insensitivity Syndrome Occurs when the cells of genetic males are insensitive to androgen. Such males are born with what appear to be female sexual organs.

Anosmia A condition in which some portion of the sense of smell is lost.

Antisocial Personality Disorder A disorder involving lack of conscience, inability to form close ties to others, and high impulsiveness.

Anxiety Fear involving the expectation of some unspecified danger.

Anxiety Disorders Psychological disorders centering around the occurrence of anxiety, (including phobias and obsessive-compulsive disorders).

Appearance-Reality Distinction The ability to distinguish between the current appearance of an object and its enduring nature.

Aptitude Tests Tests designed to measure the capacity to profit from specific types of training.

Assessment Centers Procedures for measuring a wide range of traits and characteristics, often used for identifying individuals with leadership or management potential.

Assimilation According to Piaget, the tendency to understand new information in terms of existing mental frameworks.

Attachment A strong emotional bond between infants and their caregivers.

Attraction The extent to which we evaluate others in a positive or negative manner.

Attribution The process through which we determine the causes of others' behavior.

Automatic Processing Processing of information without conscious awareness.

Autonomic Nervous System That part of the peripheral nervous system that connects internal organs, glands, and muscles not under voluntary control to the central nervous system.

Availability Heuristic A mental rule of thumb indicating that the more readily events or objects come to mind, the more frequent or likely we judge them to be.

Avoidant Personality Disorder A disorder in

which individuals cannot form adequate social relations with others because of a profound fear of rejection.

Axon The part of the neuron that carries information (action potentials) away from the cell body.

Babbling An early stage of speech development in which infants emit virtually all known sounds of human speech.

Baroreceptors Cells in the heart and certain veins that detect changes in blood pressure produced by the loss of water from the body.

Base Rates The frequency of some object or event in general (i.e., in a large population of events or objects).

Behavior Therapies Forms of psychotherapy derived from basic principles of learning.

Behaviorism The view that psychology should study only observable (overt) behavior.

Belief Perseverance The tendency to maintain established beliefs even in the face of evidence or information that contradicts them.

Binocular Cues Cues to depth or distance resulting from the fact that we have two eyes.

Biofeedback A procedure in which small changes in bodily processes are detected and magnified by electronic equipment into an audible or visible signal.

Biological Therapies Efforts to alleviate psychological disorders by changing the structure or function of the brain.

Bipolar Depression A mood disorder involving swings of emotion between deep despair and extreme elation.

Body Language Movements in various parts of the body reflecting various emotional reactions.

Brightness Constancy The tendency to perceive objects as having a constant brightness when they are viewed under different conditions of illumination.

Brown Fat Mechanism A regulatory mechanism within the body that converts calories to heat rather than to permanent fat deposits.

Burnout A psychological state that sometimes follows prolonged exposure to intense stress. Burnout involves physical, mental, and attitudinal exhaustion, as well as feelings of low personal accomplishment.

Cannon-Bard Theory A theory of emotion suggesting that various emotion-provoking events simultaneously produce the subjective reactions we label as emotions *and* the physiological changes which accompany them.

Case Method A method of research in which detailed information about specific individuals (cases) is used to formulate general principles about some aspect of behavior.

Cell Body The part of a neuron (or other cell) containing the nucleus.

Central Nervous System A crucial part of the nervous system, consisting of the brain and spinal cord.

Central Tendency Refers to the middle (center) of a distribution of scores.

Cerebellum A part of the brain concerned with the regulation of motor activities.

Cerebral Cortex The outer covering of the cerebral hemispheres.

Childhood The period from age two until the onset of puberty.

Chromosomes Threadlike structures containing genetic material (i.e., genes) found in nearly every cell of the body.

Classical Conditioning A basic form of learning in which one stimulus comes to serve as a signal for the occurrence of a second stimulus.

Cochlea A portion of the inner ear containing the sensory receptors for sound.

Cognitive Dissonance An unpleasant affective state that results when an individual notices that his or her attitudes and behaviors are inconsistent.

Cognitive Therapies Forms of psychotherapy that focus on changing disordered or faulty patterns of thought.

Cognitive View of Gender Identity The view that gender identity is based on children's understanding that they are male or female and their subsequent tendency to acquire behaviors appropriate to this identity.

Complex Cells Neurons in the visual cortex that respond to stimuli which move in a particular direction and which have a particular orientation in space.

Compliance A form of social influence in which individuals change their behavior in response to direct requests from others.

Componential Intelligence The ability to think analytically.

Concepts Mental categories for objects or events that are similar in enough respects to be grouped together.

Concrete Operations According to Piaget, a stage of cognitive development between the ages of seven and eleven.

Concurrent Validity The relationship between test scores and current performance on some criterion.

Conditioned Response (CR) In classical conditioning, the response to the conditioned stimulus.

Conditioned Stimulus (CS) In classical conditioning, the stimulus which is repeatedly paired with an unconditioned stimulus.

Cones Sensory receptors in the eye that play a crucial role in sensations of color.

Confirmation Bias The tendency to test beliefs or hypotheses by focusing on instances in which we expect them to be confirmed.

Confluence Theory A theory suggesting that IQ tends to decrease across the birth order within a family (first-borns tend to have a higher IQ than second-borns, and so on).

Conformity A type of social influence in which individuals change their attitudes or behavior in order to adhere to the expectations of others or the norms of groups to which they belong or wish to belong.

Confounding of Variables A situation that arises when factors other than the independent variable in an experiment are not held constant.

Consciousness Awareness of external and internal stimuli (yourself, your behavior, and the world around you).

Conservation Understanding of the fact that basic physical dimensions (e.g., area, volume, number) remain constant despite superficial changes in appearance.

Constancies Our tendency to perceive physical objects as unchanging despite shifts in the pattern of sensations these objects induce.

Constraints on Learning Refers to the fact that all forms of conditioning are not equally easy to establish with all organisms.

Construct Validity The extent to which a test measures a construct described by a psychological theory.

Content Validity The extent to which the items on a test sample the skills or knowledge needed for achievement in a given field or task.

Contextual Intelligence The ability to adapt to a changing environment.

Controlled Processing Processing of information with conscious awareness.

Corpus Callosum A band of nerve fibers connecting the right and left cerebral hemispheres.

Correlation Coefficient A statistic indicating the degree of relationship between two or more variables.

Correlational Method A method of research in which two or more variables are observed, to determine whether changes in one are accompanied by changes in the other. To the degree this is so, one varia- ble can be accurately predicted from the other.

Critical Thinking Systematic thinking in which all assumptions underlying conclusions or ideas are subjected to careful, detailed analysis.

Cross-Sectional Research Research in which individuals of different ages are compared in order to determine whether they differ in specific, predicted ways.

Cultural Bias Occurs when answering the items on a test of intelligence requires specific cultural experience or knowledge.

Dark Adaptation The process through which our visual system increases its sensitivity to light under low levels of illumination.

Daydreams (Fantasies) Imaginary scenes and events that occur while you are awake.

Debriefing Providing participants in psychological research with complete and accurate information about all purposes and procedures of the study following its completion.

Decay Theory of Forgetting The view that forgetting occurs because memory traces fade with the passage of time.

Decision-Making The process of choosing between various courses of action or alternatives.

Defense Mechanisms Efforts by the ego to disguise unacceptable impulses or wishes and so to allow their partial gratification.

Dendrites The part of the neuron that carries information (action potentials) toward the cell body.

Dependent Personality Disorder A disorder in which individuals allow others to make decisions for them and tell them how to act.

Dependent Variable The aspect of behavior that is measured in psychological research.

Depressants Drugs that reduce activity in the nervous system and therefore slow many bodily and cognitive processes (e.g., alcohol, barbiturates).

Descriptive Statistics Statistics that summarize the major characteristics of an array of scores.

Developmental Psychology The branch of psychology that studies age-related changes in all aspects of behavior and cognition.

Difference Threshold The amount by which two stimuli must differ in order to be just noticeably different.

Dispersion The extent to which scores in a distribution are spread out or vary around the center.

LIVERPOOL JOHN MOORES UNIVERSITY
Aldham Robarts L.R.C.
TEL. 051 231 3701/3634

Dissociative Disorders Psychological disorders involving profound and lengthy losses of identity and memory.

Door-in-the-Face A technique for gaining compliance in which a large request is followed by a smaller one.

Dopamine Hypothesis The hypothesis that schizophrenia stems, at least in part, from an excess of dopamine in the brain.

Dreams Cognitive events, often vivid and detailed, that occur during sleep. Most dreams take place during REM sleep.

Drive Theory A theory of motivation suggesting that behavior is ''pushed'' from within by drives stemming from basic biological needs.

DSM-III-R A framework for identifying (diagnosing) a wide range of psychological disorders.

Ego In Freud's theory of personality, the structure that holds primitive biological impulses in check until they can be satisfied in a safe and appropriate manner.

Egocentrism The inability of young children to realize that others may perceive the world differently than they do.

Elaborative Rehearsal Rehearsal involving efforts to understand the meaning of words or other materials and their relationship to information already in memory.

Electroconvulsive Therapy (ECT) A biological therapy which delivers strong electric shocks to the patient's head in order to alleviate major depression or other forms of psychological disorder.

Electroencephalogram A record of electrical activity occurring within the brain. EEGs play an important role in the scientific study of sleep.

Embryo The developing child during the first eight weeks of life.

Emotions Reactions consisting of subjective cognitive states, physiological responses, and expressive behaviors.

Encoding The process through which information is placed in a form that can be entered into memory.

Encoding Specificity Hypothesis The suggestion that cues present at the time information is encoded can facilitate recall if they are also present at later time.

Endocrine Glands Glands that secrete hormones directly into the bloodstream.

Entrapment A process whereby individuals who have obtained negative results from a decision continue with the failed course of action in order to justify the time, effort, and other costs they have already incurred.

Environmental Psychology A field that studies the impact of the physical environment on human behavior.

Episodic Memory Memory for personally experienced events associated with specific places or contexts.

Existential Therapy Therapy that attempts to change a patient's cognitions, especially the belief that life is meaningless.

Expectancy Theory A theory of motivation suggesting that behavior is induced by expectations that certain forms of behavior will yield valued outcomes.

Experiential Intelligence The ability to formulate new ideas or combine seemingly unrelated information.

Experimentation A method of research in which one or more variables are systematically varied in order to determine whether such changes affect some aspect of behavior or cognitive processes.

Extinction The process through which a conditioned stimulus gradually loses the ability to evoke conditioned responses when it is no longer followed by the unconditioned stimulus.

Extrasensory Perception Perceptions that are not based on input from our sensory receptors. Included under the heading of ESP are such supposed abilities as *telepathy* (reading others' minds) and *clairvoyance* (perceiving distant objects).

Facial Feedback Hypothesis The suggestion that changes in facial expressions can influence as well as reflect underlying emotions.

False Consensus Effect Our tendency to believe that others share our attitudes to a greater extent than is actually the case.

Family Therapy Therapy that focuses on changing interactions among family members.

Fetal Alcohol Syndrome Severely retarded growth, nervous system damage, and distortions in facial shape among newborns, stemming from heavy use of alcohol by the mother during pregnancy.

Fetus The developing child during the last seven months of pregnancy.

Figure-Ground Relationship Our tendency to divide the perceptual world into two distinct parts—discrete figures and the background against which they stand out.

Fixed-Interval Schedule A schedule of reinforcement in which a specific interval of time must elapse before a response will yield reinforcement.

Fixed Ratio Schedule A schedule of reinforcement in which reinforcement occurs only after a fixed number of responses have been emitted.

Flashbulb Memory Vivid memory for what an individual was doing at the time some emotionally arousing event took place.

Flooding Procedures for eliminating conditioned fears based on principles of classical conditioning. During flooding an individual is asked to think about fear-inducing objects or events. Since no unconditioned stimulus then follows, extinction of these fears eventually takes place.

Foot-in-the-Door A technique for gaining compliance in which a small request is followed by a larger one.

Forgetting The loss of information from memory. (In the case of long-term memory, this involves inability to retrieve information in memory.)

Formal Operations According to Piaget, a stage of cognitive development during which individuals become capable of deductive reasoning.

Free Association A procedure in psychoanalysis in which the patient spontaneously reports all thoughts passing through his or her mind.

Frequency Distribution The frequency with which each score occurs within an entire distribution of scores.

Frequency Theory A theory of pitch perception suggesting that sounds of different frequencies (heard as differences in pitch) induce different rates of neural activity in the hair cells of the inner ear.

Functional Fixedness The tendency to think of using an object only as it has been used in the past. This tendency can interfere with effective problem-solving.

Functionalism An early approach suggesting that psychology should focus on the contribution of our mental processes to our survival in a complex and ever-changing world.

Fundamental Attribution Error Our tendency to explain others' behavior in terms of internal causes (e.g., their traits or motives) when such conclusions are not really justified.

Gate-Control Theory A theory of pain suggesting that the spinal cord contains a mechanism that can block transmission of pain to the brain.

Gender Identity Children's understanding of the fact that they are male or female.

Generalized Anxiety A disorder in which individuals experience intense anxiety which is not directed toward any specific object.

Genes Biological "blueprints" that shape development and basic bodily processes.

Gestalt Therapy A form of therapy designed to increase an individual's awareness and understanding of her or his own feelings.

Gestures Movements of various parts of the body that convey a specific meaning to others.

Goal-Setting A technique for enhancing motivation (especially work motivation) in which specific, challenging performance goals are established.

Hallucinogens Drugs that exert profound effects upon states of consciousness (e.g., marijuana, LSD).

Hardiness A characteristic (or cluster of characteristics) that helps individuals resist the adverse effects of stress. Persons high in hardiness have a sense of commitment and of personal control and view change as a challenge rather than a burden.

Helplessness The belief that one cannot exert any influence over one's own outcomes.

Heuristics Mental rules of thumb that permit us to make decisions and judgments in a rapid and efficient manner.

Histrionic Personality Disorder A disorder in which an individual desires to be the center of attention at all times and cannot bear even the slightest criticism.

Human Factors The interface between human beings and the systems or equipment they use.

Humanistic Growth Groups A form of group therapy that focuses upon increasing individuals' awareness of their own feelings and their impact upon others.

Humanistic Theories of Personality Theories emphasizing human potential for growth and development.

Humanistic Therapies Therapies that seek to increase self-awareness and enhance the self-concept.

Hypercomplex Cells Neurons in the visual cortex that respond to complex aspects of visual stimuli, such as width, length, and shape.

Hypermnesia Improvements in memory over time or repeated efforts to recall previously learned materials.

Hypersomnia Sleep disorder involving excessive amounts of sleep or an overwhelming urge to fall asleep (e.g., narcolepsy).

Hypnosis An interaction between two persons in which one (the hypnotist) induces changes in the behavior, feelings, or cognitions of the other (the subject) through suggestions delivered while the subject is in an altered state of consciousness (a trance).

Hypothalamus A structure deep within the brain that plays a key role in regulating the autonomic nervous system, in emotion, and in regulating several important forms of behavior (eating, drinking).

Hypothesis The prediction about behavior or cognitive processes under investigation in psychological research.

Id In Freud's theory of personality, the structure containing our primitive urges.

Illusions Instances in which perception yields false interpretations of physical reality.

Independent Variable The factor that is systematically varied in an experiment.

Industrial/Organizational Psychology The subfield of psychology that focuses upon all aspects of behavior in work settings. Among the topics studied by industrial/organizational psychologists are the selection and training of employees, work-related attitudes (e.g., job satisfaction), performance appraisal, motivation, and leadership.

Infancy The first two years of life.

Inferential Statistics Statistical procedures that permit us to determine whether differences between individuals or groups are ones that are likely or unlikely to have occurred by chance.

Information-Processing Approach The view that human memory can best be understood in terms of the operations of encoding, storage, and retrieval.

Informed Consent Providing potential subjects with as much information as feasible prior to obtaining their consent to take part in psychological research.

Ingratiation A technique for gaining compliance based on first inducing others to like us and then making various requests.

Instinct Theory A theory of motivation suggesting that many forms of behavior stem from innate urges or tendencies.

Intelligence Traditionally, the ability to think analytically or to learn readily from experience.

Interests Preferences for participation in certain activities.

Interference The suggestion that forgetting occurs because various items or pieces of information stored in memory actively interfere with one another.

Intrinsic Motivation The desire to perform certain activities because they are pleasant or rewarding in and of themselves.

IQ A numerical value that reflects the extent to which an individual's score on an intelligence test departs from the average for other people of the same age.

James-Lange Theory A theory of emotion suggesting that emotion-provoking events produce various physiological reactions and that these, in turn, give rise to our subjective experiences of emotion.

Language A system of communication employing sounds, written symbols, and gestures.

Lateral Hypothalamus A portion of the hypothalamus that plays a role in the regulation of eating. It was once believed that this region serves as an eating center, but recent findings cast doubt on this suggestion.

Lateralization of the cerebral hemispheres Refers to the fact that the two hemispheres of the brain appear to be specialized for somewhat different functions.

Laws of Grouping Simple principles describing how we tend to group discrete stimuli together in the perceptual world.

Leadership Motive Pattern (LMP) A pattern consisting of high power motivation coupled with low affiliation motivation. Individuals showing this pattern are more successful as managers than others.

Learned Helplessness The reduced ability of organisms to learn that certain responses will yield reinforcement following exposure to a situation in which no response produces such outcomes.

Learning Any relatively permanent change in behavior (or behavior tendencies) resulting from experience.

Levels of Processing A view suggesting that the more cognitive effort we expend with respect to new information, the more strongly it will be entered into memory and the more readily it will be recalled at later times.

Limbic System Several structures deep within the brain that play an important role in emotional reactions.

Linear Reasoning Reasoning in which we compare items to determine their relative order.

Linguistic-Relativity Hypothesis The view that language shapes thought.

Loneliness Refers to the inability to attain close social contacts with others when these are desired.

Longitudinal Research Research in which the same individuals are studied at several points in time to determine whether some aspect of their behavior changes with age.

Long-Term Memory The memory system that permits us to store large (perhaps unlimited) amounts of information over long periods of time.

Love An intense form of attraction involving feelings of intimacy, passion, and commitment.

Major Depression A mood disorder in which an individual's mood swings between deep despair (depression) and a relatively neutral state.

Mania A state of extreme elation and activity.

Mean A measure of central tendency derived by adding all scores and dividing by the number of scores.

Means-Ends Analysis A technique for solving problems in which the over-all problem is divided into parts, and efforts are made to solve each part in turn.

Median A measure of central tendency indicating the midpoint of an array of scores.

Meditation A relaxation technique for countering the effects of stress in which individuals clear their minds of disturbing thoughts and then repeat a single syllable (*mantra*) over and over.

Medulla A structure in the brain concerned with the regulation of vital bodily functions (e.g., breathing, heartbeat).

Memory The retention of information over time.

Mental Set The impact of past experience on present problem-solving, specifically, our tendency to stick with methods that worked in the past, leading us sometimes to overlook more efficient means to a solution.

Midbrain A part of the brain containing primitive centers concerned with vision and hearing. It also plays a role in the regulation of visual reflexes.

MMPI (Minnesota Multiphasic Personality Inventory) A widely used test designed to measure individual differences on several traits related to psychological disorders.

Mnemonics Specific procedures for improving memory.

Mode A measure of central tendency indicating the most frequent score in an array of scores.

Modeling Therapy A form of behavior therapy in which individuals are shown others who perform actions they are unable to perform themselves.

Monocular Cues Cues to depth or distance provided by one eye.

Mood Disorders Psychological disorders involving major disturbances in mood or emotional state (e.g., depression).

Motivation An inferred internal process that activates, guides, and maintains behavior.

Multiple Personality A psychological disorder in which an individual appears to have two or more distinct personalities.

Natural Concepts Concepts used in everyday life that are not based on a concrete set of attributes. Natural concepts do not have clear-cut boundaries and often are defined by prototypes—the best or clearest examples of items or events the concept includes.

Naturalistic Observation A method of research involving careful observations of behavior in natural settings.

Nature-Nurture Controversy An ongoing debate concerning the extent to which various aspects of behavior are determined by genetic factors or experience.

Negative Afterimage A sensation of complementary color that occurs after staring at a stimulus of a given hue.

Negative Reinforcers Stimuli which strengthen responses which permit organisms to avoid or escape from their presence.

Neo-Freudians Personality theorists who accepted many of Freud's basic ideas but modified his theory in important ways and added several new concepts of their own.

Nervous System The complex structure which regulates bodily processes and overt behavior and which is responsible for all aspects of conscious experience.

Neurons Cells specialized for communicating information that are the basic building blocks of the nervous system.

Neurotic Disorders A wide range of psychological disorders which are both serious and stressful but which usually permit their victims to function in society.

Nonverbal Cues Outward signs of others' emotional states. Important nonverbal cues are communicated by facial expressions, eye contact, and body language.

Norepinephrine An important transmitter substance producing inhibitory effects within the brain but excitatory effects in other parts of the nervous system.

Normal Curve A symmetrical, bell-shaped frequency distribution. Most scores are found near the middle, and fewer and fewer occur toward the extremes. Many psychological characteristics are distributed in this manner.

Obedience A form of social influence in which one individual simply orders another to behave in some manner.

Obesity A condition in which an individual's body weight exceeds optimal levels for his or her age, height, and build.

Object Permanence Understanding of the fact that objects continue to exist even when they are removed from view.

Observational Learning The acquisition of new forms of behavior, information, or concepts through exposure to others and the consequences they experience.

Obsessive-Compulsive Disorders Psychological disorders in which, because of extreme anxiety, individuals repeat the same thoughts and actions over and over again.

Operant Conditioning A process through which organisms learn to repeat behaviors which yield positive outcomes or which permit them to avoid or escape from negative outcomes (also termed instrumental conditioning).

Opponent Process Theory A theory that describes the processing of sensory information related to color at levels above the retina. The theory suggests that we possess six different types of neurons, each of which is either stimulated or inhibited by red, green, blue, yellow, black, and white.

Osmoreceptors Receptors that detect the loss of liquid from cells of the body.

Overconfidence The tendency to overestimate one's own ability to make accurate judgments and decisions.

Panic Attack Periods (usually relatively brief) during which individuals experience extreme feelings of anxiety and a wide range of physical symptoms (e.g., shortness of breath, trembling).

Passive Touch Our sensitivity to being touched at various points on the body.

Perception The process through which we organize and interpret input from our sensory receptors.

Peripheral Nervous System That portion of the nervous system that connects internal organs, glands, and muscles to the central nervous system.

Person-Centered Therapy A humanistic therapy which seeks to enhance an individual's self-awareness and induce a more realistic self-concept.

Personality The unique but stable set of characteristics that sets each individual apart from all others.

Personality Disorders Psychological disorders involving strong and inflexible traits that interfere with the individuals' personal adjustment.

Phobias Disorders in which individuals experience intense anxiety toward specific objects.

Place Theory A theory suggesting that sounds of different frequency stimulate different areas of the basilar membrane, the portion of the cochlea containing sensory receptors for sound.

Placenta A structure that surrounds, protects, and nourishes the developing fetus.

Pons A portion of the brain through which sensory and motor information passes and which contains structures related to sleep and arousal.

Positive Reinforcers Stimuli which strengthen responses which precede them.

Positive Test Strategy Our tendency to test hypotheses by examining only instances in which we expect a positive result.

Power Motivation Concern with being in charge, having high status, and exerting influence over others.

Predictive Validity The relationship between scores on a test and later performance on a criterion.

Prenatal Period The period prior to birth.

Preoperational Stage According to Piaget, a stage of cognitive development occurring between the ages of two and seven.

Primary Aging Physical or biological changes directly related to increasing age.

Priming Refers to the fact that recent experiences which have activated certain aspects of memory may affect our current interpretation of events or stimuli.

Problem-Solving The process through which we attempt to determine the means for reaching a difficult goal.

Projective Techniques Procedures for measuring personality in which individuals are asked to interpret ambiguous stimuli.

Propositional Reasoning Reasoning in which we consider the truth of "If . . . then" statements.

Prototypes Best examples of natural concepts, for example, thinking of a chair or table for the natural concept "furniture."

Psychoanalysis A form of therapy, devised by Freud, that attempts to provide individuals with insight into repressed inner conflicts.

Psychoanalytic Theory of Personality Freud's theory of personality. It includes Freud's ideas about the nature of the human mind, basic structures of personality, and psychosexual stages of development.

Psychodynamic Perspective Freud's views concerning the nature and origin of mental illness.

Psychogenic Amnesia Sudden disruptions of memory that seem to occur in response to unbearable stress.

Psychological Disorders Patterns of behavior and thought that are atypical, undesirable within a given culture, and cause the persons involved considerable distress.

Psychological Perspective The view that psychological disorders are better understood as the result of basic processes such as learning and cognition than as forms of illness.

Psychological Tests Special devices for assessing the traits or characteristics of individuals.

Psychology The science of behavior and cognitive processes.

Psychosurgery A biological therapy that attempts to alleviate psychological disorder by performing medical operations upon the brain.

Psychotherapy Efforts to produce beneficial changes in an individual's behavior, feelings, or thoughts through establishment of a special type of relationship between the person seeking help and a trained professional.

Puberty A period of rapid sexual maturation and growth.

Punishment Refers to situations in which

negative outcomes follow specific responses.

Random Assignment of Subjects to Groups Assuring that all participants in psychological research have an equal opportunity of being assigned to any of the experimental conditions.

Range The difference between the highest and lowest scores in a distribution of scores.

Rational-Emotive Therapy A cognitive therapy that focuses on the task of eliminating irrational beliefs.

Raven Progressive Matrices One popular ''culture-free'' test of intelligence.

Reasoning Thinking in which we attempt to draw conclusions from given facts of assumptions.

Reflexes Rapid, seemingly automatic actions evoked by a particular stimulus (e.g., withdrawal of the hand from a hot object).

Reliability The extent to which any measuring device yields the same results when applied to the same quantity.

REM Sleep A stage of sleep in which brain activity resembling waking restfulness is accompanied by profound muscle relaxation and rapid eye-movements. Most dreams occur during periods of REM sleep.

Reminiscence A phenomenon in which information that can't be remembered at one time *is* remembered later.

Representativeness Heuristic A mental rule of thumb suggesting that the more an event or object resembles what we consider to be ''typical,'' the more likely or frequent it is judged to be.

Resistance Efforts by individuals undergoing psychoanalysis to prevent repressed conflicts from entering consciousness.

Reticular Activating System A structure within the brain concerned with sleep and arousal.

Retrieval The process through which information stored in memory is located.

Retrieval Cues Stimuli associated with information stored in memory which often play a key role in its retrieval (in bringing such information into conscious experience).

Rods One of the two types of sensory receptors for vision found in the eye.

Rorschach Ink Blot Test A famous projective test of personality in which individuals are asked to interpret a set of ambiguous figures created by ink blots.

Saccadic Movement Movement of the eyes from one point of fixation to another.

Schachter-Singer Theory A theory of emotion suggesting that our subjective emotional states are determined, at least in part, by the labels we attach to internal feelings of arousal.

Schedules of Reinforcement Rules determining when and how reinforcements will be delivered.

Schemas Cognitive frameworks developed through experience that affect the way in which incoming information is encoded, stored, and retrieved.

Schizophrenic Disorders Very serious disorders in which, because of disturbed thought, perceptions, and emotions, individuals lose contact with reality.

Secondary Aging Physical or biological changes related to disease, injury, or abuse of our bodies.

Self-Actualization The need to become the most fully developed person you can be.

Self-Monitoring A personality dimension relating to the extent to which individuals adapt their behavior to current circumstances or act in accordance with stable attitudes, values, and beliefs.

Self-Serving Bias The tendency to view positive outcomes as stemming primarily from internal causes (e.g., our own effort or ability) but negative outcomes as stemming largely from external causes.

Semantic Memory Memory for general knowledge not associated with specific times or contexts.

Sensation Input about the physical world provided by our sensory receptors.

Sensorimotor Stage According to Piaget, the earliest stage of cognitive development. During this period, infants gradually acquire a basic understanding of the concept of cause and effect.

Sensory Adaptation Reduced sensitivity to unchanging stimuli over time.

Sensory Memory A memory system that retains representations of sensory input for brief periods of time.

Sensory Receptors Cells of the body specialized for the task of transduction—converting physical energy (light, sound) into neural impulses.

Sex-Role Stereotypes Beliefs within a given culture about the supposed characteristics of persons of each gender and patterns of behavior that are considered appropriate for each to demonstrate.

Sexual Disorders Psychological disturbances in sexual arousal, sexual behavior, or gender identity.

Shape Constancy The tendency to perceive a physical object as having a constant shape even when the image it casts on the retina changes.

Shaping A technique in which closer and closer approximations to desired behavior are required for the delivery of positive reinforcement.

Short-Term Memory The memory system

that holds information we are currently using.

Shyness The tendency to feel tense or awkward during social interactions, especially ones involving strangers.

Signal Detection Theory A theory suggesting that there are no absolute thresholds for sensations. Rather, detection of stimuli depends on their physical energy and on internal factors such as the relative costs and benefits associated with detecting their presence.

Simple Cells Cells within the visual system that respond to specific shapes presented in certain orientations (e.g., horizontal, vertical, etc.).

Size Constancy The tendency to perceive a physical object as having a constant size even when the image it casts on the retina changes.

Size-Distance Invariance Refers to the fact that when we estimate the size of any object, we take simultaneous account of the size of its image on the retina and its apparent distance from us.

Sleep A process in which important physiological changes (e.g., shifts in brain activity, slowing of basic bodily functions) are accompanied by profound alterations in consciousness.

Social Cognition The processes through which we sort, store, and retrieve social information, often to make decisions or judgments about others.

Social Cognitive Theory A sophisticated theory of human behavior suggesting that environmental conditions, personal and cognitive factors, and behavior interact as determinants of one another.

Social Development Changes in social behavior and social relations occurring with age.

Social Influence Efforts by one or more persons to change the behavior, feelings, or thoughts of one or more others.

Social Learning View of Gender Identity The view that children acquire gender identity by imitating persons of their own sex (primarily their same-sex parents).

Social Psychology The branch of psychology that studies all aspects of social behavior and social thought.

Sociobiology A branch of biology that studies the evolution of social behavior. Sociobiologists contend that patterns of behavior that help members of a given species survive and reproduce become part of that species genetic inheritance.

Somatic Nervous System That portion of the nervous system that connects voluntary muscles to the central nervous system.

Somatoform Disorders Psychological disorders in which various physical symptoms (e.g., numbness, deafness, pain) do not stem from physical causes.

Somnambulism A sleep disorder in which individuals actually get up and move about while still asleep.

Split-Half Reliability The extent to individuals attain equivalent scores on two halves of a psychological test.

Stage Theory Any theory suggesting that all human beings pass through a set sequence of changes in an orderly and universal manner.

Standard Deviation A measure of dispersion reflecting the average distance between each score and the mean.

Standardization Administration of a psychological test to a large group of people who are representative of the population for which the test is intended.

Stanford-Binet-Test A popular test for measuring individual intelligence.

Statistical Analysis Mathematical procedures used to evaluate the results obtained in psychological research.

Statistics Mathematical procedures used to describe data and draw inferences from them.

Stimulants Drugs that increase activity in the nervous system (e.g., amphetamines, caffeine, nicotine).

Stimulus Generalization The tendency of stimuli similar to a conditioned stimulus to evoke conditioned responses.

Storage The process through which information is retained in memory.

Strange Situation A procedure used to study attachment. Mothers leave their infants alone with a stranger for several minutes. The infants' reactions to this separation and reappearance of their mothers are observed.

Stress An unpleasant emotional state in which individuals feel that their capacity to cope with the demands upon them will soon be overwhelmed.

Stressors Various conditions and factors in the external environment that induce feelings of stress.

Structuralism An early view suggesting that psychology should focus on the task of analyzing conscious experience into its component parts.

Superego In Freud's theory of personality, the structure representing conscience.

Survey Approach A method of research in which large numbers of persons answer questions about some aspect of their attitudes or behavior.

Syllogistic Reasoning Reasoning in which two premises are used to derive a logical conclusion.

Synapse A region where the axon of one neuron closely approaches the dendrites or cell body of another neuron, or the cell membrane of other types of cells within the body (e.g., muscle cells).

Synaptic Vesicles Structures found in the terminal buttons of axons, containing various transmitter substances.

Systematic Desensitization A form of behavior therapy in which an individual learns to relax in the presence of imagined stimuli or events which initially caused feelings of anxiety. As such stimuli become associated with feelings of relaxation, they gradually lose the capacity to evoke anxiety.

Taste Buds Structures containing sensory receptors for taste.

Terminal Buttons Structures on the end of axons that play an important role in the transmission of information across synapses.

Test-Retest Reliability The extent to which a psychological test yields similar scores when taken by the same persons on different occasions.

Thalamus A structure deep within the brain that receives a great deal of sensory input from other portions of the nervous system and then transmits such information to the cerebral hemispheres and other parts of the brain.

Thematic Apperception Test (TAT) A test designed to measure the strength of several important human motives (achievement, affiliation, power).

Theories Frameworks in science for explaining various phenomena. Theories consist of two major parts: basic concepts and assertions concerning relationships between these concepts.

Thinking The cognitive processes which take place as we process information from our senses and information already present in memory.

Tip-of-the-Tongue Phenomenon The feeling that you can ''almost'' remember some item of information.

Token Economies A form of therapy based on operant conditioning. Patients at mental hospitals are given tokens that can be exchanged for valued rewards when they behave in specific desirable ways.

Trait Theories of Personality Theories that seek to identify the key dimensions of human personality.

Traits Specific behavioral or psychological dimensions along which individuals differ.

Transference Strong positive or negative feelings toward the therapist experienced by many individuals undergoing psychoanalysis.

Trial-and-Error A strategy for solving problems in which all possible solutions are tried until one works.

Triarchic Theory A theory suggesting that there are actually three distinct kinds of intelligence.

Trichromatic Theory A theory of color perception suggesting that we have three types of cones, each primarily receptive to different wavelengths of light.

Type A Behavior Pattern A cluster of traits (competitiveness, time urgency, hostility) related to important aspects of health, social behavior, and task performance.

Unconditional Positive Regard Acceptance of another person, despite her or his failings or shortcomings.

Unconditioned Response (UCR) In classical conditioning, the response evoked by an unconditioned stimulus.

Unconditioned Stimulus (UCS) In classical conditioning, a stimulus which can evoke an unconditioned response the first time it is presented.

Validity The extent to which psychological tests actually measure what they claim to measure.

Variable-Interval Schedule A schedule of reinforcement in which a variable interval of time must elapse before a response will yield reinforcement.

Variable-Ratio Schedule A schedule of reinforcement in which reinforcement is delivered after a variable number of responses have been performed.

Variance A measure of dispersion reflecting the average squared distance between each score and the mean.

Ventromedial Hypothalamus A portion of the hypothalamus that plays a role in the regulation of eating. It was once believed that this region serves as a discrete satiety center, but recent findings cast doubt on this suggestion.

Bibliography

Abramson, L.Y., Seligman, M.E.P., & Teasdale, J.D. (1978). Learned helplessness in humans: Critique and reformulation. *Journal of Abnormal Psychology, 87,* 49–74.

Adams, R.J. (1987). An evaluation of color preference in early infancy. *Infant Behavior and Development, 10,* 143–150.

Ader, R., & Cohen, N. (1984). Behavior and the immune system. In W.D. Gentry (ed.), *Handbook of behavioral medicine.* New York: Guilford.

Agras, W.S., Barlow, T.H., Chapin, H.N., Abel, G.G., & Leitenberg, H. (1974). Behavior modification of anorexia nervosa. *Archives of General Psychiatry, 30,* 343–352.

Ainsworth, M.D. (1973). The development of infant-mother attachment. In B.M. Caldwell & H.N. Riccuiti (eds.), *Review of child development research,* vol. 3. Chicago: University of Chicago Press.

Aiken, L.R. (1985). *Psychological testing and assessment,* 5th ed. Boston: Allyn and Bacon.

Ainsworth, M.D., & Wittig, B.A. (1969). Attachment and exploratory behavior of one-year-olds in a strange situation. In B.M. Foss (ed.), *Determinants of infant behaviour,* vol. 4. London: Methuen.

Akil, J., Watson, S.J., Young, E., Lewis, M.E., Kachaturian, H., & Walker, M.W. (1984). Endogamous opiates: Biology and function. *Annual Review of Neuroscience, 7,* 223–256.

Allen, M.G. (1976). Twin studies of affective illness. *Archives of General Psychiatry, 33,* 1476–1478.

Allport, G.W., & Odbert, H.S. (1936). Trait names: A psycholexical study. *Psychological Monographs, 47* (211).

Altrocchi, J. (1980). *Abnormal behavior.* New York: Harcourt Brace Jovanovich.

American Psychiatric Association. (1987). *Diagnostic and statistical manual of mental disorders,* 3rd ed.—Revised (DSM-III-R). Washington, D.C.: APA.

Amoore, J.E. (1970). *The molecular basis of odor.* Springfield, Ill.: Charles C Thomas.

Anderson, C.A. (1987). Temperature and aggression: Effects on quarterly, yearly, and city rates on violent and nonviolent crime. *Journal of Personality and Social Psychology, 52,* 1161–1173.

Anderson, C.A., Lepper, M.R., & Ross, L. (1980). Perseverance of social theories: The role of explanation in the persistence of discredited information. *Journal of Personality and Social Psychology, 39,* 1037–1049.

Anderson, D.C., Crowell, C.R., Doman, M., & Howard, G.S. (1988). Performance posting, goal setting, and activity-contingent praise as applied to a university hockey team. *Journal of Applied Psychology, 73,* 87–95.

Andrews, E.A., & Braverman, N.S. (1975). The combined effects of dosage level and interstimulus interval on the formation of one-trial poison-based aversions in rats. *Animal Learning and Behavior, 3,* 287–289.

Andrews, J.D.W. (1967). The achievement motive and advancement in two types of organizations. *Journal of Personality and Social Psychology, 6,* 163–168.

Arkes, H.R., Christensen, C., Lai, D., & Blumer, C. (1987). Two methods of reducing overconfidence. *Organizational Behavior and Human Decision Processes, 39,* 133–144.

Arkes, H.R., Dawes, R.M., & Christensen, C. (1986). Factors influencing the use of a decision rule in a probabilistic task. *Organizational Behavior and Human Decision Processes, 37,* 93–110.

Arkin, R.M., Lake, E.A., & Baumgardner, A.H. (1986). In W.H. Jones, J.M. Cheek, & S.R. Briggs (eds.), *Shyness: Perspectives on research and treatment.* New York: Plenum.

Arndt, W.B., Jr., Foehl, J.C., & Good, F.E. (1985). Specific sexual fantasy themes: A multidimensional study. *Journal of Personality and Social Psychology, 48,* 472–480.

Arvey, R.D., Bouchard, T.J., Jr., Segal, N.L., & Abraham, L.M. (1989). Job satisfaction: Environmental and genetic components. *Journal of Applied Psychology,* in press.

Arvey, R.D., & Campion, J.E. (1982). The employment interview: A summary and review of recent research. *Personnel Psychology, 35,* 281–322.

Arvey, R.D., & Ivancevich, J.M. (1980). Punishment in organizations: A review, propositions, and research suggestions. *Academy of Management Review, 5,* 123–132.

Asch, S.E. (1951). Effects of group pressure upon the modification and distortion of judgement. In H. Guetzkow (ed.), *Groups, leadership, and men.* Pittsburgh: Carnegie.

Atkinson, J.W., & Litwin, G.H. (1960). Achievement motive and test anxiety conceived as motive to approach success and motive to avoid failure. *Journal of Abnormal and Social Psychology, 60,* 52–63.

Atkinson, R.C., & Shiffrin, R.M. (1968). *Human memory: A proposed system and its control processes.* In K.W. Spenct & J.T. Spence (eds.), *The psychology of learning and motivation: Advances in research and theory,* vol. 2. New York: Academic.

Bahrick, H.P., Bahrick, P.O., & Wittlinger, R.P. (1975). Fifty years of memory for names and faces: A cross-sectional approach. *Journal of Experimental Psychology: General, 104,* 54–75.

Balasm, P.D., & Tomie, A. (eds.). *Context and learning.* Hillsdale, N.J.: Erlbaum.

Balogh, R.D., & Porter, R.H. (1986). Olfactory preferences resulting from mere exposure in human neonates. *Infant Behavior and Development, 9,* 395–401.

Bandura, A. (1977). *Social learning theory.* Englewood Cliffs, N.J.: Prentice-Hall.

Bandura, A. (1986). *Social foundations of thought and action: Social cognitive theory.* Englewood Cliffs, N.J.: Prentice-Hall.

Bandura, A., Blanchard, A., & Ritter, B. (1969). Relative efficacy of desensitization and modeling approaches for inducing behavioral, affective, and attitudinal changes. *Journal of Personality and Social Psychology, 13,* 173–199.

Bandura, A., Jeffery, R.W., & Wright, C.L. (1974). Efficacy of participant modeling as a function of response induction aids. *Journal of Abnormal Psychology, 83,* 56–64.

Bandura, A., & Menlove, F.L. (1968). Factors determining vicarious extinction of avoidance behavior through symbolic modeling. *Journal of Personality and Social Psychology, 8,* 99–108.

Bandura, A., Ross, D., & Ross, S. (1963). Imitation of film-mediated aggressive models. *Journal of Abnormal and Social Psychology, 66,* 3–11.

Barber, T.X. (1969). *Hypnosis: A scientific approach.* Princeton, N.J.: Van Nostrand.

Barber, T.X., Spanos, N.P., & Chaves, J.F. (1974). *Hypnosis, imagination, and human potentialities.* New York: Pergamon.

Bargh, J.A. (1984). Automatic and conscious processing of social information. In R.S. Wyer & T.K. Srull (eds.), *Handbook of social cognition,* vol. 3, pp. 1–44. Hillsdale, N.J.: Erlbaum.

Baron, R.A. (1970). Attraction toward the model and model's competence as determinants of adult imitative behavior. *Journal of Personality and Social Psychology, 14,* 335–344.

Baron, R.A. (1977). *Human aggression.* New York: Plenum.

Baron, R.A. (1978). Aggression and heat: The "long hot summer" revisited. In A. Baum, S. Valins, and J.E. Singer (eds.), *Advances in environmental research,* vol. 1. Hillsdale, N.J.: Erlbaum.

Baron, R.A. (1983a). The control of human aggression: An optimistic overview. *Journal of Social and Clinical Psychology, 1,* 97–119.

Baron, R.A. (1983b). The control of human aggression: A strategy based on imcompatible responses. In R.G. Geen & E.I. Donnerstein (eds.), *Aggression: Theoretical and empirical reviews.* New York: Academic.

Baron, R.A. (1983c). The "sweet smell of success"? The impact of pleasant artificial scents on evaluations of job applicants. *Journal of Applied Social Psychology, 16,* 16–28.

Baron, R.A. (1986a). *Behavior in organizations,* 2nd ed. Boston: Allyn and Bacon.

Baron, R.A. (1986b). Self-presentation in job interviews: When there can be "too much of a good thing." *Journal of Applied Social Psychology, 16,* 16–28.

Baron, R.A. (1987a). Effects of negative air ions on cognitive performance. *Journal of Applied Psychology, 72,* 131–137.

Baron, R.A. (1987b). Effects of negative ions on interpersonal attraction: Evidence for intensification effects. *Journal of Applied Social Psychology, 52,* 547–553.

Baron, R.A. (1987c). Interviewer's moods and reactions to job applicants: The influence of affective states on applied social judgments. *Journal of Applied Social Psychology, 17,* 911–926.

Baron, R.A. (1987c). Outlines of a "grand theory." Review of A. Bandura, *Social foundations of thought and action: A social cognitive theory. Contemporary Psychology, 22,* 413–415.

Baron, R.A. (1988a). Attributions and organizational conflict: The mediating role of apparent sincerity. *Organizational Behavior and Human Decision Processes, 41,* 98–110.

Baron, R.A. (1989). Personality and organizational conflict: Effects of the Type A behavior pattern and self-monitoring. *Organizational Behavior and Human Decision Processes,* in press.

Baron, R.A., & Byrne, D. (1987). *Social psychology: Understanding human interaction,* 5th ed. Boston: Allyn and Bacon.

Baron, R.A., & Ransberger, V.M. (1978). Ambient temperature and collective violence: The "long hot summer" revisited. *Journal of Personality and Social Psychology, 36,* 351–360.

Baron, R.A., Russell, G.W., & Arms, R.L. (1985). Negative ions and behavior: Impact on mood, memory, and aggression among Type A and Type B persons. *Journal of Personality and Social Psychology, 48,* 434–441.

Barron, F., & Harrington, D.M. (1981). Creativity, intelligence, and personality. *Annual Review of Psychology, 32,* 439–476.

Baum, A., Gatchel, R.J., & Schaeffer, M.A. (1983). Emotional, behavioral, and physiological effects of chronic stress at Three Mile Island. *Journal of Consulting and Clinical Psychology, 51,* 565–572.

Bauman, L.J., & Siegel, K. (1987). Misperception among gay men of the risk for AIDS associated with their sexual behavior. *Journal of Applied Social Psychology, 17,* 329–350.

Baumeister, R.F., & Tice, D.M. (1984). Role of self-presentation and choice in cognitive dissonance under forced compliance: Necessary or sufficient causes? *Journal of Personality and Social Psychology, 50,* 636–643.

Baumeister, R.R. (1986). *Identity.* New York: Oxford University Press.

Baumgardner, A.H., Heppner, P.P., & Arkin, R.M. (1986). Role of causal attribution in personal problem solving. *Journal of Personality and Social Psychology, 50,* 636–643.

Baumrind, D. (1984). *A developmental perspective on adolescent drug use.* Unpublished manuscript. University of California, Berkeley.

Baumrind, D. (1985). Research using intentional deception: Ethical issues revisited. *American Psychologist, 40,* 165–174.

Bazerman, M.H., Guiliano, T., & Appleman, A. (1984). Escalation of commitment in individual and group decision making. *Organizational Behavior and Human Performance, 33,* 141–152.

Beck, A.T. (1976). *Cognitive therapy and the emotional disorders.* New York: International Universities Press.

Beck, A.T., Rush, A.J., Shaw, B.F., & Emergy, G. (1979). *Cognitive therapy of depression: A treatment manual.* New York: Guilford.

Becker, M.A., & Byrne, D. (1984). Type A behavior and daily activities of young married couples. *Journal of Applied Social Psychology, 14,* 82–88.

Békésy, G. von. (1960). *Experiments in hearing.* New York: McGraw-Hill.

Bell, P.A., & Fusco, M.E. (1986). Linear and curvilinear relationships between temperature, affect, and violence: Reply to Cotton. *Journal of Applied Social Psychology, 16,* 802–807.

Benjamin, L.T., Jr. (1988). *A history of psychology: Original sources and contemporary research.* New York: McGraw-Hill.

Bereiter, C., & Scardamalia, M. (1985). Cognitive coping strategies and the problem of "inert" knowledge. In S. Chipmen, J.W. Segal, & R. Glaser (eds.), *Thinking and learning skills: Current research and open questions,* vol. 2, pp. 65–80. Hillsdale, N.J.: Erlbaum.

Berger, K.S. (1988). *The developing person through the life span.* New York: Worth.

Bergin, A.E., & Lambert, M.J. (1978). The evaluation of therapeutic outcomes. In S.L. Garfield & A.E. Bergin (eds.), *Handbook of psychotherapy and behavior change: An empirical analysis,* 2nd ed., pp. 139–190. New York: Wiley.

Berkowitz, L. (1984). Some effects of thoughts on anti- and prosocial influences of media events: A cognitive-neoassociation analysis. *Psychological Bulletin, 95,* 410–427.

Berlyne, D.E. (1967). Arousal and reinforcement. In D. Levine (ed.), *Nebraska Symposium on Motivation,* vol. 15, pp. 279–286. Lincoln: University of Nebraska Press.

Berndt, T.J. (1988). The nature and significance of children's friendships. *Annals of Child Development,* in press.

Berndt, T.J., & Hoyle, S.G. (1985). Stability and change in childhood and adolescent friendships. *Developmental Psychology, 21,* 1007–1015.

Berndt, T.J., Hawkins, J.F., & Hoyle, S.G. (1986). Changes in friendship during a school year: Effects on children's and adolescents' impressions of friendship and sharing with friends. *Child Development, 57,* 1284–1297.

Berne, E. (1964). *Games people play.* New York: Grove.

Berry, D.S., & McArthur, L.Z. (1985). Some components and consequences of a babyface. *Journal of Personality and Social Psychology, 48,* 312–323.

Berry, D.S., & McArthur, L.Z. (1986). Perceiving character in faces: The impact of age-related craniofacial changes on social perception. *Psychological Bulletin, 100,* 3–18.

Berry, D.T.R., & Webb, W.B. (1983). State measures and sleep stages. *Psychological Reports, 52,* 807–812.

Berry, D.T.R., & Webb, W.B. (1985). Mood and sleep in aging women. *Journal of Personality and Social Psychology, 49,* 1724–1727.

Berscheid, E. (1985). Interpersonal attraction. In G. Lindzey & E. Aronson (eds.), *Handbook of social psychology,* 3rd ed. New York: Random House.

Berstein, I.L., & Borson, S. (1986). Learned food aversion: A component of anorexia syndromes. *Psychology Review, 93,* 462–472.

Bertenthal, I.B., Proffitt, D.R., Dramer, S.J., & Spetner, N.B. (1987). Infants' encoding of kinetic displays varying in relative coherence. *Developmental Psychology, 23,* 171–178.

Bertino, M., Abelson, M.L., Margolin, S.H., Neuman, R., Burkhardt, C.A., & Reid, L.D. (1988). A small dose of morphine increases intake of and preference for isotonic saline among rats. *Alcohol, 5,* in press.

Birnbaum, I.M., & Parker, E.S., eds. (1977). *Alcohol and human memory.* Hillsdale, N.J.: Erlbaum.

Birnbaum, I.M., Taylor, T.H., Johnson, M.K., & Raye, C.L. (1987). Is event frequency encoded automatically? The case of alcohol intoxication. *Journal of Experimental Psychology: Learning, Memory, and Cognition, 13,* 251–258.

Bixler, E.O., Kales, A., Soldatos, C.R., Kales, J.D., & Healey, S. (1979). Prevalence of sleep disorders in the Los Angeles metropolitan area. *American Journal of Psychiatry, 136,* 1257–1262.

Blakemore, C., & Cooper, G.F. (1970). Development of the brain depends on the visual environment. *Nature, 228,* 477–478.

Bleuler, E. (1924). *Textbook of psychiatry.* New York: Macmillan.

Boles, D.B. (1987). Reaction time asymmetry through bilateral versus unilateral stimulus presentation. *Brain and Cognition, 6,* 323–333.

Booth, D.A., Mather, P., & Fuller, J. (1982). Starch content of ordinary foods associatively conditions human appetite and satiation. *Appetite, 3,* 163–184.

Booth-Kewley, S., & Friedman, H.S. (1987). Psychological predictors of heart disease: A quantitative review. *Psychological Bulletin, 101,* 343–362.

Bornstein, M.H. (1978a). Perceptual development: Stability and change in feature perception. In M.H. Bornstein & W. Kessen (eds.), *Psychological development from infancy.* Hillsdale, N.J.: Erlbaum.

Bornstein, M.H. (1978b). Visual behavior of the young human infant: Relationships between chromatic and spatial perception and the activity of underlying brain mechanisms. *Journal of Experimental Child Psychology, 26,* 174–192.

Borstelmann, L.J. (1983). Children before psychology: Ideas about children from antiquity to the late 1800s. In P.H. Mussen (ed.), *Handbook of child development and behavior,* vol. 3. pp. 1–40. New York: Wiley.

Botvin, G.J., & Murray, F.G. (1975). The efficacy of peer modeling and social conflict in the acquisition of conservation. *Child Development, 46,* 769–799.

Bouchard, T.J., Jr. (1984). Twins reared together and apart: What they tell us about human diversity. In S.W. Fox (ed.), *Individuality and determinism.* New York: Plenum.

Bouchard, T.J., Jr. (1987). Information about the Minnesota Center for Twin and Adoption Research. Minneapolis: University of Minnesota.

Bouchard, T.J., Jr., & McGue, M. (1981). Familial studies of intelligence: A review. *Science, 212,* 1055–1059.

Bouchard, T.J., Jr., & Segal, N.L. (1985). Environment and IQ. In B.B. Wolman (ed.), *Handbook of intelligence: Theories, measurements, and applications.* New York: Wiley.

Bower, G.H., Clark, M.C., Lesgold, A.M., & Winzenz, D. (1969). Hierarchical retrieval schemes in recall of categorized word lists. *Journal of Verbal Learning and Verbal Behavior, 8,* 323–343.

Bower, G.H., Gilligan, S.G., & Monteiro, K. (1981). Selectivity of learning caused by affective states. *Journal of Experimental Psychology: General, 110,* 451–573.

Bowen, M. (1978). *Family therapy in clinical practice.* New York: Aronson.

Bowers, K.S. (1976). *Hypnosis for the seriously curious.* Monterey, Cal.: Brooks/Cole.

Bowlby, J. (1969). *Attachment and loss.* vol. 2: *Attachment.* New York: Basic Books.

Bowles, N., & Hynds, F. (1978). *Psy search: The comprehensive guide to psychic phenomena.* New York: Harper & Row.

Bradbury, T.N., & Miller, G.A. (1985). Season of birth in schizophrenia: A review of evidence, methodology, and etiology. *Psychological Bulletin, 98,* 569–594.

Bradley, L., & Bryant, P. (1985). *Rhyme and reason in reading and spelling.* Ann Arbor: University of Michigan Press.

Bransford, J.D., Sherwood, R.D., & Sturdevant, T. (1987). Teaching thinking and problem solving. In J. Baron & R. Sternberg (eds.), *Teaching skills: Theory and practice.* New York: W.H. Freeman.

Braverman, N.S., & Bronstein, P. eds. (1985). Experimental assessments and clinical applications of conditioned food aversions. *Annals of the New York Academy of Sciences, 443,* 1–441.

Brean, H. (1958). What hidden sell is all about. *Life,* March 31, 104–114.

Breland, K., & Breland, M. (1961). The misbehavior of organisms. *American Psychologist, 16,* 681–684.

Briggs, S.R., & Cheek, J.M. (1986). The role of factor analysis in the development and evaluation of personality scales. *Journal of Personality, 54,* 106–148.

Briggs, S.R., & Cheek, J.M. (1988). On the nature of self-monitoring: Problems with assessment, problems with validity. *Journal of Personality and Social Psychology,* in press.

Brockner, J., & Guare, J. (1983). Improving the performance of low self-esteem individuals: An attributional approach. *Academy of Management Journal, 29,* 373–384.

Brockner, J., & Rubin, Z. (1985). *Entrapment in escalating conflict.* New York: Springer-Verlag.

Brody, G.H., Neubaum, E., & Forehand, R. (1988). Serial marriage: A heuristic analysis of an emerging family form. *Psychological Bulletin, 103,* 211–222.

Brown, R. (1973). *A first language: The early stages.* Cambridge: Harvard University Press.

Brown, R., & Kulik, J. (1977). Flashbulb memories. *Cognition, 5,* 73–79.

Brown, R., & McNeil, D. (1966). The ''tip of the tongue'' phenomenon. *Journal of Verbal Learning and Verbal Behavior, 5,* 325–377.

Bruhn, J.G., & Phillips, B.U. (1987). A developmental basis for social support. *Journal of Behavioral Medicine, 10,* 213–229.

Bryant, J. (1985). *Testimony on the effects of pornography: Research findings.* Paper presented at the U.S. Justice Department Hearings, Houston.

Bryden, M.P., & Ley, R.G. (1983). Right-hemispheric involvement in the perception and expression of emotion in normal humans. In K.M. Heilman & P. Satz (eds.), *Neuropsychology of human emotion.* New York: Guilford.

Bryden, M.P., Ley, R.G., & Sugarman, J.H. (1982). A left ear advantage for identifying the emotional quality of tonal sequences. *Neuropsychologia, 20,* 83–87.

Buck, R. (1977). Nonverbal communication of affect in preschool children: Relationships with personality and skin conductance. *Journal of Personality and Social Psychology, 35,* 225–236.

Buck, R. (1984). *The communication of affect.* New York: Guilford.

Bushman, B.J. (1984). Perceived symbols of authority and their influence on compliance. *Journal of Applied Social Psychology, 14,* 501–508.

Buss, A.H., & Plomin, R. (1975). *A temperament theory of personality development.* New York: Wiley.

Buss, A.H., & Plomin, R. (1984). *Temperament.* Hillsdale, N.J.: Erlbaum.

Byrne, D. (1971). *The attraction paradigm.* New York: Academic.

Byrne, D., Clore, G.L., & Smeaton, G. (1986). The attraction hypothesis: Do similar attitudes affect anything? *Journal of Personality and Social Psychology, 51,* 1167–1170.

Byrne, D., & Kelley, K., eds. (1986). *Alternative approaches to the study of sexual behavior.* Hillsdale, N.J.: Erlbaum.

Byrne, D., & Murnen, S. (1987). Maintaining loving relationships. In R.J. Sternberg & M.L. Barnes (eds.), *The anatomy of love*. New Haven: Yale University Press.

Cacioppo, J.T., Petty, R.E., & Quintanar, L.R. (1982). Individual differences in relative hemisphere alpha abundance and cognitive responses to persuasive communications. *Journal of Personality and Social Psychology, 43*, 623–626.

Caldwell, D.F., & O'Reilly, C.A., III. (1982). Boundary spanning and individual performance: The impact of self-monitoring. *Journal of Applied Psychology, 67*, 124–127.

Campbell, J.P., & Dunnette, M.D. (1968). Effectiveness of T-group experiences in managerial training and development. *Psychological Bulletin, 70*, 73–104.

Cannon, W.B., Lewis, J.T., & Britton, S.W. (1972). The dispensability of the sympathetic division of the autonomic nervous system. *Boston Medical Surgery Journal, 197*, 514.

Cannon, W.B., & Washburn, A.L. (1912). An explanation of hunger. *American Journal of Physiology, 29*, 444–454.

Capaldi, E.J. (1979). Reinforcement level: An expectancy-association approach to relative reinforcement and nonreinforcement effects. In J.E. Baerwaldt and G. McCain (eds.), *The Arlington Symposium on Learning*. Stamford, Conn.: Greylock.

Capaldi, E.J., & Miller, D.J. (1988). Counting in rats: Its functional significance and the independent cognitive processes that constitute it. *Journal of Experimental Psychology: Animal Behavior Processes, 14*, 3–17.

Carlson, N.R. (1986). *Physiology of behavior*, 3rd ed. Boston: Allyn and Bacon.

Caputo, R. (1988). Uganda: Land beyond sorrow. *National Geographic, 173* (4), 468–491.

Carnevale, P.J.D., & Isen, A.M. (1986). The influence of positive affect and visual access on the discovery of integrative solutions in bilateral negotiation. *Organizational Behavior and Human Decision Processes, 37*, 1–13.

Carson, R.C., Butcher, J.N., & Coleman, J.C. (1988). *Abnormal psychology and modern life*, 8th ed. Glenview, Ill.: Scott, Foresman.

Carver, C., & Scheier, M. (1988). *Perspectives on personality*. Boston: Allyn and Bacon.

Cash, T.F. (1985). *The impact of grooming style on the evaluation of women in management*. In M. Solomon (ed.), *The psychology of fashion*. New York: Lexington.

Cattell, R.B., (1963). Theory of fluid and crystallized intelligence: A critical experiment. *Journal of Educational Psychology, 54*, 1–22.

Cattell, R.B., & Dreger, R.M., eds. (1977). *Handbook of modern personality theory*. Washington, D.C.: Hemisphere.

Ceci, S.J., Peters, D., & Plotkin, J. (1985). Human subjects' review, personal values, and the regulation of social science research. *American Psychologist, 40*, 994–1002.

Cheek, J.M. (1987). Shyness. *Medical and health annual*. Chicago: Encyclopedia Britannica.

Cheek, J.M., & Busch, C.M. (1981). The influence of shyness on loneliness in a new situation. *Personality and Social Psychology Bulletin, 7*, 572–577.

Cheek, J.M., Melchior, L.A., & Carpentieri, A.M. (1986). Shyness and self-concept. In L.M. Hartman & K.R. Blankstein (eds.), *Advances in the study of communication and affect*. New York: Plenum.

Chomsky, N. (1968). *Language and mind*. New York: Harcourt, Brace.

Chow, B.F., Somonson, M., Hanson, H.M., & Roeder, L.M. (1971). Behavioral measurements in nutritional studies. *Conditioned Reflex, 6*, 36–40.

Christensen, L.B. (1988). *Experimental methodology*, 3rd ed. Boston: Allyn and Bacon.

Cialdini, R.B. (1985). *Influence: Science and practice*. Glenview, Ill.: Scott Foresman.

Clark, H.H., & Chase, W.G. (1972). On the process of comparing sentences against pictures. *Cognitive Psychology, 3*, 472–517.

Clarke-Stewart, A., Friedman, S., & Koch, J. (1985). *Child development: A topical approach*. New York: Wiley.

Cohen, D.B. (1973). Sex role orientation and dream recall. *Journal of Abnormal Psychology, 82*, 246–252.

Cohen, N.J., & Corkin, S. (1981). The amnesic patient H.M.: Learning and retention of a cognitive skill. *Society for Neuroscience Abstracts, 7*, 235.

Cohen, S., Evans, G.W., Krantz, D.S., Stokols, D., & Kelly, S. (1981). Aircraft noise and children: Longitudinal and cross-sectional evidence on adaptation to noise and the effectiveness of noise abatement. *Journal of Personality and Social Psychology, 40*, 331–345.

Cohen, S., Evans, G.W., Stokols, D., & Krantz, D. (1986). *Behavior, health, and environmental stress*. New York: Plenum.

Colby, A., Kohlberg, L., Gibbs, J., & Lieberman, M.A. (1983). Longitudinal study of moral judgement. *Monographs of the Society for Research in Child Development, 48*, (1, Serial No. 200).

Coleman, R.M. (1986). *Wide awake at 3:00 A.M.: By choice or by chance?* New York: W.H. Freeman.

Collins, A.M., & Loftus, E.F. (1975). A spreading activation theory of semantic processing. *Psychological Review, 82*, 407–428.

Constantino, G., Malgady, R., & Rogler, L. (1986). Cuento therapy: A culturally sensitive modality for Puerto Rican children. *Journal of Consulting and Clinical Psychology, 54*, 639–645.

Conway, M., & Ross, M. (1984). Getting what you want by revising what you had. *Journal of Personality and Social Psychology, 47*, 738–748.

Coren, S. (1986). An efferent component in the visual perception of direction and extent. *Psychological Bulletin, 39*, 391–410.

Corkin, S., Sullivan, E.V., Twitchell, T.E., & Grove, E. (1981). The amnesic patient H.M.: Clinical observations and test performance 28 years after operation. *Society for Neuroscience Abstracts, 7*, 235.

Costanza, R.S., Derlega, V.J., & Winstead, B.A. (1988). Positive and negative forms of social support: Effects of conversational topics on coping with stress among same-sex friends. *Journal of Experimental Social Psychology, 24*, 182–193.

Cotton, J.L. (1986). Ambient temperature and violent crime. *Journal of Applied Social Psychology, 16*, 786–801.

Cowan, N. (1984). On short and long auditory stores. *Psychological Bulletin, 96*, 341–370.

Council, J.R., Kirsch, I., & Hafner, L.P. (1986). Expectancy versus absorption in the prediction of hypnotic responding. *Journal of Personality and Social Psychology, 50*, 182–189.

Coyle, J.T., Price, D.L., & DeLong, M.R. (1983). Alzheimer's disease: A disorder of cortical cholinergic innervation. *Science, 219*, 1184–1190.

Craig, K.D. (1979). Social disclosure, coactive peer companions and decision theory and psychophysiological indexes of pain. *Journal of Personality and Social Psychology, 36*, 805–815.

Craig, K.D., & Prkachin, K.M. (1978). Social modeling influences on pain thresholds influenced by social modeling. *Journal of Personality and Social Psychology, 36*, 805–815.

Craik, F.I.M., & Lockhart, R.S. (1972). Levels of processing: A framework for memory research. *Journal of Verbal Learning and Verbal Behavior, 11*, 671–684.

Craik, F.I.M., & Tulving, E. (1975). Depth of processing and the retention of words in episodic memory. *Journal of Experimental Psychology: General, 104*, 268–294.

Crick, F., & Mitchison, G. (1983). The function of dream sleep. *Nature, 304*, 111–114.

Croyle, R., & Cooper, J. (1983). Dissonance arousal: Physiological evidence. *Journal of Personality and Social Psychology, 45*, 782–791.

Crutchfield, R.A. (1955). Conformity and character. *American Psychologist, 10,* 191–198.

Csikszentmihalyi, M., & Larson, R. (1984). *Being adolescent: Conflict and growth in the teenage years.* New York: Basic Books.

Cunningham, M.R. (1979). Weather, mood, and helping behavior: Quasi experiments with the sunshine samaritan. *Journal of Personality and Social Psychology, 37,* 1947–1956.

Daft, R.L. (1986). *Organization theory and design,* 2nd ed. St. Paul: West.

Daly, M., & Wilson, M. (1983). *Sex evolution and behavior,* 2nd ed. North Scituate, Mass.: Duxbury.

Darwin, C. (1871). *The descent of man and selection in relation to sex.* London: John Murray.

Davidson, J.K., Sr., & Hoffman, L.E. (1986). Sexual fantasies and sexual satisfaction: An empirical analysis of erotic thought. *Journal of Sex Research, 22,* 184–205.

Davis, H.P., & Squire, L.R. (1984). Protein synthesis and memory: A review. *Psychological Bulletin, 96,* 518–559.

Davis, J.M. (1985a). Minor tranquilizers, sedatives, and hypnotics. In H.I. Kaplan & B.J. Sadock (eds.), *Comprehensive textbook of psychiatry,* 4th ed., pp. 1537–1558. Baltimore: Williams & Wilkins.

Davis, J.M. (1985b). Antidepressant drugs. In H.I. Kaplan & B.J. Sadock (eds.), *Comprehensive textbook of psychiatry,* 4th ed., pp. 1513–1536. Baltimore: Williams & Wilkins.

Davis, J.M. (1985c). Antipsychotic drugs. In H.I. Kaplan & B.J. Sadock (eds.), *Comprehensive textbook of psychiatry,* 4th ed., pp. 1481–1512. Baltimore: Williams & Wilkins.

Davis, P.H., & Osherson, A. (1977). The current treatment of a multiple-personality woman and her son. *American Journal of Psychotherapy, 31,* 504–515.

Dawes, R.M. (1976). Shallow psychology. In J.S. Carroll & J.W. Payne (eds.), *Cognition and social behavior.* Hillsdale, N.J.: Erlbaum.

Dawes, R. (1988). *Rational choice in an uncertain world.* New York: Harcourt Brace Jovanovich.

Deaux, K., & Lewis, L.L. (1987). The structure of gender stereotypes: Interrelationships among components and gender label. *Journal of Personality and Social Psychology,* in press.

DeCasper, A.J., & Fifer, W.P. (1980). Of human bonding: Newborns prefer their mother's voices. *Science, 208,* 1174–1176.

Deci, E.L. (1975). *Intrinsic motivation.* New York: Plenum.

DeJong, W., & Musilli, L. (1982). External pressure to comply: Handicapped versus nonhandicapped requesters and the foot-in-the-door phenomenon. *Personality and Social Psychology Bulletin, 8,* 522–527.

DeJong-Gierveld, J. (1987). Developing and testing a model of loneliness. *Journal of Personality and Social Psychology, 53,* 119–128.

Dement, W.C. (1975). *Some must watch while some must sleep.* San Francisco: W.H. Freeman.

DePietro, J.A., Larson, S.K., & Porges, S.W. (1987). Behavioral and heart rate pattern differences between breast-fed and bottle-fed neonates. *Developmental Psychology, 23,* 467–474.

Desor, J.F., Maller, O., & Andrews, K. (1975). Ingestive responses of human newborns to salty, sour, and bitter stimuli. *Journal of Comparative and Physiological Psychology, 89,* 966–970.

Deutsch, A. (1949). *The mentally ill in America.* New York: Columbia University Press.

Deutsch, J.A. (1972). Brain reward: ESP and ecstasy. *Psychology Today, 46,* (July).

Devalois, R., Yond, E.W., & Helpler, N. (1982). The orientation and direction selectivity of cells in macaque visual cortex. *Vision Research, 22,* 531–544.

Dickey-Bryant, L.A., Lautenschlager, G.J., & Mendoza, J.L. (1986). Facial attractiveness and its relation to occupational success. *Journal of Applied Psychology, 71,* 16–19.

DiClementi, R.J., Zorn, J., & Temoshok, L. (1987). The association of gender, ethnicity, and length of residence in the Bay area to adolescents' knowledge and attitudes about acquired immune dificiency syndrome. *Journal of Applied Social Psychology, 17,* 193–215.

Diener, E., & Larsen, R.J. (1984). Temporal stability and cross situational consistency of affective, cognitive, and behavioral responses. *Journal of Personality and Social Psychology, 47,* 871–883.

Diener, E., Larsen, R.J., & Emmons, R.A. (1984). Person x situation interactions: Choice of situations and congruence response models. *Journal of Personality and Social Psychology, 47,* 580–592.

Diener, E., Sandvik, E., & Larsen, R.J. (1985). Age and sex effects for affect intensity. *Developmental Psychology, 21,* 542–546.

Dixit, N. (1985). *The effect of verbal contact and spatial positioning on job satisfaction, job performance, and interpersonal attraction: An experimental investigation.* Unpublished doctoral dissertation, State University of New York at Albany.

Dohrenwend, B.S., Dohrenwend, B.P., Dodson, M., & Shrout, P.E. (1984). Symptoms, hassles, social supports and life events: The problem of confounded measures. *Journal of Abnormal Psychology, 93,* 222–230.

Dollard, J., Doob, L., Miller, N., Mowrer, O.H., & Sears, R.R. (1939). *Frustration and aggression.* New Haven: Yale University Press.

Donnelly, J. (1985). Psychosurgery. In H.I. Kaplan & B.J. Sadock (eds.), *Comprehensive textbook of psychiatry,* 4th ed. pp. 1563–1569. Baltimore: Williams & Wilkins.

Donnerstein, E., & Wilson, D.W. (1976). The effects of noise and perceived control upon ongoing and subsequent aggressive behavior. *Journal of Personality and Social Psychology, 34,* 774–781.

Doppelt, J.E., & Wallace, W.L. (1955). Standardization of the Weschler Adult Intelligence Scale for older persons. *Journal of Abnormal and Social Psychology, 51,* 312–330.

Dorner, G. (1976). *Hormones and brain differentiation.* Amsterdam: Elsevier/North Holland.

Doty, R.L., Shaman, P., Applebaum, S.L., Giberson, R., Sikorski, L., & Rosenberg, L. (1984). Smell identification ability: Changes with age. *Science, 226,* 141–143.

Douek, E. (1988). Olfaction and medicine. In S. Van Toller & G. Doll (eds.), *Perfumery: The psychology and biology of fragrance.* London: Chapman Hall.

Duck, S. (1986). *Human relationships.* London: Sage.

Duncker, K. (1945). On problem solving. *Psychological Monographs* (Whole No. 270).

Dutton, D.G., & Aron, A.P. (1974). Some evidence for heightened sexual attraction under conditions of high anxiety. *Journal of Personality and Social Psychology, 30,* 510–517.

Dweck, C.S., & Elliott, E.S. (1983). Intrinsic motivation. In P. Mussen & E.M. Hetherington (eds.), *Handbook of child psychology,* vol. 4. New York: Wiley.

Eagly, A.H., & Crowley, M. (1986). Gender and helping behavior: A meta-analytic review of the social psychological literature. *Psychological Bulletin, 100,* 283–308.

Eagly, A.H., & Wood, W. (1982). Inferred sex differences in status as a determinant of gender stereotypes about social influence. *Journal of Personality and Social Psychology, 43,* 915–928.

Ebbesen, E.B., Kjos, G.L., & Konecni, V.J. (1976). Spatial ecology: Its effects on the choice of friends and enemies. *Journal of Experimental Social Psychology, 12,* 505–518.

Ebbinghaus, H. (1885). *Uber des gedacthnis.* Leipzig: Dunker & Humblot.

Ebbinghaus, H. (1913). *Memory.* New York: Columbia University (original work published 1885, Leipzig: Altenberg).

Edwards, C.P. (1984). The age group labels and categories of preschool children. *Child Development, 55,* 440–452.

Eich, J.E. (1980). The cue dependent nature of state dependent retrieval. *Memory and Cognition, 8,* 157–173.

Eich, J.E. (1985). Levels of processing, encoding specificity, elaboration, and CHARM. *Psychological Review, 92,* 1–38.

Eisenberg, N., Cialdini, R.B., McCreath, H., & Shell, R. (1987). Consistency-based compliance: When and why do children become vulnerable? *Journal of Personality and Social Psychology, 52,* 1174–1181.

Eisenberg, N., & Miller, P.A. (1987). The relationship of empathy to prosocial and related behaviors. *Psychological Bulletin. 101,* 91–119.

Ekman, P., & Friesen, W.V. (1975). *Unmasking the face.* Englewood Cliffs, N.J.: Prentice-Hall.

Ellis, A. (1977). *Anger—How to live with and without it.* Secaucus, N.J.: Citadel.

Ellis, A. (1987a). The evolution of rational-emotive therapy (RET). In J. Zeig (ed.), *The evolution of psychotherapy,* pp. 107–137. New York: Brunner/Mazel.

Ellis, A. (1987b). The impossibility of achieving consistently good mental health. *American Psychologist, 42,* 364–375.

Empson, J.A.C. (1984). Sleep and its disorders. In R. Stevens (ed.), *Aspects of consciousness,* vol. 4. London: Academic.

Engen, T. (1984). *Perception of odors.* New York: Academic.

Engen, T. (1986). Remembering odors and their names. Paper presented at the First International Conference on the Psychology of Perfumery, University of Warwick, England.

Engen, T., & Ross, B.M. (1973). Long-term memory of odors with and without verbal descriptions. *Journal of Experimental Psychology, 100,* 221–227.

Engler, B. (1985). *Personality theories,* 2nd ed. Boston: Houghton Mifflin.

Epstein, J.L. (1986). Friendship selection: Developmental and environmental influences. In E. Mueller & C.R. Cooper (eds.), *Process and outcome in peer relationships,* pp. 129–160. New York: Academic.

Erez, M., & Earley, P.C. (1987). Comparative analysis of goal-setting strategies across cultures. *Journal of Applied Psychology, 72,* 658–665.

Erlenmeyer-Kimling, L., & Jarvik, L.F. (1963). Genetics and intelligence. *Science, 142,* 1477–1479.

Eron, L.D. (1987). The development of aggressive behavior from the perspective of a developing behaviorist. *American Psychologist, 42,* 435–442.

Estes, W.K. (1944). An experimental study of punishment. *Psychological Monographs, 57* (Whole No. 263).

Evans, F.J., & Orne, M.T. (1971). The disappearing hypnotist: The use of simulating subjects to evaluate how subjects perceive experimental procedures. *International Journal of Clinical and Experimental Hypnosis, 19,* 277–296.

Evans, G.W., Palsane, M.N., & Carrere, S. (1987). Type A behavior and occupational stress: A cross-cultural study of blue-collar workers. *Journal of Personality and Social Psychology, 52,* 1002–1007.

Eysenck, H. (1952). The effects of psychotherapy: An evaluation. *Journal of Consulting Psychology, 16,* 319–324.

Fantz, R.L., Fagan, J.F., & Miranda, S.B. (1975). Early visual selectivity as a function of pattern variables, previous exposure, age from birth, and conception, and expected cognitive deficit. In L.B. Cohen & P. Salapatek (eds.), *Infant perception: From sensation to cognition,* vol. 1. New York: Academic.

Farthing, G.W., Brown, S.W., & Venturino, M. (1983). Involuntariness of response on the Harvard Group Scale of Hypnotic Susceptibility. *International Journal of Clinical and Experimental Hypnosis, 31,* 170–181.

Faust, M.S. (1977). Somatic development of adolescent girls. *Monographs of the Society for Research on Child Development, 42,* (1, Serial No. 169).

Fazio, R.H., Cooper, M., Dayson, K., & Johnson, M. (1981). Control and the coronary-prone behavior pattern: Responses to multiple situational demands. *Personality and Social Psychology Bulletin, 7,* 97–102.

Fazio, R.H., Lenn, T.M., & Effrein, E.A. (1984). Spontaneous attitude formation. *Social Cognition, 2,* 217–234.

Feingold, A. (1988). Cognitive gender differences are disappearing. *American Psychologist, 43,* 95–108.

Feldman, S. (1971). The presentation of shortness in everyday life—Height and heightism in American society: Toward a sociology of stature. Paper presented at the meetings of the American Sociological Association, Chicago.

Ferster, C.B., & Skinner, B.F. (1957). *Schedules of reinforcement.* New York: Appleton-Century-Crofts.

Festinger, L. (1957). *A theory of cognitive dissonance.* Evanston, Ill.: Row, Peterson.

Festinger, L., Schachter, S., & Back, K. (1950). *Social pressures in informal groups: A study of a housing community.* New York: Harper & Row.

Fincham, F.D., Beach, S.R., & Baucom, D.H. (1987). Attribution processes in distressed and nondistressed couples: 4. Self-partner attribution differences. *Journal of Personality and Social Psychology, 52,* 739–748.

Fisher, J.D., Bell, P.A., & Baum, A. (1984). *Environmental psychology,* 2nd ed. New York: Holt, Rinehart, & Winston.

Fiske, S.T., & Taylor, S.E. (1984). *Social cognition.* Reading, Mass.: Addison-Wesley.

Fitzsimmons, J.T., & LeMagnen, J. (1969). Eating as a regulatory control of drinking in the rat. *Journal of Comparative and Physiological Psychology, 67,* 273–283.

Flavell, J.H. (1973). The development of inferences about others. In T. Misebel (ed.), *Understanding other persons.* Oxford: Blackwell, Basil, & Mott.

Flavell, J.H. (1977). *Cognitive development.* Englewood Cliffs, N.J.: Prentice-Hall.

Flavell, J.H. (1986). The development of children's knowledge about the appearance-reality distinction. *American Psychologist, 41,* 418–425.

Flavell, J.H., & Markman, E.M. (eds.), (1983). *Handbook of child psychology: Cognitive development,* vol. 3. New York: Wiley.

Flynn, J.R. (1987). Massive IQ gains in 14 nations: What IQ tests really measure. *Psychological Bulletin, 101,* 171–191.

Forsterling, F. (1986). Attributional conceptions in clinical psychology. *American Psychologist, 41,* 275–285.

Foulkes, D. (1985). *Dreaming: A cognitive-psychological analysis.* Hillsdale, N.J.: Erlbaum.

Fouts, R.S., Hirsch, A.D., & Fouts, D.H. (1982). Cultural transmission of a human language in a chimpanzee mother/infant relationship. In H.E. Fitzgerald, J.A. Mullins, and P. Page (eds.), *Psychological perspectives: Child nurturance series,* vol. 4. New York: Plenum.

Frankl, V.E. (1975). Paradoxical intention and dereflection. *Psychotherapy: Theory, Research, and Practice, 12,* 226–237.

Franks, J.J., & Bransford, J.D. (1971). Abstraction of visual patterns. *Journal of Experimental Psychology, 90,* 65–74.

Franzoi, S.L., & Herzog, M.E. (1987). Judging physical attractiveness: What body aspects do we use? *Personality and Social Psychology, 52,* 739–748.

Frazier, K. (1984–1985). Gallup youth poll finds high belief in ESP, astrology. *The Skeptical Inquirer, 9,* 113–114.

Freedman, J.L. (1986). Television violence and aggression: A rejoinder. *Psychological Bulletin, 100,* 372–378.

Freedman, J.L., & Fraser, S.C. (1966). Compliance without pressure: The foot-in-the-door technique. *Journal of Personality and Social Psychology, 4,* 195–202.

Frese, M. (1985). Stress at work and psychosomatic complaints: A causal interpretation. *Journal of Applied Psychology, 70,* 314–328.

Freud, S. (1885). On the general effects of cocaine. Lecture given at

Psychiatric Union, March 5. Reprinted in *Drug Dependence* (1970), *5*, 17.

Freud, S. (1900). The interpretation of dreams. In J. Strachey (ed.), *Standard edition of the complete psychological works of Sigmund Freud*, vol. 5. London: Hogarth.

Freud, S. (1908). Creative writers and daydreaming. In J. Strachey (ed.), *Standard edition of the complete psychological works of Sigmund Freud*, vol. 9, pp. 142–152. London: Hogarth.

Freud, S. (1914). *The Psychopathology of Everyday Life*. New York: Macmillan (original work published 1904).

Freud, S. (1917/1986). *Mourning and melancholia*. In J. Coyne (ed.), *Essential papers on depression* (pp. 48–63). New York: New York University Press (original work published 1917).

Freud, S. (1933). *New introductory lectures on psychoanalysis*. New York: Norton.

Friedman, H.S., Prince, L.M., Riggio, R.E., & DiMatteo, M.R. (1980). Understanding and assessing nonverbal expressiveness: The affective communication test. *Journal of Personality and Social Psychology, 39*, 333–351.

Friedrich-Cofer, L., & Huston, A.C. (1986). Television violence and aggression: The debate continues. *Psychological Bulletin, 100*, 364–371.

Fromm, E., & Shor, R.E. (1979). *Hypnosis: Developments in research and new perspective*. Chicago: Aldine.

Fuchs, A.R., & Fuchs, F. (1984). Endocrinology of term and preterm labor. In F. Fuchs & P.G. Stubblefield (eds.), *Preterm birth: Causes, prevention, and management*, pp. 39–63. New York: Macmillan.

Funder, D.C. (1987). Errors and mistakes: Evaluating the accuracy of social judgement. *Psychological Bulletin, 101*, 75–90.

Furmoto, L., & Scarborough, E. (1986). Placing women in the history of psychology. *American Psychologist, 41*, 35–42.

Gaines, J., & Jermier, J.M. (1983). Emotional exhaustion in a high stress organization. *Academy of Management Journal, 26*, 567–586.

Galnater, E. (1962). Contemporary psychophysics. In R. Brown, E. Galanter, E.G. Hess, & G. Mandler (eds.) *New Directions in Psychology*. New York: Holt, Rinehart, & Winston.

Garcia, J., Hankins, W.G., & Rusiniak, K.W. (1974). Behavioral regulation of the *milieu interne* in man and rat. *Science, 185*, 824–831.

Garcia, J., & Koelling, R.A. (1966). Relation of cue to consequence in avoidance learning. *Psychonomic Science, 4*, 123.

Gardner, B.T., & Gardner, R.A. (1975). Evidence for sentence constituents in the early utterances of child and chimpanzee. *Journal of Experimental Psychology: General, 4*, 244–267.

Garfield, S.L., & Bergin, A.E. (1986). *Handbook of psychotherapy and behavior change*, 3rd ed. New York: Wiley.

Garfield, S.L., & Goldenberg, H. (1985). *Handbook of psychotherapy and behavior change*, 3rd ed. New York: Wiley.

Gazzaniga, M.S. (1984). Right hemisphere language: Remaining problems. *American Psychologist, 39*, 1494–1495.

Geen, R.H., Beatty, W.W., & Arkin, R.M. (1984). *Human motivation*. Boston: Allyn and Bacon.

Geiselman, R.E., Fisher, R.P., MacKinnon, D.P., & Holland, H.L. (1985). Eyewitness memory enhancement in the police interview: Cognitive retrieval mnemonics versus hypnosis. *Journal of Applied Psychology, 70*, 401–412.

Geller, E.S. (1984). A delayed reward strategy for large-scale motivation of safety belt use: A test of long-term impact. *Accident Analysis and Prevention, 16*, 457–463.

Geller, E.S., Bruff, C.D., & Nimmer, J.G. (1985). "Flash for life": Community-based prompting for safety belt promotion. *Journal of Applied Behavior Analysis, 18*, 145–159.

Geller, E.S., Paterson, L., & Talbot, E. (1982). A behavioral analysis of incentive prompts for motivating seat belt use. *Journal of Applied Behavior Analysis, 18*, 403–415.

Gelman, R. (1978). Cognitive development. In M.R. Rosenzweig & L.W. Porter (eds.), *Annual Review of Psychology, 29*. Palo Alto: Annual Reviews.

Gelman, R. (1982). Preschooler's counting: Principles before skill or skill before principles? Unpublished manuscript, University of Pennsylvania.

Gelman, R., & Baillargeon, R. (1983). A review of some Piagetian concepts. In P.H. Mussen (ed.), *Handbook of child development and behavior*, vol. 3, pp. 170–230. New York: Wiley.

Gelman, R., & Shatz, M. (1977). Appropriate speech adjustments: The operation of conversational constraints on talk to two-year-olds. In M. Lewis & L.A. Rosenblum (eds.), *Interaction, conversation, and the development of language*. New York: Wiley.

George, S.G., & Jennings, L.B. (1975). Effect of subliminal stimuli on consumer behavior: Negative evidence. *Perceptual and Motor Skills, 41*, 847–854.

Gerrard, K.J. (1986). Are men and women really different? In K. Kelley (ed.), *Females, Males and Sexuality*. Albany: State University of New York Press.

Gillett, P.L., & Coe, W.C. (1984). The effects of rapid induction analgesia (R.I.A.), hypnotic susceptibility, and the severity of discomfort on the reduction of dental pain. *American Journal of Clinical Hypnosis, 27*, 81–90.

Gilligan, C. (1982). *In a different voice: Psychological theory and women's development*. Cambridge: Harvard University Press.

Giambra, L. (1974). Daydreaming across the life span: Late adolescent to senior citizen. *Aging and Human Development, 5*, 116–135.

Gibson, E.J., & Walk, R.D. (1960). The "visual cliff." *Scientific American*, pp. 64–71.

Gibson, J.J. (1979). *The ecological approach to visual perception*. Boston: Houghton Mifflin.

Gilbert, D.T., & Jones, E.E. (1986). Perceiver-induced constraint: Interpretations of self-generated reality. *Journal of Personality and Social Psychology, 50*, 269–280.

Glass, D.C. (1983). Behavioral, cardiovascular, and neuroendocrine responses to psychological stressors. *International Review of Applied Psychology, 32*, 137–151.

Glass, D., Snyder, M.L., & Hollis, J. (1974). Time urgency and the Type A coronary-prone behavior pattern. *Journal of Applied Social Psychology, 4*, 125–140.

Glenn, D.K., & Weaver, C.N. (1979). Attitudes toward premarital, extramarital, and homosexual relations in the U.S. in the 1970s. *Journal of Sex Research, 15*, 108–118.

Godfrey, D.K., Jones, E.E., & Lord, C.G. (1986). Self-promotion is not ingratiating. *Journal of Personality and Social Psychology, 50*, 106–115.

Goethals, G.R. (1986). Fabricating and ignoring social reality: Self-serving estimates of consensus. In J. Olson, C.P. Herman, & M.P. Zanna (eds.), *Relative deprivation and social comparison: The Ontario symposium on social cognition IV*. Hillsdale, N.J.: Erlbaum.

Gold, R. (1978). On the meaning on nonconservation. In A.M. Lesgold, J.W. Pellegrino, S.D. Fokkema, & R. Glaser (eds.), *Cognitive psychology and instruction*. New York: Plenum.

Goldenberg, I., & Goldenberg, H. (1985). *Family therapy: An overview*, 2nd ed. Monterey, Cal.: Brooks/Cole.

Goldstein, A.P., Carr, E.D., Davidson, W.S., & Wehr, P. (1981). *In response to aggression: Methods of control and prosocial alternatives*. New York: Pergamon.

Goleman, D. (1985). New focus on multiple personality. *New York Times* (May 21), pp. C1, C6.

Goleman, D. (1986). Studies point to power of nonverbal signals. *New York Times* (April 8), pp. C1, C6.

Goleman, O. (1980). 1,528 little geniuses and how they grew. *Psychology Today* (Feb.), pp. 28–53.

Goodstein, L.D., & Calhoun, J.F. (1982). *Understanding abnormal behavior*. Reading, Mass.: Addison-Wesley.

Gotestam, K.G., & Melin, L. (1974). Covert extinction of amphetamine addiction. *Behavior Therapy, 5,* 90–92.

Gottesman, I.L., & Shields, J. (1972). *Schizophrenia and genetics: A twin study vantage point.* New York: Academic.

Gottfried, A.W. (1984). Home environment and early cognitive development: Integration, meta-analyses, and conclusions. In A.W. Gottfried (ed.), *Home environment and early cognitive development.* San Francisco: Academic.

Graf, P., Squire, L.R., & Mandler, G. (1984). The information that amnesic patients do not forget. *Journal of Experimental Psychology: Learning, Memory, and Cognition, 10,* 164–178.

Graham, C.H., & Hsia, Y. (1958). Color defect and color theory. *Science, 127,* 657–682.

Granchow, J.R., Steiner, J.E., & Daher, M. (1983). Neonatal facial expressions in response to different qualities and intensities of gustatory stimuli. *Infant Behavior and Development, 6,* 189–200.

Gray, A.L., Bowers, K.S., & Fenz, W.D. (1970). Heart rate in anticipation of and during a negative visual hallucination. *International Journal of Clinical and Experimental Hypnosis, 18,* 41–51.

Gray, S.W., Ramsey, B.K., & Klaus, R.A. (1982). *From 3 to 20: The early training project.* Baltimore: University Park Press.

Greenberg, J., Pyszcynski, T., & Solomon, S. (1982). The self-serving attributional bias: Beyond self-presentation. *Journal of Experimental Social Psychology, 18,* 56–67.

Greenberg, J., Williams, K.D., & O'Brien, M.K. (1986). Considering the harshest verdict first: Biasing effect on mock juror verdicts. *Personality and Social Psychology Bulletin, 12,* 41–50.

Greenwald, A.G., Carnot, C.G., Beach, R., & Young, B. (1987). Increasing voting behavior by asking people if they expect to vote. *Journal of Applied Psychology, 72,* 315–318.

Gregory, R.L. (1978). *Eye and brain: The psychology of seeing,* 3rd. New York: McGraw-Hill.

Griffitt, W., & Hatfield, E. (1985). *Human Sexual Behavior.* Glenview, Ill.: Scott Foresman.

Gruneberg, M.M. (1978). The feeling of knowing, memory blocks and memory aids. In M.M. Greenberg & P. Morris (eds.) *Aspects of Memory.* London: Methuen.

Gurman, A.S., Kniskern, D.P., & Pinsof, W.M. (1986). Research on the process and outcome of marital and family therapy. In S.L. Garfield & A.E. Bergin (eds.), *Handbook of psychotherapy and behavior change,* pp. 565–624. New York: Wiley.

Hacker, A. (1983). *U/S: A statistical portrait of the American people.* New York: Viking.

Haier, R.J., Siegel, B.V., Jr., Neuchterlein, K.H., Hazlett, E., Wu, J.C., Paek, J., Browning, H.L., & Buschsbaum, M.S. (1988). Cortical glucose metabolic rate correlates of abstract reasoning and attention studied with positron emission tomography. *Intelligence,* in press.

Hall, C.S. (1984), "A ubiquitous sex difference in dreams" revisited. *Journal of Personality and Social Psychology, 46,* 1109–1117.

Hamilton, D.L., Dugan, P.M., & Trolier, T.K. (1985). The formation of stereotypic beliefs: Further evidence for distinctiveness-based illusory correlations. *Journal of Personality and Social Psychology, 48,* 5–17.

Hammersmith, S.K. (1982). *Sexual preference: An empirical study from the Alfred C. Kinsey Institute for Sex Research.* Paper presented at the meetings of the American Psychological Association, Washington, D.C.

Hansen, R.D. (1980). Commonsense attribution. *Journal of Personality and Social Psychology, 39,* 996–1009.

Harlow, H.F. (1962). The heterosexual affectional system in monkeys. *American Psychologist, 17,* 1–9.

Harlow, H.F., & Harlow, M.H. (1966). Learning to love. *American Scientist, 54,* 244–272.

Harlow, H.F., & Zimmerman, R.R. (1959) Affectional responses in the infant monkey. *Science, 130,* 421–423.

Harrington, D.M., Block, J.H., & Block, J. (1987). Testing aspects of Rogers' theory of creative environments: Child-rearing antecedents of creative potential in young adolescents. *Journal of Personality and Social Psychology, 52,* 851–856.

Harris, P.R., & Moran, R.T. (1987). *Managing cultural differences,* 2nd ed. Houston: Gulf.

Hartmann, E.L. (1973). *The functions of sleep.* New Haven: Yale University Press.

Harvey, J.H., & Weary, G. (1984). Current issues in attribution theory and research. *Annual Review of Psychology, 35,* 427–459.

Hassett, J. (1978). Sex and smell. *Psychology Today, 11,* 40, 42, 45.

Hatfield, E., & Sprecher, S. (1986). *Mirror, mirror . . . The importance of looks in everyday life.* Albany: State University of New York Press.

Hatfield, E., & Walster, G.W. (1985). *A new look at love.* Lanham, Md.: University Press of America.

Hays, R.D., Widaman, K.F., DiMatteo, M.R., & Stacy, A.W. (1987). Structural-equation models of current drug use: Are appropriate models so simple(x)? *Journal of Personality and Social Psychology, 52,* 134–144.

Hazelrigg, M.D., Cooper, H.M., & Borduin, C.M. (1987). Evaluating the effectiveness of family therapies: An integrative review and analysis. *Psychological Bulletin, 101,* 428–442.

Heggelund, P. (1981). Receptive field organization of complex cells in cat striate cortex. *Experimental Brain Research, 44,* 99–107.

Heilman, M.E., Martell, R.F., & Simon, M.C. (1988). The vagaries of sex bias: Conditions regulating the undervaluation, equivaluation, and overvaluation of female job applicants. *Organizational Behavior and Human Decision Processes, 41,* 98–110.

Helson, R., & Moane, G. (1987). Personality change in women from college to midlife. *Journal of Personality and Social Psychology, 53,* 176–186.

Herman, C., & Polivy, F. (1984). A boundary model for the regulation of eating. In A.J. Stunkard & E. Stellar (eds.), *Eating and its disorders,* pp. 145–156. New York: Raven.

Herman, C., Polivy, J., Lank, C.N., & Heatherton, T.F. (1987). Anxiety, hunger, and eating behavior. *Journal of Abnormal Psychology, 96,* 264–269.

Heslin, R., & Boss, D. (1980). Nonverbal intimacy in airport arrival and departure. *Personality and Social Psychology Bulletin, 6,* 248–252.

Heston, L.L. (1966). Psychiatric disorders in foster home reared children of schizophrenic mothers. *British Journal of Psychiatry, 112,* 819–825.

Hetherington, E.M. (1986). Introduction. In E.M. Hetherington, *Coping with divorce and remarriage.* Symposium conducted at the meeting of the Southern Conference on Human Development, Nashville.

Heuser, J.E., Reese, T.S., Dennis, M.J., Jan, L., & Evans, L. (1979). Synaptic vesicle membrane during transmitter release at the frog neuromuscular junction. *Journal of Cell Biology, 81,* 275–300.

Heuer, H., & Sanders, A.F. (eds.), (1987). *Perspectives on perception and action.* Hillsdale, N.J.: Erlbaum.

Hilgard, E.R. (1979). Divided consciousness in hypnosis: The implications of the hidden observer. In E. Gromm & R.E. Shor (eds.), *Hypnosis: Developments in research and new perspectives.* New York: Aldine.

Hilgard, E.R. (1987) *Psychology in America: A historical survey.* San Diego: Harcourt Brace Jovanovich.

Hilgard, E.R., & Hilgard, J.R. (1975). *Hypnosis in the relief of pain.* Los Altos, Cal.: Kaufmann.

Hilgard, E.R., & Hilgard, J.R. (1983). *Hypnosis in the relief of pain,* rev. ed. Palo Alto: Kaufmann.

Hilgard, J.R., & Lebaron, S. (1984). *Hypnosis in the treatment of pain and anxiety in children with cancer: A clinical and quantitative investigation.* Los Altos, Cal.: Kaufmann.

Hill, C.A. (1987). Affiliation motivation: People who need people . . . but in different ways. *Journal of Personality and Social Psychology, 52,* 1008–1018.

Hill, C.T., Rubin, Z., & Peplau, L.A. (1976). Breakups before marriage: The end of 103 affairs. *Journal of Social Issues, 32,* 147–168.

Hill, R.M. (1973). Drugs ingested by pregnant women. *Clinical Pharmacology and Therapeutics, 14,* 654–659.

Hinsley, D., Hayes, F.R., & Simon, H.A. (1977). From words to equations: Meaning and representation in algebra word problems In P. Carpenter & M. Just (eds.), *Cognitive processes in comprehension.* Hillsdale, N.J.: Erlbaum.

Hirsch, N.D.M. (1926). A study of national-racial mental differences. *Genetic Psychology Monographs, 1,* 231–406.

Hobson, J.A., & McCarley, R.W. (1977). The brain as a dream state generator: An activation-synthesis hypothesis of the dream process. *American Journal of Psychiatry, 134,* 1335–1348.

Hollenbeck, J.R., & Klein, H.J. (1987). Goal commitment and the goal-setting process: Problems, prospects, and proposals for future research. *Journal of Applied Psychology, 72,* 212–220.

Holley, J.W. (1973). Rorschach analysis. In P. Kline (ed.), *New approaches in psychological measurement.* London: Wiley.

Holmes, D.S., McGilley, B.M., & Houston, B.K. (1984). Task-related arousal of Type A and Type B persons: Level of challenge and response specificity. *Journal of Personality and Social Psychology, 46,* 1322–1327.

Holmes, D.S., & Will, M.J. (1985). Expressions of interpersonal aggression by angered and nonangered persons with Type A and Type B behavior patterns. *Journal of Personality and Social Psychology, 48,* 723–727.

Holmes, T.H., & Masuda, M. (1974). Life change and illness susceptibility. In B.S. Dohrenwend & B.P. Dohenrewend (eds.), *Stressful life events: Their nature and effects,* pp. 45–72. New York: Wiley.

Holmes, T.H., & Rahe, R.H. (1967). Social readjustment rating scale. *Journal of Psychosomatic research, 11,* 213–218.

Holtzwotth-Munroe, A., & Jacobson, N.S. (1985). Causal attributions of married couples: When do they search for causes? What do they conclude when they do? *Journal of Personality and Social Psychology, 50,* 537–542.

Honig, W.K., & Staddon, J.E.R. (eds.). (1977). *Handbook of operant behavior.* Englewood Cliffs, N.J.: Prentice-Hall.

Honig, W.K., & Urcuioli, P.J. (1981). The legacy of Guttman and Kalish: Twenty-five years of research on stimulus generalization. *Journal of the Experimental Analysis of Behavior, 36,* 405–445.

Horne, J.A. (1978). A review of the biological effects of total sleep deprivation in man. *Biological Psychology, 7,* 55–102.

Horner, M. (1970). Femininity and successful achievement: A basic inconsistency. In J.M. Bardwich et al. (eds.), *Feminine personality and conflict.* Belmont, Cal.: Wadsworth.

Horner, M. (1972). Toward an understanding of achievement-related conflicts in women. *Journal of Social Issues, 28,* 157–176.

Hovland, C.I., & Weiss, W. (1952). The influence of source credibility on communication effectiveness. *Public Opinion Quarterly, 15,* 635–650.

Howard, G.S. (1985). The role of values in the science of psychology. *American Psychologist, 40,* 255–265.

Howard, K.I., Kopta, S.M., Krause, M.S., & Orlinsky, D.E. (1986). The dose-effect relationship in psychotherapy. *American Psychologist, 41,* 159–164.

Hronsky, S.L., & Emory, E.K. (1987). Neurobehavioral effects of caffeine on the neonate. *Infant Behavior and Development, 10,* 61–80.

Hubbell, C.L., Abelson, M.L., Wild, K.D., Neuman, R., & Reid, L.D. (1988). *Alcohol,* in press.

Hubbell, C.L., Czirr, S.A., & Reid, L.D. (1987). Persistence and specificity of small doses of morphine on intake of alcoholic beverages. *Alcohol, 4,* 149–156.

Hubel, D.H., & Wiesel, T.N. (1979). Brain mechanisms of vision. *Scientific American, 241,* 150–162.

Hull, C.L. (1943). *Principles of behavior: An introduction to behavior theory.* New York: Appleton-Century-Crofts.

Hunt, D.D., & Hampson, J.L. (1980). Transsexualism: A standardized psychosocial rating format for the evaluation of results of sex reassignment surgery. *Archives of Sexual Behavior, 9,* 225–263.

Hutchings, B., & Mednick, S.A. (1977). Criminality in adoptees and their adoptive and biological parents: A pilot study. In S.A. Mednick & K.O. Christiansen (eds.), *Biosocial bases of criminal behavior,* pp. 127–141. New York: Gardner.

Hyde, J.S. (1986). *Understanding human sexuality,* 3rd ed. New York: McGraw-Hill.

Hygge, S., & Ohman, A. (1978). Modeling processes in the acquisition of fears: Vicarious electrodermal conditioning to fear-relevant stimuli. *Journal of Personality and Social Psychology, 36,* 271–279.

Isen, A.M. (1987). Positive affect, cognitive organization, and social behavior. In L. Berkowitz (ed.), *Advances in experimental social psychology,* vol. 21. New York: Academic.

Isen, A.M., & Shalker, T.E. (1982). The influence of mood state on evaluations of positive, neutral, and negative stimuli: When you "accentuate the positive," do you "eliminate the negative?" *Social Psychology Quarterly, 45,* 59–63.

Istvan, J. (1986). Stress, anxiety, and birth outcomes: A critical review of the evidence. *Psychological Bulletin, 100,* 331–348.

Istvan, J., & Matarazzo, J.D. (1984). Tobacco, alcohol, and caffeine use: A review of their interrelationships. *Psychological Bulletin, 95,* 301–326.

Izard, C. (1977). *Human emotions.* New York: Plenum.

Izard, C., Huebner, R.R., Risser, D., McGinnes, G.C., & Dougherty, L.M. (1980). The young infant's ability to produce discrete emotion expressions. *Developmental Psychology, 16,* 132–140.

Jackson, S.E., Schwab, R.L., & Schuler, R.S. (1986). Toward an understanding of the burnout phenomenon. *Journal of Applied Psychology, 71,* 630–640.

Jacobs, W.J., & Nadel, L. (1985). Stress-induced recovery of fears and phobias. *Psychological Review, 92,* 512–531.

Jacobson, S., Fein, G., Jacobson, J., Schwartz, P., & Dowler, J. (1984). Neonatal correlates of prenatal exposure to smoking, caffeine, and alcohol. *Infant Behavior and Development, 7,* 253–265.

James, W. (1890). *Principles of psychology.* New York: Holt.

Jamiesen, D.W., Lydon, J.E., & Zanna, M.P. (1987). Attitude and activity preference similarity: Differential bases of interpersonal attraction for low and high self-monitors. *Journal of Personality and Social Psychology, 53,* 1052–1060.

Janis, I.L. (1982). Decision-making under stress. In L. Goldberger & S. Breznitz (eds.), *Handbook of stress: Theoretical and clinical aspects,* pp. 69–80. New York: Free Press.

Jeavons, C.M., & Taylor, S.P. (1985). The control of alcohol-related aggression: Redirecting the inebriate's attention to socially appropriate conduct. *Aggressive Behavior, 11,* 93–101.

Jelliffe, D.B., & Jelliffe, E.F.P. (eds.) (1982). *Advances in international maternal and child health,* vol. 2. London: Oxford University Press.

Jencks, D. (1972). *Inequality: A reassessment of the effect of family and schooling in America.* New York: Basic Books.

Jenkins, C.D., Zyzanski, S.J., & Rosenman, R.H. (1979). *Jenkins Activity Survey.* New York: Psychological Corporation.

Jenkins, J.G., & Dallenbach, K.M. (1924). Oblivescence during sleep and waking. *American Journal of Psychology, 35,* 605–612.

Jenkins, W.H., Hobbs, S.A., & Hockenbury, D. (1982). Loneliness and social skills deficits. *Journal of Personality and Social Psychology, 42,* 682–689.

Johansson, G. (1975). Visual motion perception. *Scientific American, 232,* 76–88.

Johnson, T.E., & Rule, B.G. (1986). Mitigating circumstance information, censure, and aggression. *Journal of Personality and Social Psychology, 50,* 537–542.

Jones, W.H., Hobbs, S.A., & Hockenbury, D. (1982). Loneliness and social skills deficits. *Journal of Personality and Social Psychology, 42,* 682–689.

Joseph, J.G., Montgomery, S.B., Emmons, C.A., Kirscht, J.P., Kessler, R.C., Ostrow, D.G., Wortman, C.B., O'Brian, K., Eller, M., & Eshelman, S. (1987). Perceived risk of AIDS: Assessing the behavioral and psychosocial consequences in a cohort of gay men. *Journal of Applied Social Psychology, 17,* 213–250.

Kagan, J. (1984). *The nature of the child.* New York: Basic Books.

Kagan, J.N. (1988). Shyness as an inherited disposition. Paper presented at the meetings of the American Association for the Advancement of Science.

Kagan, J., Resnick, J.S., & Snidman, M. (1988). Biological bases of childhood shyness. Unpublished ms., Harvard University.

Kagen, J., & Klein, R.E. (1973). Cross-cultural perspectives on early development. *American Psychologist, 28,* 947–961.

Kahneman, D., Slovic, P., & Tversky, A. (1982). *Judgement under uncertainty: Heuristics and biases.* Cambridge, England: Cambridge University Press.

Kahneman, D. & Tversky, A. (1972). Subjective probability: A judgement of representativeness. *Cognitive Psychology, 3,* 430–454.

Kahneman, D. & Tversky, A. (1973). On the psychology of prediction. *Psychological Review, 80,* 237–251.

Kahneman, D., & Tversky, A. (1982). Psychology of preferences. *Scientific American,* pp. 161–173.

Kail, R., & Pellegrino, J.W. (1985). *Human intelligence: Perspectives and prospects.* New York: W.H. Freeman.

Kales, A., Kales, J.D., & Bixler, E.O. (1974). Insomnia: An approach to management and treatment. *Psychiatric Annals, 4,* 28–44.

Kamin, L.J. (1978). Comment on Munsinger's review of adoption studies. *Psychological Bulletin, 85,* 194–201.

Kanner, A.D., Coyne, J.C., Schaefer, C., & Lazarus, R.S. (1981). Comparisons of two modes of stress measurement: Daily hassles and uplifts versus major life events. *Journal of Behavioral Medicine, 4,* 1–39.

Kantowitz, B.H., & Sorkin, R.D. *Human factors.* New York: Wiley.

Kass, F., Spitzer, R.L., & Williams, J.B.W. (1983). An empirical study of the issue of sex bias in the diagnostic criteria of DSM-III axis II personality disorders. *American Psychologist, 38,* 799–801.

Kaufman, A.S. (1983). Some questions and answers about the Kaufman Assessment Battery for Children (K-ABC). *Journal of Psychoeducational Assessment, 1,* 205–218.

Kaufman, A., Baron, A. & Kopp, R.E. (1966). Some effects of instructions on human operant behavior. *Psychonomic Monographs Supplement, 1,* 243–250.

Kazdin, A.E. (1982). The token economy: A decade later. *Journal of Applied Behavior Analysis, 15,* 431–445.

Keinan, G. (1987). Decision making under stress: Scanning of alternatives under controllable and uncontrollable threats. *Journal of Personality and Social Psychology, 52,* 638–644.

Kelley, H.H. (1972). Attribution in social interaction. In E.E. Jones et al. (eds.), *Attribution: Perceiving the causes of behavior.* Morristown, N.J.: General Learning.

Kelley, H.H., & Michela, J.L. (1980). Attribution theory and research. *Review of Psychology, 31,* 457–501.

Kelley, K., & Byrne, D. (1983). Assessment of sexual responding: Arousal, affect, and behavior. In J. Cacioppo & R. Petty (eds.), *Social Psychophysiology.* New York: Guilford.

Kelsey, F.O. (1969). Drugs and pregnancy. *Mental Retardation, 7,* 7–10.

Kenrick, D.T. (1987). Gender, genes, and the social environment. In P.C. Shaver & C. Henrick (eds), *Personality and Social Psychology Review,* vol. 6, pp. 6–27. Beverly Hills: Sage.

Kenrick, D.T., & Stringfield, D.O. (1980). Personality traits and the eye of the beholder: Crossing some traditional philosophical boundaries in the search for consistency in all the people. *Psychological Review, 87,* 88–104.

Kenshalo, D.R. (1978). Biophysics and psychophysics of feeling. E.E. Carterette & M.P. Friedman (eds.), *Handbook of perception,* vol. 6B. New York: Academic.

Kermis, M.D. (1984). *The psychology of human aging.* Boston: Allyn and Bacon.

Kertesz, A. Anatomy of jargon. In J. Brown (Ed.), *Jargonaphasia.* New York: Academic Press, 1979.

Kiesler, D.J. (1966). Some myths of psychotherapy research and the search for a paradigm. *Psychological Bulletin, 65,* 110–136.

Kiesler, D.J. (1985). Meta-analysis, clinical psychology, and social policy. *Clinical Psychology Review, 5,* 3–12.

Kihlstrom, J.F. (1985). Hypnosis. *Annual Review of Psychology, 36,* 385–418.

Kingsbury, S.J. (1987). Cognitive differences between clinical psychologists and psychiatrists. *American Psychologist, 42,* 152–156.

Kinnaird, K., & Gerrard, M. (1986). Premarital sexual behavior and attitudes toward marriage and divorce among young women as a function of their mothers' marital status. *Journal of Marriage and the Family, 48,* 757–765.

Kinsey, A.C., Pomeroy, W., & Martin, C. (1948). *Sexual behavior in the human male.* Philadelphia: W.B. Saunders.

Kinsey, A.C., Pomeroy, W., Martin, C., & Gebhard, P. (1953). *Sexual behavior in the human female.* Philadelphia: W.B. Saunders.

Klaus, M.H., & Kennell, J.H. (1976). *Material-infant bonding.* St. Louis: C.V. Mosby.

Klatzky, R.L. (1984). *Memory and awareness: An information-processing perspective,* 2nd ed. San Francisco: W.H. Freeman.

Klayman, J., & Ha, Y-W. (1987). Confirmation, disconfirmation, and information in hypothesis testing. *Psychological Review, 94,* 211–228.

Kleinke, C.L. (1986a). Gaze and eye contact: A research review. *Psychological Bulletin, 100,* 78–100.

Kleinke, C.L. (1986b). *Meeting and understanding people.* New York: W.H. Freeman.

Kleinke, C.L., Meeker, F.B., & LaFong, C. (1974). Effects of gaze, touch, and use of name on evaluation of "engaged" couples. *Journal of Research in Personality, 7,* 368–373.

Kluver, H., & Bucy, C. (1939). Preliminary analysis of functions of the temporal lobes in monkeys. *Archives of Neurology and Psychiatry, 42,* 979–1000.

Knapp, M.L. (1978). *Nonverbal communication in human interaction* 2nd ed. New York; Holt, Rinehart & Winston.

Kobasa, S.C. (1979). Stressful life events, personality, and health: An inquiry into hardiness. *Journal of Personality and Social Psychology, 37,* 1–11.

Kchlberg, L. (1976). Moral stages and moralization: Cognitive developmental approach. In T. Lickona (ed.), *Moral development and behavior: Theory, research, and social issues.* New York: Holt, Rinehart & Winston.

Kohler, I. (1962). Experiments with goggles. *Scientific American,* pp. 62–72.

Kolata, G. (1985). Obesity declared a disease. *Science, 227,* 1019–1020.

Komaki, J.L. (1986). Toward effective supervision: An operant analysis and comparison of managers at work. *Journal of Applied Psychology, 36,* 271–279.

Kraeplin, E. (1919). *Dementia praecox and paraphrenia.* New York: Krieger.

Kuchik, A., Vibbert, M., & Bornstein, M.H. (1986). The perception of smiling and its experiential correlates in three-month-old infants. *Child Development, 57,* 1054–1061.

Kunst-Wilson, W.R., & Zajonc, R.B. (1980). Affective discrimination of stimuli that cannot be recognized. *Science, 207,* 557–558.

Kupfer, D. (1977). REM latency: A psychobiologic marker for primary depressive disease. *Biological Psychiatry, 11,* 159–174.

Laird, J.D. (1984). The real role of facial response in the experience of emotion: A reply to Tourangeau and Ellsworth, and others. *Journal of Personality and Social Psychology, 47,* 909–917.

Lamb, M.E. (1976). Twelve-month-olds and their parents: Interaction in a laboratory playroom. *Developmental Psychology, 12,* 237–244.

Lamb, M.E. (1977). Father-infant and mother-infant interaction in the first year of life. *Child Development, 48,* 167–181.

Lange, J.D., Brown, W.A., Wincze, J.P., & Zwick, W. (1980). Serum testosterone concentration and penile tumescence changes in men. *Hormones and Behavior, 14,* 267–270.

Langer, E.J., & Abelson, R.P. (1974). A patient by any other name . . . : Clinician group difference in labeling bias. *Journal of Consulting and Clinical Psychology, 42,* 4–9.

Larkin, J.E. (1987). Are good teachers perceived as high self-monitors? *Personality and Social Psychology Bulletin, 13,* 64–72.

Larry P. v. Riles. (1975). 495 F. Supp. 96 (N.D. Cal. 1979).

Larsen, R.J. (1984). Theory and measurement of affect intensity as an individual difference characteristic. *Dissertation Abstracts International, 85,* 2297B. (University Microfilms No. 84-22112.)

Larsen, R.J. (1987). The stability of mood variability: A spectral analytic approach to daily mood assessments. *Journal of Personality and Social Psychology, 52,* 1195–1204.

Larsen, R.J., & Diener, E. (1987). Emotional response intensity as an individual difference characteristic: A review. *Journal of Research in Personality, 21,* 1–39.

Larsen, R.J., Diener, E., & Crapanzano, R.S. (1988). Cognitive operations associated with individual differences in affect intensity. *Journal of Personality and Social Psychology,* in press.

Larsen, R.J., Diener, E., & Emmons, R.A. (1986). Affect intensity and reactions to daily life events. *Journal of Personality and Social Psychology, 51,* 803–814.

Lashley, K.S. (1950). In search of the engram. *Symposium of the Society for Experimental Biology, 4,* 454–482.

Lashley, K.S., Chow, K.L., & Semmes, J. (1951). An examination of the electrical field theory of cerebral integration. *Psychological Review, 58,* 123–136.

Latham, G.P., & Baldes, J.J. (1975). The practical significance of Locke's theory of goal setting. *Journal of Applied Psychology, 18,* 824–845.

Lazarus, R.S., Delongis, A., Folkman, S., & Gruen, R. (1985). Stress and adaptational outcomes: The problem of confounded measures. *American Psychologist, 40,* 770–779.

Lazarus, R.S., & Folkman, S. (1984). *Stress, appraisal, and coping.* New York: Springer.

Leary, M.R., & Maddux, J.E. (1987). Progress toward a viable interface between social and clinical-counseling psychology. *American Psychologist, 41,* 904–911.

Leibowitz, S.F. (1983). Hypothalamic catecholamine systems con-

trolling eating behavior: A potential model for anorexia nervosa. In P.L. Darby, P.E. Garfinkel, D.M. Garner, & D.V. Coscina (eds.), *Anorexia nervosa: Recent developments in research.* New York: A.R. Liss.

Leippe, M.R. (1985). The influence of eyewitness nonidentifications on mock-jurors' judgements of a court case. *Journal of Applied Social Psychology, 15,* 656–672.

Lempers, J.D., Flavell, F.R., & Flavell, J.H. (1977). The young children: Reasoning about duration. *Child Development, 48,* 435–444.

Lepper, M., & Greene, D. (eds.). (1978). *The hidden costs of reward.* Hillsdale, N.J.: Erlbaum.

Lerner, R.M. (1975). Showdown at generation gap: Attitudes of adolescents and their parents toward contemporary issues. In H.D. Thornburg (ed.), *Contemporary adolescence: Readings,* 2nd ed. Belmont, Cal.: Brooks/Cole.

Lewin, K. (1947). Group decision and social change. In T.N. Newcomb & E.L. Hartley (eds.), *Readings in Social Psychology.* Holt, Rinehart & Winston.

Levine, J.M., & McBurney, D.H. (1982). *The role of olfaction in social perception and behavior.* Paper presented at the Third Ontario Symposium on Personality and Social Psychology, Toronto.

Levinson, D.J. (1986). A conception of adult development. *American Psychologist, 41,* 3–13.

Ley, R.G., & Bryden, M.P. (1979). Hemispheric differences in processing emotions and faces. *Brain and Language, 7,* 127–138.

Lichenstein, S., & Fischoff, B. (1980). Training for calibration. *Organizational Behavior and Human Performance, 26,* 149–171.

Lidz, T. (1975). *The origin and treatment of schizophrenic disorders.* London: Hutchinson.

Lieberman, M.A. (1983). The effects of social supports on response to stress. In L. Goldbert & D.S. Breznitz (eds.), *Handbook of stress management.* New York: Free Press.

Liebert, R.M., Sprafkin, J.N., & Davidson, E.S. (1982). *The early window: Effects of television on children and youth,* 2nd ed. New York: Pergamon.

Limber, J. (1977). Language in child and chimp? *American Psychologist, 32,* 280–295.

Linden, L.L., & Breed, W. (1976). The demographic epidemiology of suicide. In E.S. Schneidman (ed.), *Suicidology: Contemporary developments.* New York: Grune & Stratton.

Linn, M.C. (1985). The cognitive consequences of programming instruction in classrooms. *Educational Researcher, 14,* 14–16.

Locke, E.A., Frederick, E., Lee, C., & Bobko, P. (1984). Effects of self-efficacy, goals, and task strategies on task performance. *Journal of Applied Psychology, 69,* 241–251.

Locke, S.E. (1982). Stress, adaptation, and immunity: Studies in humans. *General Hospital Psychiatry, 4,* 16–25.

Loftus, E.F. (1979). *Eyewitness testimony.* Cambridge: Harvard University Press.

Loftus, E.F., Miller, D.G., & Burns, H.J. (1978). Semantic integration of verbal information into a visual memory. *Journal of Experimental Psychology: Human Learning and Memory, 4,* 19–31.

Logan, G.D. (1980). Attention and automaticity in Stroop and priming tasks: Theory and data. *Cognitive Psychology, 12,* 523–553.

Logan, G.D. (1985). Skill and automaticity. *Canadian Journal of Psychology, 39,* 367–386.

Lord, C.G., Lepper, M.R., & Preston, E. (1984). Considering the opposite: A corrective strategy for social judgement. *Journal of Personality and Social Psychology, 47,* 1231–1243.

Lord, C.G., Ross, L., & Lepper, M.R. (1979). Biased assimilation and attitude polarization: The effects of prior theories on subsequently considered evidence. *Journal of Personality and Social Psychology, 37,* 2098–2107.

Lord, C.G., & Zimbardo, P.G. (1985). Actor-observer differences in the perceived stability of shyness. *Social Cognition, 3,* 250–265.

Lovaas, O.I. (1973). *Behavioral treatment of autistic children.* Morristown, N.J.: General Learning.

Lovaas, O.I. (1977). *The autistic child: Language development through behavior modification.* New York: Irvington.

Luborsky, L. (1984). *Principles of psychoanalytic psychotherapy: A manual for supportive-expressive treatment.* New York: Basic Books.

Luborsky, L., Singer, B., & Luborsky, L. (1975). Comparative studies of psychotherapies: Is it true that "everyone has won and all must have prizes?" *Archives of General Psychiatry, 32,* 49–62.

Luborsky, L., Woody, G.E., McClellan, A.T.O., Brien, C.P., & Rosenzweig, J. (1982). Can independent judges recognize different psychotherapies? An experience with manual-guided therapies. *Journal of Consulting and Clinical Psychology, 30,* 49–62.

Luchins, A.S. (1942). Mechanization in problem solving. *Psychological Monographs, 54* (Whole No. 248).

Lumsden, C.J., & Wilson, E.O. (1981). *Genes, mind, and culture: The coevolutionary process.* Cambridge: Harvard University Press.

Luthans, F., Paul, R., & Baker D. (1981). An experimental analysis of the impact of a contingent reinforcement intervention on salespersons' performance behaviors. *Journal of Applied Psychology, 66,* 314–323.

Lynch, G., & Baudry, M. (1984). The biochemistry of memory: A new and specific hypothesis. *Science, 224,* 1057–1064.

Lynn, S.J., & Rhue, J.W. (1986). The fantasy-prone person: Hypnosis, imagination, and creativity. *Journal of Personality and Social Psychology, 51,* 404–408.

MacGregor, J.N. (1987). Short-term memory capacity: Limitation or optimization? *Psychological Review, 94,* 107–108.

Major, B., & Konar, E. (1984). An investigation of sex differences in pay expectations and their possible causes. *Academy of Management Journal, 27,* 777–792.

Malamuth, N.M. (1984). Violence against women: Cultural and individual cases. In N.M. Malamuth and E. Donnerstein (eds.), *Pornography and sexual aggression.* New York: Academic.

Malamuth, N.M., Check, J.V.P., & Briere, J.H. (1986). Sexual arousal in response to aggression: Ideological, aggressive, and sexual correlates. *Journal of Personality and Social Psychology, 50,* 330–340.

Manuscia, G.K., Bauman, D.J., & Cialdini, R.B. (1985). Mood influences on helping: Direct effects or side effects? *Journal of Personality and Social Psychology, 46,* 357–364.

Marks, G., & Miller, N. (1987). Ten years of research on the false-consensus effect: An empirical and theoretical review. *Psychological Bulletin, 102,* 72–90.

Marr, D. (1982). *Vision: A computational investigation into the human representation and processing of visual information.* San Francisco: W.H. Freeman.

Marshall, G.D., & Zimbardo, P.G. (1979). Affective consequences of inadequately explained physiological arousal. *Journal of Personality and Social Psychology, 37,* 970–988.

Maslach, C. (1982). *Burnout: The cost of caring.* Englewood Cliffs, N.J.: Prentice Hall.

Maslach, C., & Jackson, S.E. (1984). Burnout in organizational settings. In S. Oskanp (ed.), *Applied social psychology annual,* vol. 5, pp. 135–154. Beverly Hills: Sage.

Maslow, A.H. (1970). *Motivation and personality.* New York: Harper & Row.

Mason, A., & Blankenship, V. (1987). Power and affiliation motivation, stress, and abuse in intimate relationships. *Journal of Personality and Social Psychology, 52,* 203–210.

Masters, W.H., & Johnson, V.E. (1966). *Human sexual response.* Boston: Little, Brown.

Matlin, M. (1983a). *Cognition.* New York: Holt, Rinehart & Winston.

Matlin, M.E. (1983b). *Perception.* Boston: Allyn and Bacon.

Matteson, M.T., & Ivancevich, J.M. (1983). Note on tension discharge rate as an employee health status predictor. *Academy of Management Journal, 26,* 540–545.

May, R. (1977). *The meaning of anxiety.* New York: Norton.

Mayo, C., & Henley, N.M. (eds.) (1981). *Gender and nonverbal behavior.* Secaucus, N.J.: Springer-Verlag.

McAdams, D.P. (1982). Intimacy motivation. In A.J. Steward (ed.), *Motivation and society.* San Francisco: Jossey-Bass.

McArthur, L.Z., & Apatow, K. (1984). Impression of baby-faced adults. *Social Cognition, 2,* 315–342.

McBurney, D.H., & Collings, V.B. (1984). *Introduction to Sensation and Perception,* 2nd ed. Englewood Cliffs, N.J.: Prentice-Hall.

McCain, B.E. (1986). Continuing investment under conditions of failure: A laboratory study of the limits to escalation. *Journal of Applied Psychology, 71,* 280–284.

McCanne, T.R., & Anderson, J.A. (1987). Emotional responding following experimental manipulation of facial electromyographic activity. *Journal of Personality and Social Psychology, 52,* 759–768.

McCarley, R.W., & Hobson, R.W. (1981). REM sleep dreams and the activation hypothesis. *American Journal of Psychiatry, 138,* 904–912.

McClelland, D.C. (1961). *The achieving society.* Princeton, N.J.: Van Nostrand.

McClelland, D.C. (1975). *Power: The inner experience.* New York: Irvington.

McClelland, D.C., Ankinson, J.W., Clark, R.W., & Lowell, E.L. (1953). *The achievement motive.* New York: Appleton-Century-Crofts.

McClelland, D.C., & Boyatzis, R.E. (1982). Leadership motive pattern and long-term success in management. *Journal of Applied Psychology, 67,* 737–743.

McConkey, K.M., & Kinoshita, S. (1988). The influence of hypnosis on memory after one day and one week. *Journal of Abnormal Psychology, 97,* 48–53.

McFall, R.M., & Twentyman, C.T. (1973). Four experiments on the relative contributions of rehearsal, modeling, and coaching to assertion training. *Journal of Abnormal Psychology, 81,* 199–218.

McGrath, J.E. (1976). Stress and behavior in organizations. In M.D. Dunnette (ed.), *Handbook of industrial and organizational psychology.* Chicago: Rand McNally.

McGrath, M.J., & Cohen, D.B. (1978). REM sleep facilitation of adaptive waking behavior: A review of the literature. *Psychological Bulletin, 85,* 24–57.

McLean, A.A. (1980). *Work stress.* Reading, Mass.: Addison-Wesley.

McNeal, E.T., & Cimbolic, P. (1986). Antidepressants and biochemical theories of depression. *Psychological Bulletin, 99,* 361–374.

McReynolds, W.T. (1980). Learned helplessness as a schedule-shift effect. *Journal of Research in Personality, 14,* 139–157.

Medin, D.L., & Smith, E.E. (1984). Concepts and concept formation. *Annual Review of Psychology, 35,* 113–138.

Medin, D.L., & Wattenmaker, W.D. (1986). Category cohesiveness, theories, and cognitive archeology. In U. Neisser (ed.), *Categories reconsidered: The ecological and intellectual bases of categories.* London: Cambridge University Press.

Medin, D.L., Wattenmaker, W.D., & Hampson, S.E. (1987). Family resemblance, conceptual cohesiveness, and category construction. *Cognitive Psychology, 19,* 242–279.

Melchior, L.A., & Cheek, J.M. (1985). *Testing cognitive explanations of shyness.* Unpublished manuscript, Wellesley College.

Melzack, R. (1976). Pain: past, present, and future. In M. Weisenberg & B. Tursky (eds.), *Pain: New perspectives in therapy and research.* New York: Plenum.

Meredith, H.V. (1975). Relation between tobacco smoking of pregnant women and body size of their progeny: A compilation and synthesis of published studies. *Human Biology, 47,* 451–572.

Mervis, C.B., & Rosch, E. (1981). Categorization of natural objects. In M.R. Rosenzweig & L.W. Porter (eds.), *Annual Review of Psychology, 32,* 89–115.

Messick, S., & Jungeblut, A. (1981). Time and method in coaching for the SAT. *Psychological Bulletin, 89,* 191–216.

Mewborn, C.R., & Rogers, R.W. (1979). Effects of threatening and reassuring components of fear appeals on physiological and verbal measures of emotion and attitudes. *Journal of Experimental Social Psychology, 15,* 242–253.

Michelini, R.L., & Snodgrass, S.R. (1980). Defendant characteristics and juridic decisions. *Journal of Research in Personality, 14,* 340–350.

Milgram, S. (1963). Behavioral study of obedience. *Journal of Abnormal and Social Psychology, 67,* 371–378.

Milgram, S. (1964). Group pressure and action against a person. *Journal of Abnormal and Social Psychology, 69,* 137–143.

Milgram, S. (1965). Liberating effects of group pressure. *Journal of Personality and Social Psychology, 1,* 127–134.

Milgram, S. (1974). *Obedience to authority.* New York: Harper.

Miller, D.T., & Ross, M. (1975). Self-serving biases in the attribution of causality: Fact or fiction? *Psychological Bulletin, 82,* 213–225.

Miller, G.A. (1956). The magical number seven plus or minus two: Some limits on our capacity for processing information. *Psychological Review, 63,* 81–97.

Miller, L. (1987). The emotional brain. *Psychology Today, 22,* 35–42.

Miller, N., Maruyama, G., Beaber, R.J., & Valone, K. (1976). Speed of speech and persuasion. *Journal of Personality and Social Psychology, 34,* 615–624.

Miller, N.E. (1978). Biofeedback and visceral learning. In M.R. Rosenzweig & L.W. Porter (eds.), *Annual Review of Psychology,* vol. 29. Palo Alto: Annual Reviews.

Miller, N.E. (1980). Applications of learning and biofeedback to psychiatry and medicine. In H.I. Kaplan, A.M. Freedman, & B.J. Sadock (eds.), *Comprehensive textbook of psychiatry,* 3rd ed., pp. 468–475. Baltimore: Williams & Wilkins.

Miller, N.E. (1983). Behavioral medicine: Symbiosis between laboratory and clinic. In M.R. Rosenzweig & L.W. Porter (eds.), *Annual Review of Psychology.* Palo Alto: Annual Reviews.

Milner, B. (1965). Visually guided maze learning in man: Effects of bilateral hippocampal, bilateral frontal, and unilateral cerebral lesions. *Neuropsychologia, 3,* 317–338.

Milner, B. (1970). Memory and the medial temporal regions of the brain. In K.H. Pribram & D.E. Broadbent (eds.), *Biology of memory.* New York: Academic.

Minuchin, S. (1974). *Families and family therapy.* Cambridge: Harvard University Press.

Mischel, W. (1977). On the future of personality measurement. *American Psychologist, 32,* 246–254.

Mischel, W. (1985). *Personality: Lost or found? Identifying when individual differences make a difference.* Paper presented at the meetings of the American Psychological Association, Los Angeles.

Mistler-Lachman, J.L. (1975). Queer sentences, ambiguity, and levels of processing. *Memory and Cognition, 3,* 395–400.

Mitchell, T.R., & Larson, J.R., Jr. (1987). *People in organizations: An introduction to organizational behavior,* 3rd ed. New York: McGraw-Hill.

Money, J. (1985). Pornography as related to criminal sex offensing and the history of medical degeneracy theory. Paper presented at the U.S. Justice Department Hearings, Houston.

Money, J. (1980). *Love and love sickness.* Baltimore: Johns Hopkins University Press.

Money, J., & Erhardt, A.A. (1972). *Man & woman, boy & girl.* Baltimore: Johns Hopkins University Press.

Money, J., & Matthews, D. (1982). Prenatal exposure to virilizing progestins: An adult follow-up study of twelve women. *Archives of Sexual Behavior, 11,* 73–82.

Money, J., & Schwartz, M. (1977). Dating, romantic and nonromantic friendship and sexuality in 17 early-treated adrenogenital females aged 16–25. In P.A. Lee et al. (eds.), *Congenital and adrenal hyperplasia.* Baltimore: University Park Press.

Monson, T.C., Hesley, J.W., & Chernick, L. (1982). Specifying when personality traits can and cannot predict behavior: An alternative to abandoning the attempt to predict single-act criteria. *Journal of Personality and Social Psychology, 43,* 385–399.

Moreland, R.L., & Zajonc, R.B. (1982). Exposure effects in person perception: Familiarity, similarity, and attraction. *Journal of Experimental Social Psychology, 18,* 395–415.

Morgan, A.H., & Hilgard, E.R. (1973). Age differences in susceptibility to hypnosis. *International Journal of Clinical and Experimental Hypnosis, 21,* 78–85.

Morris, D. (1975). *The naked ape.* New York: Harper & Row.

Morris, W.N., Miller R.S., & Spangenberg, S. (1977). The effects of dissenter position and task difficulty on conformity and response to conflict. *Journal of Personality, 45,* 251–266.

Moscovici, S. (1985). Social influence and conformity. In G. Lindzay & E. Aronson (eds.), *Handbook of social psychology,* vol. 2. New York: Random House.

Moskowitz, D.S. (1982). Coherence and cross-situational generality in personality: A new analysis of old problems. *Journal of Personality and Social Psychology, 43,* 754–768.

Motowidlo, S.J., Packard, J.S., & Manning, M.R. (1986). Occupational stress: Its causes and consequences for job performance. *Journal of Applied Psychology, 71,* 618–629.

Munsinger, H.A. (1975). The adopted child's IQ: A crucial review. *Psychological Bulletin, 82,* 623–659.

Myers, J.K., Weissman, M.M., Tischler, G.L., Holzer, C.E., Leaf, P.J., Orvaschel, H., Anthony, J.C., Boyd, J.H., Burke, J.D., Kramer, M., & Stoltzman, R. (1984). Six-month prevalence of psychiatric disorders in three communities. *Archives of General Psychiatry, 41,* 959–967.

Nagar, D., & Pandey, J. (1987). Affect and performance on cognitive task as a function of crowding and noise. *Journal of Applied Social Psychology, 17,* 147–157.

Nasby, W., & Yando, R. (1982). Selective encoding and retrieval of affectively valent information. *Journal of Personality and Social Psychology, 69,* 147–156.

Neely, H.J. (1977). Semantic priming and retrieval from lexical memory: Roles of inhibitionless spreading activation and limited capacity. *Journal of Experimental Psychology: General, 106,* 226–254.

Nelson, C.A. (1987). The recognition of facial expressions in the first two years of life: Mechanisms of development. *Child Development, 58,* 880–909.

Nelson, C.A., & Ludeman, P. (1987). The categorial representation of facial expressions by 4- and 7-month-old infants. Unpublished manuscript, University of Minnesota.

Nelson, D.L., Bajo, M.T., & Canas, J. (1987). Prior knowledge and memory: The episodic encoding of implicitly activated associates and rhymes. *Journal of Experimental Psychology: Learning, Memory, and Cognition, 13,* 54–63.

Nelson, M.J., Lamke, T.A., & French, J.L. (1973). *The Henmon-Nelson Tests of Mental Ability.* Riverside, Cal.: Riverside Publishing.

Newsweek. (1984). How executive men and women view and use fragrances at work and at leisure. Newsweek research report.

Nisbett, R.E., & Kunda, Z. (1985). Perception of social distributions. *Journal of Personality and Social Psychology, 48,* 297–311.

Nolen-Hokesema, S. (1987). Sex differences in unipolar depression: Evidence and theory. *Psychological Bulletin, 101,* 259–282.

Northcraft, G.B., & Neale, M.A. (1987). Experts, amateurs, and real estate: An anchoring-and-adjustment perspective on property pricing decision. *Organizational Behavior and Human Decision Processes, 39,* 94–97.

O'Donnell, L., O'Donnell, C.R., Pleck, J.H., Sharey, J., & Rose, R.M. (1987). Psychosocial responses of hospital workers to acquired immune definiency syndrome (AIDS). *Journal of Applied Social Psychology, 17,* 269–285.

Olds, J. (1973). Commentary. In E.S. Valenstein (ed.), *Brain stimulation and motivation.* Glenview, Ill.: Scott Foresman.

Olds, J., & Milner, P. (1954). Positive reinforcement produced by electrical stimulation of septal area and other regions of rat brain. *Journal of Comparative and Physiological Psychology, 47,* 419–427.

Orlinsky, D.E., & Howard, K.I. (1987). The relation of process of outcome in psychotherapy. In S.L. Garfield & A.E. Bergin (eds.), *Handbook of psychotherapy and behavior change,* 3rd ed. New York: Wiley.

Orne, M.T., & Evans, F.J. (1965). Social control in the psychological experiments: Antisocial behavior and hypnosis. *Journal of Personality and Social Psychology, 1,* 189–200.

Orne, M.T., Sheehan, P.W., & Evans, F.J. (1968).Occurrence of posthypnotic behavior outside the experimental setting. *Journal of Personality and Social Psychology, 9,* 189–196.

Orne, M.T., Soskis, D.A., Dinges, D.F., & Orne, E.C. (1984). Hypnotically induced testimony. In G.L. Wells & E.F. Loftus (ed.), *Eyewitness testimony: Psychological perspectives,* pp. 171–213. New York: Cambridge University Press.

Ortega, D.F., & Pipal, J.E. (1984). Challenge seeking and the Type A coronary-prone behavior pattern. *Journal of Personality and Social Psychology, 46,* 1328–1334.

Otis, A.S., & Lennon, R.T. (1967). *The Otis-Lennon Mental Ability Tests.* Los Angeles: Psychological Corp.

Oulette-Kobasa, S.C., & Puccetti, M.C. (1983). Personality and social resources in stress resistance. *Journal of Personality and Social Psychology, 45,* 836–850.

Page, R.A. (1977). Environmental influence on prosocial behavior: The effect of temperature. Paper presented at the meetings of the Midwestern Psychological Association, Chicago.

Paivio, A. (1969). Mental imagery in associative learning and memory. *Psychological Review, 76,* 241–263.

Panskepp, J. (1982). Toward a general psychobiological theory of emotions. *Behavioral and Brain Sciences, 5,* 407–467.

Paris, S.G., & Jacobs, J.E. (1987). The benefits of informed instruction for children's reading awareness and comprehension skills. *Child Development,* in press.

Pastor, D.L. (1981). The quality of mother-infant attachment and its relationship to toddlers' initial sociability with peers. *Developmental Psychology, 17,* 326–335.

Passuth, P., Maines, D., & Neugarten, B.I. (1984). Age norms and age constraints twenty years later. Paper presented at the meetings of the Midwest Sociological Society, Chicago.

Patterson, F. (1978). Conversations with a gorilla. *National Geographic, 154,* 438–465.

Patterson, G.R. (1982). *Coercive family process.* Eugene, Ore.: Castilia.

Pavlov, I.P. (1927). *Conditioned reflexes.* Transalated by G.V. Anrep. London: Oxford University Press.

Payne, D.G. (1987). Hypermnesia and reminiscence in recall: A historical and empirical review. *Psychological Bulletin, 101,* 5–27.

Pearce, J.M. (1986). A model for stimulus generalization in Pavlovian conditioning. *Psychological Review, 94,* 61–73.

Pearce, J.M. (1987). *Introduction to animal cognition.* Hillsdale, N.J.: Erlbaum.

Peplau, R.J., & Perlman, D. (1982). Perspectives on loneliness. In L.A. Peplau & D. Perlman (eds.), *Loneliness: A sourcebook of current theory, research, and therapy.* New York: Wiley.

Perls, F.S. (1969). *Ego, hunger, and aggression: The beginning of Gestalt therapy.* New York: Random House.

Perry, D.G., & Bussey, K. (1979). The social learning theory of sex differences: Imitation is alive and well. *Journal of Personality and Social Psychology, 37,* 1699–1712.

Peterson, L.R., & Peterson, M.J. (1959). Short-term retention of individual verbal items. *Journal of Experimental Psychology, 58,* 193–198.

Petty, R.E., & Cacioppo, J.T. (1985). The elaboration likelihood model of persuasion. In L. Berkowitz (ed.), *Advances in experimental social psychology,* vol. 19. New York: Academic.

Petty, R.E., & Cacioppo, J.T. (1986). *Attitude change: Central and peripheral routes to persuasion.* New York: Springer-Verlag.

Pfaffman, C. (1978). The vertebrate phylogyny, neural code, and integrative processess of taste. In E.C. Carterrette & M.P. Friedman (eds.), *Handbook of perception,* vol. 6A. New York: Academic.

Piaget, J. (1975). *The child's conception of the world.* Totowa, N.J.: Littlefield, Adams (originally published 1929).

Piaget, J. (1954). *The Construction of Reality in the Child.* New York: Basic Books.

Piaget, J., & Inhelder, B. (1969). *The psychology of the child.* New York: Basic Books.

Pines, A. (1984). Ma Bell and the Hardy boys. *Across the Board* (July/August), 37–42.

Pines, A.M., Aronson, E., & Kafry, D. (1981). *Burnout: From tedium to personal growth.* New York: Free Press.

Powers, D.E. (1986). Relations of test item characteristics to test preparation/test practice effects: A quantitative summary. *Psychological Bulletin, 100,* 67–77.

Powers, P.C., & Geen, R.S. (1972). Effects of the behavior and perceived arousal of a model on instrumental aggression. *Journal of Personality and Social Psychology, 23,* 175–184.

Prasse, D.P., & Reschly, D.J. (1986). Larry P.: A case of segregation, testing, or program efficacy? *Exceptional Children, 52,* 333–346.

Premack, A.J., & Premack, D. (1972). Teaching language to an ape. *Scientific American, 227,* 92–99.

Premack, D. (1985). ''Gavagai!'' or the future history of the animal language controversy. *Cognition, 19,* 207–297.

Pribram, K.H. (1986). The cognitive revolution and mind/brain issues. *American Psychologist, 41,* 507–520.

Price, D.D., & Barber, F. (1987). An analysis of factors that contribute to the efficacy of hypnotic analgesia. *Journal of Abnormal Psychology, 96,* 46–51.

Price, R.H., & Lynn, S.J. (1986). *Abnormal psychology,* 2nd ed. Chicago: Dorsey.

Pyszczynski, T., & Greenberg, J. (1986). Evidence for a depressive self-focusing style. *Journal of Research in Personality, 20,* 95–106.

Pzyczynski, T., & Greenberg, J. (1987). Self-regulatory perseveration and the depressive self-focusing style: A self-awareness theory of reactive depression. *Psychological Bulletin, 102,* 122–138.

Quinn, R.P., & Staines, G.L. (1979). *The 1977 Quality of Employment Survey*. Ann Arbor: Institute for Social Research.

Rachman, S.J., & Hodgson, R.J. (1980). *Obsessions and compulsions*. Englewood Cliffs, N.J.: Prentice-Hall.

Raven, J.C. (1977). *Raven progressive matrices*. Los Angeles: Psychological Corp.

Raynor, J.O. (1970). Relationships between achievement-related motives, future orientation, and academic performance. *Journal of Personality and Social Psychology, 15,* 28–33.

Read, E.W. (1988). Birth cycle: For poor teen-agers, pregnancies become new rite of passage. *Wall Street Journal* (March 17), *211,* 1, 13.

Reber, R.A., & Wallin, J.A. (1984). The effects of training, goal setting, and knowledge of results on safe behavior: A component analysis. *Academy of Management Journal, 27,* 544–560.

Rechtschaffen, A. (1968). In H. Gastauf, E. Lugaresi, G. Berti-Ceroni, & G. Coccagna (eds.), *The abnormalities of sleep in man,* pp. 109–125. Bologna: Aulo Gaggi.

Reeves, A., & Sperling, G. (1986). Attention gating in short-term retention of individual verbal items. *Psychological Review, 93,* 180–206.

Reiser, M., Nielson, M. (1980) Investigative hypnosis: A developing specialty. *American Journal of Clinical Hypnosis, 23,* 75–83.

Reitman, J.S. (1974). Without surreptitious rehearsal, information in short-term memory decays. *Journal of Verbal Learning and Verbal Behavior, 13,* 365–377.

Rescorla, R.A. (1988). Pavlovian conditioning: It's not what you think it is. *American Psychologist, 43,* 151–160.

Rhine, F.B., & Pratt, J.G. (1962). *Parapsychology: Frontier science of the mind*. Springfield, Ill.: Charles C Thomas.

Rice, F.P. (1984). *The adolescent: Development, relationships, and culture*. Boston: Allyn and Bacon.

Riggio, R.E., & Friedman, H.S. (1986). Impression formation: The role of expressive behavior. *Journal of Personality and Social Psychology, 50,* 421–427.

Ritchie, R.J., & Moses, J.L. (1983). Assessment center correlates of women's advancement into middle management: A 7-year longitudinal analysis. *Journal of Applied Psychology, 68,* 227–231.

Rodin, F., & Slochower, J. (1976). Externality in the nonobese: Effects of environmental responsiveness on weight. *Journal of Personality and Social Psychology, 33,* 338–344.

Rogers, C.R. (1954). Toward a theory of creativity. *ETC: A Review of General Semantics, 11,* 249–260.

Rogers, C.R. (1970). *Carl Rogers on encounter groups*. New York: Harper & Row.

Rogers, C.R. (1977). *Carl Rogers on personal power: Inner strength and its revolutionary impact*. New York: Delacorte.

Rogers, C.R. (1980). *A way of being*. Boston: Houghton Mifflin.

Rogler, L.H., Malgady, R.G., Constantino, G., & Blumenthal, R. (1987). What do culturally sensitive mental health services mean? The case of Hispanics. *American Psychologist, 42,* 565–570.

Rosch, E.H. (1973). Natural categories. *Cognitive Psychology, 4,* 328–350.

Rosch, E.H. (1975). The nature of mental codes for color categories. *Journal of Experimental Psychology: Human Perception and Performance, 1,* 303–322.

Rosch, E., & Mervis, C.G. (1975). Family resemblances: Studies in the internal structure of categories. *Cognitive Psychology, 7,* 573–605.

Rosenbaum, M.E. (1986). The repulsion hypothesis: On the nondevelopment of relationships. *Journal of Personality and Social Psychology, 51,* 1156–1166.

Rosenfield, D., Folger, R., & Adelman, H.F. (1980). When rewards reflect competence: A qualification of the overjustification effect. *Journal of Personality and Social Psychology, 39,* 368–376.

Rosenhan, D.L. (1973). On being sane in insane places. *Science, 179,* 250–259.

Rosenhan, D.L., & Seligman, M.E.P. (1984). *Abnormal psychology*. New York: Norton.

Rosenthal, R.R., & DePaulo, B.M. (1979). Sex differences in eavesdropping on nonverbal cues. *Journal of Personality and Social Psychology, 37,* 273–285.

Rosett, H.L., & Weiner, L. (1985). Alcohol and pregnancy: A clinical perspective. *Annual Review of Medicine, 36,* 73–80.

Rosett, H.L., Weiner, L., Lee, A., Zuckerman, B., Dooling, E., and Oppenheimer, E. (1983). Patterns of alcohol consumption and fetal development. *Obstetrics and gynecology, 61,* 538–546.

Ross, L., & Fletcher, G.J.O. (1985). Attribution and social perception. In G. Lindzey & E. Aronson (eds.), *Handbook of social psychology*. New York: Random House.

Rothwell, N.J., & Stock, M.J. (1979). A role for brown adapose tissue in diet-related thermogenesis. *Nature, 281,* 31–35.

Rotton, J., & Kelly, I.W. (1985). Much ado about the full moon: A meta-analysis of lunar-lunacy research. *Psychological Bulletin, 97,* 286–306.

Royce, J.M., Darlington, R.B., & Murray, H.W. (1983). Pooled analyses: Findings across studies. In Consortium for Longitudinal Studies, *As the twig is bent . . . Lasting effects of preschool programs*. Hillsdale, N.J.: Erlbaum.

Rubin, D.C., & Olson, M.J. (1980). Recall of semantic domains. *Memory and Cognition, 8,* 354–366.

Rushton, W.A.H. (1975). Visual pigments and color blindness. *Scientific American, 232,* 64–74.

Russell, D., Peplau, L.A., & Cutrona, C.E. (1980). The revised UCLA Loneliness Scale: Concurrent and discriminant validity evidence. *Journal of Personality and Social Psychology, 39,* 472–480.

Sackeim, H.A., et al. (1982). Hemispheric asymmetry in the expression of positive and negative emotions: Neurologic evidence. *Archives of Neurology, 39,* 210–218.

Sadalla, E., Kenrick, D.T., & Vershure, B. (1987). Dominance and heterosexual attraction. *Journal of Personality and Social Psychology, 52,* 730–738.

Salame, P., & Baddeley, A. (1982). Disruption of short-term memory by unattended speech: Implications for the structure of working memory. *Journal of Verbal Learning and Verbal Behavior, 21,* 11–21.

Sanbonmatsu, D.M., Shavitt, S., Sherman, S.J., & Roskos-Ewoldsen, D.R. (1987). Illusory correlation in the perception of performance by self or a salient other. *Journal of Experimental Social Psychology, 23,* 518–543.

Savage-Rumbaugh, E.S., Pate, J.L., Lawson, J., Smith, S.T., & Rosenbaum, S. (1983). Can a chimpanzee make a statement? *Journal of Experimental Psychology: General, 112,* 457–492.

Savitsky, J.C., & Lindblom, W.D. (1986). The impact of the Guilty But Mentally Ill verdict on juror decisions: An empirical analysis. *Journal of Applied Social Psychology, 16,* 686–701.

Scarr, S., & Weinberg, R.A. (1977). IQ test performance of black children adopted by white families. *American Psychologist, 31,* 726–739.

Schachter, S., & Singer, J.E. (1962). Cognitive, social, and physiological determinants of emotional states. *Psychological Review, 69,* 379–399.

Schaie, K.W., & Hertzog, D. (1985). Toward a comprehensive model of adult intellectual development: Contributions of the Seattle Longitudinal Study. In R.J. Sternberg (ed.), *Advances in human intelligence,* vol. 3. New York: Academic.

Schaie, K.W., & Willis, S.L. (1986). *Adult development and aging,* 2nd ed. Boston: Little, Brown.

Schaller, G.B. (1986). Secrets of the wild panda. *National Geographic, 169,* 284–309.

Schanke, M.E. (1986). Vicarious punishment in a work setting. *Journal of Applied Psychology, 71,* 343–345.

Scheier, M.F., & Carver, C.S. (1985). Optimism, coping, and health: Assessment and implications of generalized outcome expectancies. *Health Psychology, 4,* 219–247.

Scheier, M.F., & Carver, C. (1988). *Perspectives on personality.* Boston: Allyn and Bacon.

Scheier, M.F., Weintraub, J.K., & Carver, C.S. (1986). Coping with stress: Divergent strategies of optimists and pessimists. *Journal of Personality and Social Psychology, 51,* 1257–1264.

Schlossberg, N.K. (1987). Taking the mystery out of change. *Psychology Today, 21,* 74–75.

Schneider, W., & Shiffrin, R.M. (1977). Controlled and automatic human information processing: Detection, search, and attention. *Psychological Review, 84,* 1–66.

Schoenfeld, A. (1985). *Mathematical problem solving.* New York: Academic.

Schoorman, F.D. (1988). Escalation bias in performance appraisals: An unintended consequence of supervisor participation in hiring decisions. *Journal of Applied Psychology, 73,* 58–62.

Schwartz, B. (1984). *Psychology of learning and behavior,* 2nd ed. New York: Norton.

Schwarzwald, J., Raz, M., & Zvibel, M. (1979). The applicability of the door-in-the-face technique when established behavioral customs exist. *Journal of Applied Social Psychology, 9,* 576–586.

Schweder, R.A. (1975). How relevent is an individual difference theory of personality? *Journal of Personality, 43,* 455–484.

Scoville, W.B., & Milner, B. (1957). Loss of recent memory after bilateral hippocampal lesions. *Journal of Neurology, Neurosurgery, and Psychiatry, 20,* 11–21.

Seligman, M.E.P. (1975). *Helplessness: On depression, development, and death.* San Francisco: W.H. Freeman.

Seligman, M.E.P., Castellon, C., Cacciola, J., Schulman, P., Luborsky, L., Ollove, M., & Downing, R. (1988). Explanatory style change during cognitive therapy for unipolar depression. *Journal of Abnormal Psychology, 97,* 13–18.

Selye, H. (1976). *Stress in health and disease.* Boston: Butterworths.

Sewitch, D.E. (1987). Slow wave sleep deficiency insomnia: A problem in thermo-downregulation at sleep onset. *Psychophysiology,* 200–215.

Shaffer, D.R., Smith, J.E., & Tomarelli, M. (1982). Self-monitoring as a determinant of self-disclosure reciprocity during the acquaintance process. *Journal of Personality and Social Psychology, 43,* 163–175.

Shanab, M.E., & Yahya, K.A. (1977). A behavioral study of obedience in children. *Journal of Personality and Social Psychology, 35,* 530–536.

Shapiro, D.A., & Shapiro, D. (1982). Meta-analysis of comparative therapy outcome studies: A replication and refinement. *Psychological Bulletin, 92,* 581–604.

Sheffield, F.D., Wulff, J.J., & Backer, R. (1951). Reward value of copulation without sex drive reduction. *Journal of Comparative and Physiological Psychology, 44,* 3–8.

Sherif, M. (1935). A study of some social factors in perception. *Archives of Psychology, 27* (187).

Sherman, S.J. (1980). On the self-erasing nature of errors of prediction. *Journal of Personality and Social Psychology, 39,* 211–221.

Shiffrin, R.M., & Dumais, S.T. (1981). The development of automatism. In J.R. Anderson (ed.), *Cognitive skills and their acquisition.* Hillsdale, N.J.: Erlbaum.

Shiffrin, R.M., & Schneider, W. (1977). Controlled and automatic human information processing. II: Perceptual learning, automatic attending, and a general theory. *Psychological Review, 84,* 127–190.

Shimizu, N., Oomura, Y., Novin, D., Grijalva, C., & Cooper, P.H. (1983). Functional correlations between lateral hypothalamic glucose-sensitive neurons and hepatic protal glucose-sensitive units in rat. *Brain Research, 265,* 49–54.

Shock, D. (1962). Aging in different organ systems. Data reported in R.A. Baron, D. Byrne, & B.H. Kantowitz, *Psychology: Understanding behavior.* Philadelphia: W.B. Saunders.

Siegel, J. (1984). Type A behavior. *Annual Review of Public Health, 5,* 343–367.

Simon, H.A., & Hayes, J.R. (1976). The understanding process: Problem isomorphs. *Cognitive Psychology, 8,* 165–190.

Singer, J.L. (1975). Navigating the stream of consciousness: Research in daydreaming and related inner experience. *American Psychologist, 30,* 727–738.

Sistrunk, F., & McDavid, J.W. (1971). Sex variable in conforming behavior. *Journal of Personality and Social Psychology, 17,* 202–207.

Skeels, H.M. (1966). Adult status of children with contrasting early life experience. *Society for Research in Child Development Monographs, 31,* no. 3, 1–65.

Skinner, B.F. (1938). *The behavior of organisms.* New York: Appleton-Century-Crofts.

Skinner, B.F. (1953). *Science and human behavior.* New York: Appleton-Century-Crofts.

Sleet, D.A. (1984). A preventative health orientation in safety belt and child safety seat use. SAE Technical Paper Series No. 840325. Warrendale, Pa.: Society of Automotive Engineers.

Smith, E.R., & Lerner, M. (1986). Development of automatism of social judgments. *Journal of Personality and Social Psychology, 50,* 246–259.

Smith, M.L., Glass, G.V., & Miller T.I. (1980). *The benefits of psychotherapy.* Baltimore: Johns Hopkins University Press.

Smith, S.M., Glenberg, A., & Bjork, R.A. (1978). Environmental context and human memory. *Memory and Cognition, 6,* 342–353.

Smith, S.S., & Richardson, D. (1985). Amelioration of deception and harm in psychological research: The important role of debriefing. *Journal of Personality and Social Psychology, 45,* 1075–1082.

Smith, S.S., & Richardson, D. (1985). On deceiving ourselves about deception: A reply to Rubin. *Journal of Personality an Social Psychology, 48,* 254–255.

Snyder, M. (1987). The self-monitoring of expressive behavior. *Journal of Personality and Social Psychology, 30,* 526–537.

Snyder, M. (1988). *Public appearances/Private realities: The psychology of self-monitoring.* New York: W.H. Freeman.

Snyder, M., & Monson, T.C. (1975). Persons, situations, and the control of social behavior. *Journal of Personality and Social Psychology, 32,* 637–644.

Snyder, M., Simpson, J., & Gangestad, S. (1986). Personality and sexual relations. *Journal of Personality and Social Psychology, 51,* 181–190.

Snyder, S.H. (1977). The brain's own opiates. *Chemical and Engineering News, 55,* 26–35.

Spanos, N.P. (1984). *Disavowed responsibility for action: Demonic possession, hypnosis, and multiple personality.* Paper presented at meetings of the American Psychological Association, Toronto.

Spence, M.J., & DeCasper, A.J. (1982). Human fetuses perceive maternal speech. Paper presented at the meetings of the International Conference on Infant Studies, Austin.

Spearman, C.E., (1927). *The abilities of man.* London: Macmillan.

Sperling, G. (1960). The information available in brief visual presentations. *Psychological Monographs, 74,* 1–29.

Sperry, R.W. (1968). Hemisphere deconnection and unity of conscious experience. *American Psychologist, 29,* 723–733.

Springer, S.P., & Duetsch, G. (1985). *Left brain, right brain,* rev. ed. San Francisco: W.H. Freeman.

Squire, L.R., & Davis, H.P. (1981). The pharmacology of memory: A neurobiological perspective. *Annual Review of Pharmacology and Toxicology, 21,* 323–356.

Sroufe, A. (1985). Attachment classification from the perspective of infant-caregiver relationships and infant temperament. *Child Development, 56,* 1–14.

Stampfl, T.G., & Levis, D.J. (1967). Essentials of implosive therapy: A learning-theory-based psychodynamic behavioral therapy. *Journal of Abnormal Psychology, 72,* 496–503.

Standing, L., Canezio, J., & Haber, R.N. (1970). Perception and memory for pictures: Single-trial learning of 2,560 visual stimuli. *Psychonomic Science, 19,* 73–74.

Stanley, J., & Benbow, C. (1983). Studying the process and results of greatly accelerating (especially in mathematics and science) the educational progress of youths who reason well mathematically. In S. Paris, G. Olson, & H. Stevenson (eds.), *Learning and motivation in the classroom.* Hillsdale, N.J.: Erlbaum.

Stapp, J., Tucher, A.M., & VandenBox, G.R. (1985). Census of psychological personnel: 1983. *American Psychologist, 40,* 1317–1351.

Steele, C.M., & Southwick, L. (1985). Alcohol and social behavior: The psychology of drunken excess. *Journal of Personality and Social Psychology, 434,* 18–34.

Steers, R.M. (1984) *Organizational behavior,* 2nd ed. Glenview, Ill.: Scott Foresman.

Steffen, V.J., & Eagly, A.H. (1985). Implicit theories about influence style: The effects of status and sex. *Personality and Social Psychology Bulletin, 11,* 191–205.

Sternberg, R.J. (1985). *Beyond IQ.* Cambridge: Cambridge University Press.

Stephan, C.W., & Stephan, W.G. (1986). *Habla Inglés?* The effects of language translation on simulated juror decisions. *Journal of Applied Social Psychology, 16,* 577–589.

Sternberg, R.J. (1986a). *Intelligence applied.* New York: Harcourt Brace Jovanovich.

Sternberg, R.J. (1986b). A triangular theory of love. *Psychological Review, 93,* 119–135.

Stevenson, B. (1967). *The home book of quotations.* New York: Dodd Mead.

Stewart, J.E., II. (1980). Defendant's attractiveness as a factor in the outcome of criminal trials: An observational study. *Journal of Applied Social Psychology, 10,* 348–361.

Stiles, W.B., Shapiro, D.A., & Elliott, R. Are all psychotherapies equivalent? *American Psychologist, 41,* 165–180.

Stock, W.E., & Geer, J.H. (1982). A study of fantasy-based sexual arousal in women. *Archives of Sexual Behavior, 11,* 33–47.

Storms, M.D. (1981). Theories of sexual orientation. *Journal of Personality and Social Psychology, 38,* 783–792.

Stricker, E.M., Rowland, N., Saller, C.F., & Friedman, M.I. (1977). Homeostasis during hypoglycemia: Central control of adrenal secretion and peripheral control of feeding. *Science, 196,* 79–81.

Strube, M.J., Boland, S.M., Manfredo, P.A., & Al-Falaij, A. (1987). Type A behavior pattern and the self-evaluation of abilities: Empirical tests of the self-appraisal model. *Journal of Personality and Social Psychology, 52,* 956–974.

Strupp, H.H. (1986). Psychotherapy: Research, practice, and public policy (how to avoid dead ends). *American Psychologist, 41,* 120–130.

Stunkard, A.J. (1972). New therapies for eating disorders. *Archives of General Psychiatry, 26,* 391–398.

Stunkard, A.J. (1976). Anorexia nervosa. In J.P. Sanford (ed.), *The science and practice of clinical medicine,* pp. 361–363. New York: Grune & Stratton.

Sue, D. (1979). Erotic fantasies of college students during coitus. *Journal of Sex Research, 15,* 299–305.

Sweeney, P.D., Anderson, K., & Bailey, S. (1986). Attributional style in depression: A meta-analytic review. *Journal of Personality and Social Psychology, 50,* 974–991.

Tanner, J.M. (1970). Physical growth. In P.H. Mussen (ed.), *Carmichael's manual of child psychology.* New York: Wiley.

Taylor, B., & Wadsworth, J. (1984). Breast-feeding and child development at five years. *Developmental Medicine and Child Neurology, 26,* 73–80.

Taylor, M.S., Locke, E.A., Lee, C., & Gist, M.E. (1984). Type A behavior and faculty research productivity: What are the mechanisms? *Organizational Behavior and Human Performance, 34,* 402–418.

Teevan, R.C., & McGhee, P.E. (1972). Childhood development of fear of failure motivation. *Journal of Personality and Social Psychology, 21,* 345–348.

Tegliasi, H., & Fagin, S.S. (1984). Social anxiety and self-other biases in causal attribution. *Journal of Research in Personality, 18,* 64–80.

Temoshok, L. (1987). Introduction to special issue on AIDS. *Journal of Applied Social Psychology, 17,* 189–192.

Tennen, H., & Eller, S.J. (1977). Attributional components of learned helplessness. *Journal of Personality and Social Psychology, 35,* 265–271.

Terborg, J.R. (1977). Women in management: A research review. *Journal of Applied Psychology, 62,* 647–664.

Terman, L.M. (1916). *The measurement of intelligence.* Boston: Houghton Mifflin.

Terman, L.M. (1954). The discovery and encouragement of exceptional talent. *American Psychologist, 9,* 221–230.

Terrace, H.S. (1979). How Nim Chimpsky changed my mind. *Psychology Today, 13,* 65–76.

Thigpen, C.H., & Cleckley, H. (1954). A case of multiple personality. *Journal of Abnormal and Social Psychology, 49,* 135–151.

Thomas, A., & Chess, S. (1981). Correlation of early temperament with later behavioral functioning. Paper presented at CIBA Foundation temperament conference, London.

Thomas, A., & Chess, S. (1977). *Temperament and development.* New York: Bruner/Mazel.

Thomas, A., & Chess, S. (1985). The behavioral study of temperament. In J. Strelau, F. Farley, & A. Gale (eds.), *The biological bases of personality and behavior,* vol. 1, pp. 213–226. Washington, D.C.: Hemisphere.

Thomas, M.H. (1982). Physiological arousal, exposure to a relatively lengthy aggressive film, and aggressive behavior. *Journal of Research in Personality, 16,* 72–81.

Thorndike, R.L., & Hagen, E. (1982). *Ten thousand careers.* New York: Wiley.

Thornton, G.D., III, & Byham, W.C. (1982). *Assessment centers and managerial performance.* New York: Academic.

Thurstone, E.L. (1938). *Primary mental abilities.* Chicago: University of Chicago Press.

Thyer, B.A., & Geller, E.S. (1987). The "buckle-up" dashboard sticker: An effective environmental intervention for safety belt promotion. *Environment and Behavior, 19,* 484–494.

Tjosvold, D. (1986). *Working together to get things done: Managing for organization productivity.* Lexington, Mass.: Lexington Books.

Torney-Purta, J. (1984). Annotated bibliography of materials for adding an international dimension to undergraduate courses in developmental and social psychology. *American Psychologist, 39,* 1032–1042.

Trotter, R.J., (1986). Three heads are better than one. *Psychology Today,* August.

Tulving, E., & Pearlstone, Z. (1966). Availability versus accessibility of information in memory for words. *Journal of Verbal Learning and Verbal Behavior, 5,* 381–391.

Tulving, E., & Thompson, D.M. (1973). Encoding specificity and retrieval processes in episodic memory. *Psychological Review, 80,* 352–373.

Turner, J.H. (1970). Entrepreneurial environments and the emergence of achievement motivation in adolescent males. *Sociometry, 33,* 147–165.

Turner, S.M., Beidel, D.S., & Nathan, R.S. (1985). Biological factors in obsessive-compulsive disorders. *Psychological Bulletin, 97,* 430–450.

Tversky, A., & Kahneman, D. (1974). Judgements under uncertainty: Heuristics and biases. *Science, 185,* 1124–1131.

Tyler, T.R., & Cook, F.L. (1984). The mass media and judgment of risk: Distinguishing impact on personal and societal level judgments. *Journal of Personality and Social Psychology, 47,* 693–708.

Udry, J.R., & Morris, N.M. (1968). Distribution of coitus in the menstrual cycle. *Nature, 220,* 593–596.

Valenstein, E.S. (1980). *The psychosurgery debate: Scientific, legal, and ethical perspectives.* San Francisco: W.H. Freeman.

Van Essen, D.C., & Maunsell, J.H.R. (1983). Hierarchical organization and functional streams in the visual cortex. *Trends in Neuroscience,* September.

Vitkus, J., & Horwitz, L.M. (1987). Poor social performance of lonely people: Lacking a skill or adopting a role? *Journal of Personality and Social Psychology, 52,* 1266–1273.

von Bekesy, G., (1960). *Experiments in hearing.* New York: McGraw-Hill.

Von Senden, M. (1960). *Space and sign.* Trans. by P. Heath. New York: Free Press.

Voss, J.F., Greene, T.R., Post, T.A., & Penner, B.C. (1983). Problem-solving in the social sciences. In G.H. Bower (ed.), *The psychology of learning and motivation: Advances in research theory,* vol. 17, pp. 165–213. New York: Academic.

Wagner, D.A. (1986). Child development research and the third world: A future of mutual interest? *American Psychologist, 41,* 298–301.

Wagner, R.K., & Torgesen, J.K. (1987). The nature of phonological prossessing and its causal role in the acquisition of reading skills. *Psychological Bulletin, 101,* 192–212.

Wakefield, J.C. (1987). Sex bias in the diagnosis of primary orgasmic dysfunction. *American Psychologica, 42,* 464–471.

Wallace, B., & Fisher, L.E. (1987). *Consciousness and behavior,* 2nd ed. Boston: Allyn and Bacon.

Wallace, R.K., & Benson, H. (1972). The physiology of meditation. *Scientific American, 226,* 84–90.

Walters, G.C., & Herring B. (1978). Differential suppression by punishment of nonconsummator licking and level pressing. *Journal of Experimental Psychology: Animal Behavior Processes, 4,* 170–187.

Wason, P.C. (1968). On the failure to eliminate hypotheses—A second look. In P.C. Wason & P.N. Johnson-Laird (eds.), *Thinking and reasoning.* Baltimore: Penguin.

Watson, J.B. (1924). *Behaviorism.* Chicago: University of Chicago Press.

Watson, J.B., & Raynor, R. (1920). Conditioned emotional reactions. *Journal of Experimental Psychology, 3,* 1–14.

Watt, N., Anthony, J., Wynne, L., & Rolf, J. (1984). *Children at risk for schizophrenia: A longitudinal perspective.* New York: Cambridge University Press.

Weaver, J.B., Masland, J.L., Kharazmi, S., & Zillman, D. (1985). Effects of alcoholic intoxication on the appreciation of different types of humor. *Journal of Personality and Social Psychology, 49,* 781–787.

Webb, W. (1975). *Sleep: The gentle tyrant.* Englewood Cliffs, N.J.: Prentice-Hall.

Wechsler, D. (1975). Intelligence defined and undefined. *American Psychologist, 30,* 135–139.

Weinberger, M., Hiner, S.L., & Tierney, W.M. (1987). In support of hassles as a measure of stress in predicting health outcomes. *Journal of Behavioral Medicine, 10,* 19–31.

Weiner, B. (1985). An attributional theory of achievement motivation and emotion. *Psychological Review, 92,* 548–573.

Weiner, B., Amirkhan, J., Folkes, V.S., & Verette, J.A. (1987). An attributional analysis of excuse giving: Studies of a naive theory of emotion. *Journal of Personality and Social Psychology, 52,* 316–324.

Weiner, R.D. (1985). Convulsive therapies. In H.I. Kaplan & B.J. Sadock (eds.), *Comprehensive textbook of psychiatry,* 4th ed., pp. 1558–1562. Baltimore: Williams & Wilkins.

Weinstein, S. (1968). Intensive and extensive aspects of tactile sensitivity as a function of body part, sex, and laterality. In D.R. Kenshalo (ed.), *The skin senses,* pp. 195–218. Springfield, Ill.: Charles C Thomas.

Weisberg, R., & Suls, J.M. (1973). An information-processing model of Duncker's candle problem. *Cognitive Psychology, 4,* 255–276.

Weiss, R.J. (1982). Understanding moral thought: Effects on moral reasoning and decision making. *Developmental Psychology, 18,* 852–861.

Weissberg-Benchell, & Paris, S.G. (1988). Young children's remembering in different contexts: A reinterpretation of Istomina's study. *Child Development,* in press.

Welch, S., Gruhl, J., & Spohn, C. (1984). Dismissal, conviction, and incarceration of Hispanic defendants: A comparison with Anglos and blacks. *Social Science Quarterly,* 257–264.

Wells, G.L., & Loftus, E.F. (eds.). (1984). *Eyewitness testimony: Psychological perspectives.* Cambridge: Cambridge University Press.

Whorf, B.L. (1956). Science and linguistics. In J.B. Carroll (ed.), *Language, thought, and reality: Selected writings of Benjamin Whorf.* Cambridge: MIT Press.

Wiesel, T.N. (1982). Postnatal development of the visual cortex and the influence of environment. *Nature. 299,* 583–591.

Wilcoxon, H.C., Dragoin, W.B., & Kral, P.A. (1971). Illness-induced aversions in rats and quail: Relative salience of visual and gustatory cues. *Science, 171,* 826–828.

Wilder, D.A. (1977). Perception of groups, size of opposition, and social influence. *Journal of Experimental Social Psychology, 13,* 253–268.

Williams, K., & Keating, C.W. (1987). Affect and the processing of performance information. Paper presented at the meetings of the Society of Industrial and Organizational Psychology.

Wilson, E.O. (1975). *Sociobiology: The new synthesis.* Cambridge: Harvard University Press.

Wilson, T.D., & Linville, P.W. (1982). Improving the academic performance of college freshmen: Attribution therapy revisited. *Journal of Personality and Social Psychology, 42,* 367–376.

Wilson, W.R. (1979). Feeling more than we can know: Exposure effects without learning. *Journal of Personality and Social Psychology, 37,* 811–821.

Winter, D.G. (1973). *The power motive.* New York: Free Press.

Winter, D.G. (1983). Development of an integrated system for scoring motives in verbal running text. Unpublished manuscript. Wesleyan University.

Winter, D.G. (1987a). Enhancement of an enemy's power motivation as a dynamic of conflict escalation. *Journal of Personality and Social Psychology, 52,* 41–48.

Winter, D.G. (1987b). Leader appeal, leader performance, and the motive profiles of leaders and followers: A study of American presidents and elections. *Journal of Personality and Social Psychology, 52,* 196–202.

Winter, D.G. (1988). The power motives in women—and men. *Journal of Personality and Social Psychology, 54,* 510–519.

Wolpe, J. (1958). *Psychotherapy by reciprocal inhibition.* Stanford: Stanford University Press.

Wolpe, J. (1982). *The practice of behavior therapy.* New York: Pergammon.

Wood, R.E., Mento, A.J., & Locke, E.A. (1987). Task complexity as a moderator of goal effects: A meta-analysis. *Journal of Applied Psychology, 72,* 416–425.

Wyer, R.S., Jr., & Srull, T.K. (eds.). (1984). *Handbook of social cognition.* Hillsdale, N.J.: Erlbaum.

Wyer, R.S., Jr., & Srull, T.K. (1986). Human cognition in its social context. *Psychologycal Review, 93,* 322–359.

Wynn, L.C., Singer, M.T., Bartko, J.J., & Toohey, M.L. (1977). Schizophrenics and their families: Recent research on parental communication. In J.M. Tanner (ed.), *Developments in psychiatric research.* London: Hodder & Stoughton.

Yonas, A., Arterberry, M.E., & Granrud, C.E. (1987). Four-month-old infants' sensitivity to binocular and kinetic information for three-dimensional-object shape. *Child Development, 58,* 910–927.

Yuille, J.C., & Cutshall, J.L. (1986). A case study of eyewitness memory of a crime. *Journal of Applied Psychology, 71,* 291–301.

Zajonc, R.B. (1976). Family configuration and intelligence. *Science, 192,* 226–236.

Zajonc, R.B. (1984). On the primacy of affect. *American Psychologist, 39,* 117–123.

Zajonc, R.B. (1985). Emotion and facial efference: A theory reclaimed. *Science, 228,* 15–21.

Zajonc, R.B. (1986). Mining new gold from old research. *Psychology Today,* February.

Zajonc, R.B., & Markus, G.B. (1975). Birth order and intellectual development. *Psychological Review, 82,* 74–88.

Zillman, D., & Bryant, J. (1984). Effects of massive exposure to pornography. In N.M. Malamuth & E. Donnerstein (eds.), *Pornography and Sexual Aggression.* New York: Academic.

Zillman, D., & Bryant, J.B. (eds.) (1986) *Selective exposure to communication.* Hillsdale, N.J.: Erlbaum.

Zillman, D., Weaver, J.G., Mundorf, N., & Aust, C.F. (1986). Effects of an opposite-gender companion's affect to distress, delight, and attraction. *Journal of Personality and Social Psychology, 51,* 586–594.

Zimbardo, P.G. (1977). *Shyness.* Reading, Mass.: Addison-Wesley.

Zuckerman, M., Klorman, R., Larrance, D.T., & Spiegel, N.H. (1981). Facial, autonomic, and subjective components of emotion: The facial feedback hypothesis versus the externalizer-internalizer distinction. *Journal of Personality and Social Psychology, 41,* 929–944.

Zuckerman, M., DeFrank, R.S., Spiegel, N.H., & Larrance, D.T. (1982). Masculinity-feminity and encoding of nonverbal cues. *Journal of Personality and Social Psychology, 42,* 548–556.

Name Index

Subject Index

(Photo credits continued from copyright page)

L. Anderson/Off-Shoot. Pg. 157; L. Migdale/Photo-Researchers Inc. Pg. 158; R. Goldstein/ Photo-Researchers Inc. Pg. 160 TL; J. Pickerell/Click, Chicago, BL; C. Noren/Photo-Researchers Inc., R; R. Morsch/The Stock Market. **CHAPTER SIX** Pg. 168; R. Shaw/The Stock Market. Pg. 171; J. Curtis. Pg. 180; D. Dempster/Off-Shoot. 184 TL, BL; D. Dempster/ Off-Shoot, R; B. Daemmrich/Click, Chicago. Pg. 187; J. Curtis. Pg. 192; M. Ryan/Off-Shoot. **CHAPTER SEVEN** Pg. 201 Top row, L-R; L. Anderson/Off-Shoot, J. Curtis/Off-Shoot, L. Villota/The Stock Market. Bottom Row, L-R; J. Perkell/The Stock Market, J. Curtis/Off-Shoot, D. Dempster/Off-Shoot. Pg. 205; D. Dempster/Off-Shoot. Pg. 210 L; G. Smith/The Picture Group, R; C. Peterson/Sygma. Pg. 217; R. Schleipman/Off-Shoot. Pg. 219; Paramount Pictures. Pg. 224; D. Dempster/Off-Shoot. Pg. 227 L; N. Weisser/Bruce Coleman Inc., R; J. Brandenburg/Woodfin Camp & Associates. Pg. 228; Dr. Ronald Cohn/The Gorilla Foundation. **CHAPTER EIGHT** Pg. 236; Dr. Lennart Nilsson. Pg. 241; T. Cordingley/Off-Shoot. Pg. 255; Courtesy Dr. Harry Harlow. Pg. 257 L; Tannenbaum/Sygma. Pg. 257 R; S. Stone/ The Picture Cube. Pg. 259; L. McIntyre/Woodfin Camp & Associates. Pg. 263 L; Aubert-Keystone/The Picture Group, R; A. Garcia/The Picture Group. Pg. 266; T. Cordingley. **CHAPTER NINE** Pg. 275 L; Comstock, C; L. Sloan/Woodfin Camp & Associates, R; J. Curtis. Pg. 281; Courtesy of Richard E. Keesey, Dept. of Psychology, Univ. of Wisconsin. Pg. 282; Keller & Peet. Pg. 284 L; J. Curtis, R; S. Grant/The Picture Cube. Pg. 286; T. Cordingley/Off-Shoot. Pg. 291; R. Morsch/The Stock Market. Pg. 294; T. Cordingley/Off-Shoot. Pg. 295; The Kennedy Library. **CHAPTER TEN** Pg. 307; The Kobal Collection/Super Stock. Pg. 312 L; Momatiuk/Woodfin Camp & Associates, TR; J. Chenet/Woodfin Camp & Associates, BR; H. Hoefer/Woodfin Camp & Associates. Pg. 314 L; C. Steiner/Sygma, C; D. Dempster/Off-Shoot, R; Comstock. 314 B; J. Earle; The Stock Market. Pg. 321; T. Cordingley/Off-Shoot. Pg. 325; B. Bower/The Picture Group. Pg. 328; Focus On Sports. Pg. 333; O. Franken/Sygma. **CHAPTER ELEVEN** Pg. 340 L; D. Schaefer/The Picture Cube, C; D. Dempster/Off-Shoot, R: M. Abramson/Woodfin Camp & Associates. Pg. 341; D. Dempster/Off-Shoot. Pg. 346 L, R; D. Dempster/Off-Shoot. Pg. 348 L; J. Curtis, C; T. Cordingley/Off-Shoot, R; T. Horowitz/The Stock Market. Pg. 354; Courtesy The U.S. Army. Pg. 358; Dr. Thomas J. Bouchard, Jr., Univ. of Minnesota. Pg. 360; D. Stoecklein/The Stock Market. **CHAPTER TWELVE** Pg. 373; Archive/Photo-Researchers Inc. Zviki-Eshet/ The Stock Market. Pg. 386; J. Curtis. Pg. 387 L, R; D. Dempster/Off-Shoot. Pg. 391; R. Huntzinger/The Stock Market. Pg. 395; R. Schleipman/Off-Shoot. **CHAPTER THIRTEEN** Pg. 404; Bettmann Archive. Pg. 405; North Wind Picture Archive. Pg. 411; D. Dempster/Off-Shoot. Pg. 414 L; MOMA Film Stills Archive, R; Kobal Collection. Pg. 416; J. Curtis. Pg. 417; Focus On Sports. Pg. 423; MOMA Film Stills Archive. Pg. 425; E.S. Beckwith/ Taurus. Pg. 428; Wide World Photos. **CHAPTER FOURTEEN** Pg. 438; J. Curtis. Pg. 443; D. Dempster/Off-Shoot. Pg. 448; D. Dempster/Off-Shoot. Pg. 449 L; T. Cordingley/Off-Shoot, R; S. Goltzer/The Stock Market. Pg. 453; D. Dempster/Off-Shoot. Pg. 454; S. Lapides. Pg. 459; T. Cordingly/Off-Shoot. Pg. 460; W. McIntyre/Photo-Researchers Inc. Pg. 462; G. Gordon/Woodfin Camp & Associates. Pg. 463 L; D. Dempster/Off-Shoot, R; B. Ullman/ Taurus. **CHAPTER FIFTEEN** Pg. 469 L; Henley & Savage/The Stock Market, C; J. Lowenthal/Woodfin Camp & Associates, R; G. Palmer/The Stock Market. Pg. 475; E. Bakke/The Picture Group. Pg. 478; D. Dempster/Off-Shoot. Pg. 480; Courtesy The American Cancer Society. Pg. 488; Courtesy Mrs. A. Milgrim. Pg. 489; Henley & Savage/The Stock Market. Pg. 491 L-r; L. McIntyre/Woodfin Camp; A. Reininger/Woodfin Camp; P. Shah/ The Stock Market; D. Lissey/The Picture Cube. Pg. 494; C. Lee/The Picture Cube. Pg. 497 L; Lougrew; The Stock Market, R; K. McCarthy/Off-Shoot. **CHAPTER SIXTEEN** Pg. 506; D. Dempster/Off-Shoot. Pg. 507; D. Dempster/Off-Shoot. Pg. Pg. TL; JP Laffont/Sygma, BL; Presse Sports/The Picture Group, R; Schachmes/Sygma. Pg. 514; Courtesy The U.S. Dept. of Transportation. Pg. 514; K. Galvin/The Picture Group. Pg. 517; C. Sorenson. Pg. 520 L; D. Fineman/Sygma, R; The Surgeon Generals Office (photo by D. Dempster). **APPENDIX** Pg. 524 L; R. Gehrz/Photo-Researchers Inc., C; McCarthy/Off-Shoot, R; S. Seitz/Woodfin Camp & Associates.

LIVERPOOL JOHN MOORES UNIVERSITY
Aldham Robarts L.R.C.
TEL. 051 231 3701/3634